DOROTHY PARKER

Marion Meade studied journalism at Northwestern University, Illinois and later received her master's from Columbia Graduate School of Journalism, New York. She has published several biographies, including the widely acclaimed *Eleanor of Aquitaine* and two novels, *Stealing Heaven: The Story of Heloise and Abelard* and *Sybille*. Specialising in biographies, she writes regularly for *MS* magazine.

'A lively book, an entertaining read and a memorable portrait.' *Spectator*

'Could be *the* definitive work on our favourite cynic.' *Time Out*

'One of the most entertaining books of its kind of the past few years ... brilliantly recaptures the literary atmosphere of the period.' *Liverpool Daily Post*

'A sparkling and scholarly biography ... riveting.' *Cosmopolitan*

DOROTHY PARKER

What Fresh Hell Is This?

·

MARION MEADE

Heinemann · Mandarin

A Mandarin Paperback

DOROTHY PARKER

ISBN: 0 7493 00108

A CIP catalogue record for this book is available from
the British Library

First published in Great Britain 1988
by William Heinemann Ltd
This edition published 1989
By Heinemann · Mandarin
81 Fulham Road, London SW3 6RB
Copyright © 1987 by Marion Meade

Printed in Great Britain by
Cox & Wyman Ltd, Reading

PERMISSIONS ACKNOWLEDGMENTS

Grateful acknowledgment is made to The National Association for the Advancement of Colored People and the Estate of Dorothy Parker for permission to reprint excerpts from various materials by Dorothy Parker including letters, poems, untitled verse and speeches. Copyright © The National Association for the Advancement of Colored People and the Estate of Dorothy Parker.

Acknowledgment is also made to the following libraries for permission to reprint material from their collections: The University of Chicago Library, Department of Special Collections; The Bancroft Library. University of California, Berkeley, Thomas J. Mooney Papers (C-B 410); The Beinecke Rare Books and Manuscript Library, Yale University, Collection of American Literature; Columbia University Oral History Research Office, Copyright © Trustees of Columbia University in the City of New York; The New York Public Library, Astor, Lenox and Tilden Foundations, Henry W. and Albert A. Berg Collection; Van Pelt Library. University of Pennsylvania, the Burton Rascoe Collection, Department of Special Collections; the Harry Ransom Humanities Research Center, the University of Texas at Austin; Dallas Public Library. the Margo Jones Collection: The Newberry Library, Malcolm Cowley Papers; Princeton University Library. F. Scott Fitzgerald Collections. Box 51; Fales Library, New York University; The Houghton Library. Harvard University; Bentley Historical Library, University of Michigan, Arnold Gingrich Papers, Michigan Historical Collections: The John F. Kennedy Library, Boston, Massachusetts. the Ernest Hemingway Collection; Historical Society of Pennsylvania. the George Lorimer Papers; Robert Benchley material reprinted by permission of the Robert Benchley Estate and the Mugar Memorial Library.

Page 459 constitutes an extension of this copyright page.

FOR ALISON LINKHORN

Acknowledgments

Since Dorothy Parker herself left no correspondence, manuscripts, memorabilia, or private papers of any kind, I have had to reconstruct her life by talking to those who knew her and by retrieving material from various institutions, attics, trunks, and the personal files of people who considered her letters worth preserving.

Throughout her life she was secretive about her origins and gave the impression that she had no family ties whatsoever, even though her close relationship with her sister, Helen, lasted a lifetime. This biography was written with the cooperation of Lel Droste Iveson, Dorothy Parker's niece, who generously shared with me memories of her aunt and details of the family's history, as well as Parker's childhood letters, verse, and a scrapbook–photo album compiled over the course of many years. She has my deepest gratitude. I also would like to thank other members of the family who have been of tremendous help to me: Joan Grossman, Robert Iveson, Marge Droste, and Nancy Arcaro. Special thanks to Susan Cotton for the loan of the album.

Roy Eichel, the only surviving member of Alan Campbell's family, offered me photographs, reminiscences spanning nine decades, and the hospitality of his home. His wonderful cooperation was altogether a biographer's dream.

Many persons have contributed to this biography. They shared their recollections in interviews, telephone conversations, and letters; they took considerable trouble to locate photographs and correspondence, search for sheet music, draw maps, conduct tours of their homes, prepare meals, and guide me to sources I might otherwise have not known about. Without their generous assistance this book would not exist. To all of them I am greatly indebted:

Timothy Adams, Charles Addams, Stella Adler, Louisa Alger, Vera Allen, Bill Allyn, Roger Angell, Andrew Anspach, Patricia Arno, Louis Auchincloss, Julian Bach, Don Bachardy, Lisa Bain, Shirley Booth Baker, Fredericka Barbour, Margaret Barker, Vita Barsky, Charles Baskerville, Lois Battle, Saul Bellow, Nathaniel Benchley, Leonard Bernstein, Rebecca Bernstien, Paul Bonner, Jr., Gardner Botsford, Clement Brace, Frederic Bradlee, Fanny Brennan, Heywood Hale Broun, Joseph Bryan III, John Carlyle, Lester Cole, Dorothy Commins, Marc Connelly, Norman Corwin, Malcolm Cowley, Alyce Cusson, John Davies, Helen Walker Day, Sylvia Statt DeBaun, Lucinda Dietz, Harvey Deneroff, Helen Deutsch, Eric Devine, Rita Devine, Honoria and William Donnelly.

Anne Edelman, Henry Ephron, Arpad Fekete, Leslie Fiedler, Ben Finney, Moe Fishman, Nina Foch, Sally Foster, Pie Friendly, Arnold Gates, Bernard Geis, Martha Gellhorn, Brendan Gill, Margalo Gillmore, Ruth Goetz, Frances Goodrich, Milton Greenstein, Thomas Guinzburg, Albert Hackett, Emily Hahn, Curtis Harnack, Harold Hayes, Sig Herzig, Rust Hills, Henry Beetle Hough, Ian Hunter, Mary M. James, Gordon G. Jones.

E. J. Kahn, Jr., Virginia Rice Kahn, Eleanor Kairalla, Donald Klopfer, Howard Koch, Don Koll, Parker Ladd, Ring Lardner, Jr., Geraldine Leder, Queenie Leonard, Clara Lester, Miranda and Ralph Levy, Phebe Ann Lewis, Michael Loeb, Joshua Logan, William Lord, Nancy Macdonald, Gertrude Macy, Bob Magner, Chris Marconi, Sister Miriam Martin, Samuel Marx, Bruce Mason, Walter Matthau, Vera Maxwell, William Maxwell, Mary McDonald, Laura McLaughlin, Mickey Medinz, Paul Millard, J. Clifford Miller, Jr., Alice Leone Moats, Betty Moodie, Dr. Christopher Morren, Wright Morris, Cathy Morrow, Kate Mostel, Lewis Mumford, Alice Lee Myers.

Adeline Naiman, Robert Nathan, Anne Noll, Paul O'Dwyer, Emily Paley, Judith and Lewis Parker, Paul Pascarelli, Kenneth Pitchford, Robert Phelps, Noel Pugh, Ben Rayburn, Dame Flora Robson, Dorothy Rodgers, Helen Rosen, Peg Ross, Robert Rothwell, Yvonne Luff-Roussel.

Allen Saalburg, Joseph Schrank, Lee Schryver, Budd Schulberg, Jim

Seligmann, Madeline Sherwood, Frederick Shroyer, Steven Siegel, Stan Silverman, Sisters of Charity, Frances Scott Fitzgerald Smith, Toni Strassman, Shepperd Strudwick, Pete Steffens, Leland Stowe, Bob Tallman, William Targ, Marian Spitzer Thompson, Helen Thurber, Helen Townsend, Lester Trauch, Harriet Walden, James Waters, Robert Weinberg, E. B. White, Robert Whitehead, Elinor Wikler, Richard Wilbur, Meta Carpenter Wilde, Dr. Susan Williamson, Noel Willman, Jeanne Ballot Winham, Mildred Wohlforth, Dana Woodbury, Robert Yaw III, Naomi Yergin, Curt Yeske, Lois Moran Young, Jerome Zerbe.

To the libraries and librarians who helped collect and copy Parker's papers and in other ways assisted me in documenting her life, I am most grateful:

The New York Public Library, the New York Historical Society, Boston University, Columbia University, New York University, Yale University, Library of Congress, University of Southern California, Atlanta University, Queens Public Library, Pennsylvania State University, Walter Hampden–Edwin Booth Theatre Collection and Library, Gettysburg College, Brandeis University, Enoch Pratt Free Library, University of Oregon, University of Michigan, Wisconsin Center for Film and Theater Research, University of California, Dallas Public Library, University of Iowa, Greenfield Community College, Hamilton College, Harvard University, Princeton University, New York Genealogical and Biographical Library, New York Society Library, Virginia Military Institute, Pacifica Tape Library, Smith College, Indiana University, Temple University, University of Texas, American Academy and Institute of Arts and Letters, University of Chicago, Southern Illinois University, Historical Society of Pennsylvania, State University of New York (Buffalo), University of Virginia, Newberry Library, Cornell University, Academy of Motion Picture Arts and Sciences, American Film Institute, Museum of Modern Art Film Department, Ninety-second Street Young Men's and Young Women's Hebrew Association, Museum of the City of New York, Virginia Commonwealth University, Samford University, International Ladies' Garment Workers' Union Archives, Joint Free Public Library of Morristown, N.J., Leo Baeck Institute, State of Alabama Department of Archives and History, and the Mercer Museum.

For providing work space in the Frederick Lewis Allen Memorial Room during the initial stages of my research, I am grateful to the New York Public Library.

Under a Freedom of Information Act request, the Federal Bureau of Investigation released to me more than nine hundred pages of material on Dorothy Parker and Alan Campbell over a four-year period.

Several publishing companies offered valuable assistance. I would like to express my appreciation to The Viking Press and W. W. Norton and Company for giving me access to their Dorothy Parker files. *The New Yorker* and the *Saturday Evening Post* supplied inventories of her writings that had appeared in their magazines. The library at Condé Nast Publications, Inc., allowed me to spend as many hours as I wished searching bound volumes of *Vogue* and *Vanity Fair* for her earliest published work.

A number of writers, editors, and filmmakers were kind enough to offer leads and practical advice or to share information they had gathered for projects of their own: Billy Altman, April Bernard, John Dorr, Bryan Gallagher, John Keats, Nancy Milford, William Nolan, Victor Navasky, Stanley Olson, Aviva Slesin, Caroline Seebohm, and Roy Winnick. Several conversations with Richard Meryman led me to an investigation of alcoholism and two years of attendance at Alanon meetings. James Gaines helpfully loaned tapes he had made with certain individuals (now deceased) for *Wit's End*, his excellent book about the Round Table. Maxine Haleff arranged interviews for me in New York and personally conducted other interviews in California. I am especially indebted to Richard Lamparski for allowing me to quote from the revealing interview he taped with Parker the year before her death, as well as his unstinting help in supplying me with leads in Hollywood.

Vanessa Levin generously donated her services as a research assistant. My thanks for her work on behalf of the book in New York and Hollywood and for her moral support.

I am enormously grateful to my friend Minda Novek, who shared with me her fund of expert knowledge about the Algonquin Round Table and listened patiently while I nattered on about Dorothy Parker year after year.

Two friends have helped sustain me throughout the writing of the book with affection, job leads, meals, research, unfailing encouragement, but perhaps most importantly, with their wonderful humor. To Dorothy Herrmann, author of *S. J. Perelman: A Life,* and to Prudence Crowther, editor of *Don't Tread on Me: The Selected Letters of S. J. Perelman,* I owe gratitude and the memory of a great deal of laughter.

It would have been extremely difficult to complete this work without the practical help of Maria Stowe and Earle Resnick. I have been fortunate to know both of them.

Finally, I would like to thank my forbearant editor at Villard Books, Diane Reverand, for the understanding she has shown me, and my agent, Lois Wallace, who could always be depended upon for wise counsel and cheerful encouragement.

Contents

Introduction

THE ALGONQUIN HOTEL

Summer 1927

It did not look special. Other hotels on West Forty-fourth Street had American Indian names and walnut-paneled lobbies bathed in Edwardian gloom. The difference was not even in the extravagant price of the blue-plate special (half spring chicken, two vegetables, French fried potatoes—$1.65) or the fact that the hotel's regular guests included Mary Pickford and Henry Mencken. The reason for its uniqueness stemmed from a single article of furniture, a large round table that occupied the center of the Algonquin's main dining room.

Those who took the trouble to stroll through the hotel lobby around noon and stop near the portière leading to the Rose Room could get a good view of the table, quite likely glimpse George Kaufman's pompadour or the beaky nose of F.P.A., and perhaps hear Alexander Woollcott snarl one of his famous insults at Heywood Broun or Harold Ross. People who waited long enough finally saw a tiny brunette woman emerge from the elevator and breeze into the dining room. No one needed to identify her as Dorothy Parker because everyone knew this was where she lived, where she met her friends, where the luncheon circle she had helped make a national legend dined every day. If the fabled Algonquin Round Table was indeed the country's literary Camelot, as some liked to insist, then she was its Guinevere.

The summer of 1927 marked the eighth anniversary of the day she first brought Robert Benchley and Robert Sherwood to the Algonquin Hotel, all of them working together down the street at *Vanity Fair*, poorly paid editors grateful to attend a free luncheon welcoming Woollcott back from the war. Although none of them realized it at the time, that animated party in June 1919 was the first gathering of the Round Table. Dorothy, content to observe, had scarcely uttered a word. She looked meek and fragile in every way, childlike, not quite five feet tall with a mop of dark hair demurely tucked under the brim of her embroidered hat and huge dark eyes that seemed to plead for the world's protection. She wore glasses, but not in public. She had never smoked a cigarette or drunk more than a sip of a cocktail. The taste of liquor made her sick. She still lived in her childhood neighborhood on the Upper West Side and visited her married sister on Sundays.

In the intervening eight years, she had been dubbed the wittiest woman in America, her quips preserved, repeated, and printed so that by 1927 scarcely a snappy line uttered anywhere was not attributed to her. *Enough Rope*, her first volume of poetry, was a current best seller. Although she had achieved her great popularity for light verse, she also demonstrated a gift for writing short fiction and criticism.

As a public personality, she had a positive genius for creating the impression that she was a one-of-a-kind flapper—sophisticated, urban, intellectual. Born in the final years of the nineteenth century, she spun her dreams in the turbulent twenties and became a model and inspiration for the women of her time. The truth was that she was obliged to invent herself as she went along. She was a born rebel who enjoyed thumbing her nose at the rules that women were expected to obey:

> They say of me, and so they should,
> It's doubtful if I come to good.

In competition with men, she pursued a career with skill and accomplishment and demanded to be treated as an equal. She smoked and drank in public. She wrote and said exactly what she thought, expressing herself in racy English that caused eyebrows to shoot up. Her favorite word contained four letters. The word she used almost as frequently also had four letters.

Her way of looking at life was incurably pessimistic. Confronted by the unknown, she immediately prepared for the worst. Ordinary occurrences—the doorbell or a ringing telephone—made her wonder "What fresh hell is this?"

She was a married woman who insisted on being called *Mrs.* Parker and who was said to keep a husband few had seen in a broom closet and to practice free love. Scandalous stories of extramarital affairs and abortions persisted in circulating, but that was largely because she made no attempt to deny the rumors, since they were true. She called herself a slut and exclaimed to Edmund Wilson, "I am cheap—you know that!" The vigor with which she flaunted her sexuality offended more than a few people, among them Ernest Hemingway who composed a vicious poem about her. But she bestowed a royal raspberry on her critics one and all:

> But now I know the things I know,
> And do the things I do;
> And if you do not like me so,
> To hell, my love, with you!

She was thirty-three—"Time doth flit. / Oh, shit!"—and declared that living had taught her two important truths: Never trust a round garter or a Wall Street man. She disdained the American obsession with money, hated the idea of owning property or stocks, and sought only enough money "to keep body and soul apart." She preferred to live in a hotel, she explained, because all she needed was room to lay a hat and a few friends. She had visited everyplace worth visiting, from Hemingway's favorite writing cafés on the Left Bank to the Long Island house parties Scott Fitzgerald memorialized in *The Great Gatsby*; she appeared to be acquainted with nearly every person worth knowing, possess every ware worth owning.

In the golden age of "Ain't We Got Fun," a song she especially loathed, the country was entering its eighth year of Prohibition, and social pleasure was measured by alcohol. Having fun meant getting drunk. Having a lot of fun meant getting very drunk. By current standards, Dorothy was enjoying the time of her life. Her days and nights were packed with adventures tailor-made to fit the public's fantasies about the New York literary high life and unfolded with fairy-tale predictability. At twilight, she called Algonquin room service to send up ice and White Rock, and her suite became the scene of an informal cocktail party, a ritual she called "having a few people in for drinks." The few often swelled to several dozen, including Irving Berlin, Tallulah Bankhead, and Harpo Marx. No invitations were issued and everybody brought an offering from their bootlegger. Her personal taste ran to Haig & Haig, but she also was known to drink

"White Hearse," as she called all rotgut Scotch whisky, and practically anything in a pinch except gin, which, plain or mixed, made her ill.

After the party broke up, she attended the theater with friends or lovers, sometimes one and the same, then swung uptown to Forty-ninth Street and her favorite speakeasy, where she met her best friend, Robert Benchley. In Tony Soma's smoky basement, they sat at tables covered with white cotton cloths and drank right-off-the-ship whiskey from thick white coffee cups. There was no ventilation, no music, very little to eat except steak or chicken sandwiches. The club had no established closing hour. Only after the last patron had left, whether at 3:00 A.M. or 6:00 A.M., did Tony lock up.

After downing two stiff highballs, Dorothy talked happily about how she would love to pick up a stray dog because she'd never owned enough dogs. "Three highballs," she admitted, "and I think I'm St. Francis of Assisi." On Sixth Avenue, she once kissed a cab-horse because he looked tired standing there, and she liked him. She announced that she'd kiss that horse again if she ever ran into him, even go to Atlantic City with him if he asked her. "I don't care what they say about me. Only I shouldn't like to have that horse going around thinking he has to marry me."

The surroundings in which she felt most comfortable were hotels and saloons, not necessarily in that order. There were thousands of speakeasies in Manhattan. Clubs lined the streets of the forties and fifties between Fifth and Sixth avenues, and Dorothy was a regular patron in a great many of them. Her nightly rounds often included such stylish drinking establishments as Texas ("Hello, suckers!") Guinan's, Club Durant, and Jack and Charlie's. After the midtown clubs began to empty, she circled up to Harlem to hear jazz at the Savoy Ballroom, then sped back downtown to join Benchley for a nightcap at Polly Adler's brothel before calling it a day.

It was inevitable that sometimes she awoke suffering from what she termed the "rams" and felt scared to turn round abruptly for fear of seeing "a Little Mean Man about eighteen inches tall, wearing a yellow slicker and roller-skates." She certainly was acquainted with the rams—as well as the less acute strain known as German rams—but had learned that the disease was never terminal. Usually she was able to trace its onset to a stalk of bad celery from last night's dinner. At lunch, downstairs at the Round Table, she laughed and insisted that her hangover "ought to be in the Smithsonian under glass." There was no possible way, she protested, that two or three sidecars, give or take a bottle of champagne, a couple of Benedictines, and

Lord knew how many Scotches, could leave a person in such filthy condition.

A few weeks earlier, in May 1927, Charles Lindbergh's flight from Long Island to Paris presented the country with an old-fashioned hero. It was the type of heroism popular in the nineteenth century but out of style in the 1920s, which put no great store by heroes. That year Dorothy expressed the cynical spirit of the decade with these lines:

> Oh, hard is the struggle, and sparse is
> The gain of the one at the top,
> For art is a form of catharsis,
> And love is a permanent flop,
> And work is the province of cattle,
> And rest's for a clam in a shell,
> So I'm thinking of throwing the battle—
> Would you kindly direct me to hell?

In her verse rang the voice of the twenties, its hysterial insistence on having fun, its pretense that nothing was really worth believing in anymore. Two years later, all of that crashed along with the stock market.

At the close of her life, Dorothy harshly portrayed herself as "just a little Jewish girl trying to be cute." She was referring not only to herself at the Algonquin Round Table and her reputation as the country's foremost female wit in the 1920s. Her memories had strayed back to a very different past, another incarnation almost, the distant years before she had transformed herself into Dorothy Parker. In the twenties, at the pinnacle of fame, her name was synonymous with sophisticated humor and a Times Square hotel, but she did not start out in this land of literary romance, nor did she end there.

DOROTHY PARKER

Chapter 1

THE EVENTS LEADING UP
TO THE TRAGEDY

◆

1893–1903

One of her earliest memories was of ice-green water. She was hurrying toward the sea, then a sudden loop in the road revealed vast waves frothing lacily on the sand.

And another memory: She was gazing out the window, content to watch the fall of the rain, when without warning her heart beat "wild in my breast with pain."

She was supposed to have been born in New York City, but instead she showed up prematurely at the seashore on August 22, 1893. That summer, as always, her family was living at West End, New Jersey. The Rothschilds had their routines. As soon as the children's schools closed in June, they packed up household and servants and left the city. Henry Rothschild, who had his business to attend to, joined them on Sundays.

They prided themselves on renting a house at West End, which was next door to Long Branch, a seaside resort that had been the favorite spa of presidents from Grant to Arthur and that presumed to call itself "the Monte Carlo of America." West End, slightly less exclusive, was favored by the Guggenheims and other immensely rich Jewish families. ("My God, *no*, dear! We'd never *heard* of *those* Rothschilds!" as Dorothy was later to say.) Nevertheless, *these* Rothschilds knew the fashionable places to summer, and they had enough money to be among the select.

They loved Cedar Avenue with its huge gingerbread houses, the swings and screened porches, everything that accompanied living at the shore in summer. They ate big meals for breakfast, and before it grew too

3

hot, they waded into the surf, taking care to obey the swimming flags, red for gentlemen, white for ladies. The water was always icy. Later they slowly promenaded along Ocean Avenue carrying parasols, strolling past the big hotels that had recently begun to charge four dollars a day, American plan, gawking at the casinos where derbied dice rollers and roulette spinners displayed gardenias in their buttonholes. They would not have dreamed of entering; they were not those kind of people. In the evenings, bands played Sousa marches and favorites from *H.M.S. Pinafore*. At West End, everybody attended the concerts. Nearly every day there was sailing and lawn tennis, and shore suppers at the beach—the best roasted clams, corn fritters with hard sauce, huckleberry pie, and it all tasted wonderful. That year a financial panic was battering the economy. In New York, on the Lower East Side, where the Rothschild money originated, people lined up on the sidewalks for free bread and soup. At the shore, people talked about the flies, but otherwise they had few complaints about their lives.

On a weekend toward the end of August, a hard rain hit the shore. Water hurtled down in spears. The thunder blasted like fireworks. Trees were ripped up by the wind. By Monday morning, the storm had passed. Since the weather promised to be good, Henry Rothschild felt confident leaving his family to go back to town. Summertime was his busiest season.

Shortly thereafter, Eliza Rothschild went into labor. The evening after the baby came, the shore was pounded by a West Indian cyclone that knocked the chimney off their roof; the flagpole cracked and crashed, and the walls rocked on their foundation. At any moment it seemed like the house would collapse and crush them. After a terrible night, the children ventured forth to discover that not a bathhouse was left standing on the beach, and the old iron pier had been washed out to sea like a sand castle.

When Henry Rothschild returned to Cedar Avenue, he found a baby and a house that needed a new chimney.

Dorothy's paternal grandparents came from Prussia, swept across the Atlantic in the wave of German-Jewish emigration after the abortive 1848 revolution. Samson and Mary Rothschild, a couple in their twenties, were concerned about the future and were afflicted, as were so many others, by

New World fever. They heard about the marvels of America and began to dream radiant dreams. Being rural people, they decided to bypass New York and to seek a small town where an ambitious young man could establish himself, where people had money to spend on quality goods. Samson and Mary settled in Selma, Alabama, where their first child, Jacob Henry, Dorothy's father, was born in 1851. A few Jews lived in the area but none in Selma, which was primarily populated with English stock. Samson sold fancy goods—embroideries, laces, all the trimmings that Southern women treasured so highly. He peddled his finery by wagon. They had two more sons, Simon and Samuel. The Rothschilds learned to speak English with a southern accent, imitated the courteous manners of their neighbors, and suffered the anti-Semitic remarks that unthinking customers made.

Samson worked tirelessly for ten years. He prospered to some extent, but he still felt restless, dissatisfied. He was nearly forty. A few southern Jewish merchants understood that war might be likely one day and formulated business strategies to their advantage. Whether Samson was equally farsighted or whether he simply became fed up with Selma is impossible to know. He packed up and moved his family to New York City in 1860.

There being little demand for embroideries during the Civil War, Samson switched to men's wear. By 1865, he was listed in the city directory as the proprietor of a "gents furnishings" store at 294 Broadway. Elsewhere in the city lived German Jews like August Belmont, who had changed their names, become rich men, and lived in absurdly ornate palaces on Fifth Avenue. Those were not the addresses Samson dreamed about. He felt lucky to move his family, now expanded by the births of Hannah and Martin, from Avenue B to sensible and better houses in East Thirteenth Street and then to pastoral West Forty-second Street. Based on his personal experience and immigrant faith, Samson believed that you get what you want by hard work. Like his biblical namesake, he was a hardy specimen, a proud, vigorous, physically strong man who lived into his eighties; even then it was his mind that first failed him, not his body. Armed with self-confidence, he had just the qualities suitable for earning his bread by persuasion fused with the flamboyance required to make a sale. The founding father of these "folk of mud and flame," as Dorothy called them, was undisturbed about "fiddling" for his dinner, however crude he may have seemed to subsequent generations.

5

Samson's eldest son had a personality similar to his own—hearty, aggressive, and industrious. Jacob Rothschild was smart and highly ambitious, but sometimes his ambitions tended to run along alarming lines. Jacob disliked his given name. During adolescence, he began calling himself Henry, his own middle name, which must have sounded more American to him. In the course of his life, his first name passed through several incarnations, but he never tampered with his last name. There may have been Rothschilds who were butchers, but others were lords and bankers. It was an aristocratic name. Everything else he inherited from Samson was open to the winds of revision.

In 1868, the family rented half of a modest, two-family dwelling at 124 West Twenty-seventh Street, not far from stylish Madison Square, where the best stores and restaurants were located. Some months after the Rothschilds moved to the new house, the neighboring flat was occupied by a machinist named Thomas Marston, his wife Caroline, and their three children Eliza Annie, Frank, and Susan. Henry (né Jacob) Rothschild is recorded in the census taker's book as eighteen years old. Eliza Annie Marston is nineteen. Living in the same house, seeing each other every day, they fell in love.

Even to a romantic young woman, Henry's religion must have presented an insurmountable obstacle. By the standards of both families, marriage was unthinkable. Eliza Marston had been born in 1851 into a family of highly skilled English gunsmiths. Although, in the twentieth century, certain Marstons decided that their forebears arrived on the *Mayflower*, the plain fact is that Eliza's grandparents, Stanhope and Elizabeth Marston, came to New York in the late 1830s with three children and two of Stanhope's younger brothers.

This was not a family that went its individual ways. The men worked together, sharing what amounted to an obsession with firearms, lived in neighboring streets, and named their children for each other. As early as 1853, when Eliza was two, Stanhope and his brother William already held a number of important patents and had systematically set about making themselves rivals of Colt and Deringer. The Marstons manufactured percussion pepperboxes, pistols, and revolvers at a two-floor plant on Jane Street, where they employed 140 workers. That same year their breech-loading and self-cleaning rifles, on display at the Crystal Palace Exhibition, were greatly admired by Horace Greeley, who later visited Jane Street and wrote a glowing description of the Marston arms.

If the Marston brothers had been no more than small-potatoes gunsmiths in England, they were destined to prosper in America. By the outbreak of the Civil War, they were making rifles and carbines for the government in an immense four-story factory on Second Avenue called the Phoenix Armory. To New Yorkers it was a familiar, visible landmark, too visible for the Marstons' own good. In the summer of 1863, during the draft riots, a mob of some four thousand protesters aimed straight for the armory, shattered its windows with the biggest paving stones they could find, and finally forced the doors, despite the police squads assigned to its defense. When the armory went up in flames, most employees escaped through a rear entrance, but those cut off by the fire panicked and jumped to their deaths. The Marstons rebuilt the Phoenix Armory and continued to rake in wartime profits.

Eliza's father did not distinguish himself in the family business, despite his being Stanhope's eldest son, his only son after the deaths of the two younger boys. Tom Marston worked at Phoenix Armory as nothing more than a machinist, possibly because, unlike his father and uncle, he lacked a technical gift for inventions. As a skilled laborer he earned ample wages to exist comfortably and presumably had no higher aspirations. Tom and Caroline lived modestly, perhaps even frugally. Since rents were low and concessions of a month or two free rent common, nearly every spring they would pile their household goods on a cart and shuttle the family to a new flat, never far distant from the armory. Every morning Tom walked to his job, every evening he returned to Nineteenth Street or Thirty-second Street, or whatever street they happened to be living on that particular year. When his son Frank was nearly grown, he was duly apprenticed to a printer. Whatever the Marstons' expectations for their daughters, they were not interested in a match with a German Jew. When the situation between Eliza and Henry Rothschild became too obvious to ignore, the Marstons took action to solve the problem. They moved.

. . .

Eliza Marston was a young woman of iron will and independent mind. To be a single woman sentenced to spending the rest of her life with her parents or as a spinster aunt was unimaginable. She wanted marriage, children, and a home of her own, but she decided to forgo these experiences if they were not to be shared with Henry. She found a job teaching in a public school, not a usual step in her day.

As the years passed, both Eliza's brother and sister married and departed. She remained at home with her parents, outwaiting time and opposition. The summer of 1880, when she was nearly thirty, Eliza and Henry finally married.

When Dorothy was a child, at West End and other summer resorts, she would ask new playmates, "What street do you live on?"; never, "What town do you live in?" It did not occur to her until much later that people might live elsewhere than in New York. Her favorite image of the city was seeing it in the rain, smelling with sensual pleasure the odor of wet asphalt, picturing the empty streets "black and shining as ripe olives." Other places she lived would give her a sense of serenity, but New York meant uncertainty. She never knew what was going to happen next.

No. 214 West Seventy-second Street was a four-story townhouse with striped awnings hooding the windows on the street and red roses in the backyard. A decade earlier the area had been open fields, but by 1894 it had been transformed into one of the city's most exclusive residential districts. It was bisected by a broad, tree-lined parkway layed out in the style of a Parisian boulevard and accordingly named the Boulevard (until 1901 when the avenue was renamed Broadway). Prestigious Seventy-second Street was flanked by private residences, a few august apartment houses like the Dakota, and a collection of churches designed by eminent architects. The Rothschild house stood on the south side of Seventy-second, only a few doors from its intersection with the Boulevard, a corner dominated by the Hotel St. Andrew and an elite men's club called the Colonial. Both of these immense buildings were as gaily swaddled with American flags as Fourth of July bandstands.

Dorothy was Eliza and Henry's fourth and last child, their second daughter. Harold, Bertram, and Helen were twelve, nine, and six when she was born. She later attributed her sense of estrangement from them to the age difference. Their house was spacious, but there was little room to spare with four children, Eliza's widowed father, and four or five Irish servants, the latter group apparently given to high-spirited insubordination and sudden departures. Her parents would, Dorothy said, "go down to Ellis Island and bring them, still bleeding, home to do the laundry. You know, that didn't encourage them to behave well."

If Henry had once been found undesirable as a son-in-law, he was now a prosperous gentleman, respectable and respected. Lean and strikingly good looking as a youth, he had since acquired a stomach but still cut a dashing figure with his handlebar mustache and a gold chain across his vest. He behaved like other well-to-do bourgeois. A coachman drove him to his office in the Lower Broadway business district. In the evenings he dressed for dinner and afterward might visit the Progress or Criterion clubs, where he would pass a dignified hour with brandy and cigars. He served on the board of trustees of Mount Sinai Hospital, one of his few remaining concessions to his Jewish roots. Now known as J. Henry Rothschild, he had reached a proud middle age in which the fruits of struggle and American capitalism had combined to give him his heart's desire.

Ready-to-wear cloaks—styling, producing, and selling them—were the chief passion of Henry's life. It was an extremely competitive field, more notable for bankruptcies and nervous collapses than for philosophic contemplation or the reading of great literature. Beginning as a stock clerk at a time when cloaks were still custom-tailored or imported, Henry had foreseen the possibilities of manufactured women's apparel and had associated himself while still in his twenties with the former owner of a retail cloak shop, Meyer Jonasson. The pioneering Jonasson, also a German Jew, saw no reason why fine cloaks could not be mass produced. He had need of a bold young man with ideas and energy, and in no time at all Henry was established as a partner in the firm. By the time Dorothy was born, Meyer Jonasson & Company had been a household name, the General Motors of the cloak and suit industry, for nearly fifteen years. The garment industry called J. Henry Rothschild "the greatest salesman of them all," a man whose name was synonymous with "personal magnetism, good fellowship, and loyalty to his friends."

While Jonasson and other German Jews controlled the manufacture of cloaks, they relied for labor upon tens of thousands of Jews who had emigrated from Eastern Europe in the 1880s and 1890s and settled in a half square mile on the Lower East Side. The second-generation Germans welcomed these Russian and Polish co-religionists as they would have greeted a plague. The immigrants, they believed, gave all Jews a bad name: They were filthy and diseased, had no objections to crowding ten to a room in tenements that stank of onions and urine, and were grateful to work eighty-five hours a week doing piecework for pennies. At 358 Broadway, Henry Rothschild proudly conducted out-of-town buyers through the Jonasson factory, which appeared to be a model of sanitation and employee comfort. In fact, practically none of the work was performed on the premises. It was farmed out to small contractors who operated the sweatshops where Jonasson's garments were made up by the newly arrived immigrants.

Jewish New York, by the 1890s, was a dual universe. One half was the uptown refuge of the Rothschilds, with its cheeky Irish maids and seaside houses, the other was Jewtown's Essex and Hester streets with its old-world samovars and menorahs, its rag peddlers and Pig Market, its hives of cutters, pressers, basters, finishers, and embryonic anarchists. Henry Rothschild, family legend says, had a holiday ritual. Every Christmas Eve, it was his habit to ride through the streets of the Lower East Side in his coach. In his lap lay a stack of white envelopes, each containing a crisp new ten-dollar bill. These tips he distributed to the neighborhood police officers.

Conflicts and a sense of shame persisted throughout his youngest daughter's life. Never once was she heard to refer to the invisible backdrop of her early life, the humid, steamy pressing rooms where the temperatures reached 120 degrees. It was not only her father and his Philistine friends she would disdain, it was also the whole disorderly Rothschild tribe. The aunts and uncles were dedicated wisecrackers who loved a boisterous time. At family gatherings, the table would be in an uproar—choleric Sam unable to enjoy his money; Simon, who never took a job or a woman seriously; practical Hannah, who always made sure that telegrams arrived on Dorothy's birthday; dapper Martin, having wooed and won a Catholic heiress, trying to pass for one of *those* Rothschilds; Dorothy's cousins Ethel, Harold, and Monroe. They ate and argued and laughed. They traded funny stories at the tops of their voices. Even their depressions could be apocalyptically clangorous. From another perspective, the Rothschild horseplay might be interpreted as healthy merriment. To Dorothy, her relatives were absurd, noisy figures, "silly stock" whom she shrank from acknowledging as part of her emotional geography. As an adult, she was careful to speak quietly and regally, possibly so that no one would ever mistake her for a Rothschild. She had, one of her friends remembered,

> lovely speech, a little drawl that was very attractive, very upper-class. It was finishing-school talk, but not the Brearley accent, not the West Side private-school accent, it was her own. She talked like a woman who as a little girl had attended a very good singing school. That was what made her use of the words *fuck* and *shit* so amusing, because you simply did not expect it.

Eliza Rothschild was forty-two when Dorothy was born. Seven years earlier she had put infants and feedings behind her and must have taken care to avoid another pregnancy. Approaching menopause, unhappy about growing old, she quietly subtracted three years from her age.

In the innocent world that Dorothy was born into, Grover Cleveland was president, little girls wore middies and brown stockings, little boys sailor suits. Although manners were expected of both sexes, mealtimes at the Rothschild table were often rowdy because it was a lively, affectionate family much given to laughter and activity. Dorothy, at an early age, mastered the art of spitting through her teeth, and Bert and Harry liked to dare their sisters to hold ice cream under their tongues, contests that invariably ended with the girls shrieking.

Their lives had slow, familiar rhythms. In winter they rode sleighs and drank hot chocolate. July and August were spent at the shore. None of their residences had either electricity or telephone. All housework was performed by servants, and the Rothschild girls were brought up in the expectation that people would serve them.

In 1897, their summer at West End was cut short by Thomas Marston's death. Back in the city, Eliza conferred with her lawyer and composed a will that divided her estate of fifty-two thousand dollars into four equal trust funds for the education of her children.

The following summer, when Dorothy was five, the Rothschilds looked forward to unbroken months by the sea. All day long, week after yellow week, the sun throbbed against the dunes, their world all striped into bands of pale-blue sky, crystal water, and the sand the color of straw. The band played medleys of Strauss waltzes. In mid-July Eliza fell sick with persistent diarrhea that grew worse. She also had coughing fits that left her so weak she could barely speak afterward. A Dr. Simmons was summoned to Cedar Avenue. For several days Eliza kept to her bed. A curious silence permeated the house. Even the children played quietly. On July 20, a thunderstorm clattered at the windowpanes. The children remained inside all day, restless in the silent house. Later that evening, or perhaps the next morning, Dorothy learned that Eliza had gone off to a place called "the Other Side"—terrible words to her. She was told that Eliza would not come back, but surely they would meet again, because Eliza was waiting there for Dorothy.

Dorothy screamed her head off, but Eliza did not reappear. Afterward, it occurred to her that the last sound her mother must have heard was the friendly hissing of the rain falling from the sky. That was a comfort to her because the rain always had seemed magical to Dorothy.

It rained every day the rest of that week. The family accompanied the coffin from the funeral parlor in Long Branch, across the gray water on the ferry, then uptown to the Bloomingdale Reformed Church near their house. It was still pouring on Saturday when they gathered on a muddy knoll at Woodlawn Cemetery and watched the coffin sink into the soggy ground. Due to the swiftness of Eliza's demise, an autopsy had been performed. Her death certificate gave the cause of death as "diarrhea with colic followed by weakness of the heart. Postmortem showed artery disease." As some of Dorothy's adult behavior suggests, she could never rid herself of the guilty suspicion that she somehow had caused Eliza's death.

Her mother, Dorothy said, "promptly went and died on me." Her short stories were understandably devoid of loving mothers—indeed, there is not a one in the whole lot. Hazel Morse's mother in "Big Blonde," a "hazy" woman who had died, most closely resembles her own situation with Eliza. Many of her mothers are either indifferent or actively abusive to their children. Camilla, in "Horsie," dismisses her newborn daughter with the chilling words, "Good night, useless." Fan Durant, a woman intimidated by her husband, can't prevent his disposing of the children's pet while they sleep.

Most autobiographical in Dorothy's gallery of mothers is Mrs. Matson, in "Little Curtis," who adopts a four-year-old boy for questionable motives, then treats him so sadistically that one could almost applaud matricide. In the story of young Curtis, first called "Lucky Little Curtis," Dorothy drew on her experience with the second Mrs. Rothschild.

Eleanor Frances Lewis, a retired teacher, was forty-eight, the same age as Henry Rothschild. Never married, she lived with a younger brother a dozen blocks from the Rothschilds. Coming from working-class people—her father had been an upholsterer—she had managed by thrift, hard work, and living as a maiden aunt in the homes of her brothers to accumulate a nest egg of nearly five thousand dollars, plus her investment of five shares in a teachers' building and loan association.

For Henry, Eliza's death had been a catastrophe. He alternately struggled to remember and to forget her. Finding unbearable the memories associated with the house on Seventy-second Street, he quickly sold it and moved to a rented house a half-block away, then six months later gave that up and purchased an exquisite limestone row house on West Sixty-eighth Street near Central Park. By this time, Henry had met and decided to marry Eleanor Lewis, the second Christian schoolteacher he liberated from spinsterhood. The new house symbolized his determination to build a new life for himself and to have someone care for his children. On the first business day after the start of the new century, January 3, 1900, Henry and Eleanor were married at City Hall. The bride stated that it was her first marriage. So did the groom, an unconscious mistake on Henry's part or else the clerk's pen slipped.

None of the Rothschild children liked Eleanor, and Dorothy hated her. Never would she be able to understand or forgive her father for what appeared to be his unaccountably hasty betrayal of Eliza. Harry, Bert, and Helen, now eighteen, sixteen, and thirteen, expressed their coldness by addressing their stepmother as "Mrs. Rothschild." Although she urged them to call her mother, explaining that "Mrs." hurt her feelings, they had no interest in soothing her feelings. Dorothy refused to address her at all. "I didn't call her anything. 'Hey, you,' was about the best I could do." It is not difficult to imagine the size of the problem facing the new Mrs. Rothschild. Henry, sensing his wife's frustration, bought her jewelry and groped for special ways to please her.

Henry had remarried to make a bad situation better; he had only succeeded in making matters worse, and now it seemed he could do nothing right. On Sundays, he took Eleanor and the children on excursions to the Bronx, where they visited Eliza's grave at Woodlawn. "That was his idea of a treat," said Dorothy. It was a five-minute walk from the cemetery entrance to Myrtle Plot. The moment he caught sight of the marker wreathed with its stone flowers, emotions overrode dignity, the grief came rushing back, and he would start crying. "Whenever he'd hear a crunch of gravel that meant an audience approaching, out would come the biggest handkerchief you ever saw, and in a lachrymose voice that had remarkable carrying power, he'd start wailing, 'We're all here, Eliza! I'm here. Dottie's here. Mrs. Rothschild is here—' " At these moments Dorothy hated him.

Judging by her numerous poetical references to graves, coffins, and the Dead—a term that essentially meant Eliza—the Woodlawn outings had consequences that would have astounded Henry, for they provided food for his daughter's ripening fantasies. While he blubbered and waved his hankie, she observed him and inwardly smiled to think how her mother "would laugh, could you have heard the things they said." Unlike her husband, Eliza would not permit herself, living or dead, to make a fool of herself. Dorothy imagined her with hands crossed, lying quietly underfoot in shiny wood and eavesdropping on the dramas taking place above.

When Dorothy was six, she idealized her mother. Twenty-five years later, carrying the same pictures in her head but no longer able to disguise her angry feelings, she decided the dead "do not welcome me" and furiously denounced them as "pompous."

Dorothy and her sister attended Blessed Sacrament Academy, a private parochial school run by the Sisters of Charity. Academically, it was one of the city's finest schools and had the added advantage of being located close by in a double brownstone on West Seventy-ninth Street. She walked there with one of the housemaids. She never forgot the laundry smell of the nuns' robes, the desks covered with oilcloth, Sister Dionysius's cold-eyed glances, the haughtiness of her classmates.

Helen had no trouble fitting in, but she was that sort of person. Dorothy had no intention of belonging. She referred to the Immaculate Conception, which struck her as sounding a little fishy, as "spontaneous combustion" and felt enormously pleased at having thought up the joke. She made a special effort to criticize everyone and sought reasons to find them ridiculous. "They weren't exactly your starched crinoline set, you know. Dowdyest little bunch you ever saw."

There was another girl who hated Blessed Sacrament. Mercedes de Acosta, the daughter of a wealthy Spanish-Cuban family, had a married sister who was suing her husband for divorce. The newspapers were full of sensational stories about the suit, which prompted the children at school to gossip maliciously that Rita was trying to sell her son to her husband for a million dollars. Mercedes, squaring off against her persecutors, traded taunt for taunt, in which endeavor Dorothy was only too eager to aid and abet. Before long, the nuns had cast them as the school troublemakers, parts the two scrappy little girls played with relish. Eighty years later, a student who had been three grades ahead of them at Blessed Sacrament could still remember the pair behaving so badly that their teacher suffered "a breakdown." Dorothy was reputed to be just as devilish out of school. She even invented a secret language that drove her parents very nearly out of their minds.

All day long the nuns talked about Jesus. When she arrived home from school Dorothy found Eleanor bustling right out to interrogate her.

"Did you love Jesus today?" she asked Dorothy.

Despite her piety, there must have been times when Eleanor felt like strangling the miserable brat. Instead, she admonished lucky little Dorothy to count her blessings: Didn't she have everything a child might want? Eleanor naturally was talking about herself, the lonely woman reincarnated into a prosperous man's wife and the mistress of a dream house. Even though marriage had brought unexpected miseries, precisely because it had brought them, she had to work hard to deny them and prescribed gratitude as a worthy attitude. Dorothy laughed when Eleanor turned her back, and sometimes before she had.

Dorothy did not feel lucky. Eleanor made her say prayers and lectured her about regular bowel movements. The nuns were mean, her friends few, her brothers too grown up to play with her. One day she glimpsed Harry, or else it was Bert, swaggering down the street with a friend, who pointed at her and asked, "That your sister?"

"No," her brother said.

She remembered this snub with great bitterness for the rest of her life.

After her birthday in August, there was Christmas to look forward to: working herself into a frenzy of anticipation, crossing out the days on her calendar, then finally Christmas dawn and crawling downstairs groggy with sleeplessness. But to find what? That Santa Claus and Jesus and Eleanor had remembered her with a pair of galoshes she needed anyway, a board game called Dissected Wildflowers, a copy of *Sylvia's Summer in the Holy Land*, and "a fountain pen that ceased to function after the third using."

The struggle with Eleanor had evolved into trench warfare. Dorothy found further reasons to resent her and to wish the woman dead. Her weapons were the time-honored methods of sulfurous stares, extended silences, and responses that were at best grudging. These tactics drove Eleanor into a tizzy, but they provided a kind of stability to Dorothy's life. After three years of hostilities, there came an unexpected cease-fire. She was trying to dream up more imaginative tortures when one morning in April 1903, she woke to learn that Eleanor had just fallen dead of an acute cerebral hemorrhage.

Now Dorothy had two murders on her conscience. The sudden deaths of Eliza and Eleanor became the twin traumas of her early life, her ticket to self-pity, a passe-partout to self-hatred and an unalterable conviction that she deserved punishment—the source of the negativity with which she grappled so unhappily—and so happily—thereafter. Reaffirmed was her perception of the world as a horrible place where people keeled over and died without warning. Nature had no right to be so mean. Therefore, she decided,

> There's little in taking or giving,
>   There's little in water or wine;
> This living, this living, this living
>   Was never a project of mine.

Eleanor willed various amounts to her own family and gave fifty dollars apiece to Harry, Bert, and Helen. As a final gesture to lucky little

Dorothy, she left "such articles of jewelry as have been given me by my husband since my marriage to my step-daughter Dorothy Rothschild," in the value of three hundred dollars.

After Eleanor's untimely death, the house was empty of mothers. Next came the dogs.

Chapter 2

PALIMPSEST

•

1903–1914

The Rothschilds were determined to enjoy good times. Henry, fifty-two, abandoned his lifework in the garment industry, which was changing irrevocably bit by bit. The sweatshop system slowly was expiring under the spotlight of exposés and public indignation. Increasing boldness by the cloakmakers' union threatened to send wages soaring. Henry heartily denounced these omens as violations of God's plan. When Meyer Jonasson & Company faltered, he briefly entered partnership with another cloakmaking giant, then threw up his hands altogether and switched to the comparatively sedate cigar business.

The family now lived in a large brownstone around the corner from Blessed Sacrament, everyone being haphazardly cared for by two housemaids, Annie and Mary. Dorothy's most passionate interest in life at this period was collecting pictures of Maude Adams. Once she sent the actress a letter that began "Dearest Peter," and received one of the much-coveted silver thimbles inscribed *A kiss from Peter Pan.* Then came a minor but memorable change: The Rothschilds acquired an assortment of what would become the most aggressively spoiled dogs in New York. It is impossible to overemphasize the importance of these mixed French bulldogs and Boston terriers named Rags, Nogi, and Bunk, who would be reincarnated in countless hounds throughout Dorothy's life. From the first, the family regarded this trio of equivocal breeds as humans disguised as animals, endowing them with a full complement of neuroses and then grumbling accordingly.

By this time, Dorothy's brothers and sister were almost adults. Harry and Bert worked in wholesale garment houses. Bert was engaged to a long-legged colt of a girl named Mate (nicknamed "Tiny" because of her height). As a wedding gift, Henry offered them the choice of five hundred dollars in cash or a flat; Bert and Tiny chose the apartment. Helen, too, was busily preparing to move forward into the great world. Henry's expectations for his daughters were at once conventional and reflective of his personal conception of women. Despite the tradition of female professionalism in the family, if his marrying two educated women can be called a tradition, he was certainly no believer in vocations for women. He preferred to marry superior women, which for him meant primarily Christian and only secondarily a woman with sufficient intelligence to earn a living as a teacher. (The family success story in this respect was Martin Rothschild, who had wed Elizabeth Barrett of the Great Bear Springs Water family.) For all Henry's acceptance of Eliza and Eleanor as working women, he saw himself as a kind of knight who had rescued them from the misfortunes of spinsterhood. For his daughters, he invested in first-class Catholic educations, which, he hoped, would ensure a predictable outcome: marriage into wealthy Christian families.

A sensible young woman like Helen needed no parental instructions. She zipped around on a merry-go-round of dances, picnics, and golfing parties, happily pursuing young men of suitable families, preferrably those better off than the Rothschilds. To follow any other course would have been considered self-destructive. Especially high on her list of prospects was the scion of a well-known New York baking company, whom she had met at a skating party. George Droste, Jr., did not happen to be Jewish (although he was German), but then convent-educated Helen did not really think of herself as Jewish either.

Dorothy, a bedazzled spectator, found these rites of passage spellbinding. Describing her sister a long while later, she said, "She was a real beauty, my sister; sweet, lovely, but silly." What she meant by silly she didn't bother to explain, but certainly this was not her opinion as a girl. On the contrary, she adored, admired, and envied Helen, whose undisputed good looks and popularity seemed to embody ideal womanhood, a model that Dorothy aspired to copy but secretly feared a useless endeavor.

If Helen Rothschild was exceptionally glamorous, it was, alas, all too obvious to Dorothy that her own pubescent plainness was going to remain a permanent condition. In a photograph taken at age twelve, she appears to be nine or ten. She was short for her age and thin. She achieved a final growth of four feet eleven inches and remained underweight into her twenties. To make matters worse, she had hollows under her eyes, stringy hair, poor eyesight, and the kind of listless appetite that elicited constant admonitions to eat up. Since she had a heart murmur, the Rothschilds took care to cosset her in a manner befitting a child of delicate constitution.

As early as 1905, she seems to have found a place of her own in the family: She was the artistic member. Later she liked to define herself negatively as "one of those awful children who wrote verses," but she neglected to mention that her efforts were encouraged and rewarded with enthusiastic praise. "Wonderful to say the least," Helen called the verses. Nor was the writing of poetry viewed as a charming, not very noteworthy accomplishment appropriate for a sickly female child—not at all. Henry himself loved to compose verses that he referred to as his "pomes." His favorite theme was the antics of the dogs, and even though the verses sound childish, they also are charming. His lovingly amused descriptions suggest a sort of Thurberian view of the species:

> This morning Rags near' got
> a "licking"
> 'Cause, he "kicked" at meat
> & wanted "chicking"
> But Mary pleased him
> with chicken hash
> And begged me to do nothing
> rash
>
> So once more His Lordship
> is all right
> And got the better of the
> fight
> He looks at me as much
> to say
> When Dora gets back I'll
> have my way

Not the least self-conscious, he struck off this doggerel at his office desk on the backs of sheets of Royal Company stationery and, no doubt, felt pleased with his handiwork.

The paternal portrait reflected in his verses is so greatly at variance with Dorothy's descriptions that they might be two different men. Both in his verse and in the letters exchanged between him and his daughters, he exudes warmth, humor, and generosity, and his affection for Dorothy cuts like a warm stream across the middle of her childhood. His idea of child-rearing owed little to his second wife, little perhaps to his first either. He was far from being a disciplinarian. In his household, children were indulged—in return he expected them to "get ahead." Feelings, negative as well as positive, could be spoken of openly. Eccentricities, too, appear to have been tolerated, even appreciated if they were amusing. Expression of needs was encouraged. He told them that if they ever needed money, "do not fail to ask for it," and they did not fail. He was lavish with the word *love*, fond of playful teasing, an admirer of peppery behavior, and tolerant of scenes, because he himself was given to emotional extravagance. His was, above all, a house of much laughter.

In contrast, there is Dorothy's version of reality. Her lugubrious account of a deprived childhood has a plot that plods along like a gothic novel—innocent heroine victimized by heartless father, malevolent step-mother, and a Greek chorus of batty nuns—and is largely false. This romance was doubtless a therapeutic invention that enabled her to settle old scores. Underneath lay concealed another fiction, never articulated but internalized so completely that it became an implant in her deepest self—an unloved orphan, which was how she experienced herself, must be clever and amusing in order to ensure survival in the world. Therefore, behaviors ordinarily frowned upon might very well be excused, or considered virtuous, if a person happened to be an orphan. The poor orphan from whom she learned these rules of the game was William Thackeray's antiheroine Becky Sharp.

On the verge of adolescence, acutely self-conscious, she felt there was something wrong with her, and so it was necessary to create a Dorothy Rothschild she liked better. She started by changing her handwriting, a spiky scrawl that wandered uphill and down. There began to emerge glimpses of the beautiful rounded script that would be her adult hand. Similarly, her search for a better Dorothy Rothschild made her intent on erasing everything in her makeup that she considered ugly. Her method of elimination was to write over the original by reshaping herself in the form of a fictional character whom she admired. Since the psychic wounds she had suffered as a young child could never be rubbed out, she was stuck with both images, her psyche a palimpsest of two drafts, original Dorothy and final Dorothy, the new standing shakily atop the old.

When she was eleven, she first read *Vanity Fair* and felt inspired for life: In her sixties, she claimed that she still reread Thackeray's novel "for comfort," but the only example of comfort she could cite was thrilling to the line about George Osborne "lying on his face, dead, with a bullet through his heart." Thackeray's subtitle for *Vanity Fair* was *A Novel without a Hero*, but for Dorothy it was a novel with a heroine, the exact sort of person she wanted to be. She fell upon the character of Rebecca Sharp like a long-lost alter ego. Not that Becky can be called a completely healthy model; she was in every respect an outlaw, female insubordination personified, and even Thackeray disapproved of her. Antisocial as she was, Becky proved to be an extremely healthy blueprint for Dorothy. Courageous Becky, thumb glued to her nose, was able to confront and defy adversity head-on. Her fictional experiences seemed metaphors for Dorothy's emotional experiences and, perhaps following Becky's example, Dorothy might triumph too. In effect, her identification with Becky Sharp urged her beyond those early traumas.

"They say when your writing goes up hill, you have a hopeful disposition. Guess I have," she wrote to her father in 1906, when she was yet unsure whether there was anything about which to feel hopeful. Unlike Becky, who seemed naturally built for landing on her feet, Dorothy had to struggle with crippling handicaps in developing ego strength. She was forced to learn mental toughness. Taking her own inventory at the age of thirty, she listed the three things she could count on having until she died: laughter, hope and—there was always a palimpsest memory—"a sock in the eye."

.   .   .

Her twelfth summer was the most carefree of her later childhood.

In June 1905, Helen took her to the Wyandotte Hotel in the resort town of Bellport on the south shore of Long Island, where George Droste's family had a year-round house. While not wishing to deny his daughters a summer at the shore, Henry Rothschild felt badly about the two-month separation and made them promise to alternate writing every day. They faithfully complied, Helen with fairly lengthy letters and Dorothy, more often than not, with postcards that fulfilled the letter of the agreement if not the substance. She went bathing in the cold surf, played a lot of croquet, and made excursions to East Quogue on the train and to Patchogue in the Drostes' pony cart. Nearly every day there was sailing, and once a young man from Helen's crowd who owned an automobile took Dorothy on a spin along the country roads.

Her chief anxiety was about the dogs. There was no danger of a chowhound like Rags starving himself in her absence, but she feared he might pine away and be gone when she returned. She sent him loving messages, read *St. Nicholas* magazine from cover to cover, and compiled lists of gifts she wanted for her birthday. At eight-thirty she went to bed, whispers of the dark ocean coming in through the open windows. Helen reported to their father: "The kid is fine and enjoying herself greatly— she looks well and eats a lot." Some of Helen's girlfriends were having "a horrid time" because "there are hardly any fellows here," and Helen too found Bellport "pretty slow." But Dorothy was having a splendid time.

> Dear Papa,
> We are all well and having a good time. When you send my things down, will you please send my pink and green beads. They are in my dressing-table in a "Home, sweet home" box. I hope the animals are well.
>
> > With love,
> > Dorothy

> Dear Papa,
> I received your poetic effusion about Nogi and the snowballs, and will try to see if I can do any better.

I am having a lot of fun,
Tho' my neck and arms
are burned by the sun.

Doesn't "tho' " look poetic?

Dorothy

Dear Rags,
Hope you are well and having a fine time.

Dorothy

Dear Nogi,
Ditto.

Dorothy

Dear Papa,
Bert and Tiny arrived last night. They brought me some Cailler's chocolate, which was very nice of them, only I hate it. But they didn't know I hated it, so it was very nice of them, after all.

I hope that Nogi and Rags are well. Please remember me to Harry, Mary and Annie.

With love,
Dorothy

Her father wrote to her:

Say, Miss Dorothy, will you kindly tell
If the "Push" at Bellport are all well
All well here—but a little sad
Your coming home will make all glad
Rags and Bunk have got the blues
As they seek in vain for your little (2) shoes

All day, too, nothing but rain
Enough to give everybody a pain
We are all saving for to pay
For beautiful things for your birthday

A Postscript—for I forgot
To send my love to the whole lot

Rags is fine, he is all right
His behavior is "out of sight"
And as he walks along the floor
He too wishes the summer o'er
Mary now is his only chum
But what he wants is Dora "the Bum"

You seem always able to please him
And unlike Helen do not tease him
I scolded him for calling you "Bum"
But he winked his eye
As he ate his pie
And he said—"I wish she were 'hum' "

For her twelfth birthday Helen threw a party on the Wyandotte lawn
and invited fifteen young ladies. By Dorothy's exact account of the affair,
they played croquet, then had their pictures taken. There is a faded photograph of the group posing under enormous trees. Dorothy, skinny, is
dressed in white blouse and dark tie, her hair pulled back and tied at the
base of her neck, and she looks solemn. After the cake and ice cream, they
played Blindman's Buff and Cops and Robbers for the rest of the afternoon.
She was extremely pleased with the light blue beads Henry had sent, also
with the books and the bead loom. She politely thanked Bert for his dollar
and poem. "One came in handy, and the other was very good," she wrote
to her father.

The next summer, she and Helen were back at Bellport, at the white
hotel with its tall gateway that spelled out WYANDOTTE in wrought-iron
filigree. This time, though, the days seemed endless and sultry—"It's
terribly hot here," she complained. The boats still bobbed like toys at the
end of the Wyandotte dock, the plumy oaks still arched a dark canopy over
Rector Avenue, the corn fritters and chicken sandwiches still tasted better
than at home, but she mentioned no playmates, no parties.

Her sister was madly in love and sometime during the summer became
engaged to George Droste. He was twenty-three years old, conspicuously
good-looking, and determined to enjoy life. (Their daughter Lel, putting the

matter kindly, would describe him as a professional playboy, who never worked at much of anything but once broke his leg doing a legendary high kick at a party.)

Helen owned a camera. In her photo album unfold page after page of laughing young women in long white dresses and slim, elegant youths in knickerbockers and straw boaters tilted gaily on their heads. After eighty years, the browning snapshots do not dull the brightness of those summer vistas, the weedy meadows and the sand bleached white against the black water. Dorothy, who naturally was excluded from the romantic outings and from the polkas at the Saturday night dances, had other activities to keep her occupied. Entering a dress-up contest for the best advertisement looka-like, she won a vase that she described to her father as "awfully pretty," but because her tone suggests that it was hideous, she saw no point mention-ing the costume that had merited it. From the first, her letters sounded a bit homesick and more than a bit wistful.

> Dear Papa,
>
> This morning I received
>   your "pome."
> How did you do it
>   all alone?
> When you come down
>   on Sunday, Pa,
> No, nothing rhymes
>   except cigar.
>
> Well, I must tell
>   you, anyway
> Bring down St. Nich'las'
>   next Sunday.
> This "pome" looks "kinder
>   good to me."
> With love to Rags
>   from Dorothy.

In practically every one of the three dozen letters and cards to him, she wondered "how is Rags?" and assured her father that she felt "well" and was enjoying "a good time," but there was nothing to suggest she was. The exuberance of the previous year was missing. Left to her own devices, she moped around and spent many solitary afternoons on the Wyandotte's cool verandah, reading and thinking. Her father expected her to have "a good time." Clearly she had no wish to disappoint him. But just as clearly, 1906 was Helen's big summer.

By the fall of 1907, the Rothschilds were scattered. Helen was married, and Bert and Tiny were occupied with their baby son. Dorothy, now fourteen, was eager for adventures of her own. In September, she enrolled in a boarding school, Miss Dana's, thirty miles away in Morristown, New Jersey. One of George Droste's younger sisters was a student at Miss Dana's.

The overwhelming majority of Dana students were Episcopalians and Presbyterians, a few were Roman Catholics, but none were Jews. Henry solved the problem of admissions with a decisive lie. Dorothy's records indicate that her parents attended the Episcopal church.

In a blitzkrieg preparation, Mary and Annie were set to rounding up the required articles, including a golf cape and a hot-water bottle, and laboriously marking each item with Dorothy's full name. Despite an admirable curriculum, the school did nothing to contradict Dorothy's secret belief that she was an outsider. The typical Dana girl, Dorothy was to write, "was congenitally equipped with a restfully uninquiring mind," and in years to come she claimed to be able to spot a Dana graduate a block away by her "general air, no matter how glorious the weather, of being dressed in expectation of heavy rains." Dorothy took courses in algebra, Greek and American history, French, Latin, physiology, and advanced English. Her best marks were in Bible study and piano, her worst in gym. The fact that she received A's in deportment provides the only clue to the Teutonic principles of discipline practiced at the school.

At the end of the following March, she stopped attending classes. Whether this was due to illness or to some other cause, the records give no clue. She failed to return to Miss Dana's in the fall of 1908, nor did she matriculate in any other school. At age fourteen her education ended, abruptly and inexplicably. As an adult, upon request only, she would list her educational credits as Blessed Sacrament and Miss Dana's, careful not to specify that she had graduated from neither. In the company of close friends she was quick to bury the subject with a joke and say that she had "carried the daisy chain in the college of hard knocks." It was her best camouflaged deprivation. The sole time she publicly alluded to the fact that she never finished high school was when she remarked to a newspaper reporter while a visiting professor at California State College, "Because of circumstances, I didn't finish high school. But, by God, I read."

Dorothy and her father migrated from the luxurious Red House on Riverside Drive to Amsterdam Avenue and then to a somewhat less distinguished building on West Eightieth Street. Of all the Rothschild children, she alone remained with Henry and provided the companionship he required. To Dorothy at fourteen, this cloistral arrangement must have seemed natural, but by the age of twenty it had grown exceptionally deadening. There was not a sign of the personal autonomy that became her trademark. She found herself in the unenviable position of a caretaker who is totally dependent on her charge.

In the summers, she and Henry visited Helen at Bellport, but more often they spent endless, boring weeks at resort hotels in Connecticut, which Henry seemed to enjoy. Retired by 1910, he fussed over his investments, some of which would prove to be unwise. He suffered from heart disease and secondarily from chronic worry about Dorothy's oldest brother. Harry, unlike Bert, was not much interested in "getting ahead" and didn't give two cents about keeping jobs. Whenever Henry got him one, he would manage to get fired. Irresponsible about spending money, lacking self-control, he was the object of Henry's scorn, the target of his cajoling and bullying, an errant boy-man whom he felt compelled to rescue time after time. No sooner had Bert and Tiny married than Harry told his father to go jump in the lake and finally left home—he was twenty-five—and went to live with them. Subsequently he vanished altogether and was remembered in family legend as "the black sheep" who most likely had gone to the bad.

The spring of 1911 began a wrenching year. Dorothy's Uncle Sam, long subject to problems with his nerves, became insane and had to be committed to a sanatorium, where he soon died. Six months later, Hannah Rothschild Theobald died suddenly of a cerebral hemorrhage at the age of fifty. Then, in the winter of 1912, Martin and Lizzie Rothschild went abroad for a holiday and stayed on until April. The couple, who had remained childless, liked to live in lavish high style. As befitted persons of consequence, they had booked for their return trip first-class passages on the maiden voyage of the world's most luxurious steamship. On the fifth night after leaving Southampton, the *Titanic* struck an iceberg.

On the first lists to be posted, Lizzie Rothschild was noted as saved, but Lord [*sic*] Martin Rothschild's name appeared on neither the safe nor the known-dead lists. Henry clung to hope. The following evening, in drenching rain, he stood at pier 54 as the *Carpathia* was being moored; the gangplank lowered and the first of the seven hundred survivors (out of two thousand passengers) began to straggle down. There at last was a dazed Lizzie in her fur coat, but no Martin. Her husband, she told them, had escorted her to a lifeboat and then stayed behind on the boat deck. For two hours she had bobbed about under the stars, watching while the *Titanic* slipped lower in the water, then upended and glided beneath the surface. When the *Carpathia* had appeared in the gray light of dawn, she had climbed up its swinging ladder and collapsed on the deck. For several hours the *Carpathia* had searched for small boats among the icebergs, but Lizzie had known it would be useless. Martin, she said, was at the bottom of the ocean.

Henry was only sixty when the *Titanic* sank, but Martin's death triggered a state of decline in him, leaving him full of dismal thoughts about how swiftly his family had flickered out. Now he acted feeble beyond his actual years and expected everyone to fetch and carry for him, unaware that he was being burdensome. The most important person in his life became Dorothy, who had patiently to bear the brunt of his petulance day after day. She was unable to make Helen and Bert understand that she was nearly twenty and expected more from life. Henry continued to make sentimental pilgrimages to the Lower East Side, never failing to show up at Christmas to distribute holiday tips, and he liked to take along Helen's small son, Bill. By the end of 1913, he was keeping to the apartment and at Christmas lacked the energy to visit the old neighborhood—too bitter cold to be gadding about just to hand out a few dollars. On Christmas Eve he felt so poorly that the doctor had to be sent for. Three nights later, he died of a heart attack.

The New York Times obituary that credited J. Henry Rothschild as a pioneer of the wholesale cloak and suit industry would have pleased this son of a fancy-goods peddler. To his funeral came former colleagues, his club friends, and board members from Mount Sinai Hospital. He was laid alongside Eliza in Woodlawn Cemetery, where his unornamented stone seems carelessly chosen next to his wife's.

New York in 1914 was gripped by dance fever. In restaurants and tea-rooms, even in cafeterias, people were tangoing and Castle-walking. At home they rolled back the rugs and turkey-trotted to phonograph records. For those eager to learn the syncopated dances, newspapers published diagrams of the latest steps, and schools began to spring up all around the city. It was at one of these dance schools that Dorothy Rothschild found employment with the only moneymaking skill she possessed—playing the piano. She purchased quantities of sheet music and practiced "The Floradora Glide" and "Everybody's Doin' It (Doin' What, Turkey Trot)." She also had to master the various steps because the school expected her to help out with student instruction. Working at a dance school scarcely seemed like a respectable occupation for a gentlewoman—that year the Yale prom forbade the tango—but she didn't care whether people approved or not.

"After my father died, there wasn't any money. I had to work, you see. . . ." This was Dorothy in her favorite role: orphan vulnerable to the indignities of an unjust world. Then, as later, she enjoyed thinking of herself as poor. It seems probable that much of Henry's fortune had melted through speculations, but it was unlikely he had left her penniless. What he did leave is a mystery because the New York Surrogate Court has no record of either will or intestate proceedings.

Abruptly the old life vanished. The apartment she had shared with her father was given up, its contents sold or dispersed to Bert and Helen. There were some lovely crystal glasses that Helen wished to keep. She considered it important to save family photographs and letters and the verses written by her father and sister. Dorothy had no interest in artifacts from her first twenty years.

The first months after her father's death she must have lived with her brother—or else Helen and George took her in. Neither situation would have been to her liking, because Bert and Tiny had a particularly lively six-year-old son and an obnoxious parrot who flew free about the apartment. Though Helen had no parrot, she did have a five-year-old boy and a husband whom Dorothy considered to be "the most horrible, disgusting, outrageous German, the worst kind of German." Any extended stay with her relatives would have been intolerable.

She spent the summer of 1914 at the dance school, not unhappily, for the job was fun and she met plenty of new people. At the same time that she was memorizing song hits, she was also trying to write the light verses that were immensely popular before the war. When she subsequently admitted that she had "fallen" into writing, it was strictly the truth. There was a good reason she never planned to become a writer, but rather blundered into it. She regarded poetry and fiction as literature, a serious business requiring special gifts. Her self-view had always been constricted and her concept of her abilities even more limited, although her fantasies would always be grandiose. She invented herself as a writer as she went along. At this age, she had a keen interest in the theater. She said she had been stagestruck and had entertained vague theatrical ambitions, but what shape these might have taken she never made plain, perhaps had not imagined herself. As for verses, they did not qualify as genuine writing. If her father could do them, couldn't anybody?

Beyond the fact that her rhymes had been a means of pleasing him, she now wrote because it was fun and because everybody seemed to be doing "very nice light verse." She was careful about rhyming the first and third lines of quatrains and fussed over masculine and feminine endings. Such work "didn't do any harm, and it was work that didn't roughen our hands or your mind; just as you can say of knitting," which she also enjoyed. All the New York papers (and in 1914 there were more than a dozen) published light verse, but the Mount Everest of verse publishers was the *New York Tribune*, where Franklin Pierce Adams conducted a column called The Conning Tower. F.P.A. printed only the wittiest contributions and never paid a penny for any of them. It was considered a great honor to be published anonymously by Adams and to receive an invitation to his annual dinner, where he bestowed a gold watch on the poet he most admired.

There is no way of knowing how many submissions Dorothy made to The Conning Tower, *The Saturday Evening Post*, to all the likely markets, and how many rejections she received. Her typical subjects epitomized trivia: wrong telephone numbers, bloopers made at the bridge table, the pros and cons of nutmeg in rice pudding. In late 1914, she wrote a poem that poked fun at married women summering at resort hotels, those same hotels where she had stayed with Helen and later with her father. She had quietly and contemptuously observed the upper-middle-class matrons, imprisoned in their banalities and self-righteous bigotries. All the long summer afternoons, fixtures on shady hotel porches, they had chattered about the same diets, the same servants, the same unexamined frustrations. In winter, these women transferred their perorations and fancy sewing to city parlors, where they served tea and peppermint creams and triangular sandwiches made from the remains of last night's chicken. Again and again in her writing Dorothy would return to these women, and for good reason. She feared becoming one of them.

> "My husband says, often, 'Elise,
>   You feel things too deeply, you do—' "
> "Yes, forty a month, if you please,
>   Oh, servants impose on *me*, too."

> "I don't want the vote for myself,
>   But women with property, dear—"
> "I think the poor girl's on the shelf,
>   She's talking about her 'career.' "

Her rapid interleaving of colloquial fragments was an original and amusing technique, but such parallelisms allowed for little progression of ideas, and the nine individual stanzas in "Any Porch," despite their bite, soon grew repetitious. Nonetheless, she had nothing to lose by sending it to the new Condé Nast magazine, *Vanity Fair*.

One morning the mail brought a letter of acceptance and a check for twelve dollars. She dressed up in her best suit and hat and splashed herself with cologne. By the time she reached *Vanity Fair* and marched into the office of editor Frank Crowninshield, she had picked up an impressive head of steam. She told him:

"Any Porch" was "the first thing" she had ever written.

Her father had died just "a month or two" earlier. She was an orphan.

She was working at a dance school, even though she lacked "the faintest idea" how to teach, couldn't distinguish the lame duck from the bunny hug, and was expecting to be fired any day.

She was "tiring" of a musical career, which she had learned was not a bowl of cherries.

"A literary life" would suit her far better.

Could Mr. Crowninshield give her a job?

Crownie, as he was called, who had come from a distinguished New England family and spent his youth abroad, was one of the most notorious snobs in New York. People seldom found this an offensive quality in him, for he was full of seeming modesty and charming self-deprecations. He was a gentleman of wit and urbanity—tall and slender with an elegant mustache, watchful brown eyes, and a carnation in his buttonhole. Never had he touched alcohol or tobacco or had a sexual relationship with a woman to anyone's knowledge (although he had no objections to others' indulging), and he scorned modern conveniences such as telephone directories, saying of someone, "But how will we ever get in touch with him? He's not in the Social Register." When Crownie needed to hire secretaries, he never inquired about typing and shorthand skills; what mattered to him was that a woman be well-bred and come from a "good" family. Sizing up Dorothy, he must have been impressed because he gave her an enigmatic smile and promised to keep her in mind; for what he did not say.

Her stratagem unsuccessful, she continued to work at the dance school. A few months later, Crownie informed her that there was a position open on the staff of *Vogue*, *Vanity Fair*'s sister magazine, at a salary of ten dollars a week. It was her chance and she took it.

Her father had once written a poem that told her of a brightly lit place.

> If to your Papa you are good
> You shall have both clothes and food
> You shall live on milk and honey
> And never know the need of money

Hadn't she been good to Papa? And now see what had happened: His fantastical paradise of milk and honey was going to be hers. She tentatively inaugurated her new freedom by moving into a boardinghouse at 103rd

Street and Broadway, a location that lay precisely equidistant between Bert's apartment and Helen's. For eight dollars a week, she received a room the size of a pantry and two meals—and the idea that perhaps she could become a famous writer.

"I thought," she said, "I was Edith Sitwell."

This was her turning point. With the sale of "Any Porch" to *Vanity Fair*, she passed out of her father's refracted world and stepped onto the stage of the real Vanity Fair, where all wares seemed to be for sale, all trophies inevitable, all her silvered daydreams made real.

Chapter 3

VANITY FAIR

•

1915–1919

It was easier for a camel to navigate a needle's eye than for an ambitious woman to achieve literary grandeur on *Vogue,* which had precious little interest in nurturing another Edith Sitwell. All the magazine needed for its copy department was a person sufficiently familiar with the English language to spell decently and write picture captions. Since *Vogue*'s fortnightly issues were overstuffed with photos and pattern illustrations, there was always a stack of art waiting for captions.

At first Dorothy felt thrilled to be working there. For a page of underwear she chose a line from Shakespeare, "Brevity is the soul of wit," to which she applied a fashionable twist: "From these foundations of the autumn wardrobe, one may learn that brevity is the soul of lingerie." Producing this drivel proved to be a tedious, thankless task. Before long she lost her determination to sound literary and tried to relieve her frustration as best she could. She took one look at a photograph of a model wearing a tarted-up but very expensive nightgown that seemed meant for a courtesan and decided to tweak the noses of both *Vogue* and its readers. This time she borrowed from a nursery rhyme: "There was a little girl who had a little curl, right in the middle of her forehead. When she was good she was very very good, and when she was bad she wore this divine nightdress of rose-colored mousseline de soie, trimmed with frothy Valenciennes lace." To presume that *Vogue* readers might be having sex was surely an idea to set Palm Beach and Newport reeling. Dorothy was able to breeze her prose past the copy desk. Only at the last moment, in proofs, did someone catch and exterminate the subversive caption.

Edna Woolman Chase, the editor of *Vogue*, remembered Dorothy as "a small, dark-haired pixie, treacle-sweet of tongue but vinegar witted," whose carryings-on created disturbances in the office. Mrs. Chase reigned over her staff in much the same way as Catherine the Great ruled Russia. An autocrat, she insisted that employees appear for work in hats, white gloves, and black silk stockings, even though she was the world's biggest tightwad when it came to salaries. Idleness, and that included personal conversations during business hours, was forbidden. Her standards for conduct were rigorous. When an editor once tried to kill herself by diving in front of a subway train, Edna Chase was pained by her vulgarity. If a *Vogue* editor was forced to resort to suicide, she should have enough sense to swallow sleeping powders instead of leaving messes for the city sanitation department.

Since Dorothy always had a compulsion to bite the hand that fed her, the magazine soon became a natural target for her sarcasm. She ridiculed the office paintings, its marble tables and raw silk curtains, the uniformed maid who tiptoed around dusting desks and arranging fresh flowers. The book cases in the plush reception area contained fake books, she discovered, and later she described the waiting room as looking like the entrance to a whorehouse. In the women's washroom she paid close attention to conversations, which she later recounted to Frank Crowninshield. "To whom should one properly address oneself for towels?" And: "How *could* Mrs. Astor think chinchilla appropriate for mourning?"

The magazine kept her busy. In addition to writing captions she also was responsible for proofreading and fact-checking. Sometimes it would be six o'clock before she left the office and headed uptown to her rooming house, where she had grown friendly with several of the male lodgers. One of them was Thorne Smith, the future humorist and author of *Topper* who was at this time working as an advertising copywriter. In the winter of 1916, notable for the lowest temperatures within memory, Dorothy and her new friends would troop upstairs after supper and keep themselves amused. "We used to sit around in the evening and talk. There was no money but Jesus we had fun."

In the meantime she continued to submit verses to *Vanity Fair*, whose offices were conveniently located on the same floor so that she could easily stroll past Crowninshield's desk and drop off her latest effort. That nothing met his standards is clear because the single poem he did publish during this period, "A Musical Comedy Thought," is not especially good. Then she decided to take a plunge into free verse and came up with a concept that Crownie found exceptionally clever. "Women: A Hate Song" opened with a startling declaration: "I hate Women. They get on my Nerves."

It happened to be true. She much preferred the company of men. If being one of the fellows was pleasant, being the only female among males was her ideal situation. Since she had a gift for evisceration, "Women: A Hate Song" enabled her to enjoy an orgy, happily lashing all the women she had never been able to stand. Those she hated most virulently were the ones who sewed their own clothing, the ones who scanned the newspapers for recipes and were forever telling her that they had to hurry home to see about dinner. "Oh," she exploded, "how I hate that kind of woman." By the sixth stanza she had managed to make mashed potatoes out of nearly every female alive in 1916 except Dorothy Rothschild. Crowninshield suggested that she sign the poem with the pseudonym "Henriette Rousseau."

If the anthem of hate allowed her to abuse women, her next contribution to *Vanity Fair* was a truculent article that revealed equal scorn for the other sex. In "Why I Haven't Married," published later that year, she gleefully carved up the males she had dated, denounced them as idiots, and claimed they were the reasons she remained unwed. If these truly were representative of the men she had encountered, her feelings are easy to understand. There was a classic chauvinist who thought women belonged at home—hardly anyone in 1916 believed they didn't—a Greenwich Village radical, and a lush in whose affections she would always rate third, after "first and second, Haig and Haig." After skewering half a dozen men with the collective appeal of a dish of boiled turnips, she went on to present a final portrait, one of special interest because he was the only man to merit her praise. Paul, extolled as a "Vanished Dream," she judged to have the makings of an ideal husband. He was utterly confectionary, "an English-tailored Greek God, just masterful enough to be entertaining, just wicked enough to be exciting, just clever enough to be a good audience." In a moment of absentmindedness, however, this bonbon had married "a blonde and rounded person whose walk in life was upon the runway at the Winter Garden." The smitten Dorothy assured *Vanity Fair* readers that she would never get over the loss of this sublime creature.

In reality, the impeccably dressed god had not married a chorine at all. He was an eligible bachelor. Having only recently made his acquaintance and still feeling awed, she could not predict what he might do. She was merely sure of what he was not likely to do, and that was to marry her.

During the summer of 1916, drawn as always to those ubiquitous hotel verandahs, she had spent her vacation in Branford, Connecticut. It was at a hotel there that she had met and fallen in love with the unobtainable—or so she assumed. Sexually, her basic taste ran to men who were exceptionally good-looking but who were, if not exactly dumbbells, at least her intellectual inferiors, the male equivalent of the beautiful show girl to whom she had married off her god in the pages of *Vanity Fair.* Tall, slender, and blond, he was as pretty as some picture-book prince. He dressed well, as princes are wont to do. Of course princes also are apt to be dullards, but this man had demonstrated a capacity for wicked behavior, and he also seemed clever and entertaining. While he did not appear indifferent toward her, there were other women pursuing him and he naturally was busy playing the field. Dorothy began to prepare herself for rejection.

Edwin Pond Parker II was twenty-three and worked as a stockbroker at Paine Webber. He came from Hartford and had been in New York only long enough to establish himself in Wall Street, the beginning of a promising and substantial career.

He was a descendant in the ninth generation of William Parker, who had arrived in Hartford from England in 1636. The ministry became the Parker family's profession, although the Ponds also were clergymen. Ed Parker's grandfather, the Reverend Edwin Pond Parker, had been pastor of the Second Church of Christ in Hartford for nearly sixty years. He was not only the state's leading Protestant clergyman and one of Hartford's most distinguished citizens, but also he was a magisterial and dominating presence in his own family. Ed's father, Harris, had declined to enter the ministerial path, instead choosing the sporting goods business, but people in Hartford continued to associate the Parkers with Congregational clergy and to recognize the house on South Beacon Street as the old reverend's residence. The weight of all this had shaped young Ed Parker into a galloping atheist and something of a rebel.

At Branford, he was quick to poke fun at his pious Parker and Pond forebears, whom he derided as fanatics who most likely had burned their share of witches. Dorothy, sensing his scorn for religion and God, impulsively confessed that her family had been Jews, information that Ed Parker promptly dismissed as irrelevant. He could not imagine why it concerned her.

Aside from his disdainful attitude toward the church, he had a wild streak that proved irresistible to Dorothy. In an autobiographical story, she would recall their courtship:

> She liked him immediately. . . . She was enormously amused at his fast, slurred sentences, his interpretations of apt phrases from vaudeville acts and comic strips; she thrilled at the feel of his lean arm tucked firm beneath the sleeve of her coat; she wanted to touch the wet, flat surface of his hair. He was as promptly drawn to her.

She began calling him Eddie; he called her Dear.

In the city, they soon fell into the habit of spending their evenings together, and now her friends at the rooming house saw little of her. Eddie was fond of the theater, not the serious dramas she enjoyed but musicals that offered bevies of scantily dressed beauties. Since he had money, they inevitably wound up dining and drinking at expensive restaurants. She did most of the dining; he did all of the drinking. In fact, he drank hugely, steadily, which brought no objections from her because she noticed that the more he drank the funnier he got. His drinking amused her, and she treated his repeated references to hangovers as jokes because he never appeared really ill, only unsteady on his feet. What she liked best about him was his exhilaration, a cockiness that she chose to interpret as a sign of health and energy.

She hated the taste of liquor herself and refused to touch it.

During that fall and winter, she freely poured into Edwin Parker her whole self, all the love she had to give. Even though their involvement continued to deepen, she was far from convinced that anything serious would come of it. As a love-starved and insecure young woman, she over-looked defects in a man she judged her superior because her attention was focused on her own shortcomings. Since he possessed physical beauty and an impressive pedigree, the sense of myopia unavoidably deepened. Eddie, in contrast to other men she had met, professed to admire independent women who were able to hold jobs and look after themselves. Never did he speak of incarcerating a wife in a suburban backwater, nor could she imagine him sitting before a fire on a wintry evening reading aloud from "The Song of Hiawatha." On the contrary, he was always ready to raise hell and tear up the town.

Nevertheless, she took care to minimize her professional ambitions around him for fear of disturbing his masculine sensibilities. She also continued to feel uneasy about his family, especially his grandfather. That he made fun of the Parkers made no difference. If these patricians ever learned of her Jewishness, she could just imagine their dismay, how quickly they would snatch him back to their black-robed bosoms.

Many years later, in a hard mood, she told friends that she had wanted to marry Eddie because he had a nice, clean name. The people to whom she made this admission were Jewish; while they loved her enough not to take offense, they could not help lifting their eyebrows: Did she think *their* names were unclean? It was not a comparable situation at all, she protested, because their Jewish names sounded acceptable in some inexplicable way that Rothschild did not.

The truth was that in 1916 her desire for independence evaporated, along with her fantasy of becoming Edith Sitwell, and she longed to be a wife like all the other women she knew. Making bright conversation with her boardinghouse comrades had grown exhausting and she realized for the first time that it required effort to be a good sport with men. All she wanted was to be alone with Eddie, as if he and he only was the remedy for her maladies. She began to see marriage breaking on her horizon like a rainbow that promised sunlight and safety.

Though it was true that she detested the name Rothschild, Eddie's name would have meant nothing to her had it not been attached to a man she adored. Edwin Pond Parker II resembled a package encased in shiny wrappings. At twenty-three, dazzled and in love, she did not pause to wonder very much about its contents.

In the spring of 1917 the future resolved itself. On April 2, President Woodrow Wilson, reelected five months earlier on promises to keep the country out of war, delivered a war message to a joint session of Congress and received a standing ovation. Immediately Eddie Parker began to talk about enlisting, although the idea of killing anyone, even a German, made him uncomfortable. He planned to volunteer as an ambulance driver. No sooner did he make this decision than he asked Dorothy to marry him. Under the circumstances, it seemed like the sensible thing to do.

Some time that spring he escorted her to Hartford to meet his family. Dora and Harris Parker were polite to her, as were Eddie's little brother Harris, Jr., and his sister Ruth, herself recently engaged and preparing for her wedding. Despite their cordiality, Dorothy was quick to notice that they were treating her like a New York Jew on the make, an outsider with stylish suits and advanced ideas about careers for women. They had an endless supply of unflattering remarks to make about her hometown, telling her that they visited New York once or twice a year but were always glad to get home because they wouldn't live down there if Dorothy gave them the place. They guessed she was pretty happy to get away for a few days. They further put her in her place by raving about the Reverend Parker, a real author who had written countless books and hymns and frequently lectured on literary topics. The Reverend Parker, she learned, was an intimate friend of Samuel Clemens.

Having cemented a cool smile to her lips, Dorothy struggled to keep from strangling on her indignation. At last, Eddie's eighty-one-year-old grandfather appeared to inspect her. After arriving at his son's house on Evergreen Avenue on the arm of his second wife, Laura, he called the family into the parlor for prayers. Dorothy's head was bowed when she heard him intone, "Oh Lord, grant to the unbeliever in our midst the light to see the error of her ways. . . ." In the next breath he referred to her as "a stranger within our gates." Stupefied at his mean spirit, she was harshly reminded of the chasm separating New England Congregational pulpits and the Lower East Side sweatshops. If she had felt no harmony with the Jews, it was now clear that she had even less in common with these Hartford Brahmins, "toadying, in sing-song, to a crabbed god."

In the following weeks, she hid her rage by making fun of the Parkers and by clinging ever more tightly to Eddie. Her questions became relentless: Did he love her? Did he understand how truly she loved him? how sadly she would miss him? His responses seldom satisfied her. Since he was planning to marry her, he failed to understand what further proof of his love she wanted.

On the last day of June 1917, they were married in Yonkers, New

41

York, a small city in suburban Westchester County. On the marriage license application, Eddie listed his occupation as stockbroker and Dorothy gave hers as "none." In view of their antagonism toward religion, it is interesting that they observed the usual sacraments. A Reverend J. M. Ericsson performed the ceremony before three witnesses, obliging strangers whom the minister had hastily rounded up. After her humiliating treatment by the Parkers, she refused to have them at her wedding. No Rothschild was present either, nor did she and Eddie invite any of their friends. Soon afterward he joined the 33rd Ambulance Corps, 4th Division, and departed for Summit, New Jersey. One can imagine how disoriented Dorothy must have felt: She had been a bride "for about five minutes" before her husband had gone off and she found herself alone again.

Even before Eddie left, Dorothy had begun developing herself as a writer. Her earliest journalism, while written in the first person, was rooted almost entirely in what she, or her editors, hoped would sell rather than in her own experiences or memories. With her gift for making clever observations, she was able to tell a kind of truth but it was not uniquely hers. *Vanity Fair* had asked for several more free-verse hate songs—she attacked relatives, actresses, and men—and Edna Chase had agreed to try her as a special-features writer. One of her articles dealt with fashionable breeds of dogs, other pieces covered home decoration, hair and beauty care, knitting, and weddings, themes that have always been the staple fare of fashion magazines. Dorothy's treatment of these subjects was unusual because she played with them and invariably wound up mocking them. When she wrote about interior decoration, recklessly titling the piece "Interior Desecration," she made people furious. Chase never forgot that "more than one decorator swallowed hard and counted ten before expressing his feelings about it." The flak resulted less from Dorothy's cynical observations about furnishings than from her offensive portrait of an hysterical and unmistakably homosexual decorator. Mrs. Chase, who apparently had not thought to question the article prior to publication, was not amused.

Whenever *Vogue* needed a guinea pig, Dorothy volunteered. She tested beauty preparations, diets, and exercise regimens, and she agreed to submit her head to a permanent wave at a time when such procedures were still hazardous. Chase had to admit that getting the permanent had taken "rare courage," but it was also clear that Dorothy was developing into a problem writer.

At *Vanity Fair*, Frank Crowninshield could not help noticing Dorothy's work, and he also must have realized that she was training herself to write the Frank Crowninshield genre. This called for, above all, a good sense of what was clever and entertaining. The formula, subsequently summed up by Robert Benchley as the Elevated Eyebrow School of Journalism, was by no means simple to master. You could write about practically any subject you wished, no matter how outrageous, so long as you said it in evening clothes. Crownie had no objection to serious topics and would publish, for example, a report on the Russian Revolution, but it had to be showered with references to debutante dinners, Grolier bindings, and French literature, then adorned with drawings by his favorite illustrator, Fish. Finally, it would be sandwiched between a survey of the polo season and "How to Be Idle Though Rich," but at least it would be published.

In some ways the Frank Crowninshield genre was more china-painting than writing. It took Dorothy only a few months to get the hang of Crownie's style. Then she spent the next decade trying to unlearn it.

Unlike *Vogue*, *Vanity Fair* seemed more like a playpen than an editorial office. Visitors had been known to whistle, throw paper darts, and play charades. Crowninshield proudly likened his private office to "a combined club, vocal studio, crap game, dance-hall, sleeping lounge, and snack bar," and it was apparent that the magazine flourished on chaos. *Vanity Fair*, barely four years old, had already become publishing's most fabulous success story, a financial winner that carried more advertising than any other monthly with page after glossy page of Rolls-Royces, diamond necklaces, and other gewgaws for the conspicuously wealthy. Crownie, however, could not have cared less about advertisers. His dedication was to the theater—and to painting, literature, dance, poetry, music, and satire—and he was as obsessive about exploration as Henry the Navigator was, fervently cruising the capitals of Europe and the drawing rooms of Southampton to seek out the most heretical work being done. When he had unearthed a work he feared too esoteric, he would tell his staff, "Remember, there's an old lady sitting in Dubuque, and she has to be able to understand everything we print," but he was the first to ignore this old publishing cliché. To the American public he would introduce a long line of innovators, from Picasso and Matisse and Beaton to Colette, Huxley, and Millay. Dorothy was determined to enter this exciting, elite club.

From their first meeting, Crowninshield had been immensely taken with Dorothy and his admiration had continued to grow. He would describe her as wearing

> horn-rimmed eyeglasses, which she removed quickly if anyone spoke to her suddenly. She had, too—perhaps the result of nervousness—a habit of blinking and fluttering her eyelids. She had a fondness for *Chypre*, as a perfume, and for flat-heeled shoes, sometimes for black patent leather pumps with black bows, She walked, whatever her shoes might be, with short, quick steps. Her suits, in the winter, at any rate, were tailor-made. Her hats were large and turned up at the brim. Green, as a colour, seemed to appeal to her greatly, whether in a dress, hat, or scarf.

More important, seldom had he encountered anyone, man or woman, with so sharp a tongue and so keen a sense of mockery. Even though she could be difficult, this was to be expected in such an excessively opinionated person. He concluded that "her peceptions were so sure, her judgment so unerring, that she always seemed to hit the centre of the mark."

In the fall of 1917, after she had been slaving in Edna Chase's kingdom for two and a half years, Crowninshield arranged for Dorothy's transfer to *Vanity Fair*, noting that Chase had "turned her over to my tender care" as if she was a sickly moppet. He forgot to add that Edna Chase was by no means unhappy to be rid of someone who showed signs of developing into a genuine enfant terrible.

The next few months, having no idea what to do with Dorothy, Crowninshield gave her routine editorial tasks and also published several more of her hate songs. At the end of the year, he had a daring idea. P. G. "Plum" Wodehouse, the magazine's drama critic, had coauthored a hit musical comedy and wished to take an indefinite leave of absence. Crowninshield decided to name Dorothy as Wodehouse's successor. Not only did this reflect his faith in her, but also it happened to be a brilliant promotional gimmick for *Vanity Fair*.

Dorothy could not have been more amazed. She had spun out her line in hope of reeling in a modest-sized fish and instead had hauled up a whale.

From the beginning, she set out to make herself noticed. In her first column, New York's only woman drama critic described herself as "a tired business woman" who was "seeking innocent diversion"—which was the reason she had chosen to review a batch of five musical comedies. With the exception of Wodehouse's *Oh, Lady, Lady!,* where she deemed it politic to lay praise on thick, she proceeded to slice up the rest with a poison stiletto. Since it is always more fun to revile than extol and because abuse was practically reflexive with her, she made it her modus operandi. One show, for example, got her recommendation as an excellent place to do knitting and "if you don't knit, bring a book." With another, she refused to print the names of author or cast, declaring that she was "not going to tell on them." There was a show she ignored entirely, instead reviewing the performance of a woman seated next to her who had been searching for a lost glove. Certain chorus lines were damned for consisting of "kind, motherly-looking women," the locations of her seats criticized, and certain prominent producers chastized for low taste.

Altogether her debut in the April 1918 issue was a bravura performance that assured maximum pleasure to *Vanity Fair* readers and maximum annoyance to Broadway entrepreneurs.

If the beginning of Dorothy's reputation as a wit can be pinpointed, it would be that spring, for it was then, when she was twenty-four, that she began to attract the attention of an audience broader and more sophisticated than the readership of a fashion magazine. What makes that particular column so interesting is its rejection of the prevailing standards for female writing and thinking. She had chosen to present herself not so much as a bad girl but as a bad boy, a firecracker who was aggressively proud of being tough, quirky, feisty, a variation on the basic Becky Sharp model, and she managed to carry it off with terrific style and humor. She was putting on an act, but it was an act that seemed as if it might sell. Now she began to see what shape her future might take.

. . .

Life as a married woman was turning out to be dull as mud. Dorothy left the boardinghouse and moved to an apartment in a handsome building on West Seventy-first Street, the block directly behind the brownstone that Henry Rothschild had owned when Eliza was alive. Dorothy's new, non-Jewish name may have completed the superficial obliteration of Dorothy Rothschild, but choosing to live a few hundred yards from the Rothschild house, the place where she had spent her most secure years, might be construed as an indication of her ambivalence toward this disloyalty. She made no effort to turn the flat into a home because once Eddie returned they would be moving anyway. Her suits hanging next to his civilian clothes in the closet, the kitchen bare of food and drink, she took her meals in restaurants and continued to live in much the same transient fashion as she had at the rooming house.

Although she would not admit it, she had an acute aversion toward homemaking. Granted, she had not been brought up to concern herself with such matters, but most women in 1918, even those raised with servants, were nonetheless able to care for themselves in an emergency. Dorothy was not. So phobic was her reaction to domesticity that she would have starved before boiling herself an egg. Throughout her life, she would eat bacon raw claiming she had no idea how to cook it. The mechanics of laundry would be equally mysterious—when she removed her underwear, she threw the soiled lingerie back into the drawer with the clean and let a maid, if there was one, figure it out.

These days, hungry for company, she took to dropping in on her sister, who recently had given birth to a second child, a daughter also named Helen, nicknamed Lel. Helen Droste's marriage show signs of erosion. Dorothy had never been crazy about her brother-in-law, but now it seemed clear that Helen was far from contented with the party-loving George. Dorothy, playing with her niece, would talk of having a baby when the war ended, when her husband returned.

Eddie's company remained in the States. It moved from New Jersey to Pennsylvania, then south to North Carolina before shifting to Jersey again. Dorothy wrote him nearly every day, but she never felt satisfied with her letters. Had she been able to express herself fully she would have poured out her loneliness, but she knew that Eddie, with his low tolerance for teary confidences, would not appreciate gloomy mail. To cheer him up, she related amusing incidents that had taken place at the office and sometimes enclosed copies of her verses, which had begun appearing regularly in the magazine. She yearned to receive love letters but had to content herself with his postcards, usually addressed to "Mrs. Edwin P. Parker, 2nd," in care of *Vanity Fair*. His messages were marvels of brevity that began "Dear" and ended abruptly "Ed," while sandwiched in between were one or two lines that might have been written to anyone.

Several times when he was based near New York, she rushed to visit him, but their reunions were not particularly successful. The shyness they showed toward each other dismayed her. In fact, Eddie seemed so distant that she felt as if they were not married at all, which made her cry. The sight of her woebegone face had the effect of deflating Eddie further, first making him impatient and then angry. She saw him as unreasonable, and there were fearful quarrels in hotel rooms.

Eddie's drinking must have contributed to the instability of their relationship, although it was an issue that Dorothy found impossible to address because Eddie refused to admit he had a problem. In his company, he was considered a hard drinker, and after the morning when he had appeared at reveille white-faced, hung over, and looking as if he had arisen from the grave, his friends began to call him Spook, a nickname that stuck. One weekend when the company was based at Syracuse, he received a furlough and boarded the night train to New York. Eager to begin celebrating, he finished a pint of whiskey and promptly passed out. When he came to at Grand Central the next morning, he staggered off the train and bought another bottle, then drank in earnest for the remainder of his leave. Some of Eddie's friends felt sorry for his wife.

In May 1918, his division crossed to France on an Australian troop carrier and was rushed to the British front for additional training. In July, when the long-awaited counteroffensive began, he got his baptism during the Soissons offensive and after that was never far from the front lines. He took part in the Saint-Mihiel fighting and the battle of Meuse-Argonne. The fighting was more savage than First Lieutenant Edwin Parker could ever have imagined. While he had not wished to be a combatant, he discovered that transporting the wounded had special horrors. Ambulance drivers made their runs at night, lumbering without lights over shell-pitted roads, driving and making repairs under intense bombardment. Shifts of twenty-four and thirty-six hours were standard. Eddie drove to the first-aid stations behind the trenches and waited while the litter bearers loaded the wounded into his machine; then he set off for the nearest field hospital, picking his way through the darkness and dodging supply convoys and shell holes. Arriving at the hospital, it was not unusual to find that he had been driving a hearse, and he soon trained himself to have as few feelings as possible about the bloodstained shapes in his rear van.

One night as he was returning to the hospital, a shell exploded on the road, and before he could slam on his brakes, the machine hurtled into the crater, where it remained for almost two days. When help came, the van held four corpses. Eddie was fortunate to escape with only minor physical injuries.

During his four months at the front, hard liquor was all but impossible to obtain but other painkillers were not. Dorothy later said that "they had dope in the ambulance," and she named morphine as the substance to which her husband became addicted. While opiates were not as a rule carried in the ambulances themselves, they certainly were available at field hospitals and dressing stations. No doubt, Eddie was not the only one to get through the war with the aid of drugs.

Dorothy continued to gain prestige as a critic. The public loved her and repeated her witticisms; theatrical producers viewed her as a piranha and dreaded the sight of her tiptoeing down the aisles. It was what she had dreamed of. Very quickly she learned that play reviewing offered unlimited opportunities for bellyaching, one of her favorite pastimes. After only a few months on the job, she informed her readers that "sometimes I think it can't be true. . . . There couldn't be plays as bad as these. In the first place, no one would write them, and in the second place, no one would produce them." Since bad plays were the rule, however, her life was becoming "a long succession of thin evenings." By summer she was calling her job "a dog's life." In the autumn when the new season began it turned out to be true; some weeks there were nine or ten premieres, and she had to race from theater to theater. Very little of what she saw proved amusing. "It may be," she wrote grimly, "that a life of toil has blunted my perception of the humorous."

More than pressure and bad plays was agitating her. Her nerves raw from worrying about Eddie, she found herself easily distracted. Ushers with flashlights, latecomers, even the sound of applause irritated her. "It isn't only one sort of fiend that makes my evenings miserable," she grumbled, for she also felt like lashing out at umbrellas, opera glasses, and rattling programs. Worst were the pairs of happy lovers she noticed at musical comedies, couples who reminded her of herself and Eddie. "They always behave in the theatre as if they were the only ones in the house." Their hand-holding and "interchanging of meaningful glances" made her feel terrible, and in a fit of sour grapes she wished that she could have them barred from Broadway theaters.

One of the editors at *Vanity Fair* had hung a detailed map of France above his desk with flags indicating the exact positions of the American army. Dorothy noticed that his daily ritual was to check the morning papers as soon as he got to his desk, then to shift the locations of the flags. Since she disliked this editor, a posturing and immensely pompous man who wore a pince-nez attached to a black ribbon, and since "I didn't have anything better to do," she decided to give him a twitch or two.

Arriving at the office early, she rearranged his flags to show the kaiser winning. Then she sat down at her desk, put on her glasses, and pretended to work. Albert Lee, attributing the falsified map to German spies, would spend the rest of the morning correcting the flags. Bedeviling Lee was highly satisfying to Dorothy, well worth the loss of a half hour's sleep.

The armistice was signed on November 11. She attributed the fact that her sixteen-month marriage had been racked by tension to global rather than personal debacle and counted on the future being different. When she learned that Eddie had been reassigned to occupation duty in Germany, she felt terribly disappointed.

After the first of the year, she received a picture postcard of Cochem castle, a popular Rhineland tourist attraction on the Mosel River.

"Dear," he wrote to her, "if you can send me a cake of working soap I think I can arrange to buy this castle." As usual, the card was hastily signed "Ed."

He failed to mention, perhaps did not know, that Koblenz was his destination, nor did he say a word about loving or missing her, or even wishing-she-was-there. Instead he sounded absurdly cheerful. She began immediately to imagine him loose in Germany, roustabouting with his cronies or the fräuleins and surely consuming quantities of white wine. It was another seven months before she saw him again.

Chapter 4

CUB LIONS

•

1919

In the summer of 1919, New York teemed with returning veterans who were taking up jobs they had left or just beginning careers deferred by the war. Among the newcomers determined to make his mark in the literary marketplace was twenty-four-year old Edmund "Bunny" Wilson. He had postulated for himself a twofold strategy for success: get something in print and, if possible, get it in *Vanity Fair*. Around this time, Dorothy had been given the additional duty of reading manuscript submissions, stacks of them. Previously the processing of unsolicited manuscripts had been done by Albert Lee, whose system of elimination had been swift and efficient: He attached rejection slips and returned them unread to their authors. Dorothy felt obliged to read the pieces before rejecting them. From time to time, she came across writing that showed promise. When Wilson submitted some prose he had written for the *Nassau Literary Review* while an undergraduate at Princeton, she brought it to Crowninshield's attention. He invited Wilson to come in for a talk.

Wilson, nicknamed "Bunny" in the nursery by his mother, had curly red hair that was already thinning. He sought acceptance for his writing but was particularly needy in other respects. Having only recently worked up the courage to purchase his first condom in a Greenwich Village drugstore, he looked forward to remedying his lack of sexual experience. When he met Dorothy at *Vanity Fair*, there may have been more than one idea on his mind. As they shook hands, he shyly looked her over. Even though she was *Mrs.* Parker, she must have impressed him as a woman who might possibly

51

be available. Despite his attraction, he felt put off—so he would claim—by what seemed to him an excessive use of perfume. A demon with an atomizer in her hands, Dorothy had a lifelong habit of spraying her head and shoulders with clouds of scent. It made her feel feminine and secure. Friends of hers remember that she always smelled delicious, but Wilson was clearly overwhelmed by the fragrance. "Although she was fairly pretty and although I needed a girl, what I considered the vulgarity of her too much perfume prevented me from paying her court." Having hit upon a plausible excuse for rejecting Dorothy, before she could reject him, he went on to complain that "the hand with which I had shaken hers kept the scent of her perfume all day," but evidently he was not sufficiently distressed to think of washing his hands.

The randy Bunny Wilson was not the only one to find Mrs. Parker attractive—and not the first to find her intimidating either. Her appearance without a male escort at first-nights and her pugnacious literary style gave people the impression she might be approachable, although any man who tried found himself face to face with the old-fashioned manners of a Victorian matron. Dorothy was too much the war bride ever to consider infidelity. The notion of sleeping with other men revolted her almost as much as the thought that Eddie might be seeking the bed of some German woman.

During the months while she was waiting for him to come home, changes were taking place at *Vanity Fair*. All winter Crowninshield had talked about offering the managing editorship to Robert Benchley, a writer who had been contributing humorous pieces for nearly five years, but nothing had come of the idea. Benchley, who had spent the war writing publicity for sales of war bonds as well as free-lancing, was now growing impatient. When a friend resigned as associate editor of *Collier's*, Benchley had a chance for the job. He used this as a lever to force a decision from *Vanity Fair*. Publisher Condé Nast decided to interview him. He told Benchley that the magazine definitely required changes. In his opinion, it needed to be upgraded with serious articles.

Benchley, realizing this was his big chance, agreed that more serious pieces seemed a sensible change. He was hired at one hundred dollars a week.

When Dorothy came to work on Monday, May 19, she found Benchley sharing her office, already hard at work. Somebody had placed a welcoming bowl of roses on his desk. With considerable formality, he addressed her as "Mrs. Parker," and she naturally responded by calling him "Mr. Bench-ley." At noon, Crowninshield invited him to the Coffee House, his luncheon club, which excluded women. For the remainder of the day Benchley was absorbed in writing an article. A few minutes after five, he set out for Grand Central Station to catch the 5:37 train for suburban Crestwood, New York.

Robert Charles Benchley was not at all the sort of person Dorothy had been expecting. He looked like a prudish, domesticated, twenty-nine-year-old Boy Scout who played mandolin duets with his wife, went to bed at ten, and spent Sundays clipping his hedges. Such was the case.

He was five feet ten and a half inches tall, slender with thinning sandy hair, blue eyes, and a pale face. His serviceable suits came off the racks at Rogers Peet. Since he believed strongly in taking care of his health, he wore long woolen underwear and galoshes. He suffered from hay fever in season and had a nervous habit of biting his fingernails all year round. He neither smoked, drank, nor swore, and never had he been unfaithful to his wife.

Benchley came from a family of middle-class, small-town New En-glanders who had settled in Worcester, Massachusetts, before the Revolu-tion. Although one of his ancestors became a lieutenant governor of the state in the 1850s, none of the Benchleys had been particularly gifted at making money. Robert Benchley's father never got beyond clerking for the city's mayor, a position he held for thirty years. Charlie Benchley's lack of ambition was most likely related to his fondness for drink, an addiction that took ingenuity to indulge because his wife, Jennie, personally collected his paycheck and doled out his carfare without an extra cent. Of her two children, Jennie Benchley preferred her older son, Edmund. Robert, thir-teen years younger, idolized Edmund too. When Robert was eight, Edmund was killed in the Spanish-American War. Told of her son's death, Jennie blurted out, "Oh, why couldn't it have been Robert?"

To atone for those words, Jennie treated her remaining child like a prince. She even tied his shoelaces for him until he entered high school. To avenge himself on his mother, Benchley waged passive war on the female sex for the rest of his life.

If the flora and fauna of Benchley's homeland had been alcoholism and rejection, he grew up seemingly untouched by misfortunes of any kind. During his adolescence, a wealthy woman who claimed to have been his brother's secret fiancée offered to pay for his education at Phillips Exeter

Academy, followed by four years at Harvard. In college, where he became one of the best-liked students on campus, Benchley was editor of the *Harvard Lampoon* and a star of the Hasty Pudding shows. Two years after he graduated, in the class of 1912, he married Gertrude Darling, a Worcester girl whom he had known since elementary school. By the time he arrived at *Vanity Fair,* he seemed to be a well-adjusted family man with his personality and his life set as if in concrete. Though the couple had a small son and Gertrude was pregnant again, Benchley had yet to earn enough to support his family. He still entered the purchase of each newspaper and every postage stamp in his pocket expense book.

It was a mystery to Dorothy why Crowninshield had selected Benchley to be managing editor and how—or even if—he had written all the loony pieces that had been appearing regularly in the magazine. On the basis of his writing, she had imagined him to have a delicious sense of the absurd, some rare and extravagant madness that she described as "a leaping of the mind," and that others would describe as "almost-logic, the same chilly, fascinating little skid off the hard road and right up to the edge of the swamp." Yet on first meeting her new colleague, Benchley's lunacy was not obvious to Dorothy.

Several days passed. Just as she was growing accustomed to sharing her office with the methodical Mr. Benchley, Crowninshield brought in another new employee and assigned him a third desk in the room. Never before had Dorothy laid eyes on anyone quite like this individual. He was a giant—six foot seven inches, stooped, rail-thin, with cavernous brown eyes and a nailbrush mustache. Robert Sherwood, a twenty-three-year-old veteran who had served in the Canadian Black Watch and had been gassed and wounded, was plainly ill because he filled the office with his gasps as he struggled for breath. Communication was difficult because he refused to speak. When a stenographer came in to take dictation from him, he sat on the floor and turned his back on the woman.

Nobody knew what Sherwood was supposed to do. Applying for the job, he had appeared in his Black Watch uniform, and Crownie, no doubt impressed by the kilt, had hired him for a three-month trial period at a salary that was only five dollars more than the secretaries were earning. He gave him the vague title of drama editor, but told Benchley that he was to be picture editor. Eventually Sherwood decided that his real job was to be "a sort of maid of all work."

He made Dorothy and Benchley so uncomfortable that before long they began lunching together just to discuss the problem. She put forth the theory that Sherwood was a "Conversation Stopper" and that, in her experience, trying to talk to a "Stopper" was like "riding on the Long Island railroad—it gets you nowhere in particular." She also thought he looked tough and sinister. Benchley wondered how Crowninshield could have saddled him with a freak whose military exploits even remained a mystery. With so much of Sherwood to shoot at, how could the Germans have managed to hit him in both legs? He suspected that Sherwood must have been lying on his back, waving his feet in the air. The truth about Robert Sherwood did not occur to either of them. He was merely struck dumb in their presence.

Several days later, as Dorothy and Benchley were leaving for lunch, they were surprised to find Sherwood waiting for them outside the building. Hesitant, he asked whether they would mind if he walked down West Forty-fourth Street with them—not *with* them actually but *between* them— for he was in need of protection. "In those days," Dorothy recalled, "the Hippodrome, a block from the office, had engaged a troupe of midgets and Mr. Sherwood . . . wouldn't go down the street unless Mr. Benchley walked on one side of him and I on the other, because, with his six feet 7 inches, he was afraid the midgets might tease him if he were alone." Looking like an ambulatory pipe organ, the editors set off down the street, but the midgets ran squeaking alongside yelling "Hey, Legs!," warning him to duck when he crossed under the Sixth Avenue El, and demanded to know how the weather was up there. At Sixth Avenue, having outrun "the nasty little things," Dorothy and Benchley felt obliged to invite Sherwood to join them for lunch, and the ice was finally broken.

Back at the office, Dorothy whispered to Benchley that she was having second thoughts. Sherwood was "nice." Benchley agreed that he was "one of the nicest guys I ever saw." After that things began to change.

Upon closer acquaintance, Dorothy discovered that Sherry was "pretty fast." He wore his straw hat at a rakish angle, tried to make dates with the receptionist, and admitted to lifting a few in Broadway cabarets. One day when he acknowledged having a hangover, Benchley expressed alarm and disapproval. Dorothy sprang to Sherwood's defense, declaring that she had once attended a cocktail party.

Benchley was doubly shocked. "Mark my words," he warned her, "alcohol will coarsen you."

Dorothy could see nothing wrong with drinking an occasional cocktail.

Colored photographs of corpses appeared on the walls at *Vanity Fair*. While the atmosphere at the magazine had always been lively, now it was becoming downright rowdy. At first Crowninshield was pleased to note that his three editors had taken "an enormous shine to one another." What he failed to understand was how much clowning was actually taking place. After Benchley told Dorothy about his enjoyment of two undertaking magazines, *The Casket* and *Sunnyside,* she decided to become a subscriber. Whenever a new issue arrived in the mail, the two of them stopped working to admire the pictures of cadavers, then they read aloud the humor column, "From Grave to Gay," and howled with laughter.

Dorothy found the magazines hilarious. "I cut out a picture out of one of them, in color, of how and where to inject the embalming fluid, and had it hung over my desk." But in Crowninshield's memory, there was not one but an entire row of brightly colored anatomical plates above her desk, and he asked her to remove them. "I dared suggest that they might prove a little startling to our occasional visitors, and that, perhaps, something by Marie Laurencin might do as well." Dorothy responded to his suggestion with "the most palpable contempt."

Already Crownie's la-dee-dah mannerisms were beginning to grate on Benchley's New England nerves, but Dorothy said that she felt sorry for Crownie. He was "a lovely man, but puzzled," and she had to admit that "we behaved extremely badly."

After several weeks of this, Crowninshield privately began to think of the magazine as a lions' den with himself in the uncomfortable position of tamer. No doubt his editors were still cubs, "amazing whelps" he called them, whose teeth were not yet sharp and whose claws had not grown long, but they seemed to be animals nonetheless. Later on he described their antics more benignly: "Indeed I believe that in no period of their lives did the three find more enjoyment, make more friends, or work as hard, or as easily." In the early summer of 1919, the problem was that the cubs weren't working particularly hard and sometimes they weren't working at all. They were expected in the office at eight-thirty but often showed up late, then spent the mornings in enthusiastic personal conversations, took long lunch hours at Child's, and went home early. Whenever it was necessary for Sherwood to leave the office, even though the midgets had left town, he would say, "Walk down the street with me," and all three would nip out for some air. Dorothy remembered that "Mr. Benchley and I would leave our jobs and guide him down the street. I can't tell you, we had more fun."

Condé Nast was far from entertained. He instructed the business manager to enforce the company's tardy rule with a memo warning that latecomers would be required to fill out a slip explaining why they were late. Benchley was the first to receive one. His reply, hundreds of words in tiny handwriting covering a slip of paper the size of a playing card, unfolded a sorrowful tale of how he had arrived early, heard that the Hippodrome's elephants had got loose, offered to round them up, chased them up to Seventy-second Street and down West End Avenue to the Hudson River docks where they were trying to board the boats of the Fall River Line, and finally herded them back to the Hippodrome, thereby averting a major marine disaster but unfortunately causing him to be eleven minutes late for work.

This was his first and last tardy slip, but the battle lines had been silently drawn up, with the whelps on one side, Condé Nast on the other, and a nervous Crowninshield in the middle.

At the end of June, Nast and Crowninshield departed for a two-month trip abroad and left Benchley in charge of publishing two issues of the magazine with the assistance of Dorothy and Sherwood. What made Nast imagine this would be a sensible plan is hard to fathom. On the day of sailing the editors appeared at the *Aquitania* with a floral horseshoe, the tackiest one they had been able to buy, and offered exuberant bon voyage wishes to their bosses. Liberated, they trooped back to the office and immediately began to go haywire. Naturally they kept hours that suited them. They also took steps to upgrade Sherwood's position and salary. Unable to authorize a raise, Benchley did the next best thing and assigned him several articles to write. The first piece he turned in was a piece of juvenilia better suited to a college humor magazine than the country's most sophisticated monthly, but Benchley purchased it for seventy-five dollars, a higher price than some well-known contributors were getting. When the editor of the men's fashion department went on vacation leaving a half-finished column, Sherwood completed it with predictions that best-dressed men would soon be wearing waistcoats trimmed with cut jade and peg-topped trousers. This cracked Benchley up, and he and Dorothy sent it off to the printer. Nobody, they assured each other, ever read the stupid column anyway.

. . .

In June, Dorothy received an invitation to attend a luncheon at the Algonquin Hotel, a party hosted by two theatrical press agents to welcome Alexander Woollcott, *The New York Times*'s drama critic, back from the war.

Woollcott was a fat, bespectacled man of thirty-two whose smallish features tended to sink like raisins into a pudding of jowls and double chins. A master of the insult, he already had acquired a considerable reputation for bitchiness. It was said that entering into conversation with him was like petting an overfed Persian cat who had just sharpened its claws. Those who found his personality uncomfortable dismissed him as a one-man freak show, but to his intimate friends—and in time they would be a cult numbering in the hundreds and ranging from Eleanor Roosevelt to the Marx brothers—he was an acquired taste. They would vie with each other to find the right words to describe his personality: "Old Vitriol and Violets," James Thurber dubbed him; Louisa M. Woollcott, said Howard Dietz; a New Jersey Nero in a pinafore, according to Edna Ferber. George Jean Nathan called him "the Seidlitz powder of Times Square" but the only epithet to capture the whole man was George Kaufman's one-word label, "Improbable."

A native of Red Bank, New Jersey, he was the maternal grandson of a founder of the Phalanx, a Fourieristic commune that was a lesser known but more successful counterpart of Brook Farm: Owing to his father's frequent absences, Woollcott grew up in genteel poverty among his mother's people at the Phalanx. After graduating in 1909 from Hamilton College, he worked briefly as a teller with the Chemical National Bank of New York while trying to obtain a reporter's job on *The New York Times.* His literary style leaned heavily on the side of lavender and old lace, but he successfully resisted all impulses to improve it. If not one of the worst writers in America, he surely ranked among the top ten. Even his friends made fun of his style and were genuinely surprised to realize just how atrocious it actually was. (Even more surprising was the amount of money he earned by it.) In 1912, the *Times* appointed him drama critic, a position in which his taste for overripe adjectives seemed acceptable.

Still a virgin in his early twenties, a repressed, bewildered, presumably homosexual male who adored dressing in women's clothing and fantasized becoming a mother, he must have been terrified at the thought of sex with either gender. When he developed mumps at twenty-two and his physician warned that the illness in adult men might affect potency, Woollcott apparently decided to use this as a convenient means of resolving the troubling issue of his sexuality. Thereafter he played the role of a "semi-eunuch" who was physically incapable of consummating the sex act. As a substitute for sex, he indulged himself by wearing scarlet-lined opera capes, insulting friends with greetings like "Hello, repulsive," and eating enormously and exquisitely until his weight swung up to a blimpish 255 pounds.

Since Woollcott enlisted as a medical orderly as soon as war was declared, Dorothy had never encountered her colleague from the *Times* on opening nights. The hosts of the welcome-home luncheon, John Peter Toohey and Murdock Pemberton, sent her an invitation simply because she was *Vanity Fair*'s critic. They apparently did not think to invite Benchley and Sherwood. Dorothy, who went nowhere without them, insisted they accompany her to the Algonquin, where a long table had been decorated with American flags and a green felt banner that intentionally misspelled Woollcott's last name.

Some thirty-five guests showed up, nearly all of them theatrical reporters, critics, and columnists from the daily papers, just the sort of people whom press agents might be expected to court. The most important journalist at the table was Franklin Pierce Adams, a mythical figure to Dorothy, who never missed reading The Conning Tower. Not only did he publish the type of verse she was laboring to write, but several times a week he ran a parody of *The Diary of Samuel Pepys*, recounting in mock Elizabethan English his flirtations, his frailties, the opening nights he attended, the books he read, and the celebrities he habitually met. To be mentioned in F.P.A.'s column was a distinction of the highest order.

Adams was a personal friend of Woollcott's. In Paris they had served together on the staff of the American Expeditionary Force's weekly newspaper, *Stars and Stripes*, as had another of the guests, former Private Harold Ross, the paper's managing editor. Ross had developed a love-hate relationship with Woollcott, whom he thought of as "a fat duchess with the emotions of a fish." On their first meeting, Ross viewed Sergeant Woollcott with suspicion when he had come strutting into the *Stars and Stripes* office.

"Where'd you work before?" Ross asked.

"*The New York Times*," Woollcott pronounced in his most pompous voice. "Dramatic critic."

Ross broke into raucous laughter. No real man would work at a sissy profession like drama critic.

"You know," Woollcott said to him, "you remind me a great deal of my grandfather's coachman."

To this Ross would never be able to think of a suitable retort because there was none—he would always look as if he had tumbled off the train from Sauk Center. None of the *Stars and Stripes* writers would have won beauty prizes. F.P.A.'s beak nose and long, scraggly neck once led Irvin Cobb, seeing a stuffed moosehead, to exclaim, "My God, they've shot Frank Adams." Harold Ross's looks were pitiful. His hands, feet, ears, and mouth were too big, his gray eyes too small, a thicket of stiffish, mouse-colored bristles shot out of his scalp, and a large gap separated his two upper front teeth. When Ross once asked Woollcott for dental floss, Woollcott called out, "Never mind the floss, get him a hawser."

A westerner from Colorado, a miner's son who had dropped out of school at fourteen, Ross had bummed around the country working on a dozen newspapers before he enlisted. He had planned to return to the West Coast, charter a boat, and, like Jack London, take a restorative cruise to the South Seas, a project at once exotic and worthy of a real man. Definitely not among his plans was living in New York, which he considered a terrible place. While in Paris, Woollcott had introduced him to Jane Grant, a *New York Times* society reporter who had come over with the YMCA, and Ross had fallen in love. Now he lived in the Village and edited a new weekly magazine, *The Home Sector*, which was a stateside version of *Stars and Stripes* for veterans, and Jane Grant was back at the *Times* with a promotion to hotel news editor. They were engaged.

Another couple at Woollcott's luncheon had already married and spent their honeymoon in France as war correspondents: Heywood Broun and Ruth Hale. Dorothy had met Broun one summer long ago at the shore. He was a distant memory of heat and sand, a Horace Mann student who was an acquaintance of her sister. She was pleased to see Broun and liked his wife, supposing them to be a modern couple successfully negotiating the shoals of marriage by having produced a child and still pursuing their separate interests.

Frank Adams, best man at their wedding, had called them "the clinging oak and the sturdy vine," for Ruth was a militant feminist who had balked at the word *obey* in the Episcopal marriage service and threatened to call the wedding off. Tight-lipped when anyone addressed her as Mrs.

Broun, she declared that she was not and never would be anyone but Ruth Hale. Her husband, a thirty-one-year-old *Tribune* columnist, was a large, anxious, slovenly man, who bore a physical resemblance to a laundry bag. His sense of fashion was certainly odd. In Paris, learning of General John Pershing's decree that all war correspondents must wear uniforms, Broun outfitted himself at the Galeries Lafayette department store in what he believed to be appropriate attire: pink riding breeches, fedora, and raccoon coat. Pershing, noticing him at an inspection, disheveled and unlaundered with his puttees sagging about his ankles, stared in bewilderment before asking, "What happened? Did you fall down?" How Broun managed to survive a war is unclear. His phobias included trains, automobiles, and elevators. He was also a hypochondriac who took his own pulse to make sure he was still alive.

At the Algonquin, Dorothy remained silent, shyly blinking at everyone from under the brim of her Merry Widow hat, virginal, self-conscious, and extremely well turned out in one of her good suits so that she looked like a Park Avenue princess slumming. She could not decide whether or not she even liked Woollcott and his friends. A few months earlier she had written a scathing article about men whose war service had taken place far behind the front lines, scorning them as "the numerous heroes who nobly accepted commissions in those branches of the service where the fountain pen is mightier than the sword." Finding herself in the company of "fountain-pen lancers" made her feel so uncomfortable that she usually clammed up and concealed "the fact that my husband went to the front—it made him seem like such a slacker." Nobody at Woollcott's party knew the article was hers because she had used a pseudonym, but nevertheless she felt biased against them.

In years to come efforts were made to resurrect what, if anything, of significance had taken place that day, who had said what and to whom, but by then nobody remembered much. The only certainty was that Aleck Woollcott had held center stage recounting his wartime adventures at length and that the others were good-natured about allowing him to spout off. All his stories began with "When I was in the theater of war . . ." and finally Arthur Samuels cut him short. "Aleck, if you ever were in the theater of war, it was in the last-row seat nearest the exit." Despite the presence of three professional women, the climate of the luncheon was very much that of an old boys' get-together where talk of war or money would have been inevitable in any case. For Woollcott and the other veterans, it had been the best of all possible wars, but now they were concerned about their futures. In the summer of 1919, a time of great expectations and endless possibilities, they all wanted to retrieve careers, make contacts, get their books published and plays produced, be rich and famous, rise like cream to the top of the New York bottle. Therefore, they had come prepared to listen to Woollcott's bragging and laugh at everybody's jokes, just as if they were at a Booster Club bash in Toledo. Besides, it was an ideal way to spend a June day when the weather was fine and nobody felt much like working in the first place.

"Why don't we do this every day?" somebody said as the luncheon began to break up. Since it sounded like a good idea, a polite murmur of approval was heard.

Walking back to the office with Sherwood and Benchley, Dorothy did not seriously expect they would do it every day. For that matter, there seemed to be no good reason to do it ever again.

Shortly after Eddie's return in August 1919, Robert Sherwood photographed the Parkers seated side by side on a park bench. Eddie is wearing a civilian suit and a lopsided smile. Dorothy looks haggard with her mouth set in a grim line. Their bodies are not touching.

The war had taken visible toll of her husband. His features had roughened, become puffy; the sweet, angular boyishness was missing and so was the playful energy she had found so appealing. Anxious to see his family (his sister had died in childbirth while he was overseas), he had gone to Hartford for a while. When he returned to New York, he was in no great hurry to resume his career. Although he seemed glad to be home, he also appeared subdued, indifferent, restless.

Since the fall theater season was just getting under way, there were many evenings when Dorothy had to work. She came home only long enough to change into dress clothes before going downtown again. She expected Eddie to accompany her. Sometimes he did, if the show happened to be a musical. Serious plays bored him. On Sundays they visited the Drostes, where he enjoyed playing with Helen's children.

At first, when Dorothy came home from the office weary and eager to pour out her headaches, Eddie was quick to commiserate. She felt able to relax, even cry if she felt like it. Before long he greeted a long face with impatience, wondering why she was bawling again when there never was anything the matter. She explained that she enjoyed crying just for the sake of it, but this made no sense to him. If she was crying, he would slam out, returning hours later when they would make up in bed.

In time, his addiction to morphine could no longer be concealed. When he finally agreed to seek treatment, it turned out to be a more complicated process than she had expected. It meant, she recalled, probably exaggerating, "one sanatorium after another." Although she managed as well as she could, her husband was a tortured man and living with him could be harrowing. It was rumored that on more than one occasion she returned home from *Vanity Fair* to find him stretched out on several chairs with his head in the oven of their gas stove.

The return of Nast and Crowninshield at the end of August put a noticeable crimp in the high spirits of the cub lions. To show their affection, they festooned Crownie's office with streamers of crepe paper and hung a welcome-home sign. He was not pleased.

The next morning Dorothy arrived late, but Benchley breezed in even later because Gertrude had gone into labor and he had taken her to the hospital. After lunch, he failed to return to the office. Again the next day no work got done because Dorothy and Sherry were busy offering congratulations on the birth of Robert Charles Benchley, Jr., and listening to Benchley's stories of his experiences at the hospital. Dorothy, possessive about him, did not like to be reminded that he had a second life in which she had no part. Not that she had any desire to be Gertrude Benchley, who was stuck in Crestwood with a little boy and a new baby while her husband was away all day in the city enjoying himself with women like herself. This was exactly the sort of marriage that had always terrified Dorothy. Curiously, her indignation was aroused not at the thought of Gertrude's entrapment, but at the thought of Mr. Benchley's, a perception of his marriage that he did nothing to discourage. What she couldn't bring herself to wonder was why he had chosen it. Instead, she preferred seeing him as a helpless victim, either of circumstance or of Gertrude, most likely the latter. Although she had yet to meet Mrs. Benchley, she already had formed a picture of her as a frumpish, housecoated female who smelled of germicidal soap, looked for buttons to sew before they fell off, and slept in curlers.

That fall was a time of growing tension, as Dorothy tried to please one man at home and other men at the office. However hard she tried, she could not seem to succeed in either place. She failed to understand why Crowninshield fussed about copy deadlines since she worked harder and longer than he had any right to expect. If she was sometimes tardy, it was for good reason because she spent many evenings at the theater. Aside from her drama column, she did additional theater pieces as "Helen Wells," contributed verse, composed captions for Fish's drawings, read manuscripts, and helped with editing and proofreading. In her opinion, the Nast organization not only should have felt more appreciative, it also owed her a raise. When she asked for one, Crowninshield promised that he would speak to Nast after the first of the year.

The other cub lions felt equally dissatisfied. In unguarded moments, they grumbled about their wages so loudly that eventually somebody in the office reported their complaints to Condé Nast. Immediately a memo was circulated warning that discussion of salaries was against company policy and cause for discharge. No sooner had the memo reached their desks than the three of them retaliated with a memo of their own. They resented "being told what we may and what we may not discuss," and they also protested against "the spirit of petty regulation" that had made possible such an edict in the first place. Then they lettered placards spelling out their salaries and took perverse pleasure in strolling through the office with the provocative signs swinging around their necks.

A flabbergasted Nast responded to their home-grown union by doing nothing. However, Crowninshield became seriously alarmed and entreated them not to exhaust the publisher's patience.

Still boiling, but trying to keep a low profile around the office, they allowed themselves to blow out steam over lunch. From time to time, they ate at the nearby Algonquin, whose name they had familiarly shortened to "the Gonk." After his party in the summer, Aleck Woollcott had continued to lunch there and nearly always invited friends to join him. Many of those who had attended his lunch had been dropped because he found them boring. Whenever the *Vanity Fair* editors came by, they were welcomed, as were two newspaper reporters, Marc Connelly and George Kaufman, who had not been present at the June gathering. Connelly, who wrote theater news for the *Morning Telegraph*, was a cheerful, bald man of twenty-nine and had the manner of a talkative leprechaun. Born across the river from Pittsburgh in McKeesport, he had been living in New York for three years, since his ambition was to become a playwright. Nightly, after his paper went to press, he strolled uptown with George Kaufman to discuss ideas they might transform into salable plays.

Kaufman, Woollcott's assistant and a *Times* drama reporter, was a shy, nervous man who also came from Pittsburgh. He was a year older than Connelly, but aside from an interest in the theater, no two men could have been less similar. Kaufman's demeanor breathed gloom: narrow face, glasses, a high pompadour of dark hair, and a long skinny body about which he felt so self-conscious that he refused to be seen in a bathing suit. His phobias were disabling, his hypochondria of textbook dimensions. He had a horror of being touched and after a single year of marriage was unable to have sex with his wife, Beatrice, although apparently he experienced fewer problems with prostitutes.

Before long, Woollcott was coming to the Algonquin regularly, and manager Frank Case began automatically reserving a table for him. Since the hotel was patronized by celebrities such as Mary Pickford and Booth Tarkington, it was understandable that Case would not be impressed by the Woollcott contingent. To him they were "just a crowd of unusually agreeable folk." Plainly, "none of them had any money," which no doubt was the reason he directed the waiter to leave complimentary popovers and celery and olives on their table. The group took on a mangy aura on those days when they were joined by Heywood Broun, who usually looked like a one-man slum. Once, outside the hotel, a sympathetic passerby handed him a dime.

Case was astute in his judgment about their financial status. The *Vanity Fair* editors filled up on popovers and ordered eggs, the cheapest entrée on the menu. They reserved their energy for vilifying Nast, whose bookkeeper mentality they found disgusting. As they all were aware, Nast's obsession in life was sex, a commodity he pursued with greed and aggression. It evidently mattered little to him if the woman was call girl, manicurist, or socialite. They suspected that he was using Frank Crowninshield to sponsor his entry into New York high society, and still worse, using his connections to find women. Benchley's horror of libertines and social climbers made him label Nast's organization as the ultimate "whited sepulchre." Sherwood was quick to point out that employees were "treated like serfs" and "paid that way, too," but that Crownie was not to blame because he himself was handled like a poor relation.

To take their minds off Condé Nast, they began to talk about writing a play together, perhaps a musical. Searching for a story, they came up with the idea of a man who is bored with his witty, glamorous wife and who chooses instead to have an extramarital frolic with the least splashy woman imaginable, a mouse who wants to breed and keep house, the two types of women corresponding exactly to Dorothy and Gertrude Benchley. Having found a twist, they began trying to develop an outline. "All we have to do is write it," Benchley recorded optimistically in his diary, next to a reminder that he was four hundred dollars in debt.

The day before Christmas, Crowninshield summoned Dorothy into his office for a private talk. He made clear to her that she should not expect a raise, for he was displeased with the quality of the magazine in general and her work in particular. Unemotional, officious, his meticulously pressed gray suit matching his silvering hair, Crownie's usual gentle manner drained away in niggling complaints. Even though she assumed that he was voicing Nast's objections, she felt thoroughly upset. She did not understand how her mentor, the man who had admired her outspokenness, could now be denigrating what he once had endorsed and promoted.

"*Vanity Fair* was a magazine of no opinion," she later said, "but *I* had opinions." She always remembered that day with great bitterness.

Chapter 5

THE ALGONQUIN ROUND TABLE

•

1920–1921

On the second Sunday in January 1920, Crownie invited her to tea at the Plaza Hotel. Since it was a cold, snowy day, he asked the headwaiter to brighten up the table with roses. First, he told her that he admired her extravagantly and always would and that he would be honored to publish anything she might care to write. He was sure that she would be famous some day. Then he announced that Plum Wodehouse was returning to *Vanity Fair*, so that her services were no longer required, unfortunately.

Dorothy, meanwhile, had remained silent. She was waiting for him to bring up the names of Florenz Ziegfeld, David Belasco, and Charles Dillingham, three powerful producers who had recently trotted onto Broadway stages a flock of turkeys, to which Dorothy had speedily applied euthanasia. All three men, coincidentally advertisers in the magazine, had subsequently complained to Condé Nast. But Crownie was letting that matter pass. He was silent too about the angry phone call he had received from Billie Burke, the actress wife of Flo Ziegfeld who recently had appeared in Somerset Maugham's comedy *Caesar's Wife*. Dorothy's review of the show had noted that Burke coyly threw herself around the stage as if giving an impersonation of exotic dancer Eva Tanguay. Burke had taken umbrage at that comment and very likely her husband had encouraged her to make a fuss. Crownie had wound up apologizing to Billie Burke.

Crowninshield's gallantry in awkward situations was well known. His gentlemanly enthusiasm for discretion took precedence over truthfulness, and as a result, the real reason for Dorothy's dismissal was left unstated.

He then suggested that if she wanted to work on "little pieces at home," they could work out a satisfactory rate.

Though Dorothy was livid, she did not press for further explanations. The only thing left for her to do was to reject his proposal and order the most costly dessert on the menu.

After leaving the Plaza, she steamed home to telephone Benchley, who came into the city on the next train. Dorothy, Eddie, and Benchley hashed over and over the events of recent weeks until late into the night. Robert Sherwood had been fired after being told that the woman who gave music lessons to Nast's daughter would be taking over his duties. Dorothy's dismissal seemed genuinely unfair and undeserved because she had praised many productions and many individual performers, including Billie Burke. The upshot of their discussion was that Benchley decided to quit and wrote his letter of resignation when he arrived at the office the next morning. He labeled the magazine's action in Dorothy's case as "incredibly stupid and insincere," but apart from that, he added, his job wasn't attractive enough to keep him there without Dorothy Parker and Robert Sherwood.

His resignation stunned Crowninshield. In his opinion, writers came a dime a dozen but a decent managing editor, which he considered Benchley, was hard to find. When he understood that Benchley was serious, he agreed to accept the resignation and predicted he would become famous some day, one of the treacly severance speeches so typical of the man. Later, Edmund Wilson overheard him remark that it was a pity Benchley had overreacted and that the way he had carried on about Mrs. Parker had been absurd.

Dorothy was deeply moved by Benchley's allegiance, which she would call "the greatest act of friendship I'd known," and unquestionably it was a generous action for a man with a wife and two children to support. There was something fiercely loyal in Benchley's temperament, something beyond normal devotedness. This was not the first time he had left a job because a colleague was being mistreated. Benchley edited a Sunday rotogravure section for the *Tribune* in 1918. The paper's managing editor was his friend and Harvard classmate Ernest Gruening, whom the *Tribune* suspected of being pro-German, perhaps because of his name or his pacifist leanings—a pacifism Benchley shared. When Gruening was fired without a chance to clear himself, Benchley resigned the same day. Whether or not Dorothy knew of this incident, she still would have regarded his resignation from *Vanity Fair* as a sign of special fidelity.

On that Monday nothing could subdue the exuberance of the cub lions. As they laughed and boasted and ranted about Condé Nast, even the prospect of unemployment appeared trivial. After a giddy lunch at the Algonquin, they strolled back to the office, where they began telephoning people they knew to advertise their availability. Still full of high spirits once the office closed, they ploughed through the snow-covered street to the Gonk, where they were joined by Aleck Woollcott and Gertrude Benchley, who had offered no objections to her husband's decision. Over dinner, questioned by interested reporters who had heard rumors of a walkout at *Vanity Fair*, they began to discuss their plans for the future. Benchley thought that it would have been pleasant if they could have continued at *Vanity Fair*, "but it probably is better for all of us to do things for ourselves." Why shouldn't they become successful free-lancers who could write what they liked, instead of working for people like Condé Nast? There was no telling what they could do on their own. Now it might even be possible for Dorothy and Benchley to work on the play they had been talking about.

By midnight Monday, Dorothy had stopped worrying. Getting fired might be a mercy. The next morning, she was sure of it. *The New York Times* carried a news story, sympathetically worded by Woollcott, announcing her dismissal from *Vanity Fair*. It was the sort of invaluable publicity that the unemployed can't buy. Attention to her plight continued. Before the week was out, she received a second plug when Frank Adams wrote in The Conning Tower: "R. Benchley tells me he hath resigned his position with 'Vanity Fair' because they had discharged Dorothy Parker; which I am sorry for."

The trio went through the motions of working. In the lobby of the building, they hung a poster that asked people to make CONTRIBUTIONS FOR MISS BILLIE BURKE, though nobody did. They amused themselves by pinning red discharge chevrons on their sleeves and parading raffishly around the office. Dorothy was proud to recall that "we behaved very badly."

Later that same week the manufacture, sales, and transportation of liquor was banned in the United States, thus marking the start of thirteen years of Prohibition. It was an historical event of no particular interest to Dorothy, who to be sociable would accept a gin daisy at a party but nurse it all evening. Benchley, an ardent prohibitionist, hailed the ratification of the Eighteenth Amendment as "too good to be true" and insisted that the country was taking a "step toward Utopia."

Since just about the only people remaining on *Vanity Fair*'s editorial staff were the secretaries, Crowninshield asked Edmund Wilson to read a few manuscripts as a tryout. He apparently passed the trial because Crownie suggested he fill in for Benchley, which meant that he was given the duties of managing editor with neither the title nor the salary. Dorothy and Benchley, recalled Wilson, "joked about my being a 'scab,' but were kind about showing me the ropes and took me for the first time to the Algonquin." At lunch they regaled him with office gossip. Their attempts to poison his mind fell on fertile ground because ever after he would think of Crowninshield as a "born courtier who lacks an appropriate court" and of Condé Nast as "the glossiest bounder I have ever known."

On January 25, Dorothy and Sherwood cleaned out their desks and departed; Benchley's contract required him to remain until the end of the month. Dorothy's first free-lance job was writing subtitles for a movie, D. W. Griffith's *Remodeling Her Husband*, which was being directed by Lillian Gish. When she went up to the newly opened Griffith studio in Mamaroneck, New York, she took Sherwood with her because she hoped that Gish might have work for him as well. Sherry was far more interested in moving pictures than she, but unfortunately Gish did not need him.

Her screen-writing job lasted a week. For a scene in which James Rennie is having his nails manicured in a barber shop, she borrowed from Hamlet's speech to Horatio and wrote: "The divinity that shapes our ends." Since this was more or less on a par with her caption writing for *Vogue*, she may have felt the work uncomfortably regressive. In any case, she sought no further movie work.

At the beginning of February, she moved into an office with Benchley in the Metropolitan Opera House studios, near Times Square. It was a single, jerry-built room on the third floor, little more than a triangular section of hallway that had been partitioned off. It was heated, had a window overlooking Broadway, and cost thirty dollars a month, which was actually no bargain considering its size. "An inch smaller," joked Dorothy, "and it would have been adultery."

There was no adultery—nor would there ever be—but they were unquestionably a couple. In 1920, friendship between a woman and a man was not unheard of, but it was uncommon when both people were married, for it was imagined that a spouse would provide all the companionship a person needed. In the case of Dorothy and Benchley, neither of whom were able to confide fully in their mates, they complemented each other psychologically, indeed were kindred souls. Robert Sherwood, who had been obliged to figure all this out during his months at *Vanity Fair*, described their relationship as intellectual. Nevertheless, he could see that Gertrude was terribly jealous, a reaction that was hardly surprising since they completely excluded her from participation in their friendship.

In the new office, they behaved like impoverished pseudo-newlyweds who were setting up housekeeping. They furnished their cubbyhole with a pair of grubby kitchen tables, three chairs (one for a guest), a hat rack, and their typewriters, all the necessary paraphernalia of writers, and they decorated the walls with their collection of undertaking photographs. Benchley brought in his boyhood diaries and left them open for Dorothy, or anyone else, to browse through. On a bulletin board, they left notes for each other. Before long the office began to fill up with untidy heaps of undertakers' magazines and yellowing newspapers. They talked about having the door lettered with the words UTICA DROP FORGE AND TOOL CO., ROBERT BENCHLEY, PRESIDENT—DOROTHY PARKER, PRESIDENT, but abandoned the idea, also about applying for the cable address PARKBENCH, but decided the likelihood of anyone sending them a cable was slim. Outside it was a nasty winter with drifts of dappled gray snow and piles of garbage that lay uncollected for a week, but it was cozy in their hideaway, and they delighted in playing house.

Friends were constantly dropping in. Marc Connelly's job on the *Morning Telegraph*, a paper printing so much theatrical news it was known as "the chorus girl's breakfast," was not particularly taxing. When he needed a convenient place to pass the time, he would come in to visit or to amuse himself by reading Benchley's diaries. "There was always a laugh to be had with Bob or Mrs. Parker because they didn't care what they said or did. They would lean out of their window and shout 'ya, ya' to people walking along Broadway. Somehow they managed to get pieces done but it was hard to understand how." Another visitor impressed by the fun they were having together was Charles Baskerville, an up-and-coming artist who was illustrating some of Dorothy's verse for *Life*. Mrs. Parker, he remembered, "was gay and jokey and, oh, was she cute."

Very quickly Dorothy found herself another position as drama critic. *Ainslee's* was a literary magazine, respectable enough but steps beneath *Vanity Fair* in both class and circulation. They gave her a monthly column called "In Broadway Playhouses," where she was permitted to express her opinions as bitchily as she pleased. She found that she could tap out the reviews with little thought while reserving her energy for the assignments she was getting from more prestigious magazines. During much of the winter she worked on a long piece about the Ouija-board craze for *The Saturday Evening Post*, then went on to contribute four major articles to the *Ladies' Home Journal*. She also made up her quarrel with *Vanity Fair*, at least with Crowninshield, who had asked her to coauthor a book with him. *High Society* was to be a snobby little satire giving hints on how to deal with "dowagers, dinners, debutantes, dances, and the thousand and one diversions of persons of quality," with drawings by Fish and captions by Dorothy, Crowninshield, and George Chappell. When she visited the *Vanity Fair* offices to see Crownie or to chat with Bunny Wilson, the secretaries whispered among themselves that the real reason for her dismissal was that she had suggested Billie Burke had thick ankles. While Dorothy had forgiven Crownie, her hatred of Condé Nast had not abated. One day, when she and Wilson encountered him in the lobby of the Algonquin, all parties were at pains to reveal no hard feelings. Nast told her he was planning an ocean cruise. "And Dorothy," he said, "I wish you would come with me."

"I wish I could," she replied. But when Nast had walked on, she turned to Wilson and burst out, "Oh, God, make that ship sink!"

After her winter of hard labor money had piled up in her bank account. Benchley too was thriving as an advertising copywriter and book reviewer for the *World* at a hundred dollars a column. In April, after Robert Sherwood became assistant editor of *Life*, the humor magazine offered Benchley the position of drama critic, a job that paid a hundred dollars a week plus seven cents a word for additional contributions. About this time, he learned that his rented Crestwood house was to be sold. He and Gertrude found a house they wanted to buy in nearby Scarsdale, but it cost $17,500 and required a $4,200 down payment. A friend offered to loan him bonds as collateral and he borrowed two hundred dollars from Dorothy, which he used to open an account at the Lincoln Trust Company. He then asked the bank to lend him four thousand dollars on the bonds, gave Dorothy back her two hundred dollars, and made up the difference from his paycheck. It was a magical transaction that took place in less than an hour, but the magic to Dorothy was that she had two hundred dollars.

The *Life* job brought significant changes in Benchley's habits. He had kept commuter's hours and hustled back to the suburbs in time for dinner each night. With eight or ten plays opening in a week, he was lucky if he averaged one meal a week with Gertrude on the new job. Often he changed into his evening clothes in a ten-cent cubicle in the men's room at Grand Central. After a show, if his deadline was close, he stayed in town and slept on the sofa at Dorothy and Eddie's apartment or at Sherwood's.

Throughout the spring, Dorothy's intimacy with Benchley deepened. She told him that she dreamed of doing serious writing—short stories, perhaps a novel, and of course the play they had talked of writing together. He told her about his interest in the Queen Anne period and how he wanted to write a history of the humorists who had lived at that time. Despite their successes since leaving *Vanity Fair*, they continued to feel insecure about money. They worried about responsibilities they no longer wanted and the costs exacted by one's foolish choices. In both of their lives, many things were not going perfectly, but it was lucky they knew each other. With a good pal, they knew they would be all right.

An exclusive luncheon club, whose membership he controlled and where he could be the centerpiece, was a delicious idea to Aleck Woollcott. He adored a captive audience at lunch, and, in fact, had a compulsive need for company at all meals. He felt most comfortable when surrounded by friends who tolerated his affectionate abuse, giving as good as they got. No doubt his communal beginnings at the Phalanx accounted for some of this. Now he began to promote subtle changes in the little group that turned up regularly for lunch at the Gonk. The previous fall they had been simply a bunch of writers who wanted a convenient place to eat and "that's about all," as George Kaufman later explained. Aside from the professional advantages of having an opportunity to trade shoptalk, meeting for lunch at the Algonquin proved to be relaxing and the food was good. Even though they came in every day, they attracted little attention from either the management or other customers. The Algonquin's main restaurant, opposite the lobby, was the Rose Room, where it was not unusual to catch sight of theatrical celebrities such as John Barrymore or Douglas Fairbanks. The writers, however, ate at a long table in the Pergola Room (now the Oak Room), a smaller dining room that was decorated with murals depicting the

Bay of Naples. From the outset they tended to be cliquish; nobody sat at their table without an invitation and they referred to themselves as "the Board" and to their lunches as "Board Meetings."

Frank Case appeared unwilling to accept them as full-fledged adults. At that time "none of the boys or girls had done anything in particular," he wrote. Nor was he convinced they ever would, though naturally the "big man" of the group was F.P.A. because he had the largest salary and a column that could bestow fame on anyone lucky enough to land in it. The rest of the group impressed Case as nothing more than hardworking hopefuls. Woollcott, despite his affectations, was beginning to achieve some popularity. Broun and Benchley were highly regarded journalists but without big followings. Nobody had heard of George Kaufman, who was earning four thousand dollars a year at the *Times*. Case noticed among the men at Woollcott's table "a young girl" who shook wisecracks out of her sleeve. She would "simply sit, now and then saying something at which the others would laugh and that was the end of it." How was he to have known, he protested, that she was a wit? As for Harold Ross, Case must have examined him with an air of incredulity because he described him as "a sort of adopted child, taken in on approval before the final papers were signed."

The most striking fact about the writers was their vitality and the intense pleasure they seemed to take in one another's company. They were always laughing and joking, clearly having a terrific time. Unfortunately, the jokes never earned them any money. Two press agents who sometimes ate with them were Herman Mankiewicz and Murdock Pemberton. After lunch one day, as everyone was leaving the hotel, Mankiewicz shook his head sadly as he watched them disperse. He said to Pemberton, "There goes the greatest collection of unsalable wit in America."

But not for long. Soon they were naming their own price and it was Frank Case, for all his seeming indifference, who proved instrumental in helping them. Not only did he provide a free clubhouse, he also was responsible for an Arthurian table and a concept that lent itself to the creation of a legend. In her book *The Vicious Circle*, Case's daughter Margaret wrote that "the Algonquin Round Table came to the Algonquin Hotel the way lightning strikes a tree, by accident and mutual attraction." Before long her father noticed the size of the group expanding as they pulled up chairs from other tables, overflowed into the aisles and to adjoining tables, and created traffic problems. For practical reasons Case decided to move them to a front table in the Rose Room. That failed to solve the problem either, for even more people showed up to eat with them. Next he seated them at a large round table in the rear of the dining room and gave them a waiter of their own. The sheer size of the table and its location at center stage, plus the fact that Woollcott frequently entertained prominent persons, drew stares from other customers, even those who were important themselves. They fell over themselves to see if Minnie Maddern Fiske was sitting at the round table. Some began asking Georges the headwaiter to identify people who were lunching at the round table: Was that Mencken? H. G. Wells? A cartoonist for the *Brooklyn Eagle*, Edmund Duffy, published a caricature of the group and he labeled it the Algonquin Round Table. The name stuck. Newspaper columnists were hungry to publish quips that had originated at the Round Table. All this was good for the restaurant's business, as Frank Case was pleased to notice. He must have decided the boys and girls were growing up, because before long he stopped providing them with free popovers and celery.

Charter members of the Round Table were Aleck Woollcott, Heywood Broun, Frank Adams, John Peter Toohey, Robert Benchley, George Kaufman, Marc Connelly, Robert Sherwood, Harold Ross, and Dorothy. Throughout the early twenties the number of regulars kept climbing and eventually reached thirty or more. At one time or another, Frank Sullivan and Charles MacArthur were participants, as were Herman Mankiewicz, Harpo Marx, Donald Ogden Stewart, Murdock Pemberton, and Deems Taylor. So were Arthur Samuels of *Harper's Bazaar*, novelist Alice Duer Miller, playwright Laurence Stallings, and poet John V. A. Weaver.

A comparative latecomer was Edna Ferber, a writer best known for her popular stories about a traveling saleswoman who peddled ladies' underwear. Ferber was small and homely, thirty-four claiming to be thirty-two, a fiercely driven woman who called herself "a stagestruck Jewish nun." She dreamed of writing novels that would explore colorful periods in American history, but when she first came to the Round Table in 1921, she had yet to produce such successful works as *Show Boat*. She had known Woollcott for some years and wrote him a plaintive request: "Could I maybe lunch at the Round Table once?" After that, she was included in the group, even though her appearances at the hotel were infrequent. A compulsive worker who preferred to lunch at her desk, she socialized with the group after business hours. When Ferber showed up, she could parry and thrust with the best of them. On one occasion, Noël Coward had been invited. Both he and Ferber were wearing double-breasted suits.

"You almost look like a man," remarked Coward.

"So do you," she replied.

Another writer often associated with the Round Table but seldom seen there was Ring Lardner, a highly paid sportswriter and humorist who had been born in Niles, Michigan, and covered baseball for the *Chicago Tribune*. Lardner was an almost pathologically silent man in his mid-thirties with bulging eyes and an expressionless face. For many years a heavy drinker, he had developed into a full-fledged alcoholic. His pattern was periods of abstinence alternating with binges that lasted weeks or sometimes months. By 1920, having left the *Tribune* for a job as a syndicated national columnist with the Bell Syndicate, Lardner was earning thirty thousand dollars from his column alone and decided to move east. Eventually he purchased a house in Great Neck, New York, where he lived with his wife, Ellis, and their four sons, and where he also worked, coming into the city only for business or drinking. Although Lardner had mixed feelings about the Round Table, they honored him with an intensity that bordered on reverence and considered him a master of the short story. They also envied him because, Broun said, "he wrote what he wanted to." Edmund Wilson suspected that they badly needed "such a presiding but invisible deity, who is assumed to regard them with a certain scorn."

In addition to Dorothy, there were a number of women who joined the table: actresses Margalo Gillmore, Tallulah Bankhead, and Peggy Wood; writer-wives Ruth Hale and Jane Grant; and novelist Margaret Leech, who had a tongue second only to Dorothy's for its sting. Lovely, blond Peggy Leech stared at Frank Adams when he arrived at lunch one day after a tennis match. His shirt was unbuttoned to reveal tufts of black curly hair.

"Well, Frank," she said, "I see your fly is open higher than usual today."

Before long, the Round Tablers hated to part after lunch. "Conversation was like oxygen to us," Marc Connelly said. "We breathed each other in our remarks." Unable to get through a weekend without seeing each other, some of the men began meeting on Saturday nights to play poker in a second floor suite at the hotel. The Thanatopsis Literary and Inside Straight Club convened on Saturday afternoons, played throughout the night, and sometimes the marathon continued into Monday morning. Regulars were F.P.A., Broun, Ross, Woollcott, and Kaufman, and joining them were others who practically never ate in the Rose Room—*World* editor Herbert Bayard Swope, silk merchant Paul Hyde Bonner, and Raoul Fleischmann of the baking-company fortune. Ring Lardner sometimes sat in. His minimalist conversation was practically limited to "Hello," "I raise," "I'm out," and "Good night." One night, Marc Connelly was losing so badly that he flew into a tantrum and ripped up his cards. Lardner only said, "Childish." George Kaufman won most often and came up with the funniest retorts. When Raoul Fleischmann claimed he was fourteen before realizing he was a Jew, Kaufman said, "That's nothing. I was sixteen before I knew I was a boy." When a player bragged about tracing his ancestry back to the Crusades, Kaufman told him, "I had such an ancestor, too. Sir Roderick Kaufman. He also went on the Crusades—as a spy, of course."

Eddie Parker, now back at Paine Webber on Wall Street, had freed himself from morphine but had returned to alcohol, a more respectable addiction. After leaving his office each day, he generally went to a speakeasy while Dorothy, feeling abandoned, waited and smoked cigarettes. Sometimes it was 9:00 P.M. before he showed up, by which time she would have spent several hours picturing him run over or dead. He would be safely but unpleasantly drunk, his alcoholic high having already come and gone, "leaving him loud and querulous and bristling for affronts," as she described a fictional character based on him. Did she know what was wrong with her? he would ask. Immediately she would pull up a chair and give him her undivided attention, always being a dependable audience for any recital of her faults.

Since she blamed herself for the problems of the marriage, she was continually looking for ways to fix them. She decided there was nothing to be lost by a change of scenery, that is to say, by trying the ever-popular geography cure for ailing relationships. They moved south to midtown.

The Parkers rented a flat on the top floor of a shabby, three-story, red brick building at 57 West Fifty-seventh Street, on the corner of Sixth Avenue. It was a commercial property occupied by artists who needed studio space but generally lived elsewhere. Certainly there was little about the place to recommend it as a residence. The high girders of the Sixth Avenue elevated train cast a shadow over the building. Even on the brightest days, the El gave a gloomy aspect to the neighborhood, an unfashionable area of tenements and stores. Each time a train went crashing by, the noise was so deafening that all conversation had to halt. At first, this was disconcerting, but in time, as reality ate away bit by bit at their illusions, as the Parkers edged toward new crises, the racket assumed an appropriate symbolism, providing perfect sound effects for their marital battleground.

Excited by the promise of a Bohemian life, Dorothy was not in the least bit put off by the cramped, somewhat drab quarters. Neither she nor Eddie were domestic. In those days, none of the Round Tablers placed a high value on expensive appointments, and as Marc Connelly mentioned, their apartment had "a chair for everybody," which was all that anyone expected. Dorothy was satisfied with their new home. Sculptor Sally James Farnham, who owned a pet monkey, had a studio on their floor. Downstairs was the Swiss Alps restaurant, and down the block a drug store that sold decent gin made from pure alcohol.

Along with the flat, they acquired a Boston terrier that they christened Woodrow Wilson for patriotic reasons and a canary that Dorothy called Onan because he spilled his seed on the ground. The Parkers, who had difficulty caring for themselves, did not really need the responsibility of pets, but to Dorothy, no real family could possibly be complete without animals. It was a sign of her determination to cure the marriage that she chose a dog like her beloved Rags. Unfortunately, the Parker household bore little resemblance to the elaborate establishment maintained by Henry Rothschild, nor were there servants to look after the dog. No doubt Dorothy realized that pets need air and exercise and that Woodrow Wilson deserved to be trained and housebroken, but she was unable to manage it. She forgot to take him out, and Eddie, involved in affairs of his own, also seemed incapable of establishing a routine for the dog's care. In the end, Woodrow Wilson had to make the best of it. When Charles Baskerville visited the apartment to show Dorothy some drawings, he noticed that the floorboards had begun to warp.

In September, she and Eddie planned a New England vacation. On their way north, they stopped at Hartford to visit his family. By this time, Dorothy had fallen into the habit of disparaging her in-laws, as well as the whole city of Hartford, which had to be inhabited by bigots simply because the Parkers lived there.

At Birches, Maine, there was little to do but fish. Every day, even when the water was rough, they went out on the lake to catch trout, salmon, and chub. Dorothy took a conservationist's approach to fishing. She threw back practically everything they managed to pull in and insisted that Eddie do likewise. She could not bear watching the fish expire. She told him that they had got on the line by mistake and must be put back in case their children needed them. Although exercise held no appeal, the beauty of the island inspired her to take a few hikes. She was delighted to catch a glimpse of a porcupine. Since the water proved too cold for swimming, she never got a chance to wear her new bathing suit and joked about bequeathing it to a hard-up Ziegfeld ingenue. In their room at night a fire was lit, which sounds cozy and romantic, but there was no hint of any sexuality in her relations with Eddie. Writing to Benchley, she did not trouble to camouflage her dissatisfaction.

> Some children here have the whooping cough,
> If we don't get it, we'll be in soft.
> The desk clerk's manner is proud and airy,
> Nevertheless, we think he's a fairy.
> There are some people right next door
> Who turned out to be a terrible bore.
> There always must be some kind of a hitch
> Isn't Nature (finish this line for yourself
> and get a year's subscription to the Boston
> Post.)

The main hitch, of course, was Eddie, but she had no need to explain that to Benchley. She did mention that "we'd like a dash of hootch. In fact, we'd like it very much," but since she seldom drank it is unlikely that she was referring to herself. It seems more likely that Eddie was making an effort to go on the wagon in healthful surroundings, in which case the vacation would have been a strain for both of them. She openly admitted her homesickness for Benchley and barraged him with postcards that she signed "Flo [Ziegfeld] and Billie [Burke]" and "Condé [Nast] and Clarisse [Nast's estranged wife]." Repeatedly, she reminded him how much she missed him and wished he were there "and that's the god's truth."

Beginning in 1920, when the Round Table was forming, Dorothy became friendly with illustrator Neysa McMein, who had a studio across the hall from Dorothy. Neysa was five years older than Dorothy, an emancipated, frankly ambitious woman from Quincy, Illinois, who had been increasingly in demand to draw covers in pastel for top magazines and commercial advertisers. She looked like a Brunhild—tall, blond, athletic, with a classically beautiful face, masses of touseled, tawny hair, and a grin that dissolved into easy laughter. Neysa was not particularly witty and seldom came up with the mots that flew whenever the Round Tablers assembled, but she took pride in acting as their appreciative audience. Considering the assorted emotional disorders in the group, she was probably the least neurotic person among them, a straightforward woman with a talent for aggressive self-promotion. In her skylighted studio the Round Table established its second home by dropping in each afternoon between four and seven, until it had become an annex to the Algonquin. Sometimes Dorothy skipped lunch at the Rose Room because it was expensive, but Neysa's open house became a regular stop on her daily circuit.

The studio's big main room was painted a pale, dirty beige, sparsely furnished, and cluttered with a comfortable jumble of coats, overshoes, and sporting equipment. Neysa never permitted guests to interrupt her work and generally ignored people after greeting them. Even when the place grew crowded and so noisy that conversation was almost impossible, the centerpiece was always Neysa seated at her easel on a raised platform, hair uncombed, faced smudged with pastels, her smock held together with safety pins. In addition to the Round Table, her guests included people from the theater and Tin Pan Alley, the same show-business celebrities whose names appeared in F.P.A.'s column. On a typical day, Dorothy might find Charlie Chaplin, Paul Robeson, Ethel Barrymore, Jascha Heifetz, and playing duets on Neysa's piano, Irving Berlin and George Gershwin.

Not every visitor to Neysa's place succumbed to its appeal, and some hated it. Anita Loos, newly arrived in New York, thought that Neysa was "phony" and dismissed her celebrated guests as being without much interest "except for Dorothy Parker and Herbert Bayard Swope." She sized up Dorothy as a "lone wolverine," a woman who had "no belief in friendship" and associated with the Round Table only because she had nothing better to do. As for Woollcott and the rest, Loos never altered her opinion of them as willfully sophisticated suburbanites unable to admit their mediocrity. In *But Gentlemen Marry Brunettes,* her heroine, Lorelei Lee, remarks that the geniuses who eat at the Algonquin "are so busy thinking up some cute remark to make, that they never have time to do any listening."

At Neysa's studio the liquor flowed freely. She became proficient at manufacturing gin. In her tiny bathroom she installed a still, a complicated piece of apparatus which required frequent repair by Connelly and Benchley but which nevertheless was much envied by friends who wanted one for their own apartments. Dorothy, intrigued by the still, liked to escort unknowing strangers to the bathroom, where she conducted a personalized tour of the machinery.

One afternoon she encountered Gertrude Benchley at Neysa's. Most of the time Gertrude remained secluded in Scarsdale with the children, but occasionally she hired a babysitter and came into town to attend the theater with her husband.

It had become almost second nature for Dorothy to make wisecracks at Gertrude's expense. She characterized her as the sort of woman who might eat her young; anyone who found Gertrude attractive must have a vast acquaintance among the astigmatic—she always looked as if she were rushing from a burning building. Though Gertrude was not fond of Dorothy either, whenever they chanced to meet, they both behaved cordially for the sake of appearances and Robert Benchley. At Neysa's, Dorothy began making suitably sympathetic inquiries about the Benchley children, so many that Gertrude slowly lowered her guard. When Dorothy later volunteered to pilot her to the bathroom to view the famous still, Gertrude willingly followed. In the bathroom, Dorothy began to freshen her makeup, then noticed Gertrude's face and presented her with a compact.

"Have some powder on your nose," she suggested.

"I never use make-up," Gertrude said, stating the obvious.

When Dorothy insisted, Gertrude gave in and began applying the powder, only to notice a strange transformation taking place. She looked more closely at her reflection in the mirror. Her nose seemed to be turning bright red. Dorothy had given her a cake of rouge.

"That's not funny!" she shrieked.

Dorothy's reputation as a funny woman was born at the Algonquin but it developed at Neysa's. In the opening years of the twenties, when New York humor was quickening its pace, nobody had faster reactions than she did. She had learned all there was to know about speedy repartee in her father's house, where it had been a staple at every gathering of the Rothschild aunts and uncles, although nothing would have induced her to advertise that bit of personal history. To her Round Table friends like Marc Connelly (who had the impression her father had been a Talmudic scholar, an impression Dorothy never bothered to correct), her tongue seemed born quick and deadly, like a knife already implanted before anyone could catch a glimpse of the blade. There was nothing cheerful or kindly about her barbs; they were meant to be sharp, nasty, and vengeful. She took pleasure in galloping to the punch line before her victims got there. She could be witty on paper, but her forte was oral agility. She was truly at her best in conversation, where she presented the routine she had perfected: demure, deadpan expression, the disparity between a patrician voice modulated to just above a whisper and her inexhaustible repertoire of obscenities.

Wicked put-downs seemed to flow effortlessly. Hearing that a friend had hurt her leg while visiting London, she voiced a naughty suspicion: Probably the woman had injured herself while sliding down a barrister.

Wasn't the Yale prom wonderful? she said. If all the girls in attendance were laid end to end, she wouldn't be at all surprised.

At a Halloween party, she hoped they would play ducking for apples. There, but for a typographical error, was the story of her life.

Bidding good night to a friend, she promised to telephone soon, then immediately cracked that the woman spoke eighteen languages but couldn't manage to say no in any of them.

She excelled at punning word games. When asked to use the word horticulture in a sentence, she answered, "You may lead a horticulture, but you can't make her think."

She was developing a bad habit of flattering people to their faces and then condemning them behind their backs. "Did you ever meet such a shit!" she would exclaim. Such denunciations amused some people, shocked and disturbed others, and still others like Edmund Wilson simply reconciled themselves to accepting her capacity for "treachery." Dorothy acknowledged her compulsion to embrace and denounce by saying, "I cannot keep my face shut" around idiots. It may have been wicked but "as God hears me, I am perfectly justified."

It also got laughs. She once began ripping apart someone who had just left a party. A friend of the departed begged her to stop. The poor woman was a nice person who wouldn't hurt a fly.

"Not if it was buttoned up," Dorothy retorted.

. . .

Eddie had accepted her career before and during the war but now discovered that it had assumed unexpected and baffling dimensions: He was married to a woman who was becoming a celebrity. Not only was he temperamentally unsuited to the position of consort, but Dorothy's friends, with the exception of Benchley, who knew how to make everyone comfortable, made him feel conspicuously out of place. Parkie was, Marc Connelly decided, "a quiet, pleasant young man who was out of his element. He couldn't keep up with Dottie." At a party at Ruth Hale and Heywood Broun's, Dorothy introduced him to Rebecca Bernstien, Broun's assistant at the *Tribune*. "I'm almost certain it was his first public appearance after returning from the army. Dorothy said, 'I want you to meet my little husband.' There stood a shy, slim, blond young man who impressed me as having been well brought up and nice enough to know but he seemed very embarrassed and had little to say. I thought to myself that it was shabby of her to introduce him in that way." Parties where Adams, Kaufman, and Benchley were busy trotting out their routines for each other tended to make most people appear dim-witted. Eddie felt totally inadequate. It was just a matter of time before he refused to socialize with the Round Table. "I didn't see him after that," Bernstien said. "I don't even remember people referring to him very much."

However invisible Eddie may have seemed, he was present in spirit at the Round Table. Dorothy began to concoct funny stories about him, almost as if he were a Mack Sennett character who careered from one perilous episode to the next, dropping his drawers as he went. Practically every day, in her comic scenarios, dreadful accidents sought him out: He almost got run over; he broke his arm while sharpening a pencil; he narrowly avoided plunging into an open manhole while reading *The Wall Street Journal*. Dorothy's delivery was deadpan as she strewed banana peels in his path. Her friends broke up hearing about the various pickles Eddie blundered into. Soon they looked forward to hearing about the hapless Parkie's latest misadventure and egged her on by inquiring about the state of his health. This was her cue: Had they heard about so-and-so's funeral, she asked. Since she and Eddie arrived early at the mortuary, he decided to pay his respects to the deceased. Kneeling before the coffin, he inadvertently brushed against a knob, gears whirred, a door popped open, and before either of them could react both casket and corpse had disappeared into the flames of the crematorium. They ran out a side door before anyone noticed. It had been a ghastly experience for poor Eddie.

In the earliest days of the Round Table nobody strained to make an impression. Conversation was relaxed and stories flowed unrehearsed. It never occurred to them that their remarks might be worth recording for posterity, although Frank Adams occasionally printed those that had tickled him.

In fact, Frank Adams could be considered the Boswell of the Round Table. He unapologetically filled his column with plugs for their various activities and kept a running chronicle of the most mundane aspects of their lives:

> . . . so to Mistress Dorothy's and found A. Woollcott there in the finest costume ever I saw off the stage; spats and a cutaway coat, and a silk high hat among the grand articles of his apparel.

> . . . so to a great party at Neysa's, and had some talk with Miss Ruth Gillmore and D. Parker.

> . . . and so to dinner with R. Benchley and Mistress Dorothy Parker, and then with her to see "Back to Methusaleh."

> To luncheon and found there Mrs. Dorothy Parker and Rob Sherwood and he feeling ill, and was for taking train to Pelham, but I drove him there with D. and she back to the city with me, very pleasant and no chatterer at all.

> . . . and so uptown, and met Mistress Neysa McMein and Dottie Parker, and they asked me to walk with them and look in windows, which I promised to do if they would not beg me to buy them this or that, and they said they would not, but they teased for everything they saw, from emerald necklaces to handkerchiefs. But I was firm and bought them never a thing.

So Dorothy, it seemed, idled away her afternoons window-shopping and partied through the nights but never was she glimpsed sweating over a typewriter—to the old lady in Dubuque, this was the perfect fantasy of the literary life, the very embodiment of New York sophistication.

Sometimes Frank Adams could not resist repeating his own jokes for his newspaper audience. One Monday, after spending the weekend with Harold Ross in the country, he reported to the table that they had gone tobogganing. What did Ross look like tobogganing, they asked.

"Well," Adams answered, "you know what he looks like *not* tobogganing."

Ross, a favorite target of their ribbing, never got off a memorable crack himself. Benchley's appearance at the table usually meant gentle humor and a comic description of his daily vicissitudes. Hurrying out of a restaurant, he asked the uniformed man at the door to get him a taxi. The man informed him frostily that he happened to be a rear admiral in the United States Navy. "That's all right," Benchley said, "then get me a battleship."

A wag passing Marc Connelly's chair at the Round Table patted his bald, pink head. "Your head," he remarked, "feels just like my wife's behind." Connelly reached up to touch himself. "Why, so it does," he replied.

Woollcott's standard repartee relied heavily on insults. "Shut up, you Christ killer," he hissed at George Kaufman, who rose to his feet and threw down his napkin. This was the last time, Kaufman said, that he was going to tolerate slurs about his race. He was going to leave, "and I hope that Mrs. Parker will walk out with me—halfway."

Dorothy spoke infrequently. One of her greatest talents, decided Charles Brackett, was to make a perfect comeback or to say nothing. Peggy Wood noticed that "she didn't waste them on nobodies," while Frank Sullivan compared her to W. C. Fields in that her funniest jokes were lost because their obscenity made them unprintable. Marc Connelly thought her best lines were spontaneous. In the street she approached a taxi.

"I'm engaged," the cabbie said.

"Then be happy," Dorothy told him.

The Round Tablers were having the time of their lives. Very quickly they had become essential to one another, the way a shining new love drives out all other thoughts. Theirs was a special affection, magical, fierce, childlike. They were remarkably tolerant of each other's pathologies, which in some cases they shared, and rivalry was curiously absent. Eating lunch soon became the least part of it. They met for breakfast and dinner, slept together, worked cooperatively, and went on group vacations (and on Neysa's honeymoon after she married a mining engineer). They patronized the same physician, Woollcott's doctor, who built a lucrative practice administering to their ailments, dispensing diet and sleeping pills and offering his all-purpose remedy for hangovers, colds, and indigestion—high colonic irrigations. The Round Table also acquired its own unofficial psychotherapist.

Always showing off for each other, they could be reasonably confident of receiving attention and appreciation. Their meetings were boisterous enough to attract disapproving stares from outsiders, but they took no notice. They were always their own best audience and needed no one else. If they listened endlessly to each other's jokes, they also paid attention to each other's routine headaches, though they tended to hide the big troubles. They were quick to offer comfort. Before long, they began to devour each other's essences, cannibalizing the lives of the group as raw materials for their own writings. Dorothy was perhaps the first to do so.

Their pleasure in each other's company had another side. If they found themselves apart for any length of time, they suffered from separation anxiety. Marc Connelly remembered that sometimes after leaving the Rose Room, they would reassemble at somebody's apartment and then spend the rest of the afternoon discussing where they were going to eat that evening. Noël Coward was amazed to run into the same group of them three times in one day, in three different places. "But don't they ever see anyone *bloody* else?" he said.

Marc Connelly could see nothing strange about all this. "We just hated being apart," he said.

It also was true that not one of them could tolerate being alone, which is a different thing entirely. In fact, the existence of such a group made it possible for them as individuals to avoid loneliness and self-examination. Their habit was to shove the troublesome parts of life, all the painful stuff they found hard to acknowledge, under Frank Case's big table and pull the cloth down.

One morning in June 1921, Dorothy was visiting the offices of *Life*, when she was introduced to Donald Ogden Stewart, a new acquaintance of Benchley's and Sherwood's. At noon they went to lunch at the Plaza Hotel for a change. When Sherwood returned to work afterward, Stewart accompanied Dorothy and Benchley back to their office. They strolled down Fifth Avenue in the sunshine with Stewart feeling euphoric and thinking that he had found two people who understood him so completely that it probably wasn't necessary to explain his ideas or even to finish his sentences. That day, he said later, he fell in love with both of them and would remain so for the rest of his life. Stewart was in his mid-twenties, a likeable, attractive Ohioan who had come to the city only six months earlier from Columbus and established himself and his widowed mother in a tiny Village apartment. Bespectacled and prematurely balding, insecure and obsessed with money and success, he was a 1916 Yale graduate who dreamed of becoming a millionaire, but his brief experience in the business world had proved him a misfit there. A meeting in St. Paul with Scott Fitzgerald, another ambitious, impoverished Ivy Leaguer who felt like an outsider, had been fateful. The success of Fitzgerald's recent novel *This Side of Paradise* had inspired Stewart to try his luck at a writing career. When he met Dorothy and Benchley, he had sold several humor pieces to *Vanity Fair* and *The Smart Set,* but he remained nervous about his ability to earn a living as a satirist.

Dorothy found him amusing. Like herself, he was fascinated by wealth. He was, she noticed, eager to be "an enlivener of the incessant dull hours of the rich." Even though he could not resist presenting himself as a "gay dog," she sensed his serious side. She also praised his writing. Whenever an editor criticized him or rejected a piece, she was quick to take his side and dismiss the editor as dog excrement. If he had a hangover, she pretended to have a worse one. It was this kind of warmth and attention that Stewart badly needed.

If he felt any sexual attraction toward her, it must have been quickly suppressed. He thought she was "absolutely devastating" with her petite figure and gorgeous big eyes, an "imp-at-large," but she also was a married woman—however unhappily made no difference—and he fell into the same comradely relationship with her that Benchley had. Soon Stewart was a regular visitor at Dorothy's apartment and at Neysa's studio. He never was at his ease at the Round Table, because he felt obliged to say something funny, nor did he enjoy exchanging the type of barbs that Woollcott doted on. His friendship with Dorothy and Benchley provided him with constant sustenance. The others struck him as basically unfriendly. Before he joined them for lunch at the Algonquin, he fortified himself with several cocktails.

. . .

The more engulfed she felt by the unpalatable aspects of her marriage, the more extravagantly did she unfold her serial accounts of Eddie's misadventures. The pratfalls she described to the Round Table were actually rooted in reality; chaos was his norm. Like most addicts, he leapfrogged naturally from crisis to crisis and created trouble out of thin air, then professed himself surprised at finding himself in a mess. It was not that Eddie nearly fell into manholes because he was accident prone, but rather that he was accident prone because he was an alcoholic. Whether or not Dorothy understood she was dealing with a sick man is not clear. Her preoccupation with him grew until he became the focus of her existence and nearly all her sentences began with the word *he*. She spoke of him endlessly and compulsively because she was unable to do otherwise.

If Eddie's misfortunes fit an alcoholic archetype, her behavior likewise began to fall into the common patterns of those who live with alcoholics. When not trying to control his drinking by urging him to stop, she was busy covering up for him: The mornings he could not go to his office, she was the one who reported him ill; when he passed out, she put him to bed; when he was sick, she held his head. Increasingly her energy was sapped by efforts to keep him on the track, until she began to lose sight of the dangers facing herself.

Throughout 1921, she ground out bushels of fluff for *Life* or *The Saturday Evening Post*, much of it humorous light verse that appealed to the same audience who gobbled up Scott Fitzgerald's frothy flapper stories. Fluff was short, silly, easy to write, and it paid the bills. Typical of her verse at this period was "Song for the First of the Month":

> Money cannot fill our needs,
> Bags of gold have little worth;
> Thoughtful ways and kindly deeds
> Make a heaven here on earth.
> Riches do not always score,
> Loving words are better far.
> Just one helpful act is more
> Than a gaudy motor car.
> Happy thoughts contentment bring
> Crabbed millionaires can't know;
> Money doesn't mean a thing,—
> *Try to tell the butcher so!*

She judged such early work to be inferior; never would any of it be included in her collected writings.

Articles, by virtue of their length, required concentration, which she often lacked. When assignments failed to get done, letters had to be written, charm turned on, convincing excuses offered. To Thomas Masson, an editor at the *The Saturday Evening Post* and an admirer of her work, she wrote shameless alibis.

> I am ashamed to offer you excuses again, but this has been a ghastly week for us. My husband has had an attack of appendicitis, and they are not sure yet what is going to happen about it. They are still freezing it, which is a pleasant process, and they think they may still get it to listen to reason that way.

Most likely Masson, who had worked with Dorothy at *Life*, knew her well enough not to be taken in by the sad story of Eddie's frozen appendix, but he did consider her the best woman humorist in the country. At first she had completely fooled him with her luminous eyes and enthusiastic promises. Then, Masson recalled, "you sit around and wait for her to finish what she has begun. That is, if she has begun. The probability is that she hasn't begun."

When he inquired about her progress, she would say that the idea they had agreed upon was rotten. Be that as it may, she was working on it anyway. Next, he would be driving through Connecticut when he would stop at a speakeasy and see Dorothy drinking with Heywood Broun and Marc Connelly. Did she pretend that she didn't see him?—certainly not. Her greeting would be warm, her manner unconcerned. If not for the fact that she was recovering from a near-fatal illness, she said, she would have finished his piece long ago. Masson could never bring himself to reproach her. Months later, after he had given up, she would send him the article.

Tom Masson found her exasperating because he felt she was "a born artist" who could easily win an important place in American literature if only she settled down and wrote. But "she refuses to write," he reflected sadly. "All of her things are asides."

· · ·   ·

Eddie blamed her for everything. He called her a nag who made his life miserable, so that it was necessary for him to get drunk. By now she was accustomed to walking on eggs with him, never able to predict when a casual remark or an unthinking glance would be misinterpreted and send him spinning into rage or melancholia. Inexplicable as it seemed to her, he would be friendly in one breath, spitting abuse in the next.

Margalo Gillmore, eating one day at the Round Table, watched the expression on Dorothy's face and thought that it reminded her of a cocker spaniel. "She had eyes like one of those lovely, sad dogs, eyes with deep circles under them." Gillmore decided that she must have been weeping into her pillow all night to get eyes like that.

Although Eddie frequently threatened to leave, she couldn't or wouldn't take him seriously. Nor did she consider leaving him. Marriage was supposed to be forever, a view Eddie presumably shared because he did not carry out his threats. They struggled on as best they could.

Unhappy as she was in her marriage, she did not notice other couples having a better time of it and there were some whom she judged to be doing far worse.

Robert Sherwood introduced her to Scott Fitzgerald and his bride shortly after their marriage, when they were honeymooning at the Biltmore Hotel and working strenuously to carve out daring reputations for themselves. The management requested their departure. Dorothy already knew Scott slightly, having met him in 1919 when he was working at a ninety-dollar-a-week job for an advertising agency and living in a dismal room in Morningside Heights. Penniless, talking about a novel he wanted to write, he had regaled Dorothy with stories about someone he planned to marry, referring to her as "the most beautiful girl in Alabama *and* Georgia," even though he was in the midst of a torrid liaison with an English actress. Eventually he had drifted back to the Midwest, but he had returned to the city after selling his novel to Scribner's, and with him he had brought his Zelda Sayre.

Dorothy suggested to Edmund Wilson that they meet for lunch with the Fitzgeralds. They went to the Algonquin, where they sat not at the Round Table but at one of the banquettes. Dorothy quickly broke the ice.

"This looks like a road company of the Last Supper," she said.

She believed Scott to be a gifted writer, but found his wife ordinary. She chewed gum and looked like a Kewpie doll. "She was very blonde with a candy box face and a little bow mouth, very much on a small scale and there was something petulant about her." If Zelda didn't get her way, she turned sulky.

Whatever Zelda may have lacked as an individual, the Fitzgeralds impressed her as a couple, looking robust with health, as though they had "just stepped out of the sun." When they moved into a flat around the corner from her building, she visited them. It was hard to understand how Scott got any writing done because the place was a mess, with overflowing ashtrays and unmade beds. Their lives seemed to consist of an endless round of parties and hangovers. If Scott's drinking rivaled Eddie's, Zelda's consumption was impressive too. Toward the end of the year, despite earnings of twenty thousand dollars, Scott told Dorothy that he was completely broke. She lent him a hundred dollars. Not long afterward, Scott admitted that the money had disappeared. He suspected Zelda had hidden it. They fought constantly and themselves predicted their marriage couldn't succeed.

While most of Dorothy's wedded friends were less noisy about their troubles than the Fitzgeralds, their marriages seemed no better. Benchley— or Fred, as she had begun to call him—was in a dreadful mess. George Kaufman had stopped sleeping with Beatrice. Frank Adams bedded a succession of young women, whose names he flaunted in his column for his wife and a million New Yorkers to read over their morning coffee. Dorothy could find nothing inspiring about the marriages of Heywood Broun and Harold Ross. Ruth Hale and Jane Grant, paragons of feminist strength, may have kept their maiden names, but they spent much of their time running households and entertaining their husbands' friends, exactly like those oppressed wives who had relinquished their names.

Another marriage that had gone sour was her sister's. After a dozen years and two children with George Droste, Helen had finally made the difficult decision to call it quits. Ever since the Droste bakery had been sold to the National Biscuit Company, George had been assured of wealth whether he cared to work or not; mostly he did not. While Dorothy's contact with Bert and Mate was increasingly infrequent, she remained close to "Mrs. Drots." She confided in her about the troubles with Eddie and was equally familiar with Helen's discontentment and George's infidelities. Her sister had never supported herself, but was accustomed to money and maids. How she might manage on her own was problematic. Helen also feared that if she divorced George he might remarry, sire more children, and disinherit Bill and Lel. The obvious solution was not to divorce him, but that meant Helen would never be able to remarry either. To Dorothy it seemed inconceivable that she and Helen, born well-off and having made so-called good marriages, could be working their way down to poverty. Life was growing increasingly complex for the daughters of J. Henry Rothschild.

Being alone terrified her. It was fine when she felt happy, but if she happened to be melancholy she got "the howling horrors." With her Round Table friends, who made her feel funny and lovable, the howling horrors could be kept at a distance.

She closed the year 1921 at a New Year's Eve party given by Ruth Hale and Heywood Broun in the brownstone they had newly purchased on the Upper West Side. It was a large, noisy gathering, some two hundred guests crowded into the first floor, which had been emptied of furniture and filled up with folding chairs so that anyone who wished to could practice the old custom of jumping into the new year. In place of food Ruth and Heywood provided nutrition by brewing up a huge vat of gin and orange juice, which was replenished several times during the evening.

"A great party and merry as can be," wrote F.P.A., noting that the house had been aglitter with celebrities. "Saw there Mistress Claire Sheridan in the prettiest pink dress ever I saw her wear. . . . Saw H.G. Wells, too. . . . Miss M. Leech there too and Mistress Pinna Cruger, one prettier than the other; but I loved Mistress Dorothy Parker the best of any of them, and loath to leave her, which I did not do till near five in the morning, and so home."

Chapter 6

PAINKILLERS

•

1922—1923

She could never quite remember the day when she discovered that a drink could make her feel better. It was not hard to remember when Robert Benchley made that discovery: the evening of the championship fight between Jack Dempsey and Georges Carpentier. She had been celebrating Dempsey's four-round victory at Tony Soma's speakeasy with Robert Sherwood and Scott and Zelda, when Benchley came in and joined them. Although he drank nothing stronger than coffee, it was not unusual to find him at Tony's, where he was apt to get preachy, always tut-tutting Dorothy about her Tom Collinses and grumpily sermonizing that alcohol made people act unlike themselves. That evening, however, was different. At the urging of his friends, he agreed to sample an orange blossom. When the waiter placed the drink on the white tablecloth, Benchley took a tentative sip, pulled a face, then put the glass down carefully before pronouncing his verdict.

"I hope this place is closed by the police," he said.

One rainy night several weeks later, having meanwhile broadened his sampling of medicinal spirits from orange blossoms to whiskey sours, he left Tony's with Don Stewart. Coming toward them down West Forty-ninth Street they saw a man holding an umbrella over his head. Stewart ducked under the umbrella.

"Yale Club, please," he instructed the astonished pedestrian.

Off they went, leaving Benchley with his mouth open. He could not deny being impressed. After he graduated to rye, he expressed astonishment that the smell reminded him of his Uncle Albert and said that what he always thought had been his uncle's distinctive odor had actually been whiskey fumes. Perhaps the smell also brought back memories of his father.

Dorothy and Benchley became a regular twosome at Tony's, where they drank from thick white china cups so heavy that they bounced on the floor without breaking. As a rule, Tony's customers behaved fairly well, but Dorothy and Benchley in their cups would become rambunctious. When another customer showed them a watch that he claimed was indestructible, they offered to test it: They promptly slammed it against the tabletop, then threw it on the ground and began to stomp on it. Finally the dismayed owner was able to rescue his timepiece and held it up to his ear.

"It's stopped!" he cried.

"Maybe you wound it too tight," they replied together.

Although Dorothy still found the undisguised taste of liquor disgusting, she did continue to explore drinking. Gin, she learned, could not be trusted because it made her miserably sick. After a good deal of experimentation, she found that Scotch whisky, without water, was generally quick, safe, and reliable. Eddie urged her to drink, even though Haig & Haig was selling for twelve dollars a quart at current bootleg prices, because he hoped it might lessen her endless scoldings about his drinking. Finally, she agreed. As she later revealed in a short story, drinking together meant an hour or two of cockeyed wild times, before the situation got out of hand. She turned censorious, he called her a lousy sport and an old crab, then he stalked out in a fury. Sometimes he stayed out all night and refused the next day to say where he'd been. Worse were the mornings when she woke with bruises, and she once suffered a black eye.

Whenever she drank with Eddie, the alcohol tended to make her jittery. She did find that drinking without him was enjoyable and that Scotch helped her to function better. It seemed almost miraculous how little sips, spaced regularly throughout the day, could act as an effective tranquilizer.

The best drinking company was Benchley or other Round Tablers like Heywood Broun, who had a habit of fueling himself all day long from his hip flask. Their easy masculine camaraderie allowed her to banish the most recent squabble with Eddie from her thoughts, and there was always one to forget. The liquor made her feel cheerful and loose, clever remarks spun spontaneously from her lips, until everyone was falling down with laughter and she felt appreciated and loved.

Never did Dorothy appear drunk. But she was seldom completely sober either.

In the spring of 1922, she was temporarily distracted from her marital troubles when the Round Tablers presented an amateur musical. A hit revue called *Chauve-Souris,* was running at the Forty-ninth Street Theater. The Round Table decided to rent the theater on a Sunday evening when the house was dark and to stage their own show, which they planned to call *No Sirree* Dorothy's contribution, the lyrics for a song called "The Everlastin' Ingenue Blues," was sung by Robert Sherwood and a chorus line of actresses that included Tallulah Bankhead, Helen Hayes, Winifred Lenihan, and a petite brunette named Mary Brandon, whom Sherwood married later that year. Benchley improvised a monologue he had dreamed up in a taxi on his way to the theater. It was a committee report delivered by an assistant treasurer called in to pinch-hit for the regular treasurer who was ill. Though this assistant was a bad speaker, he became caught up in the spell of his own oratory and got carried away. The audience seemed to find Benchley's "Treasurer's Report" quite droll. Musically, *No Sirree* must have been an intriguing oddity, for Deems Taylor wrote the music, Irving Berlin conducted the orchestra, and Jascha Heifetz provided offstage accompaniment.

According to Laurette Taylor, who reviewed *No Sirree!* for *The New York Times,* it was silly and totally amateurish, a criticism that was beside the point. The Round Tablers had a wonderful time. Afterward, the cast and audience, all friends of theirs, adjourned to Herbert and Maggie Swopes' for a party that broke up at four in the morning.

After that single performance of *No Sirree,* Benchley said, "My whole life changed its course." Irving Berlin and his partner, Sam Harris, thought his monologue was hilarious and wondered if he might want to repeat "The Treasurer's Report" in the next edition of *The Music Box Revue.* Benchley was incredulous. He hadn't even written it down. He wondered whether appearing as a performer might be a conflict of interest for a drama critic. As a joke, he asked for five hundred dollars a week. Harris was silent for a moment, then answered, "Well, for five hundred dollars you'd better be awfully good." A surprised Benchley promised them he would think it over.

He and Dorothy spent so much time together that people thought of them as a couple. Edmund Wilson believed their relationship was "special" and "rather peculiar" in that Dorothy seemed to regard Benchley as "a kind of saint," but Wilson did not suppose them to be sexually involved. Others assumed they must be. When a gossip columnist printed an item insinuating they were having an affair, Benchley was so upset that he sought out Parkie and apologized for the columnist's malice. Even some of the Round Tablers had their suspicions. One evening when Aleck Woollcott was entertaining the son of William Allen White by taking the Harvard freshman to a first night, he began to point out celebrities in the audience. The young man seemed most interested in Benchley, whom he noticed sitting with a dark-haired woman.

He whispered to Woollcott, "And that, I suppose would be Mrs. Benchley."

"So I have always understood," Woollcott replied, "but it *is* Mrs. Parker." Later he attempted to excuse this bit of nastiness by claiming that he had not yet known either of them long enough to understand the "lack of romantic content" in their relations.

Actually, theirs was very much a romance of the unconsummated, nineteenth-century variety, when the poetic notion of soul mates was not considered extraordinary. Dorothy's devotion was sororal. Benchley was her precious companion and closest confidant—and she also loved him. There was nothing remarkable about this because his male friends also found him lovable. Don Stewart said it was hard *not* to love Benchley, because he made people feel warm and clever. "If he had been a woman," Stewart declared, "I would have married him."

If Stewart had been married to Benchley, he would have seen little of his spouse. How serious an issue Dorothy was between the Benchleys is unknown, but Gertrude would have a lot bigger problems than Mrs. Parker.

That spring, it became clear that Eddie wanted to end their marriage. As Dorothy would recount in "Big Blonde,"

> Each time he left the place in a rage, he threatened never to come back. She did not believe him, nor did she consider separation. Somewhere in her head or her heart was the lazy, nebulous hope that things would change and she and Herbie

settle suddenly into soothing married life. Here was her home, her furniture, her husband, her station. She summoned no alternatives.

Suddenly Eddie painted New York City as Gomorrah. He thought that if he returned to Hartford, perhaps he would be able to pull himself together and make a fresh start. Apparently Dorothy refused to take him seriously because she expressed her reaction in a poem that imagined their life together away from the city. The verse is mockingly titled "Day-Dreams":

> We'd build a little bungalow
>   If you and I were one,
> And carefully we'd plan it so
>   We'd get the morning sun.
> I'd rise each day at rosy dawn
>   And bustle gaily down;
> In evening's cool, you'd spray the lawn
>   When you came back from town.

She promised to buy a cookbook and learn to cook, and even if the casserole turned out burnt and dry, she knew he would be understanding. She would sew and scrub. If her mind required cultivation she would join a women's club.

> If you and I were one, my dear,
>   A model life we'd lead.
> We'd travel on, from year to year,
>   At no increase of speed.
> Ah, clear to me the vision of
>   The things that we should do!
> And so I think it best, my love,
>   To string along as two.

A thumb of the nose was her answer to Hartford, and then the ball was back in his court. After so many furious but empty threats, she did not believe he would actually leave. They continued to string along as a couple. Memorial Day found them in Hartford visiting his family. Dorothy took with her a draft of a lengthy article, some nine or ten months overdue, that she had been promising *The Saturday Evening Post*. It was about out-of-town visitors in New York. Guilty about her tardiness and feeling frantic, she found that the trip provided incentive because she was able to base some of the provincials in the piece on the Parkers and their friends. In a seizure of inspiration, she dispatched it to the editor:

> Maybe it's the New England influence—we are up with my in-laws for over the holiday—but this simply won't turn out funny. I don't dare keep it any longer, and so I'm taking a shot at sending it anyway. I look for the worst—
>
> Hopefully,
Dorothy Parker

George Horace Lorimer must have been pleased because "Welcome Home" was published a few weeks later.

There was no trip to Connecticut for the Fourth of July. They spent a tense holiday in the city and went to dinner with Frank Adams. Quite soon after this the final explosion took place, and Eddie left for Hartford by himself. With the exception of Benchley, the Round Tablers did not receive an accurate account of the parting. Their assumption, which Dorothy did not bother to correct, was that the separation had been amicable, with Parkie begging her to come along and Dottie naturally refusing because she could not leave the Algonquin to live in a place where people had the mentalities of fruit flies. Not until seven years later, when she dealt with the scene in her fiction, did she describe her husband's anger and her bewilderment over the impossible actually happening. One day she came home to find him stuffing clothes into a suitcase. When he insisted that he was finished, she did not attempt to talk him out of the decision.

As she had written in "Day-Dreams," she honestly felt they would be better off apart. But that had been theory and had nothing to do with the emotions that now swept over her, a sadness that she took good care to conceal. Wishing to avoid pity, she proceeded to face her friends well-armored. She pretended that nothing of particular significance had taken place. When some people suggested that Parkie would surely return, she spikily insisted they were wrong and in any case she didn't care. Privately, she was dwelling on her estranged husband in an obsessive way. Any day she was able to chase him from her thoughts successfully, with the help of Scotch, she counted as a victory.

In August, she passed her twenty-ninth birthday with little pleasure or enthusiasm. Twenty-nine was dangerously close to thirty, which meant to her that the best years of her life were already behind, and all she had to show for them was a failed marriage. Her considerable achievements seemed trivial and suddenly unsatisfying.

Even though Dorothy became known for writing about uniquely female experiences, the theme of her first attempt at short fiction was male oppression, and the oppressed male was Robert Benchley. That she would write about him rather than herself was hardly surprising and certainly not coincidental. In her verse as in her fiction, she always wrote about herself or else drew portraits of people she knew, describing them so vividly that everyone in her circle knew exactly to whom she was referring. She was almost incapable of doing purely imagined characters or situations. In 1922, not yet prepared to expose herself, writing about her own failed marriage proved far too difficult. It was logical for her to address Benchley's problem, with which she strongly identified anyway.

By the end of the summer, after many months of meticulous work to perfect the story, she finally finished "Such a Pretty Little Picture." It begins with a man standing in his yard in summer, clipping his hedges, the evening cool with the smell of grass and the funny before-supper quiet of a suburban street. He is daydreaming. Mr. Wheelock is a wimp, an undistinguished man who has no first name and needs none because both his wife and daughter call him "Daddy." He secretly longs to flee:

> Some summer evening like this, say, when Adelaide was sewing on buttons, up on the porch, and Sister was playing somewhere about. A pleasant, quiet evening it must be, with the shadows lying long on the street that led from their house to the station. He would put down the garden shears, or the hose, or whatever he happened to be puttering with—not throw the thing down, you know, just put it quietly aside— and walk out of the gate and down the street, and that would be the last they'd see of him. He would time it so that he'd just make the 6:03 for the city comfortably.

Mr. Wheelock, like James Thurber's Walter Mitty, contents himself with fantasies and continues to clip his hedges, while his wife and daughter look on from the porch and neighbors passing by remark on what a pretty domestic picture the family makes.

In this tale, Dorothy sensitively developed a character living out the most common, banal of circumstances. Nothing Mr. Wheelock does surprises us, for he is us, the part of us that knows sometimes we cannot do anything we like with our lives, because it is just not possible. While her portrait of Robert Benchley was incomplete, the general outline conformed to his situation and it was uniquely his truth.

She sold "Such a Pretty Little Picture" to *The Smart Set*, a nonconformist literary magazine, coedited by Henry Mencken and George Jean Nathan, which doted on realistic stories that spoke out against the ignorance and pretensions of the so-called average American. Even though it published superior writers such as Eugene O'Neill and D. H. Lawrence, the pay was modest, probably less than fifty dollars. A dozen years later, when Burton Rascoe was editing a *Smart Set* anthology and asked permission to include the story, Dorothy replied that "its mother thinks it's the best thing she ever wrote, which would make it about on a parallel (oh, all right!) with the work of Carolyn Wells's middle period."

Writing fiction was a torturous process for her. When she insisted that it took her six months to complete a story, it was often the case. Instead of making a first draft, she thought out each paragraph beforehand and then laboriously wrote it down in longhand sentence by sentence. She may have been careless about many aspects of living, but she was obsessively careful, a perfectionist, in her writing. Nothing pleased her and she couldn't "write five words but that I change seven." She named her characters from the obituary columns or the telephone book. The notion of jotting down ideas and phrases in a writer's journal appealed to her and she managed to start one "but I could never remember where I put the damn thing." Finally she typed out the story on her typewriter, a tool that frustrated and mystified her, as did all machines. Once, stymied in a struggle to change a ribbon, she abandoned the machine in disgust and quietly resolved the problem by buying a new one.

"Such a Pretty Little Picture" marked the beginning of her literary career, but pride in her achievement was overshadowed by the departure of Eddie, by the emptiness of the flat, and the vague but unmistakable whiff of failure. Since her obsession had arisen and walked away, there was only herself to look after, a person she had never believed worth much trouble. From another perspective, her situation had dramatically improved overnight because now she was released from a variety of humiliations. There was an opportunity to heal herself, if she desired. She did not.

Accustomed to chaos, she hardly knew what to do with herself without Eddie and felt compelled to replace him immediately. Marc Connelly said that "when they were living together I don't think she had any lovers. But after Eddie left, then the men were in and out of her house like mail." But not at once. First, Dorothy fell in love.

When she met Charles Gordon MacArthur, he was a twenty-seven-year-old newspaperman with curly brown hair, an elfin grin, and charm that left few people of either sex unaffected. Everyone who knew him, said Aleck Woollcott, "always lights up and starts talking about him as if he was a marvelous circus that had once passed his way." MacArthur's beginnings were rooted in poverty and violent religiosity. He was the son of a mother who died early of exhaustion and an Elmer Gantry–like evangelist father who could smell a sinner ten miles away on a windless day. Chasing the ungodly from Scranton, Pennsylvania, to Chicago, to Nyack, New York, where he finally settled down, William Telfer MacArthur believed he owned a direct line to the Almighty. Having convinced himself that his six children must be in the sulfurous grasp of Lucifer, he would line them up, MacArthur recalled, "beseech God in a firm voice to forgive us, uncover our backs and whale the hell out of us. He kept a strap soaked in vinegar to make it a finer instrument of the Lord." At fourteen, he was sent to Wilson Academy in Nyack, a seminary with a curriculum that leaned heavily on prayer and Bible study and with an aim to train boys for the ministry and missionary work. After his mother died in 1913, he ran away to New York City and found employment as a salesman in the necktie department of Lord & Taylor.

From there he moved to Chicago and got jobs on newspapers. During the Pershing expedition to Mexico, MacArthur joined the First Illinois Cavalry, and in the World War he served in France with the Rainbow Division. Afterward he returned to Chicago, where he became a reporter on the *Herald-Examiner*. By the early 1920s, he and his friend Ben Hecht had become the highest-paid newsmen in the city.

In 1922, he went to work for the *New York American*, but by this time his ambition was to become a playwright. He met Aleck Woollcott in New York. As drama critic for the *World*, Woollcott, who had appointed himself keeper of the gateway to theatrical and literary fame, immediately began to regard MacArthur as a fabulous personal discovery. Adoring his wild sense of humor, admiring him extravagantly (as he would his next enthusiasm, Harpo Marx), Woollcott affectionately christened MacArthur "Baby Vomit" and brought him around to the Algonquin to meet his friends.

Since playing matchmaker was one of Woollcott's favorite avocations, he naturally thought of bringing together Charlie and the woman who was, in his words, "a blend of Little Nell and Lady Macbeth," and whose lacy sleeve had "a bottle of vitriol concealed in its folds." Knowing that "our Mrs. Parker," as he possessively called her, was alone and could use cheering up, he benevolently presented Charlie to her in the manner of a retriever laying a catch at his owner's feet. Since Woollcott knew that MacArthur had a wife, his gift was not entirely an act of generosity.

MacArthur, in common with Dorothy, had married his first love only to see it turn out badly, which was one reason he was living in New York but his wife was not. Two years earlier, at the *Herald-Examiner*'s water cooler, he had met Carol Frink whose duties as the paper's so-called Girl Reporter included covering beekeepers' conventions or dressing up as a Western Union messenger and delivering telegrams. Frink, a petite blonde with a tiny waistline and hair cut in an Ivanhoe pageboy, was loaded with so much pep that she once turned cartwheels down Michigan Avenue, which struck MacArthur as delightful. A few months later they were married by his father and spent their honeymoon at Coney Island. Frink's ambition to quit her job and write a novel was encouraged by her husband, who appreciated bright, literary women. In due course he bought her a typewriter, a raccoon coat, and agreed to finance a retreat in the Michigan woods, which she believed a necessary condition for serious writing without interruption.

By 1922, their relationship must have been fraying badly because Frink was not with MacArthur when he moved to New York. While they were separated geographically, the estrangement was far from final. Charlie continued to write her regularly, signing his letters "Charliecums" and similar baby-talking diminutives. Still, he was an unhappy man. Aside from knowing by now that Carol had little talent for writing fiction, he also suffered from loneliness and felt considerable antagonism toward his new

home. New York, unlike Chicago, which he considered a reporter's paradise, struck him as a phony, smart-aleck town more suitable for press agents
than for newspapermen. Newspaper reporters customarily were hearty
drinkers, but MacArthur drank more than most. Soon he was putting away
a quart of Scotch every night. He was not a good-natured drunk. Hanging
around subway entrances, he would yell, "God damn New Yorker! Deny
you're a lousy New Yorker!" More than one lousy New Yorker punched him
in the mouth. Once, on a spree with his writer friend Gene Fowler, he began
to feel sorry for the lonely dogs at the ASPCA pound and decided something
should be done for them. Buying birthday cakes at a fancy French bakery,
he delivered the sweets in a taxi. "My good man," he announced to the
ASPCA porter, "we've come to jubilate with your charges."

The attraction between Dorothy and Charles MacArthur was immediate and intense, a case of, Marc Connelly thought, "a two-ton truck meetin'
another two-ton truck. That was a collision on the highway there." She
made no secret of the fact that she found him the answer to her prayers
or that she was captivated by his sense of humor and a playful recklessness
reminiscent of Eddie Parker when she first had made his acquaintance.
Soon they were seen constantly in each other's company, at theater open-
ings, at a party Irene Castle gave for her husband, at Tony Soma's and
numerous other speakeasies (and they were once caught by federal agents
in a raid). In the late afternoons they usually could be found at Neysa's
studio, where Anita Loos caught a glimpse of Dorothy looking like a woman
very much in love. It seemed clear to her that Dorothy's "crush" was
ill-advised, because MacArthur struck her as a playboy "not to be pinned
down by any one girl."

Dorothy, meanwhile, was busily composing love poetry for Charlie
who was, she wrote, her "one love," a man for whom she wore her heart
"like a wet, red stain" on her sleeve for all to see. The Round Tablers, who
first had received the news of the affair with amusement, were now amazed
at Dorothy's innocence. Not only was she serious about Charlie but she
seemed to expect that he would reciprocate the intensity of her feelings.

MacArthur found her irresistible. She was the type of woman to whom
he had always been drawn, even though he probably realized that this type
was not necessarily what he needed. To him she was a pretty, successful
writer with a Rabelaisian wit and a manner that seemed to be frankly
sexual. There is no reason to believe that he regarded her as much more
than a casual flirtation. He had disliked being married and now, technically

single again, he was enjoying himself. In New York a few months, he had already established a reputation as a woman-chaser who bounced from bed to bed. Neysa McMein presented him with a rubber stamp that printed I LOVE YOU, a convenience in his many conquests, and Marc Connelly summed him up as "just a bird looking for the right twig to land on." Dorothy chose to ignore the fact that he never remained on any twig for long.

She was distraught when she saw him with other women and could not help bursting into tears, expecting that the sight of her pain might convince him of how deeply she loved him. "Lips that taste of tears," she wrote, "are the best for kissing." Charlie did not agree. He was losing interest in her.

To Dorothy's consternation, she realized that she was pregnant. She had once dreamed of bearing Eddie's child and only common sense had mercifully outrun her desire for maternity. She felt reluctant to let go of either her lover or her baby. Procrastinating, she worked on a *Post* piece about novelists who, like Scott Fitzgerald, make fortunes writing about the rebellious younger generation. She lived from day to day in bewildered agony, alternately denying and accepting the certainties of her situation. "It's not the tragedies that kill us," she believed. "It's the messes. I can't stand messes." Her untimely pregnancy, a tragedy, also qualified as a sorry mess. She found herself, at the age of twenty-nine, married, pregnant, and carrying the child of another man, also married. Reluctance to abort the fetus only partially accounted for her paralysis. She seems to have been waiting, hoping that Charlie would return to her, hoping like a small child herself that painful choices would magically dissolve and allow them to dramatically shed their legal spouses before riding away into the sunset with their love child.

In the fall she was busy rehearsing for another Round Table theatrical production. Encouraged by the success of *No Sirree*, the group was mounting a full-scale revue at the Punch and Judy Theatre where they hoped for an extended run. Dorothy and Benchley collaborated on a one-act drama, *Nero*, whose plot had little to do with Roman emperors but whose characters included Cardinal Richelieu playing solitaire, Generals Lee and Grant, Queen Victoria, and the New York Giants winning a pennant. *The Forty-niners* had other sketches concocted by Ring Lardner, Heywood Broun, and Howard Dietz and was staged by George Kaufman and Marc Connelly. Despite the considerable talent involved, it was a grab bag of hit-and-miss sketches, mostly miss. *The Forty-niners* opened on a rainy evening in early November and ran fifteen performances before closing. Frank Crowninshield said that maybe he missed the point "but was it all supposed to be taking place in an insane asylum?" Even Woollcott was embarrassed and admitted that the show "wasn't fun. Not at all."

Dorothy, in the meantime, could delay no longer. After the revue folded, her doctor performed a legal hospital abortion. There was no problem about obtaining one, so long as she had the means to pay. Her guilt and anguish were exacerbated by the doctor, who was upset to discover in the operating room that she was further along than she had known or had admitted to him. Either from the physician's remarks or perhaps from glimpsing the fetal material, she became convinced that the embryo's hands were already formed, confirming her suspicion that she had done something truly wicked.

For a while afterward, she numbly resisted the temptation to speak about the experience, but, in time, the truth became known to her friends. It was a subject she brought up periodically, usually late at night at Tony's, when she had drunk a great deal and verged on brimming over with great emotional cloudbursts. Then, with little discrimination, she would unburden herself to her drinking companions, mostly males who classified abortion stories as woman talk and wished she would go home and sleep it off. Despite herself, she went on talking, haunted by the memory of the operation.

Cruel stories began to make the rounds of the speakeasies. She was quoted as saying that the experience served her right for having put all her eggs in one bastard. Another piece of gossip reported that MacArthur had contributed thirty dollars toward the cost of the abortion, which had prompted Dorothy to declare that it was like Judas making a refund.

On Christmas Day eight plays opened. It made her angry to imagine that others were at home checking on the fires caused by their Christmas tree candles or strolling to the ice box for a nibble of cold turkey, but she had no tree or turkey, no comfortable fireside where she might warm herself. Her apartment, despite the presence of Woodrow Wilson and Onan, seemed the saddest, loneliest place on the face of the earth, and to top it off she had to "wrap her shabby garments about her and rush out into the bitter night, to see as many as possible of the new plays."

Most of the time she was tired and depressed. Her tears could be stirred by almost anything—a stray cat, the horses on Sixth Avenue, their heads drooping. She began sleeping all day until it was time to dress and go out for the evening. Scotch, she found, only made her sleepy, and when she woke up, she felt worse than ever. Reveries, visions of serenity, slithered into her head and stuck there. She could not pinpoint any one moment when she first decided to kill herself. Instead it seemed as if the idea had been a possibility as long as she could remember, like an ache that could be ignored most of the time but then began to throb unexpectedly. In truth, she had no great passion for violence. What she objected to was existence, its futility, its complicated surges of sadness that always left her feeling more surprised than angry. Taking herself through a single day presented no burden, but having to repeat the effort day after day was tiresome.

She became intrigued with suicide and began to research the subject like a bloodhound sniffing out a scent. She took the trouble to pore over daily newspapers in pursuit of suicide accounts, hoping to find useful details. Far from frightening her, the universe of self-inflicted destruction seemed cozy and reassuring, almost spellbinding. Somehow she managed to get through a bleak holiday.

At 412 West Forty-seventh Street, Jane Grant and Harold Ross's newly purchased brownstone, there was a tree hung with gifts for their friends. Ruth Hale and Heywood Broun gave their annual New Year's Eve party. Dorothy joined an informal bridge class with Jane, Peggy Leech, and Winifred Lenihan. They began meeting once a week at each other's homes to brush up on their game. She kept her expression cheerful at parties while she continued privately to obsess on ways to kill herself. She wondered how people actually went about it.

When the time finally came, it was easy. Midway through January, on a gray Sunday when mountains of dirty snow melted at the curbs, she slept until late afternoon, as was her habit. It was unusually quiet in the flat because the Sixth Avenue elevated trains ran less frequently on Sundays. The room smelled of perfume, whiskey, and dog droppings, all aromas to which her nose had become inured. Feeling wretched, she huddled under the bed clothes with a bottle and a glass, drinking until she could delay getting up no longer. That evening she was supposed to go to the theater. When she did get out of bed, she hurriedly dialed the Swiss Alps restaurant to order up a meal and then pottered off to the bathroom where her eyes alighted on a discarded razor that Eddie had left behind, an object that must have been in plain view for six months. Whiskey, she would write in "Big

Blonde," "could still soothe her for most of the time, but there were sudden, inexplicable moments when the cloud fell treacherously away from her."

She cut the long bluish vein on her left wrist, then quickly slashed at the right one.

Some time later, when the Swiss Alps brought her dinner, she was slumped unconscious on the bathroom floor and rushed by ambulance to Presbyterian Hospital.

When Dorothy was sufficiently recovered to receive visitors, she prepared her performance. Even though she looked wan and still felt weak from crying, she greeted her Round Table friends with a cheerful grin and her customary barrage of four-letter words. Pale-blue ribbons were gaily tied around her bandaged wrists, and she waved her arms for emphasis as if she were proudly sporting a pair of diamond bracelets from Cartier's. Had she been candid about her despair, they might have been forced to acknowledge the depth of her suffering and probably would have responded in a manner more suitable to the occasion. Playing it for laughs, she gave them an easy out.

By the time she left Presbyterian, her self-mutilation had found its place in Round Table lore as one of her unpredictable eccentricities, a gesture not to be taken wholly seriously since she had the foresight to arrange for her own rescue by the Swiss Alps. This version enabled them to shrug off Dorothy's unhappiness. Marc Connelly was not the only one who had the mistaken impression that "it was a little bit of theater, a young lady's romantic concept of Victorian melodrama. Coffins and all that, you know." According to Margalo Gillmore, "some people believed she did it because she wanted attention, although I didn't understand that because she had a lot of attention."

Convalescing at home, she was finally well enough to entertain the bridge group. Jane Grant and the others knew she had tried to kill herself but Dorothy chose not to mention her bandaged wrists, which she had tied with black velvet ribbon and oversized bows.

"What's the matter, Dottie?" someone finally asked.

"I suppose you might as well know," she answered defensively. "I slashed my wrists. Eddie doesn't even have a sharp razor." It was the sort of tough talk that discouraged expressions of sympathy.

Toward the end of January, Eddie returned from Hartford and quietly moved in with her. Dorothy agreed to try again because it seemed to be a logical solution, but she was not optimistic about their future. Charles

MacArthur had returned to Chicago, there was no man in her life, and she felt grateful to have someone there. On Valentine's Day it snowed almost all day and the city looked wonderful through swirling snowflakes. That evening they made their way through the snow-silenced streets of the Upper West Side to attend a dinner at Frank and Minna Adams's apartment. The only other guests were Frank Case and his wife Bertha. Everyone made a special effort to make Parkie feel at home and to regard them as a couple again.

Soon afterward Neysa McMein did an oil painting of Dorothy. She was, Neysa declared, "a design" that was perfect in proportion and linear beauty. She insisted that in her experience no more than five women in a hundred could be called designs. Since Dorothy had always considered her figure badly proportioned, she may have suspected Neysa of pulling her leg but she did agree to pose for the painting, which subsequently was exhibited at the Chicago Art Institute and won an award. Dressed in a simple frock with a demure white collar, she looked at once younger and older than her twenty-nine years. She seems noticeably thin and pale, fragile, her hands clasped tensely on her knees. Her eyes seem to be regarding the world with the dulled cynicism of a woman who knows a great deal more than the viewer.

Feeling the need for reforms in her life, she resigned her theater column in *Ainslee's*, the literary magazine she joined after *Vanity Fair*. After five years as a drama critic, she saw relatively few plays she did not detest. She was beginning to run out of nasty cracks and to repeat herself. The magazine replaced her with a writer who aped her literary mannerisms, an irony because Dorothy was now eager to abandon them. Nineteen twenty-three marked a major turning point in her prose. Until that year, she had taken as her themes subjects that reflected not so much her own preoccupations as the country's. Throughout the first years of the decade, she was sensitive to the mood of contemporary America. Since that mood tended to be one-dimensional and frivolous, so was her work. For her light verse, she mined and remined familiar terrain—cynical flappers, mothers from Montclair obsessed with Junior's tonsils, self-conscious young marrieds desperate to be thoroughly modern, America's obsession with prosperity and mediocrity. Much of what she wrote was mediocre. Nearly everything she wrote found a buyer, in itself a comment on the quality of her work.

What seemed acceptably cute in 1921 made her wince in 1923, and mortified her by 1925. Still, the dozens of hokey verses and prose pieces that she continued to publish initially established her reputation as a humorous poet. Critic-friends such as F.P.A. and Heywood Broun held a high opinion of her verse and so did enthusiastic editors like George Horace Lorimer, who was willing to pay top dollar because it sold his magazine. The content of her verse began to change drastically, as she now marched past her readers a procession of macabre images not generally associated with popular humor. Satin gowns turn into shrouds, decomposing corpses clinically observe the activity of worms, the living dead ghoulishly deck themselves with graveyard flowers. There were alarming glimpses, no more than a series of snapshots, of the tragedies that would be recognized by twentieth century women as peculiarly their own: the gut-searing loneliness of the women who have "careers," the women who don't marry, the women who do but divorce; the women deprived of maternal warmth and comfort who are condemned to seek love forever in the barren soil of husbands and children and even animals; women howling primitively for nourishment, flanked on one side by rejecting mothers and on the other by rejecting lovers. Her verse began to acknowledge the timeless subject of female rage.

As the weeks passed, her mental condition became more vigorous, as if the experience of almost dying had cathartically released pent-up energies and purged her depression. Sometimes she felt as if she had died, except that she continued to walk around, holding herself tall "with my head flung up" and carrying "between my ribs . . . a gleaming pain." She began writing another short story, "Too Bad," this time evidently feeling more confident of herself because she was able to leave Benchley's life as a fictional subject and move on to her own experiences for the first time:

> "Like your pie, Ernie?" she asked vivaciously.
>
> "Why, I don't know," he said, thinking it over. "I'm not so crazy about rhubarb, I don't think. Are you?"
>
> "No, I'm not so awfully crazy about it," she answered. "But then, I'm not really crazy about any kind of pie."
>
> "Aren't you really?" he said, politely surprised. "I like pie pretty well—some kinds of pie."
>
> "Do you?" The polite surprise was hers now.
>
> "Why, yes," he said. "I like a nice huckleberry pie or a nice lemon meringue pie, or a—" He lost interest in the thing himself, and his voice died away.

Grace and Ernest Weldon are a childless couple who have been married seven years and are regarded by their friends as models of marital devotion. In reality, they are uncongenial strangers who happen to share the same bed. Warily cheerful, unbelievably polite, they have passed far beyond the point where either of them cares enough to fight, drink, or hate, and they have absolutely nothing to say to each other. The Weldons, unlike the Parkers, do not drink and are in no sense people who lead unusual lives. Otherwise, the alliances are identical. When the Weldons split up, their friends find it incomprehensible and can only murmur trite condolences: It's too bad.

Just as Dorothy eventually portrayed the early years of her marriage in "Big Blonde," she recounted its demise in "Too Bad," which appeared in the July 1923 issue of *The Smart Set*. The fact that she wrote and published this story while still living with Eddie indicates it was a public announcement, not only to her Round Table friends but perhaps also to Eddie and his family. The concealed message was that while they were not yet ready to part, they had given up.

For the rest of the year, they preserved appearances. In contrast to the frenzied years, they lived peaceably, and once they had accepted the hopelessness of their situation, began to behave like schoolchildren showing their best manners. An understanding of who had been at fault was important to Dorothy. In seeking causes, she blamed the Rothschilds and went on to flagellate herself because as a half-Jew she should have known better than to have married a Gentile, particularly a Gentile above her station. In the peculiar poem inspired by this analysis, she hastened to absolve Eddie from any responsibility in the matter:

> Who was there had seen us
> Wouldn't bid him run?
> Heavy lay between us
> All our sires had done.

In the anti-Semitic "Dark Girl's Rhyme," where her self-loathing suddenly bobs to the surface, Eddie's forebears are portrayed as far from perfect but her own people are dark, very nearly evil, "devil-gotten sinners" dismissed by the Gentile world as fools. Eddie's rejection of her was only natural. She ignored such factors as their immaturity and the emotional fissures caused by a world war. She also pushed aside the devastating injuries done to their marriage by alcohol and morphine dependencies, which enabled her to avoid asking two crucial questions: What caused her attraction to an addict in the first place, and what was it about her that drew unstable men? She never acknowledged her need for the chemically addicted. It seemed a random event rather than a pattern. Since she could not confront the issue, it was always there, the prepared trap into which she would stumble again and again.

The healing scars on her wrists almost defied detection. As they faded, so did her earlier sense of despair. Suddenly she seemed to be having fun and prospering, earning decent money from *Life* and *The Saturday Evening Post* for verse and long feature articles. She guessed that it would be a long time before she made, as she wrote, "a few million—I figure, by the way things are running now, I ought to have it piled up somewhere around the late spring of 2651." She and Benchley had given up their office. Though she was working from her apartment, they continued to take a close interest in each other's writing and even collaborated on an advertising brochure for Stetson hats. In "What a Man's Hat Means to Me," she was in her usual droll form:

> I don't say that I am one of those big business women that make anywhere between ten and twelve dollars a month, in their spare time, by reading character from the shape of the hair-cut or the relative positions of the mouth and the ear. In fact, if I were to sit down and tell you how often I have been fooled on some of the most popular facial characteristics, we'd be here all afternoon. All I say is, give me a good, honest look at a man's hat and the way he wears it, and I'll tell you what he is within five pounds, or give you your money back.

That winter she became friendly with the tall, dark-haired poet Elinor Wylie, whose work Dorothy admired. Most likely, they met for the first time at one of Mrs. Simeon Ford's poetry dinners, rather hoity-toity literary affairs at which writers were served an excellent meal in exchange for an after-dinner recitation. ("Everyone," Mrs. Ford would remind her more retiring guests, "must sing for his supper.") During dinner, conversation turned enthusiastically to Walt Whitman, with one of the guests declaring that the two greatest people who had ever lived must have been Whitman and Jesus Christ. Wylie, asked for her opinion, named John Milton as her favorite poet. Amid cries of general horror and disapproving murmurs of "She says she likes Milton!" (all of which had to be repeated loudly for the deaf Mrs. Ford), the fan of Whitman and Jesus turned to Wylie and said, "I thought you were a *good* poet. You haven't been influenced by *Milton*!" To which Wylie promptly replied, "You admire Jesus Christ, but you don't behave like him, do you?" Dorothy could not help liking Elinor at once.

Wylie, reputedly a femme fatale, was thirty-seven. Her personal life had been marked by a number of tragedies, including the suicides of a brother and sister, and also by the juiciest sort of scandal. She had been born Elinor Hoyt into a socially prominent Philadelphia family. In 1906 she married a handsome, well-born schizophrenic named Philip Hichborn and bore a son. Four years later, leaving behind her infant, she ran away with Horace Wylie, a married Washington attorney and lived with him in Europe under an assumed name. Wylie suffered from periods of despondency. Once, the story goes, she appeared at the apartment of Katherine Anne Porter, saying that she planned to kill herself and Porter was the only friend she wished to bid farewell. An annoyed Porter replied, "Well, good-bye Elinor," and shut the door. Having finally married Wylie, she had divorced him and now planned to marry the poet William Rose Benét.

If the Ford parties were made bearable for Dorothy by the presence of Elinor Wylie, sometimes she encountered less welcome people such as Mercedes de Acosta, a face out of the past. The little rich girl who had been Dorothy's ally at Blessed Sacrament was the author of a novel and two books of verse. A twenties jet-setter who numbered among her intimate friends Eleanora Duse, Marlene Dietrich, and Sarah Bernhardt, Mercedes had married, but it appeared to be a marriage of companionship because her affairs with women were an open secret. Despite their common cause against the nuns at the age of seven, Dorothy was far from appreciative at seeing Mercedes, nor did she wish to be reminded of Blessed Sacrament, where she had spent some of the worst years of her life.

Sailboats from the Manhasset Yacht Club dotted the choppy green water of the Sound when Dorothy made her first visit to the pleasure domes of the very rich. The modest resort towns along the ragged southern shore of Long Island had been familiar to her since childhood, but the north shore constituted an entirely different world. It was not called the Gold Coast for nothing. On East Shore Road in the town of Great Neck, Herbert and Maggie Swope rented an ornate old mansion overlooking the bay. Across an empty field was Ring Lardner's house, while Scott and Zelda Fitzgerald lived on nearby Gateway Drive. It was the Swopes' house that Dorothy made her weekend headquarters throughout most of the twenties.

Herbert Bayard Swope was considered by his contemporaries to be the foremost newspaper reporter of his generation. He was big and overbearing, with the velocity of a human hurricane, the tastes of a Roman emperor, and hair the color of carrots. Cocksure, bouncing from one enthusiasm to the next, he was a compulsive talker and namedropper. The Round Tablers held a high opinion of the man, which had nothing to do with the fact that at one time or another he had employed most of them. Woollcott, F.P.A., Deems Taylor, even Benchley for a brief period, were all *World* columnists, as was Heywood Broun who said of Swope that if he sounded like a big bluff that was only ten percent right. "He is a big bluff but in addition to that he's got the stuff." Having the stuff meant that Swope had won the first Pulitzer Prize for reporting in 1917 for his work as a war correspondent and had gone on to become executive editor of the *World* three years later. Although the paper did not belong to him, he often behaved as if it did and its owner Ralph Pulitzer didn't seem to mind. When Swope retired from the *World* in 1928, at the age of forty-six, he sold his interest for six million dollars.

Swope and his wife liked to live on a lavish scale. At Great Neck they turned their house into a summer playground for friends and assorted gatecrashers. Their parties served as the inspiration and model for Scott Fitzgerald as he began writing *The Great Gatsby* that summer. Seldom were formal invitations issued. People jumped into their cars and drove until, somehow, they ended at the Swopes' door. The world and its mistress, as Fitzgerald wrote, gathered at Gatsby's house and "twinkled hilariously on the lawn." They chatted endlessly about theater gossip and antiques; they drank and passed out and revived, and they talked stock tips and horse racing. Some of those who accepted Herbert Swope's hospitality in Great Neck paid him, as they did Jay Gatsby, the subtle tribute of knowing little about him.

Across the way, sipping Canadian ale on his porch, Ring Lardner observed the Swope pageant with annoyance. He seemed irked that his neighbor was running "an almost continuous house party." There were large numbers of people roaming the woods because the Swopes liked to organize treasure hunts that sent guests scurrying through the shrubbery in search of sapphire cufflinks and other gewgaws. Sometimes the city folks got confused and forgot where they were staying, "for they wander in at all hours demanding refreshment and entertainment at the place that happens to be nearest at the moment," Lardner complained. Maggie Swope, who smugly called her house "an absolutely seething bordello of interesting people," showed no trace of concern for her censorious neighbors. Scott Fitzgerald happily described Great Neck as "a very drunken town full of intoxicated people and retired debauchees + actresses," and thought it was wonderful. Others claimed that anything could happen there. Despite Lardner's grumbling that the town was becoming a "social sewer," his complaints seem forced and he too was probably enjoying the spectacle.

The Long Island season began in the spring and continued until Thanksgiving. During these months it was Dorothy's habit to arrive at the Swopes' on late Saturday afternoon and settle down on the verandah overlooking the circular driveway with a glass of imported Scotch, all of the Swope liquor having been tested and certified by a competent pharmacist. There she waited for the other guests to assemble. At that hour, it was not unusual to find that her host and hostess had not yet risen for the day, but she generally had plenty of company. Frank Adams might be there, as would Ruth Gordon and her husband Gregory Kelly, Robert and Mary Sherwood, and Ethel Barrymore; Heywood Broun and Aleck Woollcott would be organizing a croquet game; invariably she found an assortment of politicians, gamblers, and poets. Often Dorothy got into conversation with a close friend of Swope's, a man with a thatch of white hair who she learned was Bernard Baruch. Despite their talks, he continued to mystify her. She knew that he was speculator-rich, negotiated armistices, and kept going to Washington to see President Coolidge, but still she could not figure out exactly what he did. There were two things that would always bewilder her, she joked: how zippers worked and the exact function of Bernard Baruch.

At the Swopes', tea was served at six or seven, dinner at midnight. No guest of his, Swope boasted, went to bed before three in the morning, although some of them passed out long before that. Maggie Swope engaged two shifts of servants and spent a thousand dollars a week on groceries. If ever Dorothy felt hungry in the middle of the night, she could order a steak or a bottle of champagne. When she awoke on Sundays at noon and rang for breakfast, it was brought on a tray with pink breakfast china that matched the pink linen napkins, along with an assortment of newspapers. The Swopes' stylish yet vulgar way of living attracted and disgusted Dorothy, who hated their money but wished it was hers. She never wore out her welcome at their house because the only unforgivable sin in their eyes was dullness. Dorothy, never dull, was the perfect guest, who could always rise to the occasion. Seated once next to Governor Albert Ritchie of Maryland, she listened politely as a series of questions were addressed to the governor about the state of the union. When this high-toned colloquy was interrupted by a drunk's noisy belch, she turned to the offender and said she would ask the governor to pardon him.

Dorothy repaid the Swopes' hospitality by giving them a dog. Their collection of pedigreed pets included an imported English pug that had been a gift from Baruch, two Pekinese, and several German shepherds. Her contribution to their menagerie of purebreds was a cur she rescued on Sixth Avenue after she saw a truck driver kicking it aside. Scooping up the filthy animal, she took her to Neysa's studio, gave her a bath, and named her Amy. The dog proved to be a good-natured coquette whose only bad habit was a perverse craving for Neysa's rose madder paints, so Dorothy decided that Amy would be happier living in the country, perhaps in fancy country like Great Neck. The idea of Amy the mongrel installed in the Swopes' kennel pleased her greatly.

Other estates where Dorothy became a regular weekend house guest included Ralph Pulitzer's mansion in Manhasset and Averell Harriman's family seat, Arden House, on the Hudson River. On one visit there, Dorothy took the precaution of bringing along a box of candy because she found the food inedible. Once each summer the banker Otto Kahn permitted Aleck Woollcott to plan an entire weekend and dictate the guest list. Woollcott was free to invite whomever he wished, so long as they were not stupid or boring. Dorothy and fifty or sixty others who happened to be in Woollcott's good graces at the moment trooped out to Kahn's 126-room French chateau at Cold Spring Harbor, Long Island. Addie Kahn, having checked Woollcott's guest list, would flee to New York, leaving her husband alone to entertain "your zoo." At Kahn's nine-million-dollar monument to the golden age of capitalism, Dorothy and the Round Tablers consumed fountains of mint juleps and gin rickeys, played Ping-Pong and charades and wild, emotional games of croquet that knocked over garden furniture and broke windows in the greenhouse. Their behavior at meals was not much better. "Can I order from the menu?" Frank Adams asked the footman

standing behind his chair. "Or do I have to take the blue-plate special?"
Kahn, presiding over the table in the grand ballroom with his dachshunds
at his feet, only smiled.

Being a professional guest had decided drawbacks, and there were
times when Dorothy accepted invitations against her better judgment. Only
after she had arrived and realized her mistake too late did she begin
groaning to herself: "I knew it would be terrible. Only I didn't think it
would be as bad as this. This isn't just plain terrible; this is fancy." She
would be stuck for fifty-six hours with people she abhorred and forced to
sleep in a room that reminded her of an iron maiden and drink highballs
so lethal that she feared a drop on her bare skin would scar her for life.
What she hated most were hostesses who announced that maybe Dorothy
would consent to recite "some of her little things for us" after dinner.
Dorothy gritted her teeth. "Maybe she would," she muttered under her
breath. "And maybe there was no war."

Long Island weekends ended on Monday mornings when Dorothy
caught an early train to the city. In a bad mood or hungover, she blamed
her condition on the Long Island Railroad, which forced her to climb off
the train at Jamaica in Queens and board another train. "No matter where
I go," she complained, "I always have to change at Jamaica." She bet the
readers of *Life* that if she embarked on a nonstop transatlantic journey she
would be required to change at Jamaica. It was terrible.

So was going back to her flat under the eyesore El on Sixth Avenue.

Eddie, meanwhile, continued to live with her. During the summer of 1923,
they spent a week together in Vermont, and now and then he accompanied
her to Swope weekends. Like the rest of the Round Tablers, Dorothy and
Eddie had become passionate croquet players. Eddie usually teamed up
with Frank Adams, while Dorothy joined Neysa McMein's team. When
darkness fell, the Swope guests flooded the lawn with their car headlights
and went on playing until dinner was served at midnight. As fervent as
Dorothy could get about the game, she felt this was going too far. Watching
from the Lardner porch, she shook her head. "Jesus Christ," she exclaimed.
"The heirs of the ages."

For a change, things were running smoothly for her. She no longer
wrote for *The Saturday Evening Post*, because after a boring weekend at

George Horace Lorimer's Pennsylvania estate Dorothy had made unflattering remarks that had got back to him. She continued to contribute regularly to *Life* and also began working for the Bell Syndicate, which paid exceptionally well. She and Neysa teamed up to produce a series of syndicated pieces about celebrities. She interviewed and wrote a profile of the famous person while Neysa sketched a portrait. These assignments hardly felt like work because many of their subjects—Charlie Chaplin, Irene Castle—were people they knew. When assigned to interview Luis Angel Firpo, the Argentinian heavyweight who was preparing to fight Jack Dempsey, they went to Atlantic City where Firpo was training and made a party of it.

Although Dorothy had few memories of her childhood or her mother, she intuitively disliked the Jersey shore, felt uncomfortable about spending even so much as a day there, and sometimes apologized for having had the bad luck to be born in West End. "I was cheated out of the distinction of being a native New Yorker, because I had to go and get born while the family was spending the Summer in New Jersey, but, honestly, we came back to New York right after Labor Day, so I nearly made the grade." On this occasion, she persuaded Benchley to join them. Flanked and shielded by her two friends, she advanced on the New Jersey coastline as if she were a doughboy revisiting Argonne Forest. Firpo's house resembled "one of those Atlantic City chalets that looks as if a cuckoo ought to spring from the door every half hour and call the time." Dorothy was a Dempsey fan but she decided that the "Wild Bull of the Pampas" was "a very nice boy." After watching him train for a while, they went off in search of fun and wound up at the greyhound races. In contrast with Great Neck, Atlantic City was filthy and the ocean looked so unappetizing they did not bother to go swimming. It was "a horrible dump," Benchley declared, crowded with "the worst bunch of people I have seen outside of Coney Island."

In the fall Charles MacArthur returned to the city and his old job at the *American,* and he rejoined his friends at the Round Table. Dorothy resigned herself to the fact that she could not avoid him, especially since he had become chummy with Benchley. At the end of September, when Jane Grant, Harold Ross, and Aleck Woollcott finally threw a housewarming party for their new communal house on West Forty-seventh Street, she and Charlie got together with Harpo Marx to rent a street carousel so that the neighborhood children might have rides.

Dorothy continued to feel bitter about the abortion, but, since it was a bitterness she could not direct toward MacArthur, she deflected it onto others. Robert and Mary Sherwood were expecting a child. Nearly everyone at the Round Table found the tiny Mrs. Sherwood a thoroughgoing bully and a bore, a veteran whiner who tyrannized her husband with petulant demands to earn more money. Throughout her pregnancy, she spoke aggressively and incessantly about her symptoms and her plans to have a Caesarian. At the theater, whenever the stage action became too intense for her delicate condition, she conspicuously rose and cakewalked up the aisle, until Dorothy's patience was exhausted. Compelled to offer congratulations after a daughter was finally born, Dorothy wired, GOOD WORK, MARY. WE ALL KNEW YOU HAD IT IN YOU, and sent the telegram collect.

Benchley, enjoying new celebrity as an actor, was appearing nightly in the *Music Box Revue.* He and singer Grace Moore were the hits of the show. Many theatergoers agreed with Heywood Broun when he wrote that "nothing of the season made me laugh as hard as 'The Treasurer's Report.' " Benchley had not given up his job reviewing plays for *Life,* which meant that he often had to be in two places at once. Finally he worked out a system: After going on stage at the Music Box at 8:50, for eight minutes, he dashed to the night's opening where Dorothy or Don Stewart or Gertrude were covering the first act for him and explained what he had missed.

A few weeks later, without warning, he collapsed with a violent attack of arthritis. In due course, he became virtually disabled and needed crutches to get around. At the Music Box, he left the crutches in the wings and tottered on stage to deliver his monologue.

Gertrude Benchley, assessing the situation from Scarsdale, concluded that working two jobs was grueling, even if one of them required only sixty-four minutes a week. She noted that her husband rarely got home to the country before one in the morning and left for the *Life* office shortly before eight. Clearly this placed a great strain on his health. Dorothy, who had been paying close attention to the facts, did not make Gertrude's assumptions. She knew exactly what had gone wrong with Benchley. She knew who had made it go wrong. The only thing she did not know was what he planned to do about it.

Chapter 7

LAUGHTER AND HOPE AND
A SOCK IN THE EYE

◆

1923–1924

Catastrophes fascinated her. In later years, living in California when summer forest fires were ravaging thousands of acres, she felt horrified at the magnitude of the holocaust, yet traveled many miles to view the blaze. At the sight of the horizon rolling endlessly in flames, she hid her face behind her hands and peered through her fingers. "Think how frightened all the little animals are," she exclaimed, "the little squirrels, the little rabbits, all the little birds." It was Dante's inferno, it was Armageddon, it was the end of the world. She could scarcely believe her good fortune. "Do you think we could get any closer?" she asked the friend who had brought her. In 1923, similarly spellbound, she quietly watched Benchley's marriage from behind crossed fingers. Not only had she made his domestic woes her chief literary material, but events in Scarsdale also influenced her feelings and subsequent decisions about her own marriage.

In the face of considerable evidence to the contrary, she persisted in regarding him as a slice of packaged white bread, unambiguous and predictable. She could not believe he would leave Gertrude. Both Dorothy and Benchley were genuinely confused. The crux of the matter was loyalty to people and concepts. Decent people, she had declared in "Such a Pretty Little Picture," "just didn't go away and leave their wives and family that way." Tutored and propagandized by the nineteenth century, she believed that to be God's truth, but she also suspected it was a lie because plenty of ordinary people were running away from their families in 1923. They were taking new spouses or sleeping with people who would never become their wives, or, like Eddie, just allowing themselves to be sucked up by their pasts and returning to hometowns they once had fled in revulsion. They were like Frank Adams, whose entanglement with Esther Root had made him spurn his long-suffering wife Minna after twenty years. It was impossible for Dorothy to believe that Benchley might be capable of a rebellion such as infidelity. "Good Lord," she had written of Mr. Wheelock in "Such a Pretty Little Picture," "the last thing he wanted was another woman."

But her pretty little picture had begun to fade.

Robert Benchley had evolved a pessimistic theory. Each of us, he believed, whether we like it or not, tends to become the type of person we hate most. The idea was thoroughly repulsive to Dorothy. All the same, she had to admit there was something in it that spoke a simple truth. Like all of us who can be more clearsighted about our friends' stupidities than our own, she could see the accuracy of the thesis at work in Benchley's life. Only too well did she understand what he feared becoming—a weakling, a failure, a self-pitying drunk—for she felt the identical fears for herself.

The previous summer, while hesitating over whether to accept Irving Berlin's offer to perform, Benchley stopped at the Western Union office in the Biltmore Hotel, a building that was near Grand Central Station and through which he passed regularly. One day he struck up a friendly conversation with a nineteen-year-old Western Union telephone operator.

By the time the third *Music Box Revue* opened on September 24 with Robert Benchley as a headliner, the stagestruck young woman no longer worked at Western Union for seventeen dollars a week. Although her name was listed in the playbill, she had no lines, nor did she sing or dance. She was a show girl and, as show girls customarily do, she wore spectacular costumes and impersonated things. In the show's opening number, "The Calendar," she was the month of November. In other sketches, she played a nightgown and a fish. In the space of a few weeks, having exceeded her wildest dreams, she had risen from phone operator to the stage of an Irving Berlin hit. The person to whom she owed her discovery was a prominent, exceptionally kind drama critic who appeared to be crazy about her.

Dorothy thought that Benchley's protégée was "very inferior," reported Edmund Wilson. It was an opinion shared by other scandalized Round Tablers, in fact by practically everyone who knew Benchley. That he would make a fool of himself over an unimportant woman bewildered them. Never for a moment did anyone publicly question the morality of his having a beautiful teenage mistress—to have objected on that ground would have been the ultimate vulgarity—but rather it was the Proustian ferocity of his obsession that shocked them. Was Benchley going to end up a besotted Charles Swann and want to marry her? His behavior suggested that possibility. Inexperienced at adultery, he was full of extravagant compliments and delighted in explaining to Dorothy why he found the show girl admirable. She had majesty; she entered a room, he said, with the presence "of a queen." He described her to Edmund Wilson as resembling a grand duchess. When Wilson finally met her, she told him that she was planning to audition for a "leg and fanny show." Wilson decided she was a floozy, "quite a pretty blonde with thick ankles, who, however, I thought, had something of that hard-eyed prostitute stare, the result of there being no coherence or purpose in a woman's emotional life."

Had there been purpose in her life it would have been frustrated. Dorothy, a worldly-wise twenty-nine, could have told her about wayward married men:

> Lady, lady, should you meet
> One whose ways are all discreet,
> One who murmurs that his wife
> Is the lodestar of his life,
> One who keeps assuring you
> That he never was untrue,
> Never loved another one . . .
>   Lady, lady, better run!

Dorothy had no advice to give Benchley's new companion, who was not the sort of female she could value or befriend. She appreciated her no more than she did Gertrude, whom she also considered to be a ninny and undeserving of Benchley. On the other hand, neither the show girl with her lack of sophistication nor Gertrude with her suburban matron mentality presented any competition for Dorothy's unique relationship with Benchley. She continued to be his confidante and hand-holder.

Several times a week Dorothy made a point of dropping in at the Music Box to hear Benchley deliver his monologue, the perfect starting point for an evening's round of partying. Recently she had discovered the pleasures of champagne and promptly composed a paean to her new drink: "Three be the things I shall never attain: / Envy, content, and sufficient champagne." Apparently, there were plenty of evenings when she did obtain sufficient champagne. After a performance of the *Music Box Revue*, remembered Don Stewart, "Irving Berlin came with us up to Dorothy's apartment where we celebrated my twenty-ninth birthday and with the aid of champagne helped Irving write the last two lines of a new song called 'What'll I Do?'" She genuinely enjoyed the parties, even if she did wake up feeling wretched the next morning. A doctor had warned a friend of Bunny Wilson's that if he continued to drink his toes might fall off and that very night he went to a party and got drunk again. In his place, Dorothy would have done the same thing.

Their lives held so many worries and potential worries; sobriety held no allure whatsoever. She worried about Benchley, who ached in every joint and went on stage with temperatures of 103. These ailments may or may not have been connected with his emotional distress, but his doctor diagnosed them as grippe and latent arthritis. Whatever the cause, he was increasingly incapacitated. The conflict could not have been more clear: He was in love, but he could not abandon Gertrude and his children. His attitude was that both women had claims on him, that neither would scarcely know how to tie her shoes without him. There was a period of several months when Benchley was seeking a way out of his predicament, caught at some crossroads between show business and suburbia and agonizing about what to do. During this time, Dorothy conceived the idea of writing a play about Benchley and his attachment to a chorus girl.

In January 1924, Dorothy accompanied Neysa McMein and Irving Berlin on a winter holiday to Miami Beach. When she returned, she and Eddie parted for a second time. He went back to Hartford, and it seemed likely that this second attempt at separation would be permanent, though they continued to be in contact. Since he planned to trade on Wall Street and would be in New York from time to time, he wanted to keep the flat for himself (and, in fact, paid the rent for another two years). Dorothy stayed for several months before moving to the Algonquin Hotel, where she rented a furnished suite.

Henry Mencken called the Algonquin the most comfortable hotel in

America. "The distance from the front door to the elevator is only forty feet," he wrote, "an important consideration to a man whose friends all drink too much, and sometimes press the stuff on him." The hotel offered Dorothy hot water that was actually hot and a front desk to call if she ever needed anything. She quickly discovered that the simplicity and lack of responsibility connected with hotel living suited her taste perfectly. The limited space also pleased her. Among institutional furnishings she felt free and organized. The Algonquin, of all hotels, was already a second home to her: She had only to ride an elevator to take her place at the Round Table, just as she had once walked across the hall to reach Neysa's parties. She had not outgrown her need to be in close proximity to the Round Tablers' hangouts.

Installed in her new home, she settled down to work. Writing had become her salvation. Although she had never written a play, she had done dramatic sketches and songs for the Round Table productions and saw no reason why she could not write a full-length show. Unlike her work habits for fiction, when she wrote so slowly that her typewriter practically spun cobwebs, she found herself tearing off page after page of typescript.

When she had completed a first act, she showed it to Philip Goodman, an advertising man turned theatrical producer who had made a fortune with two recent hits, including *Poppy* with W. C. Fields. Dorothy had a social relationship with the gourmandizing Goodman and occasionally visited his home for dinner. As a result of his recent successes, Goodman was riding a winning streak and felt confident about his ability to pick winners. He expressed generous praise for what Dorothy had written so far; no doubt, he was intrigued by the idea of a *roman à clef* about Benchley and his personal problems. He cautioned her that the manuscript needed work and suggested she team up with an experienced playwright. If she liked, he would hunt around, maybe find somebody like Elmer Rice for her. Dorothy could only nod enthusiastically. Aware of Rice's considerable accomplishments, she knew that he was being called America's Ibsen. She had praised *The Adding Machine* as an important play. For these reasons, she doubted if he would be interested in her project. Her excitement mounted, nevertheless, while she waited for Goodman to arrange a match.

Goodman's daughter Ruth, fourteen at the time, recalls meeting Dorothy in front of the Fifth Avenue building where her father had his offices. "I was sitting outside in the car with my mother when an enchanting little woman came to the side of the car with my father. She was in a blue serge dress with an Eton jacket and a very neat little blouse, extremely soignée, and she was holding on to a Boston terrier she had on a leash, a very feisty little animal. She sat between my mother and me on the backseat and was confidential about her dog. She didn't want him to hear what she said, and it was one of those side-of-the-mouth undertones as she discussed how impossible he was, how rude he was to her friends. I couldn't possibly imagine what he put her through each day."

If Dorothy knew Elmer Rice by reputation, so did he know of her, and what he'd heard were reports of self-indulgence and dissipation. Mrs. Parker was, everyone said, temperamental and unreliable. But Rice had a family to support and he needed money. *The Adding Machine*, despite its artistic success and a two-month run, had left him broke. He now needed to finance himself while working on another expressionistic tragedy about mechanized society, *The Subway*. Apart from the money, Rice enjoyed the technical aspects of playwriting and had no objections to accepting a routine assignment at play-doctoring. After reading Dorothy's first act, even though it seemed clear that she had only a dim notion of how to write for the stage, Rice could not help being impressed. Her characters were sharply defined and "the dialogue was uncannily authentic and very funny." The problem was that "the characters, suburbanites all, just went on talking and talking." Her first act, completely formless, ran as long as an entire play. Not without some misgiving, he decided to accept the job.

Rice's worries proved groundless. They quickly developed a good work routine with Dorothy doing practically all the writing while Rice concentrated on scene construction and plot development. The collaboration could not possibly have run more smoothly. Since Rice found it difficult to write at home with two small children present, he had recently rented a studio. He and Dorothy met there every few days to go over her playscript, page by page and line by line, with Rice suggesting places that needed cutting or rewriting. Once they had polished a section, they moved on to the next scene and discussed it in detail. Then Dorothy, inspired and full of awe for Rice, went home to write.

She felt "so proud" that Rice had agreed to work with her. "I was just trembling all the time because Elmer Rice had done so many good things, and here was I, a small cluck." It was impossible to believe that any play in which he had a hand could possibly fail. She also gained confidence from Philip Goodman's belief in his own infallibility. With two hits to his credit, suddenly feeling affluent enough to move from Riverside Drive to Park Avenue, he waxed expansive by saying that success in the theater was not a mystery but simply a matter of being smart. Most producers were saps who failed due to stupidity. With Goodman and Rice on her side, Dorothy felt extremely optimistic.

Working hard, incredibly hard by her standards, she was punctual about her appointments with Rice and diligent in producing promised scenes on schedule, altogether as heavenly a writing partner as anyone could wish. Rice found her "unfailingly considerate and, of course, amusing and stimulating." More to the point, he was beguiled by this "tiny creature with big, appealing eyes" and upper-class manners, and could scarcely believe the gossip about her lethal tongue. She was the picture of elegant breeding. In his memoirs, as if he had not already made his feelings clear, he felt compelled to add chivalrously that their relations had been "cordial and easygoing, but entirely impersonal." Not entirely, because he had wooed her persistently and excessively.

Dorothy was not particularly attracted to Rice physically because he was not her type. She preferred tall, slim, cinematically beautiful blonds. Rice was a dour six-foot, red-haired, bespectacled Jew, who had been born Elmer Reizenstein and had changed his name because he thought Rice would look better on a marquee. He must have reminded her of a childhood she had no wish to recall and of her father, who would have dearly loved to change his name from Rothschild to Ross but lacked the nerve. She found Rice to be a gloomy individual, which mystified her because later she pointed out that he had had great success. Against her inclination and better judgment, she finally went to bed with him, but it was one of those cases in which she realized her mistake at once. They were far less compatible sexually than artistically. Dorothy got little pleasure from their several encounters because in years to come she could not resist describing Rice to friends as "without question the worst fuck I ever had." Once having begun the affair, the problem became delicate: how to end it without wounding his feelings or, far more important, without jeopardizing her play. When she chose, Dorothy could be skilled at evoking protective feelings in men, and in this situation she probably delivered her orphan-of-the-storm impersonation. However she went about rejecting Rice, it worked.

Her affair with Rice left no scars and taught her something useful about herself. As she noted ruefully in "Ballade at Thirty-five," she was invariably attracted to men who would reject her. On the other hand, once a man began to pay her excessive attention she tended to quickly lose interest:

> This, no song of an ingénue,
>   This, no ballad of innocence;
> This, the rhyme of a lady who
>   Followed ever her natural bents.
>   This, a solo of sapience.
> This, a chantey of sophistry,
>   This, the sum of experiments—
> I loved them until they loved me.

That was, she explained, as Nature had made her.

According to Elmer Rice, Dorothy's play owed its merit more to her shrewd observations and pungent lines than to the plot. "It was a simple tale of a suburban householder who, bedeviled by a sweetly dominating wife and an insufferable brat, finds solace in the companionship of a neighbor, a former chorus girl; but habit and convention are too strong, and the spark flickers out."

It is possible to see how Dorothy subtly redrew the characters from "Such a Pretty Little Picture"—the doormat Mr. Wheelock becomes Ed Graham, his shrewish wife is renamed Harriet, and Sister remains Sister— and then went on to introduce a serpent into their suburban Eden. She is Belle Sheridan, an ex–chorus girl, now married to an alcoholic playboy who, having brought her to "Homecrest" (forty-seven minutes from Grand Central) has now tired of her and spends his time trysting with other women in the city. The Sheridans live next door to the Grahams. Ed is afraid of his wife, who constantly denigrates him as a useless fool and refuses to let him play his mandolin or smoke his pipe in the house. Belle is equally unhappy in her marriage, and both are extremely lonely. One day Belle, who plays the piano, invites Ed to bring over his mandolin. They play duets, they talk, they laugh, and they kiss. As the evening progresses, they give in to their attraction for each other and to their mutual neediness and impulsively decide to run away together. It's possible, Ed insists, to begin life all over again.

When he goes next door to pack, he speedily loses his nerve and terrifies himself by wondering what they will do once they get to the city. Go to a hotel? Register as husband and wife? Make love? Will he be able to satisfy a beautiful woman like Belle when his only sexual experiences have been with his wife?

At the last moment, when Belle notices his fear, she decides to go alone, perhaps secretly relieved knowing she won't be burdened with him but grateful that he helped her decide to leave her husband. "Don't you worry about me," she cries out. "I'm fine. Why, the minute I decided to break away I knew it was what I'd ought to do all along. It was just three years out of my life, that's all. Now I'm back where I belong." This is Belle's creator speaking about her own marriage, for, in many ways, Belle Sheridan is evocative of Dorothy's actual experiences with Eddie, as well as her imagined fears of what her life would have become if she'd accompanied him to Hartford. Belle's superficial characteristics—her mentality, her theatrical clothes, her statuesque figure—all seem to be based on Benchley's mistress, however.

In the final scene, Dorothy wants to show that her hero's experience with the chorus girl has changed his life too, by giving him more confidence in his masculinity. Now he talks back to his wife and spanks his daughter. As the curtain falls, he is seen sitting defiantly in his living room puffing on his pipe and strumming "that Blue Danube song" on his mandolin.

Constantly on Dorothy's mind was the issue of choice, not only as the essence of her play but a practical predicament for her and Benchley. Should she reconcile with Eddie? Should Benchley leave his family for a woman he loved? Was the correct decision for her also right for him as well? How many times they had debated these questions. It was their own existential refrain, a piano and mandolin duet they had been practicing for years. At stake, for both of them, was nothing less than their identities and their fears that living, or rather misliving, would transform them into the types of people they most despised.

The play was a love letter to Robert Benchley, who had helped her to wrench free of a dying marriage. Like Belle Sheridan, Dorothy felt "so sure" that she had made the right choice. Her advice to Benchley was "Don't do it! You stay here!" because she was convinced that his family "would always be on your mind." She wanted freedom for herself, but needed him to remain a father and husband, solid and leanable, upholding the traditional values of family sanctity.

By early summer the finished play was delivered to Philip Goodman, who scheduled it for the coming season. It was duly copyrighted under the title *Soft Music* and all concerned with the project were feeling pleased as they looked forward to a lucrative run in the fall.

Reality, by this time, had surpassed fiction in terms of strangeness. In the play, Dorothy had recorded some of the changes in the way people were viewing marriage and the family. Belle Sheridan returns to the city and her theatrical life, while Ed remains in Homecrest, unhappy but faithful to his commitments. It was an indecisive but wholly appropriate ending for the mid-twenties, when marriages ordained to last forever were splitting apart at the slightest pressure, and startled people were sitting in the wreckage, their futures in doubt. When institutions taken for granted kept blowing up in people's faces, a reevaluation was clearly indicated. It was no coincidence that one of Dorothy's characters chooses to abandon marriage as a dangerous way of life while the other sticks around and tries to make minor repairs. Unlike Ed Graham, this was not the choice that Benchley finally made.

On the surface, nothing had seemed to change in his relationship with Gertrude, nothing mentioned about harsh realities such as separation or divorce. Gertrude later admitted that her husband hated Scarsdale and that making the trip home each night was "too much for him," but she was quick to point out that he called her once or twice a day, as if that had made up for his absence. "People asked me if we were going to be divorced," an idea she scornfully dismissed as "absurd." Benchley himself later summed up his philosophy for James Thurber by saying that "a man had his wife, whatever their relationship might be, and that was that. The rest was his own business."

Benchley was determined to have his freedom, and the solution that he devised called for a caper more inventive than anything Dorothy had dreamed up for *Soft Music.* By all accounts, other than his own and Gertrude's, he left the suburbs and appeared there only as an occasional visitor. After his arthritic attack, his physician is said to have given him a choice between commuting to Scarsdale and continuing in the *Music Box Revue*. Since Benchley was contractually obligated to Irving Berlin and Sam Harris, he insisted that he had no choice and promptly rented an apartment on Madison Avenue. Gertrude had to be content with the assurance that he would come home on weekends. If she liked, she was welcome to commute into the city every evening and join him at the theater. If this seemed to offer a fair compromise, it was nothing of the sort because it was a man's solution. As any mother responsible for the care of small children knows, dashing into the city at the end of the day and returning home after midnight would be an exhausting schedule on any regular basis. As for Benchley's vow to join Gertrude in the country on Sundays, he became so reluctant to attend those Sunday dinners that he could not bring himself to board the train. His marriage operated according to the rules he set forth, and Gertrude, presumably, came to realize that she had been granted a Victorian divorce, with all the legal rights of a wife but none of the conjugal privileges of companionship. In exchange for Benchley's discretion with his mistresses, she looked the other way, and they began to live a lie.

The Music Box Revue closed in June 1924 after a nine-month run. The following Monday morning Benchley appeared at the *Life* office and asked Robert Sherwood for an advance on his salary as drama critic because he owed back rent on his apartment. Sherwood was shocked. Like most of Benchley's friends, he had assumed that Benchley was growing rich and salting away his wealth in savings bonds, so that he would be free to work on the serious books he talked about writing, "which shows how much I knew," Sherwood later commented.

As Dorothy knew, Benchley had been spending every penny of his acting salary of five hundred dollars a week. By then, he had been on a spree for nearly a year, and he remained on it throughout the rest of his life. One of the poems she published in *The New Yorker* was called "For R.C.B." It emphatically summed up her approval of the new Benchley, who said the hell with conscience:

> Life comes a-hurrying,
>   Or life lags slow;
> But you've stopped worrying—
>   Let it go!
> Some call it gloomy,
>   Some call it jake;

> They're very little to me—
>> Let them eat cake!
> Some find it fair,
>> Some think it hooey,
> Many people care;
>> But we don't, do we?

Dorothy and Benchley tried to strengthen each other by proclaiming how little they cared for public opinion, but it was wishful thinking and, in the long run, not helpful to either of them. It is not surprising that Gertrude's initial dislike of Dorothy was hardening. Mrs. Benchley was determined to make no overtly hostile statement, but could not resist an occasional acid aside. In retrospect, she told an interviewer, Dorothy "wasn't a very nice person—well, no. I won't say that. Whenever she came up here, she never helped with the dishes—fled upstairs." A cardinal sin in Gertrude's book was coming to dinner and not offering to help with the washing up. (It never occurred to Dorothy to wash up her own dishes.) Nor did Gertrude truly understand why Dorothy had separated from Eddie Parker. She professed to be puzzled that "she *was* fond of him" and yet there were "so many [men] after that."

About this time Dorothy was confronted by a curious situation when her best friend and her ex-lover decided to live together. One night Benchley encountered Charles MacArthur near the punch bowl at a cocktail party and impulsively said that if MacArthur ever needed a place to stay he could share his apartment.

"I'm a late sleeper," warned MacArthur.

"Delighted to hear it," Benchley replied.

Once MacArthur moved into the fourth-floor walk-up on Madison Avenue, where the two men lived for the next three years, Dorothy could not escape his presence without giving up the company of Benchley. As a result, the three of them were often together.

While finishing up the play, Dorothy had put aside other assignments, which now were due or overdue. Always reluctant to refuse offers of money, she had responded favorably to one from publisher George Palmer Putnam, who had cooked up an unusual idea for a serialized mystery novel. Nineteen well-known writers had been invited each to contribute a chapter. Dorothy had unthinkingly accepted, perhaps hoping that when the time came, she would be able to dash off her chapter effortlessly. No writing, even froth, came easily to her. Carolyn Wells had written the first chapter of *Bobbed Hair*, Woollcott the second, and now the collaborative murder story had a plot whose complications almost defied description and, alas, had magically progressed to chapter seven. It was Dorothy's turn.

Her standard, well-practiced evasions did not work with Putnam, who was publishing the serial monthly in *Collier's* before it appeared as a book and breathing impatiently down her neck. She was further distracted by Benchley's surgery for his arthritic problems and his subsequent departure for Nantucket to recuperate. After he had gone, the traffic in and out of her Algonquin suite seemed to grow unusually heavy. A number of people had the habit of dropping in and ordering a club sandwich from room service. There was a continual parade of waiters coming and going with pots of coffee. None of this commotion contributed to her concentration. After taking her out to dinner and a show one night, MacArthur reported to Woollcott that she had finally finished the chapter but only after Putnam had threatened to call out the police and fire departments.

A snapshot taken that summer found its way into Aleck Woollcott's photo album: Dorothy posing with Aleck, Art Samuels, Harpo Marx, and Charlie, who is seated cozily at Dorothy's side, their shoulders touching, the faintest of smiles on their mouths, smiles of complicity. Her continuing intimacy with MacArthur, who had become romantically involved with comedienne Beatrice Lillie, is interesting in view of other writing she was now doing. As friendly as she had become with him, she had not forgotten or forgiven his rejection of her or the pain he had caused her. The result was a bitter story, her third, this one dealing with the subject of abortion. In "Mr. Durant," she ventured to characterize MacArthur as a middle-aged monster of a husband and father who tyrannizes his family as well as his mistress and who gets rid of his children's dog while they sleep. The need to write this story must have been intense because she faced the problem of disguising the identities of Charlie and herself. In the story she exaggerated herself as a naïve, pathetic twenty-year-old stenographer in a rubber plant, a classic victim. Despite her off-beat theme and an extremely hostile portrayal of unfaithful husbands who impregnate their mistresses, she sold the story to Henry Mencken for his new magazine, *The American Mercury*, and it was published in the September issue. While she had painted MacArthur as a brutally insensitive man, this did not seem to interfere with their cordial relations. Possibly he chose not to recognize himself in "Mr. Durant."

The Democratic National Convention convened at Madison Square

Garden in June. Suddenly the city was crowded with visitors and cars, new revues were opening to cash in on the convention trade, Fifth Avenue was festooned with flags, and women were wearing the new summer styles: nude-colored stockings, floppy hats, and blue-and-pink chintz dresses that looked like flowered wallpapers. At the *World*, Herbert Swope had installed a radio in his office, and the Round Tablers listened to the convention proceedings on the wireless, or sometimes they dropped by the Garden to hear the speeches. The Democrats finally nominated John W. Davis of West Virginia, but these historical events held little interest for Dorothy, who stuck close to her rooms on the second floor of the Algonquin, regulated her drinking, and got out quantities of work. Like every writer she knew, she wrote when she was not drinking—and she drank when she was not busy working. "We drank our heads off, but we worked like holy hell." Despite a spell of sultry, sticky weather, so unseasonable for June, she felt better than she had in a long while. After finishing "Mr. Durant," she began collaborating with George Kaufman on a one-act play, the first and only occasion they ever worked together.

Famous Players–Lasky had purchased the film rights to the Kaufman-Connelly stage hit *Beggar on Horseback*. As part of the deal, they asked Kaufman to supply a curtain-raiser, a live playlet to be performed on the same bill as the film. Why Kaufman chose Dorothy instead of Connelly as his collaborator is puzzling, because they were not fond of each other. He felt put off by her obscenities, which he considered unladylike and offensive. She thought he was "a mess" and could see "nothing in that talent at all," although she grudgingly admitted that he could be funny now and then. Somehow they managed to contain their disdain long enough to produce *Business Is Business*, a forty-minute, four-scene farce that satirized a shoe manufacturer's obsession with making money. Kaufman at this time happened to be preoccupied with lampooning big business, and Dorothy's contempt for commercialism was solidly underpinned by her experiences with J. Henry Rothschild and Eddie Parker. *The New York Times* thought it was a clever play with "scintillating ideas" and "some amusing lines," but it is impossible to know for certain because neither author liked it enough to keep a copy.

Many of her friends were away. She saw little of Don Stewart, who had written a comic novel, *The Crazy Fool*, the leading characters of which were based more or less on herself and Benchley. Neysa, married and pregnant, had taken a summer place in Mamaroneck. Aleck Woollcott, writing a biography of Irving Berlin and claiming he needed solitude to work, spent a month on Neshobe Island in Vermont. When she next saw him, he was talking about buying the wooded island as a communal summer retreat for the Round Tablers. She kept running into Harold Ross and Jane Grant who turned up at party after party, passing a hat for a weekly magazine they wanted to publish. Everywhere they went they carried a dummy of the magazine until people were bored seeing and hearing about it. They were looking for investors and hoping to raise fifty thousand dollars from friends, but nobody was biting. None of the Round Tablers believed Ross capable of starting a magazine about New York. Woollcott thought the idea sounded "crazy" and flatly refused to listen. Dorothy listened but had no cash to invest. At a party given by Ruth and Raoul Fleischmann, Jane delivered an enthusiastic pitch that succeeded in whetting Raoul's interest. By nature a gambler who owned several racehorses and did minor speculating in Wall Street, Fleischmann reluctantly agreed to contribute twenty-five thousand dollars and office space in a building he owned on West Forty-fifth Street.

While trying to raise the remaining twenty-five thousand dollars, Ross went ahead and assembled a small staff. He also badgered his Round Table friends to suggest a name for his magazine. Among those under consideration were *Manhattan, New York Weekly, Our Town,* and *Truth* but none of them sounded quite right. Then one day, when press agent John Peter Toohey was lunching with them at the Round Table, the subject came up again. Looking up idly from his plate, he asked what kind of magazine Ross had in mind. A magazine about New York, Ross told him. Well, Toohey replied, then call it *The New Yorker,* and he returned to his meal.

An elated Ross wrote a prospectus, a model of simplicity and clarity, that described the kind of reader he wished to reach and the kind he did not: "*The New Yorker* will be the magazine which is not edited for the old lady in Dubuque. It will not be concerned in what she is thinking about." No disrespect was intended "but *The New Yorker* is a magazine avowedly published for a metropolitan audience. . . ." By this time, Raoul Fleischmann was developing cold feet; he had checked with a number of experienced publishers who warned him that he had been impulsive and, in fact, rather foolish. Ross had gulled him. Increasingly disturbed, he complained as if he had been the victim of a scam. To pacify him, Ross needed to acquire some impressive window dressing for his project, and he needed it quickly. He hastily assembled a board of editors that included Dorothy, Marc Connelly, Edna Ferber, Aleck Woollcott, and George Kaufman. In this raid on the Round Table, he was unable to get Frank Adams and Heywood Broun because they were under contract to the *World*, and Benchley and Sherwood had contracts with *Life* that would not permit their association with a rival publication. After a short time, Ferber and Woollcott withdrew because they were reluctant to have their names associated with a magazine doomed to failure.

Ever since Dorothy learned that Ross was intending to publish a sophisticated magazine, she had been smiling because he seemed wildly miscast in such a role. For most of the years she had known him, he'd been editing the *American Legion Weekly*, whose readers probably were the old men in Dubuque. In recent months, he had been working for the humor magazine *Judge*, but not so long ago she had heard him talking about starting a shipping newspaper, something he had referred to as the *Marine Gazette*. In her opinion, he was "almost illiterate," a wild man who had "never read anything and didn't know anything." His ignorance was a Grand Canyon among ignorances, so deep that one was compelled to admire it for its sheer size. Never would she forget the evening he took her to see Nazimova in *The Cherry Orchard*. "At first he sat silent. Then he said, and over and over throughout the evening, in the all-but-voiceless voice of one who comes suddenly upon a trove of shining treasure, 'Say, this is quite a play—quite a play!' He had not seen it before. He had not heard of it."

With this "monolith of unsophistication" at its helm, the future of *The New Yorker* augured poorly. Allowing Ross to use her name for his advisory board may have been a fraud ("the only dishonest thing I ever did," he said later about this phony board) but it meant nothing to Dorothy, who was preoccupied with *Soft Music*. Unlike Ferber and Woollcott, she didn't particularly care if her name was connected with a flop. Ross explained that the advisory board might be called upon to offer editorial advice or contribute an occasional piece, but he warned that payment was out of the question. He planned to reimburse writers with stock in his company. He also wanted contributors to write under pseudonyms so that the magazine would be able to project a unique character.

Hearing all this, Dorothy reacted by speedily putting Ross's *New Yorker* out of her thoughts.

. . .

In July, after Benchley returned to the city, Dorothy amused herself by accompanying him to the brothel operated by Polly Adler on West Fifty-fourth Street. The idea of drinking champagne in a bawdy house delighted her and she liked Polly. So did Benchley, who opened a charge account and began keeping a black kimono there. Though he played backgammon with the madam for the services of her women, which were currently going for twenty dollars a throw, he had begun thinking of Polly's as a second home where he slept or even worked. Polly Adler was devoted to Benchley, who, she said, "lighted up my life like the sun." She made certain that he received the finest treatment. In the mornings, he woke to find that Polly's personal maid, Lion, had pressed his suit, washed his socks and underwear, and was waiting to serve him breakfast in bed.

Dorothy and Benchley thought that Polly's house could use a touch of culture, and they were pleased to offer their assistance. They drew up a shopping list of classical and contemporary books for her bookshelves. In due course, Polly's patrons had at their disposal a nice selection of literary works.

At the age of thirty-four, Benchley was busy sowing his wild oats. Since he and Charlie MacArthur had been rooming together, they had become inseparable. There were times when Dorothy found herself ex-cluded from their escapades as they bounced around the city like teenagers. They once chased the aristocratic Charles Evans Hughes down Madison Avenue, spraying him with cries of "Yah, yah, Secretary of State." Dorothy could not enter into this sort of adolescent, alcoholic male bonding, proba-bly luckily for her.

In September, Philip Goodman discovered that life as a Broadway producer was not all roses. His new musical, *Dear Sir,* was practically laughed off the stage on opening night when a horse in the cast defecated on stage, distract-ing performers and audience alike. Although the show had music and lyrics by Jerome Kern and Howard Dietz, the critics decided that the production was indeed manure, and it folded after fifteen performances. Goodman, unnerved, ordered production temporarily suspended on *Soft Music* and indicated he would probably abandon it altogether.

Shortly after the failure of *Dear Sir*, Goodman suffered a second blow when his next offering, *The Mongrel*, directed by Dorothy's friend Winnie Lenihan, also proved mediocre and had to be withdrawn. By now, Goodman was devastated and decided that he wouldn't proceed with Dorothy's play unless he was able to find someone willing to coproduce and stage it. To her relief, he finally persuaded Arthur Hopkins to be his partner. Hopkins, an Ohioan by birth, taciturn by temperament, was a veteran producer with many successes to his credit, among them such quality dramas as *Hedda Gabler* and *Anna Christie*. At first, the addition of Hopkins did not displease Dorothy. Nor did she object when Goodman and Hopkins changed the name of the drama from *Soft Music* to *Close Harmony*, even though the latter seemed to her no great improvement over the former. But once rehearsals began, she became increasingly worried about Hopkins's directorial technique, because he seemed to have none.

Each day at noon, after the cast had been put through their paces by the stage manager, Hopkins drifted in and leaned against the proscenium arch. He looked on almost indifferently, rarely if ever interrupting, and occasionally took an actress or actor aside for a few moments of whispering. After a while—a very short while—he departed for the day. It had been explained to Dorothy that Hopkins believed performers should work out their own readings and stage business, but watching him in action was far from reassuring. She caustically dubbed his directorial style "the Arthur Hopkins honor system of direction."

While Dorothy worried, Hopkins leased one of New York's most expensive theaters, the Gaiety, for the sum of four thousand dollars a week and announced to the papers that *Close Harmony* would open on December 1. This further alarmed Dorothy, who knew from her experience as a drama critic that attendance is always poor before Christmas. When she voiced her doubts to Hopkins, he brushed them away.

"Whenever you open this play," he assured her, "it will run for a year."

Close Harmony had its out-of-town preview in Wilmington, Delaware. Dorothy and Elmer Rice accompanied the cast, who were traveling in a reserved parlor car. A private compartment had been set aside at one end of the car for the writers and producers, but at the last minute they were joined by several of the actresses, including Georgie Drew Mendum, who had been cast as the Gertrude Benchley character. Dorothy disliked Mendum almost as much as she did Mrs. Benchley. A garrulous descendent of two theatrical royal families, the Barrymores and the Drews, she was in the habit of regaling people with stories about dear Jack and dear Ethel, as well as other members of the clan. On the train she talked nonstop. Elmer Rice remembered that since the train did not have a dining car, there was no escape from her. He and Dorothy and the two producers fidgeted and stared out the window at the New Jersey farmland. "We were trapped, elbow to elbow, knee to knee," Rice said.

When the train pulled into Wilmington, everyone disembarked and began straggling down the platform toward the taxi stand. Dorothy, watching them leave, remained near the train door with Goodman and Rice.

"Let's go to Baltimore," she said.

Without a word, they grabbed their suitcases and climbed back on the train just as it was pulling out. Only then did her bewildered companions begin to object. What could she be thinking of, because there was plenty to do that evening in Wilmington.

"I'm terribly sorry," she said, "but I just couldn't look at them anymore."

It was after eight when they arrived in Baltimore, starving. Goodman telephoned Henry Mencken, who invited them to his hotel for drinks and dinner. Not only did Dorothy respect Mencken as an innovative publisher, but also she had a personal reason for feeling warm toward him: he had published every short story she had written thus far. On this particular evening, she was disappointed to find him coarse and insensitive. Even allowing for the immense quantities of alcohol they were consuming, Mencken acted badly. When he began to tell jokes about blacks, Dorothy bristled and decided to leave. She refused to spend the night in Baltimore and made Rice take her to Wilmington, even though it meant riding a milk train that got them there at three in the morning.

The next day, exhausted and hung over, she sat in the darkened theater with Arthur Hopkins during dress rehearsal and decided that the play was insipid. Hopkins appeared to be studying the bouncing breasts of Wanda Lyon, the actress playing Belle Sheridan.

"Dorothy," he said, "don't you think she ought to wear a brassiere in this scene?"

"God, no," she replied. "You've got to have something in the show that moves."

On opening night, the first laugh of the evening was hers, in response to a wry telegram she received from Benchley. THAT OLD FILLING HAS JUST COME OUT, it read. After that, the laughs came from the audience who chortled straight through until the curtain fell. The next day, when she saw that the local critics had hailed the show a winner, she began to hope again. During her years as a drama critic, she had complained incessantly about tedious opening nights, but watching people on stage speaking words she had written was another matter entirely. It was "the most exciting thing in the world." When *Close Harmony* opened in New York the following week, she was still feeling euphoric and confident of success enough to throw an opening-night party at the Algonquin.

Despite excellent reviews and hosannas for "Miss Dorothy Parker, who is known as New York's brightest girl," customers were slow to buy tickets. The third week, after a matinee when the house was practically empty, Dorothy sent a telegram to Benchley that read, CLOSE HARMONY DID A COOL NINETY DOLLARS AT THE MATINEE. ASK THE BOYS IN THE BACK ROOM WHAT THEY WILL HAVE. By guaranteeing the Gaiety Theater four thousand dollars a week, Hopkins could not afford to carry the play. A week later, he posted the closing notice. The play had run twenty-four performances and grossed less than ten thousand dollars. Hopkins subsequently assigned touring rights to another producer, who changed the play's name to *The Lady Next Door* and opened it in Chicago the following summer. There it played fifteen weeks, followed by another ten weeks in smaller Midwestern cities, to fine reviews and substantial houses. As Elmer Rice later wrote, "These things are inexplicable." Ring Lardner was also puzzled. Writing to Scott Fitzgerald in Rome, he reported that *Close Harmony* was a good play that had gotten great notices and still it failed. To Dorothy the failure seemed nothing short of astonishing, an enormously bad joke that she could not comprehend and would be unable to talk about. In years to come, when asked about it, she supposed that "it was dull," and yet "how do you know about your own."

Philip Goodman, who had enough of the theater, went to Paris for the winter. He and Hopkins may have been relying on the enthusiastic support of the Round Table to ensure success and a long run. Perhaps they also had counted on its being a spicy open secret that the play concerned Robert Benchley, but audiences were not privy to this titillating bit of rialto gossip. Benchley had the unenviable task of reviewing a work based on his own messy domestic life, but with which he could not admit any connection. He found the play deeply moving, especially the scene in which James Spotts-wood and Wanda Lyon play a mandolin and piano duet to the tune of "The Sunshine of Your Smile," and decided it was "just about as heartbreaking a thing as we have ever seen on the stage." On the evening that he attended *Close Harmony* the audience apparently began to laugh during this scene and he took it badly. In his *Life* review he inferred that they must have severe personality disorders and singled them out "for special and painful extermination next Monday morning, rain or shine." If he saw anyone so much as daring to grin during the scene "you will receive, on leaving the lobby, one special souvenir crash on the skull which will make it awfully difficult for you to laugh at anything again. That's final." *Close Harmony* was, in his opinion, closer to "magnificent tragedy" than to comedy.

Both Dorothy and Benchley felt murderous but as usual they veiled their anger with humor. Dorothy wished she could be a pirate so that she might cut out the hearts of everyone she hated. After the play closed she wrote a revealing poem for *Life* and called it "Song of Perfect Propriety":

> Oh, I should like to ride the seas,
>   A roaring buccaneer;
> A cutlass banging at my knees,
>   A dirk behind my ear.
> And when my captives' chains would clank
>   I'd howl with glee and drink,
> And then fling out the quivering plank
>   And watch the beggars sink.
>
> I'd like to straddle gory decks,
>   And dig in laden sands,
> And know the feel of throbbing necks
>   Between my knotted hands.
> Oh, I should like to strut and curse
>   Among my blackguard crew. . . .

Given the chance, she would do all that and more. Certainly she felt capable of destroying those who had injured her.

> But I am writing little verse,
>   As little ladies do.

Chapter 8

"YESSIR,
THE WHADDYECALL'EM BLUES"

•

1925

During that winter of 1925 there seemed to be no end to the number of men passing through her life and her hotel suite. Their names were "ever written on the pages of my heart—and, by the way, my dear, what *was* your name?" Chiefly, these visitors were in transit. It was the period that Marc Connelly was thinking of when he likened her apartment to a mailbox. Connelly's description of one of those lovers could serve as a portrait of all:

> She fell in love with some of the goddamnedest terrible people. John What-the-hell-was-his-name—society boy with the famous brother, you'd know the name if I could remember it. He and his brother were very, very, very East Hampton. Handsome guy, pretty good tennis player. He was a wealthy mucker and quite a bastard. We were all delighted when she shook him off—he was dandruff. Have you got a list of her beaux? Not a full list? Well, I wouldn't think so.

After months of hard work she was pleased to be idle. She wanted to have fun, which meant dating sizable numbers of rich, good-looking men. No doubt she felt genuinely enthusiastic about some of them, but these affairs were certainly nothing more serious than crushes. The string of men offered the illusion of accomplishment and helped to obscure the fact that Eddie Parker had dropped out of the picture by now. She insisted on being called Mrs. Parker, wearing the title as grandly as if it had been inherited. Whenever impertinent people inquired why she continued to call herself Mrs., she answered defensively that there *had been* a Mr. Parker once. Although she thought of Eddie in the past tense, neither of them had decided to obtain a divorce, and he remained her legal husband until 1928. Among those who remembered his existence was Gertrude Benchley, who professed from her outpost in Scarsdale to find the banishment of Parkie and his replacement by a bunch of Long Island playboys incomprehensible. "She dedicated one of her books 'to John,' but by the time the book came out it was quite another John! Lucky it was a common name like that."

Dorothy learned that there were special benefits to be derived from her celebrity as a playwright, even from being a failed playwright. An attractive, successful woman who had passed the age of thirty, who no longer expected men to respect her so-called purity, was able to wield a type of power over males, not genuine power, of course, but a counterfeit that seemed real. Suddenly swarms of men seemed eager for her company, for no other reason than that she was Mrs. Dorothy Parker. She had her pick of polo players, low-brow moguls who had never heard of James Joyce, gentleman stockbrokers, and all the assorted frog-princes who congregated in Great Neck. Even those who found clever women terrifying, which included most of them, could not suppress the urge to pay court. Since sex seemed to be her only immediate reward for the failure of *Close Harmony*, she had every intention of milking that painful experience for its current worth. She wondered if it was worth anything, and suspected not.

> Because your eyes are slant and slow,
>   Because your hair is sweet to touch,
> My heart is high again; but oh,
>   I doubt if this will get me much.

Even though she felt drawn toward men with money, she secretly abominated them and undertook it as her mission to punish them, even those she genuinely liked, even those who worked hard for their money. Her attitude toward these men can be summed up in her treatment of Frank Case, the manager of the Algonquin Hotel, whom she seldom bothered to pay for her suite. She convinced herself that her presence was good publicity for the hotel, that in fact Case should feel fortunate to have her living there rent-free. One Christmas when friends asked if she planned to hang up a stocking, she said, "No, but I'm going to hang up Frank Case," which she had, in fact, been doing all year.

She also derived satisfaction from hanging up wealthy men, thinking of them as rich Neanderthals who could well afford to pay for the privilege of being seen around town with one of New York's most sought-after women. There were times, however, when her gorge rose and she could not control her contempt. At Ralph Pulitzer's estate in Manhasset one evening, she stared for a long while at the face of a man sitting across from her. Then she turned to her friend Peggy Leech and blurted out, "He looks just like a pig, doesn't he, Peggy?"

Donald Stewart thought that any man who got emotionally involved with Dorothy "would have found out, little by little, that she wasn't really there." At first this wouldn't be apparent because she was always so much fun to be with, but eventually it would become clear that "it was *her* emotion; she was not worrying about *your* emotion." While striking fancy poses and whipping herself into an emotional frenzy got her adrenaline moving, that white-hot heat also served a serious purpose; it generated salable verse and enabled her to deposit checks into her bank account. In this respect, she was no more calculating than Scott Fitzgerald who, in April, published his novel *The Great Gatsby*, which he had extracted from his and Zelda's eighteen-month residence in Great Neck. His characters were modeled on people he had met at the Swopes', who were some of the very same men winding up in Dorothy's bed at the Algonquin and, eventually, in her verse. Both Dorothy and Fitzgerald were adept at sucking the juices out of people. All those pretty playboys had their practical uses. Once she had melted down and recycled them, they behaved much like men in Pasadena or Tulsa and were instantly recognizable to readers of her verse.

In the humorous verse she wrote in the mid-twenties, men were little loves who sweetly, if naïvely, presented her with "one perfect rose," never considering that she might instead have preferred a good solid Rolls-Royce. Like exotic insects under glass, men became her subject of special study. She was prepared to announce conclusions about the entire species. Men were incapable of passing up a speakeasy, a poker game, or a golf course, which meant that they often neglected to call at the precise time they had promised, while women wasted their time waiting for them. In fact it sometimes seemed that "all your life you wait around for some damn man!" Furthermore: They were seldom capable of experiencing sexual attraction for a woman who wore glasses, unable to suppress their boasting about others with whom they slept, and perhaps most distressing, totally incapable of accepting a woman as she was. When younger, Dorothy wrote, she had done her best to indulge men in their fantasies, had even tried to change herself to suit their rattlebrained theories. Now, in her thirties, she understood that if you scratched a lover you would find a foe. It was safest, therefore, to look upon the male sex as a temporary entertainment because

> By the time you swear you're his,
> > Shivering and sighing,
> And he vows his passion is
> > Infinite, undying—
> Lady, make a note of this:
> > One of you is lying.

In the winter of 1925 it was she who was doing most of the lying.

That year, Seward Collins fell in love with a cabaret singer named Lee Morse from her phonograph records, and then contrived to meet her. Her big hit was "Yessir, the Whaddyecall'em Blues." Even though her fans liked hot tunes, she preferred romantic ballads, some of which she wrote herself. One night after a party Collins took Bunny Wilson and his wife, Mary, and several other friends to the club where Lee Morse was singing, and they wound up drinking unidentifiable, practically undrinkable liquor that was served in ginger ale bottles. When Lee Morse joined them, she confided to Mary Wilson and Alice Seldes that she was waiting for a marriage proposal from Sew, not because she planned to accept but because she wanted to be asked. Alice, knowing the twenty-six-year-old Collins to be an immature and vulnerable bachelor, warned him about Lee Morse. Before long, however, Collins stopped seeing her because he had fallen in love with Dorothy.

Seward, always called Sew or Sewie, was born in Pasadena in 1899, into a well-to-do family who owned a chain of cigar stores. They sent him to Princeton where he became friends with Edmund Wilson and John Peale Bishop. In 1920, after Wilson took over Benchley's job at *Vanity Fair*, he brought in Collins as a regular contributor. Later, when Wilson moved to

The New Republic, he continued to assign articles to Collins, whose background and liberal political views paralleled his own. By the time Collins met Dorothy, he was eager to use his wealth to further his publishing ambitions and was negotiating to buy a literary journal called *The Bookman.* His claim to fame fell into the area of sexology rather than literature because he owned a collection of obscene English literature said to be the largest in the world.

Collins took extreme pride in his erotica, although those who remember it say that by today's standards it would be rated tame. What it lacked in sophistication, it more than made up for in quantity, for he was a compulsive buyer. A spectacular number of boxes and trunks were stored at his country house in Connecticut. The really wild items he kept in his Manhattan apartment, which was a virtual gallery of old and new masters. Running into Sewie at a speakeasy, Marc Connelly remembered, generally meant an invitation to stop by later for a nightcap and a look. It was not uncommon for Collins to arrange formal showings, where he would display recent acquisitions.

Dorothy had known Collins casually for several years but paid him slight attention. Not only was he six years her junior, but he was undistinguished physically, being of medium height and pale, mousy coloring. He had an ingratiating smile and was a talker, which annoyed some people, but his friends found him witty and amusing. When Edmund Wilson drew up an imaginary guest list for an ideal party, he put Sewie and Dorothy near the top.

Despite Collins's infatuation with Lee Morse, he was very much aware of Dorothy, very admiring, and flirted discreetly. His interest in sexology did not mean he personally was sexually emancipated. In contrast to Benchley, for example, who was too busy copulating to gaze at pictures of people doing it, Collins was strictly a spectator who, according to Marc Connelly, always comported himself like a gentleman around women and who behaved "like a nice guy." Nice guys did not impress Dorothy.

That spring he backed her into a corner at a party and smothered her with excessive compliments. He seemed exactly the sort of man she had meant when she wrote, in "Experience," that "some men fawn and flatter." Not long after that, someone at *The Bookman,* Collins no doubt, enthused over the prettiest spring hat in New York. "It was on the head of no less a beautiful person than the pleasant Dorothy Parker, maker of plays and verses and dramatic criticism. It was large and low and green—pale green, along the side was a sheaf of pussy willows. There's a hat to square yourself with, sir." Seeing Dorothy's intense eyes next to the pussy willows knocked all thoughts of Lee Morse out of his head for good.

The Bookman also reported that Dorothy was working on a play and would soon embark on a novel, inaccurate information supplied by Dorothy herself. On the evening she had blabbed all this to Collins, the night she was wearing the pussy willow hat, she had been in the company of Elinor Wylie. She had spoken about a new novel she had started, and Dorothy, not wishing to be outdone, had fabricated a fictitious work schedule on the spot. She couldn't get rid of Collins fast enough. He was one of those naïfs who assumed writers must always be busy writing, just as dentists were forever drilling. Routine though his questions may have been he greatly irritated her.

Meanwhile, the first issue of *The New Yorker* was published on February 21. Jane Grant admitted that she and Ross were "not proud" of its debut. F.P.A. expressed disappointment: "To H. Ross's, and he showed me a copy of the New Yorker, which is to be issued on Tuesday, but most of it seemed too frothy for my liking." James Thurber called it, without exaggerating, "the outstanding flop of 1925." Ross had been expecting his board of editors to help out with contributions and found their lack of assistance disheartening. The first issue appeared without the Round Tablers, nor were they present in succeeding issues. The single exception was Dorothy, who contributed drama reviews for the first two issues under the byline "Last Night." Despite the pseudonym, there is no doubt of their authorship: ". . . we bashfully admit that we wept, and lavishly; but on the other hand, it is but fair to admit that we are that way. All you have to do is drop a hat, and if we are in any kind of form we will break down and cry like a little tired child."

For the second issue, again out of the goodness of her heart, she turned in another theater review, as well as a poem, "Cassandra Drops Into Verse," and a short story, "A Certain Lady." Then, except for some unsigned verse in July, she was not heard from until September, when she sent in the poem "Rainy Night."

During the *The New Yorker*'s first year, she regarded her contributions as charitable donations, certainly not what she considered serious work. In any case, she wanted to be paid.

Writing, she decided, was turning out to be a nasty profession. "And what do you do, Mrs. Parker. Oh, I write. There's a hot job for a healthy woman." It was a pity she hadn't the foresight to have taken a course in interior decorating, she said. Why anybody would choose a career as a writer mystified her, and she swore that if she had a choice she would prefer to clean out ferry boats, peddle fish, or be a Broadway chorus boy. The problem was, "I wish I didn't have to work at all. I was made for love, anyway." Since that was not to be, she wished that she knew how to write prose that would earn a lot of money. Poetry was not the answer. "This is a fine thing to be doing, at my age, sitting here making up sissy verses about broken hearts and that tripe," and getting a dollar a line for it. What she actually wanted was payment "in chunks, not drips."

Despite her jokes, the painful truth was that sometimes she found herself exceedingly hard up. "She was ignorant about money," a friend said. "All she knew was that she needed it." Given her attraction-repulsion about money, the way she went about practicing economies was peculiarly her own. She continued to give the Algonquin IOUs in lieu of her rent. Since she was always asked out to dinner, meals were not a problem. She was even able to arrange the expense of entertaining so that it cost her nothing but the price of club soda and ice. Most afternoons around five, people came in for drinks. A frequent visitor at the ritual cocktail hour was painter Allen Saalburg, who would drop in with his wife, the fashion designer Muriel King. "Dottie needed to have people around her all the time but she never had any money. So everybody would bring a bottle and put it down some place, to show they had earned their right to be there. She welcomed almost anybody."

Her chief expenses were for necessities: clothing, perfume, Johnny Walker cigarettes, and liquor. And now she hired a part-time maid. Ivy (whose surname has been lost) was a young black woman who supported herself and a small son. She was said to be an accomplished cook, but, since Dorothy seldom ate at home, she had no use for Ivy's culinary skills. In the morning Ivy would arrive and brew coffee. If Dorothy was still asleep, as was generally the case, Ivy moved softly around the suite, tidying up the dirty glasses from the previous evening and washing and ironing Dorothy's designer nightgowns. By noon, she was ready to move on to her other employers. Sometimes, if Dorothy was giving a more formal cocktail party, Ivy would return to pass drinks. While she seems to have performed these minimal duties perfectly well—Dorothy swore she would never entrust her laundry to anyone else—Dorothy still professed to find her inadequate. It pleased her to have people around who lent themselves to dramatization, as Eddie had. For the moment, Ivy was the chosen one. With characteristic deviltry, Dorothy complained freely about her, until Ivy became infamous as a slovenly, abnormally inefficient horror whom Dorothy lacked the heart to discharge.

When Dorothy's Boston terrier, Woodrow Wilson, died, she grieved extravagantly for him. He had reminded her of Rags, and after Eddie left, he had been her constant companion wherever she went. Although it could never be said that Dorothy had actually trained him, the dog had somehow learned to comport himself decorously in speakeasies, parlors, and offices. Though Woodrow Wilson's passing left a gap in her life, she could not bring herself to take the disloyal step of replacing him.

Throughout the spring of 1925, restless and dissatisfied, she began to draw closer to the Round Tablers again. Benchley was often away. Frequent excursions to the hinterlands to deliver "The Treasurer's Report" on the vaudeville circuit had become a necessity, because he had grown accustomed to earning a large salary, living a spendthrift life, and piling up debts. In his absence, Dorothy turned for companionship to Frank Adams, who was currently single again. Dorothy had always liked Minna Adams, a former "Floradora girl" who had been unable to bear children and instead babied her husband and her cat Mistah. Dorothy had taken no sides in their breakup.

For as long as she had known F.P.A., he had chased women, although his amorous techniques overflowed with hostility. At a party when he made advances toward a statuesque ingenue, she accused him of caring only about her body. Adams promptly agreed and cautioned her to take good care of it because when it was gone she would have nothing left. Sometimes he gave a titillating kick to his affairs by mentioning the women in his column as Mistress so and so.

Edna Millay had introduced him to Esther Sayles Root, an accomplished woman in her early thirties who studied music. Adams had fallen in love. The affair turned serious and resulted in his divorce. They planned to marry.

In the interim, Adams depended on women friends like Dorothy to fuss over him, even though his behavior was more highstrung and grouchy than ever and he was not the most cheerful of companions. Dorothy went out of her way to humor him. At a dinner they attended at George and Beatrice Kaufman's, he whined into her ear throughout the meal about the necessity for paying his income tax, but Dorothy was able to supply little consolation. Filing tax returns often slipped her mind, and she claimed to have once told a tax collector that she had stayed home all day on March fifteenth but nobody came. When Dorothy coaxed Adams into joining a card game, he groused about disliking hearts and, to prove it, promptly lost eighteen dollars. On another occasion, a party to which she had not been invited, she obligingly trotted around to his apartment and helped him dress.

One Sunday, Dorothy made plans with Adams and Edna Ferber to motor into the country and stop at a rustic inn for luncheon. Among the Round Table regulars, she disliked Ferber second only to George Kaufman, because she categorized Edna, along with Kathleen Norris and Fannie Hurst, as a writer who manufactured potboilers. In later years she found the idea that Ferber was actually making a fortune from her overstuffed novels to be insufferable and roundly denounced her as an oil well gushing dollar bills. "I understand Ferber whistles at her typewriter. And there was that poor sucker Flaubert rolling around on his floor for three days looking for the right words."

When she and Adams arrived at Ferber's apartment, they found her in bed pleading illness, although to Dorothy she did not appear sick. She was wearing a frothy pink bed jacket that would have been sensational on a Ziegfeld Follies vamp but looked seriously silly on a woman as homely as Ferber. The sight amused Dorothy, who told F.P.A. afterward that Ferber "was not so ill that she did not look lovely, with the pink maribou flowing like water." Adams was fond of Ferber, but that did not prevent him from printing Dorothy's catty crack in The Conning Tower.

Before long Dorothy's most persistent suitor was Seward Collins, who trailed after her as if he were a beggar at a moveable banquet, an approach guaranteed to lower himself in her esteem. Sewie's dependency and Dorothy's lack of respect for him supplied plenty of gossip for the Round Table, even though her friends agreed that he was precisely the sort of person she needed. To them, he was a well-heeled intellectual who wanted to marry and look after her. To Dorothy, Sewie was a fool, but in superficial ways he seemed to be suitable. He showered her with attention and presents and even paid some of her bills. She was sublimely indifferent because, once again, she had gravitated toward an ill-considered, unsatisfying relationship, having lately conceived a great affection for a married man.

Deems Taylor was the most eminent music critic in the country, a small, blond man with a bespectacled face and crinkled smile who resembled an affable gnome. Physically, he was as far removed as a man could possibly be from the movie-idol types she preferred. His tongue, as efficient as a buzz saw when it came to slicing fools into small pieces, was a match for hers. She first met him in 1920, but even before that, she had known him by reputation as "Smeed," one of the most gifted writers of light verse to appear in The Conning Tower.

One thing she liked about him was that he disliked working as much as she did and put off assignments until the last minute. Even so, he was the most prolific, versatile person she had ever known. Apart from criticism, he was also a gifted composer, a skilled cabinetmaker, architect, painter, and illustrator. His personal life had been chaotic. During the war he married a journalist named Jane Anderson, a brilliant, strikingly beautiful, unstable woman, and both of them worked as war correspondents for the *London Daily Mail.* By the time Jane returned from Europe she had become lovers with writer Gilbert Seldes, and that ended their marriage. Now Taylor was married to Mary Kennedy, a Broadway actress with whom Dorothy was acquainted. In fact, Mary had been among those performing "The Everlastin' Ingenue Blues," the song that Dorothy and Deems had written for *No Sirree.* Lately Taylor had grown dissatisfied with his life. Not only had he resigned his position on the *World* because the job left no time for serious composing, but he and Mary had embarked on a trial separation before deciding whether or not to end their marriage.

When Dorothy first began the affair with Deems, he was only one of many men with whom she was involved, but soon her interest began to focus on him exclusively. With the neediness that invariably consumed her whenever she fell in love, she grew increasingly demanding of his affection and his time. Taylor, probably unprepared for such a development, began to back off and the romance soon began to suffer difficulties.

Things were going badly when the Round Tablers and their friends gathered to attend Frank Adams's wedding to Esther Root on May 9. The ceremony was performed at the home of friends who lived near Greenwich, Connecticut. A number of the wedding guests arrived in extremely low spirits, because it looked as if *The New Yorker* would fold. Five months after its birth, the magazine's original capital was depleted and it seemed unlikely to survive the summer season, customarily a slow period even for prosperous publications. Raoul Fleischmann had been advised that the wisest course would be to suspend publication until the fall, but Harold Ross and Jane Grant were convinced that this would mean ruin for the magazine. They had begun to seek capital elsewhere. In the midst of Adams's nuptial festivities, Fleischmann arrived with a miraculous last-minute reprieve and announced that he had persuaded his mother to invest $100,000, enough to assure the summer issues at least.

For Dorothy, F.P.A.'s wedding day was marked by an excess of champagne and caviar and unpleasant quarreling with Taylor. When Elinor Wylie and Bill Benét invited her to spend the night at their New Canaan home, she left. She squeezed into a taxi with Elinor and Bill, as did a number of the other wedding guests: Edna Millay, her husband Eugen Boissevain, her former lover Arthur Davison Ficke, and his new wife, Gladys. By the time they reached New Canaan, the fare had risen considerably from the agreed-upon price, which ended in a violent quarrel. Exhausted, everyone settled in the dining room for food and drinks to restore their nerves before heading up to bed. Dorothy remained downstairs, having a nightcap with Elinor and Arthur Ficke, when Elinor asked her to say aloud some of her verses for Ficke. Even though Dorothy had not the slightest desire to recite poetry at that hour, she made a polite effort to oblige. To her astonishment, Arthur Ficke began to offer unsolicited advice and told her that her verse could use work. Dorothy knew that Millay once had been in love with Ficke and still referred to him as her spiritual adviser, but Dorothy certainly felt no affinity toward the man and was not concerned about her spiritual development. To her, he was nothing more than an ex-lawyer and a third-rate sonneteer. His presumption that she would accept a tutorial was an added affront, because she felt competitive with Millay and hated critics' calling her an imitator of Millay's light verse.

Incensed, she excused herself and went up to bed. Just as she was dropping off to sleep, Wylie and Ficke rushed in because Elinor wanted to show the scars on Dorothy's wrists, apparently to convince him that Dorothy had indeed taken suicide seriously. Dorothy burst into tears.

In some ways, Deems Taylor acted as a positive influence on her. His decision to resign from the *World* and devote himself to creative work impressed her deeply, inspiring her to consider carefully her own future. When she told Seward Collins that she was working on a novel, it had been a partial lie; writing a novel had been on her mind. With Taylor's example before her, she returned to the idea, or at least to thinking about it.

In many other ways, her relations with Taylor proved a source of familiar misery, terrain she had traversed in her affair with Charles MacArthur. Both of these married men were associated with the Round Table, thus falling safely, but incestuously, into the category of extended family. Neither of them was legally or emotionally available to her, even though their marriages had tailed off to the point where they seemed to be. Dorothy was aware that Taylor felt undecided about a divorce. Depressed, her mood degenerated into morbidity. A poem she wrote in June suggests how insubstantial and unsafe rejecting men made her feel:

> The first time I died, I walked my ways;
> I followed the file of limping days.

She sensed herself plunging into that same torment again:

> The next time I died, they laid me deep.
> They spoke worn words to hallow my sleep.
> . . . .
> And I lie here warm, and I lie here dry,
> And watch the worms slip by, slip by.

Harold Ross agreed to publish "Epitaph," even though death and decomposition were scarcely subjects that his readers found screamingly funny. Indeed, the poem was not the least bit entertaining. Ross ran it without her byline.

In addition to documenting her pain in her writings, she also needed to share unhappiness with her friends, particularly with Benchley. At this time he was abroad with his family, vacationing after his extramarital liaison had turned cold. Adams was also in Europe on an extended honeymoon, and Aleck Woollcott, who had limited tolerance for hearing about the entanglements of heterosexual love, confided in Murdock Pemberton that the messiness of Dorothy's affairs left him sick at his stomach and that if he ever decided to have an affair, he would choose a waitress.

As it turned out, the person most sympathetic toward Dorothy's troubles was Ring Lardner. Encountering him at F.P.A.'s wedding, she aired her problems with Taylor and complained that she wanted to begin a novel but couldn't find the necessary solitude. Lardner was in the middle of an extended drinking spree that had begun in early May and continued until the middle of July. Impulsively, he invited "Spark Plug" Parker, as he liked to call her, to be his houseguest. The visit would cheer her up, he promised, and she would have complete privacy to write.

Arriving in Great Neck with her typewriter, she walked into a situation that did not bode well for concentration. As Lardner admitted afterward, he was "constantly cock-eyed." He would stay up the whole night drinking, then sleep throughout the next day. He did no writing himself, nor did he plan to, because he had stockpiled eight weeks' worth of columns before going off the wagon. Ellis Lardner, withdrawing as usual from his drinking, stayed out of the way and tried to live as separate an existence as she could decently manage.

To Dorothy's dismay, the Lardner household was anything but quiet. There were four active children, not to mention friends and neighbors who seemed to be dropping in constantly. One evening when Herman Mankiewicz turned up, in a mood to barrel around the North Shore drinking and raising hell, Lardner proposed a visit to a popular speakeasy in Manhasset. Ellis chose to stay home. When Dorothy and her two companions arrived at Rene Durand's restaurant, the smoke-filled bar was crowded with its usual clientele of big burly Irishmen. After a few drinks, Mankiewicz remembered he was once a marine and began to pick fights with some of the customers, until it was necessary for Lardner to nose in and extricate him from a fistfight. With some difficulty, he and Dorothy finally hauled him back to the house and put him to bed. The next day, after declaring that he had to hurry back to town to finish an article, Mankiewicz braced himself for the trip with a succession of highballs and did not leave until five o'clock. This was an ordinary day at the Lardners.

After a week, during which Dorothy had accomplished nothing, she decided it would be best to depart. Back in the city, she complained that her stay had been perfectly horrible. Ring had lured her to his home with the promise of privacy, but there he had pursued her all hours of the day and night so that finally she had been forced to leave, just to escape being seduced. She neglected to mention that she had found Ring's advances flattering, just as she found him sexually attractive, and that she had left the Lardner house only after she had slept with him. Before long, her indiscreet remarks were reported back to Ellis Lardner, who considered them unkind repayment for her hospitality.

Long afterward, when Ring was dead, she told practically every one of her close friends that she once had been his mistress, which may have been a genteel term to describe what had gone on between them, but also was a considerable embellishment of what was really a midsummer diversion. At the time, emotionally involved with Taylor, she probably had chalked it up to drinking and proximity and the sort of carousing that went on in Great Neck during the season. Lardner had been drunk her entire stay, but Dorothy also knew what everyone else knew—that, despite his great devotion to Ellis, he liked to chase other women.

Soon after her return from Great Neck, the relationship with Taylor began to improve, perhaps because Mary Taylor had gone to Europe and left the field clear. Taylor was spending the summer near Stamford, Connecticut, where he and his wife owned a farm. He was busy composing a tone poem, *Jurgen*, which was based on a satirical novel by James Branch Cabell and which had been commissioned by the New York Symphony for an autumn premiere. Dorothy visited him and stayed the rest of the summer even though rural life held no appeal for her. The small tumbledown house, which the Taylors intended to restore as a summer home, was still primitive. It lacked electricity, plumbing, and a telephone, but had an abundance of wasps and poison ivy. She heard from Don Stewart, who had once borrowed the house to write, that a rat had bitten him on the nose while he was asleep. Nevertheless, it was largely a happy time for her and she managed to settle down to work. Whether as a result of the orderly regime or the example of Taylor's labors, her state of mind grew less muddled during her residence at the farm.

Her original idea was to write about her family and to set the opening of the novel in her early life, perhaps in the period of her father's marriage to Eleanor Lewis or possibly later at the time of his death, the two events that she considered of the greatest consequence. The first of these themes concerns a child of five, modeled on herself, who has been adopted by a wealthy childless couple. The mother is a terrible figure, an oblivious woman who is determined to squeeze all the life out of the child, not from misdirected affection but rather from her own gross character defects and her inability to love.

The second theme draws on her father's last years. The Old Gentleman, as she calls him, lives with one of his two daughters, exploits her shamefully, and appears indifferent to the hardship he has brought into her existence. He is, admittedly, ill, but he also is excessively selfish and tyrannical. The mood of the writing is as somber as the mustard-colored wallpaper and the heavy, tapestried furniture in the daughter's parlor. Other characters bear resemblances to Helen and George Droste and to Bert Rothschild and his wife, Tiny. There also is a sketch of Dorothy's oldest brother, Harry. Unwilling to offend Bert or Helen, she took pains to disguise them. She added twenty years to her father's age and made him eighty-four at his death. It almost seems as if the portrait drew from an even earlier time when her grandfather Thomas Marston had lived with the Rothschilds, but it is not likely that she actually remembered any details about this period.

After sitting all day at her typewriter, she felt entitled to spend her evenings drinking Scotch and socializing with Round Tablers who owned summer homes in the area. A short drive away was the ninety-seven-acre farm that Ruth Hale had purchased with her own money and named Sabine Farm, after Horace's estate in the Sabine Hills outside Rome. The only word for Ruth's place was *squalid*. The two-hundred-year-old house was a wreck, not at all like Deems's home, where his skill as a carpenter had created at least a facsimile of civilization. Sabine Farm, recalled Ruth's son Woodie Broun, "looked as Horace's place must have looked after the Goths, Gauls, and Vandals had passed over it several times." Dorothy, disgusted at the sight of a brown, worn-out toothbrush in the bathroom, had refused to acknowledge the possibility that Ruth might actually be using it to clean her teeth and insisted that it must be a broomstick she rode on Halloween. In addition to Ruth, Murdock Pemberton lived in a second house on her property, Heywood Broun had bought a place down the road, and Peggy Wood and John Weaver owned land in North Stamford.

One evening at Ruth's, they were sitting around the fire drinking with actor Ed McNamara. Dorothy was talking about Deems when she saw a pack of rats come running out of the wall like Olympic gold medalists, pounce on something, and then speed away. Breaking off her story, she stiffened with horror. Although she loved all animals and could put up with the most eccentric behavior so long as a creature walked on four legs, she had never cared for rats and in fact feared them. When she looked over at Ruth and McNamara, they were paying no attention to the rats. They were just sitting there calmly and smiling as they waited for her to continue. A few minutes later, the rats again came sprinting toward her, until they were just a few feet away. She was sure they could not be real; on the other hand, she had not drunk enough to be experiencing the DTs. After she finished her anecdote, she said, "Does anyone but myself see giant rats in this room?"

Ruth and Ed had been planning to say, "What rats, Dottie?" but a glance at her stricken face changed their minds. They confessed that they had been summoning the famished rats by quietly tossing bread pellets against the wall.

Several times she visited New York to look after her business affairs. For a change she was making money. *Close Harmony*, after reviews that compared her to George Kelly, was now in its third month in Chicago and doing excellent business. In New York, *Business Is Business* could be seen at the Criterion Theatre with *Beggar on Horseback*. On one of her trips to the city, she ran into Eddie, whom she had seen little of since his return to Hartford. In a jubilant mood, he told her that he was making money in Wall Street and had in fact cleaned up seven thousand dollars during the previous week. When he insisted on buying her a gift, she agreed to accept a dog, a seven-week-old Airedale she took with her back to the farm. On another trip she bumped into Harold Ross, who was in a far from jubilant mood. He was struggling to keep *The New Yorker* going with a tiny, inexperienced staff and an office that had only one typewriter. In August, circulation fell to twenty-seven hundred copies. Ross said, "I thought you were coming into the office to write a piece last week. What happened?"

Dorothy replied, "Somebody was using the pencil."

At the end of July, she was in the city to greet Benchley, who returned alone from Europe. In an unhappy, cranky mood, he complained about the sticky weather and wished he had remained in Cap d'Antibes with his family. Dorothy planned to stay for the weekend, just long enough for a reunion with her best pal, but she hung around until the following Wednesday. She attended a few shows, even though everything she saw looked stale, and she spent many hours at Tony Soma's with Benchley, catching him up on her news and listening to his stories of good times in Paris with Don Stewart and a likeable friend of Stewart's, a newspaper stringer by the name of Ernest Hemingway. At Tony's one night, she learned that Frank Sullivan was struggling to find material for The Conning Tower while F.P.A. was on his honeymoon. She mailed him two poems the next day. "If you can't use these, give them to some poor family," she wrote Sullivan, who was greatly moved by her generosity because The Conning Tower paid nothing for verse.

On this trip, she spent time with Charles MacArthur, whose new girlfriend, Helen Hayes, was away on tour. After dining together one night, they made a circuit of the speakeasies, the consumption of innumerable highballs constituting an evening's entertainment for both of them. As the evening progressed, they began to quarrel. Charlie, as Benchley later told his wife, "bawled the life out of her." His condemnation proved more than she could bear, because the following day she hurried back to Stamford and told Taylor that she felt like killing herself.

Frank and Esther Adams, who had just returned from Italy, appeared on Saturday and insisted that she go for a drive with them to visit actress Fay Bainter. Dorothy was in good form that afternoon. When Bainter expressed affection for her husband and mentioned that she had been married seven years, Dorothy replied, "Don't worry, he'll come back in style again." Despite the jokes, she continued to feel depressed.

As the summer drew to a close, Dorothy was forced to acknowledge that her affair with Taylor had reached its conclusion because Mary Kennedy Taylor returned from Europe and Deems began to see her again. Appearing to accept this turn of events, Dorothy bowed out gracefully. Since she and the Taylors socialized in the same circles and could hardly avoid each other, their relations remained cordial. The following year the Taylors had a child, and their marriage survived until the mid-1930s.

Chapter 9

GLOBAL DISASTERS

•

1926

BARTENDER: What are you having?
PARKER: Not much fun.

All around people seemed to be having fun, but recently Dorothy had begun to suspect that there might be a "flaw in paganism" and even thought she knew what it might be:

> Drink and dance and laugh and lie,
>   Love, the reeling midnight through,
> For tomorrow we shall die!
>   (But, alas, we never do.)

After returning from Stamford, she continued to feel as low as mud. She drank more but with an aggressive quality that had not been present before. At Tony's, she started out by ordering Scotch with plain water, then called back the waiter and defiantly switched her order to straight Scotch, which she swallowed with alarming speed. Touchy and foul-tempered, she bit off people's heads. When Johnny Weaver remarked that he was glad to see her looking so well, she snapped, "Where the hell are you looking?"

Her friends had seen her in bad shape, but never like this, when it took so little to kindle her rage. People, she wrote, "can say what they like about me," but they should remember that she was not a troublemaker. "I make my own living, and I don't have to ask favors off of anybody." If trusted friends chose to insult her, they knew what they could do and where they could do it. "Tiffany's window, see?" Into these diatribes she injected bits of autobiography about her heart murmur, the respectability of her upbringing, and the handsome houses her family had owned, vague references that were more relevant than anyone suspected. Finally she would subside, whispering that she wished she were dead.

Whenever friends named the things she might live for, she refused to listen. "When she would be really blue," said Allen Saalburg,

> she would begin talking about how worthless life was. Marc [Connelly] once got down on his knees and took her hands in his. He started telling her how valuable she was, how wonderful life could be, how everybody had troubles, and she should cheer up. She didn't say anything, but after he had left she said, "What a silly old fool." And she was right. He had been sort of silly, because he overplayed it in a theatrical way. Nothing he'd said were the things that might have impressed her.

Knowing that she was edging close to danger scared her. The story that she began to write was an almost-verbatim account of her irascible behavior and an apology for it, an attempt to articulate her mood and an effort to dissipate it. In a speakeasy at three in the morning, a woman wearing a petunia-colored hat is overheard throwing a fit as she unleashes a tearful monologue, the gist of which seems to be that life is not worth living. She is good and drunk. Her companion, a man described as owning ice-blue hair and who probably was a thinly disguised portrait of Seward Collins, keeps trying to placate her but is unable to get a word in. In this story, she was eager to put a comic face on her fears. Harold Ross thought that "Dialogue at Three in the Morning" was amusing enough to publish in The New Yorker for, on its most superficial level, as a portrait of a drunk wallowing in willful self-pity and paranoia, it had meaning for Prohibition readers.

At a party one night, Peggy Leech introduced her to a doctor she was dating. Alvan Barach was thirty, an earnest young intern from Newcastle, Pennsylvania, who had taken his degree at Columbia Medical School, read Bergson and Goethe, and wrote poetry and fiction as a hobby. In 1925

Barach had yet to begin his lifelong specialty in pulmonary medicine and his work leading to the development of the oxygen tent. He taught at Columbia and privately practiced psychotherapy. In spite of his attraction to the Algonquin writers, he felt somewhat out of place. His idea of cocktail-party conversation was a discussion of Tolstoy's ideas; theirs was not. During the evening, he rose up and initiated a comparison of Dostoyevsky with Tolstoy that provoked indulgent smiles from Woollcott and the others, who thought he was laying it on a bit thick. Undeterred by their amusement and Marc Connelly's repeated interruptions, Barach pressed on without taking offense. Dorothy observed him approvingly. His manner had a purposefulness that impressed her; she called his office the next morning to make an appointment for a consultation.

Barach decided that she had a lot of "tender expectancies" that were not being fulfilled, but the problem in need of most urgent attention was her drinking, which he felt had reached pathological proportions. While he tried to emphasize the subject in their sessions, he was met with almost total resistance. Dorothy found it impossible to participate in any productive way. As is often the case at the beginning of psychiatric treatment, her symptoms became exacerbated and she felt more depressed than ever. Yesterdays blurred into todays and she forgot the day of the week. Drinking no longer produced an automatic high. In fact, she now had to work at it, increasing the dosage to get the same sensation. What frightened her most were those times when the effects of the whisky suddenly deserted her without warning and she would be swamped by anxiety so powerful that she seemed to be sinking in her tracks, literally unable to move forward or backward. She felt misery was crushing her "between great smooth stones." Terrified to discover that Scotch could not be trusted, she began to view it as an old friend who had inexplicably refused to do her a simple favor.

As she drifted from drink to drink, her anguish mounting, she also had to deal with parting from the dog Eddie had brought for her. The Airedale kept growing until she joked about entering him in a horse show. Even more troublesome was his habit of eating the Algonquin's furniture. Dorothy called him "a veritable addict" who could make a whole meal out of a sofa and when he ran out of sofa turned to a chintz-covered arm chair for a light snack. "It was eventually decided—and maybe you think that tears weren't shed over that decision!—that he was not the dog for apartment existence." She presented him to friends in the country, but felt miserable over the loss.

As Dr. Barach urged her toward sobriety, Dorothy was meantime investigating a different kind of insurance policy. She discovered Veronal, a popular sodium barbital–type sedative, and took it when Scotch failed to put her out. In New York State, Veronal was available by prescription only, but she learned this was not the case in New Jersey. She made a special trip to Newark, where she tramped from drug store to drug store buying Veronal, as well as sundries such as talcum powder and emery boards so that her purchases would not arouse suspicion. She concealed this cache of pills in the drawer of her dressing table. Knowing it was there made her feel better.

She failed to mention the Veronal to Dr. Barach. While she was willing to give him a chance to repair her, she remained secretly unconvinced that she was worth the trouble. One night when she returned to the hotel, drunk but not high, she carried the Veronal bottles into the bathroom and filled a glass of water. It took a long time to swallow the tablets because they kept sticking in her throat. Then she laid herself down on the bed and waited. According to Dr. Barach, she saved herself by hurling a glass through the window at the last moment. Dorothy herself suggested later in "Big Blonde" that the attempt failed because she had not taken a sufficient dosage and also because Ivy (called Nettie in the story) discovered her in time.

After two days she returned to consciousness at the Harkness Pavilion of Presbyterian Hospital, where her first thoughts were rage at Barach for daring to interfere. Then the tears fell "as if they would never stop." When the nurses said she was lucky to be alive, she thought the opposite was true. She felt unlucky to have failed. She also needed a drink badly.

She didn't get one, because now that Barach had her in the hospital, he insisted she dry out and knew there was no earthly way of her getting a drink. After a few days, he was astonished to notice that she was tight. On his 4:00 P.M. rounds, she would be sober, but, when he stopped again at six, it was clear that she had been drinking. Investigation revealed that every day at five she had a visit from Heywood Broun, who by this time was also a patient of Barach's. As always, Broun carried with him a hip flask of gin, and Dorothy persuaded him to share it. She could not wait to find out if alcohol would again be her friend; the prospect of not being able to get drunk filled her with terror.

After the first week, she felt bored and eager for company. When Frank Sullivan stopped by, he found her with "the insides of her arms black and blue from the saline injections they had pumped into her, but putting up a brave front." Benchley tactfully acknowledged this latest attempt to terminate herself by cloaking his emotion in banter. He warned her that if she didn't stop it she would make herself sick. From a chair next to her bed, he began to unburden himself as though he were the one who had caved in. By now, his love affair had become an emotional and financial strain. He owed the Shelton Hotel so much money he couldn't afford to move. When Edmund Wilson appeared shortly afterward, she reported that Benchley was at the end of his rope. The hospital, she joked, "was getting the room across the hall ready for him." The last subject she wanted to discuss was herself. Instead, she began describing other patients on the floor: a girl who tried to teach her rug weaving and a genuine vicomte who presented her with an anthology of French poetry and a turtle that ran away. Wilson noticed that she looked thinner and "her intelligence and sensibility came back into her eyes."

After her release from the Harkness Pavilion, she kept regular appointments with Dr. Barach. Treatment at twenty-five dollars an hour was expensive, but Dorothy seldom (perhaps never) got around to paying and the doctor did not press her. Her recovery depended upon her ability to control her drinking. Making Dorothy understand this was difficult because she remained unconvinced of her alcoholism. Having lived with Eddie, she considered herself an expert on drunks. It was hard to dissociate the problem from his rampages. She decided her own afflictions had nothing in common with Eddie's. Dr. Barach did not insist that she give up alcohol, only cut down. It was his opinion that reasonable amounts were harmless and furthermore he believed that people who drank moderately probably lived longer than abstainers. Dorothy promised to curb her consumption and for some weeks liberally diluted her Scotch with ice and White Rock club soda, and then nursed it.

As before, she tried to make light of her impulse to self-destruction, although this time psychiatric treatment made it harder to accomplish. In verse, she compiled a consumers' report for those contemplating suicide and rated the various methods of killing one's self: Razors, as she knew from experience, were painful, and drugs caused vomiting and cramps. Other methods she had not actually tested had to be dismissed on hearsay as hopelessly unreliable: Given the inadequacy of what was available to an aspiring suicide, Dorothy figured she might as well go on living. When "Résumé" was published in The Conning Tower, some people admired the way she had transformed a near-fatal experience into dark humor. As might be expected, Dr. Barach was not among them.

Even though Barach was a convivial man who enjoyed partying with the Round Table and was a regular weekend guest at the Swopes in Great Neck, his overall view of the group tended to be critical. He told Dorothy that the tragedy of life was not so much what people suffered, but what they missed. In his opinion, she and her friends were missing a great deal. Their need to spend so much time together was a measure of their insecurity, he thought. Their compulsion to be entertaining and their reluctance to discuss anything for more than a few minutes—and then never in depth—forced them to neglect the purposeful, striving side of their natures. By developing her instinctual drives at the expense of her serious nature, by then compounding the problem by partying and drinking, she was losing the energy to progress as a writer. While it was valuable to live in the moment and to enjoy her impulse for pleasure, he believed she should also acknowledge the opposite principle of purpose and restraint, to appraise her life as she was living it.

Perhaps influenced by Barach, Dorothy suddenly began to knock the Round Table. She talked bitterly about how the group had spoiled her and how she regretted having wasted so much time trying to dream up witticisms when she could have been doing serious work. Although those close to her listened to these critical remarks without much enthusiasm, they had to agree that a new way of life would be in order.

Dorothy turned to Seward Collins. Having kept him at a distance during her affair with Deems Taylor, she now decided to sleep with him. Despite the fact that he was always available (therefore weak and unexciting), she knew that he meant well and was eager to coddle her. In her precarious state, it must have been reassuring to have him around. As one of her friends later observed, Collins regarded her as a madonna, while she treated him like a dust mop and wiped up the floor with him. What motives Collins had for entering into this arrangement are unknown.

Collins not only had plenty of money, but he was also a generous lover. He bought her a beautiful wristwatch studded with diamonds. Of even greater value to her was his know-how when it came to marketing her work, what little there was of it. It is very likely that he had a hand in her resurrecting a passage from the novel she had begun in Stamford, the section depicting her father's death, and shaping it into a short story. Whatever her original intention for this piece of writing, it was able to stand alone satisfactorily. She titled it "The Wonderful Old Gentleman" (with the pointed subtitle, "A Story Proving That No One Can Hate Like a Close Relative") and immediately sold it to the *Pictorial Review*, where it appeared in January 1926.

In February, still lying on Dr. Barach's couch and trying to get straightened out, she met Ernest Hemingway. He was in New York to break his contract with Boni and Liveright because they had rejected a novel he had written. For some months now, she had been hearing favorable things about Hemingway from Don Stewart, who had been his friend for several years, and also from Benchley, who had met him in France the previous summer. She knew that Hemingway was working on a semiautobiographical novel about bullfighting, in which one of his characters was based on Stewart and another on Benchley. All this had predisposed her toward the man before she ever set eyes on him.

Hemingway intended to stay a week. He arranged to move from Boni and Liveright to Scribner's, who agreed to bring out both *The Torrents of Spring* and *The Sun Also Rises*. He was pleased to have Scott Fitzgerald's editor, Max Perkins, as his new editor. After his business had been taken care of, he lingered for a second week of partying, drinking, and getting acquainted with the local literary crowd. Dorothy ran into him often. All that she knew of his writing was *In Our Time*, a recent collection of short stories. His stark prose had impressed her even though the book had caused, she recalled, "about as much stir in literary circles as an incompleted dogfight on upper Riverside Drive." What interested her more than his fiction were his views about the process of writing itself, a task that by now she had come to view as painful. In talking to him, she soon learned that their methods of composition had much in common. He told her that writing did not come easily for him; invariably, he would set down a word or a sentence, scratch it out, then have to begin all over. For Dorothy, the discouraging slowness of her work—the isolation, the claustrophobic silence—was enough to make her flee, and often she did.

When she wondered if Hemingway ever found writing unpleasant, he said he did but dismissed this as too obvious to worry about. Writing was hard and dirty work, he said; you had to accept this and not expect conditions to improve, because they wouldn't. He also told her that sometimes he would rewrite a single page sixty or seventy times without feeling satisfied. The whole secret of writing was to work like hell.

Dorothy managed to overlook the fact that Hemingway's pronouncements were a touch condescending and his judgments not unique; he was not the first novelist to rewrite a page sixty times. Still, she valued his views for their common sense and also found him to be an especially engaging person whose masculinity was magnificent. She would not have agreed with Zelda Fitzgerald, who, about this same time, branded him as a phony and witheringly described *The Sun Also Rises* as being about "bullfighting, bullslinging, and bull————." In New York, charming and modest, Hemingway was at his most agreeable. His blowhard side, soon to grow more prominent, was not yet evident to Dorothy, who felt eager to know him better and pursued his friendship like everyone else.

Hemingway proved to be a most attractive delegate from the expatriate paradise that she had heard so much about. She was an avid and soon envious listener to his stories about how American writers were living and working in Paris. She found enchantment in his repeated accounts of the Dingo bar, the Closerie des Lilas, a café where Hemingway did his writing, and the flat over a sawmill he shared with his wife, Hadley, and an infant son whom he called Bumby. Everyone in her crowd was fascinated by him, but nobody took a closer interest or asked more questions than Dorothy.

Within a few days, she made up her mind to go abroad to live. It was an impulsive decision, characteristic of her love of drama, but it managed to catapult her out of her gloom so successfully that none of her astonished friends or Alvan Barach attempted to dissuade her. In later years, she explained her move to France by noting that "everybody did that then," Paris being a fashionable address for writers who took their work seriously. By 1926 the exchange rate had become so favorable that it would be possible for her to live there more cheaply, certainly more grandly, than in New York.

Her real motives were personal. After the painful times she had experienced recently, she wanted to forget and hoped that a new environment might enable her to cure herself, or at least to insulate herself from dangerous habits and unsafe relationships. She wanted to believe that in France she could somehow become a different person, a real writer like

Ernest Hemingway, and envisioned herself in the comfortable cafés of the Left Bank writing diligently.

Once her decision was made, she lost no time and booked passage for the February 20 sailing of the *President Roosevelt,* the same ship on which Hemingway was returning to France. In her impatience to be off, she allowed herself only one week in which to tidy up her past and arrange for her future. Seward Collins probably paid for her passage. The problem of how she might scrape up enough money to support herself abroad resolved itself with remarkable swiftness when she decided to collect the verse she had written for The Conning Tower and *Life* and publish them in book form. Collins most likely originated this plan; Dorothy herself had strong doubts about it. She thought her poems were "not good enough for a book" and had no wish to make a fool of herself by calling public attention to the fact. Yet Horace Liveright immediately expressed enthusiasm for the idea. Their friendship did not affect his business judgment; he believed that Boni and Liveright could make a decent profit on a volume of light verse. Liveright had recently contracted with another light-verse writer, Sam Hoffenstein, for a similar collection and saw no reason not to publish a pair of poetry volumes. Among the items hastily thrown into Dorothy's steamer trunk were folders of clippings and carbon copies of her published verse. She planned to select those poems she considered good enough to include in the book she had tentatively titled *Sobbing in The Conning Tower* once she got settled in Paris.

At the last minute, Benchley volunteered to shepherd her to Paris, but second class on the *Roosevelt* was fully booked. All the United States Lines could offer was a promise of cancellation. He had difficulty convincing Gertrude that the journey was absolutely necessary—and indeed it was not. For a while, it looked as if Gertrude might exact a price by insisting he take nine-year-old Nat along for company, chaperonage that Benchley was doubtless not anxious to have. In the end, she relented and gave permission. Benchley could joyride across the Atlantic with Dorothy and Hemingway without any strings attached, but he had to come straight home on the next boat.

As soon as he could get away, Collins was also planning to join Dorothy abroad. Always happy for an excuse to visit France, his chief source of erotica, he looked forward to a buying spree.

Dorothy, along with Benchley and Hemingway, boarded the *Roosevelt* in Hoboken at midnight in the midst of a blizzard, none of which was particularly reassuring to Dorothy; since the *Titanic*, she had always been inclined to associate ocean travel with her uncle Martin's death. The final day had passed feverishly with farewell celebrations and a trip to the bootlegger to buy Scotch for the crossing. By the time she reached Hoboken, countless shakers of cocktails had been emptied, several additional stops had been made en route to buy bootleg champagne, and the bon voyage party had expanded to include Elinor Wylie and Bill Benét, Marc Connelly, and Dorothy's sister and brother and their families. Friends sent a dozen steamer baskets of fruit, which she would never eat. According to Hemingway, who had fallen in and out of love with Wylie that day, he was good and pie-eyed, and so was everyone else.

Despite the champagne, Dorothy felt apprehensive. When the boat was getting ready to depart, she and Benchley ventured out on the icy decks to the slippery rail and looked over. To cheer her up he began to tell stories so silly and tasteless that she could not help smiling. He joked about throwing the children's life preservers overboard, then started a story with, "God, what a night to go out in the storm!—and I wouldn't mind if the crew wasn't yellow." Benchley could always make her feel better. Once they were under way he learned that the steamship line had no available rooms in first class after all and planned to put him in a maid's room adjoining a bridal suite. The next day Dorothy discovered that some scoundrel among the bon voyage revelers had stolen all her Scotch. On the fourth day, Benchley said he felt just as he had felt when he'd once had the crabs. On the sixth day out, he realized he did have pubic lice.

Still, the crossing turned out to be a good time. The *Roosevelt* was a comfortable ship with excellent food. Despite squally weather, there was only a slight roll to the sea. Dorothy slept late, then played bridge in the afternoons with Hemingway and Benchley. They all took their meals together at the officers' table, where Hemingway made a serious production out of consuming saltpeter. He told them it was necessary to control sexual appetites. While Dorothy refrained from showing her amusement to his face, she did continue to giggle about it to friends for months afterward. Benchley wrote to Gertrude that Dorothy was "quite all right now that she is relieved of the strain, and there hasn't been a fight yet." She arrived in Cherbourg in fine spirits.

In Paris it felt like spring. The weather was unseasonably warm, all in all a perfect introduction to the city Dorothy had been daydreaming about. Everything enchanted her. It made no difference that nothing much seemed to be happening there and that the few people she knew were about to depart. Hemingway had spoken incessantly about his eagerness to return to Austria, where he had left his wife and son, but then, as though he were in no rush to leave, he offered to show Dorothy and Benchley the sights. The reason for his lingering was actually a *Vogue* editor with whom he was having an affair. The girlfriend, Pauline Pfeiffer, did not join them, nor was she ever mentioned. There were a couple of convivial meals at the Closerie des Lilas with Scott and Zelda, who, having spent the winter in the Pyrenees so that Zelda could take a cure for colitis, were now stopping briefly in Paris before heading south to the Riviera where they had rented a villa. Benchley too, after ridding himself of crabs and buying presents for his family, soon left. By this time, Seward Collins had arrived.

Sewie rapidly took charge of arranging a journey to southern France and Spain. Invited to join them were Collins's good friend Gilbert Seldes, a critic who had been managing editor of *The Dial*, and his wife Alice. The couple had arrived there some weeks earlier. Collins announced that the Seldeses and Dorothy should consider themselves his guests because he planned to foot the bill for a deluxe tour. Dorothy made no objection. Her unspoken understanding with the rich was that it was part of God's foreordained plan for them to give and her to receive, with no obligation on her part to feel guilt or gratitude. Before she settled down to work, she wanted to see Europe. With Collins paying the bills, she could save money. Shortly before their departure, the false spring suddenly ended with snow, and she was happy to head South.

During the previous weeks, Hemingway's enthusiasm had helped to form her ideas about Spain. The realization that his sensibilities might be quite different from her own and that she was going to hate Spain began soon after they reached Barcelona. So thoroughly had his tales of the *corrida* mesmerized her, that she had somehow managed to overlook the fact that animals were involved. From expensive seats in the shade, she watched with interest at first. When the first bull came rushing out, the matador moved in and began to work the bull with his cape. Then the bull charged the picadors and the crowd was noisy around her when suddenly the bull's horns disappeared into the belly of a picador's horse. Horrified to see the horse's intestines spurting into the sand, Dorothy rose and stalked toward the nearest exit with a bewildered Collins coming after her.

Revolted, sick to her stomach, she cursed Collins, whom she seemed to hold responsible for the Spanish national sport and refused to return to her seat. She could not understand why he had brought her to witness the killing of defenseless animals when he knew she could not bear their slightest mistreatment. It made no difference that bulls sometimes killed matadors, and for that matter she hoped they did because she found matadors disgusting.

The rest of Spain proved to be equally unpleasant. On the train to Madrid, a guard patrolling past their compartment noticed Gilbert Seldes kissing his pregnant wife on the forehead and reproached him in Spanish for vulgar behavior. Collins, the only one of them who understood anything of the language, warned the guard to mind his own business, then copied down his badge number and threatened to lodge a complaint once they reached their destination. At the Madrid railroad station, in a bizarre reversal, the guard reported Collins and had him hauled down the platform and taken to a police station. Dorothy and the Seldeses trooped helplessly behind. By the time Collins had been released, with a warning to behave himself in the future, they all were furious and marched straight to the American consulate, where they were advised to forget the incident and continue their sightseeing.

By this time, Dorothy was convinced that Spain was a dreadful country. She was appalled by its poverty and backwardness; she hated its narrowmindedness and believed its treatment of animals barbarous. The only way she could express her disgust was to ridicule the Spanish. She said that their national anthem seemed to be "Tea for Two," a popular international hit that year, being played ad nauseum in hotel lounges. There was now additional tension among the group because Dorothy had grown to dislike Gilbert Seldes, who was dominating their itinerary. At Hendaye, before they crossed the frontier, Seldes "did not have a stitch of Spanish to his name," but by the time they had reached Aragon "he was helping the natives along with their subjunctives. It was enough to make me, in a word, sick."

They spent Easter in Seville, where the solemnity of Holy Week was thoroughly spoiled for Dorothy by chilly temperatures and the repulsive habit of Spanish men of pinching women's bottoms. It got so bad that she hated to walk on the streets. To make matters worse, she discovered that Sewie was not a lover who improved with extended contact.

They returned to Paris, to a round of expatriate-colony parties, invitations to which arrived by pneumatique, and to a city that spring seemed to have bypassed, despite its budding horse chestnut trees. Dorothy mockingly described Paris as "*la belle, la brave, la* raw, *la* rainy." The place was "as cold as a son-of-a-gun," as gray and cheerless as Hartford. She and Collins moved into the Lutetia, a large hotel on the Boulevard Raspail near the Luxembourg Gardens. Sewie and his mania for dirty postcards got on her nerves and she was no good at controlling her tongue. They continuously argued. In the midst of a quarrel one day, she pulled off the diamond watch he had given her and flung it out the window, whereupon he ran down five flights to the street to rescue it. Her disdain was complete when he returned the watch to her. He decided to go home. Dorothy did not care.

It rained every day for three weeks. Ordinarily, she enjoyed rain, but not every day. The dark weather made the city sad and dingy and depressed her. Once or twice Hemingway came to visit her. Sitting in the Lutetia, they watched the passage of a funeral procession moving quietly down the rain-swept boulevard. For Dorothy, rain and death entwined were events so awful that she had to make jokes, and she did so. Hemingway lifted his eyebrows at her seeming callousness, but she did not bother to explain herself and merely remarked that the funerals of strangers left her unmoved. When Hemingway, who was leaving shortly for Spain, asked her impression of the country he loved so greatly, Dorothy unthinkingly launched into a massive attack on the place. Her comments deeply insulted him. Furthermore, he was offended by her choice of traveling companions. He did not care for Collins, to whom he facetiously referred as the man who had shot Abraham Lincoln, and he had a long-standing feud with Gilbert Seldes, who had once turned down a story of his and supposedly written a rejection letter advising him to stick to journalism. Hemingway concealed his hurt feelings but privately added Dorothy's name to his catalogue of people he disliked.

During the two months she had been abroad, she had written nothing except two poems for *The New Yorker*, and now it was time to work on her book. She assembled a rough draft of an eighty-eight-page manuscript at breakneck speed. Nearly all the verse had been published in *Life* and The Conning Tower and their subjects ranged from dogs to domestic crises with Eddie when she still had hopes for their marriage, from her mother to popular Broadway actress Marilyn Miller. Critical examination of the poems dissatisfied her. Too many struck her as undistinguished or self-consciously cute, there was no unifying theme, and even the title *Sobbing in the Conning*

Tower displeased her. Once she had omitted everything she disliked, very little remained, certainly not enough for a book. She began to write substitutions.

During the summer she worked hard and finished a bundle of new poems, including "Indian Summer," "Men," and "Inventory," and sent them in batches to Harold Ross and Bob Sherwood. These new verses were punchy, cynical, and invited laughter. There was a biting candor about them, a combination of fragility and toughness almost bordering on vulgarity, that was highly distinctive compared to those written by other women poets. Slowly Dorothy could see a central theme of death emerging—the death of loved ones, but more frequently the end of love or the death of dreams. All the verses were by no means successful in her opinion, but she had built up the percentage considerably and now felt far happier about the project.

Among those she had retained from the original batch was one called "News Item," which had appeared in The Conning Tower. It was the sort of poem she did so well and so effortlessly:

> Men seldom make passes
> At girls who wear glasses.

Those nine words seemed quite innocuous to her at the time. Later, to her utter amazement, it would be "News Item" that people remembered while they forgot or ignored or never knew any of her other work, and she cursed the impulse that ever led her to republish it.

Since the French economy suffered a depression at the time and the official rate of exchange had fallen to thirty-six francs to the dollar, Dorothy lived comfortably on very little. She did potboiler articles for *Life* and three short stories for *The New Yorker,* but the only one of particular interest is "Oh, He's Charming!" The story depicts a tea-party encounter between a celebrity novelist and an admiring female reader who is thrilled to meet him socially. Dorothy's novelist character, with his swollen head, his arrogant manner, and insulting dismissal of writers such as Sherwood Anderson and Ring Lardner, strongly suggests Ernest Hemingway. As much as she admired him as a writer and experienced the pull of his personal charm, she must have felt a spurt of dislike for him. While Dorothy counted Hemingway and James Joyce as two of her favorite authors, she was never sufficiently impressed by either to forgo mockery. Joyce, whom she passed on the streets or glimpsed in restaurants, was known to be excessively taciturn. "I guess," Dorothy later remarked to Elmer Rice, "he's afraid he might drop a pearl."

That summer several of her closest friends visited Europe. Aleck Woollcott and Charles MacArthur passed through Paris on their way to the Riviera. Don Stewart and his new wife, a Santa Barbara debutante named Beatrice Ames, turned up en route to Cap d'Antibes on their honeymoon. For a while, the Fitzgeralds were in town so that Zelda could have her appendix removed, but they too returned to the south of France. All of Dorothy's friends seemed to be either just going to, or just returning from, Antibes. They all raved about the Murphys, a wealthy American couple with three young children who lived in Paris and in Antibes, where they were renovating an elegant house they called Villa America. Shortly after her return to Paris in May, Dorothy had met them and liked them very much. Gerald Murphy, who graduated from Yale in the class of 1911, was a tall, redheaded man whose wealth came from the New York leather goods store, Mark Cross. The family business held no attraction for Murphy, who studied landscape architecture and later painting and once called the Mark Cross store a monument to the useless. In 1921, he had married Sara Wiborg, the daughter of a millionaire manufacturer of printing ink, and brought her to Europe, where they were drawn to artistic people such as Pablo Picasso, Cole Porter, and Scott Fitzgerald. Their many friends considered the Murphys to be an ideal couple who knew how to live with exceptional style and grace. Dorothy did not know them well, but they impressed her as fine people, even if they were extremely rich.

Although reluctant to admit it, she was beginning to feel lonely. There were few people to converse with because her grasp of French remained poor. She was able to understand the language only if the speaker was "reasonably adept at pantomime" and could read it "at glacier speed, muffing only the key-word of every sentence." As the months passed there were too many meals alone and too many drinks, so that she had put on weight. In need of fun, she made a brief excursion southwards via Carcassonne and wound up in Monte Carlo, where the casino refused to admit her because she was not wearing stockings. "So I went and found my stockings, and then came back and lost my shirt." On this trip she bought herself a Scottish terrier whom a previous owner had named Daisy. It wasn't the name Dorothy would have selected, but she soon realized it made no difference, for Daisy couldn't be bothered answering no matter what anybody called her. On the other hand, Daisy was unusually smart. "Why, that dog is practically a Phi Beta Kappa. She can sit up and beg, and she can give her paw—I don't say she will, but she can." Having a dog again cheered her greatly and made Paris more bearable.

Still, it was a relief when autumn came. One day, when she went to the Guaranty Trust Company to collect her mail, she realized that the American tourists had gone home. Now some of her friends began drifting back to the city. Road-weary Don and Bea Stewart arrived from Munich and moved into a nearby hotel with their new schnauzer, continuing their honeymoon while Don wrote articles for the *Chicago Tribune*. Dorothy got on well with Bea, who had a nice sense of humor and was fond of having a good time.

While it was pleasant to have company, she continued to invest most of her energies in her writing. She overhauled the autobiographical story about a mother and her adopted child that she had begun the previous summer as part of her novel. Having plundered a partial manuscript again, the novel no longer amounted to much. The adopted child, quite likely a little girl in her original drafts, became a boy named Curtis. The story reverberates with Eleanor Rothschild's admonitions to Dorothy about counting her blessings. Dorothy titled this story "Lucky Little Curtis" and mailed it to *Pictorial Review*, the same magazine that had published "The Wonderful Old Gentleman." She did not submit either of these stories to *The New Yorker* because she did not regard the magazine as an appropriate market for serious fiction. She further dismissed it because Harold Ross paid writers so little.

Early in October, Dorothy went to a birthday party that Don gave for Bea at Prunier's restaurant. Hemingway showed up alone. He effectively wrecked the party mood by announcing that his marriage had broken up and he was now living by himself in a studio lent by Gerald Murphy. He supposed that he would be getting a divorce to marry Pauline Pfeiffer. This news considerably upset Don Stewart, who admired Hadley Hemingway as one of the finest women he knew, nor could he hide his disapproval that the breakup had occurred over another woman.

Shortly after this, the poet Archibald MacLeish and his wife, Ada, hosted an evening party at a sumptuous flat on the Avenue du Bois de Boulogne that some wealthy friends had loaned them. Among the guests was Hemingway, so depressed over his temporary separation from Pauline that he was seriously considering suicide. The Stewarts were also present but not Dorothy, who did not know the MacLeishes at that time. Hemingway had brought a poem with him he'd written about Dorothy and insisted upon reading it, although nobody encouraged him once he had read the title: "To a Tragic Poetess—Nothing in her life became her like her almost leaving of it." The poem opened with an extremely harsh attack that accused Dorothy of cowardice. Apparently its author had no sympathy for those who want to kill themselves but lack the nerve to carry through. There were further ridiculing references to her affair with MacArthur and the subsequent abortion, and her scorn for Spain and bullfighting were not passed over either:

> Spaniards pinched
> the Jewish cheeks of your plump ass
> in holy week in Seville
> forgetful of our Lord and His passion.
> Returned, your ass intact, to Paris
> to write more poems for the New Yorker. . . .

Then, offering a contrast to Dorothy, he went on reverentially to present several supposedly genuine tragedies that had been suffered by various Spaniards whose courage he deeply appreciated. The poem was in exceptionally bad taste, racist as well as sexist in that it contained anti-Semitic slurs against both Dorothy and Gilbert Seldes.

At the MacLeishes', Hemingway's audience was not amused. Don Stewart, who thought it was "viciously unfair and unfunny," immediately jumped up and protested. "I told him what I thought of his poem"; that turned out to be the end of their friendship. As might be expected, Stewart and his wife took pains to shield Dorothy from all knowledge of what had taken place at the MacLeish party, and apparently none of the others present spoke of the incident either. The poem was eventually published, but not until after her death. If Dorothy found the sudden estrangement between the two men peculiar, she asked no questions. Unaware of Hemingway's cruelty toward her, she continued to regard him as an innovative writer and a person with many estimable qualities.

She was beginning to change her mind about living abroad. She had spent nearly half a year on her own and proved to herself that she could still labor with discipline. She had a good deal to show for those nunnish months, but accomplishments were not enough. In early November, when the Stewarts booked their sailing, she knew that she could not face the prospect of being alone. Taking her Scottie with her, she went home with Don and Bea.

Her first week in New York she was merry as could be. The transatlantic crossing, she joked, was "so rough that the only thing I could keep on my stomach was the first mate." Frank Adams wanted to hear all about Ernest Hemingway. How old was this fellow anyway?

"Well, I don't know," she told him. "You know, all writers are either twenty-nine or Thomas Hardy."

Back in her old suite at the Algonquin, at her favorite table at Tony's with Benchley, she trundled her new Scottie all over town and told stories about life in Paris. When the New York *Telegram* offered her a job as drama critic, she pretended to debate whether or not to accept. "What would Lincoln have done?" she wondered. It was obvious Lincoln would have refused and so did she. One night Thornton Wilder took her to hear a concert of old English ballads. The singers sang without accompaniment and then thoroughly mystified her by sitting down at a table as if they were going to play cards. She kept "expecting them to deal." It was an intensely boring evening. She went to a Saturday night party at Ruth Hale and Heywood Broun's house where she reminisced at length with Elinor Wylie and congratulated an elated Frank Adams, whose first child had been born that evening.

Next morning she woke unusually early for her. West Forty-fourth Street was Sunday silent. She dressed and went down to the lobby. By eleven o'clock, she was ringing the bell at Elinor Wylie and Bill Benét's house on East Eighteenth Street. When a surprised Elinor opened the door, Dorothy said that something really bad was happening to her, if Elinor knew what she meant, which she did. "She spent the day with us from eleven AM till five PM, saying she was going to kill herself that night & as she'd already made two attempts—wrists and veronal—it was not very soothing to [the] nerves." For several hours Elinor talked to her, then she was joined by her husband and both of them "begged, reasoned, kidded, scolded & did all we could."

Wylie and Benét somehow got through to her. Relenting, she promised Elinor not to do anything "for the present." The next day Elinor wrote to her mother that "we were queer ones for her to come to, in a way. I supposed she thinks we are experts on the subject!"

The bad time passed away fairly quickly, but it shook her confidence. She had imagined herself strong again, since she had been able to write so much that year. She worried that her periods of creativity were going to be nothing more than intervals between suicide attempts. It was a chastening thought.

After her brief treatment with Dr. Barach, she did not continue psychotherapy. Many years later, she mentioned to Oscar Levant that once she had told Barach about hating her father, she could think of nothing further to say and wondered how other patients managed to fill up the time, a problem the garrulous Levant found impossible to comprehend. Citing the eleven-year analysis of Lillian Hellman and the case of Heywood Broun, who went in and out of treatment "like a revolving door," she expressed doubt about therapy because, she said, "I've never seen a cure."

Instead, she continued to place her faith in Scotch. Any substance that made her feel good was as velvet to her—and Scotch had the further advantage of being portable.

About this time, Edmund Wilson ran into her on the street. He was surprised to see her looking fat, bloated, puffy-eyed, and he thought her hairstyle, cut into a ragged bob, was unbecoming.

"Why dontcha ever come to see me, yuh damn fool?" she said to him.

One evening they went out together. Dorothy insisted on going to Tony's because "Mr. Benchley is sunk tonight, and I promised I'd go up there and see him." Wilson felt annoyed but not surprised because the Round Tablers, in his opinion, did not know how to get along with anybody but one another and only felt safe in their regular hangouts. His account of this boozy evening is a sad update on Benchley's life: ". . . He was getting worse and worse in debt (his syndicate stuff began to show it—overdrafts on Scarsdale bank), he would rush out to Chicago, where the mistress was playing, to lecture. . . ." Benchley had taken great pains to help the young woman. Robert Sherwood later told Nathaniel Benchley that the elder Benchley had taught her how to behave, to enter a room, and even tutored her in French. As it happened, Benchley's youthful protégée was able to profit quite nicely from his coaching in speech and deportment. She went on to become a dramatic actress whose distinguished career spanned forty-five years on American and British stages.

Arriving at Tony's, Dorothy and Wilson found Benchley leaning against a wall in the hall. They ordered the first of many rounds of Tom Collinses and settled down for an evening of serious drinking. Wilson did not find the reunion enjoyable. Dorothy flattered him excessively, "which always inspired me with misgivings," and Benchley nervously drummed his fingers on the table until the people opposite requested him to stop. Wilson found their clowning to be embarrassing and their jokes about children "cruel and disgusting." Suddenly he remembered that Dorothy always referred to his infant daughter Rosalind as an "it." Wilson was further upset by Benchley's heavy drinking and "his red grossening face," perhaps because he himself was in the process of developing a serious problem with alcohol. Writing in his diary about the evening at Tony's, Wilson noted disapprovingly that Benchley "had got to a point where he no longer went at all to plays he reviewed for *Life*," as opposed to previous years when he at least showed up at some of them. Although Wilson allowed that Benchley had "some admirable qualities," he would never agree with E. B. White or James Thurber, who idolized him as one of America's finest humorists, surpassing even Mark Twain, and he also failed to understand why Dorothy regarded him as "a kind of saint."

It took only a short time for her to slump back into the old nocturnal rituals: smoky cocktail parties in her suite with Ivy passing drinks, a few hours at some revolting play, then on to Tony's to drink and argue about "life, sex, literature, the drama, what is a gentleman, and whether or not to go on to Helen Morgan's club when the place closes."

In December, Boni and Liveright published her book of poems under the title *Enough Rope*, which she had adapted from Rabelais's "you shall never want rope enough." The handsome volume bore a gray-and-yellow dust jacket and a price tag of two dollars. It was dedicated to Elinor Wylie, whose personal copy Dorothy inscribed with the words *With love, gratitude, and everything.* After the publication of *Enough Rope*, everything would be different.

Chapter 10

BIG BLONDE

•

1927–1928

Well before the spring of 1927, it was clear that something out of the ordinary was happening. *Enough Rope*, already in its third edition with the end not yet in sight, was making publishing history by becoming a best seller, an almost unprecedented achievement for a volume of poetry.

Suddenly, Dorothy found herself inundated with invitations to literary luncheons that were held in hotel ballrooms "filled with people who looked as if they had been scraped out of drains"—women in draped plush dresses and pince-nez and men who were "small and somewhat in need of dusting." She quickly learned to avoid these gatherings of "literary Rotarians" by pleading "a return of that old black cholera of mine." She had to be extremely vigilant even with friends. She was horrified to learn that Horace Liveright planned to merchandise her as "another A. A. Milne," an author whom she found repulsive. She managed to veto the idea, but not in time to prevent Robert Benchley from going about the city saucily calling her "Dotty-the-Pooh."

Enough Rope received impressive reviews. The *Nation* said that in the book's best lyrics "the rope is caked with a salty humor, rough with splinters of disillusion, and tarred with a bright black authenticity." The *New York Herald Tribune* praised her work as "whisky straight," an unfortunate metaphor considering her drinking problem. *Poetry* observed that she had in fact carved out her own niche in American literary humor with poetry that was fashionably chic, " 'smart' in the fashion designer's sense of the word." A few disapproving reviewers couldn't wait to slap her down on the very same grounds, calling *Enough Rope* flapper verse that seemed to them slangy, vulgar, and frivolous. All in all, *Enough Rope* could not have suited more perfectly the tastes of readers in the year 1927.

By far the most thoughtful assessment came from Edmund Wilson, who believed that even though "few poems in this book are completely successful," the best of them were extraordinarily vivid and possessed a frankness that justified her departure from literary convention. It was incontestable that her verse gave off the essence of the Hotel Algonquin. He wrote in *The New Republic* that "her wit is the wit of her particular time and place." Her writing had its roots in contemporary reality, which was precisely what he had been pleading for in poetry. Dorothy had emerged as "a distinguished and interesting poet," he wrote, an opinion later seconded by John Farrar in *The Bookman*, when he called her a "giantess of American letters secure at the top of her beanstalk," who wrote "poetry like an angel and criticism like a fiend."

Any kind of praise made Dorothy uncomfortable. Even though she was extremely gratified by the book's reception, she dismissed compliments and tended to downplay her new popularity. When *McCall's* magazine invited her to join Edna Millay, Edward Arlington Robinson, and Elinor Wylie in contributing to a Christmas feature that would be titled "Christmas Poems by America's Greatest Poets," she was perfectly happy to oblige and threw together "The Gentlest Lady." Not for an instant did she fancy herself among America's greatest poets, if indeed the editors of *McCall's* were competent to make that judgment, which she must have questioned. As she later wrote in *The New Yorker*, "There is poetry and there is not." Her writing, she believed, fell into the latter group. Once Hendrik Van Loon said to her that if a reader has any doubt about a poem, then it isn't one. Dorothy had nothing but doubts about her work. Regardless of *McCall's*, she felt that her true aptitude might lie in fiction. Her intention was to give up verse and concentrate entirely on short stories, but this raised other problems. How could she quit writing poetry now? She was too famous.

Anarchism was a theory she understood naturally. During the summer of 1927, she published a poem in *The New Yorker* that she appropriately titled "Frustration":

If I had a shiny gun,
I could have a world of fun
Speeding bullets through the brains
Of the folks who give me pains;

Or had I some poison gas,
I could make the moments pass
Bumping off a number of
People whom I do not love.

But I have no lethal weapon—
Thus does Fate our pleasure step on!
So they still are quick and well
Who should be, by rights, in hell.

Among those she hated were the powerful who had no qualms taking advantage of the weak. It was a revulsion against mistreatment of all creatures, human and animal, that dated back to her earliest days. That summer, her own past (heretofore fairly well concealed) suddenly began to interlock with disturbing current events, and she became absorbed in a political cause. Like Katherine Anne Porter and Edna St. Vincent Millay, she was drawn to this particular issue because of her conviction that a shocking miscarriage of justice was taking place. She entered the fight with the intention of stopping the execution of men she believed innocent, but by its conclusion, her experiences had thoroughly radicalized her. She would remain unalterably committed to radical principles for the rest of her life, even when it meant sacrificing her livelihood.

To a large degree, her reputation had been built on tough talk and a whiplash tongue, a style that was synonymous with taking little seriously. Not only the public but some of her closest friends wrongly concluded that her feelings could not be altogether sincere. Certainly she had indicated absolutely no interest in organized politics before 1927. Women won the vote in 1920, but not once had she taken the trouble to cast a ballot. Politicians of both parties bored or appalled her, and not until after the election of Franklin Roosevelt was she heard to speak kindly of any candidate. Little wonder that those who saw newspaper photographs of policemen bundling her off to jail were astonished.

The explanation for all this was simple: It was not the American political system that succeeded in firing her imagination, but foreign-grown philosophies that most Americans found extreme and distasteful.

Her first memories of course were of a family whose every comfort depended upon a system that was merciless about squeezing the lifeblood out of helpless people. Whether or not she ever saw the inside of a sweatshop is immaterial, because she surely absorbed the essence of the conflict between bosses like J. Henry Rothschild and the cloakmakers he employed. In 1927, she began to recover pieces of her past and apply them to the present.

Three decades of rage came roaring to the surface.

As soon as she stepped off the train at South Station two detectives pounced on her, asking if she was from New York and to state her business in Boston. Since she was decked out in creamy-white gloves, smelled of gardenias, and was obviously a gentlewoman if not an aristocrat, they let her pass.

Boston was under martial law. Across Prison Point Bridge, in Charlestown, Nicola Sacco and Bartolomeo Vanzetti waited in their death-house cells. The two Italian-American anarchists, fish peddler and shoemaker by professions, had been tried and found guilty of the murders of a paymaster and a guard in South Braintree, Massachusetts, on April 15, 1920. What had begun as an obscure, routine murder trial had developed into an international cause célèbre. Seven years of legal maneuvering—a tortured stew of motions, petitions, and reviews—had held off the electric chair until all legal remedies had been exhausted. Sacco and Vanzetti were to die at midnight.

At three o'clock, Dorothy arrived at 256 Hanover Street in the North End and climbed two dark, narrow flights of stairs. Sacco-Vanzetti defense headquarters was located in a poor Italian neighborhood where peddlers' carts made splashes of color with big ripe peaches, plums, and pears. Rookie policemen, nice-looking youngsters who seemed self-conscious, were stationed on the sidewalk. The thermometer read in the low eighties and the shabby two-room office was stifling. On the wall a poster announced JUSTICE IS THE ISSUE!, and alongside somebody had tacked up a remark being attributed to Judge Webster Thayer: I'M GONNA GET THOSE ANARCHIST BASTARDS GOOD AND PROPER.

Heading the defense committee were Mary Donovan, formerly an industrial inspector for the Massachusetts Department of Labor, and Gardner "Pat" Jackson, a journalist who handled publicity. For both of them, Sacco and Vanzetti had become the center of their existences. On this afternoon, August tenth, discouraged beyond measure, they were almost ready to concede that the months of unrelenting letter writing and pamphleteering had been wasted. At that moment, Governor Alvan Fuller was debating at the State House on Beacon Street whether or not to grant a last-minute reprieve. Demonstrations and strikes had erupted all over the world, but in Boston the thousands of protesters that Donovan and Jackson expected to turn out were nowhere to be seen. By mid-afternoon there had rolled in only a single bus whose gaudy, red banner proclaimed SENT BY THE SACCO-VANZETTI DEFENSE COMMITTEE OF NEW YORK. Aboard were a dozen Communist Party workers.

Dorothy had changed into an embroidered dress with a matching scarf, high-heeled ankle-strap shoes, and a Hattie Carnegie cloche; her gloves were spotless and she moved in a cloud of perfume. Donovan and Jackson stared at her as if she were an apparition. They did not stare long because an hour later she found herself leading a file of demonstrators down Beacon Street. A convoy of men in shirt-sleeves and women wearing cotton house-dresses, sensible shoes, and black armbands marched behind her in a single line. Many of them carried placards. Dorothy had only her handbag, tucked properly under one arm. The marchers were mostly local Party members, among them several well-known New York writers: *New Masses* editor Michael Gold and Sender Garlin from *The Daily Worker*. The only person she knew was John Dos Passos, who explained that he was covering the execution for the *Worker* and who squeezed into the queue ahead of her. Soon everyone started to sing "The Internationale," then "The Red Flag." Dorothy mouthed the words.

Across the street, near the Shaw Memorial, a crowd rapidly collected. Four or five policemen stood there, twirling their clubs and observing the promenade with sleepy interest. Before long two police wagons tore up the street with their sirens screaming. The captain got out and ambled over.

"It's against the law to do this," he warned. "I'll give you seven minutes to go away."

Dorothy kept on walking and singing.

Arise, ye prisoners of starvation!

At the end of the block she turned and started back. The seven minutes passed. Nothing happened.

Arise, ye wretched of the earth!

Another long seven minutes ticked by. The number of gogglers across Beacon Street had grown to several hundred. The crowd wanted a glimpse of Dorothy Parker, who was being exotically identified as "the Greenwich Village poetess." They stretched their necks and looked her clothing up and down while they sucked at bottles of soda pop, as if they were watching an American Legion parade. To her, the worst of it was the name-calling: "Bolsheviki!" "Guinea lover!" "New York nut!" "Red scum!" Some people addressed Dorothy by name. One man warned her the police were coming. She'd better run.

"I don't mind being arrested," yelled Dorothy, seething.

When finally a whistle shrieked and the police came directly at the line, the marchers broke rank and some began to run. Two policemen herded Dorothy toward a patrol wagon but she refused to get in. When the captain ordered her, she insisted on walking the three blocks to the Joy Street Station.

The police held her arms, hustling her roughly down the middle of the street. Her high heels caught on the cobblestones. When her scarf slipped to the ground, they would not stop so that she could retrieve it. As they yanked her arms, she began to curse them. Behind her followed along a dogged crowd, shouting "Hang her!" "Give her six months!" "Kill her!" At the station, she was booked and then a sour-looking matron with a gold tooth took away her cigarettes and led her to a cell.

Before long, Ruth Hale came to bail her out. Behind Ruth stood a flustered, panting Seward Collins. Sewie, never at a loss for words, said that he felt terrible because he had arrived late and missed the glory of being arrested. The sight of him angered Dorothy. There was still time, she told him. It was not too late to go back to the State House and get himself arrested.

There were reporters waiting for her outside. She responded to their questions by lobbing out the wisecracks they expected of her.

"I thought prisoners who were set free got five dollars and a suit of clothes," she said, to loud laughter.

"Is this your first arrest, Mrs. Parker?"

It was, and she had found it disappointing. Her fingerprints had not been taken, "but they left me a few of theirs. The big stiffs!" She pushed up a sleeve to show that bruises were already forming.

The execution had convulsed Boston. Overhead she saw planes circling, as if the city anticipated a full-scale invasion by the Red Army. Every policeman and fireman was on twenty-four-hour duty; grim-faced squads patrolled public buildings. Near Prison Point Bridge, streets had been roped off, and state troopers blocked the intersections. The Charlestown prison was fortified with machine guns, tear gas, and double guards wearing bulletproof vests. Dorothy persuaded a newspaper reporter to take her into the prison and once inside found that nobody paid any attention to her. She strolled around freely looking at the machine guns and patting the noses of the troopers' horses. In the cell blocks, prisoners were screaming, "Let them out! Let them out!"

As the evening wore on, Dorothy sat in the pressroom and observed. Dozens of telegraphers and reporters played cards and smoked, scavenging for the tiniest crumbs of news to put on the wires. The more cynical were eager-beavering ahead and filing execution pieces, as though Sacco and Vanzetti were already dead. When the warden barreled in to say he'd just heard from the governor and the execution was off, telegraph keys began to cackle madly. Five minutes later, the warden ran back—it was on—midnight, and that was final. There was a round of applause. Dorothy found a telephone and called defense headquarters. She may have been talking too loudly because she was spotted by a deputy warden who went haywire, called her an enemy spy, and threatened to have her driven out of town. Luckily for her, the man had more important things to worry about. At eleven-thirty, Warden Henry burst in again. Off again, for twelve days. That *was* final. Like a man whose wife has just had a baby, he passed around a box of cigars.

Meanwhile, a pair of detectives in a Ford spent the night opposite Hanover Street headquarters. A reporter who noticed them keeping watch and asked what they were doing was told that they had received a straight tip on a bomb plot. They were watching for the bombers: "Two women from New York. Ruth Hale and Dorothy Parker."

Dorothy arrived at Municipal Court the next morning, August 11, to discover the hallway outside the courtroom jammed with yesterday's prisoners.

They were flipping through the morning papers in search of news of their arrests and singing "The Internationale." The corridor sounded like a musical version of *Potemkin*, with courthouse guards breaking in periodically with a chorus of "shut ups." Several comrades brought Dorothy papers showing photographs of herself and John Dos Passos. Not only had they made the headlines, but she was disgusted to notice that some papers had allotted them almost as much space as they had Sacco and Vanzetti.

She pleaded guilty and received a five-dollar fine for loitering and sauntering.

Several days later, Dorothy and Ruth were at the dock when Vanzetti's sister, Luiga, arrived on the *Aquitania*. It was clear at once that Luiga would be worthless to the defense; she had only come, she said, to guide her brother back to the Catholic faith so that he would be prepared to meet his maker.

Dorothy remained briefly in New York, trying to persuade her friends to join the protesters. She had no trouble talking Sewie into contributing thirty-five hundred dollars, which was used to purchase full-page ads in *The New York Times* and other major papers. Benchley had already testified before the Lowell Committee about an indiscreet remark of Judge Thayer's in the Worcester Golf Club locker room; later, he filed a writ of protest with the court. Heywood Broun used his *World* column to write movingly on behalf of the condemned men, and Ruth Hale was as deeply involved with the defense committee as Dorothy was. Don Stewart wasn't interested and made no attempt to understand. Dorothy found the indifferent behavior of other friends extremely vexing. "Those people at the Round Table didn't know a bloody thing. They thought we were fools to go up and demonstrate for Sacco and Vanzetti." She supposed them ignorant because "they didn't know and they just didn't think about anything but the theater." That was no excuse in her opinion.

On her return to Boston, she spent long hours at Hanover Street helping with whatever tasks needed to be done. She worked in the back room, where Gardner "Pat" Jackson was always typing at the long oak table, and soon developed a little-girl crush on the tweedily handsome Coloradan who had been a reporter on the *Boston Globe*. Since the opportunity for personal conversation was limited, and she was too shy to approach him directly, she dropped breathless notes full of superlatives into his lap as she left the room. Pat Jackson was, she wrote, a very great human being, precisely the kind of perfect man she had always wanted to spend her life with. "These adoring businesses," as Jackson described the notes, were embarrassing and he did not reciprocate because, "I had my work to do."

Plenty of visitors milled through the office. The weekend before the new execution date saw the arrival of a number of prominent writers: Susan Glaspell, Edna St. Vincent Millay, Mary Heaton Vorse, Upton Sinclair, and Katherine Anne Porter. John Dos Passos returned. They picketed the State House, got themselves arrested, and defense headquarters promptly bailed them out at twenty-five dollars each. It had become almost a routine.

Throughout the day, the defense workers sometimes drank to steady their nerves, and each evening they tottered out to eat spicy spaghetti at one of the Italian restaurants along Hanover Street. Mother Gaboni's, third floor back, was rated the best. Mother Gaboni, a fine cook, had two bootlegger sons and served big jugs of home-made red wine. Since red wine gave Dorothy a mighty high, she jokingly referred to it as the "Red Badge of Courage."

The pressroom felt like an oven because all the windows had been nailed shut for fear a bomb would be thrown in. At eleven o'clock Dorothy telephoned Pat Jackson to tell him that there was a rumor, erroneous as it turned out, that the killings might be held up. As Jackson remembered it, on the night of the execution Dorothy "was able to get admitted to the prison for last words with Sacco and Vanzetti," but this memory is confirmed by no other source. Near twelve-thirty, the Associated Press reporter who had been chosen by lot to witness the electrocutions returned to the pressroom with the details. "No features," he announced. "Entirely colorless." Neither man had confessed. Sacco's last words were "*Viva l'anarchia!*" and somebody asked if *anarchia* was spelled with a *k*. Vanzetti shook hands with everyone, then like a gentleman thanked the warden for his many courtesies, and lastly said he forgave everyone. Correction: He forgave some people.

The insensitive remarks of the reporters seared Dorothy: "The little infant Jesus!" "Ain't they lambs, those Reds?" Listening to them sickened her.

At Hanover Street, the telephone rang and rang, but nobody picked it up. Finally, the rooms were hushed. Dorothy sat with Jackson, Vanzetti's friend Aldino Felicani, and a few others. None of them spoke. For a long time they sat staring at their knees. Then, Jackson hoisted himself up and said he was going for a walk. Felicani followed him.

After a while Dorothy staggered down the stairs. The empty street in the gray hour between night and morning breathed coldness. It was August 23. The day before had been her thirty-fourth birthday.

During the autumn after the execution of Sacco and Vanzetti, new people entered her life, and because they contrasted so strongly with what she had witnessed, she welcomed them. The ideas she had heard in Boston had struck a live nerve somewhere, and now she began proudly calling herself a socialist. "My heart and soul are with the cause of socialism," she announced. The odd choice of company she began to keep did not reflect her politics however. Some of her new friends were bankers and Wall Street businessmen, some of them millionaires, but all of them conspicuous capitalists whose political consciousness had not been raised. Although Dorothy still had the run of the Swopes' place and regularly visited other estates along Long Island's North Shore, she got to know the new bunch through Benchley and Stewart: John Hay "Jock" Whitney, his sister, Joan Whitney Payson, Pierpont and Marise Morgan, and Robert and Adele Lovett.

These attractive, moneyed socialites found the circles in which they had grown up too stuffy for their tastes. Amusing writers like Dorothy and Benchley were much in demand. Their talent and gaiety were considered charming, and their company welcomed in drawing rooms and on trips. The previous spring, Jock Whitney had taken Benchley to see the Grand National in England. Stewart and Benchley liked this crowd very much. Dorothy, who tended to trust their judgment, went along with these associations, which she would later deride as products of the natural social-climbing instincts of indigent writers. Still, these friendships had undeniable advantages because the rich could be generous suppliers of cottages on their estates for little or no rent, memberships in racquet and tennis clubs, and gifts of money and stocks.

Dorothy's closest friend in the group was Adele Quartley Brown Lovett, daughter of investment banker James Brown, wife of Robert A. Lovett (a partner in Brown Brothers Harriman & Company and secretary of Defense in the 1950s), and mother of two children. Famous for her dinner parties, Adele Lovett was a witty and elegant blond clotheshorse who cultivated the Round Table writers and made a big effort to befriend Dorothy. Dorothy gave the impression of reciprocating Adele Lovett's esteem for several years, even dedicating a book to her, although Adele and her Brahmin manners grated on her nerves. Finally, as an indignant Lovett said herself, she "dropped us like hot potatoes." The truth was that Dorothy tolerated her wealthy friends and even gave the appearance of enjoying their company. There was a wonderful tawdriness to be found in their drawing rooms, where she was sure to meet "over-eager portrait-painters, playwrights of dubious sexes, professional conversationalists, and society ladies not yet quite divorced." Their stupidities were of course ideal targets for all manner of wisecracks and gossip. Dorothy appreciated the rich for their houses, cars, servants, and clothes, but, with a few exceptions, she invariably found them dull, silly, and almost totally ignorant.

About this time she met John Wiley Garrett II, an investment banker with the private banking firm of Hallgarten & Company. Garrett was the same age as Dorothy, although she sometimes described him as "a very good-looking young man indeed," or as "a graceful young man ever carefully dropping references to his long, unfinished list of easy conquests," so that it seemed as though he were significantly younger. He was born on December 3, 1893, in St. Louis, attended the Kent School, and graduated from Williams College in 1915. During the war, he served in France as a captain in the 103rd Field Artillery, and immediately afterward began working in Wall Street. He sailed and played golf and tennis, and he belonged to The Leash and Downtown Association and the American Legion. Politically he was about as far right as he could get, a stereotype of a reactionary Republican. (During the Depression, Edmund Wilson remembered him as someone upon whom he might base a fictional character who thought President Hoover was doing a fine job.)

Dorothy broke off with Seward Collins and fell in love with John Garrett, who looked like a romantic lover and had a voice as "intimate as the rustle of sheets."

. . .

On October 1, she took over the "Recent Books" column in *The New Yorker*, under the pseudonym "Constant Reader." Need of money was her reason for assuming the responsibility of a regular weekly assignment. She started out cautiously and the reviews were relatively benign during the early weeks. As a reviewer, she did poorly with quality books, usually slopping adjectives like "beautiful" and "exquisite" all over the page. By the end of the first month, reviewing a memoir by President Warren Harding's mistress and the mother of his illegitimate child, Dorothy had worked herself into a properly bilious mood. An effort had been made to suppress Nan Britton's creation because police had invaded the printing plant to seize the plates. "Lady," Dorothy was dying to tell the author, "those weren't policemen; they were critics of literature dressed up."

It was the rare column that did not contain something to make readers laugh: *Crude* is the name of Robert Hyde's first novel, she reported. "It is also a criticism of it." Margot Asquith's latest book, she chortled, has "all the depth and glitter of a worn dime," and she went on to speculate that "the affair between Margot Asquith and Margot Asquith will live as one of the prettiest love stories in all literature." Dorothy was probably at her most pugilistic with how-to books. Confronted with a work about happiness, titled *Happiness* and written by a Yale professor, she described the book as

> second only to a rubber duck as the ideal bathtub companion. It may be held in the hand without causing muscular fatigue or nerve strain, it may be neatly balanced back of the faucets, and it may be read through before the water has cooled. And if it slips down the drain pipe, all right, it slips down the drain pipe.

Constant Reader's best-known review was of A. A. Milne's *The House at Pooh Corner*. Milne's whimsy had always nauseated her. When she came to the word *hummy*, her stomach revolted. "And it is that word 'hummy,' my darlings," she wrote, "that marks the first place in *The House at Pooh Corner* at which Tonstant Weader Fwowed up."

Almost from the outset, she set a precedent of being late with her copy, which was due at *The New Yorker* on Fridays. On Sunday mornings, some-one from the magazine would telephone. Dorothy, reassuring, said that the column was finished except for the last paragraph and promised to have it for them within the hour. Throughout the day, the same routine would be repeated several times. Occasionally, she would claim she had just ripped up the column because it was awful. At that point, she would start writing.

She joked that her lateness was unavoidable because she had to begin a column by typing her name and address in the upper left hand corner of the paper (if it did not look perfect she would retype it sometimes as often as eleven times) and because she first had to study the typewriter keyboard to see how many words could be formed from the letters in the word *Corona* (fifteen if she used the dictionary). Naturally, time flitted by like a steamroller, and the first thing she knew the morning was shot and the noon whistles were blowing. The whistles meant lunchtime for most people, but not for her because, "I have an editor. I have an overdraft at the bank. I have a pain in the eye."

While she was unquestionably accomplished when it came to stalling, the missed deadlines at this time were due to the fact that she had undertaken more work than she could comfortably complete. In this period of fertility, when not even an attack of mumps slowed her down, she wrote some of her best stories, among them "Arrangement in Black and White," a rather bold attack on racism that appeared in *The New Yorker,* and the comic but deadly serious monologue she called "A Telephone Call," published in *The Bookman.* She continued to produce verse, and she also agreed to accept a second regular assignment, an editorial column for *McCall's* that required her to write a chatty personal essay about New York or any subject she cared to write about each month.

She was leading a hectic social life and staying up late, drinking a lot, but handling it well. Only occasionally did she suffer from incapacitating hangovers, which she jokingly referred to as "the rams."

Most of the time, she kept her hangovers to herself and insisted that she felt "perfectly fine," a phrase she repeated so regularly that she finally used it as the title for a short story.

Dorothy settled into a nonsexual friendship with Seward Collins. Recently, Sewie had gone into partnership with Burton Rascoe to purchase *The Bookman* and now was pestering her to contribute fiction. There had been a brief, friendly interlude with Howard Dietz, the MGM publicity director who was trying to break into theater as a songwriter. Their involvement did not get publicized out of deference to Dietz's wife Betty, but in any case it soon ended. In fact, she was sweeping all males from her life except John Garrett, with whom she had begun an affair. Although Garrett practically had a neon sign emblazoned across his forehead that blinked I

DON'T WANT TO GET MARRIED, Dorothy couldn't see it. She adored "his boyishness and gaiety and sweetness." There was no denying he was striking, very tall and slim with dark brown hair, broad shoulders, and elegant clothes. At the age of thirty-five, he had never wed. He was a flirt who enjoyed being pursued and competed for by flotillas of women, especially those who were married or divorced. He also liked nothing better than to play them off against each other. In his Murray Hill flat overlooking a garden, there was a considerable collection of cigarette cases and monogrammed dressing gowns, which had been presented to him by hopeful women.

Enamored once again with a handsome, Gentile, corporate type, wearing Roman numerals behind his name, who was in no other way remarkable, she found John Wiley Garrett II as fascinating as she once had found Edwin Pond Parker II. Although decently educated, he was a man whose interests were limited to business and sports. He shared neither her radical tendencies nor her love of literature. Later, trying to remember what they had talked about, she retained a foggy impression that he spoke about the war and about his clubs at Williams, but she couldn't be certain because "we were both pretty fairly tight" most of the time. Alcohol transformed him into a fascinating lover, but the reality was that they had nothing in common.

In the early months of the affair, although she never mentioned John by name, she knitted the private details of their relationship into a number of columns and stories. She had a friend, she wrote in *The New Yorker*, "who is trying to make a lady of me, and the first step in the uphill climb has been the gaining of my promise to keep from employing certain words," which was why she couldn't reveal her true opinion of Sinclair Lewis's latest novel. In the end, she coyly identified the forbidden word as *rotten* but only because the magazine would not print her favorite word, *shit*. John, incidentally, seems to have resented her position as literary critic and complained that she never wrote about anything that people read, so the next week she reviewed something he did read, the tabloid comic strips. He further complained that her drinking and late hours were a bad influence on him.

His behavior maddened her, especially his habit of breaking his promises to telephone. She would sit by the phone waiting and agonizing, resisting the impulse to phone him; when women phoned men, she wrote, "they know you are thinking about them and wanting them, and that makes them hate you." She decided that men "hate you whenever you say anything you really think. You always have to keep playing little games." For fear of losing him, she tried to contain her jealousy, but she continued to distrust him.

At Christmas she could not deny feeling unhappy. "Sunk I am. And in a big way. It is my conviction that civilization is about to collapse." John's faithlessness was scarcely news, but she had hoped to break the pattern. What surprised her was his promiscuity and his stamina for deception. He was not a bit ashamed of himself and took few precautions to conceal his exploits, which Dorothy rightfully interpreted as provocative behavior. One evening Heywood Broun and Rebecca Bernstien, who were to dine with them, plowed up the stairs to Garrett's apartment only to find themselves with front-row seats to a confrontational scene between John, Dorothy, and a musical-comedy actress. "It was a screaming match," Bernstien remembered, "except that it was Dorothy who was doing all the screaming. I can't remember the exact obscenities she used but she was very, very graphic."

"Let us leave," Broun whispered. They shut the door and crept away.

The winter of 1928, after a four-year separation, she finally filed for divorce from Eddie. To avoid publicity, she slipped into Hartford and, before a committee of the Superior Court, testified at a private hearing in which she cited several unpleasant episodes from her married life. The committee recommended that she be granted a divorce on the ground of intolerable cruelty. Eddie declined to contest. They did not see one another on the day of the hearing, nor did they ever meet again.

Several months after the divorce, Eddie married Anne O'Brien, a probation officer employed by the Hartford Juvenile Court. They moved to the small town of Haddam, Connecticut.

Five years later, on January 7, 1933, Eddie died of Ipral (a barbituric acid derivative) poisoning. The medical examiner gave the cause of death as a self-administered overdose of a sleeping powder but concluded it was accidental. A different cause was cited by Eddie's physician, who attributed the death to "an acute septic condition resulting from surgical procedure." His patient, he said, recently had several teeth extracted. Eddie fell into a coma and was taken to St. Francis Hospital, where he died two days later without regaining consciousness. He was thirty-nine. His obituary noted that he had once been a stock trader with Paine Webber but mentioned no recent employment. *The Hartford Courant* emphasized two facts about the deceased. One was his distinguished ancestry as a grandson of the Reverend Dr. Edwin Pond Parker, pastor of the South Congregational Church and friend of Mark Twain. The other was his first marriage to Dorothy Parker, the "well-known poet."

On the day the divorce became final, Dorothy spent the evening with John Garrett at Jack and Charlie's speakeasy, where later they were joined by Heywood Broun and writer Mildred Gilman, at that time Broun's secretary and assistant. Gilman recalls that Dorothy went to pieces.

> Even though she hadn't seen Eddie Parker for years, and never said a good word about him, this was a terrible time for her. She carried on and kept running off to the ladies room to cry, and the men kept sending me after her because she had this tendency toward committing suicide, and she also had a habit of giving all her money to the ladies-room attendant. After this happened three or four times, I was getting bored stiff. Finally, John rose in all his Wall Street finery and announced emphatically that *he* had to go to the gentleman's room, to which Dorothy muttered, "He really has to use the telephone but he doesn't want to admit it."

That spring she tried to temper her drinking with highballs that were just little ones, "awfully weak; just cambric Scotch," and talked about needing more dogs. May marked the publication of *Sunset Gun*, her second volume of verse. Boni and Liveright did a hefty first printing of ten thousand copies, along with a fancy numbered and autographed special edition of 250 copies that was priced at $7.50. Dorothy switched titles at the last moment from the rather cheerful *Songs for the Nearest Harmonica* to the darker *Sunset Gun*, a reference to the cannon that is traditionally fired at the end of the day when the flag is lowered. Reviews were, if anything, even more enthusiastic than for *Enough Rope*. In the *Saturday Review*, Bill Benét repeated the question some people were asking: "Is it as good as *Enough Rope*?" Benét emphatically believed it was and went on to call *Sunset Gun* "a moth-gray cloak of demureness hiding spangled ribaldry, a razor-keen intellect mocking a head dark with desperation." As for its author, "Long may she wave!"

In *Sunset Gun* Dorothy included a concise poem written for *The New Yorker* before she met John Garrett, which she called "Three-Volume Novel," although in the collection she downgraded it to "Two-Volume Novel":

> The sun's gone dim, and
> The moon's turned black;
> For I loved him, and
> He didn't love back.

She dedicated *Sunset Gun* to John, but the situation remained as unsatisfactory as ever. She was not prepared to send him packing, nor could she accept him as he was. Her emotional dependence on him was contrasted by the autonomy she exhibited in other areas of her life. She left the Algonquin, where Round Table lunches had become less frequent, and moved into a furnished flat on East Fifty-fourth Street, off Fifth Avenue, two flights above a piano store. She paid seventy-five dollars a month for a living room, a tiny bedroom, and a kitchenette with all the usual useless conveniences. Only the ice box interested her, because the White Rock needed to be chilled.

Dorothy's nightly cocktail parties took place as always at her new apartment. One evening, when a large crowd had assembled, Mildred Gilman happened to enter Dorothy's bedroom to get to the bathroom at about the same time as Robert Benchley went in to make a telephone call. Dorothy noticed and later saw them coming out of the bedroom together. Jumping to conclusions and furious at Mildred, whom she supposed to have lured Benchley into the room, she waited until Mildred had left before informing Heywood Broun that his secretary was a slut. When this got back to Gilman, a divorcée with a small son, she was so upset that she asked Benchley to tell Heywood the truth. She also wondered why Dorothy would have fabricated such a mean story. Benchley, too, found it baffling.

> She is quite given to telling of assaults on John by various ladies (I have never heard you included in the list, but have heard only part of the list) but this [is] the first time that I have ever been made the hero. It sounds like one of Dottie's

vivid word-pictures to illustrate my helplessness in the clutches of any attractive woman. . . . Incidentally, you don't suppose for one minute that, if I had any reason to believe that you had designs on my person, you would have left that room inviolate, do you?

Allen Saalburg remembered Dorothy as "half-soused a good deal of the time, and that's when her worst qualities came out." A certain amount of the respect she commanded was rooted in "very strong fear. People were afraid of being jumped on from behind."

Dorothy had experienced abdominal pain in the winter and wondered if she might have appendicitis, but the discomfort was slight. Instead of reporting it to Dr. Barach, she bought a book about appendicitis and self-diagnosed the symptoms as a fancy hangover, "just the effects of that new Scotch of mine which, friends tell me, must have been specially made by the Borgias." One Monday afternoon toward the end of May, she suddenly developed severe pain and began running a temperature. This time she did send for Barach, who diagnosed acute appendicitis and sent her to Presbyterian Hospital, where she was operated on the same evening.

When Aleck Woollcott came to visit,

> I found her hard at work. Because of posterity and her credi-
> tors, I was loath to intrude, but she, being entranced at any
> interruption, greeted me from her cot of pain, waved me to
> a chair, offered me a cigarette, and rang a bell. I wondered
> if this could possibly be for drinks. "No," she said sadly, "it
> is supposed to fetch the night nurse, so I ring it whenever I
> want an hour of uninterrupted privacy."

She gave her address as Bedpan Alley and requested a typewriter, insisting that the size of the hospital bill made it necessary for her to write her way out of the place. Ignoring the fact that she had two best-selling books in print—and loath to shell out the fruits of her success to Presbyterian Hospital—she tried to think of someone who might want to underwrite an extravagance like an appendectomy. Bea Stewart assumed the hospital expenses would not be a problem, since they had rich friends who would be pleased to help out.

"No rich people," Dorothy cautioned. Dorothy never took money from people she disliked.

Dorothy agreed that John Gilbert would be the logical candidate to approach. Although he earned ten thousand dollars a week in Hollywood, he did not qualify as "rich people" by her definition. Gilbert responded to Bea's telegram by promptly wiring the money, which she asked the telegraph office to pay out in one-dollar bills. Stuffing the cash into a paper bag, she marched into Dorothy's room and tore open the bag to let the green leaves blow around like a hurricane in a cabbage patch. The nurses failed to find this amusing.

"Is this insanity?" one of them asked sourly and stalked out.

"It's a form of it," Bea replied.

After three weeks at Presbyterian, Dorothy faced a month's convalescence at home. She was miserably bored. Before long she was wishing that she owned an electric train. "Hell, while I'm up, I wish I had a couple of professional hockey teams." To kill time she read fiction, which reminded her of her own failures in that genre. Despite everything, her ambition still was to write a novel. Real writers, in her eyes, seldom limited themselves to short fiction. More than ever, she felt a need to prove herself a real writer. Short-story collections never sold well because literature was measured by the yard and people wanted their money's worth. She began to work on a story that would not be quite long enough to qualify as a novella, but was two or three times the length of anything she had attempted so far. It was possibly the finest story she ever wrote. To read it is to envisage her laying down a sentence, laboriously shaping it until it seemed simple, then going on to the next sentence and doing likewise, so carefully crafted is this story.

It can be described as a parable of a woman who loses her way, condemned to live and wander. Hazel Morse is a wholesale dress model, good sport, wife, ex-wife, swell drinker, animal lover, unsuccessful suicide, and big blonde. The story readily suggests Dorothy and presents a fictionalized account of some bad things that had happened to her. "Big Blonde" is perhaps the most intensely autobiographical of all her fiction. Certainly, it was no accident that she opens the story in the garment industry, where Hazel has been employed as a model for many years and where she has perfected her good-sport role with dress buyers from Des Moines and Houston. Like her heroine, Dorothy had her own origins in the garment business; although Seventh Avenue was a world she despised, it was as familiar to her as breathing.

After tinkering with the story off and on for the rest of the year, she allowed Seward Collins to publish it in *The Bookman* as a favor, because she might have placed it in a more distinguished magazine. When "Big Blonde" appeared in February 1929, it brought her unanimous praise. F.P.A.'s reaction in The Conning Tower typified the enthusiasm:

> ... So had a beaker of milk with O. Hering the architect, and so home and read a tayle of Dorothy Parker's in the February Bookman, called "Big Blonde," the best short story I have read in so long a time that I cannot say. I would nominate that lady for a membership in the Dudless Writers' Club, a sacred society, whose only other member I can think of at this moment is A. E. Housman.

Her friends, naturally, loved "Big Blonde." So did a great many others, however. The prestigious O. Henry competition selected it as the best short story of 1929.

The publication of "Big Blonde" marked a leap forward in her literary reputation. It also sealed the end of her relationship with Collins, who, in due course, committed professional suicide. He and his literary magazine continued to win respect for another two or three years before taking a nose dive when he began publishing political ideas that seemed to parallel Mussolini's. It was whispered that he had become a fascist. In addition to his admiration for the Nazis, his fascination with psychic research and his claims to be receiving messages from other worlds did not reassure people either. In 1952, Edmund Wilson informed her that Sewie had died.

"I don't see what else he could do," she said, as if he had killed himself. In her eyes he had, long ago.

Technological progress, aside from the Lindbergh flight, left Dorothy cold. She never learned to drive and refused to purchase a radio, obstinately declaring "there is no force great enough to make me," and she found movies boring. A motion picture theater was "an enlarged and magnificently decorated lethal chamber to me." All the same, she began to revise some of those judgments slightly when Benchley filmed *The Treasurer's Report* for the William Fox Studio and a few months later acted in a second short, *The Sex Life of the Polyp*, which were the first films to use sustained talking for more than a minute. Dorothy thought he was magnificent. She also enjoyed watching a filmed conversation with George Bernard Shaw, but the ear-splitting sound tracks of other talkies made her feel like shouting at the screen, "Oh, for heaven's sake, shut up!"

Three months later, she was sitting in a Culver City office building, staring at palm trees. Later, she said need of money lured her to Hollywood. Not only did the deal seem too good to pass up, but film writing also looked like easy money. She remembered thinking, "Why, I could do that with one hand tied behind me and the other on Irving Thalberg's pulse." Thanks partly to Howard Dietz, MGM offered her a contract paying three hundred dollars a week for three months, which added up to a tidy little sum. The disturbing part of the deal was living three thousand miles from New York. Still, the film company wooed her with excessive flattery, praising her wit and talent and telling her how much they needed clever writers like herself. A telegram arrived from John Gilbert: I HEAR SWELL NEWS ABOUT YOUR HAVING GONE MOVIE THAT'S GRAND WHEN ARE YOU ARRIVING.

Before she left for California, she gave an interview to the *Brooklyn Eagle* in which she excused her defection. "It always takes more to live on than what you earn," she said, adding that she was "always hampered by money." She also stated that she abhorred movies, hoped the entire film industry would collapse, and predicted she would hate Hollywood because it was full of palms, which "are the ugliest vegetable God created." After a week in Hollywood she realized that she really did hate the place, but by then it was too late.

Her first assignment was writing dialogue for a melodrama, *Madame X*. The job got off to a bad start when she glimpsed an MGM publicity release that referred to her as "the internationally known author of *Too Much Rope*, the popular novel." She was further dismayed to meet Irving Thalberg, production head of MGM, and realize that he had no idea who she was or why she had been hired.

"Now let's see," he said to her. "What was it you wanted to do for us?"

Her office was located at the end of a hall. "It was a lovely office but the air was oppressive, and even though I opened the windows and opened the doors, it was still depressing." Her desk had the unmistakable fragrance of an outhouse. After days of sniffing and holding her nose, she learned why. The previous occupant had been growing mushrooms in a bottom drawer by a correspondence course with liquid manure guaranteed to produce mushrooms in any climate on earth. Other writers seemed reluctant to visit her cubicle. She felt isolated. When a sign painter arrived to letter her name on the door, she felt like bribing him to print GENTLEMEN instead.

Everything she had heard about Hollywood turned out to be true. Living was ridiculously expensive. At first she stayed at the Ambassador Hotel in a ten-dollar room that she thought was worth three. After she received her first paycheck and could afford to move, she lived with screenwriter Arthur Caesar and his wife, who had a big house in Beverly Hills. The parties she attended were pompous affairs, full of old fogies who had to be in bed by ten-thirty. A newspaper reported that at one gathering, she let off steam by yelling, "Come on, you so-and-sos, get a little action on this." California weather made her sleepy, the brilliant flowers smelled like rotten, old dollar bills, and she suspected the enormous vegetables had been grown in dirty trunks. On Thanksgiving Day, when it was too hot to wear a coat, she wished she were at home where it was cold and a turkey sat in the oven at her sister's house.

She hoped that three months in Hollywood might cure her obsession with John Garrett, the curious sensation she had of honestly not knowing "where John leaves off and I begin." Separation from her had not changed him. When she telephoned, he sometimes pretended they had a poor connection or claimed he couldn't talk on account of having visitors. Nothing had changed.

There was no lack of friends with whom she could commiserate in Hollywood. Gerald Murphy was there with Sara and the children. Murphy, an expert on Early American spirituals, had been recruited by MGM as a music consultant to King Vidor on the all-black picture *Hallelujah*. The Murphys agreed that the town was unappealing, and so did Bunny Wilson, who was living in a beach cottage in Santa Barbara and writing a novel. In early December, when Benchley arrived to act in three Fox pictures, he also found that he hated Hollywood. They turned into marathon complainers. On December 17, Dorothy was shattered to learn that Elinor Wylie had died the previous evening of a stroke; even Benchley's presence could not dent her grief. "Dottie is so low that she hardly speaks even to me," he reported to Gertrude.

Two months passed. Through no fault of her own, she had not written a single word for *Madame X* because nobody instructed her what to write. Instead, she wrote dialogue for an untitled film (whose plot remained a secret too). When she had finished, she sent it to Irving Thalberg for approval. Eventually, the pages came back with a message from his secretary: "Mr. Thalberg said to tell you that you have to be careful in writing for the pictures. You always have to think of the Little Totties." Dorothy was ready to explode.

"God," she moaned, "and how I hate children!"

Given her frustration, it is not clear why she signed two more contracts in early January committing herself to work on *Five O'Clock Girl* and the Cecil B. DeMille film *Dynamite*.

For *Dynamite*, she was asked to write a song, even though the picture was not a musical. Since the success of *The Jazz Singer*, producers were insisting that even nonmusicals use a song for exploitation purposes. To Dorothy's mind, the theme-song craze had got out of hand with such foolishness as "Varsity Girl, I'll Cling to You," for *Varsity Girl*, but she was determined to give MGM what she imagined might please, and she concocted a snappy lyric entitled, "Dynamite Man, I Love You," which was swiftly pronounced unacceptable. At her wit's end to know what they wanted, she made up her mind to ask DeMille himself what the picture was about, although getting in to see him was "like riding a camel through the eye of a needle."

"Mr. DeMille, just tell me what this picture is about," she croaked, fearful lest she waste a second of the producer's precious time.

DeMille treated her to a lengthy saga about a socialite who, in order to gain an inheritance, needs a husband and makes up her mind to marry a man who has been accused and convicted of a murder, unjustly of course, and is awaiting the end in a prison cell, with time hanging heavy on his hands and nothing for solace but his guitar, not knowing a last-minute reprieve awaits him, the whole sorry goulash wanting nothing more than a catchy tune for the poor devil to sing. By the time he got to the end, Dorothy's eyes had rolled upward and backward into her head.

"Mr. DeMille, the details of these pictures must be . . . my goodness, it's just staggering."

DeMille said, "Ah, yes, zebras in *The King of Kings.*"

In her office, she began flipping through a Bible to find out why zebras should be in a film about the life of Christ. She wondered if she had heard wrong. Perhaps DeMille had said Hebrews.

Next time she saw DeMille, she said, "Mr. DeMille, what were you doing with zebras?"

He said, "Oh, the zebras. They were pulling the chariots of Mary Magdalene." He paused. "Terrible, they kick so easily but their legs broke."

"Of course," Dorothy said. "I should have known that," and tottered back to her office where she quickly wrote, with composer Jack King, a lovely ballad, "How Am I to Know?" When it was accepted, she informed Thalberg that she was going home. She demanded, and received, train fare back to New York. So eager was she to make her getaway that she left the home of Arthur Caesar without saying good-bye.

Back in New York, she allowed herself to be swept away by the enthusiasm of two men who had founded The Viking Press, Harold Guinzburg and George Oppenheimer, long-time admirers who convinced her that it would be a crime if she didn't write a novel. Guinzburg was the type of intellectual whom Dorothy could respect, a sensitive, rather scholarly man who was exceptionally solid in his knowledge of literature. In contrast, "Georgie Opp" was extroverted—a snappy dresser, a bit of a smart aleck, a man who took pride in knowing everybody worth knowing and in cultivating those he didn't. He loved women (as friends) and set about forthwith fawning over Dorothy, flattering her shamelessly. The upshot was that she agreed to produce a novel in time to head Viking's spring 1930 list, an astonishing promise for someone who spent three or four months on a short story, but she was counting on it being possible if she went abroad again.

There seemed to be nothing holding her in New York, because her affair with John was over. She had a romantic's view of broken love affairs. When an interviewer once asked if she thought it silly to kill oneself over unrequited love, she opened her eyes wide. "No," she said. She took the same approach to the writing of novels. The solution for both was foreign travel.

When she learned that Muriel and Allen Saalburg were planning to sail in April, she made up her mind to go over with them.

Chapter 11

SONNETS IN SUICIDE,
OR THE LIFE OF JOHN KNOX

◆

1929 – 1932

During a brief stay in London, she bought a pugilistic, prizewinning Dandie Dinmont terrier named Timothy, who was fourteen months old and would have been the sweetest dog in the world if not for his habit of picking fights with almost every animal that crossed his path. Dorothy took Timothy to Paris, where she had not been at the Hôtel Napoléon more than a few days before she began to feel sick.

Luckily, the Saalburgs knew of a physician, as it happened one of France's most eminent surgeons, and they offered to accompany her to the examination. Afterward, the doctor came out to the reception room and gestured broadly to them with both arms to indicate the enlargement of the patient's liver. Dorothy blamed the language difference for her difficulty in understanding the diagnosis and would mysteriously refer to her condition as "a dainty complaint—something the matter with my liver." For six weeks she felt "sick and blue and lonely." Work was out of the question, and drinking was strictly forbidden. Confined to her hotel room with only the Dandie Dinmont for company, she had visits from the Saalburgs and also a sick call from Ernest and Pauline Hemingway, who were living with their infant son near the church of Saint-Sulpice and who were, she said, "something swell to me," although later she admitted disliking Pauline.

When she began to feel better, she went on a shopping spree and bought a summer fur coat made of cream-colored unborn lamb, which had "all the warmth and durability of a sheet of toilet paper." She also ordered a number of trailing chiffon dresses and stocked up on nightgowns, chemises, and slips with matching panties for herself as well as her sister. Afterward, looking at her purchases, she realized they were "some of the most ill-advised clothes ever assembled. They were just what somebody with an afflicted liver *would* have picked out." Her most costly mistake proved to be the summer fur, which she would wear only four times before shipping it home to Helen, who had little use for it either.

At the end of June, Benchley arrived with his wife and children. Against her better judgment, Dorothy agreed to join them in a rented car on a grueling four-day journey to Antibes, where they planned to visit the Murphys. Around Gertrude, Benchley seemed strangely silent. "He simply can't speak, in the presence of his bride, and who could? O my God, *what* a woman, oh, my God, *what* a woman!" She found it hard to believe he was the same man, so subdued was his behavior around his family. Before long, Nat and young Bub were driving her crazy. When Robert Junior had been a baby, Dorothy had been quite taken with his chubbiness and fondly nicknamed him Annie, because he reminded her of the Irish maid once employed by the Rothschilds. "Annie," his baby fat gone, had matured into a normal, high-spirited ten-year-old who bickered and competed with his older brother. According to Benchley's diary, crisis followed crisis: Dorothy left her passport in a restaurant, Timothy barked at every dog along the roadside, young Bub "gets in nettles making p.p." The children's rowdiness forced Benchley to offer a prize "to first boy not to be amusing."

Gertrude regarded travel for children as an opportunity for education. Assuming the role of teacher and tour guide, she pointed out Roman ruins and conducted spelling contests. At one point, almost unhinged by the racket, Dorothy told Gertrude that she was considering surgery to reduce the size of her breasts. What prompted her to cook up such a peculiar confidence would be interesting to know. On the other hand, as she wrote to Aleck Woollcott, "I have a collection of Mrs. Benchleiana that will knock your justly prize right eye out."

At Villa America, Sara and Gerald installed the Benchley family in one of their guest houses and put Dorothy and Timothy in the other, the *bastide*, which resembled a picture-book Normandy farmhouse with plumbing and electricity and exquisite decorations. It stood surrounded by fig trees laden with purple fruit, which was fine, she said, "except that I hate figs in any form." The weather was glorious and suddenly Dorothy felt fired with "deferred health and twilit energy." She began swimming two kilometers a day; she devoured the accounts of murders and dismemberings in the Nice papers; and she played with the Murphy children—eleven-year-old Honoria, eight-year-old Patrick, who had a stomach ailment requiring a special diet, and ten-year-old Baoth, who named a chicken after her. When the chicken turned out to be a rooster, Baoth shrugged philosophically and said, "What is that of difference?" Dorothy's hair grew long and she began to gain weight.

From Antibes, Dorothy sent *The New Yorker* three poems and two short stories. She was barreling ahead on her novel, to which she had given the intriguing title *Sonnets in Suicide, or the Life of John Knox.* Numerous pages got torn up, and what was left failed to please her entirely but, she said, "it's an awful pile of work, just the same." Daily she prayed, "Dear God, please make me stop writing like a woman. For Jesus Christ's sake, amen."

Among the old friends she saw were the Fitzgeralds, who had rented a villa near Cannes. Zelda, who seemed tired and more remote than usual, was gravitating toward her ultimate breakdown, but Dorothy was unaware of her problems. It was Scott, jittery, argumentative, and often obnoxiously drunk, who seemed to be in poor shape. Jealous of the hospitality that Sara and Gerald were lavishing on Dorothy, he wrote petulantly to Hemingway that the Murphys were putting on their most elaborate performance for her benefit but she didn't seem to appreciate it.

At Villa America she was content to live quietly. Everyone told her that the Riviera social scene that summer was terrible because every "tripe" was there, including Rosie Dolly and Peggy Hopkins Joyce. Still, she never knew who might turn up. Adele Lovett came over for four days, just to see Benchley she claimed, but left in disgust because he was tied up with his family every minute. Jack Gilbert and Ina Claire arrived on their honeymoon. Benchley, walking along the street in Cannes, came face to face with his former mistress, who was in the company of her current boyfriend, and she cut him dead. That evening, shaken by the encounter, he managed to give Gertrude the slip, and he and Dorothy sallied forth to get "absolutely blotto."

Dorothy had dutifully cut back on her drinking, but that night she got so drunk that she wound up in bed with a good-looking international polo star, the heir to a carpeting fortune. "The lucky man was Laddie Sanford," she wrote Helen, "and we wouldn't know each other even if we ever did see each other again. And I don't even feel embarrassed about it, because I can't tell you how little sex means to me now. Or at least I can't tell you how little I think sex means to me now. And polo players wouldn't count, anyway."

Unfortunately, the drunken encounter with Sanford triggered her memories of John Garrett. Before leaving New York, despite her suspicion that he was involved with at least two other women, she felt pleased when he told her that he too would be in France that summer. She must cable her address so they might rendezvous somewhere for a week or two, he insisted. Although she read of his arrival in the *Paris Herald*, she failed to hear from him and finally wired to say she wished they could be friends. He responded with a collect telegram: DELIGHTED WIRE ALWAYS, three words whose studied ambiguity seemed downright spooky to her.

Knowing that he was close by and ignoring her shattered her earlier contentment. Sometimes Yvonne Roussel, tutor to the Murphy children, would catch sight of Dorothy in the garden "looking a little lost." Suddenly she felt bewildered and miserable. "I don't know how much I have built up for myself of his boyishness and gaiety and sweetness—even of his good looks. I honestly can't remember what it was like to be alone with him; I couldn't possibly recall any of our conversation." She was mourning the loss of a fantasy, but a part of her enjoyed the unhappiness of her position, for she believed that a broken heart was no disgrace; indeed it was rather romantic.

In early August she checked her funds and was disagreeably surprised to discover she had only forty dollars left. She knew that Harold Guinzburg was in Paris with his wife, Alice, and she lost no time in speeding back there to discuss a further advance. To prove to Guinzburg how conscientious she had been, she brought along as much of the typed manuscript of *Sonnets in Suicide* as she had completed to date. Even though it was a stupendous stack of work, the partial manuscript began to look puny to Dorothy at the last moment, so that she decided to fatten it up by inserting carbons of old articles and letters from friends.

Dorothy was incapable of asking anyone for money. Pride would not allow her to beg. What she would do instead was to look woebegone, wring her hands, and confess that she simply had no idea what she was going to do because she was broke and feeling scared about it. What usually happened was that the offer of a loan would be forthcoming, which she could then be prevailed upon to accept. On this occasion, she managed to convey her predicament to Guinzburg, who sympathetically doled out an amount sufficient for her to remain in France and finish the book. Afterward, alone in the Paris flat loaned to her by the Saalburgs, a good dingy hovel she called it, she plunged into depression. She found herself "looking thoughtfully at the Seine," although prior to that time she had never seriously considered suicide by drowning. In this agitated frame of mind, she began to torment herself and indulged in a bit of typical pathology—she made the mistake of sending Garrett a pleading letter that confessed her longing to see him and concluded by asking what she should do, as if she expected him to offer helpful advice.

His reply, another collect cable, could not have been more insulting: LOVED LETTER DEAR SO HAPPY YOU ARE WELL.

Young Patrick Murphy was gravely ill. In Dorothy's absence, Villa America had been transformed from a paradisiacal retreat to a house of anxiety and horror when his affliction was diagnosed as tuberculosis. Later, the Murphys' doctors traced the incubation of the disease back to February, when the family was living in Hollywood and employing a chauffeur who subsequently proved to be tubercular. Sara and Gerald were determined that their son must be cured, even though no known cure for tuberculosis existed at that time, only methods of prolonging the patient's life by cold mountain air and a rich dairy diet. Just as they had poured their energies into creating a magical life for themselves, they began to rechannel that same passion for living well into a counterattack on a fatal illness. At once, they dismantled Villa America in preparation for moving their whole establishment—children, servants, and pets—to Montana-Vermala, a health resort for tuberculosis patients near Sierre in the Swiss Alps.

Dorothy prepared to return home, although she dreaded living in New York, where she seemed to do nothing but drink and entertain "horrible" people in the afternoons. During the weeks before the Murphys left, she traveled to Paris to interview Ernest Hemingway for a *New Yorker* profile. *A Farewell to Arms* had just been published to superlative reviews and had jumped to the top of the best-seller list. To her disgust, the restrictions he put on her made a decent story practically impossible. He would not permit her to mention his family in Oak Park, his divorce from Hadley, "or anything he ever did or said," she later complained. In trying to respect his wishes, she was reduced to filling the space with compliments about his writing, but the gushy, fan-magazine tone of "The Artist's Reward" was less her fault than Hemingway's.

Her departure plans were suddenly revised when Sara and Gerald asked her to accompany them to Montana-Vermala, as a favor, because Sara found her a comfort to have around. Dorothy immediately cabled Benchley for advice, but "the big shit" was away or never answered or both, she said, "so I came anyhow." That is what she guessed Benchley would have done. Staying was not in her best interests; in fact, it was probably the worst decision she could have made. The first project of hers to be abandoned was *Sonnets in Suicide*, even though she cabled Viking to assure Guinzburg that she was WORKING HARD, as if saying it would somehow make it true. He answered that he expected *Sonnets* to be a best seller and to mail the manuscript special delivery when it was completed and also include an autobiographical blurb for the dust jacket.

By the third week of October, the Murphys had vacated Villa America. Only Dorothy remained to gather up Timothy and the four Murphy dogs, plus the rest of the baggage, which consisted of eleven trunks and seventeen hand pieces, and follow along behind. Shepherding the baggage caravan entailed three changes of trains and the greasing of several palms to pass the animals through customs at Geneva, but otherwise she accomplished the trip without incident. She had always considered Switzerland "the home of horseshit," she wrote Benchley, and saw no reason to revise her opinion. Montana-Vermala was built on the side of a "God damn Alp," from which she had no idea how she would descend; before she risked her life a second time on the funicular, she would prefer to remain among the bacilli.

The Swiss Family Murphy, as she had dubbed them, were installed in a row of six rooms at the Palace Hotel (all the sanatoriums were called Splendide or Royale) and Dorothy's room was located on the floor above. Standing on her terrace, staring at the peaks, she remembered how strongly she had always hated mountains. She overheard a woman in the next room dying audibly one night. Day or night, she froze because there was no way to keep warm. Indoor temperatures had to be maintained at practically subarctic levels for the patients. Dorothy's pretty Parisian clothes remained in her trunk while she bundled up in tweed suit, overcoat, and woolen muffler. Out of doors, where it was warm in the sun, she removed either the coat or the muffler.

Dorothy tried not to think about Harold Guinzburg and George Oppenheimer. When she received a panicky telegram from them saying that the spring catalogue was closing December 15 and they had to know immediately if *Sonnets in Suicide* would be ready, she did not reply.

Once the children were in bed at nights, Dorothy joined Sara and Gerald in their room, where Gerald had arranged a makeshift bar and would ceremoniously put out a bottle of wine, a bag of cinnamon, some lemons, and a spirit lamp. Huddled in their mufflers and talking in whispers because Patrick's room was next door, they drank the wine out of hospital tumblers and spoke of past good times and absent friends, especially Benchley. "Ah, old Boogles Benchley," Gerald sighed. "Ah, old imaginary good lucks. Let's cable the old fool to come over." On Sara's birthday they celebrated with cake and champagne and presents for everybody, including dogs, canaries, and Coquette, the parrot Dorothy bought for the children, which turned out to be a vicious creature. Afterward Dorothy went back to her room and cried.

On alternating days, Patrick received pneumothorax treatments, a procedure in which a hollow needle was inserted through his ribs into the pleura and gas pumped through it to make the lung collapse, so that if one lung was isolated perhaps the other could be saved. The thought of it made Dorothy shudder. "Christ, think of all the shits in the world and then this happens to the Murphys!"

Apart from one or two glasses of wine at bedtime, amounts that scarcely counted as drinking in her opinion, Dorothy tried to stay on the wagon. Hard liquor was not recommended at those altitudes, but some days she didn't care; getting drunk was a necessity. One of those days she frightened Patrick and Honoria when she narrowly missed killing their canary. She offered to help Honoria clean the bird's cage, but her hands were so unsteady that she dropped it.

Liquor, she found, did little to lighten her somber mood, which she described to Benchley as like having the "slow, even heebs." At times she caught herself examining a clean white towel that the hospital had thumbtacked above the washstand. "It's a good thing to look at. You can go all around the edges very slowly, and then you can do a lot of counting the squares made by the ironed-out creases." She felt bushed—her favorite word for exhausted—without having done anything at all, and she also felt curiously cut off from the world at the foot of the mountain. The Wall Street crash, for example, might have taken place on another planet. Since she owned no stocks, the trouble in the market had no effect on her finances, which suffered from major depressions year in, year out, but she wrote anxiously to friends asking if anyone they knew had been wiped out.

On Thanksgiving Day the Palace Hotel served veal for lunch, not unusual because nine meals out of ten featured veal. Afterward, Dorothy wrote a homesick, eleven-page letter to her sister saying how much she missed "youse guys." Christmas proved more cheerful because company arrived: John Dos Passos and his bride, Katy, Ernest and Pauline Hemingway, and Pauline's sister, Virginia Pfeiffer. They celebrated an all-American Christmas with a tree and a goose that Ernest had shot especially for their dinner. The bird was roasted in the hospital kitchen and served with mashed chestnuts and a flaming brandied pudding decorated with holly. The guests were eager to spend their days on the ski slopes, where Hemingway taught Honoria and Baoth how to herringbone and sidestep. Dorothy, who viewed a ski slope with the same enthusiasm as she did an electric chair, declined to accompany them.

In the evenings, Dos Passos recalled, Dorothy made "her usual funny cracks with her eyes full of tears," and he described them eating cheese fondue and drinking the local white wine while laughing their heads off, which suggests that the merriment was a bit forced. For five or six days the Christmas visitors brought a respite of sorts, but after they departed the little group was alone again, and Dorothy began to bombard Benchley with cables and letters. She wrote,

SEE BY PARIS HERALD HOOVER SAYS NO NEED OF PESSIMISM EVERYONE HERE GREATLY ENCOURAGED STOP LOVE AND HOW ARE YOU.

YOU COME RIGHT OVER HERE AND EXPLAIN WHY THEY ARE HAVING ANOTHER YEAR.

And the plain truth:

DEEPLY SUNK LOVE YOU SOMETHING TERRIBLE.

The atmosphere of death in Montana-Vermala was inescapable. She dreaded going out for a walk and dreaded meeting people who stopped to admire Timothy. Some of them told her that they had a Dandie Dinmont at home, but of course they would never see home again. No doubt the

Murphys sensed her mood, because when she talked about going home for a while, they made no attempt to dissuade her. She decided to spend a month in New York to take care of business and collect her five-hundred-dollar O. Henry prize for "Big Blonde" before rejoining Sara and Gerald. Mid-January 1930, she and Timothy braved the terrifying funicular descent down the mountainside on the first leg of their journey home.

When the *De Grasse* docked at the end of January, Benchley was on hand to welcome her. A crowd of newspaper reporters trailed them back to the New Weston Hotel, where they jammed themselves into Dorothy's suite and began asking questions that immediately irritated her. She felt far from comical, but they expected to be entertained. Curled up on the sofa, with Timothy blinking soberly next to her, she insisted that she was not a wit but "only a hardworking woman, who writes for a living and hates writing more than anything else in the world." She intended to stay a month, she said, before returning to Switzerland to finish a novel whose subject she did not care to reveal. She tried changing the subject to the economic situation and wondered whether people were nicer now that they were poorer, but the press seemed uninterested in serious subjects. When somebody asked what she thought of the New York skyline, she'd had enough of dumb questions and snapped, "Put a little more gin in mine!" as she shooed them out.

A few days later, Sara Murphy's sister threw a welcome-home party for Dorothy. The chief topic of conversation was of course the illness of Patrick Murphy. Archibald MacLeish, meeting her for the first time, reported to Ernest Hemingway that her reputation for being affectionate with her right hand and murdering people with her left had always made him fear her. When she began to talk about the Murphys, "she took me in about eight minutes. She may be serving me up cold at this minute for all I know but I doubt it and if she is it doesn't matter."

After the months in Montana-Vermala, she had to reaccustom herself to the quick pace of Manhattan life. While she was away, her friends had been busy: Don Stewart wrote a successful comedy that opened on Broadway in February and so did Marc Connelly, whose biblical play with an all-black cast had finally found a producer. With *The Green Pastures*, Marc finally proved he could accomplish a work of consequence without George

Kaufman. Between attending first nights and meeting with Harold Guinzburg and George Oppenheimer, who were growing concerned by now,
Dorothy tried to resurrect *Sonnets in Suicide* but knew it was useless. It
would never be finished, and she began to grow angry at herself for listening
to those who had encouraged her to start the book in the first place. "Write
novels, write novels, write novels—that's all they can say. Oh, I do get so
sick and tired, sometimes." A poem required days to write, a short story
perhaps several months, but a novel seemed to last forever. The process
seemed unnatural, for she had neither the taste nor the endurance for
marathons. Knowing that most of her friends, writers like Benchley and
Lardner for whom she had the highest regard, were also sprinters did not
make her feel any happier about acknowledging her limits.

That winter she drank with Benchley at Tony's. Aleck Woollcott
purchased an apartment on the East River (named Wit's End by Dorothy),
where she turned up on Sunday mornings for his weekly breakfast party
and kept his guests entertained with her wry observations. Outwardly she
appeared calm, but actually she was an emotional wreck. March passed
without her booking a return passage to Europe or solving the problem of
the novel. It would have been sensible to tell Guinzburg that even though
she wished desperately to write it she was "quite incapable of it—I'm a
short-distance writer." Almost from the start, she realized that the autobiographical material was "too painful" and that, moreover, a novel would take
a very long time to complete because she wrote so slowly. This was the
reason she had so little to show for her months abroad. Leveling with
Guinzburg was impossible or perhaps never crossed her mind. Instead, she
panicked and drank a bottle of shoe polish. While it failed to kill her, the
shoe polish made her quite ill, and she was hospitalized.

Since *Sonnets in Suicide* had almost proved a prophetic title, Oppenheimer and Guinzburg were quick to reassure her of their understanding.
Submitting to *force majeure*, Viking accepted the fact that no Dorothy
Parker novel would top the best-seller list in 1930, even though Guinzburg
did not give up hope that eventually she would fulfill her contract. To make
the best of the situation and to recoup Viking's investment, he scooped up
thirteen of her short stories and sketches and announced the publication
of a collection, called *Laments for the Living*, published in June, on Friday
the thirteenth. The book's centerpiece was "Big Blonde." It also included
"Mr. Durant" and "The Wonderful Old Gentleman," as well as some minor

pieces, like the tiresome "Mantle of Whistler," which Viking threw in as filler.

At the end of May she left for Montana-Vermala. GOODBYE DARLING, George Oppenheimer cabled to the *Leviathan*, AND ALL LOVE WRITE ME SOON.

The painful issue of the unfinished novel was resolved, but probably her greatest accomplishment in New York was that she made no effort to contact John Garrett. She had finally been able to accept his rejection. Garrett did not marry until 1945. He and his wife, Madeleine, had no children, but after his retirement, when he was living in Martha's Vineyard, he became director of the Edgartown Boys Club. In the summer of 1961, at the Martha's Vineyard airport, he sent his chauffeur into the airline office to pick up some tickets, then fired a gun into his mouth and blew his head apart.

She found Switzerland in summertime, especially the lakes, to be extravagantly beautiful, even though she still detested the Alps and continued to regard Montana-Vermala as a village of death houses. It did not surprise her to learn that the country's per capita consumption of alcohol was the highest in Europe.

In her absence, Patrick's condition had improved so greatly that the Murphys left the hospital. They now lived in a chalet about a mile away and had purchased a house in town, which they refurbished as a nightclub, decorated with mirrors and red stars and named Harry's (after Harry's American Bar in Paris), a legitimate business open to the public and featuring good food and a dance band from Munich. Bars always comforted Dorothy, and Harry's was one of the bright spots of her summer, a place familiar and fun that reminded her of home.

At the end of July, Benchley came over for a visit. They met him at Sierre with a car. After several welcoming rounds of Cinzanos at the depot bar, they motored up to the village because he was no more enthusiastic about the funicular than was Dorothy. His arrival put them all in a bright mood, but for Dorothy it was pure pleasure. Though he stayed at the Regina Hotel while she was at the Murphys, they immediately fell into their old routine of drinking and talking until dawn. At noon, they woke with hangovers and met for lunch at Harry's to greet the new day with a drink.

She was working diligently on a story for *Cosmopolitan*, about a pair of nervous, quarreling newlyweds on their honeymoon. She expected the handsome payment of twelve hundred dollars for "Here We Are." During the afternoons, she spent several hours at her typewriter before rushing out to Harry's to meet Benchley and the Murphys. One evening after Dorothy and Benchley closed up Harry's and the local casino, they walked along the dark, silent streets when it suddenly occurred to him that somewhere in the desolate village there might be a lonely Harvard man. If he were condemned to live in this mining camp, Benchley declared, nothing would be more inspiring than to hear football songs, and so they began to sing "With the Crimson in Triumph Flashing," a serenade more for themselves than for any Harvard men in the neighborhood.

A week later, they made a trip to Venice with Sara and Gerald, staying at the lavish Grand Hotel and enjoying the Venetian sights. They visited glassblowing factories and stared at Titians; they ate lunch at Florian's and swam at the Lido in the afternoons. For practically every other meal, they dined on scampi. Late in the evenings, when they had run out of amusements, they entertained themselves with a Ouija board. At first they received fairly routine messages from an American woman named Alice who claimed to have died while traveling in Europe but soon a personality who identified herself as Elinor Wylie came through and began to make ghoulish announcements about various crimes and a few poisonings. Alarmed, they abandoned the Ouija board.

The last two days of the holiday were spent in Munich, where they drank beer at the Hofbrauhaus, attended a "not so hot" play, and went sightseeing in the rain. Gerald shopped for records by an unknown singer named Marlene Dietrich from a film called *Der Blaue Engel* and Dorothy bought a dachshund, Eiko von Blutenberg, whose lineage was so noble that "he has no sense and therefore is at ease in any drawing room." He was accustomed to a diet of bratwurst because he turned up his royal nose when she offered him a dog biscuit. After they put Benchley on the sleeper for Paris, she took Eiko back to the Regina Palace Hotel and began considering a change of name—perhaps something a little less formidable. Eventually she renamed him Robinson, which was probably a tribute to the Swiss Family Robinson. Montana-Vermala seemed less lonely with the haughty Robinson trotting at her ankles.

In the meantime, *Laments for the Living* had been published. Sales started off exceedingly well and the book went through four editions during the first month, but Dorothy thought she deserved critical success as well. The first batch of reviews she received from George Oppenheimer were, on the whole, quite good, but a few scorned her stories as slight. It was on the uncomplimentary critiques that she fastened. All the reviews, she cabled him, SEEM TO ME BEYOND WORDS AWFUL AM SICK THAT MY BOOK FOR YOU IS SO BAD PRETTY DISCOURAGED ABOUT EVER WRITING AGAIN. She wondered whether an intelligent reviewer had given her a decent notice. Oppenheimer replied, "They are dancing in the streets, Mrs. Parker, and drinking magnums of champagne in your honor and yet you sit there and say you will never write another book for shame." Her neediness was so great that even Oppenheimer's glib reassurances sounded good. He hoped that she would write eight or nine books, so that The Viking Press could pay its rent and "George can have enough money to go to Europe and see you," because he missed her so unmercifully that he "couldn't even go near '21' without shedding tears."

Apart from the story for *Cosmopolitan*, she completed only a few poems, one of them a memoriam for a tubercular woman of her acquaintance, aged twenty-five, who had recently died.

Once Benchley left, there were visits from other old friends that brought less pleasure. At the end of August, Scott Fitzgerald spent a week in Montana-Vermala; Zelda had entered treatment at a psychiatric hospital near Geneva, and his preoccupation with her schizophrenia and his family's disintegration had left him insensitive to the agonies of others. One night at Harry's, talking about the disappointments life had dealt him, he turned to Sara and said, "I don't suppose you have ever known despair." Dorothy was furious at him. After Scott, Don and Bea Stewart arrived. Later Stewart admitted finding the town far more oppressive than he had imagined from Dorothy's descriptions. Despite her jokes and Gerald's Marlene Dietrich records, the Stewarts suffered from bad dreams and insomnia, and after a few days they hurried back to Paris.

But not before Dorothy quarreled with her old friend: Ever since she had published a *New Yorker* profile of Hemingway the previous year, Stewart had been simmering with indignation over her praise for a man who had vilified her, even if she knew nothing about it. Dorothy had commended Hemingway as a writer who, unlike others, would never traffic with the gentry who lived on the North Shore of Long Island, and Stewart had assumed those words meant him. In fact, she was probably thinking of herself and Benchley, and of the whole Round Table, who at one time or another had kowtowed to the Lovetts and the Whitneys. It pained Stewart to read her adulatory remarks about his former friend, with whom he had quarreled for her sake, and he told her that the piece had "hurt like hell." Dorothy swore she had not been thinking of him, and after many cognacs, the misunderstanding was finally smoothed over. Despite Hemingway's cordiality whenever they happened to meet, his private feelings remained hostile because the following year he composed another poem about her:

> Little drops of grain alcohol
> Little slugs of gin
> Make the mighty notions
> Make the double chin—
> Lovely Mrs. Parker in the Algonquin
> Loves her good dog Robinson
> Keeps away from sin
> Mr. Hemingway now wears glasses
> Better to see to kiss the critics' asses—

It seemed to be the season for quarreling. One morning at breakfast she got embroiled in a ridiculous but upsetting dispute with Gerald, who had reprimanded Baoth with a severity so stinging that Dorothy found it intolerable to witness. When she asked him not to be so hard on the boy, Gerald advised her to mind her own business. It *was* her business, she replied, because she thought he was being mean to his son, and she had a right to express her opinion. Finally she threatened to leave, and Gerald agreed it might be for the best.

While that quarrel was predictably mended, she found the conflicts unsettling. In fact, the atmosphere seethed with tension and festering angers. Patrick's ordeal had left its mark on the health of both his parents—Gerald suffered from depression and Sara, in poor physical health since her son had fallen ill, developed a gall-bladder disorder. In October, Sara traveled to Cannes for treatment and Dorothy came along as a companion for Honoria, but almost as soon as they reached the Hotel Majestic, she changed her mind about remaining with the Murphys. AM NEARLY GONE WITH LONELINESS AND DISCOURAGEMENT, she cabled Oppenheimer. It was melodramatic but true. From Cannes she cabled Benchley that it would be ALL RIGHT WITH ME IF NEVER SEE ANYONE UNDER SIXTY AGAIN and asked him to send her a kind word.

After booking passage on the *Saturnia,* she wired Viking for a thousand dollars. A few days later, apologizing for being a pest, she requested another thousand because she was having difficulty paying her bills and promised Harold and George repayment from the money *Cosmopolitan* owed her for "Here We Are." She remembered to cable birthday greetings to her sister, and finally, to Benchley, she reported that the *Saturnia* would be sailing from Cannes on November 15 and

ARRIVING NEW YORK SO FAR AS I CAN MAKE OUT SOME TIME IN
EARLY APRIL . . . AND WILL I BE GLAD TO SEE YOU DEAREST FRED.

Getting away from it all had been fine, she wrote, but "when the day comes that you have to tie a string around your finger to remind yourself of what it was you were forgetting, it is time for you to go back home." Unfortunately, her bank account was so overdrawn that it looked "positively photographic," and as a consequence she had to find walking-around money in a hurry. She wanted to retire to a vine-covered cottage in the country where she could "spend the rest of my life raising cheques," but that idea lacked practicality, and soon she was working for *The New Yorker* again. In January, her Constant Reader column appeared for the first time in two years, opening with "Maybe you think I was just out in the ladies' room all this time," and in mid-February, when Benchley went to Hollywood for two months, she agreed to take his place as the magazine's theater critic. She found the job of play reviewing just as unpleasant as ever. Her first review concluded with a plea, "Personal: Robert Benchley, please come home," an appeal that might just as easily have been voiced by Gertrude Benchley.

Benchley led a classic double life. His domestic and extramarital arrangements confined Gertrude to Scarsdale, where she seemed content to raise the boys and paste Robert's newspaper clippings into scrapbooks. After breaking with the chorus girl, Benchley had a lengthy affair with actress Betty Starbuck. After that his love life grew too complex to document easily. In addition to the prostitutes he patronized at Polly Adler's, he made routine overtures to countless women and very often met with success. At any given time, there were four or five women openly claiming to be madly in love with him. Ending these infatuations proved difficult sometimes. The wife of a well-known banker was so eager to continue sleeping with him that she once crawled through the transom of his room at the Royalton Hotel. In 1931, he began a long-term relationship with Louise "Louie" Macy, a Smith College graduate who worked as a saleswoman at Hattie Carnegie's fashionable shop. Their first dates were threesomes that included Dorothy, which caused Louie to conclude that Mrs. Parker was one of his lovers. The adoring Louie would do practically anything for him, including the selection of Gertrude's Christmas gifts at Hattie Carnegie. Benchley treated her—all his women for that matter—with a protective courtliness that verged on the Victorian. Escorting her home at the end of an evening, he shook her hand and said, "Thank you very much. I had a wonderful time." This performance misled Louie's sister Gert so completely that it was years before she realized that Louie's relationship with Benchley had been sexual.

Soon after Dorothy's return to New York, she met a reporter who worked for the *New York Sun*, a husky, sandy-haired man with a cheerful manner that put people at ease. His name was John McClain, and he was twenty-seven years old. A native of Marion, Ohio, he had played football at Brown where he had been one of the so-called Iron Men, players who never needed a substitute. He returned to Ohio for graduate work at Kenyon College. In spite of his education, McClain remained on the bottom rung of the ladder in New York journalism. He frequently was assigned to cover shipping news and strove for promotion to the *Sun*'s regular ship reporter. For the time being, he scraped along on little money, rode the subway to work, and lived on Morton Street in the Village, where the flat he shared with two other young men seldom knew heat or hot water.

In more ways than one, McClain was a hungry man, determined not to live in a cold-water flat any longer than necessary. Among his assets were blond good looks and a well-built, athletic body, in which he took great pride. He kept fit with regular workouts at a gym. A friend later described him as pink and white, "the male equivalent of a Rubens nude," while another observer graphically portrayed him as "a bohunk." So often had women told him he was good in bed that he had come to believe it. He realized that one way to infiltrate New York's smart circles might be on the arms of well-known women. Not bothering to bandy words among his friends, McClain bluntly announced his premeditated campaign of fornicating his way to a more satisfying life. His first success was torch singer Libby Holman. Before long, he was frequenting saloons like Tony's and Moriarty's, where his winning demeanor and convivial drinking skills made him popular with the literary crowd.

McClain knew Dorothy by reputation only, because his arrival in the city had coincided with her absence from it. One night they were introduced at Tony's, and McClain set out being seductive and ingratiating. While he may have been genuinely attracted to her, it was probably also true that had she not been a celebrity he wouldn't have glanced twice at a woman ten years his senior. At that particular time she was looking far from her best anyway. Her face remained lovely—at times she still resembled an adolescent—but her body was bloated from alcohol and her chin was doubling. This failed to deter McClain, who escorted her back to the Algonquin and settled down for the night.

Afterward, he bragged to friends about his success. He boasted that Dorothy had assured him he was a good lover and added that she knew some tricks herself, which he enumerated as if she were a neighborhood tart.

Meanwhile, Dorothy assumed that John McClain's desire was genuine and rejoiced at her good fortune. At first they had enjoyable times together because he was star-struck, awed by the glamour of her life, and eager for introductions to people in the literary community.

One of her regular drinking companions was John O'Hara, whom she had known since 1928 as a reporter and rewrite man on the *New York Herald Tribune.* Dorothy believed his short stories showed unusual promise and steadfastly championed him to editors as a coming major writer, at a time when others doubted he was exceptional. Although O'Hara was not physically attractive to her—he had bad teeth and acne—she enjoyed his company late at night when he joined her at Tony's. She assured him he would never be happy because he was a genius, and she further bet him that if Ernest Hemingway read some of his stories he would want to cut his own throat. "I am sorry to be compelled to add," O'Hara wrote to his brother, "that Mrs. Parker was tight, but I understand she has told other people the same thing about me," and he was right. O'Hara admired John McClain whose dashing self-assurance and success with women represented the type of male O'Hara wished he could be.

William Faulkner, another friend of Dorothy's, impressed her as a vulnerable country boy in desperate need of her protection. She introduced him to the Round Table and her *New Yorker* friends, and she further made sure he received a welcome in the drawing rooms of rich people like Adele and Robert Lovett. In the fall of 1931, when Faulkner was staying at the Algonquin, she gave a cocktail party in his honor. He turned up late with an old friend of his, Eric Devine, by which time most of the guests were gassed. So was the hostess, who proudly passed around manuscript pages from *Light in August*, the novel he was working on at the time. Eric Devine recalled that John McClain was so firmly glued to Dorothy's side as to leave no doubt about the intimacy of their relations.

With or without McClain, Dorothy and Robinson went out every night. Some people felt sorry for poor Robinson who would try to sleep under a table in the smoke and noise of Tony's at two or three in the morning. Given her love for animals, Frank Sullivan thought, "she could have been a little more considerate." He might have been more disapproving had he known that when Dorothy took her nightly sleeping pills she sometimes fed one to Robinson so that he wouldn't wake up too early the next day.

Occasionally there was an evening memorable for its serenity. Once she and John were drinking double Scotches at Tony's with a group that included Benchley, Vernon Duke, and Monty Woolley, when the conversation turned sentimentally to Paris and the city's special beauty in springtime. "Oh," somebody sighed, "to be in Paris now that April's there!" What a great title for a song, Duke recalled remarking, whereupon the obliging Tony Soma escorted them upstairs to a delapidated piano, and Duke composed the music for "April in Paris," while everyone hummed along quietly.

With a new man in her life, Dorothy felt compelled to slim down and smarten up her appearance. As she had done with John Garrett, she telephoned McClain every day to arrange their meeting later in the evening. She expected to be the only woman in his life, but this John behaved remarkably like the old one and soon began to vocalize his martyrdom. He felt smothered, resented her demands, and began to invent engagements. Increasingly, he told Dorothy that he was fatigued after work, then he had to work out at the gym, and after that he was exhausted and simply wanted to crawl back to his flat and tumble into bed. To his friends McClain grumbled that Dorothy refused to leave him alone and it took all of his ingenuity to escape her.

At the outset, some of Dorothy's friends sized up McClain as a social climber and a sponge who had no qualms about taking advantage of her. Bea Stewart despised him, and others tried to caution Dorothy, but she disregarded their warnings. She was even able to find humor in John's social aspirations and his gargantuan appetite for women who owned penthouses and luxurious country estates. He was only twenty-seven and she made up her mind to be tolerant of his imperfections.

At one of her cocktail parties, to which McClain had been invited, she waited expectantly for him to suggest dinner together. He said nothing and finally asked if he might use her telephone. Everyone in the room could hear him confirming a dinner engagement elsewhere, and off he went. Dorothy broke the tension with a quip and a shrug.

"I have no squash courts," she said. "What can I do?"

What she did was to write about her lover, although he proved less inspiring than his predecessors. *Death and Taxes*, a collection of verse published that year by Viking, was mostly written before she met McClain, but a few of the poems apply to him: "Every love's the love before / In a duller dress." She entertained her friends with postmortems on the latest outrage he had perpetrated. After a quarrel, when he called her a lousy lay and slammed out, she said that his body had gone to his head. She described him as a male prostitute, who mistook her for a stepladder so that he could climb into the beds of famous women. When she once learned that a wealthy Long Island socialite had invited him to her home for the weekend, Dorothy predicted that he would be back "as soon as he has licked all the gilt off her ass."

Depressed, Dorothy described 1932 as "this year of hell" and again attempted to kill herself, this time with barbiturates, after preparing a last will and testament and setting it aside for Benchley's attention. "Any royalties on my books are to go to John McClain. My clothes and my wrist-watch to my sister, Helen Droste, also my little dog Robinson— Dorothy Parker." But her resolve to die was not particularly solid. On a Thursday evening at the end of February, she made her departure with sleeping powders, but it was apparently the will of God that she be shipped back like an undelivered letter, to the Hotel Algonquin, 59 West Forty-fourth Street, New York City, return receipt attached. On Friday afternoon, feeling like a cadaver but nonetheless very much alive, she managed to call Dr. Barach and explain what had happened.

With stoic patience, Barach began to question her about how many powders she had actually taken. Not enough, it turned out. Evidently he did not suppose her to be in serious danger, because he only reserved a room at Presbyterian and arranged for an ambulance.

The newspapers had a field day with the story of Dorothy's overdose, even though Dr. Barach tried to minimize the incident by saying it was of so little consequence that he had no plans to visit her in the hospital. His inference that knocking herself out might have been an accident was understandably dismissed, because by this time she had an Olympic-sized track record as an attempted suicide.

Since she dreaded returning to the Algonquin, she welcomed an offer to convalesce at the country estate of one of her women friends. Every care was lavished upon her. She was coddled twenty-four hours a day and surrounded by so much solicitude, so much harping about her health, that before long she felt suffocated. A few days later she sent friends a martyred telegram: SEND ME A SAW INSIDE A LOAF OF BREAD, and propelled herself back to Manhattan where she resumed her nightly rounds and her drinking.

The relationship with John had become impossible. After her suicide attempt, he announced to many that he considered it a typical female scheme, staged in the hope that she could tie him to her. He professed to have lost respect for her.

Not long afterward, they broke off for good. Subsequently McClain made a reputation for himself on the *New York Sun* with a bylined ship-news column, "The Sun Deck." In the late 1930s, he went to Hollywood, where he worked as a screenwriter and shared a house with Benchley, who had become a close friend. During the war he served with valor in the Navy, then distinguished himself as drama critic of the New York *Journal-American*. In 1951 he married for the first time, and when his wife died, he remarried; both marriages were happy. During his last years he suffered from cancer of the mouth and died (just a few weeks before Dorothy) of a liver ailment at the age of sixty-three.

It was a rough year. The world beyond Tony's and the Algonquin darkened: In March, there were eighty-six bread lines in New York, one third of the

welve-year-old Dorothy Rothschild at the Soldiers and Sailors Monument in Riverside Park, January
(HELEN IVESON, ROBERT IVESON, MARGARET DROSTE, SUSAN COTTON)

Sunday outing in Riverside Park, 1906. Dorothy poses with brother Bert, her dog Rags, sister Helen,
ster-in-law Mate. Absent is oldest brother Harry, who would subsequently cut himself off entirely from
mily. (HELEN IVESON, ROBERT IVESON, MARGARET DROSTE, SUSAN COTTON)

3) A widowed J. Henry Rothschild in 1899, six months after the death of his wife Eliza. Radiating prosperity and his customary confidence, he was known in the garment industry as "the greatest salesman of them all" *(Crerand's Cloak Journal).* (HELEN IVESON, ROBERT IVESON, MARGARET DROSTE, SUSAN COTTON)

4) A boyish Edwin Pond Parker II, nicknamed "Spook" by friends in the 33rd Ambulance Company, because hangovers made him look pale as a ghost, in 1917. Already dependent on alcohol, Eddie (second from left, top row) became further scarred by his war experiences in France and turned to another means of escape when liquor was not available. "Unfortunately," Dorothy said, "they had dope in the ambulance" *(Esquire).* (SOURCE: UNKNOWN).

"Harry" Rothschild, the greatest salesman of them all, whose personal magnetism, good fellowship and loyalty to his friends have kept him busy welcoming newcomers to Blumenthal Bros & Co.'s, at Third and Mercer streets.

Dorothy and her husband, photographed by Robert Sherwood in October 1919, after Eddie's return the war. His features have coarsened, he is struggling with morphine addiction, and to Dorothy, who had been married "for about five minutes," he had become practically a total stranger. (COURTESY OF STON UNIVERSITY LIBRARIES)

6) Dorothy and Robert Benchley pose demurely with their employers in 1919: *Vanity Fair* editor Frank Crowninshield, *Vogue* editor Edna Chase, and publisher Condé Nast. Dorothy and Robert Sherwood, behind the camera, would soon be dismissed, and Benchley would resign in sympathy. "It was the greatest act of friendship I'd known" *(Paris Review)*. (COURTESY OF THE BOSTON UNIVERSITY LIBRARIES)

7) Two revealing portraits of Dorothy in the early twenties: In 1921 (above) she still looks like a vulnerable, naïve adolescent, but in Neysa McMein's 1923 oil painting (left) her face has aged and her expression has grown tense. In the interval between the two portraits, she separated from Eddie, had an affair with Charles MacArthur complicated by pregnancy and abortion, and attempted suicide by slashing her wrists. Alcohol was becoming a problem. (ABOVE, COURTESY OF SAM SCHAEFLER; LEFT, COURTESY OF CULVER PICTURES).

8

8) Charles MacArthur and Dorothy with Arthur Samuels, a wigless Harpo Marx, and an unusually thin Alexander Woollcott, 1924, probably partying at one of the Long Island mansions where they liked to spend weekends. (SUSAN MARX).

9) Dorothy sunbathing in Miami Beach, January 1924. The rest of the group includes Ray Goetz, William Emmerich, Neysa McMein, and Irving Berlin. (NEW YORK NEWS, INC.)

10) Painting of the Round Tablers and friends playing poker was commissioned by Paul Hyde Bonner. Seated counterclockwise around the table are Dorothy, Franklin P. Adams, Henry Wise Miller, Gerald Brooks, Raoul Fleischmann, George Kaufman, Paul Hyde Bonner, Harpo Marx, Alexander Woollcott, and Heywood Broun. Standing are Robert Benchley, Irving Berlin, Harold Ross, Beatrice Kaufman, Alice Duer Miller, Herbert Bayard Swope, George Backer, Joyce Barbour, and Crosby Gaige. (THE HAMPDEN-BOOTH THEATRE LIBRARY AT THE PLAYERS)

9

13) Dorothy and ▮ Benchley (at righ▮ guests of the Murphy ▮ at Cap d'Antibes i▮ 1929. Standing ▮ cabana with tow▮ Honoria and ▮ Murphy. Dorothy sw▮ kilometers a d▮ worked diligently on a▮ "Dear God," she ▮ "please make ▮ writing like a wom▮ Jesus Christ's sake, ▮ (PROPERTY OF MR. ▮ WILLIAM M. DO▮

11) Singing "The Internationale" on Beacon Street, Boston, during a demonstration to protest the execution of Nicola Sacco and Bartolomeo Vanzetti, August 10, 1927. Marching ahead of Dorothy in her embroidered dress and white gloves is John Dos Passos. Minutes after the picture was taken, she was arrested. Next morning she pleaded guilty to a charge of loitering and sauntering and paid a five-dollar fine.

12) Dorothy dressed for an evening on the town around the time she fell in love with John Garrett and divorced Eddie Parker. Snapshot was taken by Heywood Broun's assistant, Mildred Gilman, during a typical evening of partying and making rounds of the speakeasies. (MILDRED GILMAN WOHLFORTH)

Dorothy in Montana-Vermala, Switzerland, late
where she had accompanied the Murphy family
eir son Patrick developed tuberculosis. Although
the atmosphere of death in the sanatorium town
sed Dorothy, her sympathy for Sara and Gerald's
ny kept her with them off and on for more than a
 cheer herself up she bought a Dandie Dinmont
terrier and derived pleasure from characterizing
Switzerland as "the home of horseshit."

(PROPERTY OF MR. AND MRS. WILLIAM M. DONNELLY)

14

15) *New York Sun* reporter John McClain, described by a friend as resembling a male Rubens, with Dorothy during their affair in 1931.
(BRENDAN GILL)

16

WE ARE PUSHED FOR MONEY.

16) Dorothy and her dachshund, Robinson. Duri early thirties she was one of the two most socially sc after women in New York (the other was Fanny Bric her nightly rounds of parties and speakeasies, Dorc was usually accompanied by Robinson, who slept elegantly curled up beneath her chair. (HELEN IVESON ROBERT IVESON, MARGARET DROSTE, SUSAN COTTON)

17) Thirteen-year-old Alan Campbell on the boar in Atlantic City with his mother, Horte Campbell, ar aunt Beulah Eichel. Across the face of the photogra Alan printed *We are pushed for money.*
(AUTHOR COLLECTION)

lan Campbell and a radiant, girlish Dorothy shortly after their marriage in 1934. The newlyweds
ently arrived in Hollywood to become a screen-writing team at Paramount Pictures.
SY OF PARAMOUNT PICTURES CORPORATION)

19

19 Dorothy and Alan arriving in New York on the *Champlain*, October 1937, after returning from the Spanish Civil War. Horrified by her observations in Valencia and Madrid, Dorothy promptly volunteered her services to aid Spanish children. (WIDE WORLD PHOTOS)

20) Dorothy and Lillian Hellman with Fernando De Los Rios, Spanish Republic ambassador to the United States, at a lunch benefit homeless children in December 193 a passionate supporter of the Loyalists, Dor helped to raise an estimated $1.5 million fo refugees from Franco. (CULVER PICTURES)

20

At Marc Connelly's Hollywood house in the late thirties, Dorothy is shown chatting with William
...ner (standing), Faulkner's woman friend, Meta Carpenter Wilde, and his agent, Ben Wasson.
...ner, unlike Dorothy, did not allow his screen-writing work to interfere with his fiction.
ESY OF THE DRAMATISTS GUILD FUND)

Dorothy and Alan enjoying cocktails at the Café Deux Magots in July 1939. That summer Paris was
...sted with American tourists eager to party and spend money, even though their sleep was broken by
...one of German planes circling overhead. World War II began on September 1. (COURTESY OF JOHN DAVIES)

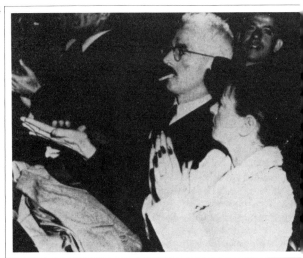

23)   Dorothy next to Dashiell Hammett, applauding a speaker at a meeting in Hollywood, late 1930s. Hammett's aversion toward her increased until he refused to stay under the same roof.
(COURTESY OF THE ESTATE OF LILLIAN HELLMAN)

24)   Dorothy seated between her sister Helen (right) and unidentified woman in Hollywood, 1943. Dorothy proudly conducted Helen on a tour of the movie capital and introduced her to stars such as Marlene Dietrich. "Everyone makes a swell fuss over Dot," Helen wrote to her son.
(HELEN IVESON, ROBERT IVESON, MARGARET DROSTE, SUSAN COTTON)

25) Dorothy and Alan's second wedding, August 17, 1950, in Hollywood. Dorothy explained the remarriage by telling wedding guests, "What are you going to do when you love ʌe son of a bitch?" The marriage, however, failed to last even a year. (WIDE WORLD PHOTOS)

26) Dorothy and Alan with Donald Ogden Stewart at Los Angeles Airport in the late 1930s, before embarking on one of their frequent cross-country air trips between Hollywood and their farm in Bucks County, Pennsylvania. Dorothy is carrying her ever-present knitting bag. (DONALD OGDEN STEWART, JR.)

27) Alan and Dorothy reunited after a[n] eleven-year separation, outside Alan's bungalow in Norma Place, Hollywood, 1[ ] He is behind the wheel of his new green Jaguar, confidently purchased in the hop[e] a script slated for Marilyn Monroe would [lead] to a rebirth of their career as a screen-wr[iting] team. (PAUL MILLARD)

28) A grinning Dorothy, holding her p[oodle] Cliché, after deciding to remain with Al[an,] Hollywood, June 1962. On the table are [the] heaped review copies that she received f[or her] monthly book column in *Esquire*, a task [that] became increasingly difficult to carry ou[t.] Unemployment insurance—and the sale [of] review copies—helped support them du[ring] lean times. (© 1962 <u>LOS ANGELES TIMES</u>)

27

28

work force was unemployed, and the average family income plunged to sixteen hundred dollars a year. Every week the papers carried stories about people who had lost hope and jumped to their deaths from rooftops or spent their last nickel on razor blades to kill themselves. Everyone seemed to be scared or desperate or suffering in some way, although it was hard to guess the country's financial deterioration by the way some of Dorothy's affluent friends continued to frolic. They still rose at the crack of noon to gossip with the manicurists who arrived to do their nails. Dorothy later ridiculed them in a short story, "From the Diary of a New York Lady," which she pointedly subtitled, "During Days of Horror, Despair, and World Change."

> Can't *face* deciding whether to wear the blue with the white jacket or the purple with the beige roses. Every time I look at those *revolting* black nails, I want to absolutely *yip*. I really have *the* most horrible things happen to me of anybody in the *entire* world. *Damn* Miss Rose.

That winter, to escape the painful memories she now associated with her Algonquin suite, she moved to the Lowell, at 28 East Sixty-third Street, a fairly new residential hotel that had been decorated in the fashionable Art Deco style. Her comfortably furnished flat even had a big easy chair in which she liked to curl up and read, but living there was far beyond her means. It had been nine months since she had done any work for *The New Yorker*; only once in the past year had she managed to complete a short story, and she was flat broke. She owed money to practically everybody she knew and was obliged to accept alms from many she did not. The Lowell seemed glad to have her as a tenant, perhaps because the publicity offset the drawback of seldom receiving her rent.

In the months that followed the barbiturate incident, convinced that the two most beautiful words in the English language were "cheque" and "enclosed," she began to give diligent attention to her shaky financial position. Though difficult to acknowledge, she knew writing poetry did not provide enough revenue to sustain the high life to which she had grown accustomed, and she decided to abandon it, at least for the time being. Harold Guinzburg was eager to publish a second volume of short stories, but she had to write them first, a task that had grown no easier for having been absent from her typewriter for so long. To break through a writer's block that was proving as deep as the Grand Canyon, she formulated a desperate solution. She asked some of her friends to become duennas; more specifically, they were to park at the Lowell for three or four hours and look busy, with what "I don't really know, to make me speed up and feel ashamed of myself when I incline to be lazy." As always, she rewrote so extensively that progress was slow, but she also began to produce some fine work: "Horsie," "Lady with a Lamp," "Dusk Before Fireworks," "Advice to the Little Peyton Girl," and "Diary of a New York Lady."

When she was asked to compose an introduction to a collection of Jim Thurber's cartoons, *The Seal in the Bedroom and Other Predicaments,* she was delighted to comply. Not only had she taken a fancy to Thurber as a drinking companion, but also she admired his drawings, which she liked to present as Christmas gifts to her friends. In her eyes, his strange men, women, and dogs resembled "unbaked cookies"; she understood them perfectly because they seemed to expect so little from life. Like herself, they were people who "remember the old discouragements and await the new." Whenever she looked at one of Thurber's hounds, she went soft with sentiment. Nobody, she decided, could have dreamed up dogs like those unless he felt as she did about animals. The awesome fact was that Thurber actually owned fourteen dogs.

In mid-July, the Murphys closed Villa America and moved their family to the States, although they continued to spend holidays abroad. After the death of Gerald's father, the Mark Cross Company had lacked leadership, and he decided to re-enter the family business. After a brief stay in East Hampton, Long Island, and a reunion with Pauline and Ernest Hemingway in Montana, they finally settled down in a Bedford Village, New York, house and a Manhattan apartment. Dorothy continued to ridicule Adele Lovett and other well-off friends, whom she satirized cruelly in "Horsie" and "Diary of a New York Lady," but she never joked about the Murphys, because she loved them.

In the meantime, she found herself the object of surprising and unwanted attention. George Oppenheimer, dissatisfied with the publishing business and ambitious to become a writer, had been working on a play whose central character's personality was modeled on herself. Other characters were supposed to be Robert Benchley and Donald Stewart. At the outset, he had been collaborating with Ruth Goodman, daughter of producer Philip Goodman, but she withdrew from the project leaving him to muddle along on his own. While Dorothy continued to tolerate Oppenheimer, she had few illusions about his skill as a dramatist, did not take kindly to the idea of seeing herself on stage, and strongly suspected that the play would mean more "fresh hell," all of which proved to be precisely the case. *Here Today*, bearing the subtitle "A Comedy of Bad Manners," opened in September with Ruth Gordon playing Dorothy and George Kaufman directing. Dorothy attended opening night with Bennett Cerf. Throughout the performance he noticed her wriggling in the seat, enraged at the stage caricature of herself and muttering threats against Oppenheimer's life. Afterward, she and Cerf went backstage, where she threw her arms around the playwright and assured him she had enjoyed the play.

"Oh, you caught me so perfectly!" she declared. "It was absolutely wonderful! How did you do it?"

Here Today mercifully ran only five weeks, although it would remain a favorite with summer stock companies for the next twenty-five years.

Here Today was the least of her concerns. Robinson had been attacked by a large dog and injured so seriously that it had been necessary to hospitalize him. She tried to hide her anxiety with jokes. The owner of the other dog refused to take responsibility and even had the temerity to claim that Robinson provoked the attack. Dorothy was indignant. "I have no doubt that he was also carrying a revolver," she said vehemently to Aleck Woollcott. As comfort until the dachshund recovered, friends gave her a huge stuffed English sheepdog.

Robinson failed to pull through, however. Dorothy, who had been exceptionally attached to him, grieved inconsolably. Earlier that year, when *Vanity Fair* asked her to sit for a full-length portrait by Edward Steichen, she insisted that Robinson must be included in the shot. Steichen photographed her seated in an ornate high-back chair with her hands demurely tucked into a muff. On the floor behind the chair, Robinson was gazing off loftily into the distance, as if the whole business was beneath his dignity. The result was a lovely photograph, one of the very few to show her smiling broadly.

In the hope of alleviating her bereavement after Robinson's death, Sara Murphy proposed a trip to Paris. Dorothy, feeling she deserved a vacation, asked Viking Press for a thousand-dollar advance on her next book. At the end of October, the two women sailed on the luxurious *Europa*, the interior decor of which combined Buckingham Palace, the Munich Hofbrauhaus, and Radio City Music Hall. They would be away for a month.

Although traveling first class, Dorothy soon began spending time in third. Aboard ship was the mother of Tom Mooney, the West Coast labor leader who had been convicted of a bombing and was serving a twenty-three-year sentence in San Quentin. Dorothy sought her out and learned that she was traveling to Russia with a delegation of American Communists. Mary Mooney, Dorothy decided, had the presence of a queen, or at least the manners that queens ought to have. She was a big, chunky Irish woman, eighty-four years old, wearing a string of shiny green beads and an emerald green scarf over an old wool sweater.

A few days later, when the Communists announced a meeting in the third-class dining hall, Dorothy took the opportunity to attend. She carefully examined the stocky women with short hair and the serious black men wearing gold-rimmed glasses. They seemed terribly young and earnest, but their speeches about Tom Mooney and others struck her as "much too long and much too muddy and with many—too many—sweeping allusions to the woiking class and the bawss class." It was their style she found objectionable, not the content of the speeches, with which in fact she was in total agreement. This marked her second exposure to the American Communist Party. The first, during the Sacco-Vanzetti demonstrations five years earlier, had been completely accidental. Aboard the *Europa*, however, she deliberately went in search of the Party. Even though she found fault with Party rhetoric, her reaction to the meeting was significant. She immediately composed a letter to the *New York Sun* praising Mary Mooney as "the best person on this ship, and I wish that were higher praise." The letter, published in the *Sun* and picked up by other papers throughout the country, left no doubt where Dorothy stood on the subject of Tom Mooney. She believed him innocent.

In the company of old friends, Dorothy felt happier than she had in months. The first night in Paris, she and Sara had a long dinner with the Murphys' close friend Dick Myers. For the next three weeks, they did nothing but ramble around the city, attending cocktail parties and teas and dining at Lipp's and all her favorite restaurants.

When she arrived home on December 1 a few pounds heavier, she had to admit that she had done absolutely nothing abroad but relax and amuse herself. In merry spirits, she telephoned Frank Adams at his office. "How now, Mr. Pepys, would you like a poem for keeps?" she asked and then proceeded to dictate a poem to him over the phone.

That fall, Dorothy spent at least four hours a day at her typewriter. Once dusk began to settle, however, she chafed at this hermetic life and began telephoning friends, asking where they were going to be later in the evening. Certain stops were mandatory: Tony's, "21," Benchley's suite at the Hotel Royalton. She was welcome at the Village home of Howard and Betty Dietz or at Polly Adler's or in the clubs in Harlem—everywhere—regardless of her condition. "She and Fanny Brice, they were the queens of the town," recalled Ruth Goodman Goetz. "They divided New York between them." One evening Dorothy dropped in at a cocktail party hosted by producer Courtney Burr, who was starting rehearsals for a Bea Lillie revue, as yet untitled. He hoped one of the forty or fifty guests he had invited might come up with something clever.

Dorothy walked in late and tight. She was dressed to kill in a black Lanvin gown, feathered cloche, and opera-length gloves and smelled like the ground-floor perfume department at Bergdorf's. When Burr introduced her to one of the show's authors, she shifted to automatic pilot and began to ladle compliments upon the writer comparing him to Congreve, Oscar Wilde, and Noël Coward. A native of Providence, Rhode Island, Sidney J. Perelman had worked for the Marx Brothers on *Monkey Business* and *Horse Feathers* but was still struggling to establish a firm toehold in the theater. Twenty-eight, of medium height with blue eyes and wire-rimmed glasses, he was married to Laura West, the sister of another aspiring writer, Nathanael West, who currently was employed as the manager of the Hotel Sutton. Sid Perelman later wrote that "Dorothy Parker was already a legend when I first met her in the autumn of 1932."

When Courtney Burr asked the assembled guests to think of a good name for his revue, all eyes naturally swiveled to Dorothy, who suggested *Sing High, Sing Low*. But no, wait a minute, she added, that wasn't sparkling enough. How about *Pousse-Café*? There were approving nods and murmurs of "oh, I love it" and "just darling," but when Dorothy glanced around she noticed Perelman looking glum.

"What do *you* think of *Pousse-Café*, Mr. Perelman?" she asked.

Perelman, with enthusiasm that was clearly feigned, pronounced her title "great" but wondered if it really carried enough punch. When Dorothy countered with *Aces Up*, he called her suggestion "marvellous" but continued to look doubtful.

"I just wonder, though," he said, "if we can't find something a *tiny* bit sharper, less static . . ."

"Well, goodness me," she said, spraying him with a smile. "What ever shall we do? Our wrist has been slapped by the house genius there, who feels that we're a bit dull-witted. Of course, *he's* in a position to know, isn't he, leaning down from Parnassus—"

By this time, some of the guests had begun drifting uneasily toward the door, and a nervous Burr was trying to switch Dorothy off, decharge the atmosphere, and get his party moving again, to no avail. She was just warming up. Perelman made his escape, vowing that if he ever again ran into Dorothy Parker, legend or no legend, "I'd skewer her with one of her own hatpins."

The next day, sober and remorseful, Dorothy was stricken to recall dimly that she had been rude to Perelman. She lost no time in sending him a dozen of the most expensive roses she could buy with a note of abject apology. Courtney Burr's untitled show was eventually christened, by someone other than Dorothy, *Walk a Little Faster*, and it ran 119 performances. The friendship between Dorothy and Sid Perelman survived for thirty-five years.

Chapter 12

YOU MIGHT AS WELL LIVE

•

1933–1935

It looked as if her sex life had died. Since she and John McClain had parted, she had "put sex carefully away on the highest cupboard-shelf, in a box marked 'Winter Hats—1916.'" Not that there weren't plenty of ravishing men around, most of them willowy young actors who were thrilled to escort her wherever she wished to go and to see that she got back to the Lowell and tucked safely into bed if she passed out. If they had no interest in sleeping with women it made no difference because, as she often said, she needed good fairies to protect her. One night, she was invited to a costume ball where all the divine young men were dressed up to look like divine young women. Lubricated by several highballs, Dorothy observed the dancers from a balcony, but every so often she leaned over the railing and looked down at the dance floor, muttering in despair. Water, water everywhere and not a single drop to drink. When she could contain herself no longer, she shouted, "Come on up, anybody. I'm a man!"

That August she turned forty. On the night of her birthday she walked into Tony's with her head defiantly armored in a football helmet, a gift from Adele Lovett's husband. In the distance loomed all the birthdays to come, the unfolding of solitary years, until she felt like a prisoner trapped in a cage of her own construction.

> Long I fought the driving lists,
> Plume a-stream and armor clanging;

Link on link, between my wrists,
Now my heavy freedom's hanging.

During the spring, she met Alan Campbell at Tony's one night. Bench-ley introduced them, although Alan was not a friend of his. Alan Campbell was a personable young actor, who had published a few stories in *The New Yorker* and whom Benchley knew only well enough to say hello and how are you. A few months later, Dorothy ran into him again at Howard Dietz's house, and she was surprised to learn they had other mutual friends. She was immediately impressed by Alan's golden good looks, the fine bone structure, the fair hair and dazzling smile that made it seem as if he had just stepped indoors on a June day. He resembled Scott Fitzgerald when Scott had been young and healthy, before he began drinking heavily, and some people thought him far better looking. Alan, like Scott, had a face that was a touch too pretty for a man, the kind of features that caused people to remark he would have made a splendid woman. He was typecast by producers as a classic juvenile. His looks projected the image of a stunning man clad in a blazer, carrying a racquet, bursting through the doors of a stage drawing room, asking, "Tennis, anyone?" That cliché could have been written for Alan. His only physical flaw was a habit of chewing his nails.

He was twenty-nine, eleven years Dorothy's junior. While he never actually lied about his background, some people got the idea that his father had been a wealthy Virginia tobacco man, and he could not bring himself to correct the mistake. His real background was similar to Dorothy's, a mixture of Jewish and Gentile. In Alan's case, his father was of Scottish descent. His mother's family, the Eichels, were Jewish emigrés from the Alsace region of France who fought in the Civil War and afterward settled in Richmond, Virginia, where Alan's grandfather was known to be the finest butcher in the city.

When Alan's mother, Hortense, was eighteen, she eloped with Harry Lee Campbell, a six-foot-tall Baptist who worked for a company that sold leaf tobacco. He was reputedly a drinking man. For much of their fifteen-year marriage, they alternated living with their families. When Alan was born in 1904, they were staying at the spacious Eichel house on East Clay Street. It was an unhappy marriage. Clara Lester, who cooked for the Eichel family, remembered Horte's restlessness. "She'd pick up and go off, and nobody knew where. Anybody goin' anywhere would say to Horte, 'You goin' my way?' and off she'd go. Her husband was jealous and he drank." After the Campbells divorced, Horte and Alan continued to live with Horte's family.

Alan's mother, who worked as a clerk at the Internal Revenue Service, never remarried. Content to raise her beautiful son, Horte made him the center of her existence and devoted herself to obtaining the very best for him: dancing classes, scholarships to a prep school, summer camps patronized by Richmond's elite families, and an education at Virginia Military Institute, where he became one of the most popular boys in his class. Although Alan majored in civil engineering, he also revealed a definite talent for the artistic. His writings and drawings appeared regularly in campus publications and he played the leading feminine parts in dramatic club productions. J. Clifford Miller, Jr., who was three years behind Alan at VMI, recalled that in one play he "was dressed in an evening gown and was so well made-up that in spite of his very obvious arm and leg muscles, he got a lot of whistles from the cadets when he appeared as a very pretty young lady." For two years after graduation, he lived at home and worked for the state highway department. Roy Eichel remembered his nephew's unhappiness:

> All at once, one night, without saying a word to anybody, he disappeared. Later we figured out that when nobody was looking he had packed a suitcase, which he lowered out of his bedroom window on a rope during the night. Then he walked down the stairs to the backyard, picked up the suitcase, and went off to the station where he caught a train for New York. Of course Miz Campbell carried on like a lunatic.

A few weeks later, finally learning of his whereabouts, Horte dispatched Roy to New York on a special mission to bring her son home. Alan, determined to become an actor, refused.

His first theater job was in the Schubert costume department, but he soon got small parts with Eva Le Gallienne's repertory company. In 1928, he played Laurette Taylor's son in *The Furies*. By the time he met Dorothy he had appeared in a dozen Broadway shows, including the hit musical *Show Boat* and Noël Coward's *Design for Living* with the Lunts. Alan also began to write and sell fiction, mostly about the theater, which was the subject of many of his *New Yorker* stories.

From the start, Dorothy and Alan were extremely taken with each other. He said years later that she was "the only woman I ever knew whose mind was completely attuned to mine." They were very much alike, not only in their Jewish-Gentile backgrounds, but in their likes and dislikes, their fears, and their critical judgments. "No one in the world has made me laugh as much as Dottie," he said. He could never predict when or where she would open her mouth and quietly utter five or six priceless words. One evening at the home of Dorothy and Richard Rodgers, dinner guests were happily and lengthily denigrating Clare Boothe. Her sole defender at the table was Ilka Chase, who protested that Clare was always loyal to friends. Moreover, added Chase, Clare was always kind to her inferiors.

"And where does she find them?" asked Dorothy, without looking up from her plate or missing a bite.

Quite apart from his uncritical appreciation of her wit, it was obvious to him that she needed someone to look after her. The disorderly way she lived was deplorable, but Alan took it for granted that a writer of her stature should be ignorant of cooking, shopping, and keeping her bank account in order, indeed coping with any mundane matter. He was quick to notice every detail of her appearance and to make tactful suggestions for improvement. Even though she had excellent taste in clothing, her grooming was occasionally less than impeccable. Alan felt strongly that a woman in her position should look elegant, and he was going to make sure she did. Not only did he supervise dieting and shopping for a new wardrobe, he redid her makeup and also designed an exceptionally becoming hairstyle—long soft bangs with the rest of her hair sleekly pulled back into a twist. She liked the style so much that she kept it for the rest of her life. Alan was, said Ruth Goodman Goetz, "your instantaneous, quick-witted interior decorator. Alan bought her clothes, fussed with her hairstyle and her perfume. I don't know if he actually set her hair or not, but he may have. Dottie was delighted to have this handsome creature around."

Meanwhile, she was suffering from serious problems that seemed incapable of solution by anything as simple as a new coiffure. Sunk deep in one of the moods that she called "a Scotch mist," she drank heavily and sometimes had blackouts. Writer Joseph Bryan III, a childhood friend of Alan's from Richmond, remembered running into him at a dance.

"Come along at once," Alan said. "Dottie Parker is here and she's dying to meet you."

Bryan followed him to the edge of the dance floor, where Dorothy was holding court on a gilt chair. To his amazement and delight, she seemed thrilled to see him, complimented him extravagantly on a recent *New Yorker* profile, and insisted he take a seat next to her. After a time, she wondered whether he might be interested in collaborating on a play with her—he said he would be—and wanted to know how soon he could start. When they agreed to meet the next morning, Bryan left the dance floating on a pink cloud. Next day, on the stroke of eleven, he appeared at her hotel and asked the doorman to ring her.

> She was a long time answering, but finally he said, "Mr. Bryan, madam . . . Mr. *Bryan*. . . . " He turned to me: "Will you spell it, sir?" I spelled it, and he repeated, "B, R, Y, A, N, madam. . . . Yes, madam." He turned to me again: "Mrs. Parker asks what you wish to see her about." I don't know how I made myself heard over the noise of my heart cracking, but I must have succeeded, because presently I found myself in the elevator, even though I was already achingly aware that she'd have no recollection of our glittering plans from the evening before. It proved to be worse than that: she had no recollection even of our having *met*.
>
> I saw Dottie many, many times afterwards . . . but never once was that first evening ever mentioned. For all that she retained of it, it had never happened.

A few weeks later, another embarrassing incident occurred. Dorothy had agreed to support Fiorello La Guardia's candidacy for mayor of New York City. At a press conference arranged by Beatrice Kaufman, a horde of reporters arrived at Dorothy's apartment and began to interrogate her about politics. One of the better political jokes of the year had been hers: When Benchley brought her the news that Calvin Coolidge was dead, she responded, "How can they tell?"

Firsthand witnesses claimed that Benchley shot back, "He had an erection." But the punch line was generally omitted in deference to Benchley's image as a one-hundred-percent clean-cut family man.

On the afternoon of the La Guardia press conference, crouched in a chair, Dorothy was either drunk or hung over. She refused to talk about La Guardia, or any other subject, and declared that "I'm having a filthy time." Reluctant to acknowledge that she had never voted, she said that maybe she once had voted for a surrogate judge but could no longer remember. When asked about the election, she replied, "Maybe we'd better have another round of drinks. I'll tell Ivy," and added angrily, "This is not going so well, I feel miserable."

The Viking Press was preparing to issue her second volume of collected fiction. The original title, *The Infernal Grove*, had been discarded and donated to John O'Hara, who also finally vetoed it in favor of *Appointment in Samarra* for his first novel. Dorothy's book finally appeared as *After Such Pleasures* from John Donne's "Farewell to Love." Viking reprinted several of her best stories ("Horsie," "Dusk Before Fireworks"), some of her earliest work ("Too Bad," written in 1923) and popular soliloquies such as "The Waltz." An excited Edmund Wilson recommended the book to Louise Bogan: "You should read it, if you haven't—I'll send you my borrowed copy, if you promise to send it back." Wilson's praise was typical of the critical reaction, which should have delighted Dorothy, but the pleasures of success were overcast by the debilitation that always accompanied a "Scotch mist."

Prohibition was repealed. After thirteen years, the sale of alcohol became legal again on December 5, 1933, and the speakeasy era, in which Dorothy learned to drink, would soon fade to a memory. Even though Prohibition had never interfered with her drinking—quite the opposite— she enjoyed the new freedom, particularly in Alan's company, as they made the rounds of her favorite saloons. One night they were drinking at Tony's when their voices began to rise. Alan got up and angrily stamped out. Dorothy, left fingering the silverware, looked around and smiled at the people sitting nearby. "I don't know why he should get so angry," she said to Emily Hahn, "just because I called him a fawn's ass."

Ordinarily, Alan did not react to such provocative remarks. Having grown up with drinking parents, he instinctively understood that in these situations somebody had to be responsible and usually it was himself. He knew what Dorothy badly needed was somebody to take charge, and Alan took great pleasure in being a manager. On a practical level, he endeared himself by sobering her up, making excuses, and getting her out of jams whenever necessary. There were some problems about which he could do nothing but shake his head in astonishment, however. By this time, her debts had grown so sizable that it seemed she could never repay them if she lived to be a hundred. Her method of handling money and debt was careless. She disposed of her earnings by reckless spending until nothing was left and then panicking, at which point she would shoot off an apologetic telegram to Viking, asking that five hundred dollars be deposited in National City Bank.

Part of her financial distress was due to generosity. She was quick to give away money to any friend who needed it. When John O'Hara faced a domestic crisis and required fifty dollars in a hurry, she wrote a check and ordered him never to mention the matter again, because she was so deeply in debt that fifty dollars made no difference. She also helped her sister, who was working as a salesclerk at Gimbel's. George Droste died in 1932, and Helen recently married Victor Grimwood, a retired schoolteacher in his sixties and a sportsman who was the author of a book on fly fishing. Sometimes the Grimwoods were hard up. Dorothy agreed to cosign a bank loan for Victor, a kindness that did not prevent her from complaining about him behind his back. The members of her family, she grumbled, "seem to have retired from active work of any kind. That is, all except my brother-in-law, who has a dandy business. He makes ships' models. Of course, it's a little dull at the moment, but it'll come back."

Attracting a man as young as Alan pleased Dorothy, but she also felt extremely sensitive about the difference in their ages. For the most part, she carried off the situation by never mentioning Alan's true age and pretending he was merely a few years her junior. Only among her closest friends did she joke about it. When Howard Dietz once needled her about Alan being too straitlaced for her, she agreed but wondered what could be done about it. "Oh yes," she said, "we could send him to military school." Instead of dwelling on his youth, she preferred to emphasize the fact that he was a Southerner and affectionately began referring to him as "the Colonel."

Dorothy went out of her way to help the Colonel. In January 1934, presumably as a result of introducing him to her close friends Ellen and Philip Barry, Alan was cast in Barry's new play, *The Joyous Season*. That same month Dorothy made up her mind to leave the Lowell and moved into an apartment building at 444 East Fifty-second Street, which afforded an unbroken view of the garbage in the East River and was located, as she said, "far enough east to plant tea." At first she found the new apartment oppressive, but after Philip Barry's play had closed, the Colonel began spending most of his time there with her. By spring they were more or less living together.

With a new home and a new lover, it seemed only natural to buy a dog, and she acquired a Bedlington terrier. "I picked him out because Bedlingtons are trained to root up gardens and hunt otters, and my New York apartment was simply infested with otters." No animal of Dorothy's was exposed to the concepts of obedience training or housebreaking, and Wolf proved no exception. To compound the problem of owning an un-trained puppy, Alan insisted that Wolf should have a friend, and they decided to get a second, fully grown Bedlington, Cora. One night they were at the Murphys' Beekman Place apartment with John O'Hara, wait-ing for the arrival of Ernest Hemingway. After four hours, he had not shown up and the Bedlingtons grew restless. So did O'Hara, who felt antagonistic toward Sara because he suspected that she disliked him. As he gleefully reported to Hemingway later, "I had the pleasure of watching first one dog, then another taking a squirt on Mrs. Murphy's expensive rugs."

That spring Dorothy saw a good deal of Scott Fitzgerald, who was living in Baltimore while Zelda underwent treatment at Johns Hopkins. Scott was busy revising *Tender Is the Night* for an April publication date. Dorothy had not seen him for several years, although the previous fall, she had impul-sively written to him, when Ring Lardner had died of a heart attack at the age of forty-eight. She and John O'Hara were sitting over coffee in the Baltimore Dairy Lunch late one night while Dorothy read the latest issue of *The New Republic* containing Scott's obituary of Ring. Dorothy could not help weeping. O'Hara irritated her by repeating, "Isn't it swell?" until she finally told him, "The Gettysburg Address was good too." Writing in what appears to be crayon, she scrawled a tipsy note to Scott: "I think your piece about Ring is the finest and most moving thing I have ever read," and she signed it "Dorothy Parker, N.Y. City," as if she and Scott were complete strangers.

He telephoned to thank her, but they did not meet again until April, when Zelda's paintings and drawings were exhibited at a Manhattan art gallery. Dorothy, who attended the exhibition with the Murphys and Adele

Lovett, dutifully made several purchases. She paid thirty-five dollars for two watercolors, one of them a portrait of Scott wearing a crown of thorns and the other a dancer who resembled Zelda. She was shocked to find the prices pitifully low. Zelda had talent, she thought, but the painful qualities of the work and the dominating color of blood red upset her. She knew she would never hang the pictures in her apartment.

During this period, while Zelda was temporarily living at a rest home on the Hudson River, Scott made frequent visits to New York, where he stayed at the Algonquin or the Plaza. His pockets stuffed with catalogs for Zelda's exhibit, he turned up at Tony's or telephoned Dorothy, eager to ramble around all night partying and asking for introductions to women. Jim Thurber obliged. Dorothy did not, but she once invited him to join her, John O'Hara, and O'Hara's former wife, Helen. To O'Hara's dismay, as they were seeing Helen home, Scott began making passes in the cab, and she did not bother to fight him off. When the taxi pulled up at her door, Scott immediately climbed out and escorted her inside, even though he was so drunk that he needed the doorman's assistance to walk.

"He's awful," Dorothy protested to O'Hara. "Why didn't you punch him?"

O'Hara replied that Helen was entitled to behave as she liked.

Years later Dorothy confided in a friend that she had slept with Scott, but added that it had been nothing more than a fleeting affair. Since he was an alcoholic like herself, she could feel compassion for him, but he made her uncomfortable for the same reason. She despised in him the very qualities she hated in herself—sniveling self-pity, the way they both wasted their talent, their lack of self-discipline. And, like herself, Scott could be tiresome when he was drinking. It is not impossible that they slept with each other once or twice in some unplanned encounter when both of them were drunk. However, given her deepening involvement with Alan at this time, the fact that they were living together and spending most of their time in each other's company, it seems unlikely that she went out of her way to have affairs.

Some of her friends wondered what sort of erotic relationship she was having with Alan. Some were pleased to speculate that there was little physical intimacy at all. In order to make such remarks, they had to ignore the obvious, which was that "in addition to their friendship they had a real physical love for each other so strong that it was startling to see," as one friend said:

Before meeting Dorothy, Alan's involvements with the opposite sex had been with older women, with whom he slept or lived and whom he treated like daughters. He'd once, for example, lived with actress Estelle Winwood. Sid Perelman classified Alan as a homosexual, temporarily non-practicing. Other friends tended to agree with Ruth Goetz who said, "All the time I knew Alan I never saw him do anything overtly homosexual. I sensed, however, that somewhere in his past there had been homosexual friendships."

Regardless of what people said, it was increasingly clear that Dorothy loved Alan and that he loved her. With her history, her seeming knack for selecting those very men incapable of loving back, this development seemed excellent progress. Marc Connelly was one friend who welcomed Alan. "When Dottie fell in love, she fell in love. She didn't swim in a fishpond, you know; she went into the ocean. Alan was a nice boy, a good boy. She was very much in love with him, and so he was welcome."

Although Alan's wit was not in the same class as Dorothy's, his conversation was rarely dull. He had an engaging sense of humor and a highly developed idea of fun. One evening when they were drinking in a Village bar, another customer, whose appearance was decidedly effeminate, began to interrogate Dorothy about her literary tastes. Did she prefer this author or that author? Did she ever read fairy tales?

"My dear," she replied, "let us not talk shop."

Alan laughed so hard he almost fell on the floor. Later that evening, still feeling merry, he suggested that they have themselves tattooed. They had themselves decorated at one of the Bowery tattoo parlors with matching blue stars in the insides of their upper arms. Afterward, Dorothy complained that she would be condemned to wearing long sleeves for the rest of her life.

After Dorothy's tattoo was revealed in a gossip column, the *New York Daily Mirror* dispatched a reporter to find out where it was located. Sheilah Graham, a young Englishwoman, arrived to find Dorothy having cocktails with Alan and John O'Hara. Shyly, Dorothy pushed up the sleeve of her dress to show Graham her arm and apologized for the boring location of the star. It was so tiny that Graham had trouble distinguishing the design. Dorothy offered Graham a drink, said she liked her, and assured her they would become close friends. She urged her to call again, an invitation Graham took seriously. After she had stopped by several times, always informed that Mrs. Parker was out, she realized that Dorothy had been making a fool of her.

That summer Alan was offered a job playing juveniles with the Elitch Gardens stock company in Denver, which meant a separation of several months. Dorothy decided to go along with him; they could rent an apartment together, and she could write while he was busy at the theater. Alan insisted that it would be a wise move to buy a secondhand car and motor across the country. He promised the trip would take only four days, and Dorothy began to dream of their romantic progress toward the western sun, riding through fields of windswept grain. Among those who saw them off on the morning of June 8 was Marc Connelly, who recalled that their car, a 1929 Ford that resembled a sitz bath, "was the most goddamnedest most-loaded vehicle you ever saw. There was more junk in it, completely unnecessary stuff," not to mention the two Bedlingtons. When they reached Newcastle, Pennsylvania, Dorothy stopped to telegraph the Murphys, who were sailing for Europe the next day.

> THIS IS TO REPORT ARRIVAL IN NEWCASTLE OF FIRST BEDLINGTON
> TERRIERS TO CROSS CONTINENT IN OPEN FORD. MANY NATIVES NOTE
> RESEMBLANCE TO SHEEP. COULDN'T SAY GOODBYE AND CAN'T NOW
> BUT GOOD LUCK DARLING MURPHYS AND PLEASE HURRY BACK. WITH
> ALL LOVE, DOROTHY.

The trip west delighted Dorothy. She decided that the finest people who existed operated filling stations and that most Americans west of Pennsylvania lived entirely on catsup. Wolf sat on her lap the whole trip; Cora annoyed Alan. On the fourth day, having just crossed the Nebraska–Colorado state line, they decided it would be fun to wire Don Stewart in Hollywood:

WE ARE IN JULESBURG, COLORADO, IN OPEN 1929 FLIVVER WITH
TWO BEDLINGTON TERRIERS. PLEASE ADVISE.

Stewart had no suggestions and replied,

I HAVE NEVER BEEN IN JULESBURG, COLORADO.

    Arriving at Elitch Gardens, they stepped into more "fresh hell." The
telegram to Stewart had been signed with both their names and apparently
he showed it to a Hollywood journalist. "We got out of the car into a swirl
of reporters, camera men, sports writers, and members of the printers'
union," Dorothy recalled. They naïvely assumed they would be able to live
together as in New York but immediately realized their mistake. "Eyebrows," Connelly said, "shot up to the tops of the cathedrals. I don't know
why they expected to go out to Denver and get away with having an affair."
When they heard phrases like "living in sin," they both lost their heads.
Before Dorothy could stop him, Alan's southern chivalry had bounded to
the forefront, and he boldly declared that they were married, lies that led
to further lies because naturally the reporters then wanted details about
where and when. Improvising, Alan said the wedding had taken place last
October by a justice of the peace in Westbury, Long Island. Dorothy told
other reporters that the ceremony had been performed at her sister's house
in Garden City. When the wire services searched the vital statistics of North
Hempstead Township, they could find no registry of the marriage, nor had
the municipal clerk issued a marriage license. When they called Helen's
home, Victor Grimwood said it was news to him, in fact he was quite sure
no ceremony had been performed at his house.

    There seemed to be only one way to save face. A few days later, on
the evening of June 18, they drove across the state line to Raton, New
Mexico. It was nearly midnight by the time they located a justice of the
peace. In an effort to conceal the marriage, Dorothy gave her name as
Dorothy Rothschild, age forty, and Alan said he was Allen [sic] Campbell,
age thirty-two (he was only thirty). The next day, back in Denver, Dorothy
sent her sister a wire from one of the dogs:

COMMUNICATION HAS BEEN IMPOSSIBLE IN APPALLING CONFUSION.
BUT MANAGED UNANNOUNCED DRIVE TO NEW MEXICO YESTERDAY
WHERE PARENTS DIFFICULTIES PRIVATELY SETTLED, IT IS HOPED

FOR ALL TIME. BOTH VERY HAPPY. BEST LOVE AND MOTHER IS
WRITING.

She signed the telegram CORA. A wire-service photograph snapped the day before their marriage reveals that they were in fact very happy. Dorothy, trim, radiant, and looking closer to thirty than forty, wore a dress printed all over with daisies and seemed like an adorable Japanese doll next to Alan, who was beaming as usual.

Still, reporters continued to trail them. Dorothy began to feel persecuted. "Oh, this is the first real happiness I've had in my whole life," she cried. "Why can't they let us alone?" Her attorney, Morris Ernst, advised showing the marriage certificate but keeping well concealed the date or place it was issued, which she did. While she was at it, she threatened to bring a fifty-thousand-dollar libel suit against the *New York Post* for suggesting she had lied about having been married the previous autumn.

Otherwise she was, as she wrote in an ebullient letter to Aleck Woollcott, "in a sort of coma of happiness." Being Alan's wife was "lovelier than I ever knew anything could be." She also felt rapturous about her new status as a wife. When she heard from Scott Fitzgerald in early July, she wired him back:

DEAR SCOTT THEY JUST FORWARDED YOUR WIRE BUT LOOK WHERE
I AM AND ALL MARRIED TO ALAN CAMPBELL AND EVERYTHING ALAN
PLAYING STOCK HERE FOR SUMMER.

She sent him deepest love from both of them.

It was one of the happiest summers of her life. For only fifty-five dollars a month they leased a furnished bungalow at 3783 Meade Street, which Dorothy named "Repent-at-Leisure." For the first week or so, they attempted to keep house for themselves. Alan did the cooking and put tomatoes in every dish he prepared, while Dorothy's contribution to housekeeping was a botched effort to make the bed. She offered to help in the kitchen but failed sublimely. Alan ordered her to stay out. Once rehearsals started, the system broke down, and they had to seek help from an employment agency. They needed, Alan stated, a man who would market, cook, serve, clean, and keep the cigarette boxes filled. A man was preferred because, in their experience, maids tended to chatter, and it was essential for any servant of theirs to observe silence. His wife, he explained to the agency, must never be disturbed: She wrote.

During the first week, the newlyweds hired and fired three servants, one of whom turned out to be a nonstop talker. Dorothy disliked him so passionately that she was inspired to write a short story about him, "Mrs. Hofstadter on Josephine Street," which was probably the quickest story she had ever written. It appeared in the August 4 issue of *The New Yorker*. They finally retained a housekeeper, who insisted on calling Dorothy "honey" and who was genteelly fond of her liquor.

As for Dorothy, she was drinking less. Blaming the altitude, she explained that "two cocktails and you spin on your ass," but she also felt happy and relaxed. Expecting to hate Denver, she confessed that "I love it. I love it. I love being a juvenile's bride and living in a bungalow and pinching dead leaves off the rose bushes. I will be God damned." Ensconced in the little bungalow, she did nothing but eat, sleep, and knit socks for Alan. Some days she saw little of him because he was in rehearsal, then performed at night, including Sunday. Dorothy was fanatical about staying away from Elitch Gardens; she had once read in a movie magazine that Hollywood respected Clark Gable's wife for staying out of her husband's business. Probably this was a wise decision on Dorothy's part because she had taken to making wildly slanderous observations about the company's leading lady, telling Alan that she looked like "a two-dollar whore who once commanded five."

Some of Dorothy's closest friends did not take her marriage seriously. Aleck Woollcott, told of her happiness, only snorted sourly and replied, he had read nothing of hers lately that was worthwhile, "That bird only sings when she's unhappy." Eventually he became close to Alan. They shared many of the same obsessions and sensibilities and, to a lesser degree, they had in common confusions about gender identity. Dorothy knew that Woollcott accepted her marriage when he began playing his usual practical jokes. After Alan applied for a department store charge account and gave Woollcott as a financial reference, Aleck responded with a fake carbon copy of his reply to the store:

Gentlemen:

Mr. Alan Campbell, the present husband of Dorothy Parker, has given my name as a reference in an attempt to open an account at your store. I hope that you will extend this credit to him. Surely Dorothy Parker's position in American letters is such as to make shameful the petty refusals which she and Alan have encountered at many hotels, restaurants, and department stores. What if you never get paid. Why shouldn't you stand your share of the expense?

Woollcott and what remained of the defunct Round Table awaited Dorothy's return to New York, perhaps anticipating the excitement on Broadway that would attend the fall opening of George Kaufman and Moss Hart's new drama, *Merrily We Roll Along*, featuring a character named Julia Glenn, a wisecracking alcoholic—a woman you could talk to like a man. Word-of-mouth publicity identified her real-life counterpart as Dorothy Parker. Questioned by reporters, Kaufman admitted that there might be a trace of Mrs. Parker in the character, but he insisted he and Hart meant no offense.

Once again somebody had stolen her story. This time she could not complain that her character was distorted; the Kaufman and Hart portrayal was uncomfortably close, supplying a harsh chronicle to her drinking. As the play's stage directions noted, the youthful Julia of 1925 looked fresh and glowing, but in 1927 she showed signs of decay, and by 1934 she had acquired the typical flabbiness of the steady drinker, a woman never quite sober. Julia Glenn preferred to sleep with men much younger than herself. Unlike George Oppenheimer's *Here Today*, which borrowed mainly her mannerisms, this was not a likeness Dorothy could laugh off by going backstage and carrying off an awkward moment with a "darling, how delightful." If she had never been fond of Kaufman, now she hated him.

She was able to avoid *Merrily We Roll Along*. Alan, who felt he had earned a holiday, proposed going to California for a honeymoon after the season ended at Elitch Gardens. They could visit Hollywood and stay with Don and Bea Stewart for a few weeks. In the meantime, another idea came along. They met Rosalie Stewart, a former Broadway producer, now a Hollywood agent, who thought they should go to Hollywood as a husband-and-wife writing team and even promised to get them a ten-week contract at Paramount.

Hearing Rosalie Stewart's idea and remembering her unpleasant experience at MGM in 1928, Dorothy disdained the plan and wanted to "file the whole thing under Horseshit," but Alan felt differently. He became increasingly excited, especially when Stewart talked about a deal in which

Alan's contract would call for him to write dialogue as well as act. When Dorothy continued to drag her feet, he pointed out that the job would last only for ten weeks and that she could repay the suffocating mass of debt he called "Dottie's dowry."

They signed contracts that guaranteed Alan two hundred and fifty dollars a week and Dorothy one thousand, a discrepancy that seemed reasonable to Alan. His wife was, after all, an acknowledged literary figure, and he knew that without her Paramount would not have signed him at all. The studio's news release announced that Dorothy's first assignment would be to write an original screenplay for Lee Tracy and Carole Lombard.

For Dorothy, the film capital was symbolized by a sight she never forgot:

> Once I was coming down a street in Beverly Hills and I saw
> a Cadillac about a block long, and out of the side window was
> a wonderfully slinky mink, and an arm, and at the end of the
> arm a hand in a white suede glove wrinkled at the wrist, and
> in the hand was a bagel with a bite out of it.

Throughout the thirties, Hollywood was a combination kosher deli and El Dorado that attracted talented writers of all types: newspapermen like Ben Hecht, left-wing New York theater people such as Clifford Odets and John Howard Lawson, a contingent of *New Yorker* authors, even some of the country's most illustrious novelists and playwrights—William Faulkner, Elmer Rice, Thornton Wilder, and later Scott Fitzgerald. There was no secret about their motivations. Everybody was eager to make the proverbial hay while the sun shone, and few remained immune to the astronomical salaries being offered. What they were obliged to do in order to collect the huge paychecks was another matter.

The emigrés rented bungalows at the Garden of Allah or houses in Beverly Hills. When they gathered at parties, they stood around grumbling about how degrading their jobs were, although Sid Perelman rated screenwriting as "no worse than playing the piano in a house of call." There was good cause for complaint. Standard procedure assigned half a dozen writers to the same film, either working simultaneously or performing a frontal lobotomy on a predecessor's script. The relationship between the writer and the studio was more or less sadomasochistic. Writers held their employers in contempt, feelings that were reciprocated. Studio executives called them "schmucks with Underwoods," or the highest-paid secretaries in the world. Dorothy and Alan prepared for the worst.

The Hollywood press eagerly fed them into its meat grinder and they emerged in the press looking like chopped movie star:

> The devastating Dorothy Parker and her young husband, Mr. Campbell, were practically turtle-doves [at the Trocadero] . . .

> Dorothy Parker and Alan Campbell guests at Countess di Frasso's . . .

> Met Dorothy Parker with Alan Campbell, her young and handsome husband, at a tea given by Zoe Akins . . .

> Dorothy Parker and the handsome husband buying a house in her once despised Hollywood. New York papers please copy.

Although Alan appeared satisfied with secondary billing, Dorothy was alert to the potential dangers of a husband living in his wife's shadow. Paramount made a token attempt to credit him for being somebody in his own right. The caption accompanying a studio publicity photo announced:

> Doubly Famous: Alan Campbell, actor-author, just placed under contract by Paramount, is a double bid for fame. Plus his own accomplishments, which are several, he can rightfully brag about those of his talented wife, Dorothy Parker, also under contract to Paramount as a writer.

This was feeble but probably better than nothing. That Paramount failed to enumerate Alan's several accomplishments was unfortunate, but hardly accidental. Once it became clear to the studio that Dorothy, despite her reputation, was worthless to them without Alan, he was never offered an acting role of any kind.

Those who later claimed that Alan rode on Dorothy's coattails in Hollywood could not have been more mistaken. He was a capable, but certainly not a distinguished or original writer. He continued to write for *The New Yorker* throughout the thirties, publishing a total of nineteen short stories. In Hollywood, from the start, he showed himself to be a dogged worker determined to master a new craft. His strength turned out to be construction. He would first block out a scene, then labor to pull it together on paper so that Dorothy could follow along and inject amusing dialogue. Without her, Alan's scenes would have fallen flat, but without him there would have been no scene. As a team they were a perfect complement.

On September 3, they moved into the Paramount writers building, where they were assigned a comfortable, if seedy, office. The Lee Tracy picture did not materialize. She told the Murphys that the work they were given "stinks." One of their first scripts was *Twenty-two Hours by Air*, a story that had been kicking around the studio so long that the progress of aerial transportation had practically made it obsolete. "It is now called 'Eleven Hours by Air,' " Dorothy said. "By the time we are done, the title is to be, I believe, 'Stay Where You Are.' " (It was finally produced as *One Hour Late.*) They prepared a new screenplay for *Sailor Beware*, an adaptation of a recent Broadway play, and removed the sex from a previous version, specifically a scene in which the sailor bets he can seduce the woman. The producer considered it obscene. "But would they accept our change," Dorothy reported to Aleck Woollcott, "that triumph of ingenuity where the sailor just bets he will make another sailor? Oh, no. Sometimes I think they don't know *what* they want." What they did not want was the Parker-Campbell version, nor did they even want the screenplay's original title, because it was finally released in 1936 as *Lady Be Careful*. Dorothy and Alan also worked on a Sylvia Sidney picture, *Here Is My Heart*, followed by still another assignment memorable mainly because they were informed of neither plot nor title, only that "the male lead will be played by Tullio Carminati or Bing Crosby. So just write it with both of them in mind."

Dorothy explained to Harold Guinzburg that a few months in Hollywood would mean "no art but can clear up that national debt." The Campbells' combined salary of twelve hundred and fifty dollars a week represented a truly gigantic sum at a time when income taxes were minimal and the dollar worth six or seven times its current value. It was a relief to repay debts. At the same time, they found that living in Hollywood in a manner befitting their position was far more expensive than living in New

York. She discovered that "Hollywood money isn't money." It was "congealed snow" that "melts in your hand."

They rented a house at 520 North Canon Drive in Beverly Hills. When they received assurance that their contracts would be renewed, they decided to purchase expensive white carpets, whose impracticality made them irresistible. Christmas came and the weather felt like summer. Dorothy could not have been more delighted with their new home, as she wrote to Woollcott:

> Aside from the work which I hate like holy water, I love it here. There are any number of poops about, of course, but so are there in New York—or, as we call it, The Coast—and the weather's better here. I love having a house, I love its being pretty wherever you look, I love a big yard full of dogs. There are two additions—a four-months-old dachshund, pure enchantment, named Fräulein, and a mixed party called Scrambles who is, by a happy coincidence, the one dog in the world you couldn't love. This gap in her character causes us to lean over backwards to ply her with attentions, and so she's worse than ever. You don't know anybody who wants a half-Welsh-terrier, half-Zambi, do you?

In New York, Dorothy's pets had been welcomed, or at least tolerated, by public establishments, but she found local custom to be less broadminded. When she brought one of her dogs to the Beverly Hills Hotel, the animal misbehaved in the lobby.

The manager promptly appeared. "Miss Parker, Miss Parker!" he shouted. "Look what your dog did."

Dorothy drew herself up and gave the man a withering look. "I did it," she said and walked away with as much dignity as she could summon under the circumstances. After this, she left the dogs home.

Thanks to Alan, life on North Canon Drive was a miracle of orderliness. Not only did he take care of everything, but also he cosseted her with loving patience. There was less drinking, with a few exceptions. After they threw a splashy housewarming party, to which they invited a hundred guests and were surprised to find more than three hundred showed up, Dorothy declared that her hangover was impressive enough to be referred to as "we." Apart from her comparative sobriety, other changes could be noticed. No more did she talk about killing herself. When this became apparent to Dorothy, she was amazed.

> In May my heart was breaking—
> Oh, wide the wound, and deep!
> And bitter it beat at waking,
> And sore it split in sleep.
>
> And when it came November,
> I sought my heart, and sighed,
> "Poor thing, do you remember?"
> "What heart was that?" it cried.

"Autumn Valentine," published in 1935, was one of her last verses. No longer did she despair over princes who turned into frogs. Having always courted men capable of torturing her, having always derived creative inspiration from her suffering, she now found herself in the paradoxical position of being wed to a man who did not abuse her but who also failed to inspire serious writing. As far as is known, she composed only one poem for him and that was later, during the war, when it was history that caused her misery. In 1931, Viking had published Dorothy's third volume of poetry under the title *Death and Taxes*, which was followed five years later by a volume of her collected verse, *Not So Deep as a Well*. After 1935, however, Dorothy wrote only three known poems: the unpublished "The Passionate Screen Writer To His Love" (1937), "Threat to a Fickle Lady" (1938), and "War Song" (1944).

At MGM, William Randolph Hearst had built his mistress, actress Marion Davies, a dressing-room bungalow whose entrance was adorned with a statue of the Madonna. To Dorothy's annoyance, Hollywood insisted upon crediting her with the authorship of a popular jingle about them:

> Upon my honor
> I saw a Madonna
> Standing in a niche
> Above the door
> Of a prominent whore
> Of a prominent son of a bitch.

Dorothy, offended, declared that she would never stoop to rhyming *honor* with *Madonna*.

Despite her happiness with Alan and her abandonment of suicide as a philosophy of life, a few lingering anxieties emerged in the form of psychosomatic ailments. While living in Denver she experienced hay fever for the first time. The allergy made her uncomfortable but proved to be minor compared to the itching and scratching that began once she arrived in California, where she was afflicted with hives. Throughout the fall, the hives worsened. Despite a battery of tests, her doctor could offer no sensible answers about the cause. After Christmas, she developed intestinal hives and was obliged to spend a week at Good Samaritan—"or at least Pretty Good Samaritan"—Hospital. In time the hives passed, as such problems often do.

Dashiell Hammett was a writer for whom she had high regard. While reviewing *The Glass Key* in 1931, she described him "as American as a sawed-off shotgun." He was one of the most powerful writers of the time and had become her hero. That same year, catching sight of him at a cocktail party, she introduced herself before dropping to her knees and kissing his hand. It was meant to be funny, but Hammett was so embarrassed that, he responded with an uncharacteristic simpering reply. The woman with him stared daggers at Dorothy. Afterward, the dagger-staring woman and Hammett quarreled over what kind of a man would permit a literary critic to kneel in adoration. In the winter of 1935, Dorothy ran into Hammett's critical girlfriend at a party. After Lillian Hellman spent the better part of the evening glowering at her, they finally began to talk and realized they liked each other. The previous autumn, her play *The Children's Hour* had opened to acclaim and was named the best play of the year by the New York Drama Critics Circle. Samuel Goldwyn had brought her to Hollywood with a salary of twenty-five hundred dollars a week.

While married to writer Arthur Kober and living in Hollywood, Hellman had first met Hammett five years earlier. Despite his wife and daughters, despite his chronic womanizing, they had fallen in love and been together ever since. Lillian was a scrapper, a woman of spirit and independence and some ruthlessness who knew where she wanted to go and did what was necessary to realize her ambitions. She had reddish hair, stylish clothes, and a tough, funny way of expressing herself, but she was not a handsome woman. She had heavy features; her mouth was thin, her chin receded, and her nose was large and protrusive.

Dorothy and Lillian became good friends. In her memoirs, Hellman decided that their friendship had been remarkable because they were so dissimilar. That was true. Apart from a difference of eleven years in their ages, they led entirely different lives, were not the same kind of writer, and often disagreed on people and books. Certainly their tastes in men were different. Alan was, Hellman admitted, "a hard man for me to take;" in fact, she despised him. Although Dorothy was too polite to say so, she did not get on well with Hammett as a person. To complicate matters further, Hammett couldn't stand Dorothy. In later years, he would leave the house whenever she came to visit. Her habit of flattering people to their faces and then declaring, "Did you ever meet such a shit?" once they had left was especially perturbing to him. Hellman stood up for Dorothy by saying that it was nothing more serious than a defense sometimes adopted by frightened people. Subsequently, she decided that the explanation was too simple. She grew to believe that Dorothy's hunger for love and admiration, a craving that led to intense self-loathing, could only be released by the most violent behind-the-back denunciations.

Throughout the years of their friendship, Dorothy took pleasure in Lillian's company, but the reverse was not always so. As time passed, it became less and less true. "Dottie admired Lillian," said Ruth Goetz.

> She admired her political stance and respected her success in the theater. She was never jealous or mean spirited about somebody else's good fortune or talent. But Lillian did not admire Dottie because she had no admiring mechanism, and she wasn't generous about anything. Either she was jealous of those who were doing well or she flattered them as colleagues. She enjoyed Dottie's company because Dottie was so delicious to be around. They got on well at parties and over the dinner table, even though Lillian had no time for women. She was so frantic for male company, male adulation that I don't think she was ever a good friend to a woman. I was very surprised when I heard that Lillian was to be her executor. It seemed inappropriate because she had not really been a

friend to Dottie. To put it bluntly, in later years she had found Dottie wearisome.

As new friendships developed, several old ones began to fade as a result of distance, Alan, or death. Soon after Dorothy's arrival in Hollywood, she was stunned to learn of Ruth Hale's death. It was hard for her to believe, let alone accept. She greatly respected Ruth, whose stand on many subjects paralleled her own. An important exception was Ruth's adamant belief that married women should retain their unmarried names. With Jane Grant, she cofounded the Lucy Stone League to encourage women not to change their names. Dorothy, who regarded keeping the name Rothschild with as much distaste as Ruth would have viewed the idea of taking Heywood Broun's surname, could never personally endorse Ruth's crusade. To indicate the emotions behind her rejection, she once sent Ruth a telegram that began TO RUTH BROUN FROM DOROTHY ROTHSCHILD. . . . Despite her opposing viewpoint she could not help feeling angered at the irony of Ruth's obituary in the *Los Angeles Examiner,* a five-word record that struck her as the total failure of a feminist's life: EX-WIFE OF HEYWOOD BROUN PASSES.

All through the year she was gripped by a sense of dislocation. Waves of homesickness for New York came and went and later sent her rocketing from coast to coast. She reminded herself that nice people lived in Hollywood—she thought Bing Crosby was "swell" and James Cagney "the best person"—but nobody made up for the loss of old, dear friends. Each week she made a point of tuning in to Aleck Woollcott's radio show, *The Town Crier.* When she heard his voice, she felt "pulled apart by nostalgia" and began to cry. She also missed the Murphys, whose older son, Baoth, suddenly died of spinal meningitis at the age of sixteen.

The person she missed most was Robert Benchley, which was ironic, since he was living half of each year in Hollywood. She could have seen as much of him as she had in New York. With a successful second career as a film actor, he came to the Coast in April and lived at the Garden of Allah until September or October, when he rushed back home to cover the theater season for *The New Yorker.* If not for Gertrude and the boys, he might have spent even less time in the East.

A coolness had developed between Dorothy and Benchley. To a great extent, Alan had usurped Benchley's role of confidant, comrade, and advisor, but her withdrawal from Benchley predated her marriage. In 1933 Edmund Wilson visited one Sunday afternoon and found her entertaining Bea Stewart and Benchley's ex-mistress Betty Starbuck. Drinking gin and ginger ale and lounging around in a dowdy dressing gown, she openly ridiculed Benchley for selling out to Hollywood. She also was disgusted by an advertisement for his *New York Mirror* column that showed a little girl saying, "Oh, goody! here comes the funny man." Wilson wrote, "They were vomiting and puking over his stuff in the *Mirror.*"

In Hollywood, her contacts with Benchley were increasingly limited to social occasions.

Their plans to return East after clearing her debts seemed to have been postponed and perhaps temporarily forgotten. Indeed, they were settling more firmly in California. In 1935 they moved to 914 North Roxbury Drive in Beverly Hills, a colonial mansion with tall white columns and rolling lawn graced by magnolia and pine trees. Despite Harold Guinzburg's warnings about the folly of writers who remained in Hollywood year-round, they continued to sign contract renewals and hurtle from film to film: *The Case Against Mrs. Ames, Hands Across the Table,* and *Mary Burns, Fugitive,* as well as others Dorothy wished she could assign to oblivion. For three months in the autumn, Paramount loaned them to MGM, where they worked on *Suzy,* a gold-digger comedy about an American showgirl in London that was to showcase Jean Harlow and Cary Grant.

By now their joint salary had climbed to fifteen hundred dollars a week. Dorothy may not have taken pride in her work, but she refused to belittle her labors. "Garbage though they turn out, Hollywood writers aren't writing down. This is their best." Unfortunately, she was unable to develop the pragmatic attitude held by friends like William Faulkner and Nathanael West, who viewed film writing as a means of underwriting their other work. After a six-and-a-half-day week at the studio, Dorothy found she had little energy left. This was not true of Alan. He wrote three stories for *The New Yorker* in 1935, but Dorothy produced no fiction or verse, only a five-page introduction to Arthur Kober's book, *Thunder over the Bronx.*

As the months passed, her estrangement from New York continued to deepen. She mourned the unwilling severance of old ties, developed hurt feelings over what she interpreted as neglect by eastern friends, and told herself that New Yorkers had peculiar attitudes about friendship—if you left town for any length of time, they simply figured you were dead. She did not intend to be forgotten and sometimes felt sufficiently provoked to issue a reminder of her existence:

> Dear Harold [she wrote to Guinzburg],
>   This is small business troubles. Look, it seems that Miss Miriam Hopkins . . . did some broadcasting while in your New York, and used for her vehicle, the bitch, my "Telephone Call." I didn't hear it, because what would I be doing with a radio, but it turns out, from the testimony of kindly friends, that she did it on two occasions. I never knew anything about it—no one ever asked me about using it, let alone any matter of royalties. . . .

It is doubtful whether she realized that she had referred to her native city as "your New York." The truth was that the city felt less and less like hers. Two years earlier, in Manhattan, she was quoted as saying that she favored taxes because "rich people should be taxed for being alive." What she could not yet bring herself to acknowledge was that she was, by any standards, well on her way to becoming one of those despised people.

Chapter 13

GOOD FIGHTS

•

1936–1937

All through the middle and late thirties, Dorothy was engaged in feverish warfare, but some observers found it hard to say what side she was on. In the spring of 1936, John O'Hara paid a visit to Hollywood and stayed briefly as a houseguest with Dorothy and Alan, who were living grandly on their fifteen hundred dollars a week. His eyeballs rolled up. "They have," he recounted peevishly to Scott Fitzgerald,

> a large white house, Southern style, and live in luxury, includ-
> ing a brand new Picasso, a Packard convertible phaeton, a
> couple of Negroes, and dinner at the very best Beverly Hills
> homes. Dottie occasionally voices a great discontent, but I
> think her aversion to movie-writing is as much lazy as intel-
> lectual. She likes the life. She and Alan are with Paramount,
> writing a courtroom picture for Claudette Colbert. Don Stew-
> art, who is full of shit, has converted himself to radical
> thought, and goes to all the parties for the Scottsboro boys.
> His wife, who is more honest and whom I don't like either,
> stays home from them. . . . He is certainly scared about
> something, and it isn't only the Revolution. But he is such a
> horse's ass that it doesn't matter much. . . .

There is no mention of Dorothy's political activities, most likely because O'Hara was unable or unready to decode the signals he was receiving from his one-time mentor. When Robert Benchley wrote to his wife at the end of April, he too mentioned the new political awareness that was sweeping Hollywood. The Scottsboro case had become a cause célèbre among liberals and Communists. Everybody was eager to organize a screenwriters' union or join a committee to free the eight black Alabama youths convicted of raping two white girls. "Dottie and Alan," Benchley added, "are on *all* committees at once, and seem to be very happy about it."

What drew her attention most powerfully was news of the Third Reich's persecution of Jews. Her ambivalence over her own Jewishness was so great that she would think of herself as a "mongrel" because of her mixed origins to the end of her life. At the same time, she found anti-Semitism terrifying and had begun to take a passionate, emotional interest in what was happening politically in Germany. At a hundred-dollar-a-plate banquet that she co-hosted with Don Stewart and others, she heard a firsthand account of the situation. The dinner speaker was a professional Communist propagandist, although it is unlikely that Dorothy knew anything about Otto Katz's politics that evening. A native of Prague and a former Berlin journalist, Katz was a suave and extremely persuasive man who spoke five languages and could talk about Kafka as easily as he could about Karl Marx. In 1936, he was acting as chief of staff for the legendary Willi Münzenberg, the German Communist who had escaped the Nazis and established a new headquarters for Comintern propaganda in Paris. Münzenberg is credited with being the first to recognize the advantages to be gained by quietly recruiting the support of eminent intellectuals, cultivating the friendship of these distinguished fellow travelers by subtle means, rarely quite aboveboard. He wooed foreign sympathizers such as Clarence Darrow and André Gide to the Soviet cause. Otto Katz had figured importantly in this work. He also had helped to compile Münzenberg's *Brown Book*, an indictment of Hitler that had been translated into twenty-three languages.

During his visit to Hollywood, Katz avoided expressing himself in Communist terminology, nor did he go out of his way to publicize his association with Münzenberg, whose name probably would have meant nothing to his audience anyway. Although Katz spoke eloquently about the importance of maintaining ties of friendship with the Soviet Union, he presented his primary allegiance as the cause of combatting fascism. Don Stewart recalled that when Katz began to describe the Nazi terror, "the details of which he had been able to collect only through repeatedly risking his own life, I was proud to be sitting beside him, proud to be on his side in the fight."

When Otto Katz called for the cooperation of the film colony in fighting Hitler and preventing a second world war, Dorothy saw an opportunity to make herself useful. Together with Stewart, Fredric March, and Oscar Hammerstein II, she helped found the Hollywood Anti-Nazi League to propagandize actively against Hitler. Offices were rented, a weekly newspaper was published, and public meetings were sponsored. Stars, writers, and directors contributed donations, and the studio heads offered enthusiastic support. Don Stewart became the League's chairman, Alan its secretary, and Dorothy a member of the executive board.

Several months later, after it was rumored that the League might be a Red organization, some stars dropped out and producers withdrew for fear they were contributing to Communism. By this time, Otto Katz was back on the other side of the Atlantic, his mission successful. Despite the early dropouts, the League continued to thrive and its membership eventually reached some four thousand.

Dorothy began moving away from people who failed to take the threat of fascism seriously, those who would not be convinced "until they see what has happened." She turned to another group. The white house on Roxbury Drive soon became the scene of buffet suppers that appeared to be ordinary social functions. At some point in the evening, Dorothy introduced a Marxist lecturer or a trade unionist, sometimes a German refugee, and she urged the need for generous contributions. She gave a dinner to raise money for the defense of the Scottsboro boys. One weekend, she and Alan, along with Don Stewart and a delegation of film writers, were invited to San Francisco for a conference being sponsored by the League of American Writers. This was an openly left-wing affair, whose speakers included Harry Bridges, the Australian-born leader of the International Longshoremen's Union, and Ella Winter, the widow of Lincoln Steffens. Welcoming the screenwriters, Winter said that the movement needed their spirit and humor. She flattered Dorothy and Don by describing them as people who "in one sentence can help us more than a thousand jargon-filled pamphlets." Later, she met them at a nearby cocktail lounge and introduced them to Bridges, who promptly won them over with his humor and ability to put away respectable quantities of bourbon. Everyone relaxed and got drunk. The next day the visitors made a trip to San Quentin prison and spoke with Tom Mooney.

Dorothy had been arrested during the Sacco-Vanzetti demonstrations, but nine years later, with no attempt at concealment on her part, her leftist tendencies still baffled those who knew her well and those who believed they did. If her support on behalf of two anarchists was not taken seriously, neither did she receive respectful attention when she began to speak warningly about Franco and Hitler. To many observers (including some of her most intimate friends), the source of her radicalism was obvious: She was playing amateur revolutionary, just as she once had played amateur suicide. This was nothing but theatrics.

Even her appearance underwent an evolution. In the days when she had been broke, she had always managed to turn herself out in fine outfits from Valentino and Hattie Carnegie. Since moving to Hollywood, she had hundred-dollar underwear and nightgowns made at an exclusive Beverly Hills shop. Outwardly, however, she began to adopt the proletariat look—a ruffled peasant blouse, baggy dirndl skirt cinched in at the waist, flat-heeled shoes, a babushka wrapping her hair and tied under the chin, so that only the dark bangs stuck out. You didn't see many women looking like that in Hollywood. There were days when she showed up at Paramount dressed like a Ukrainian farm woman getting ready to climb on a tractor. For that matter, she also bore more than a passing resemblance to those 1890-style sweatshop workers jogging along Hester Street with bundles of shirtwaists riding on their heads. J. Henry Rothschild would have swooned.

Dorothy declined to explain the reasons for this transformation. As she wrote in *New Masses*, "I cannot tell you on what day what did what to me," a statement that shed little light on the subject. She did recount a childhood memory: She and her Aunt Lizzie Rothschild were watching men shovel snow outside the house on West Sixty-eighth Street when Lizzie said that it was nice there had been a blizzard—now the men had work. "And I knew then it was not so nice that men could work for their lives only in desperate weather, that there was no work for them when it was fair." She also alluded to the Sacco-Vanzetti executions by noting that at certain times of her life, she had felt "wild" with the knowledge of injustice but had not known what to do. It amazed and amused her that she had to come to Hollywood, of all the improbable places, to discover ways of fighting values she had always hated.

With more generosity than accuracy, she gave credit for her radicalization to Don Stewart, though he corrected this error in his memoirs by observing that she "had 'gone left' before I had." She felt intense rapport with Stewart, who was also losing friends and suffering for his new beliefs.

Alan was, according to Budd Schulberg, "a genuine left liberal who had a little trouble stomaching the Party," but he put aside his own beliefs when they conflicted with his wife's enthusiasms. This was not true in Stewart's marriage. Bea objected vigorously to his political activities. As Robert Benchley sympathetically commented, "Don pretty difficult in past two years, all wrapped up in his guilds and leagues and soviets." In due course, Bea divorced him and married Count Ilya Andreyevich Tolstoy, a grandson of Leo Tolstoy, whom she met in Florida, where he was managing the Marine Aquarium without a dime to his illustrious name. In 1939, Don Stewart married Lincoln Steffens's widow, Ella Winter. Throughout the thirties and forties he worked on a number of highly successful films, such as *The Philadelphia Story*, while continuing his political involvements. By 1951, he immigrated to England, blacklisted.

Dorothy, meanwhile, had begun to divide the world into two camps: those who smiled at her indulgently and the like-minded leftist friends whom she referred to as "my own people." She preferred the company of her own people, including Lillian Hellman and Dashiell Hammett. Her feelings were reflected in a tart remark she made about Walter Duranty, the *New York Times* Moscow correspondent and a journalist she disliked for his callous attitude toward the Russians: "When the train of history went around a sharp curve, he fell out of the dining car." In her eyes, history had shoved a great many people out of the dining car. Out of affection and nostalgia, she continued to maintain ties with the Murphys, the Guinzburgs, and Aleck Woollcott, but she dropped people like Adele Lovett. She felt saddest of all about Benchley. At first, eager for his support, she had counted on his understanding because he believed that the new progressive movement was good for Hollywood. He paid twenty dollars to attend a fund-raising dinner on behalf of German-Jewish refugees. Afterward, he complained to Gertrude that such affairs were "all very laudable—but expensive." As Dorothy kept inching further to the left, she soon realized he was not following, but appeared to be increasingly skeptical of her direction.

A serious break occurred the following year, when she and Benchley both happened to be visiting New York and met for drinks at "21." Cannoning him with a fusillade of leftist ideology, she espoused her views with such militancy that Benchley was taken aback and greatly angered. He reacted to what probably struck him as political arrogance by launching an indirect counterattack and told her "not to make those ingenue eyes at me," because she was no longer an ingenue. Writing to Sara and Gerald Murphy about it, he said, "Dottie didn't mind my views on her labor activities but the 'ingenue' line (so I am told) cut her to the quick." In fact, she objected violently to both. For several months, she refused to answer his phone calls or visit him at the Garden of Allah, until eventually the intercession of friends brought about a reconciliation.

Benchley's reference to labor activities meant Dorothy's fierce belief that screenwriters should be organized. She had been in Hollywood a very short time when she stopped marveling about the fairy-tale salaries studios paid to their writers. She was dismayed to learn that few writers had the credentials to command hundreds of dollars a week and that for every Parker or Loos or Hecht, someone was earning slave wages.

> I saw some of the most stinkingest practices you'd ever want to see. People—honest, hard workers were thrown out of their jobs, without warning, without justice. People were hired on what is called "spec"—which meant that they wrote without pay, with the understanding that if their work was accepted they would be paid—and then their work would be used, but they would be fired—still without pay. The average wage of a screen writer was forty dollars a week. [Well, that] would have been perfectly corking except that there was a catch to it. The average term of employment was two weeks in a year.

In the summer of 1936, a drive got under way to recruit new members for the Screen Writers Guild, the union that had been formed four years earlier but had encountered violent opposition from the studios, who refused to accord it recognition or bargaining power. Many writers considered unions beneath the professional dignity of so-called artists. Needless to say, Dorothy was not among them, nor did she have sympathy for those who later affiliated themselves with a rival, studio-supported union known as the Screen Playwrights. Expecting studios to represent the rights of writers, she was said to have remarked, "was like trying to get laid in your mother's house. Somebody was always in the parlor, watching." At a meeting where a number of well-known writers spoke out against affiliation with the Guild, she was enraged to hear Richard Schayer, a writer who had been in the business for twenty years, insist that "screenwriting is a soft racket." He saw no reason for writers to gum up the works. "Especially when the Mothership [MGM] objects," Dorothy retorted. She was furious. For the *Screen Guilds' Magazine* she wrote a toxic rebuttal to Schayer and saracastically titled it "To Richard—With Love."

> I do not feel that I am participating in a soft racket (and what the hell, by the way, is a *hard* racket?) when I am writing for the screen. Nor do I want to be part of any racket, hard or soft, or three-and-a-half minutes. . . . I have never in my life been paid so much, either—well, why am I here, and why are you, and why is Mr. Schayer? But I can look my God and my producer—whom I do not, as do many, confuse with each other—in the face, and say that I have earned every cent of it.

Her anger at writers who "wouldn't join because they were individuals, they were artists, because it wasn't genteel, because they were ladies, they were gentlemen" did not abate either. Two years later, when a writer she was trying to persuade to join the Guild said he didn't believe that creative writers belonged in unions, she saw red. "That sonofabitch telling me that *he's* a creative writer! If he's a creative writer, I'm Marie of Rumania."

To those who feared the word *union*, she wanted to say: "Now, look, baby, 'union' is spelled with *five* letters. It is *not* a four-letter word."

After settling in Hollywood, Dorothy frequently saw Sid and Laura Perelman, who were working as a writing team at Paramount. Disenchanted with the film business, the Perelmans would instantly decamp once they had completed a picture. Dorothy paid careful attention when they began extolling the virtues of the farm they had purchased in Pennsylvania. Judging from their poetic description, Bucks County was an unspoiled stretch of country north of Philadelphia along the Delaware River, a place where the eye beheld vistas on every side that refreshed the soul, a pastoral retreat of covered bridges and stone barns, gently rolling hills, and unpretentious hamlets that might have graced the Cotswolds before the advent of the Industrial Revolution. In other words, it sounded everything that Beverly

Hills was not. The Perelmans reported that even though the area had been invaded by artists and writers, property was still relatively inexpensive. There were bargains to be found if one made the effort.

These delirious references to Bucks County began to intrigue Dorothy. She found herself growing receptive to the idea of trees and grass, vegetation synonymous in her mind with suburban living. Suddenly she was struck by a gloomy thought.

"We haven't any roots, Alan," she said. "You can't put down roots in Beverly Hills. But look at Laura and Sid—they've got *roots*, a place to come home to. Roots, roots."

Alan's eyes were already misty. As he too warmed to the prospect of becoming a country squire, the interior decorator lurking within came bubbling to the surface. Nothing like their home on North Roxbury Drive would do, nothing that came equipped with washing machines and stainless-steel kitchens. Instead, he visualized a place they could refurbish to suit their tastes, the kind of old house that had character.

They visited New York in July. It was a slow, sultry journey in a baking-hot compartment. When they reached Kansas, Dorothy wired Sara and Gerald, cheerfully swearing that the next time she crossed the continent by railroad it would be in a coffin covered with an American flag. Once they had checked into the Surrey Hotel, they lost no time in heading to Bucks County to inspect the Perelmans' rustic paradise for themselves. Sid and Laura introduced them to Jack Boyle, Tinicum township's resident anarchist and former professional fur thief. He was usually planted on the steps of the post office spinning yarns, but he also peddled real estate in his spare time. Dorothy hit it off with the Irishman at once.

For the next few days, the Perelmans accompanied the Campbells on a tour of local farms for sale. The second property Boyle showed them turned out to be an extremely handsome Pennsylvania Dutch house in Pipersville. Set back from the main road, reached by a long, scenic lane that guaranteed complete privacy, the fieldstone house sat on 111 acres of land that boasted a panoramic view of the Delaware River valley. Boyle called the place Fox House, named he said for a family who had owned it since the Revolutionary War. Three maples shaded the fourteen-room house on the north side, an apple orchard luxuriated on the south, and about fifty yards away stood an immense stone barn. When Boyle announced an asking price of only forty-five hundred dollars, it seemed past belief and everybody's eyes widened. Sid Perelman declared that if the

Campbells hesitated, he and Laura would certainly scoop up the house themselves.

Boyle raised a warning hand. They should see the inside of the house first, he told them, because it needed a little work.

It did indeed. Poultry feathers and cobwebs blanketed the interior. The ceilings dripped plaster stalactites, and the woodwork crumbled beneath their touch. There was no cellar, and what remained of the rotting floors was carpeted with dead chickens—"not still corpses, not yet skeletons," Dorothy recalled. Most incredible of all, people were actually living there, an elderly Lithuanian couple who had established a rent-free colony a number of years ago and had been eking out a living cultivating a few fields and raising chickens. They did not welcome the appearance of potential buyers.

Dorothy and Alan, taking action forthwith, moved into a room at the Water Wheel Tavern and prepared to devote the remainder of the summer to buying and restoring Fox House.

In August, a reporter for the *Doylestown Intelligencer* stopped by the bar at the Water Wheel and asked the waitress if any celebrities had checked in. None that she knew of, she replied, but they did have a couple named Campbell, and Mrs. Campbell received mail addressed to Dorothy Parker. When Lester Trauch called to request an interview, Dorothy and Alan invited him to join them for dinner at the inn. Trauch showed up with another reporter, his friend Grace Chandler. Entertaining the local press, Dorothy abstemiously limited herself to one old-fashioned before dinner and a single brandy afterward. Alan turned on his full charm when he learned that Trauch, a theater lover, had enjoyed Alan's performance in *Design for Living*. He was terribly pleased to find a fan in the Pennsylvania boondocks. Running through Trauch's mind was what an odd couple the Campbells made. Alan, lithe as a dancer, appeared so much younger than Dorothy that "they might have been mother and son."

It became clear that buying the farm was going to be a lot more difficult than Dorothy and Alan had expected. Tom and John Ross, the legal firm they had retained to handle the closing, were having trouble with the Lithuanians. Even though they had been given notice to vacate the premises, they seemed strenuously determined to keep the Campbells out. They dramatized their protests by draping across the threshold of the front door the body of a dead groundhog. "It was August weather," Dorothy remembered, "and the groundhog had not too recently passed on." The squatters' delaying tactics angered Alan so greatly that he complained to Jack Boyle, who advised patience and reminded him that the old people had standing crops to harvest and chickens to ready for market.

"That's *their* problem," Alan said stubbornly. "Don't they realize it's costing Dottie and me seven hundred and fifty dollars a week to stay away from Hollywood?"

Actually, it was costing double that figure but fifteen hundred dollars a week would have been even less comprehensible to the Lithuanians, or to any of the Bucks County farmers for that matter.

After retaining an architect to proceed with the alterations, they decided to stay in the area to keep an eye on the work. Alan was growing restless at the Water Wheel, their room having become cramped because both of them had a habit of piling up books and magazines on the floor. Just as the room was beginning to resemble the basement of a public library and the maid was complaining about the impossibility of cleaning, the owner of the Cuttalossa Inn near Lumberville proposed closing his establishment to the public and renting the entire quarters to the Campbells. It seemed like an ideal solution, but the natives were appalled. "It was the Depression," said Lester Trauch, "and they must have been paying enough rent so that the Cuttalossa didn't need any other business. People thought this was insane. We didn't know exactly how much rent the Campbells were paying, but whatever it was seemed outrageous in our eyes."

In the middle of September, after an absence of three months, they left Fox House in the hands of a crew of workmen and raced back to the Coast by plane, the first of many such cross-country air trips. They were due to begin work at Selznick International on a picture that would be, they were told, a tragedy. This was unusual. During their two years in the business almost every one of their assignments had been a comedy, hardly surprising, for during the Depression comedies had become Hollywood's forte. Operating on the theory that people out of work would not pay to see movies about people out of work, studios were usually careful to portray a fantasy world devoid of economic hardship. Even when a serious property was purchased, it somehow wound up on the screen thoroughly fumigated of anything that might kindle a thought or resemble a message. Employed solely for her wit, Dorothy was constantly typecast by producers and accepted the fact that she would probably never be invited to work on serious features. However, this was about to change.

She did not expect much from David Selznick, the dictatorial thirty-four-year-old studio head. One of Hollywood's self-important young Turks, as recently as 1934 he had been kicking around MGM and RKO before forming his own independent company. His track record was not particularly impressive and he was hoping to recoup some of his losses with a film about Hollywood, a subject he believed the whole world found as fascinating as he did. The trouble with previous pictures on the subject, he decided, was a lack of credibility. Basing his idea for a plot on a 1932 film, *What Price Hollywood?*, he visualized a movie about a determined young woman, a country bumpkin, who turns up in Hollywood to break into pictures and marries a famous movie idol. The twist is that his career begins to nose-dive just as hers is ascending, until eventually the husband, an alcoholic has-been, feels there is no alternative except to swim out to sea toward the sunset. Although Selznick considered himself a gifted screenwriter and certainly the author of this tale, he believed that it would be unwise to give himself the credit for reasons of policy. Robert Carson and William Wellman developed a screenplay, as yet untitled. Selznick signed Dorothy and Alan as a second team to rewrite the script and beef up the final dialogue. In fact, he took no writer's contribution very seriously.

On her arrival in Hollywood in 1934, Dorothy had made an important discovery. Everybody seemed to believe they were writers. Guards at the studio gates expounded story ideas and messenger boys bearing interoffice memos felt no qualms about suggesting dialogue. The worst offenders in this respect were producers. Evidently, Selznick believed that a film was capable of writing itself. Some years later, he openly discounted the efforts of Dorothy and Alan, as well as Carson and director William Wellman, by insisting that ninety-five percent of the dialogue in *A Star Is Born* "was actually straight out of life and was straight 'reportage,' so to speak." That autumn he irritated Dorothy with his habit of flapping into her office around six o'clock, just as she and Alan were preparing to go home. They would spring to attention while he rejected their handiwork by beginning, "No, not this," and then they would be compelled to stay late changing it. Equally irksome were the afternoons when he would march in with a page of dialogue he had composed and fling it on her desk.

The following spring, the Campbells went to see *A Star Is Born* when it opened at Radio City Music Hall. They apparently were pleased with their work because in an interview, Dorothy pointed proudly to the script as an example of the progress Hollywood was making in respect to realism. She said happily that producers were discovering "that people, once given the chance, would be as partial to good pictures as they once were to bad ones."

Upon reflection, she felt that she had contributed nothing of significance to Selznick's Technicolor opus, which may account for her subsequent negativity when she expressed surprise that anyone considered *A Star Is Born* a memorable picture. She also liked to pretend that she had never seen the entire film: "I went to see it, all alone, for a few minutes, and I came out, all alone." Dorothy and Alan, with Robert Carson, were nominated for an Academy Award for the screenplay, but they failed to win (the award went to the writers of *The Life of Emile Zola*). Carson and Wellman picked up the film's only Oscar for Best Original Story. At the Oscar presentations, Wellman accepted the award and then rendered homage by marching it straight over to Selznick: "Take it, you had more to do with winning it than I did."

All the while, Dorothy and Alan, busy nesting, had their minds elsewhere. Rebuilding the farmhouse was exciting, and they devoted so many hours to studying blueprints that Alan later used them to paper a wall in the upstairs hall. They spent a great deal of time toying with color schemes, leafing transfixed through endless catalogues full of furniture, hardware, and Early American accessories. They intended the completed Fox House to be a dream.

Another dream also seemed to be coming true that autumn. At the age of forty-three, Dorothy found herself pregnant. It looked as if a totally new phase of her life was about to begin. Over the years she had expressed her longing to "have babies," as she put it. She and Alan were jubilant and regarded her conception as a miracle, but anxiety about her chances for carrying a baby to term made them cautious about announcing the news. Privately, she talked about little else and began to knit baby clothes.

Once she passed the first trimester in December and revealed her pregnancy to friends, she developed a baby mania. She was soon beleaguered with requests for interviews and photographs. In response to a query from Hollywood gossip columnist Louella Parsons, she and Alan wired: HOW DID YOU KNOW BEFORE WE DID? DOCTOR SAID SOMETIME IN JUNE. Some of her friends regarded this publicity as inappropriate. Frances Goodrich had known Dorothy in New York before she and husband Albert Hackett arrived at MGM to write the *Thin Man* films. Goodrich found Dorothy's behavior pathetic:

When she knew she was pregnant, she called up Hedda Hopper and Louella Parsons to give them the scoop. In God's name! Dottie Parker announcing she's going to have a baby when she's forty-five or something, nature's last attempt. And knitting for the cameras!

Despite the love Dorothy routinely lavished on her dogs, few people could imagine her as a mother. "She was great with dogs," said a friend. "A dog couldn't talk back and couldn't top her jokes. But I thought she would grow very bored with motherhood. She didn't have the staying power." Another skeptic questioned whether it was possible for her "to have anything in common with children because they didn't drink." There were jocose predictions that the baby, accustomed to imbibing in utero a liquid diet of martinis and French brandy, would emerge tight and need a cup of coffee. Nobody doubted that Alan would make an exceptional father because his rapport with children was plain to see. Thomas Guinzburg has vivid recollections from his childhood of the Campbells' visiting his parents. He remembers Alan's extraordinary ease with himself and his sister, his sense of fun and mischief, and how ready he was for a romp. "He would be with us in the kitchen, shooting with a water pistol and spraying the cook, and I thought I'd get blamed." Dorothy remained in the drawing room.

"Oh my," Guinzburg once overhead her say, "if only the Guinzburg children were as well behaved as the Guinzburg dogs."

They flew to New York for the Christmas holidays. Even though no sign whatever of trouble had arisen thus far, sometime during the week between Christmas and New Year she miscarried. Her physical recovery was fairly rapid, because less than two weeks later she attended a birthday tea at Adele Lovett's home, where she partied with Marc Connelly, John O'Hara, and Averell Harriman. Dick Myers wrote to his wife Alice Lee that she was "looking well after her mishap." She managed to contain her feelings, deliberately minimizing the seriousness of the loss to her friends. During her New York stay, the Murphys were in Saranac Lake, New York, where Patrick had taken a turn for the worse. He died at the end of January, after an eight-year battle with tuberculosis.

When faced with loss in the past, her typical response had been an attempt at self-destruction or a major depression, followed by efforts to survive by literary description. Now the situation was different. She had grown immeasurably stronger during her marriage. She had felt no suicidal impulses for several years—and Alan was there to offer comfort. Following the standard advice given in the case of failed pregnancies, she did her best to forget the incident as quickly as possible by getting pregnant again. After returning to California, she began infertility tests. During that winter, mourning one pregnancy and trying to achieve another, she worked on a second Selznick comedy, *Nothing Sacred,* and did her best to produce amusing dialogue.

By spring, Fox House was finally ready for occupancy. A new cellar, a well, and electricity had been installed. They did not have a telephone because the phone company was asking three thousand dollars to bring in the lines to Pipersville, charges Dorothy and Alan considered prohibitive. They decided it would be refreshing to live "sweet and peaceful and sequestered." The task of transforming the place into a home was left to Alan, but Dorothy agreed with his plan to pass up safe neutral tints in favor of a variety of styles and colors. The result was an unusual mixture of Colonial, Empire, and Victorian, with a few advanced touches such as indirect lighting, a style local wits derided as Pipersville Modern. Alan's efforts delighted her but were judged to be in impossibly bad taste by some of their friends, who were swift to voice their opinions. Dorothy later excused his excesses by claiming that the interior design was a deliberate protest against the theory that present-day country dwellers ought to live like Early Americans.

The house looked extremely cheerful and felt comfortable. The living room contained ten shades of red, including shrimp walls, Chinese red carpeting, and a wing chair upholstered in pink chintz with a large floral pattern. It was like sitting in the middle of a bowl of cherry Jell-O, but Dorothy admired the room and decided that the rosy tones made her look younger. The master bedroom was painted deep marine blue, a spacious dressing room was built, and space made for three dog beds so that a few of their nine animals could always sleep with them. Alan's pièce de résistance was lining the deeply recessed windows in the dining room with sheets of mirror to reflect the orchard beyond. Dorothy loved the idea but visitors rolled up their eyes at each other. They believed that Alan had ruined the old windows.

Having decorated the interior without making concessions to Bucks

County custom, the Campbells next set to work landscaping the grounds. Near the house stood a grove of trees, "a clump of sickly, straggly maples" as Dorothy described them, that blocked her view of the meadows. With little thought to the matter, she and Alan had the trees chopped down. When word of this desecration circulated among their writing friends, everyone expressed horror. Fifty years later, the cutting of the trees still had not been forgotten. Writer Joseph Schrank observed, "They weren't content to citify the house, but then they started cutting down trees. It was terrible. Dottie didn't give a damn, but the writers out there were incensed, and I remember how one playwright swore he was going to write a play about it."

Dorothy found the fuss incomprehensible. "Fifty-second Street Thoreaus," she sniffed.

Sid Perelman gazed out over the spot where the offending maples had once stood. "You must have needed the wood pretty bad," he told her.

This was the last straw. Indignant, she banned the Perelmans from Fox House for a time.

Several years later, she got her revenge on Bucks County tree lovers. At a cost of nearly thirty-five thousand dollars, Moss Hart had transformed his New Hope estate practically overnight by planting thousands of pines, elms, and maples, but Dorothy remained unimpressed. When she saw the trees, she said that it only showed what God could do if He had money.

Their first months in Fox House was a period of exceptional contentment. Alan's homemaking pleased Dorothy. She was particularly delighted with the stone statue of Bacchus that he bought for the garden, and she also admired his cleverness with tools. After she complained about the long trip between the porch and the kitchen—she had to walk the entire length of the house for a drink—he built a chest to hold bottles, glasses, and an ice bucket. It was laboriously decorated with scrolls and colored flowers, but what made it truly beautiful was the love that had gone into it.

It turned out that owning a country place was a little more complicated than they had anticipated. Hiring a man to handle the farm work was not a problem. He moved into the barn apartment with his family and planted their acreage with fodder corn, oats, and soybeans, as the government directed. Besides ploughing, harvesting, and functioning as gardener and handyman, Hiram Beer looked after the car and fed the animals. They were not so fortunate with other servants, despite Alan's boast when they first bought the farm that people could always be found to run it—not in Bucks

County, a community of mainly farmers. A succession of imported live-in couples began—none of them stuck around for long. In time, Alan was compelled to bring a man from Richmond to drive the Packard. He was, Joseph Schrank recalled, "the only black uniformed chauffeur I ever remember seeing in Bucks County."

In Alan's capable hands, Fox House operated efficiently, at least most of the time. Dorothy had little interest in the household, nor did she even spend much time out of doors. She claimed that she loved the idea of gardening—in theory. The truth was, she left it to Hiram Beer. "I'm awfully lazy about it—and the weeds are so much quicker than I am." Like the dogs, who were confused by the farm and needed coaxing to venture out to the porch, she remained at heart a city person who always found nature an acquired taste. Her idea of country life was sleeping until mid-afternoon, then spending a few hours reading, knitting, or chainsmoking until it was time to dress for dinner. Sometimes the chauffeur would run her into Frenchtown, New Jersey, the nearest town of any size, to visit her hairdresser, but Mary McDonald did not mind driving out to the farm to do her nails and hair.

Much of their social life was with the Perelmans, whose house was located in Erwinna, and with Ruth and Augustus Goetz who lived in nearby Keller's Church. [Gus Goetz was an ex-stockbroker. Several years later the Goetzes became playwrights with successful dramatic collaborations such as *The Heiress* and *The Immoralist*.] When it was the Campbells' turn to entertain, their dinner parties ran along predictable lines. Meals were served quite late, sometimes before 11:00 P.M. but more frequently later, because Dorothy enjoyed a lengthy cocktail hour. Ruth Goetz noticed that "she drank her martinis with real thirst, as if she were having ice tea on a hot day."

As the evening wore on, Alan would dance back and forth to the kitchen, where the cook was marking the time, which was transforming her meal into a blackened mess. Dorothy never ventured into the kitchen. When the dinner could be delayed no longer, she strolled into the dining room as if she were as much a guest in the house as the Goetzes or the Perelmans. By this time, everyone was so inebriated that no one cared about the meal.

At her hungriest, Dorothy managed only slight interest in food. When the Campbells were invited out, she always got down a little of anything put before her and, like a mannerly child, made a point of whispering, "Oh, that's lovely." Said Ruth Goetz, "She overthanked you when she arrived and overthanked you when she left." At Fox House, if Alan happened to be absent or the cook had quit, Dorothy didn't eat.

Houseworkers constantly disappeared. "It was the weird hours," Roy Eichel guessed. "Dottie and Alan went to bed half-drunk at four in the morning and then slept until the next afternoon. They expected their help to stay up till dawn cleaning up and then to be awake whenever they got up. They had a terrible time keeping people because nobody wanted to live like that." It was not unusual for weekend guests to come downstairs on Sunday morning and find the cook gone. Before they knew it, they were preparing their own breakfast and Dorothy's as well.

In the winter of 1936, during a brief trip to New York, Dorothy met Alan's mother, who had come up from Virginia. Horte Campbell was outraged over her son's marriage to a woman only twelve years younger than herself. As Marc Connelly remembered, she was so mad "about his marrying this horrible creature that her southern pride near could have blown up the entire United States," and he watched "the little forks coming out of Horte's eyes" whenever she looked at her daughter-in-law. Throughout the visit, which Dorothy likened to "a cycle of Cathay," Horte kept muttering that the rigorous climate was killing her. The other Mrs. Campbell also took pleasure in calling attention to her daughter-in-law's age by addressing her, sweetly, as "my little daughter." Dorothy put up a show of cordiality while privately gnashing her teeth and mocking Horte's southern accent, saying that she was the only woman alive who pronounced the word egg as if it had three syllables.

After they moved to Bucks County, Horte complained of feeling lonely in Richmond and insisted she could be helpful to Dorothy and Alan if she were to live at the farm. It was not hard to figure out what was on her mind. She schemed to stay in the house during their absence once when they flew back to Hollywood for an assignment. Dorothy said, only half-jokingly, "She fired our farmer—and oh boy, are they hard to replace—fired our servants, and set fire to the drawing room." To ward off further trouble, she proposed buying Horte a house of her own in Bucks County, which at least would prevent her from camping at the farm. In time, a cottage was found a few miles away in Point Pleasant. It was a modest house compared to Fox House, but otherwise perfectly suitable for a single person. Horte felt it lacked grandeur and enjoyed referring to it as her "rotten lil ole shayukah," pronouncing shack in three syllables. Dorothy fumed, "The fact that Alan and I bought her the 'shayukah' at great expense, and kept it going at greater, means nothing."

Nor did the gift of the house solve the problem of Horte's interference in their lives. Quite the opposite: Living nearby merely enabled her to drop in whenever she liked, although in the winter she usually returned to Virginia. Her presence sometimes annoyed Alan more than Dorothy. Lillian Hellman and Dorothy were once knitting before the living room fireplace while Alan and his mother were upstairs quarreling. As the afternoon wore on, it began to snow, and Dorothy heaped more wood on the fire until it was built high. The silence in the room was broken only by bloodcurdling shouts and recriminations that drifted down from the second floor. Dorothy sighed but made no comment. Suddenly, the racket stopped and Alan came pounding down the stairs. When he appeared in the living room, he immediately began to vent his anger on their fire.

"It's as hot as hell in here," he said balefully.

"Not for orphans," Dorothy replied.

One morning a young man knocked at the back door of Ruth Goetz's house in Keller's Church. He introduced himself as a Communist Party organizer for Bucks County, who had got her name from the rolls of the New York office. "From now on," he told her, "you'll be paying your dues to me every month." After she handed over her fifty cents, he asked directions to Pipersville, specifically to Fox House. Until then, Ruth was unaware of Dorothy's connection with the C.P.

Subsequently, the same young man appeared regularly in the neighborhood to collect dues and to conduct informal meetings. Usually the group consisted of Dorothy and Ruth with their husbands, who, Ruth recalled, "looked upon us as if we were mad women. Alan was absolutely agreeable and Gus always said, 'Well, if that's the way you feel—' We believed there was a war coming, and we were all very concerned about politics at that time." Sometimes Sid and Laura Perelman appeared but from no particular desire to study Marxism. Laura, open-minded about the subject, indicated willingness to learn, but Sid was very apparently bored.

Ruth Goetz believed that Dorothy's allegiance to the C.P. lasted about two years. She recalled a particular meeting when "this poor inexperienced boy thought he was going to have a grouping of the faithful for his lecture on Karl Marx. It turned out to be a slim evening for him, because we all asked difficult questions." Long before Stalin drew up his nonaggression pact with Hitler in 1939, she was busy knitting socks for the British army. Dorothy also carried a knitting bag, said Goetz. "We both were knitting for England. Our affiliation with the Party was over."

Dorothy did not, in fact, share Ruth Goetz's disgust about Stalin's purge of his political enemies. Dorothy endorsed the verdicts. In April 1938, she and Alan were among one hundred and fifty American artists and educators who signed a statement declaring that the evidence presented during the Moscow trials established "a clear presumption of the guilt of the defendants." Furthermore, the signers urged support for the Soviet Union, because it was struggling to free itself from "insidious internal dangers."

It is impossible to determine the degree of Dorothy's involvement with the Communist Party. A number of her nonpolitical friends were convinced of her membership, for no better reason than she subscribed to the *Moscow News*. Ring Lardner, Jr., a member of the C.P.'s Hollywood section, recalled that she and Alan joined together. "It was quite brief. They belonged to a special group that was sheltered [by the Party] and kept away from meetings. Shortly afterward, they went off to Paris. I don't think they picked up the membership after they came back to Hollywood." Writer Budd Schulberg, he said, "recruited them."

Schulberg, another Hollywood Party member in the late thirties, said that he did not remember specifically recruiting Dorothy nor did he know for certain that she was a member. "Everyone at that time knew she was sympathetic," he said. He added that "there were people who made contributions without actually joining. There was a gray area."

There was no doubt about her feelings. She believed that Communism was the great crusade of her time, the U.S. Communist Party the one movement from which great deeds might emerge, the only political party where there was love, even rapture, to be got and given. She was vulnerable to such systems. During the 1930s, she lent the Party the prestige of her name. She joined more than thirty organizations, including the Friends of the Abraham Lincoln Brigade, the Southern Conference for Human Welfare, the League of Women Shoppers, and the International Workers Order. She contributed money to these organizations, which would later be described as Communist fronts, and permitted them to list her as a sponsor on their letterheads and fund-raising appeals. She was convinced they were worthy causes. It never occurred to her to ask probing questions about their origins or how the collected money was actually spent.

While there is much to suggest that she joined the Communist Party, there is no conclusive evidence to prove that she actually did so. Some claim that she became a secret member, and it is easy to imagine how enticing she would have found such an idea. When the Federal Bureau of Investigation subsequently attempted to establish her membership, their efforts failed. In 1947, reviewing its files on her, the Bureau put together a nineteen-page memorandum that summarized her activities during the previous decade. After a biographical blurb taken from *Who's Who in America* and a list of her publications, also copied verbatim from *Who's Who*, the memo went on to address the subject, "Evidence of Communist Party Membership and Affiliation." The following six pieces of evidence were presented:

> On May 6, 1937, an anonymous outside source advised that Dorothy Parker was among those who had contributed to the Communist Movement.

> A report received by the Bureau from G-2, dated October 23, 1940, described Dorothy Parker as a Communist Party member, writer for New Masses, member of the "Stinkers Committee," and a signer of the "Let Stalin Alone" letter.

> Time Magazine in its publication of January 6, 1941, in an article on "The Revolt of the Intellectuals," described Dorothy Parker as an ally of the Communists in 1938 although not a Communist herself. She was called a fellow traveler who wanted to help fight Fascism.

> The Washington Times Herald of September 8, 1941, carried an article saying that Congressman Martin Dies had accused Leon Henderson, director of the Office of Price Administration, of being a Communist. He referred to Henderson's argument with a photographer at his home when the photographer

271

tried to take a photograph of a nationally prominent Communist. The article said that Henderson identified the Communist as being Dorothy Parker.

xxxxxxxxxxxxxxxxxxxxxxxxxxxxxxxxxxxxxxxxxxxxxxx
xxxxxx* said that he had been advised by xxxxxxxxxxxx
xxxxxxxxxxxx* that Dorothy Parker had broken all her ties
with the Communist Party.

xxxxxxxxxxxxxxxxxxxxxxxxxxxxxxxxxxxxxxxxxxxxxxx
xxxxxxxxxxxxxxxxxxxxxxxxxxxxxxxxxxxxxxxxxxxxxxx.*

Nineteen forty-seven, the year that this memo was compiled, was a dangerous time for those holding leftist beliefs. Membership in a list of supposedly subversive organizations drawn up by the Attorney General's office branded people disloyal and therefore unemployable. In Hollywood, the film industry quaked when Congressman J. Parnell Thomas served forty-five actors, writers, and directors with subpoenas commanding their presence before the House Un-American Activities Committee. Of this number, nineteen unfriendly witnesses—quickly labeled the Hollywood Nineteen—refused to cooperate. Ten who were eventually cited for contempt of Congress served prison terms.

Lillian Hellman provided an account of Dorothy's experience with HUAC in her memoirs. She claimed that when the subpoena arrived, she offered to accompany her to the hearing. Dorothy looked puzzled and asked "Why, Lilly?" Hellman interpreted this to mean that she regarded the ruling classes as nothing more than people who had more money than she did. Hellman went on to commend Dorothy's hauteur before the Committee, as if she were telling them, "Yes, dear, it's true that I'm here to observe you, but I do not like you and will, of course, say and write exactly that."

As with so many of Lillian Hellman's memories, this simply was not true. Dorothy was not among those who received a pink slip in 1947, nor was she summoned as a witness in the HUAC hearings during the early fifties, because the government must have known that it had a weak case. Dorothy herself made two rather emphatic statements on the subject. In

*Material deleted by the Federal Bureau of Investigation on the grounds that it falls under one or more of the Freedom of Information Act's nine exemptions (e.g., unwarranted invasion of privacy, damage to national security).

1937, she wrote that she belonged to no political party, her only group affiliation having been with "that not especially brave little band that hid its nakedness of heart and mind under the out-of-date garment of a sense of humor." Fourteen years later, she denied having ever been a Party member, although it is easy to understand that the circumstances under which she made the statement might have warranted the stretching of the truth.

In 1937, after the Communist Party decided to form alliances with nonrevolutionary groups like the Democratic party, Hollywood began to resemble a tropical rain forest that teemed with lush varieties of political ideologies and activities. In this steamy atmosphere of the Popular Front, the distinctions between Communism and home-grown American liberalism tended to blur.

An interesting paradox began to develop in the C.P. On the one hand, it was a fairly accessible organization—all that was required to obtain information was listening. Even the indifferent—and Dorothy was far from indifferent—had difficulty avoiding both the C.P. gospel and C.P. members. All over town they could be encountered at Chasen's or Screen Writers Guild meetings or the studio commissaries.

At the same time, an air of secrecy had grown up around the Hollywood C.P. Chiefly, this seems to have been a result of the Party's doctrine of expediency—the notion that there was little to gain if they frightened the people they wanted to influence by waving radical ideas under their noses. As C.P. functionaries have since explained, it was standard procedure for Party members active in politics or union organizing, particularly in the Screen Writers Guild, to avoid open participaton in Party work. Contributing to the secrecy was the fact that the Hollywood C.P. did not issue membership cards. Ring Lardner, Jr., later stated that the organizatonal secretary probably kept a list of members in order to record dues payments, but most likely even that used pseudonyms or partial names. Lardner and Dalton Trumbo ridiculed the C.P. cards reading "Ring L." and "Dalt T." that HUAC produced at the 1947 hearings of the Hollywood Ten.

The fact that some found the melodrama of belonging to a secret society appealing does not seem remarkable in an industry whose product was fantasy. Ring Lardner recalled that during telephone conversations he made from his MGM office, he referred to Party meetings as poker games. Meetings were generally sheltered events held in private homes, where people sat around with drinks in their hands, so that the gathering would look like a cocktail party if an outsider happened to barge in. One writer stashed his library of Marxist literature in a secret compartment of his bar. Others concealed their political activities from wives or lovers. Lillian Hellman wrote that, despite her attendance at three or four C.P. gatherings with Dashiell Hammett, with whom she was living at the time, he never divulged whether or not he was a member. She suspected that he joined in 1937 or 1938, but she never asked "and if I had asked would not have been answered," a state of affairs that she attributed to the peculiar nature of their relationship.

The main person to connect Dorothy with being a secret member of the Party was Martin Berkeley, an ex-Communist screenwriter (*My Friend Flicka*) who appeared as a cooperative witness before HUAC in 1951 and managed to win a good deal of publicity by naming 158 individuals whom he claimed had been C.P. members in the thirties. Berkeley testified that he knew exactly when—mid-June 1937—the Hollywood section of the Party had been organized because it had taken place at his home, since his place had a big living room and ample parking facilities. Among those who showed up, he said, were five prominent writers: Dorothy Parker, Alan Campbell, Donald Ogden Stewart, Lillian Hellman, and Dashiell Hammett. He went on to say that after the meeting at his house he never saw any of those five writers again. Curious, he asked his Party superior about their whereabouts and was told they had been assigned to a group known as "party members at large," that he had seen the last of them as far as organizational meetings were concerned. A member at large, Berkeley explained to the Committee, meant that "you are pretty important and you don't want to be exposed." It was his guess that the important writers had ended up meeting secretly with Party functionaries like John Howard Lawson or V. J. Jerome to receive instructions but otherwise had no contact, for their own protection as well as for that of the Party.

Accusations such as Berkeley's destroyed Dorothy's career during the fifties. Unable to find work as a screenwriter, she paid dearly for her transgressions, real or invented, but she never called attention to her plight, never singled herself out as exceptional or in any way worthy of admiration, in contrast to Lillian Hellman who felt compelled to exalt her behavior. Dorothy declined to speak of her politics, past or present. When an interviewer once tried to question her about the political consciousness in Hollywood during the 1930s, she affected not to understand the question. "I haven't the faintest idea about the politics of Hollywood, and you make me laugh when you speak of them."

Living in Pennsylvania and working in California meant the expense of supporting two establishments, but the money continued to roll in. In May 1937, Dorothy and Alan signed a five-year contract with Samuel Goldwyn at a combined weekly salary of fifty-two hundred dollars. The new contract was respectfully reported by the press, for that amount was remarkable by anyone's standards and close to the upper limit of salaries being paid to screenwriters. Returning to Hollywood on June 7, they moved into the Beverly Wilshire Hotel, where Alan abruptly—and inexplicably—began to institute economies. Contending that the hotel was expensive and noisy, he rented a house in Beverly Hills and hired a single servant. This about-face toward spartan living failed to please him either. He described their new quarters at 710 North Linden Drive as "hideous."

At first they liked the studio. As the name plates on the doors of the Writers' Building attested, Sam Goldwyn made a practice of hiring top-quality writers. In the office next to theirs was their friend Lillian Hellman.

The picture that Dorothy and Alan had been signed to work on was called *The Cowboy and the Lady*, a romantic comedy intended for Merle Oberon and Gary Cooper. It had already run through several titles and an equal number of writers, including Anita Loos and John Emerson, but the Campbells were entrusted with writing the final draft. They soon discovered that while Goldwyn wanted only the most important writers, his disregard for their work was no different than other Hollywood producers'. When the new script failed to satisfy him, they were yanked off the project and reassigned to *The Goldwyn Follies*, a musical blockbuster that was to make use of beautiful women, outstanding comics, Gershwin music and lyrics, and George Balanchine dances. All that it lacked was a decent script. Once again a band of writers had preceded Dorothy and Alan, who, remembering their fifty-two hundred a week, struggled to devise still another version. While Goldwyn seemed pleased, he thought it could use a fresher finish and eventually showed their draft to Ben Hecht, who talked him out of it and into a completely new one written by himself. When *The Goldwyn Follies* did poorly, Dorothy and Alan cackled with glee. Hecht had claimed the sole writing credit for himself.

Finally, Goldwyn shifted them to another project that had been worked over by practically every writer on the lot. *You Can Be Beautiful* was supposed to tell the story of an entrepreneur like Elizabeth Arden or Helena Rubenstein, a woman who revolutionizes the beauty business. For the movies, she had to be beautiful and happy. When Dorothy was asked for a new twist, she proposed making the heroine plain as a pancake, a contented duckling who is transformed into an unhappy beauty. Garson Kanin remembered Goldwyn's reaction:

> "God *damn* it, Dottie!" he thundered. "You and your God damn sophisticated jokes. You're a great writer. You're a great poet." He paused, frowning in an effort to recall something. He quoted, " 'Men never make a pass at girls wearing eyeglasses.' That's a great poem and you wrote it. You're a great wit. You're a great woman, but you haven't got a great audience and you know why? Because you don't want to give people what they want."
>
> Dorothy's wide, innocent face looked up at him. "But Mr. Goldwyn," she said softly, "people don't *know* what they want until you *give* it to them."
>
> "You see that?" said Goldwyn to the world. "You just did it *again*. Wisecracks. I told you there's no money in wisecracks. People want a happy ending."
>
> Dottie rose. "I know this will come as a shock to you, Mr. Goldwyn," she said, "but in all history, which has held billions and billions of human beings, not a single one ever had a happy ending."
>
> She left the room.
>
> Goldwyn surveyed those of us who remained. "Does anybody in here know what the hell that woman was talking about?"

No doubt they did but nobody dared try to explain it.

Back in the summer of 1936, the Screen Writers Guild had disbanded, but it looked as if it was about to rise phoenix-like from its ashes. Dorothy threw herself wholeheartedly into making sure it did. Even though the studios believed the Guild had died, a handful of people had kept it alive for the past year by meetings at private homes, Dorothy and Alan's among them. An unpublished poem Dorothy wrote during the days of clandestine organizing was titled "The Passionate Screen Writer To His Love." Its opening stanza provoked grins among screenwriters in 1937 and Marc Connelly carefully preserved it among his papers:

> Oh come, my love, and join with me
> The oldest infant industry.
> Come seek the bourne of palm and pearl,
> The lovely land of Boy-Meets-Girl,
> Come grace this lotus-laden shore,
> This Isle of Do-What's-Done-Before.
> Come, curb the new, and watch the old win,
> Out where the streets are paved with Goldwyn.

The Guild had been waiting for a favorable ruling by the Supreme Court on the constitutionality of the Wagner Act. When this happened on April 12, the Guild lost no time in drafting a petition for a National Labor Relations Board hearing. The studios had insisted all along that writers were artists, therefore ineligible to unionize. The hearing would be a test case to see whether or not writers could be considered labor.

Less than two weeks after Dorothy's return to Hollywood, the Guild held its first open meeting at the Hollywood Athletic Club. More than four hundred writers showed up. Despite Red-baiting charges that the Communists were responsible for reforming the Guild, the slate of officers and board members elected that evening demonstrated a nice balance between conservatives, liberal Democrats, and those known to be left-wingers. Dorothy was elected to the board.

The union organizing went on for more than a year until the National Labor Relations Board ruled in June 1938 that screenwriters did indeed qualify as workers under the Wagner Act. A certification election held that same month allowed them to choose either the Screen Writers Guild or the more conservative Screen Playwrights as their representative. The Screen Writers Guild won by a vote of more than four to one.

Though the Guild did not win its first contract until 1941, nine years after the organizing had begun, the battle had been won. Dorothy thought that "the bravest, proudest word in all the dictionaries" was *organize*, but she was realistic enough to believe "that if a screenwriter had his name across the Capital Theatre in red, white, and blue letters fifty feet tall, he'd still be anonymous."

Chapter 14

BAD FIGHTS

•

1937–1941

Hollywood offered an uncommonly rich lode of raw material for satire. Although Dorothy loathed the place, she was unable to write anything about it. Instead, she merely looked on while friends published their observations in books for which she often composed laudatory reviews. Nathanael West finished *The Day of the Locust*, Budd Schulberg wrote *What Makes Sammy Run?*, and Sid Perelman reeled out sulfurous pieces ridiculing the movie titans who "forgather in their knotty-pine libraries beside the murmurous Pacific" while cigar smoke "wreathes their Renoirs." Scott Fitzgerald, who was eventually inspired to write *The Last Tycoon* about the legendary Irving Thalberg, arrived in Hollywood during the summer of 1937. Seeing him again triggered Dorothy's guilt about abandoning her fiction writing.

Dorothy's former drinking companion looked pale and his hair had begun to thin, but he was unquestionably functional. He explained with great pride that he had been on the wagon for ten months. He moved into the Garden of Allah, where he lived chastely and consumed huge quantities of Coca-Cola. Scott was struggling to deal with serious troubles. Zelda had been diagnosed as incurable and would probably remain hospitalized for the rest of her life. Since he was barely earning a living lately, he was delighted when his agent secured him a six-month contract at MGM, where he was to be paid a thousand dollars a week.

Dorothy tried to head off his reproaches about her lack of productivity by taking the offensive and warning him that screen writing was exhausting work. When she spoke about the impossibility of serving two masters,

Fitzgerald scoffed and retorted that he planned to get up early and write before reporting to MGM. He wrote to Max Perkins that Dorothy's trouble was laziness. What he failed to realize was how much of her energy was directed into the Communist Party and the Screen Writers Guild. What he did know of these activities only made him suspicious. Having always found her basically self-concerned—a "spoiled" writer, he said—he did not believe that her conversion to Communism had any effect on her "supremely indifferent" attitude toward others.

Dorothy sought to lure Fitzgerald into radical politics by inviting him to social-cum-political functions. One of the memorable events of that summer was Ernest Hemingway's arrival in July with a documentary film about the Spanish war. Dorothy made sure that Scott was invited to the private benefit screening at the home of Fredric March. The politically concerned element in the movie business turned out in force to see *The Spanish Earth,* a film that Hemingway had shot with Dutch director Joris Ivens and for which he also had written and recorded the narration. Frankly partisan in its support of the Spanish Republic, it demonstrated the anguish of the people and the way that war had affected their lives. After a screening at the White House for the Roosevelts, Hemingway was now hoping to obtain commercial distribution by one of the major studios as well as contributions for the purchase of ambulances. He promised that a donation of one thousand dollars would put an ambulance in action at the front in only four weeks. Dorothy, who had invested five hundred dollars in the film, was one of the few guests to buy an entire ambulance.

Lillian Hellman later wrote that after the screening Dorothy and Alan invited Hemingway, Fitzgerald, and a number of other friends to their house for a nightcap. According to Hellman, she accepted the offer of a lift from Fitzgerald, whom she described as acutely melancholy, perhaps even suffering delirium tremens, because he drove along at ten miles an hour with his hands trembling on the wheel. Pulling up at Dorothy's house, he expressed fear about going in because he was on the wagon and terrified of Hemingway. "It's a long story, Ernest and me," Hellman reported him as saying. She replied that he mustn't be afraid. They entered the house hand in hand at the precise moment that Hemingway, who was standing with his back to the door, decided to heave a highball glass against the stone fireplace. The sound of the smashing glass sent Fitzgerald into shell shock. Hellman shepherded him into the kitchen, where Dorothy and Alan were fixing drinks and Dashiell Hammett was getting drunk. Hellman recalls that her appeals to Hammett to help poor "Mr. Fitzgerald" proved useless and that Hammett remarked that Ernest had no gift for portraying women but only displayed them in his fiction in order to admire them, but she was unable to recall anything more about the evening. She and Scott never met again.

But this account is not true. Hellman herself wrote that she first met Hemingway in Paris a few months later, which is confirmed by the recollection of other individuals. Moreover, on the day of the screening, Hemingway and Fitzgerald had enjoyed a convivial luncheon together with Robert Benchley, who sent Gertrude a report of their reunion. There was no indication that this meeting was anything but warm and good-humored. The morning after *The Spanish Earth* was shown, Fitzgerald sent Hemingway a telegram of congratulations.

Not long after this, Dorothy's proprietary interest in Scott's political education came to an end. She invited him to a dinner dance sponsored by the Screen Writers Guild at the Coconut Grove nightclub. As organizer of the fund-raising dinner, she reserved a large table for her personal guests, including Scott, and danced often with him during the evening. When he was alone at the table, he noticed a pretty blonde nearby and began to cast admiring glances in her direction. This was Sheilah Graham, the reporter who had interviewed Dorothy about her tattoo, now an up-and-coming Hollywood gossip columnist. In Sheilah Graham, Scott would try to find a replacement for Zelda.

Dorothy and Alan made a precipitous and disgusted departure from Hollywood in early August. After two months of frustration, they learned that Sam Goldwyn was not planning to extend their option and that their ballyhooed five-year contract would yield only $52,000 instead of a projected $1.3 million. While they had not really counted on becoming millionaires, neither had they envisioned a mere ten weeks of employment for which they would receive not a single writing credit. They certainly did not expect to be cashiered without warning. Benchley told his wife, "Their jobs blew up."

In a huff, Dorothy and Alan gave up the house on North Linden Drive and hurried back to Bucks County, where they planned to be farmers. A few days later, deciding that they deserved a holiday after the recent unpleasantness, they changed their minds and set off on a European vacation. Dorothy had not been abroad since 1932 and Alan had never been, so she was eager to conduct him around the sights. When they sailed for France aboard the *Normandie* on August 18, Lillian Hellman was with them.

On the boat they befriended Martha Gellhorn, a writer who was having an affair with Ernest Hemingway and who became his third wife after he divorced Pauline. The handsome, golden-haired Gellhorn had become involved with Hemingway while covering the war in Spain for *Collier's*. They planned to meet in Paris before returning to Spain together. The Campbells hit it off immediately with Martha Gellhorn, even though her idea of shipboard fun was an energetic workout in the gymnasium. Dorothy would rather have eaten nails than exercise, but she admired Martha's fitness and thought she was "truly fine—even leaving aside her looks and her spirit and her courage and her decency—though I can't imagine why they should be shoved aside. . . ." It turned out to be an unexpectedly enjoyable crossing, except for the pouting presence of Lillian Hellman who could not manage to conceal completely her jealousy of Gellhorn and later made catty remarks about "her well-tailored pants and good boots," as if she were covering a war for *Vogue*.

Hellman, a difficult traveling companion under the best of circumstances, continued to dampen Dorothy and Alan's gaiety once they reached Paris. She disliked Alan, whom she scorned as effete and affected. She attributed to Hemingway the remark that Alan treated his wife as if he were the manager of a champion prizefighter or movie star, a remark that may or may not be apocryphal, but one which perfectly reflected her own view of their marriage. Alan clearly worshiped Dorothy; he enjoyed ministering to her and actually sought opportunities to please her, traits conspicuously absent in Hellman's own partner.

In Paris, crowded with visitors to the World Exhibition, they checked into the Hôtel Meurice and plunged into a round of partying with Sara and Gerald Murphy, Alice Lee and Dick Myers, Janet Flanner, and Fernand Léger. One evening they had drinks with Hemingway. They also saw Ring Lardner's son Jim, who wanted to enlist in the International Brigade and fight in Spain (where he was killed a few months later). Hellman tagged along, pretending to like the Murphys and trying to conceal her contempt for their manners and money. Alan tried to ignore Hellman's animosity.

That summer in Paris, Dorothy was lionized everywhere she went. The rich and famous, Hellman recalled, "invited Dottie for dinners and country lunches and the tennis she didn't play and the pools she didn't swim in." Although Hellman pretended to feel pleased when important people courted Dorothy, she was extremely jealous. Few had heard of her, nor did she have the personality or beauty to enchant them. She admitted that her own invitations were "second-class stuff compared to Dottie's admirers." In public, she expressed amusement at Dorothy's excessively good manners, the haughtiness she would exhibit toward those who were trying to purchase her good will, but privately Hellman felt otherwise. For decades she suppressed her real feelings that the rich had indeed bought Dorothy whether she was willing to acknowledge it or not.

Hellman felt awkward around Dorothy's wealthy friends. In *Pentimento*, she described them as an older generation who continued to move in a pre-Depression world that made her uncomfortable. After a few weeks of heavy-drinking nights and headachy mornings, she began to excuse herself from their compulsive partying. The Campbells saw less of her.

In her memoirs, Hellman wrote that her presence in Paris was connected with an invitation to attend a theatrical festival in Moscow. In 1981, when Martha Gellhorn tried to confirm that such an event had actually taken place, she was unsuccessful. Hellman, who liked to endow her smallest action with significance, never admitted simply to tagging along with Dorothy and Alan.

By mid-September, the weather had turned cold and rainy. One night Dorothy ran into Leland Stowe, a Pulitzer Prize–winning foreign correspondent who had just returned from Madrid. Traveling on a leave of absence from the *New York Herald Tribune*, Stowe could talk of nothing but the events he had seen in Spain. The Loyalist cause, he said later, was "the greatest, most meaningful cause in my life up to then." When he asked Dorothy if she didn't want to do something for the Spanish, she reared up defensively and replied that she didn't wish to use their food when they had so little. Stowe advised her to fill up a suitcase with tins of French food, recommending that she donate the cans to the Spanish and dine on their wretched dishes herself.

Before this conversation with Stowe, Dorothy had not planned to visit Spain, unlike others she knew who practically regarded it as a sacred pilgrimage. One of Dashiell Hammett's biographers mentions that his desire to visit the war that summer had been refused by the Party, who thought he could be of more use at home. Dorothy had not sought Party approval for the simple reason that she was not eager to risk having her head blown off. "I couldn't imagine what it was like," and when she tried to imagine going to war she felt "scared stiff." Before she parted from Stowe, his words began to have an effect. She was "licked, and I went, and I did." Alan hurried out to buy canned goods.

During their ten days in Spain, they spent part of the time in Madrid, where they looked up Martha Gellhorn and Ernest Hemingway. "Dottie Parker is here and very nice," Gellhorn wrote to her mother, "and we had a marvelous dinner at [Herbert] Matthews." The city had been under siege for nearly a year. Despite the evacuation, a million people still lived there, the trams and restaurants crowded, the shops doing business. Dorothy learned that there was little action on the front, but the city did not seem quiet to her. All day long she could hear the dull boom of the big guns and the irritable crackle of the smaller machine guns. She had to keep reminding herself that "gunners no longer need to shoot for practice." Surprised to see that people were going about their business without hysteria, she calmed down and even went shopping like a tourist, purchasing a sheaf of war posters as souvenirs. A government employee acted as escort and interpreter because she was anxious to speak to people she met on the streets. When she asked a woman living with seven children in a bombed-out house why she had not left, she received a reasonable reply: She was waiting for her husband to come home from the front on furlough.

After a few days, Dorothy and Alan journeyed to Valencia, the capital of Republican Spain. Shortly after their arrival, the city suffered its worst air raid of the war. On a bright Sunday morning, five German planes unloaded sixty bombs on the area around the port. Afterward, Dorothy went to view the damage for herself. She never forgot the hills of rubble on which she noticed a broken doll and a dead kitten, the two small girls trying to push past guards to the house where their mother probably lay buried. That evening she and Alan visited one of the big popular cafés, where she stared mesmerized at a baby wearing a blue ribbon in her hair and where the waiter outdid himself to find a few pieces of grayish ice for the vermouths they ordered.

During their stay, Valencia was raided four times. She preferred night raids because she could anesthetize her fear to some extent by pretending it was a ballet with "scurrying figures and the great white drafts of the searchlights." In the daytime she could not avoid seeing the terror on people's faces. Most wrenching to watch were the children. She saw them on the streets with their mothers, visited the homeless in children's refugee camps, observed them in schools drawing pictures of sailboats, and stared at the faces of those who were starving. "They don't cry. Only you see their eyes. While you're there and after you're back, you see their eyes."

On October 11, she and Alan flew to Paris, which seemed like another planet—shops shocked the eye with creamy yellow butter and Brie, and charcuteries offered beefsteaks adorned with sprigs of parsley. Practically the first person they ran into was Lillian Hellman. After giving her an excited account of their trip, it was natural for them to encourage her to go. They offered advice about what to take and who to see. So persuasive were they that Hellman departed for Spain only a few days later. Describing her travels in *An Unfinished Woman,* Hellman devoted some thirty pages to her role in the Spanish war, including the time her foray into the street during an air raid elicited a compliment from Hemingway: "So you have *cojones* after all."

Despite her *cojones,* Hellman failed to mention that Dorothy and Alan had preceded her to Spain. Instead, she emphasized Dorothy's rich friends. In Hellman's version, Alan never got to play any role except a *cojones*-less swish. Martha Gellhorn, comparing Hellman's visit to Dorothy's, remembered that she and her friends pooled their canned goods to cook a decent dinner for Hellman, only to find that she arrived empty-handed. "Miss H. brought nothing but herself and unlike Dottie she was not funny," she wrote and called the reunion "a dull, grumpy dinner."

After her experiences in Spain, living on the farm made her feel restless. She wrote an article about the war for *New Masses* and began the first of several short stories. She gave newspaper interviews saying that she wished to do something for the American hospitals in Spain and declared that the Loyalist government "has to win," even though she secretly believed its cause was hopeless. "You knew darn well it was going to happen, even when you were there." At parties, she tried to contain her anger against people who asked, "Why did you want to go all the way over and get into that messy thing for? A person like you!"

In Pipersville, the enemy was "Mrs. Camp Bell," as she had begun calling her mother-in-law. Horte had no desire to hear about Spain and pointedly ignored that part of their trip. Dorothy was apoplectic. She imagined Horte lounging under a magnolia tree and waving a fan while Alan was being "bombed and shelled and machine-gunned and sniped at," and decided that her mother-in-law didn't give a damn about her son.

"Well," Horte said to Dorothy, "that old war wasn't goin' on while you were there, was it?"

"Oh, no, they stopped the war while your son was there."

"Well, I tho't so," Horte replied.

A few days after her return, Dorothy received a letter from the North American Committee to Aid Spanish Democracy, a group that the House Un-American Activities Committee later said was a Communist front organization. Sheelagh Kennedy knew about Dorothy's trip and thought she might be interested in the women's subcommittee they were organizing to undertake a campaign on behalf of Spanish children. The nonpolitical group would be a purely humanitarian effort to help refugee children facing another winter of starvation. She wondered if Dorothy might want to offer aid or advice. Dorothy, still shaken by memories of the children, replied promptly.

> Dear Miss Kennedy,
>   I want with all my heart to do anything I can in the campaign to aid Spanish children.
>   I am living here in the country, but it is a very little way from New York, and I could come in any time you might want me.
>
>   Sincerely yours,
>   Dorothy Parker

The voluminous files of this group, preserved in the Rare Book and Manuscript collection at Columbia University, are full of solicitation letters to women of means, who were likely prospects for cash donations, tickets to cocktail parties, or a loan of their homes for fund-raising parties. While many letters were mailed out, acceptances were predictably few. Sheelagh Kennedy must have been overjoyed to hear from Dorothy. She promptly telegraphed Fox House to thank Dorothy for the letter and to invite her to a meeting the very next day. Within two weeks, Dorothy had become national chairman.

In her honor, Sheelagh Kennedy arranged a luncheon that drew an enthusiastic crowd of notables, including the Spanish ambassador. Dorothy, in her address to the guests, discovered that public speaking terrified her. She managed to get a laugh by saying that she had been "scared green" in Spain, but she said she believed herself to be the only person in the country to feel frightened. She went on to praise the courage of the Spanish people. In months to come, Kennedy scheduled speaking dates for her, even though she continued to suffer intense nervousness. She believed her speeches were banal and repetitious.

But the people at the women's division thought she was wonderful, that how she sounded made little difference when her talks raised so much money for Spain.

From the first, it was clear that volunteer work was going to make heavy demands on her time, a good deal more than she had bargained for. Her holidays were taken up by fund-raising parties. She and Alan spent New Year's Eve in the Village at a charity ball for Spain because Dorothy had promised to be there. Two weeks later, they were back in the Hollywood rat race, this time working at MGM. Dorothy promptly christened their new employer Metro-Goldwyn-Merde.

When Sid and Laura Perelman gave up a job at MGM because Laura was pregnant, the Campbells were hired as their replacement. The picture was a Nelson Eddy and Jeanette MacDonald musical, an adaptation of Victor Herbert's operetta *Sweethearts*. MGM offered Dorothy and Alan two thousand dollars a week, which was double the Perelmans' joint salary, but a comedown from their last ill-fated job working for Sam Goldwyn. Even though their agent, Zeppo Marx, had managed to sweeten the deal by persuading MGM to pay the cost of their transportation from the East Coast, Dorothy did not feel the least bit appreciative.

With relish, the Perelmans proceeded to brief them on producer Hunt Stromberg's special eccentricities and the difficulties they might expect to encounter in his unit. Stromberg insisted that everyone attend a story conference so that he personally could bring his new writing team up to date.

On Monday, January 17, 1938, Dorothy, Alan, and Sid, who remained on the payroll, presented themselves at Stromberg's office. Perelman was curious to see at close range how his friends would function in "an industrial setting," far from Bucks County's parlors. Dorothy sank into the shadows of a deep armchair, put on her glasses, and brought forth her knitting from a reticule. Alan revealed himself to be "the drive train of the duo, toothy, voluble, bubbling with suggestions, charming the birds out of the trees," while Dorothy subtracted herself from the meeting, turning down her attention to a level where she appeared to be in need of oxygen. Hunt Stromberg, zigzagging back and forth with his shoelaces untied and dragging, rambled on. He puffed on one or another of his collection of pipes and had a disquieting habit of flinging around wooden matches, some of them still lit, with little regard for ash trays. Perelman pondered the article that Dorothy was knitting. Since it was gray and measured about seven feet in length, he decided it must be a carpet, most likely a staircase runner. Every now and then Stromberg interrupted his discourse to stop at Dorothy's chair.

"I'd say we were making pretty good progress, eh, Dorothy?"

Dorothy's spectacles kept sliding down her nose. Looking up uncertainly, she made an attempt to return from outer space. "Oh, I *do* think it's altogether marvelous, don't you?" This slid from her lips in a breathless rush, after which she submerged into a coma once more.

Perelman recalled how Stromberg, still in full flow, finally managed to set a fire under Dorothy. It happened on the third day of the conference when Perelman, surreally bored, was not fully awake. He became conscious of Stromberg's trailing shoelaces and his pipe, then spied an odd cloud that was beginning to wreathe Dorothy's head, almost a nimbus halo. It dawned on Perelman that it must be smoke when he heard Alan's voice.

"Dottie!" Alan screamed. "You're on fire."

But Perelman could see that

> it was just kapok, the stuffing in her chair that was touched off by one of Stromberg's matches, and it smoked and smoldered a bit after we yanked her out and rolled her on the floor. People ran in, throwing Lily Cups of water on the cushions, but the damage was piffling. The damage to the chair, that is—the damage wrought by *Sweethearts* is still being dealt with by therapists, I presume.

Sweethearts worked out remarkably well for the Campbell bank account, because they became mired in a script that failed to suit Stromberg and the job dragged on until July. In a letter to Harold Guinzburg's secretary, Alan complained about their difficulties. After many weeks of work, he said, "We have no story." He consoled himself by purchasing "a wonderful sofa . . . at bargain prices" from friends who were leaving town. Sheelagh Kennedy enriched the U.S. Post Office and Western Union with requests that Dorothy sponsor tea dances, cocktail parties, musicales, and champagne dinner dances, all of them taking place in New York. There was a serious milk shortage, and the Women's Division felt sure it could collect a thousand dollars if Dorothy appeared. Usually Dorothy sent regrets, but she did fly in for a weekend in March. She stayed at the Waldorf Towers and spoke at a meeting to raise money for powdered milk and ambulances. As always, she disliked her performance and afterward apologized to Kennedy for "my bad speech and hurried exit." In May, during a Newspaper Guild strike in Los Angeles, she marched in a picket line outside the *Hollywood Citizen-News*.

During the years 1938–1941, their joint salary stabilized at two thousand dollars a week. Among the films they worked on were *Crime Takes a Holiday* and *Flight into Nowhere* (both Columbia Pictures), *Trade Winds* (United Artists), and *Weekend for Three* (RKO). Several other films were never produced. In 1941, when Sam Goldwyn bought the film rights to Lillian Hellman's successful Broadway drama *Watch on the Rhine*, Hellman asked several friends to write additional dialogue, including Dorothy and Alan and her former husband, Arthur Kober. Kober later claimed that their contribution was so insignificant that having their names on the picture was absurd but Alan Campbell was "a little guy who needed the credit," and therefore all three names were used.

Alan's reputation as a "little guy" persisted. Many in the industry chose to regard him as an illegitimate writer riding on his famous wife's coattails. The truth was otherwise. Alan was beginning to get a few assignments on his own. Budd Schulberg believed that he was badly maligned, that Dorothy could not have held a job without him. "Her work habits were terrible, but Alan was extremely disciplined. He dragged her along. At United Artists, I watched how they worked. Alan would say, 'We start at nine A.M.'—and they would start. After he'd blocked out a scene, he'd tell her, 'We need a real zinger here,' and then Dottie would come up with lines to improve his dialogue. In his own right he was a really good screenwriter, maybe because he'd once been an actor, but nobody gave him credit."

It was fortunate that Alan had plenty of patience, because Dorothy could be a surly collaborator. While they were writing *Sweethearts* at MGM, the neighboring office was occupied by Frances Goodrich and Albert Hackett. When the door was open, they could hear Dorothy and Alan composing dialogue out loud.

"And then what does *he* say?" Alan asked.

Dorothy's answer was soft but audible. "Shit."

"Please don't use that word," Alan muttered. Turning back to his typewriter, he continued, "All right—and then what does *she* say?"

"Shit."

"Don't use that word!"

According to Albert Hackett, Alan did all the typing. "He also did all the work. He pushed Dottie." Often she would be in a complaining, critical mood. She spoke disdainfully about the money they earned, saying that they spent every penny—their paychecks melted like ice cubes. People in Hollywood got on her nerves too. At a party, she listened politely as British actor Herbert Marshall made repeated references to his busy "shedule." When she could stand it no longer, she burst out, "I think you're full of skit."

Despite her complaints, she never seriously suggested they leave Hollywood.

> You could have the most remarkable house. You could have
> a pool, if you wished. I don't swim. My goodness, you could
> have so many things. And you said to yourself while you were
> there, "For heaven's sake, I might as well live as good as I
> can while I have to be here."

Occasionally she enjoyed a wonderful laugh, as when a producer once asked her, "Now listen—are we extracting the milk of the theme?" Since extraction was tough work, she never belittled the sweat that went into screen writing. To an interviewer who suggested the work was demeaning, she quickly protested, "No, it wasn't dreadful. It was a terrible bore. It was a strenuous bore. You sat there and you sat there and you sat there. That's what it was."

After work, Alan drove them to the house they had purchased in the provinces, way out in Coldwater Canyon. She had been charmed by the place at first sight, because its authentic bar had once been part of an old San Francisco saloon. It was a comfortable small house with a large garden, perched on the side of a hill. She made no objection to the pink satin drapes and cabbage rose wallpaper Alan installed in the living room. They lived there off and on for two years. One day, she looked out the window and told Alan they would have to move immediately because there was "a suicide light" rippling on the hill behind the house.

They hastened back to the Garden of Allah, where the light did not make her think that it might be refreshing to be dead.

A newspaper reporter asked her if she would care to say a few words about her life.

By all means. It was "terrible."

Didn't she enjoy anything?

Certainly. "Flowers, French fried potatoes, and a good cry."

In the spring of 1939, Madrid fell to the Fascists, and President Roosevelt recognized the Franco government. Even though the war in Spain had been lost, the refugee situation remained grim. A half-million Spanish Republicans, having fled to France, were stranded on the French side of the frontier. Money had to be raised in America so that something could be done for them.

Dorothy was able to collect thousands of dollars in a single evening by inviting Hollywood friends to her home and calling it a party. Since she had a tendency to assume personal responsibility for world catastrophe, she gave herself no credit. She insisted that she was not doing enough to help while she complained simultaneously that raising money was "the dirtiest of all jobs." Public speaking still made her miserably nervous.

As conditions in Europe worsened during 1939, she grew more agitated about Hitler. Nazis obsessed her, and she affected to spy storm troopers behind every tree. Many people in America were unwilling to listen. Her habit of appealing to people's emotions sometimes struck them as paranoid and hysterical.

In Boston, at a Foreign Policy Association luncheon, Dorothy portrayed the Germans as demons. One of the guests, chalking her remarks up to exaggeration, thought it was a pity a more objective speaker had not been invited. In Washington, at a party for the Loyalists at the home of New Deal economist Leon Henderson, Dorothy arrived in an expensive fur coat. Sitting on a baby grand piano, she first talked calmly about the war, but soon could not keep from boiling over into angry tears. The living room was packed wall-to-wall with dry-eyed, embarrassed guests who stared at her. She began to scold. "If you had seen what I saw in Spain, you'd be serious too. And you'd be up on this piano, trying to help those people." A humorist in the year 1939 was whistling sad songs, she decided, because nothing was funny in the world anymore. Twenty-five years later, talking about the Spanish defeat remained difficult for her because, she said, "I die hard."

The Spanish Children's Milk Fund, as her group was now called, mailed out letters and signed Dorothy's name. Among those regularly solicited for contributions or labor were writers once associated with the Round Table. Robert Benchley, asked to emcee a benefit, scribbled a curt refusal. The relentless letters annoyed Edna Ferber, whose crusty all-purpose RSVP stated that she did not wish to be a patron, purchase a box seat, attend the Coq Rouge cocktail party, or support a Stars for Spain benefit, but she was enclosing five dollars for two tickets, which she did not intend to use. Bill Benét, invited to a luncheon honoring Dorothy, sent his acceptance in verse:

> Though the world grows darker
> And life grows starker,
> I'm all for a luncheon
> For Dorothy Parker.

Meanwhile, Dorothy went on appearing at rallies even though there were times when she had to wire the Milk Fund, ". . . would you send me brief encouraging wire as to what my speech is to be about." If the number of extant form letters is any measurement, great quantities of mail went out, all of this correspondence carried on by the industrious Milk Fund staff. Dorothy, who was in Pennsylvania or California, never saw the letters, a situation she would be at a loss to explain when an investigating committee questioned her about it in the 1950s.

The terrible year of 1939 was a year of personal failure for Dorothy and Alan. They collaborated on a play, an adaptation of a comedy by the

Hungarian playwright Miklos Laszlo. When they finished, *The Happiest Man* was practically a new work. The happy man of the title works for a plumbing supply company, has everything in life he wants, then the company suddenly fires him after eighteen years. Dorothy sprinkled the script with polemics, which got watered down in the end and lost some of their bite, but it was an amusing play that looked like it would reach Broadway without problems. Otto Preminger was asked to direct, Paul Muni and Burgess Meredith to play the leads. Then, for no apparent reason, producer Max Gordon dropped his option. In despair, Dorothy and Alan themselves took a six-month option and tried to get it produced. Not until 1942 did she acknowledge defeat and admit that *The Happiest Man* had gone "completely by-by."

Again, the dream of theatrical success eluded her. The closest she got to Broadway was journeying to Baltimore for the out-of-town opening of Lillian Hellman's new play, *The Little Foxes.* The title, taken from the Song of Solomon, had been Dorothy's suggestion. As if that was not frustrating enough, the Algonquin Hotel was suing her about a party she had given for Philip Barry after the opening of his new play, *Here Come the Clowns.* The unpaid bill sent Frank Case to court claiming that her guests had eaten 182 dinners and drank 730 cocktails. The court awarded the Algonquin $488.22, which Dorothy probably had never intended to pay since she always regarded the hotel as one of her patrons. Apparently, Case thought she had become rich. She told a newspaper columnist that, despite her salary, she was forced to sell her house and move to a hotel because she gave away nearly everything she earned. "Dot," Charles MacArthur remarked to Janet Flanner, "will never be happy until she is on relief."

In 1939, she became pregnant again. She took no care to curtail her activities and seemed not to care whether she lost the baby. Perhaps by this time she sensed that she would abort no matter the precautions she took, which was precisely what occurred. Afterward, suffering from a lingering, low-grade depression, she insisted she must have diabetes mellitus, until her doctor managed to convince her it simply was not true.

The miscarriage marked an important turning point in Dorothy's relations with Alan. Their marriage was never the same again, once the structural defects in its foundation slowly began to expose themselves. Entirely apart from the fact that Alan loved her deeply, he had seemed to be an ideal partner in many ways, both prescription and placebo for her ailments when she was forty. He made plausible the middle-aged woman's idyll of rejuvenation by a young lover, the alcoholic's prayer for alliance with a devoted fixer, the orphan's longing for a protective mother. On a fantasy level, Alan was practically perfect, except for the fact that he was not rich. Secretly, Dorothy had always resented his lack of a private fortune. On one occasion, after she had roundly abused him before a gathering of friends, someone reminded her that he was a charming, handsome man who adored her. What more did she want from the poor guy? "Presents," she growled. One of her most popular verses, written in 1923, expressed a belief from her childhood, that love was better when it was attached to money:

> Why is it no one ever sent me yet
> One perfect limousine, do you suppose?
> Ah no, it's always just my luck to get
> One perfect rose.

She had received many perfect roses from Alan but he was never able to present her with a limousine that her own labor had not helped to finance. She knew that his income since their marriage had depended entirely on being her husband. She also suspected that without her, his career as a screenwriter would dry up and blow away. Even though she needed him badly, he needed her even more desperately, but this subject they were unable to broach, let alone discuss. Still, for the first five years of their marriage, this trade-off and their endless mutual dependencies had been obscured by Dorothy's fruitless quest for a baby.

Marrying a thirty-year-old husband had allowed her to roll back the clock and pretend that she was his contemporary, thereby enabling her to plan for a baby as might any thirty-year-old bride. Like most Faustian bargains, this one held for a while.

She had sex faithfully, whether Alan felt like it or not, and she spent the better part of five years hanging around gynecologists' waiting rooms. Submitting herself to every infertility treatment known to medical research had resulted in at least two pregnancies (if there were more there is no record), followed by two spontaneous abortions, which had caused her a surprising amount of physical discomfort, but she had persevered without complaint.

While most people thought Alan would make a splendid father, and he himself expressed eagerness for children, Dorothy was not fully convinced. As each of her pregnancies advanced, as she began to gain weight and take on pouter-pigeon proportions, she detected subtle shifts in his feelings toward her, changes that provoked her own ambivalences about having a child. As early as a few weeks into a pregnancy, she felt roly-poly and unattractive, which accentuated the age difference between herself and Alan. The process of reproduction, by which she hoped to recall her youth, also made her look and feel her actual age and exacerbated her fears about losing Alan to a younger woman.

Another aspect of their marriage that pregnancy threatened to disturb was their child-mother relationship. A genuine child in the family would have presented Dorothy with a sibling rival. Beneath Alan's superficial enthusiasm for the idea of fathering, she detected a whispered message that he was not as interested in caring for two children as everyone assumed.

They claimed to be eager for a child, yet they never considered the obvious alternative of adoption.

After the miscarriage, her weight pushing one hundred and fifty pounds, she neglected her grooming and moaned that she wanted to shut herself in a room and push the bureau across the door. When Alan suggested they take a vacation, she scorned the idea as stupid. She could not prance off on a grand tour with all the misery and suffering in the world. Once she had whined herself out, she agreed that it might not be a bad idea after all. The whole world lay before them: "We can go *any* place our fancy takes us," Alan wrote the Goetzes, and he named the possibilities: Rome, Petrograd, Budapest, Paris, Blue Ball [Pennsylvania]. They chose Paris. Dorothy perked up and wrote to her sister, "Things have been pretty bad as I think you guess and this may be a life saver."

On June 17, they sailed on the *Veendam*, a Dutch ship that developed turbine trouble and took ten days to cross the Atlantic, during which time the bars were drunk dry. Dorothy, still portly, was irritated to learn that a number of passengers had mistaken her for Gertrude Stein. When the Paris boat train lost a car and they had to sit for hours in the countryside, Dorothy and Alan got acquainted with a group of students from Amherst and Princeton who were thrilled to meet a famous author. Dorothy's appearance disappointed them, however. John Davies thought that she was "the sloppiest woman I ever met: cracked nail polish, stringy unflattering bangs, runny makeup, broad derriere, a shapeless unfashionable pleated dress with green and white flowers." Helen Walker also noticed that "she wore more makeup than was becoming. She painted her cheeks with great round circles of rouge."

Dorothy and Alan took up residence in an elaborate apartment in Avenue Saint-Honoré-d'Eylau borrowed from actress Maxine Elliott. It was decorated in the worst possible taste and to reach the apartment it was necessary to ride an ancient elevator that habitually got stuck between the second and third floors. Alan adored the place. That summer, Janet Flanner reported in *The New Yorker* that Paris was suddenly experiencing "a fit of prosperity, gaiety, and hospitality." She described magnificent costume balls and garden parties, the air filled with music and the smell of money and the expensive hotels congested with American and English tourists. Still, the city seemed schizoid. Even though the chief topic of conversation was war—and everybody thought it was coming soon—nobody believed it would arrive that summer to spoil their holidays. At the same time, war was difficult to forget because the Germans sent planes over every night, and the drone of their circling made sleep difficult.

Dorothy enjoyed buying new hats and sipping cocktails at the Crillon Bar with Sara Murphy, Muriel King, Janet Flanner, and Louise Macy. Again, she and Alan got together with the students they met on the train, especially with Helen and Bob Walker. On the Fourth of July, the Walkers joined them at a reception at the American Embassy. When Dorothy was immediately surrounded by clusters of fans, twenty-one-year-old Helen Walker was intrigued to notice that Alan disappeared into a corner and left his wife to enjoy the limelight alone. Alan impressed Helen as "a darling, just the sweetest, most considerate man."

For all his sweetness, it was clear that something was amiss. Helen Walker had heard about Dorothy's miscarriage and knew she continued to feel depressed, so she made allowances for her irritability. Walker observed, "Dottie was never happy staying anywhere for very long and always wanted to keep moving." Alan was adept at managing her moods and made excuses when she became obnoxious. "One of the things that bothered me," said Walker, "was how hilariously funny she would be one minute and so bitter and angry the next—about the Spanish war, about people like Hemingway whom she considered hypocrites. Whenever she got caustic, Alan would tell us, 'Well, it's good for her to let out her anger.'"

It was a trying time. A few weeks later, after they had returned to Pipersville, Dorothy was dismayed to hear that the Soviet Union and

Germany had banded together in their nonaggression pact. The events during the following weeks—Hitler's march into Poland, the English and French declaration of war, and Russia's subsequent invasion of Poland—caused further grief. When the American Communist Party opposed the war and called the Soviet invasion justified, some of Dorothy's friends dropped out of the C.P. The pact also caused wholesale resignations from the Hollywood Anti-Nazi League, which weathered this setback by changing its name to the Hollywood League for Democratic Action. Dorothy did not pull out.

Out of loyalty to her friends, she did not publicly criticize either the pact or Stalin or the American Communist Party, nor did she abandon any of the groups to which she had lent her name. However great her private doubts, she hewed to the party line against the war until 1941 when Hitler broke the pact by invading Russia. Then, however, she made up for those two years of silence by supporting the war wholeheartedly.

Meanwhile, it was not pleasant to be a Communist or a fellow traveler in Hollywood, where she received severe censure from her liberal friends. Alan admitted to Aleck Woollcott that "a great many people have stopped speaking to us."

In the fall of 1940, Dorothy and Alan were invited to Sun Valley by Martha Gellhorn and Ernest Hemingway. On their return to Hollywood, Dorothy had a pelvic examination, which revealed the presence of uterine fibroid tumors, benign growths of fibrous connective tissues that occur commonly and usually go undetected because they produce no symptoms. Fibroids generally require no treatment, unless they begin to enlarge as did Dorothy's. She now learned that probably the fibroids were irritated by her pregnancies, and also may have affected her ability both to conceive and to carry a fetus to term.

Knowledge of the fibroids plummeted her into self-loathing, and she immediately imagined herself trying to pass for normal but "all the while containing a rock-garden planted with every flower mentioned in Shakespeare." The references to Elizabethan flowers could not conceal her sense of feeling gangrenous.

Standard treatment for fibroid tumors is removal of the uterus. Dorothy entered the hospital for a hysterectomy.

Alan expected major trouble to follow the operation. He telegraphed the farm and ordered her favorite dog, a Sealyham terrier, shipped out by rail as a cheery surprise. He was astonished to notice that Dorothy already seemed "quite cheerful" and looked happier and more radiant than she had appeared in a long time. Convalescing in a Beverly Hills house he had rented at 602 North Bedford, cared for by a team of Canadian nurses, she stressed her guilty contentment in a letter to Aleck Woollcott: "I am full of a peaceful, negative joy that that damned operation is over." Probably she also felt better knowing that the quest for pregnancy had ended, a relief that Alan seemed to share.

By the middle of December, Dorothy had recuperated. On Friday the thirteenth, she and Alan attended a dinner party at the home of Nathanael West and his wife, Eileen, who had been married eight months and had recently moved into a house in North Hollywood. It was a convivial evening among old friends, including Scott Fitzgerald, Elliot Paul, Frances Goodrich, and Albert Hackett. As their mood grew increasingly nostalgic, they began talking about the twenties and sang "The Last Time I Saw Paris."

The following Saturday afternoon, Scott fell dead of a heart attack while browsing through the *Princeton Alumni Weekly* and eating a Hershey bar. The next day the Wests were killed in a car crash, returning home in their Ford station wagon after a weekend hunting trip below the Mexican border. Fitzgerald was forty-four, West thirty-seven. Even though Scott had suffered a minor heart attack in November and "Pep" West was notorious as one of the most maniacal drivers ever to hit the Los Angeles freeway, Alan convinced himself that he had but a short while to live. Extremely superstitious at times, certain that Friday-the-thirteenth bad luck occurred in threes, he was petrified. Robert Benchley described him as "hiding under the bed."

Dorothy thought his behavior was silly. Her chief problem with death had always been the depressing thought that she had lacked competency to successfully do away with herself. Her imaginary hope was that on the "other side," she would be able to eavesdrop on the living and finally learn what they had been saying behind her back.

Both of her friends were laid out at Pierce Brothers Mortuaries. Visiting the funeral home, she walked down a long, carpeted corridor to reach Scott's casket, which had been placed on view in the William Words-worth Room. She and Alan were among the few people in Hollywood who came to pay their respects. The embalmer had worked on Scott's features to make him look youthful. Not a line showed on his face or a gray hair on his head. His hands, however, were as thin and wizened as an old man's. His flesh had craved alcohol, but, despite his reform, he had still died young. Dorothy, sober, stood beside the coffin staring a long time. Although she had been sharply critical of Scott, even telling several friends that she thought he had turned into a horse's ass, she was struck by the isolation of the room, the absence of mourners or flowers, and Hollywood's complete disinterest in his death. To mind came Jay Gatsby's funeral and the words spoken by the bespectacled character that Scott had named "Owl-eyes."

"The poor son-of-a-bitch," she said softly.

Later, when her remark made its way around the film industry, few recognized it as a quote from Fitzgerald's novel. It was assumed that she had delivered some pithy eulogy over his coffin.

During 1939 and 1940 she began to make Alan the scapegoat for the death of her motherhood dream, and he felt obliged to accept the blame. Up to this point in their marriage she had wanted to be a good wife. Granted, she was not a conventional one, but she had behaved no differently than any male writer of comparable reputation. She had married in the expectation that Alan would appreciate her intellectual gifts and take for granted that her comfort came first. She also wanted him to be her partner, collaborator, and equal. Marriage to her had given him entrée to some of the most respected literary and theatrical figures of the time, helped him to achieve self-assurance as a writer, and enabled him to live on a scale that he probably would never have achieved on his own. She had made possible his becoming "the damnedest snob in the world," as a friend pointed out, a person who indexed people on A, B, and C social lists, who could not host a party without engaging a butler but then made a show of forgetting the man's name.

In addition to the tangible benefits she felt she had conferred upon him, she also had been loyal, his most dedicated defender and supporter. From the start of their marriage, some of her friends had ridiculed Alan. Benchley told the Murphys that an evening with Dorothy and Alan reminded him of adolescent visits to Rosemary Hall (a girls' prep school), and he always expected to find himself making fudge in Alan's room before the evening was over. While Dorothy could not avoid noticing people's smirks, she never uttered a disrespectful word against Alan. That began to change as she turned on him the full force of her abuse, both to his face and behind his back. She knew his vulnerable spots better than anyone and quickly hit pay dirt.

Suddenly there were belittling references to Alan's stage career. She would ask friends if they had ever seen Alan act. Never, she declared, had he appeared on a Broadway stage without a tennis racquet or a lime squash in his hands. Seeing him perform, she said, was like watching a Vassar girl whose coiffure seemed on the verge of collapse at any moment. In this way, she announced that criticisms of Alan could thenceforth be expressed openly, that she would in fact welcome them. When a friend admitted that Alan made her nervous, Dorothy promptly replied that she would be psychotic if he didn't.

Dorothy had a number of homosexual friends. Although presumed to be tolerant, she was secretly prejudiced and enjoyed making caustic remarks at their expense. Around lesbians, her ragging tended to be easygoing. During a dinner in Paris with Janet Flanner and her friends, the subject of legal marriage had come up. When asked for her opinion, Dorothy nodded sympathetically. Lesbians should have the legal right to marry, she said, because the children had to be considered. Far less tolerant of males, she took gleeful pleasure in being mean: "Scratch an actor and find an actress." Now, searching for the worst insult for Alan, she began to insinuate that he was a homosexual.

At a dinner party in Bucks County, she held out her hands in a dramatic gesture of defeat and announced loudly, "What am I doing with him? He's as queer as a goat." Albert Hackett heard her say, "What am I doing in Hollywood at my age and married to a fairy?" She hadn't been at one of Charles Brackett's Sunday brunches ten minutes before she noticed Alan in conversation with a group of young men at the bar and muttered: "It's the curved lips of those boys that's got him so interested." Growing reckless, she devastated her mother-in-law by inquiring; "Where's my homo husband?" When Dorothy was not referring to Alan as "that pansy," she was only slightly less vituperative and called him "that shit" or "that man." Said Ruth Goetz, "In the beginning she was sweet and tender with Alan, but as life wore on, she found his mannerisms immensely irritating. He embarrassed her. And the more embarrassed and the angrier she got, the more she drank."

Very likely her accusations were unjustified. Although Alan had mannerisms that might have been considered feminine, never at any time was he known to have a sexual relationship with a man. Nevertheless, some of their friends now began to take Dorothy's word for Alan's homosexuality or bisexuality, whether they saw evidence of it or not. They assumed that somewhere in his past, if not his present, there must have been male lovers.

Dorothy did not really believe that Alan was sneaking off to sleep with men. Presumably, what she meant to convey was that he no longer wished to sleep with her.

Alan remained stoic. Whenever guests came over, setting the stage for an evening of drinking and providing an audience for Dorothy's attacks, he faithfully concocted his secret-recipe canapés and served shakers of tequila cocktails. Dorothy's acrimonious stories about him brought a smile to his lips.

They constantly saw Sid and Laura Perelman, who took great pleasure in gossiping about the Campbells. Sid, well known for his hostility toward homosexuals, referred to Alan as "that fag," although it is striking how much time he spent with the Campbells. He insisted this was Laura's fault, for it was she who felt life in Hollywood would be unbearable without Dorothy and Alan. Perelman functioned as a West Coast news agency speeding the latest dispatches back to the Goetzes in Keller's Church:

> Dotty has been heard to say very freely that this is the end, etc., etc. I am sure you were with us, in spirit at least, one evening not long ago when we spent an evening with them and Janet Flanner and a group of spectacular bull-dikers of the Elsa Maxwell set. The talk was strictly concerned with H.R.H. the Nizam of Hyderabad who dresses up as a faun in a tiger-skin and chases his cicisbeos around the conservatory with bull-whips. Alan was in a sheer tizzy, and although the figures have not yet come in from the outlying districts, *on dit* he came three times.

Dorothy and Alan must have enjoyed extending the privilege of house seats at their arguments to the Perelmans as much as Laura and Sid liked serving as their audience. Certain caustic scenes tended to be routine curtain-raisers: Alan's nagging about money, Dorothy's insistence they could live on the farm for ten thousand dollars a year if he fired his secretary. Alan could not believe she wanted to live at Fox House year-round; it had no heated swimming pool.

Like many who live with alcoholics, Alan had a large capacity for accepting abuse. As a child, he had perfected the skill of smiling his gorgeous white smile—there is not a single unsmiling photograph—and he reacted to Dorothy's assaults with performances of Oscar-winning quality. Adopting a common steam valve, he complained incessantly about how badly Dorothy treated him, but he did not consider leaving her. Some wondered why. Ruth Goetz called him "that poor bastard. Believe me, his life was not an easy one. She simply crucified him." Sid Perelman, speculating about when Alan would "beat the living urine" out of his wife, waited for him to snap.

Dorothy's politics had no effect whatsoever on her screen writing because, contrary to the later claims of the House Un-American Activities Committee, it was virtually impossible for any individual writer to inject messages, subversive or otherwise, into a Hollywood picture. Even if she had contemplated such an idea, Alan would never have allowed any step that might threaten their livelihood. Hollywood wealth had become necessary to support their scale of living.

Communism did have a prominent influence on her creative work, what little there was of it at this period. By now, with great relief, she had given up writing verse. She had chafed under the charge that she was a second-rate Edna St. Vincent Millay, an accusation that she was all too ready to accept as true. She bitterly described herself later as a person who had slogged along in Millay's footsteps "unhappily in my own horrible sneakers." She was the first to call attention to her failure as a serious poet, insisting that her verse was bad because it had been fashionable.

In the late thirties, she continued to write fiction, and it was into this work that the Communist Party philosophy marched in heavy boots. Editors like Harold Ross were appalled.

After the publication of "Mrs. Hofstadter on Josephine Street" in 1934, three years passed before she completed another story for *The New Yorker*. Although she had never been a prolific contributor, three years between submissions was an unusually long interval. When she finally did offer a story, it was heavily laced with the Party line and not particularly successful. Unlike Budd Schulberg, whose novel *What Makes Sammy Run?* was attacked by the Party for being insufficiently proletarian, a criticism that led to his dropping out of the C.P., Dorothy had no conflicts over artistic integrity. Without prompting, she was inspired to produce dutifully proletarian stories. "Clothe the Naked" is a dull, heavy-handed manifesto: Big Lannie, an impoverished black laundress who does washing for "secure and leisured" white matrons, is raising her blind grandson, Raymond. When Big Lannie dresses the boy in cast-off clothing she has begged from an employer, an elegant suit and pair of shoes that had belonged to Mrs. Ewing's husband, he goes outside for a promenade in the grand clothing and is almost beaten to death by white workmen.

Dorothy's best work was inspired by her own experiences: the urban, after-dark landscape she shared with Hazel Morse in "Big Blonde"— smoke-filled speakeasies, moneyed men, Scotch, and the inevitable night-cap of Veronal. Both Dorothy and Hazel employed black maids who could be counted on to rescue them when they had overdosed on sleeping powders. Dorothy, being neither black nor southern, a laundress nor a grandmother, knew practically nothing about Big Lannie, except what she could imagine, which was not a great deal.

The New Yorker rejected "Clothe the Naked." It was the first submission of Dorothy's that Harold Ross had turned down since the magazine's beginning, and he apparently had difficulty informing her of his decision. She was, after all, among the four or five writers who had, as Brendan Gill has noted, "helped to invent what the world came to call the '*New Yorker*' short story. . . ." Unsure how to proceed, Ross talked the problem over with Harold Guinzburg, who advised waiting before either of them notified Dorothy. The blow would be softened if Guinzburg could tell her it had been sold to another magazine. When he submitted the story to *Harper's*, the story was turned down again.

Meanwhile, a month had passed and Dorothy was getting worried. She fumed at Ross's silence. It took the magazine three weeks to reject stories by mediocrities, she complained, and they might at least extend her the same courtesy. Her mood was not improved by the publication of a nasty profile in *Cue* magazine, which might have been libelous had it not been so accurate. Clearly, her so-called friends in New York had been blabbing because there were references to Ed Parker's suicide attempts, John Gilbert's sexual rejection of her (she was quoted as having said Gilbert was "a dear but he never wants to go to bed"), and it also recalled various humiliations at the hands of John McClain. Someone she knew had betrayed her.

Alan wrote secretly to Guinzburg and asked him to get in touch with Dorothy at once. By now, Guinzburg had been able to place "Clothe the Naked" with *Scribner's* and was able to present Dorothy with pleasant news. From the beginning of their association, he had adopted a protective attitude. Over the years, he had grown adept at handling her ego like a delicate icon. Neglecting to mention the *Harper's* rejection, he told her the story didn't really belong in *The New Yorker* and insisted it was good business for her work to appear in a first-class literary magazine like *Scribner's*, "in order to get away from the widely-held notion that you write only for the *New Yorker*, live at the Algonquin, and associate only with Woollcott and Ferber." He apologized for *Scribner's* "measly" two hundred and fifty dollars.

To Alan, Guinzburg wrote privately that "there is something wrong with the story, and I think I know what it is." Although the weakness was obvious—indigestible propaganda cooked too little to become art—Guinzburg could not bring himself to name the flaw and lamely told Alan that the story's ending was not strong enough to justify the buildup of anticipation throughout the piece. This is a curious conclusion since part of the story's failure is that its violent conclusion seems too strong for everything that has preceded it.

After rejecting "Clothe the Naked," Harold Ross grew increasingly suspicious of Dorothy as a writer. In some ways he had never trusted her and once referred to her, with an affectionate smile, as an alley cat. When James Thurber had been an editor at *The New Yorker*, Ross cautioned him to keep an eye on Dorothy because she inserted double meanings into her copy to embarrass him. He warned Thurber to query everything. Now he was on the lookout in case she was plotting to slip Red propaganda into his magazine. Their twenty-year friendship seemed in danger of deteriorating completely. Writing in *New Masses* in 1939, Dorothy described an editor who had turned down a story about the Spanish war because it favored the Republicans. "God damn it," he had said to her, "why can't you be funny again?" This nameless editor was Ross.

In 1927, Ross had made no objection to printing "Arrangement in Black and White," a story that dealt with racial prejudice, but the reason he had done so was not to his credit. He "thought it was a scream," Dorothy recalled. That, she assured herself, made no difference so long as it got published. Ten years later, "I tried to use just the same technique with pieces about Loyalist Spain that I wanted to have published. It didn't work; that's all. Fun is fun, and all that, but 'Loyalist' has become a four-letter word to editors." After returning from Spain, she submitted several stories to *The New Yorker*, only to see them rejected. If Ross could not take Dorothy seriously as a foe of international Fascism, she refused to acknowledge his policy that the magazine should not take political stands.

Her pique at Ross ended when she sent him a spare report about some Loyalist soldiers on leave whom she and Alan had met in a Valencia café one Sunday evening. Dorothy had been drinking vermouth, the six soldiers ordered coffee, and she passed around a package of American cigarettes. Talking through an interpreter, the men told her they were farmers and the sons of farmers. "Their village," she wrote, "was next to that one where the old men and the sick men and the women and children had gone, on a holiday, to the bullring; and the planes had come over and dropped bombs on the bullring, and the old men and the sick men and the women and the children were more than two hundred." After the soldiers left the café, Dorothy was touched to learn that they had paid for her and Alan's drinks. Although meeting the soldiers happened much as she described, she preferred to label "Soldiers of the Republic" as fiction. It was the best work she had done in years, an understated, powerful story that captures with tremendous clarity the life inside a crowded café where babies are still awake in the late evening and the death outside where bombs have fallen that morning in broad daylight. It transcends politics, which presumably was the reason Ross accepted it.

In its way, "Soldiers of the Republic" was as propagandist as "Clothe the Naked," but it was superior artistically. The story was so widely praised after publication that Aleck Woollcott arranged for it to be reprinted as a pamphlet.

The Viking Press was eager to publish a third volume of her collected fiction, but there was little to collect. Since *After Such Pleasures*, she had written only three stories. When Harold Guinzburg suggested padding with stories rejected from previous collections and with book reviews, Dorothy balked. She disliked nearly all her old work and stubbornly insisted that she wished to reprint nothing except "Soldiers of the Republic" and "Clothe the Naked."

In an apologetic telegram, she ruled out the possibility of another book and asked his forgiveness. She said her stay in Hollywood had lasted too long, confessed that she felt FRIGHTENED BY THE PASSING OF TIME, and begged for news of her New York friends because IT IS GOOD TO HEAR OF REAL PEOPLE DOING FINE THINGS.

Guinzburg was sympathetic. If an author wished to use her talent doing missionary work, that was her business and he did not condemn her. Her political commitment was no doubt healthy, he replied, but it was irrelevant to commercial book publishing. He scolded her for remaining in Hollywood and succumbing to "the seductions of agents, producers, and others." As an incentive, he predicted that a new collection of stories would probably earn at least ten thousand dollars in royalties, perhaps forgetting that she and Alan earned almost that much in a month.

Guinzburg, used to getting his own way, was relentless in his coaxing. In the following months he outmaneuvered her. *Here Lies* was finally published in April 1939. Dedicated to Lillian Hellman, it included "Soldiers of the Republic" and "Clothe the Naked," as well as a new story she wrote especially for the collection. "The Custard Heart" attacked her wealthy bourgeois women friends who had failed to develop a political consciousness. The remaining twenty-one stories had appeared in earlier books. Although readers found little that was fresh, the book was praised by the critics and sold well. What Dorothy herself admired most about *Here Lies* was its title. She had wanted to use it for *Not So Deep as a Well*, but the book of verse had already been printed and Guinzburg had no intention of discarding an entire printing. He had sent her a gentle telegram: WE WOULD HAVE TWENTY THOUSAND BOOKS TO GIVE TO SALVATION ARMY AND THINK OF EFFECT OF THAT.

One of the many chores that Alan gladly took care of was answering Dorothy's mail, even her correspondence with intimate friends. He signed the personal letters rather sweetly as "alandotty." Once the marriage began to be troubled, she felt uncomfortable as half an "alandotty." The more she relied on Alan, the more bitterly she resented him and the stronger became her denials that she needed him. She knew that some people believed her pathetic in this respect and could not help noticing their condescending smiles, even though she asked for their smiles by launching violent tirades against her husband.

Bridling at the funny way Lillian Hellman looked at her, she told her off, although she did it gently. She once looked up from a book she was reading and said to Hellman, "The man said he didn't want to see her again. That night she tried to climb into the transom of his hotel room and got stuck at the hips. I've never got stuck at the hips, Lily, and I want you to remember that." Precisely the opposite was true.

Suddenly, both she and Alan were eager to prove they could manage without the other. She was writing again. Within a matter of months, she completed "Song of the Shirt, 1941" and "The Standard of Living," two fine stories that also pleased Harold Ross. In the summer of 1941, she traveled to New York without Alan, a trip that Robert Benchley described as "a friendly divergence." She kept bellyaching about Hollywood and all her friends back in New York, he wrote,

> until Alan suggested she go East and shut up for a while. So she did, and now calls up every day to fight over the phone and hint about coming back, having probably fought with all her Eastern pals. Alan told her he thought she had better stay there a little longer, as he had several jobs of his own to finish before he could team up with her again.

All of a sudden Alan began to assert himself. His confidence shot up when he got a string of assignments from RKO. Most of the scripts on which he worked without Dorothy were not produced, but he was hardly to blame for it. The important achievement was his salary—$1,250 a week.

Dorothy remained away nearly two months. She spent much of the time with Sara and Gerald Murphy at East Hampton, Long Island, and hardly any at Fox House, which she seemed reluctant to visit alone. The farm was isolated and she was used to Alan's being there, tidying and fussing. While it gave her great pleasure to talk about old times with her friends and to feel she was in the middle of things again, she missed her husband and returned to Beverly Hills in July. On her birthday, she thought nostalgically of Harold Ross and mailed him an affectionate note: "Ah, look, dear Harold—today's my birthday—Dorothy."

Not too long afterward, Alfred Hitchcock engaged her to add choice material to a script already written by Peter Viertel and Joan Harrison. *Saboteur* is about an aircraft factory worker who is wrongfully accused of sabotage and includes a cross-country chase to apprehend the true criminal. Dorothy wrote the dialogue for a troupe of circus freaks—a bearded woman and Siamese twins. She and Hitchcock appear in the film together, as a couple driving along the highway in a car just as Robert Cummings is manhandling Priscilla Lane. "My," Dorothy remarks, "they must be terribly in love."

The rest of 1941 passed less pleasantly. Dorothy, in a sour mood, taunted Alan for enjoying Hollywood. She called his values low, trashy, and bourgeois, his principles "debased." Remorseful, she later admitted that she had gone too far and "behaved like a shit to him," but added tartly, "I had much right on my side, but I used all the wrong things." Again they teamed together to work on a baseball film about Lou Gehrig, *The Pride of the Yankees.* They were making good money at the Goldwyn studio when Dorothy spied an opportunity to yank the rug from under Alan's feet by getting herself dismissed from the picture. Figuring that "alan" without "dotty" would certainly have to take up begging at Hollywood and Vine, she sat back and waited for Goldwyn to fire Alan. It was a prospect that gave her great satisfaction, but something went wrong.

The studio decided to keep Alan and replace Dorothy with Helen Deutsch, a short-story writer and former newspaper reporter who was working in pictures for the first time. Deutsch had no idea what had preceded her arrival. "I was too green to know the score, although somebody told me that Dorothy Parker had got stinking drunk and had been taken off the picture. All I knew was that Alan Campbell was there every day and Parker wasn't." Alan, she decided, was "a cute guy but creepy"— he shaved after he arrived at the office and spent hours leaning out the window. When she noticed him watching the story editor, Deutsch wondered if "they weren't a couple of homosexuals and Alan was in love with him."

It pleased Dorothy to imagine herself as the victim in this situation. The studio had had the nerve to replace her with a pretty thirty-five-year-old unpracticed screenwriter who was making only three hundred dollars a week. Helen Deutsch was soon earning three thousand a week and she wrote a string of successful films including *National Velvet, Lili,* and *I'll Cry Tomorrow.* Adopting an appropriately offended attitude, Dorothy began to imagine that Alan was having an affair with Helen Deutsch. Though not true in this case, she herself had always found creative collaboration impossible without sex. It seemed as likely a theory as any, and it gave her another reason to increase her consumption of brandy.

After the bombing of Pearl Harbor and the outbreak of war in December, Dorothy became increasingly difficult to live with. She began the day with a morning eye-opener and drank steadily until bedtime or a blackout, whichever happened to come first. Alan affected not to notice. Dorothy checked herself into a hospital to dry out. Alan's uncharacteristic response contrasted with his habit of automatically jumping to her rescue, a reaction that in no way denoted acknowledgment of her alcoholism. In fact, the reverse was true. While he could hardly deny that sometimes she overdrank, he did not recognize it as an uncontrollable compulsion. He was unwilling to endorse her stopping and drank along with her so that she might have company. Without meaning to, he encouraged her drinking with his collection of recipes for unusual cocktails, with expensive ice crushers and bar paraphernalia. Joseph Bryan cannot remember Dorothy ever preparing a drink for herself. "She would just hold out her glass, and Alan would jump up to refill it."

Like many who live in alcoholic families, Alan found it natural to assume a custodial role. He accepted his wife's tendency to overreact, feel sorry for herself, and embrace the victim's role. Not only did he tolerate her selfishness, but also he shut his eyes when she showed indifference toward his interests. He was finally getting fed up. Nothing he did pleased her, and when he responded to her peevish moods with impatience she called him "a cross little man."

While Dorothy was in the hospital, Laura and Sid Perelman busily carried olive branches between the warring parties:

> Our old friend Dotnick has been in something of a spin—loaded on brandy by eleven in the morning and the like. She clearly resents Alan working with Miss Helen Deutsch, she's fed up with pictures and picture people, and by Thursday of this past week, she had got herself into such shape that she had to go off to a sanitarium for three or four days. All through this, Alan was phoning us at the studio and running in to our apartment biting his nails and telling us how unreasonable she was.

The Perelmans paid a call on Dorothy. Wan and sober, she announced her readiness to chuck the marriage and return to New York for good. They conveyed this threat to Alan, who predictably rushed to her side, humbled himself, and patched up the quarrel. "As of last night," Sid notified the Goetzes, "they were home together again, but it's hardly Paola [sic] and Francesca."

Seeing them together brought to Sid Perelman's mind the image of a cobra and a mongoose. It was more true than he realized. Ever since war had been declared, Dorothy had been testing Alan in new and provocative ways. To prove that he loved her, she wanted him to join the army. She had warned him a thousand times about the evils of Fascism. Now the whole world was in flames and "there were men getting their balls shot off, and here he was in Beverly Hills." Were she a man, she knew that she would enlist. "She would say very rough things to him," remembered a friend.

Her demand was outrageous because Alan, at thirty-eight, could easily have avoided serving in the armed forces. Despite his education at Virginia Military Institute, which had been Horte's idea, he had always shown more interest in perfecting the art of making chocolate soufflés than in warfare. He made a confession to Dorothy: He had hated military school. After practically starving to death as an actor, he was now flourishing in his career as a screenwriter and had no desire to throw it away by joining the army.

Excuses like these made Dorothy livid. She was not suggesting he go to the Ukraine and join the Red Army, only to be a patriot and defend his country.

Alan, however, was oblivious to such taunts. He couldn't go to war because he had to install a new chimney at Fox House, and that was that.

Throughout the winter of 1942, hectored almost without letup, Alan gnawed his already bitten fingernails and increased his drinking. Now that neither one seemed to be in control, some of their friends began avoiding them. Regular drinking companions like screenwriters Phoebe and Henry Ephron suddenly claimed to be spending a great deal of time in Palm Springs. Henry Ephron felt the Campbells were a bad influence. "We were working very hard and they would want to stop in every night to sit around and drink, then at the end of the evening we'd have to drive them and their car home. We just had to drop them. It came to a point where we'd put the cars in the garage and the lights out, so it would look as if we weren't at home."

But the Campbells were too absorbed in their own high drama to be hurt. Alan probably enjoyed the game as much as Dorothy. These months may well have been among the most spicy of their entire marriage. Tantalizing her, Alan told Dorothy about movie people who were being commissioned as majors or colonels and said that if he should ever decide to join up he would want a commission. This elitist idea sent Dorothy into a frenzy.

At last, in the spring of 1942, Alan made up his mind to enlist as a private. By now the battles they had waged on the subject were so plentiful that it was easy for Alan to forget that enlisting had been Dorothy's idea. Wisely, his victorious wife did not remind him. She assured Aleck Woollcott that "no one had told him what was right, except himself," that he had enlisted "without telling one soul." This scenario may have fooled Woollcott, but those who knew better were incredulous. Dorothy, having got her way, full of respect for her husband, was feeling intensely satisfied. When she repeatedly spoke of how much she loved him, she meant it sincerely.

Alan's plans stunned his mother. After confusing the issue by calling him heartless and inconsiderate, she rounded up a delegation of Point Pleasant matrons who descended on the farm like vigilantes to try to talk Alan out of leaving "that poor sick woman all alone." When this failed, Horte faked a heart attack. Dorothy, furious, reminded herself that she had never been a vengeful woman. Her philosophy was that if you had patience "the bastards will get theirs and it will be fancier than anything you could ever have thought up. But I would . . . give quite a large bit of my soul if something horrible would happen to that woman for poisoning Alan's last days here." Whether by "here" she meant Pipersville or the planet earth is ambiguous.

Among those praising Alan's decision as deeply courageous was Gerald Murphy, who presented him with a wristwatch engraved with the admiring but melodramatic inscription, QUI SENSAT ACET [He who feels, acts].

This proved far too high-toned for Robert Benchley, who wisecracked that the watch should have read WHOSE WIFE FEELS, ACTS.

Chapter 15

THE LEAKING BOAT

◆

1942—1947

In the first days of Alan's absence, she attempted to minimize her loneliness by drawing closer to her family. She first called her sister, who was separated from her second husband and living with her daughter in East Patchogue, Long Island. Informed of Alan's departure, Helen neglected to offer the sort of commiseration that Dorothy expected and instead reported how the war was affecting East Patchogue that summer. A few of the Saturday night dances had been canceled.

Dorothy next telephoned Bert, who still worked in the garment business as a dress salesman. When she dialed his home in Queens, she got her sister-in-law. Mate affected to find nothing exceptionable about Alan's enlistment because, she explained, he was a college graduate. Her son Bertram, only a year younger than Alan, would like to train in aviation, but had no college degree. When Dorothy interrupted to say that Alan had enlisted as a private, Mate changed the subject. By the time Dorothy hung up, she was cursing to herself.

Despite her fame, there had been no real alteration in the Rothschild family roles over the years. To them, she was still the clever little sister, a source of pride and pleasure. Dorothy, for her part, continued to scorn their tributes on the grounds that they could not be trusted to judge her worth or even to fathom her thinking. Despite her complaints about the Rothschilds, she in fact considered Bert "not bad," actually high praise from her, and she expressed her deep-rooted affection for Helen by her usual generosity. Her niece Lel recalled that, whenever she visited the

Algonquin as a child, her mother would warn her "not to admire anything Aunt Dot is wearing because she'll take it off her back and give it to you." During Lel's adolescence, Dorothy bought her a squirrel coat. On her marriage to Robert Iveson, she gave her the Cartier diamond watch that once had been a gift from Seward Collins. (The watch, now owned by Lel's daughter Nancy Arcaro, has become a family heirloom.)

Failing to find comfort in her family, Dorothy holed up at Fox House to redesign a life without Alan. She was determined to pull her socks up and prove her competency: "I've got to write a lot of stories—if, of course, I can. I've got the farm to keep going. I've got myself. I've got Alan's mother." It occurred to her that she should undertake some kind of factory work, perhaps welding, but quickly abandoned the idea as impractical. Still, a nine-to-five civilian job remained a possibility, a position like the one she had at *Vanity Fair* during the last war, when a regular routine had helped pass the time. Before Alan left, he strongly advised against her living at the farm because anyone "who cannot drive a car, much less make coffee" would be better off in Manhattan. He spoke to a friend who managed the luxurious Ritz Hotel about giving her a good rate on a suite. Even if she did take a place in town, she wrote Woollcott, she intended to make periodical visits to Pipersville as often as the hired man could spare the gas to meet her at the station.

Mapping out a strategy was simple. Living it was harder. In mid-September, after moving to the Ritz, she telephoned Harold Ross to ask for a job. Not a writing assignment, she explained, but a staff position. While Ross was struggling to comprehend the idea, which he did not for a moment take seriously, she went on to say that she was living at the Ritz, and she argued that it was costly but not unreasonably so, indeed there were hidden benefits that actually made it a bargain. Her logic must have struck him as sounding like a miracle on the order of the fishes and the loaves, and since publishing a weekly magazine on a shoestring always had meant looking for "Jesuses" who might save his operation, he pricked up his ears. He later joked to Marc Connelly about making her head of the design and layout department. He heard nothing further from her. When he subsequently telephoned the Ritz, he never found her in, for the good reason that she was seldom there.

. . .

Alan took basic training at the Army Air Corps base in Miami Beach, where his barracks turned out to be a deluxe hotel that had been requisitioned for servicemen. Pulling KP duty in the dining hall, he was given the job of serving dessert to men coming through the chow line. One day while trying to spoon five canned cherries into each passing tin cup, he heard someone call him stingy and order him to pour in the whole can. Alan's response was to hold up the line while he recounted to make sure he'd given the soldier no more than the regulation five. Glancing up, he was startled to see a familiar face, Broadway director Joshua Logan. Immediately Alan invited him to his room because he wanted to give him some ashtrays. Logan said he had no need of ashtrays, but Alan insisted. Everybody in Miami Beach needed ashtrays, and he had been saving these for friends. Logan, as it happened, was the first one to come along. After that, they became friendly, and before Alan knew it he was having a a good time. Miami Beach seemed like a huge Hollywood soundstage with fake palm trees and a Technicolor moon. The place was full of tall, skinny, suntanned men in starched uniforms who looked like Jimmy Stewart and boogie-woogied around Miami singing, chewing Wrigley's, boozing, and living in comradely style in hotels that had colossal swimming pools and cocktail lounges full of girls with pompadours. The Army Air Corps, as anyone could plainly see, was a party, and Alan loved parties.

In November, he wasted no time in applying for Officer Candidate School. Josh Logan, who had not initially wanted the responsibility of being an officer, changed his mind and applied as a gesture of friendship. They were both accepted. Right before OCS graduation, anticipating the revels ahead once they were officers and able to live as they pleased, they rented a small apartment across the street from their hotel and stocked it with food and liquor.

Alan, quite popular in Squadron 24, soon won the reputation of being a wit. Practically nobody was aware that he was the husband of Dorothy Parker, and some had no idea who she was. Nor did they know or much care about his job in civilian life. During a physical examination that included a routine psychiatric interview, the doctor asked for his highest earnings as a civilian.

"Five thousand dollars," Alan said.

"Five thousand dollars a year is all you made?" said the doctor.

"Five thousand dollars a week."

The doctor stared a moment before asking, "Ever had any mental illness in the family?"

Dorothy's first reaction to Alan's application to Officer Candidate School had been annoyance. When he had written to ask the birthplace of her father for the OCS application, she had gotten obstructive. Alan later recalled that "trying to get the little woman to write a letter stating any facts about her old man was a career in itself." Prior to the service, Alan would not have dared call Dorothy "the little woman." He was beginning to sound less and less like a man who seemed to be content bringing up the rear in his marriage and professional life. Dorothy noticed this with considerable misgiving.

That fall she sped back and forth to Florida and parked there for a month in December. For all her good intentions, no new fiction got started, only a trite article for *Mademoiselle* urging its readers to become men for the duration and take the jobs left vacant by servicemen. She suggested, for example, that they drive buses, something she might have liked to do, just as she also talked about wanting to enlist in the WACs or become a war correspondent. These last ideas she mentioned so often that some people mistakenly concluded she had actually applied and been rejected as a premature antifascist.

Waiting for the inspiration to begin another short story, she was dismayed to learn that Ruth Gordon was writing a play with main characters who bore an unmistakable resemblance to herself and Alan. The plot of *Over Twenty-one* concerns a famous novelist-screenwriter whose husband is struggling through Officer Candidate School at the age of thirty-nine and—the resemblance ends here—her determination to help him. This was the third time that Gordon played her, and Dorothy was getting tired of watching others profit from her life story. Even though she herself had practically elevated procrastination to an art form, she adopted an offended tone, snarling that she didn't dare write a play about her life because Ruth would very likely sue her for plagiarism.

Over Twenty-one opened on Broadway in January 1944. A great success, it was made into a film starring Irene Dunne.

Just before Alan graduated from Officer Candidate School, he and Josh Logan organized a celebration for their friends at the rented apartment. Logan later figured their guests must have consumed more liquor than usually was drunk in all of Miami at the height of the tourist season.

Unfortunately, he and Alan were scheduled to appear on a GI radio program the next morning. With Dorothy tottering along behind, they made their way to the station on one of the piers. Logan noticed that she looked wrecked—rheumy eyes, gray-green face, twitching cheeks. He felt sorry for her. Despite his preconceived notions about Dorothy's being vitriolic, she seemed to him like "a beady-eyed dumpling" who needed care. Since fifteen minutes remained until air time, he offered to run back to one of the bars along the beach and get her anything she wished—"a double Scotch, a double rye, whatever. I might even find a bottle of gin."

Despite his promises, he found it impossible to get off the pier and returned from the expedition with the only beverage he was able to buy, a bottle of Coca-Cola with a straw in it.

"How sweet," Dorothy said. "Coca-Cola. I'll try it. I've never had a Coca-Cola." Accepting the soda, she sucked tentatively at the straw, then swallowed a larger slurp. Logan was anxious to know whether it was making her feel better.

"No, but as it was going down I learned a deep, abiding truth about drinking Coca-Cola."

"What's that?"

"Never send a boy on a man's errand."

Several weeks later, Dorothy was again in Miami when another verity appeared to her. She noticed that Alan seemed unusually distant. He no longer seemed interested in her, at least he was making no attempt to cater to her.

Nedda Harrigan, Logan's future wife, was also there for the weekend, and they had another party. This time Logan observed that Dorothy and Alan seemed tense and unhappy. "They were terribly intimate, only it wasn't cozy or jolly, more like a couple of vipers. Of course we were all drinking heavily, because that was standard procedure in the air force, but she was in a bad temper and later on they had a terrible fistfight."

When Dorothy met Nedda Harrigan for lunch the next day, she had a black eye. Deeply humiliated, she refused to acknowledge the bruise and instead launched into an indignant recital of Alan's misbehavior. He and Josh, she told Nedda bitterly, didn't need them anymore because they had their war. She finally pointed to her face. "A beloved little mouse below my eye. That's not very pretty, is it? Not very pretty at all."

Nedda Harrigan urged Dorothy not to take the quarrel seriously. War was difficult for everyone, and besides, they were all in the same boat.

Dorothy disagreed. "My boat," she insisted, "is leaking."

Violence had never entered her relationship with Alan. During the years when she had vilified him as a queer and a Vassar girl, he had mildly turned the other cheek, but he now fell on her in a fury. He reminded her that he had enlisted for her sake; now she was accusing him of desertion. No matter what he did, she was never satisfied.

Dorothy took the train back to New York.

In late January 1943, on a CBS radio broadcast, Aleck Woollcott was taking part in a discussion entitled "Is Germany Incurable?" when he pushed away from the microphone and printed on a scrap of paper, I AM SICK. A few hours later he was dead of a heart attack followed by a cerebral hemorrhage. Even though Dorothy had recently visited him in Lake Bomoseen and knew firsthand of his poor health, she still took it hard.

On the evening of his death, she hurried to the Algonquin and sat in a corner with Bea Stewart and Joseph Hennessey, Woollcott's secretary. She was annoyed to notice that others had the same idea. When George and Beatrice Kaufman and a few more appeared, she nudged Bea. "We have the Round Table with us. Let's get out of here." A few days later, after a memorial service thronged by some five hundred of Woollcott's friends, Dorothy joined the bereaved Round Tablers in the Rose Room for one last drink. Among those present were the Kaufmans, Neysa McMein, Peggy Leech, and several other ghosts from the past with whom she had fallen out over the years. Looking warily around, she saw people who had been her dearest companions in the old days, friends who never had been at a loss for words, but now there was uneasy silence. They had utterly nothing to say to each other. Harpo Marx found it equally eerie and recalled that "it was the last gathering of the Woollcott crowd, and it was our strangest gathering."

Shortly after this alarming reunion, Dorothy fled New York. Somerset Maugham had invited her to spend a few weeks in South Carolina, where he was living on the estate of his publisher, Nelson Doubleday. Dorothy made the mistake of accepting impulsively. It was a curious invitation because they barely knew each other. They had, in fact, met only once at a Hollywood dinner party given by Fanny Brice. Dorothy, seated next to Maugham, found herself feeling uncharacteristically intimidated and thought that "whenever I meet one of these Britishers I feel as if I have a papoose on my back." When Maugham proposed she compose a poem for him, she cheerfully agreed to perform. A paper and pencil were requested and Dorothy wrote:

> Higgledy Piggledy, my white hen;
> She lays eggs for gentlemen.

That was very nice, Maugham said. He had always liked those lines. Giving him a cool smile, she completed the verse:

> You cannot persuade her with gun or lariat
> To come across for the proletariat.

Maugham chuckled with delight. There was no one around in South Carolina but Maugham and a number of sycophantic young men who were devoted to their host but regarded Dorothy with indifference. All Maugham wanted to do was play bridge. Although Dorothy later called him "that old lady" and "a crashing bore," she concealed her ennui and her tongue. Feeling miserable anyway, she spent three weeks playing cards with Maugham. A year later, as if to prove that virtue does indeed have its own reward, Maugham wrote, for $250, a glowing introduction to her collected works, *The Portable Dorothy Parker*.

Back in New York, her distress over Woollcott's death failed to subside with time. More than two years later, when Samuel Hopkins Adams wrote a well-received biography of Woollcott, she felt sufficiently upset to offer a dissenting opinion. In an article for the *Chicago Sun Book Week*, she scorned the book as only sporadically accurate and said that she smelled "a strange little underlay of meanness all through it." She went on to flay George Kaufman and Moss Hart for distorting Woollcott's personality in their play *The Man Who Came to Dinner*, which was, she declared hotly, a "nasty little play."

In 1943, Woollcott had been fifty-six and Dorothy turned fifty. His early death does not seem extraordinary considering his obesity and accompanying ailments, but Dorothy refused to make such connections and felt shaken by what she considered his premature passing. With great reluctance, she had stopped pretending to be Alan's age. Suddenly she regretted never having lied about her age. On the other hand, she joked, all she might have subtracted were three or four years and "what's a couple of sandspits to an archipelago?"

She disliked the bodily decay of aging, but the cause of her distress was far more complex: She was forced to reevaluate her thinking on death, a subject she had adopted long ago as her peculiar speciality. She did still enjoy making morbid wisecracks. She said she wanted a large, white tombstone because it would give her "something to live for."

She claimed it was the word *middle* in middle-age that she hated, because it branded her a frump. She wanted to skip her fifties and get to the seventies and eighties. "People ought to be one of two things, young or old. No; what's the good of fooling? People ought to be one of two things, young or dead." Suddenly the passage of time terrified her. She wondered if she really did seek death. She who had never feared death and had busily cultivated her demise was startled to realize a ghastly fact: She would not be around forever to carry on her flirtation with nonexistence. What she recognized was a truth about herself so depressing that it almost made her feel like killing herself.

Woollcott's death had angered and saddened her, but it was nothing compared to her acute shock in November 1945, when Robert Benchley died unexpectedly. Like Woollcott, he too was fifty-six. He had been visiting Gertrude in Scarsdale when he suffered a series of nosebleeds that could not be controlled. When Marc Connelly heard he had fallen into a coma, he hurried hatless and coatless to the Stork Club, a favorite saloon of Benchley's, and rushed from table to table asking patrons for their blood types. Those whose blood type matched Benchley's were immediately whisked off to Columbia-Presbyterian Hospital to provide transfusions. Benchley died from a cerebral hemorrhage, complicated by cirrhosis of the liver.

When she was notified of his death in Hollywood, Dorothy cried out, "That's dandy!" Her words offended Gertrude Benchley, whose hostility toward Dorothy had remained strong. Misinterpreting her words as indifference, she never forgave her.

Despite a breach after her marriage, Benchley remained one of the most important people in her life. She loved him in a special way. When Benchley's son Nathaniel began collecting material for a biography of his father in the 1950s, she showed little interest in the project and cooperated minimally with requests for her recollections. Probably she was convinced that any authorized biography of Robert Benchley would be well sterilized.

After Benchley's death, John O'Hara decided that "the party was over," which was not strictly true because it was already breaking up in 1929, not long after he arrived in New York. The Round Table's legend was so powerful that the group was believed to be alive fifteen years after its demise. In the minds of the nostalgic, it lasted even longer.

Whenever people asked Frank Case what had become of the Algonquin Round Table, he shrugged and replied, "What became of the reservoir at Fifth Avenue and Forty-second Street? These things do not last forever." Edna Ferber realized the party was over when she arrived at the Rose Room in 1932 and found the big table occupied by a family from Newton, Kansas. Dorothy was happy to spread malicious stories about the Round Tablers. At her mildest, she described them as a pack of hypocrites and show-offs who "came there to be heard by one another. 'Did you hear what I said last night?' "

Still, the unexpected deaths of Woollcott and Benchley had a profound effect on her and on some of the others, perhaps because it brought them face to face with their own mortality and other disagreeable subjects. In 1919, young and unproved, their goal had been to have it all—love, money, fame, and happiness. Twenty-five years later, they were still hoping for happiness and wondering why fame had failed to satisfy. To their great shock, they now were reminded that it was quite possible to drop dead without finding it. In their time, no American had been more famous—and more unfulfilled—than Alexander Woollcott. Three decades later he was forgotten, "famous mostly for being famous," as a critic aptly commented.

Robert Benchley, beloved as he had been, had seen happiness elude him. He slumped into a decline before he died. Sleeping pills kept him awake at night, and the Benzedrine he took on the set made him sleepy. Finally, he gave up the Benzedrine because he could think of no important reason for wanting to be awake. Before the war, Dorothy had attended a Hollywood party where the guests had included Benchley and Robert Sherwood. Benchley went haywire. Pointing at Sherwood, who had recently won a second Pulitzer Prize for his drama *Idiot's Delight,* he cringed in horror and cried out, "Those eyes—I can't stand those eyes looking at me. He's looking at me and thinking of how he knew me when I was going to be a great writer . . . And he's thinking *now* look at what I am." Sherwood later admitted that those might very well have been his thoughts. When Harold Ross felt obliged to fire Benchley as *The New Yorker* theater critic, he deputized St. Clair McKelway to deliver the bad news. Benchley, quickly sensing the reason for the meeting, told McKelway he understood perfectly and ordered another round of drinks.

Many of those associated with the Round Table were destined to live shorter-than-average lives. Ring Lardner, suffering from alcoholism and tuberculosis, died of a heart attack at the age of forty-eight. During his last years his face resembled a skull, and his trembling fingers could not light a match. Ruth Hale died suddenly when she was forty-seven, and Heywood Broun followed her at fifty-one.

Since all of them, with few exceptions, were what would now be termed substance abusers, the problems they suffered are not surprising. Although Dorothy was the only one to attempt suicide, the rest selected alternate roads to self-damage, just as Dorothy herself did in the latter part of her life. Woollcott gorged himself into his grave with an early-Renaissance appetite for mountainous quantities of food; he adored creamy, calorie-loaded cocktails (he claimed the Brandy Alexander was named for him) and drank untold cups of coffee, although during rare periods of moderation he cut down to nineteen cups a day.

The others simply drank. Benchley's friends choked when they watched him adding vodka to chocolate ice-cream sodas.

"Bob," Scott Fitzgerald said after he had gone on the wagon, "don't you know that drinking is slow death?"

Benchley had a ready answer. "So who's in a hurry?"

Charles MacArthur, despite a stable second marriage to the long-suffering Helen Hayes, died of an internal hemorrhage after being hospitalized for nephritis and anemia. He was sixty and looked eighty. Eventually Heywood Broun's hands shook and his nose reddened, although during the years when he had sedated himself with a flask of warm gin, his alcoholism had not been particularly noticeable. John O'Hara had recurrent drinking problems. Edmund Wilson, who was hospitalized during periods of manic-depression, also was afflicted by alcoholism. Enthroned on a divan in the Algonquin lobby, he ordered double martinis or double bourbons one after another, conducted brilliant, completely coherent conversations, but sometimes fell flat on his face when he got up to leave.

Frank Adams also drank too much, but it was the early stages of an Alzheimer's-type disorder that caused his deterioration. In the late 1930s, the rhyming wit of the *World* became the host of a popular radio panel show, *Information Please*. When it made the transition to television, he was slipping mentally and had to be replaced after two performances because of complaints that he looked like a death's-head. After Esther divorced him, which he never was able to admit, he lived at the Players Club, where it saddened fellow guests to witness his senile rambling and his intoxication. His son Timothy thought that "he aged quite prematurely. In his early sixties he looked like an old man and by the time he died at seventy-eight, he was ancient." During F.P.A.'s final years in a nursing home, where he watched television and read paperback novels, he would have been destitute had not Harold Ross and William Shawn kept him on *The New Yorker* payroll at a modest stipend.

Those Round Tablers not afflicted by alcoholism had other crippling problems that made happiness difficult to sustain. Few of them managed to find satisfaction in love or marriage. Marc Connelly, after years of frustration over his unrequited passion for Margalo Gillmore, finally married a Mack Sennett bathing beauty, Madeline Hurlock, only to watch her fall in love with one of his best friends, Robert Sherwood, who himself had been trapped in a turbulent sadomasochistic marriage with Mary Brandon. George and Beatrice Kaufman, unable to have sex with each other, adopted a daughter and then went their separate ways emotionally, and a similar type of open-marriage arrangement was chosen by Neysa McMein and John Baragwanath. In 1928, Jane Grant divorced Harold Ross, who went on to marry twice again. The Round Tablers greeted Heywood Broun and Ruth Hale's divorce with equanimity, but they could accept neither his remarriage to a dancer nor his conversion to Catholicism for her sake. Robert Benchley's farcical marriage and his endless womanizing contrasted so vividly with his basic integrity and decency that practically everyone who knew him colluded in pretending that it was not happening. No doubt the worst hypocrite in this situation was Benchley himself, who continued to masquerade as an all-American, suburban family man until the end of his life. In the thirties, he had been a favorite lover of Tallulah Bankhead. Brendan Gill recalled that "she was always praising the size of his prick and telling everybody what a terrific 'cocksman' he was. An ordinary mortal, which Benchley was not, might have thought, 'Yea! spread the word,' but he simply couldn't stand to hear it." Edna Ferber and Aleck Woollcott sidestepped messy sexual complications by choosing celibacy.

The collective excesses of the Round Tablers made Dorothy's problems appear unexceptional.

In 1943, Dorothy gave up her trips to Florida. Once Alan's squadron had been transferred to Harrisburg, Pennsylvania, and then to Long Island, she saw practically nothing of him. When he did get a furlough, she was intent on making it perfect, which is to say, she usually managed to spoil it. As she admitted in "The Lovely Leave," a short story she published in the *Woman's Home Companion,* their meetings always ended in disaster. All it took was a single bitchy word from either to start a shoot-out, then they both turned glacial, and before she knew it, the door would be slamming behind him. "When she knew he was gone, she was cool and still no longer. She ran about the little flat, striking her breast and sobbing. Then she had two months to ponder what had happened, to see how she had wrought the ugly small ruin. She cried in the nights."

She also cursed him in the nights. Once she sent a letter that seemed to be nothing but a half-dozen unrelated items of gossip about people they knew. At the end she added a postscript, suggesting he look at the first letter of each sentence to decipher her real message. The letters spelled out FUCK YOU.

She seldom visited the farm. Wolfinger's general store in Ottsville could generally count on unloading certain brands of toilet paper merely by mentioning it was used by Mrs. Parker, but now the toilet paper had to sell on its own merits. She moved to the New Weston, a residence hotel on the corner of Madison Avenue and Fiftieth Street, where she had a pleasant two-room apartment. She made it homier by bringing from the country a few pieces of furniture and one or two precious possessions—a Utrillo landscape and a cocktail shaker engraved with the words TO ROBERT BENCHLEY FROM HIS SUNDAY SCHOOL CLASS.

Meanwhile, she was not the only one of her crowd to be alone. Lillian Hellman was in pretty much the same situation after Dashiell Hammett enlisted and was shipped to the Aleutian Islands. Hellman had adjusted to his absence. She was occupied with the film version of *Watch on the Rhine* and thinking of beginning a new play. Dorothy gave the appearance of being occupied. She worked for the Spanish Refugee Appeal, now part of the Joint Anti-Fascist Refugee Committee, and she made speeches on behalf of causes as diverse as Yugoslav relief, the rescue of European Jews, and children's book week. When she volunteered to sell war bonds, the Treasury Department teamed her up with Ogden Nash and a young *New Yorker* editor just returned from New Guinea and sent them on a tour of Pennsylvania to visit schools. To E. J. Kahn, Jr., who had joined the magazine in 1937, Dorothy was a figure from another era. "At the *New Yorker* she was considered a great lady," but in his twenty-seven-year-old eyes she appeared "small and faded, too world-weary to be witty."

While Benchley was still alive, she made several trips to Hollywood. She would tell people that she was doing a picture with Gregory Ratoff, or she might name other producers. If it was true, there remains no record of such employment, no screen credits. She stayed at the Garden of Allah. In Benchley's bungalow, the bar never closed.

Dorothy insisted that Helen come out and visit. Due to wartime travel restrictions, it was an exhausting train trip that meant sitting up for several nights. Dorothy took her sister to see the standard sights. They went to Romanoff's and to the set of a Joan Crawford picture, and she introduced Helen to Marlene Dietrich and George Murphy. All the time Dorothy kept putting down the movie stars. "Everyone makes a swell fuss over Dot," Helen wrote to her son Bill. "I can't understand why she hates it so." Although Dorothy outdid herself to show Helen a good time, Helen had difficulty with the pace and found it a relief to go home. "I seemed to be continually drinking. I really stood it beautifully, too. I was surprised at myself."

In the fall of 1943, Dorothy returned to New York because Alan was due to be sent overseas, and she wanted to say good-bye. It was unbearable for her to admit that his life offered her no place. She felt deeply wounded that he was so obviously relieved to be free of her and suffered from intense, almost paranoid jealousy. His friends, the air corps, and the entire army of the United States disgusted her. It seemed as if he had gained a whole new life, but, "I have half an old one," she wrote, feeling deprived. The thought of Alan having any kind of existence separate from hers made her furious, and knowing that it was she who had forced him to enlist made it even worse.

After he left in November, she rushed back to the Garden of Allah to spend the Christmas holidays with her Hollywood friends, but she was in a smoldering mood. At nine o'clock on Christmas morning she knocked on the door of Frances Goodrich and Albert Hackett, wanting company. This was extraordinarily early for her to be up, and since she looked queasy, it was likely she had never been to bed. She told them that Alan's checkbook stubs had revealed spending fifteen thousand dollars on a bracelet for Miriam Hopkins. Since this information failed to jibe with her portrayal of him as a dedicated pederast, the Hacketts were understandably perplexed.

In the evening, she turned up with two photographs of Alan in uniform and asked the Hacketts which one they preferred. When they reluctantly made a choice, she presented them with both photos, frames and all.

Helen suffered a minor stroke that left her with diminished sensation in her hands, and then developed pneumonia. On January 18, 1944, she died at the age of fifty-seven. Bill Droste wired Dorothy of his mother's death. She wired back immediately, saying that she would be unable to get back East in time for the funeral, but wished to pay for the burial expenses. She asked Bill to order a blanket of roses to cover the coffin. He replied that, while Helen had expressly forbidden flowers, they would gladly accept her offer to pay for the funeral.

Dorothy was stunned. Her customary manner of dealing with death was to wire Toni Strassman at The Viking Press and direct her to order cut flowers to be charged to her royalty account. Her offer of flowers having been rejected, she did not know what to do. The Drostes heard nothing more from her.

"We guessed she was annoyed with us," said Marge Droste. "We didn't get the blanket of roses, and she never paid for the funeral."

Three months after Helen's death, Bert Rothschild died suddenly. Since Dorothy had not been as close to him and Mate, it was easier to bear. As for her eldest brother, nobody had heard from poor Harry in thirty-five years. She had stopped speculating long ago on whether he was dead or alive. Helen's passing threw her off balance.

William Targ, an editor with World Publishing in Cleveland, was not only an admirer of Dorothy's but an exceptionally personable man. For more than a year, he pursued her with a proposal that she edit an anthology of women writers. He was confident she could do it because the volume would require a minimum of writing, only brief critical introductions to the writers. He finally enticed her into accepting.

Whenever Targ came to New York, he called Dorothy to inquire about her progress, and they would meet for dinner at the New Weston. Claiming to be working hard, she pointed to a sheet of paper in her typewriter.

"You see that?" she said with a reassuring smile. "That's a page of your book." It was a lie, but not one that he cared to challenge, any more than he objected when she broke appointments with telegrams full of absurd excuses. She had German measles, or she had to fly to Amsterdam.

One rainy evening, she and her poodle Misty paid a call on Targ at the Warwick Hotel. As usual, she chain-smoked her Chesterfields, played with her dinner, and showed an unquenchable thirst for martinis. When it was time to leave, she was tremendously plastered. Targ wanted to take her home in a cab, but she refused. At the curb, as they began to argue, she donned her aristocratic manners. Targ pointed out that she had no coat or umbrella and it was pouring rain. Dragging the sleepy Misty behind her, she disappeared into the storm and left Targ standing there soaking wet.

Facing reality, Targ decided that "she wasn't capable of doing any work that she cared to see in print." That was a tactful way to describe it.

Dorothy felt as if she were being gnawed by "a great, grey rat," a rat whose name was Captain Alan Campbell. In London with Air Force Intelligence, Alan had yet to come within sniffing distance of a battlefield. Judging by the exhilarated tone of his letters, Dorothy concluded that he was having a lovely time. It seemed wrong somehow to be enjoying a war so much.

Toward the spring of 1944, she first began to worry about small, cryptic hints in his references to dinner party invitations and weekends spent whizzing about the English countryside to palatial homes. At first she ignored the hints, but they became impossible to disregard. Every now and then names were mentioned; she began to wonder if Alan might be sleeping with someone. She had not expected him to remain celibate all this time. Men would be men, she supposed, and "when were soldiers true?" She wrote a poem, her last, gingerly giving him permission to sleep with anybody he liked and emphasizing that he should not feel guilty about it either. She simply had one request:

> Only, for the nights that were,
>   Soldier, and the dawns that came,
> When in sleep you turn to her
>   Call her by my name.

After VE Day, Alan was stationed in Paris for a time, but he returned to London. He wrote Dorothy that he had fallen in love with another woman, a titled and wealthy aristocrat. This was supposed to be a secret because the woman was married and had three children. According to Alan she was passionately in love with him.

Dorothy was completely taken by surprise. Her immediate reaction was to panic, drink, and slide into a black hole of gloom. She consulted a psychiatrist for a time, but it failed to help, probably because she regarded therapists as quacks. In this crisis, Toni Strassman, Harold Guinzburg's former secretary who had become a literary agent, often held her hand. A kindhearted woman with no family responsibilities of her own, Strassman lived nearby and was willing to slip over to the New Weston to keep her company for whole evenings. Since Strassman knew Alan, she was a logical confidante to whom Dorothy could unburden her feelings about the English-woman, whose existence she wanted to conceal from her friends. Dorothy assured Strassman that she was having a nervous breakdown: She related anecdotes about her psychiatrist, alluded to powerful medications, and claimed to be receiving electroshock treatments. Since she looked half-dead, Strassman assumed she was telling the truth.

Only after Dorothy's fury against Alan began to flow did her depression slowly depart. She had two and a half years to come to terms with his bombshell, because he took his time returning after the war. Although he told her he planned to divorce and remarry, some of his friends wondered if he seriously meant it. They knew that he and his woman friend were fond of each other, got on extremely well, and shared a number of tastes, including an interest in furniture and decoration, but they doubted that the affair would result in marriage. Josh Logan interpreted it as a threat to remind Dorothy how much she needed him. "Alan expected her to plead with him to come home." Before the war, he had a great need to punish her, and his English romance was a ready-made way to achieve this end.

For a time, Dorothy's biggest fear was that the Englishwoman would want to marry Alan. When she decided she never wanted to see him again, she feared that the woman would not. That Alan might fall in love with another woman had not seriously occurred to her. Marriage to him had entailed a number of indignities, including the sly smiles of those who had ridiculed her for marrying a chorus boy. She had been responsible for placing him in a false light and telling people he was gay. She had built the myth of his homosexuality so carefully that she herself had nearly come to believe it. Even in the late fifties, she blithely remarked to Charles Addams, "I can compete with the girls, but not the boys." The Englishwoman was no boy.

By the fall of 1946, for reasons never clear to her, Alan's affair seemed to be wearing thin; suddenly he wrote that he was coming home. Dorothy did not answer. In desperation, he contacted Toni Strassman, asking her to act as intermediary, to reassure Dottie that he would be back soon. Dorothy's pride would not permit her to forgive him or to take him back. She decided it was time he earned his own living. She intended to divorce him.

Alan returned to New York on November 13. The following spring, he was in Las Vegas. In this rite of passage, both he and Dorothy charged mental cruelty. Despite his residence in Nevada, Alan insisted that he did not want a divorce, which no doubt was the truth. It was the war that had made them strangers and destroyed their marriage, he believed. "I'm sorry it's over," he told newspaper reporters. "We had a wonderful time." He assured his family that Dottie was still the love of his life. To his uncle he said: "I can't live without her and I can't live with her. Now what am I going to do about it, Roy?" Roy Eichel, a bachelor, could offer no advice.

The farm was put up for sale. Furnishings were divided, although there was little Dorothy wished to keep except the Utrillo and a Picasso gouache. The rest was either stored at Horte's house in Point Pleasant or moved into the city to furnish Alan's new duplex on East Sixty-second Street. Some of his decorating could not be removed—for example, the blueprint wallpaper in the upstairs hallway, labeled "A Country Residence for Mr. and Mrs. Alan Campbell," which finally began to buckle in the 1980s and had to be removed by the farm's present owner. The mirrors lining the dining room windows remained and the statue of Bacchus continued to stand sentinel in the garden.

Both Dorothy and Alan handled the divorce quite well. Throughout the unpleasant task of dismantling their marriage, they maintained cordial relations. Dorothy finally stopped referring to Alan as "a shit and a queer." Although they seldom saw each other, the Christmas after the divorce they spent a rare evening together at the theater and went to the Stork Club afterward. The name of the play was appropriate: *Crime and Punishment.*

Chapter 16

TOAD TIME

•

1948-1955

Tall with dark eyes and hair, Rosser Lynn Evans was thirty-one years old.
Alan had been responsible for introducing him to Dorothy in Miami Beach,
where Evans had been in Officer Candidate School with Alan and Josh
Logan. In 1942, she had paid Evans no attention, except to notice that he
was a two-fisted drinker who always seemed to be drunker than she was.
According to Logan, Evans not only seemed to be drunker, he was. "He
was a confirmed alcoholic who would just go silly with liquor. Once we got
him through a mapmaking examination by cheating for him. It was an awful
thing to do to the United States Air Force but he was a nice guy and we
liked him."

After the war, Evans was working in New York as a radio announcer
when Dorothy encountered him at a party. His confession that he aspired
to writing a novel caught her interest. She told him that she hoped to write
an historical play about Mary and Charles Lamb but hadn't yet found a
collaborator. Was he interested? This was her all-purpose cocktail party
conversational gambit, but it was fresh to Evans. Unable to distinguish
Lambs from lamb chops, he tried to hide his ignorance. Later he described
himself as "dazed. Me collaborate? I'd have been glad just to sharpen her
pencils."

Dorothy had no need of a pencil sharpener or an alcoholic radio
announcer with a secret passion to write. At the same time, she could not
deny that big, good-looking, available men were rare.

330

There were quite a few raised eyebrows among Dorothy's friends, who thought he was handsome—"a beautiful hunk of Victor Mature" said Bea Stewart—but not overly bright. Since he continued to wear his air-force shoes, they tagged him Li'l Abner, but the shoes had little to do with the nickname. Compared with Alan, Josh Logan said, "Ross Evans lacked talent, flair, and strength. Leaning against him must have been like leaning on a tower of Jell-O." Yet Dorothy needed to touch him. "She was constantly pawing him, couldn't keep her hands off him," another friend noticed.

Ross Evans, after graduating from Tenafly (New Jersey) High School, had worked as a messenger in the garment district before winning a swimming scholarship to Franklin and Marshall College, where he majored in English. He had married before the war but was now divorced. Unlike Alan, he had no interest in domesticity and thought of himself as an athlete, having once been diving champion at the Newark Athletic Club. He still had a muscular body, but liquor was beginning to take its toll.

Since Ross was an agreeable drinking companion, Dorothy felt comfortable with him. He was soon living with her at the New Weston. She thought him splendidly masculine, well built, and sexy and looked forward to a refurbished sex life. At the outset, like a false springtime, there was a brief flurry of activity. Then weeks and sometimes months would pass without Evans's exhibiting the slightest interest in sex, a not-unusual pattern with heavy drinkers. She took pleasure in publicly punishing him by announcing to a room full of guests at a party that "Rossie" would not sleep with her. She may not have been as troubled as she claimed. Late at night, engulfed in the pleasant fumes of Courvoisier, often falling into bed and passing out, she could not be bothered with sex either. When Evans did happen to be seized by an amorous urge, he sometimes acted on it forthwith, regardless of time and place. Once, while visiting friends, he began making love to Dorothy on their living room sofa. Dorothy thought it was funny, but apologized afterward to her red-faced hosts.

Since Evans had an urgent need to see his name in lights, he kept pressuring her to work so that he might accumulate a few joint bylines. Dorothy was in no hurry to oblige. When *Cosmopolitan* magazine sent around a scout to see if she could be talked into writing a story, she invited Aaron Hotchner up for a drink, even though writing fiction for *Cosmopolitan* was hardly something she had been longing to do. Ross, definitely a participant in the negotiations, swaggered around making highballs, attempted to speak for both of them, and frequently used the pronoun *we*. There was no doubt that he was eager to accept the *Cosmo* proposition.

Meanwhile, sophisticated in the ways of publishers demanding her blood, Dorothy was playing hard to get. She said that her writing joints had probably atrophied from disuse. As she began her third highball, she expressed doubt whether she could get back to the typewriter, it had been so long.

"Don't worry about that," Evans piped up. "*I'll* handle the typewriter." The way he loomed over her, legs bent and chin thrust out, reminded Hotchner of a paratrooper standing at parade rest.

Evans was absent the next time Hotchner came by to discuss his proposal. When he suggested having lunch downstairs in the dining room, Dorothy hesitated and explained that she was six months behind in her rent. She didn't dare leave her room for fear of running into the manager. Hotchner, feeling sorry for her, promised protection and assurances that the lobby at noontime would no doubt be crowded. As they cruised by the reception desk, however, a voice called out, "Mrs. Parker! May we see you a moment?"

Out bustled a receptionist who delivered a stack of uncollected mail, among which there turned out to be a check.

In the dining room, the captain came to the table for their order four times. Dorothy downed three highballs before being forced to select a lunch that she did not eat. She asked Hotchner if *Cosmopolitan* would accept a dual byline and described Evans as a person who kept her from drinking while she worked. The story she outlined to Hotchner was about a newly married couple, recently returned from their honeymoon, who were hosting a dinner party for his friends. Throughout the evening, which would include an elaborate dinner followed by parlor games, one of the guests (a former mistress of the man's) lengthily reveals to the wife that her husband's first wife had killed herself. Hotchner, who was being paid a three-hundred-dollar bonus for each famous author he bagged, didn't much care what the story was about so long as Dorothy delivered a publishable manuscript.

If Dorothy had never before collaborated on a short story, neither had Evans ever written one. He proved to be a mediocre writer. Refusing to listen to her voice of experience, he plunged ahead like a maddened racehorse, with a predictable result. When "The Game" was finally pronounced finished by Evans, she felt like a Lhasa Apso who had just given birth to a Saint Bernard. She watched the great creature stagger to its feet and lumber off into the pages of the December 1948 *Cosmopolitan*. Except for perhaps the first few paragraphs, there was nothing about "The Game" that suggested its coauthor was Dorothy Parker.

She had been pulling Hotchner's leg with her tale of atrophied writing joints. The truth was, she had not been as idle as she pretended. The previous year she and Frank Cavett had concocted a film treatment about an alcoholic wife. John Howard Lawson had subsequently based a screenplay on the treatment for Universal. *Smash-Up: The Story of a Woman* was a female version of *The Lost Weekend* with Susan Hayward effectively playing the Ray Milland role. It won Dorothy and Cavett an Academy Award nomination in 1947 for best original story and Hayward a best actress nomination. Hollywood gossip said that the film was based on the life of Bing Crosby's wife Dixie Lee, an impression that Dorothy did nothing to correct. Although *Smash-Up* lost the best story Oscar to *Miracle on Thirty-fourth Street*, it garnered exceptionally good reviews and served as an announcement in the picture business that Dorothy could still turn out quality work, with or without the slave-driving Alan Campbell.

Throughout their screen-writing career, Dorothy and Alan had been represented by various Hollywood superagents like Leland Hayward and Zeppo Marx. In early 1948, mobilizing herself for action, Dorothy retained another top agent, Irving "Swifty" Lazar, to negotiate a contract for her at Twentieth Century–Fox. When she packed up and headed for the Coast, Ross Evans followed closely on her heels.

Chateau Marmont is a bogus turreted castle on Sunset Boulevard, a bit seedy in appearance, but in 1947 even the Garden of Allah had begun to look arthritic. Dorothy settled snugly into California hotel life and spent the winter working on her play about the mad Mary Lamb. Recreating Charles and Mary Lamb and their friends, a collection of manic-depressive Bohemians that included Coleridge and a hopped-up De Quincey, was thoroughly enjoyable. All her characters had comforting habits—opium, laudanum, brandy, homicide—that she understood and respected. With a title inspired by the mythical shore where Shakespeare shipwrecked Viola and Sebastian in *Twelfth Night*, *The Coast of Illyria* was based on the tormented life of Mary Lamb, who had fatally wounded her mother by planting a kitchen knife in her chest during a psychotic episode, and on Mary's brother, Charles. Despite a sprinkling of humorous lines (Wordsworth is described as being "up to his rump in sunsets"), the play drew mainly on Dorothy's painful psychological relationship with Alan. On top of this personal memoir, she superimposed the lives of the early nineteenth-century siblings—a brother and sister who needed each other too desperately to ever separate, drifting toward destruction as the woman's recurrent attacks of insanity push the man further into alcoholism, attacks that in the end assure her total derangement.

In May 1948, she submitted the play to the Margo Jones repertory company in Dallas, a regional theater that presented quality productions of both new works and classics. It was July before she heard from Jones, a cautious response praising the play and expressing tentative interest in producing it. A month later it was scheduled for the 1949 season and its authors advanced a $150 royalty against five percent of the gross. Dorothy felt idiotically happy.

In 1948 and 1949, she attempted to recapture the success that she and Alan had achieved in Hollywood during the thirties. After her Oscar nomination for *Smash-Up*, she felt on top again. Suddenly there were job offers, money, a man. Lean times were over. Although Hollywood's golden age was nearing its end, no one knew it. Television was not yet being taken seriously, and Hollywood remained the movie capital of the world as well as a writers' fount of gold. Dorothy's first assignment at Fox was to adapt Oscar Wilde's *Lady Windermere's Fan* with Ross and Walter Reisch. Renamed *The Fan*, the picture was produced by Otto Preminger and starred George Sanders and Madeleine Carroll. Next, she turned her attention to an original screenplay called *Rose-Lipped Girls*, a title inspired by A. E. Housman's poem. It was never sold. Aside from the title, nothing about this script survives. About the same time, MGM purchased one of her short stories, "The Standard of Living," for twenty-five hundred dollars, and an independent producer optioned "Big Blonde," to be filmed on location in New York's garment center. Neither of these projects reached the screen.

In collaboration with Evans at Fox, she worked on a Loretta Young–Celeste Holm comedy about two nuns, *Come to the Stable*, and several other pictures for which they received no credit. Referring to a film intended for Humphrey Bogart, Evans joked, "We rarely think about the picture but when we do we think that we brought it up to gutter-level." Professionally and personally, Ross was content to accept second place, which enabled them to avoid some of the power struggles that had impaired Dorothy's relationship with Alan toward the end.

Dorothy had highly unrealistic expectations for *The Coast of Illyria*. In part these were fueled by Margo Jones, who praised it in terms usually reserved for events such as Halley's comet. Not only did she predict a Broadway production, but she also practically promised its appearance at the Edinburgh Festival of Music and Drama with Flora Robson playing Mary Lamb. In letters to Dorothy and Ross, she addressed them as "you two cuties," "you babies," and similar terms of flattering endearment, a personal style that made Dorothy hyperventilate. Nevertheless, she was an old hand at playing this game and sent sweet replies. "Now we know that everything people who know you have said about you is true," she purred, a statement open to more than one reading, and she assured Jones that when they finally met she would no doubt "hug you to death."

The Coast of Illyria opened in April 1949, for a three-week run. Arriving for the opening, Dorothy was an object of curiosity for actors and audiences alike. During intermissions, she fled the theater. She hated people coming up to her, and atheist that she was, acknowledged compliments by grunting, "Bless you," so that she would appear friendly. At the curtain, she received a standing ovation. "Cries for author were universal and genuine. A shaky Miss Parker and a pale Mr. Evans arose from sheltered corner seats in Section B," the *Dallas Morning News* reported. Ross, who had thus far seemed content to be treated as Dorothy's luggage bearer, babbled to a *Time* reporter: "We've tasted blood. We don't want to do anything ever again except write for the theater." Dallas critics called *Illyria* the best play of the season and compared it favorably to Tennessee Williams's *Summer and Smoke*, which had also received its premiere by Margo Jones.

When Dorothy returned to Hollywood, her moment in the sun over, it was to the heat of a California summer at the Chateau Marmont. Weekends, she and Evans drove to Malibu or Arrowhead, but mostly their life settled into a routine: studio jobs, revisions on *The Coast of Illyria*, discussion of ideas for another play, a modern work this time because she didn't want to be typecast as writing exclusively about the Romantics. By now, there had been an addition to their household, a boxer named Flic, who was a few months old when they got him. Flic turned out to be an affectionate but timid animal who was terrified of just about everybody and everything. Dorothy, giving him the benefit of the doubt, decided that he must have been mistreated by his previous owners and began a program of assertiveness training. It didn't work. Norman Mailer urged her to bring Flic over to meet his dog, a large, black, ferocious German shepherd, apparently on the theory that if Flic could manage to make friends with Karl, he would be cured. Dorothy admired Mailer's best-selling *The Naked and the Dead*. When he sought her out upon his arrival in Los Angeles that summer, she had found the young war novelist and his pregnant wife, Beatrice, to be amusing company. Mailer, exhibitionist as only an insecure, twenty-six-year-old first novelist can be, seemed pathetically eager to be liked. Not so with Karl, whom Dorothy and Ross agreed had a shifty look. She doubted that a confrontation would be a good idea. Mailer said she overestimated the danger and assured her that Karl would behave himself.

When Dorothy and Ross drove up to Mailer's house, Flic must have caught a whiff of Karl because he seemed reluctant to leave the car. When they finally persuaded him to enter the living room, he immediately urinated on the carpet. Everyone could hear Karl breathing noisily in another part of the house. Dorothy, nervous, got ready to bolt, but Mailer swore he could control the situation.

At last Karl was led out on a leash. Advancing pleasantly, he first eyeballed Flic and sniffed his nose. Then he exploded like a bursting watermelon, his fleshy pink jaws spraying streams of spittle. As Mailer wrestled Karl back to a bedroom, Ross tried to quiet the petrified Flic and got his finger bitten.

As they were getting ready to drive off, Dorothy watched Mailer come scampering after them, shouting and waving his arms. Although outraged, she forced herself to speak. "I said it wouldn't work," she told him. Mailer said that he was sorry, but he did not look contrite. It would be nine years before she saw him again, and then she would remember only the harrowing encounter with his dog. In her eyes there was nothing he could do to redeem himself.

During the summer Dorothy was forced to cut back her drinking. Ruth Goetz, in Hollywood with Gus to write a film adaptation of their successful Broadway play *The Heiress*, remembers Dorothy's entrance to a party at their house. She fell flat on her face in the hall and had to be scraped up and carried out feet first. In poor health, she suffered from back pains that sapped her strength and caused her to hobble around "bent and bitter." Admitted to the hospital for tests and X-rays, she was treated by a doctor who lectured her about excessive drinking. "One of her doctors," Ross

Evans reported to Margo Jones, "said he didn't like her kidneys and she later confessed that she didn't like his nose."

Bit by bit Dorothy resigned herself to the fact that *The Coast of Illyria* would go to neither Broadway nor Edinburgh, although it was a bitter truth to accept. In due course, this failure affected her relations with Ross, who turned moody and talked about wanting peace and quiet. She felt that if their life were much quieter they would be in a coma.

Evans suggested they leave Hollywood. Fearful of electricity in general and electrical appliances in particular, he proposed they relocate in a country where neither was highly regarded, nor continuously available. In Mexico, he promised Dorothy, they would be able to write creatively and live cheaply. He began to promote a town south of Mexico City, Cuernavaca, which had a semitropical climate year-round, sounded suitably exotic, and enjoyed popularity with American tourists. Before many weeks had passed, Ross's imagination had transformed Cuernavaca into the promised land. When his nagging could be ignored no longer, Dorothy condescended to spending a month's vacation in Mexico.

In March 1950, they rolled south in Evans's dusty De Soto, with the sleeping boxer sprawled across the backseat. The trip was notable for its unfriendliness. Dorothy clothed herself in her grand-duchess disguise, and Evans did an outstanding imitation of Abner Yokum. When they arrived at the plaza in Cuernavaca, Dorothy climbed out of the car and gazed around sourly.

They rented a house on the outskirts of town for three hundred pesos a month, a bargain that Dorothy scarcely appreciated. Nor did she find the local culture as entrancing as Ross did. There was a melancholy cathedral, a single movie theater showing endless Cantinflas films, and several dinky outdoor cafés whose tables were monopolized by Americans wearing unattractive beards. She ran into a few Hollywood acquaintances who were staying at the hotels. She also looked up Martha Gellhorn, who, now divorced from Hemingway, was living there with her adopted son.

Certain activities taking place in Cuernavaca that spring would have interested Dorothy a great deal had she known of them at the time. One of the residents there was busily keeping tabs on her for the Federal Bureau of Investigation, though spotty investigation turned up very little of import.

The informer was able to find out, for example, the amount of rent Dorothy paid for the house but not Ross Evans's name. The report refers to him only as "an American writer of the male sex." According to this document, which was added to her ever-growing file, "In Cuernavaca she is not known to have placed herself in contact with Mexican Communists but according to xxxxxxxxxxxxx [name deleted by FBI] PARKER is in contact with various Spanish refugees who reside in Cuernavaca; however, PARKER does not speak Spanish and it is not believed that these contacts are very intensive."

Dorothy found living in Cuernavaca stupendously monotonous. To make matters worse, after five or six weeks had gone by, she noticed Ross paying excessive attention to a woman who owned a dress shop in town. Jealous, eager for a bit of drama, she protested angrily, but he said nothing. When she threatened to leave, he answered that she could go that very day if she liked.

At the airport in Mexico City, a surly Ross stopped at the terminal entrance just long enough for Dorothy to scramble out before he gunned the De Soto's motor and pointed it back toward Cuernavaca. He said later, "This so-called Land of Enchantment hardly amused Milady." Too angry to ask where she was going, he assumed she was returning to "the land of milk and soundtracks," but Dorothy purchased a ticket to New York.

Arriving at the Plaza Hotel with her belongings stuffed into two large straw bags, she was dressed in a drindl skirt and a scruffy peasant blouse and looked like a migrant lettuce picker. Her request for a suite ignored the fact that such accommodations cost fifty-five dollars a day and she was carrying barely enough cash on her person to pay the taxi driver. Desperate to get her bearings, she could think of no more ideal surroundings in which to burn Ross Evans in effigy than the most expensive hotel in New York. Soon, she got hold of herself and began telephoning to gather together her friends, the tone of her voice promising electrifying stories of adventures south of the border.

When Bea Stewart arrived, Dorothy gave her a tour of the suite before putting on a woebegone face and launching into a recital of her afflictions: Li'l Abner was a totally inept writer who had never published a story; she had got him a byline in *Cosmopolitan;* his closest contact with movies had been Radio City Music Hall; she had got him a Hollywood screen credit, VIP treatment in Dallas, and his name in *Time* magazine. She had even given him the portrait of Scott Fitzgerald she had purchased from Zelda in 1934. She had not expected gratitude. On the other hand, she did not expect him to desert her for another woman, throw her out of her house, force her to flee the country, and—if all that were not horrible enough—he had stolen her dog too. From now on, she vowed, she planned to live by herself.

Three months later, she married Alan again in a splendid ceremony in Bel Air, California, after waking on the morning of August 17, 1950, pulling the blanket over her face, and warning him not to look at the bride. It was bad luck.

She behaved as if the surprise reconciliation had been foreordained and regarded it as a second chance. "Who in life gets a second chance?" she asked. Eager to have fun again, perhaps to be spoiled by a nice-looking man, she was willing to forget ten years riddled by conflict. Alan, oddly enough, was the one who felt uncertain about remarriage. He queried friends, "Do you think she needs me?" A woman he had been dating expressed herself bluntly and asked him, "How can you marry that old woman?" The question was beside the point; at forty-six, Alan had long ceased to consider the age difference. Announcing the news to the press, he said that he had asked Dottie to remarry him, because this was how it was done where he came from, and she had said yes. "You never know why one does these things," he added lamely. They had no plans for a honeymoon because, Dorothy said, "we've been everywhere."

Alan took charge of the wedding arrangements. He leased and hastily furnished a big house, booked a judge, and ordered a bridal bouquet. Charlie Brackett served as best man and Dorothy, in a nonethnic taffeta cocktail dress, was attended by Sally Foster and Miriam Hopkins. The reception at the Brackett home was memorable for lavish food and drink and the diversity of the guests, who included Humphrey Bogart, Howard and Lucinda Dietz, and James Agee. When somebody pointed out that a few of the guests had not spoken to each other for years, Dorothy agreed that was true. "Including the bride and groom," she murmured. Budd Schulberg described the party as "a real Hollywood wedding. Dottie had a little bouquet of violets and was busy playing the bride. She went around saying, 'What are you going to do when you love the son of a bitch?' She was a riot and yet nobody could doubt she was absolutely serious." Alan was heard to remark brightly that "now we can have dinner parties again." As the evening wore on, reported Howard Dietz, "parlor games erupted and raged for hours. All the guests who could still walk played, until Dottie got mad at Alan for guessing she was the wolf suckling Romulus and Remus when she was acting out the Brooklyn Bridge."

For Alan, the three years since the divorce had often been a struggle, but he was not a person who permitted himself to suffer visibly. For a time he had shared his Manhattan duplex with Tom Heggen, the writer whose comic war novel, *Mister Roberts*, had been transformed by Josh Logan into a successful Broadway play. In 1949, while Alan was in Hollywood, a maid found Heggen in the bathtub, dead of an overdose of sleeping pills. Alan, aware of Heggen's severe depression, refused to admit that he might have deliberately killed himself and instead insisted that Tom must have dozed off in the tub. He soon gave up the duplex and moved to California, where he found it increasingly hard to command either the assignments or the money he had received as Dorothy's partner. A Fox executive urged him to reconcile with his ex-wife, then he would hire them as a team. This did happen after the wedding. In November, they were employed for three weeks.

In the winter of 1951, he and Dorothy tried to pick up their marriage where they had abandoned it in 1942. They had dinner parties. Dorothy bought a new silver-colored poodle whom she named Misty for the dog she'd owned during the war, and she also allowed Alan to institute a regime aimed at improving her health and appearance. In January, he reported to the Murphys that Dorothy looked and felt terrific after getting a new short haircut and a permanent wave. She now had "a beautiful figure, and feels fine besides," but this impression was misleading. Their second attempt at matrimony was not proving a success. By this time, Alan must have been getting nervous.

In mid-April, two men rang the doorbell. Before they could identify themselves as FBI agents, Dorothy knew they meant trouble—because they were wearing hats, she explained afterward. They began by inquiring if she knew Dashiell Hammett and Lillian Hellman, then went on to mention other names: Donald Stewart, Ella Winter, and John Howard Lawson. Was she aware that these individuals were Communists? they asked. Had she ever attended a C.P. meeting with them?

This quiz was merely a prelude. Next came endless questions, quotations from their portable collection of newspaper clippings, references to organizations, rallies, and banquets so unimportant that she could no longer recollect them. Throughout the interrogation, Misty kept barking and jumping on the men, so that Dorothy was frequently obliged to chastise her, although not in a very firm tone because she was probably getting vicarious pleasure from the dog's refusal to behave. The agents seemed to be curious about Dorothy's feelings. They repeatedly asked how she felt about this or that group. "Frankly," she finally said, "I was going through change of life then. How would you have felt?"

On some points she replied emphatically. When asked if she had ever conspired to overthrow the government of the United States, she assured them, "Listen, I can't even get my dog to stay down. Do I look to you like someone who could overthrow the government?"

She impressed them, they wrote afterward, as "a very nervous type of person" who weighed approximately 125 pounds and dressed neatly. "During the course of this interview, she denied ever having been affiliated with, having donated to, or being contacted by a representative of the C.P." Their report was soon joined by another exhibit, a form letter mailed out over her signature on behalf of the Spanish Refugee League, which Walter Winchell's office had forwarded to FBI director J. Edgar Hoover with a note:

> Dear Mr. Hoover:
>   Mr. Winchell wondered if you knew about Dorothy Parker, the poet and wit, who led many pro-Russian groups. She and the boss were once good friends, but she became a mad fanatic of the Commy party line.

The decade-long shadow cast over the country's history by McCarthyism poisoned Dorothy's personal and professional life and eventually undermined her spirit. She could think of no better term to describe the horror of the anti-Communist inquisition than Dalton Trumbo's derisive phrase "the time of the toad," when stool pigeons played the informer to save themselves. Many friends of hers were blacklisted, denounced as traitors, subpoenaed, cited for contempt of Congress, and sentenced to prison terms. Among those close to her, Lillian Hellman managed to foil the House Un-American Activities Committee by refusing to betray friends and still escaping the consequences. Less fortunate were Dashiell Hammett and

Ring Lardner, Jr., who ended by serving prison terms. Donald Stewart and Ella Winter avoided subpoenas by moving to England. Practically all of Dorothy's friends on the board of the Joint Anti-Fascist Refugee Committee, whose national chairman she had been, went to jail after declining to turn over records to HUAC.

Dorothy's deliberately provocative behavior seemed calculated to attract HUAC's attention. At first, perhaps underestimating the dangers involved, she adopted defiance as the only sane response. In 1947, speaking at a rally to raise money for the defense of Hans Eisler (brother of C.P. leader Gerhart Eisler), she unabashedly informed the audience that she was there to "damn the souls" of the Committee and its chairman, Representative J. Parnell Thomas. The next day she read her remarks in the New York *Daily News,* along with the information that HUAC planned to subpoena her. The Committee failed to carry out its threat, and no United States deputy marshal arrived at the New Weston bearing a bright pink slip. In September of that year, when Thomas began subpoenaing people in the film industry, she journeyed to Washington in order to attend the hearings in person and did not hesitate to voice her disgust. In New York, she delivered a scorching speech at a fund-raising reception for the nineteen Hollywood directors, actors, and writers who refused to cooperate with the Committee, where she shouted, "For Heaven's sake, children, Fascism isn't coming— it's here. It's dreadful. Stop it!" Still she was not called to testify, even though she continued to characterize the Committee as a bunch of fools and to denounce the FBI as an agency that she held in "monumental scorn."

Beginning in 1949, her name came up regularly as a subversive. In that year, not only was she branded a "Red appeaser" by the California State Senate Committee on Un-American Activities, but at the espionage trial of Judith Coplon, accused of stealing government secrets to aid Russia, an FBI document naming Dorothy and Edward G. Robinson as traitors was read aloud. The accusation made her feel "very sick" because she was glad to be an American, she said. She was acquainted with no Russians—but wished she was—and had no plans to sell them secrets, for the simple reason that she knew none. Robinson denied he had ever been a Party member. No denial was issued by Dorothy, who insisted that she did not "even understand what a Communist organization is."

By 1950, the year Senator Joseph McCarthy made his first charges, the FBI had categorized Dorothy as one of four hundred concealed Communists, which they defined as a person "who does not hold himself out as a Communist and who would deny membership in the Party." The Bureau also quoted an informant as stating that Dorothy had once been considered "queen of the Communists" by her neighbors in Bucks County. The same informant reported that, although Dorothy publicly disparaged HUAC, privately she was more worried than she let on. She had been heard to declare that if the Committee questioned her about the C.P., she would refuse to answer, and she also boasted of having friends in the Justice Department who had offered to get her files removed if the need ever arose. In 1950, she found herself listed in the pamphlet *Red Channels*, a right-wing compilation of "Communist sympathizers" that the broadcasting and advertising industries adopted as a guide to employment and blacklisting. To be included in *Red Channels* could be dismissed as a gigantic joke, even as a strange kind of compliment because it also listed liberals like Leonard Bernstein and Marc Connelly. The following year, screenwriter Martin Berkeley singled her out as a top Hollywood Communist. "I was black-listed," Dorothy admitted later. While she had never actually been dismissed from a job, she knew that "I couldn't get another" had she sought employment.

In 1953, Dorothy read in *The New York Times* that Senator McCarthy planned to call her as a witness in connection with his investigation of subversive literature in the State Department's overseas libraries. This proved another false alarm—no subpoena arrived. Should she ever be called, she had decided on the course she would follow. Choices were limited to three: invoke the First Amendment and risk going to prison, take the Fifth and risk blacklisting and possibly imprisonment, or cooperate with the Committee by turning informer. Her choice was to take the Fifth. She agreed with E. M. Forster, who had written that if he were forced to choose between betraying a friend and betraying his country, he hoped he would have the courage to betray his country.

She was finally invited to mount a witness stand in 1955, and then it was strictly a local show, a New York State legislative committee investigating the alleged diversion of millions in charitable contributions to the Communist Party. Dorothy was called because one of the committee's targets was the Joint Anti-Fascist Refugee Committee, listed by the U.S. Attorney General as a Communist front. She arrived at the county court house looking smart in a mink jacket over a brown suit, a large Tyrolean-style hat, and a regal smile. Unlike other witnesses who began angrily denouncing the state senators, she controlled her temper. It was true, she told them, that she had made speeches and signed countless letters appealing for funds when she had been national chairman, but she had not composed the letters. As for what had become of the $1.5 million collected to aid refugees from Franco, she had no idea. She knew nothing about the JAFRC's finances except that the money was used "to help people who were helpless." Nor did she know if the group was controlled by the C.P.—it had never occurred to her to ask, she said. Dorothy was uniformly polite to all queries except one. Asked if she had ever been a member of the Party, she ferociously invoked the Fifth Amendment and declined to answer on the grounds of possible self-incrimination.

Shortly after she took the Fifth, the FBI closed its investigation of her. A four-page memorandum, dated April 15, 1955, and reviewing her C.P. activity since 1950, concluded with the following recommendation: "Although the foregoing information reflects CP front activity in the past three years, and the subject could technically qualify for inclusion in the Security Index, it is not felt that she is dangerous enough to warrant her inclusion in same."

The summer of 1951, with the Korean War entering its second year, was particularly frightening. In July, Dashiell Hammett was arrested after declining to reveal the names of contributors to a bail fund operated by the Civil Rights Congress, a group largely devoted to supporting the civil rights of Party members. The specter of doom had edged much closer to home than Hammett's trouble, however. In March, a man known to be a Communist Party leader was appearing before HUAC when one of the Committee members suddenly brought up the name of Alan Campbell.

> MR. TAVENNER. Allen [sic] Campbell was secretary of the Hollywood Anti-Nazi League. Have you talked to him about the affairs of the league?
>
> MR. JEROME. I decline to answer the question in the exercise of my right against discrimination.

Representative Frank Tavenner dropped Alan and went on to other individuals, but even that brief mention seemed ominous to Alan. He was shocked. In the thirties, he had gone along with Dorothy's politics simply because he was her husband, but he had rejected the Party long ago. He was terrified that he would be blacklisted and thus unable to work; indeed he must have already attributed part of his difficulty in getting a job to Dorothy's politics. Alan was not the only one to feel panic. As Sid Perelman noted, the mood in Hollywood had passed beyond simple anxiety and now rapidly approached frenzy. Many he knew worried about being interned by the FBI—"and people *are* being so jugged and blacklisted." He described the film capital as a terrible combination of a boom town gone bust and Nazi Germany in 1935. Dorothy likened the widespread fear to "the smell of a Black Plague."

During that summer, Dorothy and Alan planned no dinner parties. After a violent quarrel, Alan walked out and their marriage ended as abruptly as it had resumed. His parting comment, Dorothy later claimed, was to hand her a twenty-dollar bill and tell her not to worry because the rent was paid for a year. Unfortunately, he neglected to mention the furniture. Not long after he left, a store van drove up and movers began to strip the house systematically to the bare walls, although Dorothy was able to rescue her bed.

More disgusted than bitter, she washed her hands of Alan for a second time, swearing that this time the marriage was dead. For several weeks, she managed on her own. At the end of the summer, despite the barren rooms, she acquired two roommates, Jim Agee and his friend Pat Scallon, a pretty, fresh-complected twenty-two-year-old whom Dorothy privately christened the Pink Worm. Agee, forty-one, former film critic for *Time,* and now a highly regarded screenwriter, was enveloped in a full-blown obsession with the young woman, even though he had a family in New York. Like Dorothy, Agee was an alcoholic, but his physical condition was far worse. Earlier that year he had suffered a coronary while working on *The African Queen.* He was supposed to ease up on liquor and cigarettes, and to eat salads, fruit, and fish, the latter items seldom found in Dorothy's pantry. Agee smoked and drank as usual and showed no sign of being able to change his regimen. Dorothy told Sid Perelman that one Friday evening he had consumed three bottles of Scotch unaided, which led Perelman to speculate about the quantity *she* had consumed. Agee looked like a panhandler. Day after day he wore the same filthy, sweaty shirt and pants, the same scuffed black shoes. He badly required a barber, a dentist, and a bath. Other writers at Fox complained about having to eat lunch near him in the commissary.

Dorothy, who got on well with him, welcomed his company. She was unperturbed about his disregard for personal hygiene, having more than once found herself in a like frame of mind. For that matter, anyone who valued domestic cleanliness would not have remained long in her house. The condition of the place grew increasingly squalid as the weeks went on because arranging for maid or laundry service did not occur to her. She liked having Agee around, especially after one convivial evening when she walked into a tree in the yard, causing her to fall insensible to the ground. She figured that she might have been lying there until morning if Agee had not come along and dragged her inside.

Her ménage à trois with Agee and the Pink Worm caused the squeamish to blanch. A disgusted Sid Perelman described them as living like pigs "in a fog of crapulous laundry, stale cigarette smoke, and dirty dishes, sans furniture or cleanliness; one suspects they wet their beds." The group broke up at the end of October when Agee was stricken with a second heart attack. Once he had been released from the hospital, his wife, Mia, arrived to take charge of him. Dorothy, alone and lonely in the empty rooms, her toleration for disorder apparently having reached its limit, moved herself and Misty to a tidy room at the Chateau Marmont.

By September 1952, she was back in New York and feeling so grateful to be home that "I get up every morning and want to kiss the pavement." She leased an apartment in a residence hotel on East Seventy-fourth Street, just off Central Park. The Volney was a small, well-kept, moderately expensive hotel popular with the literary and theater crowd. Dorothy knew a number of people who had once lived there, including journalist Quentin Reynolds, who still did. It was idyllic for Misty, since there were more than forty dogs in the building. All she wanted to do now was to write a successful play and be able to "eat and live and have a roof—and buy some dresses." Soon after her arrival she wasted no time in beginning a play featuring characters who live in a hotel that closely resembles the Volney.

In California, while working on a picture about Eva Tanguay called *The I Don't Care Girl*, she had met Arnaud d'Usseau. At thirty-six, d'Usseau was a successful playwright who had a fine record as a co-writer on the Broadway stage. During the war, collaborating with James Gow, he had taken part in several commercial hits including *Tomorrow the World* and

Deep Are the Roots. In 1951, after Gow died, d'Usseau tried to write a play alone but was never able to get it produced. Like Dorothy, he did best as a team writer. When they met, it was a case of two professionals in search of a collaborator. Dorothy also felt personally attracted to the hard-working, moody, bespectacled writer, a well-known radical whose views were compatible with her own.

Their original idea, a murder mystery, was soon discarded. "We dropped it when we found we liked the murderers too much," Dorothy joked. Instead, they began talking about a social phenomenon particularly noticeable in New York but certainly not exclusive to it. "We had been thinking of the numbers of small expensive hotels, lived in by lone ladies. And there we were." Like the Volney, these apartment hotels were located in the side streets of the Upper East Side, streets so desirable that they actually had trees planted on them. Exclusive and expensive, they proudly advertised their addresses by claiming that everything interesting in Manhattan lay within convenient distance, a ridiculous boast in Dorothy's opinion because she doubted very much that the women who lived in these hotels ever went anywhere interesting. Mostly they were widows who, in Dorothy's words, "are not young. But they take excellent care of themselves, and may look forward to twenty good years, which will be spent . . . doing what they are doing in the present, which is nothing at all."

Admittedly these idle, elderly, lavender-coiffed widows sounded dreary. How many people would want to watch three acts about their barren lives? But what if a woman younger than the rest should happen to be washed ashore, someone who is aware of time slipping by and who looks around and sees in her sister guests some unhappy prophecies of her own future, someone like herself? It was interesting to imagine the complications that such a catalyst might provoke.

There is no question that Dorothy liked the Volney, despite her fierce criticism of it during the next fifteen years. It was exactly to her taste, the kind of surroundings that felt as familiar as a mother's womb. A green canopied entrance led to a dark, oak-paneled lounge where residents congregated for free tea, gossip, and sour examinations of visitors. Behind the front desk, a switchboard operator smoked and read movie magazines. At the end of the lobby was a dining room where a round table displaying fruit and pastries that seemed to be made of wax sat in the doorway. Dorothy, who always used room service for meals, seldom ate there. She paid $275 (a hefty price in 1952) for a two-room apartment that included a good-sized living room, bedroom, and pantry with a small refrigerator and a hot plate. There were other advantages as well. The management offered maid and laundry service and doormen to walk dogs and assist tipsy residents out of cabs. Once a year, the hotel redecorated and replaced the furniture and rugs that Misty had urinated upon or chewed up.

Not only did she find the Volney comfortable, but also she derived perverse pleasure from its aging clientele, who provided a butt for her ghoulish humor. It seemed as if everywhere she looked her eyes fell upon dried-up females who appeared on the brink of death. She began to wonder how the hotel would get her out should she happen to die. Obviously not by the tiny passenger elevator, which could not accommodate a coffin unless it was stood on end, an undignified position in her opinion, and she certainly would not wish to be carted away in the service elevator with the trash. Finally she came up with a solution that she confided to Quentin Reynolds, who was living on the sixth floor. They must persuade the Volney to build a chute leading from one of its upper floors to the Frank Campbell Funeral Home, a well-known mortuary located a few blocks away. "We'd arrive in good condition and the trip would take a minute," Dorothy said.

Dorothy and Arnaud d'Usseau spent the fall at the Volney writing *The Ladies of the Corridor,* whose title came from T. S. Eliot's "Sweeney Erect." To avoid problems, d'Usseau's wife, Susan, established strict rules for dealing with Dorothy's drinking. The d'Usseaus began to function as a package replacement for Alan, with Arnaud as writing partner and Susan assuming responsibility for maintenance of sobriety and management of daily affairs.

Susan was a textile designer and portrait painter. Some years before, she had operated the Book of the Day shop in Hollywood, a bookstore and art gallery that the House Un-American Activities Committee described as a Communist Party front business. Not a great beauty in her physical features, she was vivacious and good humored, an exceptional cook and hostess who knew how to make guests feel comfortable. She was fifteen years older than her husband, whom she married when he was in his early twenties. As a friend described the couple, "She educated him to be a cosmopolitan who knew what to order in restaurants and what wine went with what. Before that he had been a little boy wet behind the ears." When Arnaud presented his new collaborator, Susan promptly took Dorothy in hand and decided she must be kept off the bottle. Using a system of rewards and bribes, she decreed there would be no drinking during working hours.

After work, Arnaud brought Dorothy and Misty back to the house the d'Usseaus owned on East Fifty-eighth Street, where Susan had a home-cooked meal waiting. She fixed Dorothy a drink, allotting time enough for only one before serving the meal at the unusually early hour of six-thirty. After dinner there was entertainment in the form of guests, who had been invited to spend the evening playing charades, adverbs, Botticelli, all the parlor games that Dorothy adored. Susan, in the meantime, unobtrusively monitored Dorothy's liquor intake so that she would be pleasantly high but not so drunk that she could not work the next day.

Through the d'Usseaus, Dorothy met actor-painter Zero Mostel and his wife, Kate, both of whom she liked immediately and henceforth counted among her closest friends. Zero disliked games, but found that playing with Dorothy was amusing enough to make an exception. One night they were playing Botticelli, the game of identities in which a player thinks of a famous person, Hamlet for example, and tells the other players the initial. They have to ask questions like "Did you write music to be played on water?" and the player who is "it" has to reply, "No, I'm not Handel." When it was Dorothy's turn to ask a question, she said, "Do you chase men for business and pleasure?"—a question that stumped the it-player so thoroughly that he had to give up. "J. Edgar Hoover," Dorothy said. Her answer found an appreciative audience in Mostel who suffered from black-listing and the grilling of congressional committees. An adoring Kate Mostel thought of Dorothy as "a little flower who wasn't like the rest of us. She was a fragile, ladylike lady who had to be protected. Somebody would always do her taxes, always escort her home in a taxi, always pick up the tab in a restaurant."

Dorothy found it vulgar for a woman even to acknowledge the presence of a check on a restaurant table. When invited to friends' homes, she was content to do nothing after dinner but smoke in the parlor while waiting for after-dinner drinks to be served. Whenever she visited the Mostels, she trotted around the table before dinner and folded up the napkins into animal shapes and afterward offered to help Kate clean up. She took a single plate and polished it until Kate removed it from her hands. The Mostels, aware of her reputation for lethality, waited to be bit but found her toothless.

Kate and Zero Mostel spoiled her. Zero's brother Milton became her accountant, a hair-raising task because she kept no records and all checks were made out to liquor stores or cash. Susan d'Usseau ran errands and bought her clothes, even underwear. As a result, Dorothy was looking uncharacteristically fashionable. One reason for the rather odd clothing she normally wore was that she disliked shopping, but a more serious problem was her figure, which had begun to develop a notable alcoholic tire around the middle and made her feel self-conscious. To Norman Mailer, her clothing looked as if it had come from attics, except that Los Angeles was a city without attics, and so he never could figure out where she acquired her "congeries of black shawls and garments that gave her the appearance of a British witch." The loose, baggy garments did little for her appearance, but they were comfortable.

Susan d'Usseau was, Dorothy discovered, a rigid taskmaster, but more often than not she succeeded in keeping her sober. Dorothy did not mind being bossed around, at least not during the week, because she enjoyed Susan's personal services—and she did not even have to be married to get them. She showed her appreciation by thanking her profusely and sending her a case of champagne one New Year's. Weekends and holidays were mercifully exempt from the regimen. On Thanksgiving Day, invited to the Mostels for dinner, she showed up late with the excuse that she had seen a lost kitten huddled under a car. "That was really the drunkest I ever saw her," said Kate Mostel. "She had a crying jag and all evening talked about the kitten who had no home." The other guests decided she must have an exceptional passion for cats. Another evening at the Mostels, writer Ian Hunter threatened to kill his family cat. Angry because the animal had urinated in his favorite chair again, he asked for suggestions on the best way to dispose of it. "I expected Dottie to get hysterical," Kate Mostel said. "Instead she said to Ian, 'Have you tried kindness?' "

By the time *The Ladies of the Corridor* was completed at the end of the year, Dorothy had begun thinking of it as a feminist play that warned women "to stop sitting around and saying 'It's a man's world.' " Although the wasted lives of her characters disturbed her, she was inclined to believe that their illness was rooted not so much in age as in manlessness "and they should be better trained, adjusted to live a life without a man," a problem that she herself had yet to resolve. It is difficult to determine d'Usseau's contribution to the story since this was a drama about being Dorothy Parker at fifty-nine, living in a hotel without a man, feeling terrified, and wondering what "fresh hell" lay in wait for her. All the characters seemed to be taken from her life: Eleanor Rothschild, Alan, Horte, but mostly various aspects of herself as an alcoholic, would-be suicide, middle-aged woman seeking affection from a younger man, and as the crone she feared becoming.

Producer Walter Fried planned a first-class production for the following fall. Harold Clurman staged it with an all-star cast. In the leading roles were Edna Best, Betty Field, and Shepperd Strudwick, and an excellent supporting cast included Frances Starr, June Walker, Vera Allen, Margaret Barker, and Walter Matthau. These were exciting months for Dorothy who attended all the rehearsals. Walter Matthau remembered her as "very quiet and quite shy."

Harold Clurman found her presence unpleasant. "The first day of rehearsal, when we actually put the play on the stage and it was working out very nicely, she began to cry because there it was coming to life." He labeled her "a bleeding-heart" liberal who was "seldom far from hysteria." They clashed because she refused to give him credit for knowing anything about audiences. He assured her the play would be a hit if she agreed to cut the Betty Field–character's suicide and give the work a happy ending. Dorothy wouldn't hear of it. Making the alcoholic character suffer pleased her, and furthermore, she despised happy endings.

The Ladies of the Corridor had its premiere on October 21, 1953. Dorothy thought it would be "insane" to attend the opening, but, of course, she did. The minute the curtain lowered she crept out and accompanied the d'Usseaus and the Mostels to the home of friends for a celebration and to wait for the reviews, "and then some bastard said, 'Let's go out and get the papers.' " Some of the reviews turned out to be disappointing, "not rotten, but not good," remembered Kate Mostel, who played a small part as a chambermaid. They all did their best to comfort Dorothy, calling critic Brooks Atkinson a jerk who couldn't distinguish "shit from Shinola," but the negative comments hurt because, she said, "that play was the only thing I have ever done in which I had great pride." As she was pulling on her coat to leave, she whispered, "Does anybody need a lady pool shark?"

The Ladies of the Corridor turned out to be a near-miss. Even though *The New York Times* critic thought everyone knew old women lead pathetic lives without having to go to the theater for a reminder, still five of the eight New York reviewers admired the play. It especially impressed George Jean Nathan, who voted it the best American play of the season in the Drama Critics Circle balloting. It was, he thought, "completely honest." It also closed after six weeks.

Almost immediately, Dorothy and d'Usseau began work on a second play. The protagonist of *The Ice Age*, Gordon Corey, is a passive man of twenty-five, extremely good-looking, always tanned, married, strapped for money, and living with his mother. Even after twenty-five years, Dorothy's hatred of Horte Campbell remained intense, because she included dialogue that characterized Gordon Corey's mother as evil and stupid. After finding a job at an art museum, he is seduced by its owner, Adrian Zabel, a wealthy and cultivated homosexual of almost satanic dimensions who regards him as a perfect sex object. When Daisy Corey, Gordon's wife, accuses her husband of sleeping with his employer, he shouts hysterically that he no longer feels sexual desire for her and cannot even bear to touch her. Once the homosexual affair has driven away Daisy and their newborn child, and Adrian is planning to add Gordon to his permanent collection, Gordon bashes in his head with a piece of marble sculpture as the curtain falls.

In the fall of 1955, producer Robert Whitehead agreed to take an option on *The Ice Age* and advanced the authors fifteen hundred dollars. When the good news was reported to Dorothy, she rejoiced at getting a deal that seemed "very pretty and I love it." What she did not suspect was that Whitehead cared little for the play and did not intend to produce it. He was, however, fond of Dorothy:

> The subject of homosexuality wasn't unusual in the fifties, and by then I was getting kind of bored reading plays about people whose mothers and fathers had made them fags. It was a bad play, and I didn't want to do it, but I must have decided, "Oh Christ, I'll option it because of Dottie and then let the option drop."

That was precisely what happened. *The Ice Age* failed to enthuse Dorothy's New York agent, Leah Salisbury, because it sounded more like a political tract than a play. She dutifully tried to interest Emlyn Williams in playing the museum director, but when these negotiations failed and the Whitehead option was dropped, she made no further effort to arrange a production. By that time, Dorothy herself had grown disenchanted and was willing to let it die a natural death.

The Ice Age concluded her professional collaboration with d'Usseau as well as her intimacy with him and his wife. During the McCarthy period, the couple's lives had grown increasingly rocky. Arnaud d'Usseau had been described as a member of the Hollywood Communist Party by Martin Berkeley and others. Summoned before HUAC in 1953, he declined to discuss his political affiliations, past or present, on the basis of the Fifth Amendment and spent most of his time on the witness stand energetically engaging the congressmen in debates about anti-Semitism and racial discrimination. Susan d'Usseau, unlike her husband, was closemouthed, and her time on the stand was accordingly brief. She took the Fifth and First amendments whenever queried about Party membership and refused to answer almost every question put to her. While neither of the d'Usseaus cooperated with the Committee, neither was cited for contempt. Their marriage broke up.

Although Dorothy had needed the d'Usseaus, she resented assistance and hated the obligations that such dependency always entailed. In the end, she retaliated by writing a story about characters who loosely resembled the d'Usseaus in some respects. She portrayed the woman as the epitome of an abandoned wife who whines so bitterly and incessantly that nobody can stand to be around her, and the husband as a man who walks out on a marriage considered ideal because, his wife decides later, he was going through male menopause. Her picture of the wife was especially heartless.

Dorothy had difficulty feeling appreciative for the temporary sobriety the d'Usseaus imposed on her—even if it made possible two playscripts.

Chapter 17

HIGH-FORCEPS DELIVERIES

•

1955—1960

Dorothy's dream of Broadway fame may have been thwarted, but it brought her back to New York, forced her to plan a life without Alan, and paved the way for her return to writing fiction. For the first time since 1941, her byline appeared in *The New Yorker*.

While working on *The Ice Age*, where homosexuality had been a central motif and she had revealed a predictable lack of sensitivity in her treatment of certain types of homosexuals, she was also writing "I Live on Your Visits," which was published in *The New Yorker* in January 1955. Once again her preoccupation with homosexuality overflowed into her work. Inspired by observation of a friend's relations with her sons, the story was primarily about the sterile life of an alcoholic divorcée who lives vicariously on the visits of an adolescent son now making his home with his father and stepmother. Dorothy must have been privately appalled, because she was pitiless in exposing her friend as a drunken mother who inflicts untold damage on her child. For comic relief, however, Dorothy could not resist adding a peripheral character who drifts in and out of the story, a character whom editor William Maxwell described as "a chatterbox homosexual queen, well along in years and terribly amusing, a perfectly standard character that everybody would now recognize. My superiors stuck at the idea of writing about such a person." He was instructed to inform Dorothy that the magazine would not publish the story unless the homosexual was removed. "She agreed to this, reluctantly, and probably only because she was in need of money," said Maxwell. She certainly needed money, but her greater need was to publish fiction again. The story as printed suffers from monotonous repetition in showing the mother's unconscious cruelty. While it did not require a homosexual character, it needed a counterpoint to dilute the intensity of Dorothy's painful portrait of the mother and son. Her instinct was essentially correct.

The New Yorker published two additional stories. "Lolita" (1955) concerns the necessity for escaping from the type of possessive, manipulating mother whom Dorothy had written about in her two recent plays and in "I Live on Your Visits." In this case, she made the child a daughter, a plain, thoroughly undistinguished young woman who extricates herself from her mother by marrying a man who is successful, handsome, and very much in love with her. Lolita's mother, having happily concluded that her duckling daughter will never attract a man, is bewildered and jealous. Her only comfort is the hope that someday John Marble will leave Lolita, and she will be forced to return home.

In "Lolita," for the first time, Dorothy departed from her usual technique by writing entirely in narative. Her previous fiction had always relied heavily on telling a story through what people said to each other, her ear for recreating such conversations being uncanny. "I haven't got a visual mind. I hear things." In 1955, she vowed, "I'm not going to do those *he-said she-said* things any more, they're over, honey, they're over. I want to do the story that only can be told in the narrative form, and though they're going to scream about the rent, I'm going to do it." But her experimentation with the all-narrative form was short-lived because in her next story, "The Banquet of Crow," her scathing picture of a couple like the d'Usseaus, she returned to dialogue.

Throughout the fifties, Dorothy's relations with *The New Yorker* underwent a change. She ceased to feel a personal attachment to the magazine after Harold Ross died of cancer in 1951 and was succeeded as editor by William Shawn. Now she regarded the publication as she did any other. In her dealings with William Maxwell, she adopted a manner that he described as "very solicitous and motherly. It was unnerving." He felt that her current work lacked the sharp vernacular quality that once had distinguished her fiction. "Her style had become heavily mannered and grew more and more like a fictional King James Bible."

Dorothy's next—and last—story was written in the stately style that made Maxwell uncomfortable. In "The Bolt Behind the Blue" (1958), an unmarried secretary who is poor and plain finds herself philanthropically befriended by a rich woman. Mary Nicholl is invited to Alicia Hazleton's home for cocktails, but never for dinners, so that Alicia can show off her house and her glamorous wardrobe. The story is a study in female pretense and self-deception with the secretary swearing after she leaves that she wouldn't trade places with the rich woman for anything on earth, and Alicia Hazleton declaring she would be delighted to exchange. It was amazing, the narrator observed, that a bolt did not swoop from the sky and strike down both of them. Around this time, Dorothy complained to James Thurber and Edmund Wilson that *The New Yorker* had been rejecting her stories lately and possibly it is this one she meant. At any rate, it was published instead in *Esquire*, where she recently had begun writing a monthly column and was establishing a close personal relationship with publisher Arnold Gingrich.

In January 1957, *The New York Times* asked Dorothy to review Sid Perelman's latest book, *The Road to Miltown*, a piece that appeared prominently on the front page of the *Book Review*. It caught the eye of Harold Hayes, a young editor at *Esquire* who had long been a fan of hers. "Seeing the review made me wonder why I hadn't read anything by her lately. So I tracked her down to the Volney and asked her to do something for us." The assignment was a year-end round-up of notable books. On the strength of that article, the magazine offered her the position of regular book columnist beginning with the April 1958 issue, an honored spot that once had been occupied by writers such as Sinclair Lewis, James T. Farrell, and William Lyon Phelps. While *Esquire* was less familiar to her than *The New Yorker*, she had known Arnold Gingrich since the thirties and his wife, Jane, even longer than that, and she immediately felt at home as a contributor. Said Harold Hayes, "She was precious to the magazine, which had been going through a fairly fallow period and was just starting to come alive again. If *Esquire* was being seen anew, Dorothy Parker was one of the reasons. Whereas she may not have regarded writing the column as a great literary period in her career, her doing it was one of the great things happening to us."

Esquire gave her the first financial security she had enjoyed since the 1930s. She was paid six hundred dollars a month, with raises until the figure eventually reached seven hundred and fifty, and she could count on a check even when she missed a column. There were times when Harold

Hayes found it necessary to issue a delicate reminder that the deadline was approaching or make last-minute trips to the Volney to collect the column. She was charmed by the young North Carolinian who always treated her like a lace doily, understood that "she had a miserable time writing," and gave her full credit for being, as he said, "one of the major writers in the country, in my mind." With Hayes she allowed herself to act playful, even a bit flirtatious. One day when he telephoned to compliment her on a column, she trilled happily, "Will you marry me?" Hayes knew that she drank because sometimes on the telephone her articulation was distorted. This distressed him because "she was an elderly lady. But I certainly never considered her a drunk. Occasionally she just would have a little too much to drink—I think the old-fashioned word is tipsy."

During her five years as *Esquire*'s book reviewer, Dorothy wrote forty-six columns and reviewed more than two hundred books, a tremendous output for her but a lot less than Arnold Gingrich would have liked. Having lured her to his magazine, he continually badgered her to write more pieces—a retrospective of the Jazz Age or a piece on speakeasies, he suggested—and Dorothy politely agreed these would make splendid subjects. She hooted at his notion that the twenties had been glamorous and proposed a title that she thought was honest: "The Dingy Decade." But, recalled Gingrich, "it was so hard getting her regular columns out of her with anything reasonably resembling regularity that I never did have much hope of our getting the extra piece." The only bonus she gave him was her short story, "The Bolt Behind the Blue."

At first she struggled hard to meet deadlines, but then she could not resist playing games, perhaps unconsciously withholding copy so that she would hear from Hayes or from fiction editor Rust Hills whose name tickled her (she said it conjured up images of New Jersey suburbs), one or the other of whom might rush up to the Volney to pick up her column. More frequently, she was tardy because reading the books became a grinding effort, aside from the fact that she hated writing. The longer she sat at her typewriter, the more paralyzed she became. Gingrich recognized this problem and before long thought of her writer's block as a complicated case of childbirth. He viewed his own job as obstetrics, and often referred to the monthly operation as a "high-forceps delivery." Not that forceps always worked, but his success rate at prying copy from her beat all other publishers. There were those who believed that not even a cesarean section could make Dorothy meet a writing deadline.

Aside from Gingrich's generosity about money, he rose to her defense whenever asked why he had hired a blacklisted writer, although it was unlikely she knew about the mail that attacked *Esquire* for publishing her. Would he, a reader asked, employ a Nazi storm trooper for an editorial position? Then why was he hiring a Communist? Gingrich replied curtly that he knew nothing of Dorothy's private life, but judging by her writings for *Esquire*, if she was a Communist, then the late Senator Robert Taft was a dangerous radical and so was his father.

Arnold Gingrich was not the only person looking out for her welfare. Among those aware of her precarious financial position, nobody was more determined for her to have a decent income than Leah Salisbury, the formidable literary agent who made a point of inventing fresh angles so that Dorothy might profit from the work she had produced during her lifetime. Although she had used topflight movie agents to obtain screen assignments, she never had a literary agent until 1952 because she held them in low esteem. She acquired Salisbury by chance. Her client list included the Perelmans, the Goetzes, the Hacketts, and Arnaud d'Usseau. When d'Usseau and Dorothy began to collaborate, it seemed logical for Salisbury to represent both of them in negotiations with theatrical producers. After the partnership ended, Salisbury continued to handle Dorothy's professional affairs.

The sad truth was that after forty years as a writer she owned practically nothing tangible to show for it. All the money earned in Hollywood and from her collected works had vanished. She had been imprudent when it came to investing—she dreaded thinking about the future let alone planning for it—but that did not mean she took responsibility for her present circumstances. In 1958, she was sixty-five, an age when most people look forward to retirement. She felt that everyone expected her to toil until she sunk in her tracks like a creaking plowhorse. Although the prospect was horrible, she could not retire. She had no money.

Dorothy observed happily as Leah Salisbury wheeled and dealed on her behalf. Salisbury did not hesitate to crack down on pirates, amateur or professional, who had long been in the habit of using Dorothy's work for everything from high school dramatic productions to network television programs. Shutting down unauthorized productions and confiscating scripts and tape recordings, she warned violators that they would be lucky if Dorothy did not bring charges against them. Salisbury told Dorothy that if her material was to be adapted for the stage, it must be a first-class production that would bring her pride and happiness, in addition to the money. Dorothy agreed. Those who requested permission to adapt her stories and verse for the stage or screen were often sped on their ways with regrets that Miss Parker did not feel her material could be a success in the form they presented.

With one hand Salisbury labored to transform old writings into current income, as when she sold René Clair the film rights to "Here We Are" for four thousand dollars, and with the other she urged Dorothy to undertake new projects. As a result, Dorothy signed a contract with Bernard Geis Associates to write a biography of Ethel Barrymore, in collaboration with Barrymore's son Samuel Colt. As the Geis press release announced, Dorothy's insights into the distinguished actress would produce a lasting contribution to American letters. Bernard Geis admitted that the book, "never came close to transpiring." Along with the Barrymore book, he also signed her to write her autobiography, a project that Leah Salisbury had been pressing her to consider. To Salisbury, it must have seemed that a memoir would be a fitting subject, not only in terms of public interest but also a book that Dorothy might be strongly motivated to complete. For all her respect for her client and a tolerance for eccentricities that sometimes verged on the saintly, Salisbury was not sufficiently familiar with Dorothy's personal history to understand that the subject had been attempted fictionally in *Sonnets in Suicide* and ended in disaster.

Dorothy confided in Quentin Reynolds that "rather than write my life story I would cut my throat with a dull knife." Like some other authors, she considered publishers to be fair game, but, in this case, she must have felt guilty or sorry for Geis because she decided to return his advance. By the time she reached this decision, however, she had already spent a good deal of it. To show that she meant well, she sent a down payment on her debt. "Dear Bernie," she wrote,

> This is, as you see, only a part of what I owe you for your advance. The book—oh, I can't. I've tried and tried, I've gone away alone, I've done my damndest. But it doesn't come—I'm sorry I have to pay you back in bits and pieces—but times are like that with me—Always with gratitude and affection—

Whether she was referring to the Barrymore book or to her own memoir is irrelevant, for she could do neither. In the letter she enclosed a check for a tenth of the advance. Geis felt happy to write off the remaining ninety percent "to experience and to the privilege of being able to say I once almost published a book and a half by Dorothy Parker."

The following year, Salisbury tried to engineer another contract for Dorothy's life with editor Lee Schryver at Doubleday, but by then the Parker reputation for ripping off publishing houses had grown, and Doubleday stipulated certain fail-safe conditions. Dorothy dragged her feet in signing a contract in which payments were contingent upon delivering sections of the manuscript. Finally, Doubleday gave up. Random House publisher Bennett Cerf severely criticized her for accepting advances on books that she had no intention of writing. He considered her behavior unprincipled.

Salisbury remained undaunted. When Columbia Pictures approached her with the idea of making a film about Dorothy's life, she gave serious attention to their proposal. The story editor at Columbia, thinking big bucks, reminded her about the financial success of such movies as *The Jolson Story*. Salisbury passed along the idea to Dorothy, who was in Martha's Vineyard visiting Lillian Hellman.

> Dear Dorothy—
> Would you be interested in discussing a motion picture
> to be based on your wonderfully interesting life—don't shoot
> me, I was asked and said I'd try to find out!

Dorothy did not dignify the letter with a reply.

Lillian Hellman was eager to venture onto the musical stage with an operetta based on Voltaire's witty novel *Candide*. She wrote the book, Leonard Bernstein composed the score, and poet Richard Wilbur assumed chief responsibility for the lyrics. Initially, other lyrics were written by James Agee, followed by John Latouche. When he withdrew, Dorothy was invited to step in.

"I had only one lyric in it. . . . Thank God I wasn't there while it was going on. There were too many geniuses involved." The show's history did turn out to be chaotic. The story line underwent constant revisions, and Hellman produced a dozen versions before they got a satisfactory working script, but even then the operetta suffered from her heavy, pretentious book. Dorothy was irritated by Leonard Bernstein's presumption that he knew how to write lyrics. She complained to Hellman that he clearly wanted to handle the whole show himself. Some years later, she was still shaking her head over his mania "to do everything and do it better than anybody, which he does, except for lyrics. The idea was, I think, to keep Voltaire, but they didn't. But everyone ended up good friends except John Latouche, who died."

Her single contribution to *Candide* was the droll lyric for the song "Gavotte." Leonard Bernstein recalled that Dorothy "was very sweet, very drunk, very forthcoming, very cooperative and, in sum, a dream to work with. I expected it would take weeks of visits and phone calls to get the lyric, but amazingly we had it the next day." It is hard to imagine Dorothy writing anything overnight, but perhaps she did compose the lyric fairly quickly. The tone of Madame Sofronia's tabulating of her many woes echoes Dorothy in one of her Lord-how-I-pity-me moods:

> *I've got troubles, as I said,*
> *Mother's dying, Father's dead.*
> *All my uncles are in jail.*
> *It's a very moving tale.*

Sometimes she sounds as though she is mocking herself:

> *Though our name, I say again, is*
> *Quite the proudest name in Venice,*
> *Our afflictions are so many,*
> *And we haven't got a penny.*

In the end, though, Dorothy's connection with *Candide* did nothing to enhance her reputation or to alter her penniless state. The show was, she thought, "so overproduced that you couldn't tell what was going on at all."

Candide opened in December 1956. Despite the Bernstein score, a stunning production, and admiring reviews, the audiences stayed away and it closed after seventy-three performances.

. . .

During the late 1950s, Dorothy finally began to reap long overdue professional rewards from the literary establishment. The National Institute of Arts and Letters had recently set up the Marjorie Peabody Waite Award to honor an older person who was not a member of the Institute for achievement and integrity. In 1958, its third year, the award went to Dorothy. Lillian Hellman had added her name to the list of contenders, which also included Dashiell Hammett that year. When Dorothy received notification of the award in a letter from Malcolm Cowley, then president of the Institute, she failed to acknowledge it for some reason. After friends advised her that it was proper to send a formal letter of acceptance, she felt mortified and immediately wrote to Cowley claiming that she had been "in a state of euphoric stupefaction, never pierced by the idea that I should have answered." She wanted him to have her official reply, which was "Mr. Cowley—Good God, yes!" The award, incidentally, gave a cash prize of a thousand dollars.

At the awards ceremony, Cowley read a glowing citation that had been composed by Lillian Hellman:

> To DOROTHY PARKER, born in West End, New Jersey, because
> the clean wit of her verse and the sharp perception in her
> stories have produced a brilliant record of our time. Because
> Miss Parker has a true talent, even her early work gives us
> as much pleasure today as it did thirty years ago.

Then, Cowley recalled, an unusual reaction took place. "In 1958 standing ovations were not yet a common occurence. I think there had never yet been one at an Institute Ceremonial. But when Dorothy Parker received her award, the whole audience rose spontaneously as if to prove that, yes, they remembered her work with pleasure. I saw men and women in the audience wiping away tears."

As a result of the Waite award, Dorothy became acquainted with Elizabeth Ames, who had established the prize in memory of her sister. Ames, eager to help Dorothy, arranged still another honor, an invitation to Yaddo, the four-hundred-acre haven for artists, writers, and composers that she administered near Saratoga Springs, New York. Since 1926, Yaddo had patronized American arts and letters by operating a sort of sleep-away camp. Its impressive list of alumni included Eudora Welty, Robert Penn Warren, Katherine Anne Porter, and Aaron Copland, who, among many others, had accomplished important work there. It was hoped that Dorothy would do likewise. While she felt honored, she soon discovered that accepting an invitation to Yaddo presented problems that she had not bargained for. An all-expense-paid exile in the country did not affect her obligation to pay rent at the Volney and, worse, Yaddo did not welcome dogs. Not only would she have to board her current poodle, Cliché, so named because "the streets are carpeted with black French poodles," but she also would be separated from her pet, a far more serious hardship.

To stall Elizabeth Ames, she said that an autumn residence would do just as well as a summer one. "My driving idea is work," she wrote, "and I do so want an unbroken stretch of it, up there." She could not resist rubbing Ames's nose in the matter of the ban on dogs. "Fortunately, I know of a place where she [Cliché] has been, when I have to be away, and she has been well and happy there." She went on to offer a detailed description of the Connecticut kennel—its floor plan, menus, physical-fitness program. Of course, she reminded Ames, no kennel could provide what dogs wanted most, which was "affection. Well, you know—just like two-legged people."

The day came when Ames could be put off no further. In September 1958, Dorothy arrived for a two-month stay. She found Yaddo pretty much as advertised: a stone Victorian mansion flanked by woods, a daily routine during which no resident was to be interrupted, and a black metal lunch pail outside her door. In this setting, supposedly idyllic for productivity, she realized at once that she would be devoutly bored. The rustic silence was unnatural. Her writer's block was invigorated by the country air. The place was filled with the kind of self-conscious, pretentious writers she crossed the street to avoid. Morton Zabel, an English professor from the University of Chicago, was an exception. He struck her as having a fairly decent sense of humor. Sometimes she and Zabel would put their heads together to exchange observations about some of the guests, particularly a pair of hoity-toity young women whose artistic airs had already begun to grate on her nerves.

After Zabel returned to Chicago and Yaddo was drenched by cold autumnal rains, the estate became soggy and unbearably gloomy. She stayed in her room, pleading illness. "The two young ladies are still here," she reported to Zabel, "and I doubt if you could notice any change in their manners and ways—you might think, though, that they have got rather more so. There are two new arrivals, scraped from the bottom of that barrel, and I rather think that my illness that has kept me to my room was not entirely due to germs." In November, when her time ran out, she was overjoyed to escape Yaddo. "I can only say it was good to get back from the dreary wet days and the dreary wet people at Yaddo," she wrote Zabel once she was safely back at the Volney and reunited with Cliché. It was amazing that she lasted two months.

Dorothy managed to accomplish practically nothing at Yaddo. Having been without the distraction of a telephone for two months, one of the great attractions of Yaddo, meant nothing to Dorothy, who solved that problem long ago by simply never picking up a ringing phone. She used her time in Saratoga Springs to polish "The Bolt Behind the Blue," which *Esquire* published that December. She also must have worked on her book column, but these were tasks she would have done in any case. Although the entire experience had turned out to be a waste of time and an exceptional bore, she went out of her way to compose a gracious bread-and-butter note thanking Mrs. Ames "a million times" for her kindness. She did not wish to appear ungrateful.

The following spring, she was elected a member of the National Institute of Arts and Letters, her nomination having been proposed by Van Wyck Brooks and seconded by Louis Untermeyer and Sid Perelman. Brooks termed her a writer of "real importance, unaccountably overlooked, who should have been certainly elected years ago." That was cold comfort now, although among the dozen new members also selected that year were two equally overlooked women whose company and writings Dorothy had enjoyed since the twenties—Janet Flanner and Djuna Barnes. The Institute insisted on referring to Dorothy as a satirist, a term that usually prompted one of her cracks about "creatures like George S. Kaufman and such who don't even know what satire is," but on this occasion she took care to keep her opinions to herself. In her own eyes she was not a satirist, but if they wished to call her one, she would not argue. This time she made sure to reply in writing, cranking out a note so sloppy that it appeared to have been typed in the dark.

> Dear Miss Geffen, my typewriter trembles to tell you how truly elated I am to be a member of the National Institute of Arts and Letters. I didn't think this could ever happen to me. Now that it has—there is no living with me. Miss Geffen, I can only say, in older words—I will try to be a good queen. With gratitude,

Realizing the letter was a hopeless mess, she tried to avoid the need for redoing it by adding a postscript that blamed the typewriter:

> Please forgive the typing. My typewriter has been overcome,
> ever since it got the lovely message that I had been elected.

The afternoon of the induction ceremony found Dorothy in fragile condition because she had prepared for the event with far too many cocktails. Marc Blitzstein, another new member seated next to her, was obliged to look after her. Upon her introduction, she rose with some difficulty and made a brief speech, which consisted of only one sentence. "I never thought I'd make it!" she declared, then quickly sat down again. This left some of Dorothy's old friends in the audience blinking and trying to imagine her true thoughts, since it was impossible to believe she had ever given a moment's consideration to the institute. Afterward, Thornton Wilder reported to Frank Sullivan, "Never did I more wish for mind-reading radar than when she stood up and bowed to the assembly." As it happened, she was probably thinking of nothing because she was on the verge of passing out. Later, in the middle of the keynote address, a talk about abstract painting by Meyer Schapiro, Dorothy suddenly came to and stood to deliver her speech again. Oblivious of Schapiro, she was distinctly heard to blurt out, "I never thought I'd make it!" Blitzstein managed to subdue her with gentle shushing.

Her gaffe, said Richard Wilbur, is not pleasant to remember, "but it gives some sense of the extent of her drinking at that time: a prepared speech was given both at the right time and at a later, totally wrong, time." At a reception afterward, her behavior was fine. The star of the party was not a writer at all but Marilyn Monroe, newly married to Arthur Miller, who was there to accept a drama prize. When Louis Untermeyer offered to introduce Dorothy to Monroe, she responded with enthusiasm and wriggled her way to the head of the line.

Arnold Gingrich talked her into participating in a two-day symposium being cosponsored by *Esquire* and Columbia University, in which her colleagues on the panel were to be a trio of young male writers with big reputations— Saul Bellow, Wright Morris, and Leslie Fiedler. Flattered and swayed by the fifteen-hundred-dollar fee, Dorothy decided to accept. All she had to do was deliver a speech and comment briefly on the role of the writer in America.

The militant styles of Morris and Fiedler caught her by surprise. They began attacking the way America corrupted its writers with foundation grants, prizes, even invitations to perform like tame bears at events like this one. Clearly Morris and Fiedler were eager to bite *Esquire*'s hand. Since ingratitude had long been Dorothy's typical reaction to handouts, she felt startled and then indignant. Hearing them beef about how badly writers were treated, a subject on which she had been discoursing for forty years, she perversely rushed to the opposite side. For the first time in years, she had managed to pick up a few philanthropic plums, and she was taken aback to hear these people disclaiming prizes and writers' camps.

When it came time to deliver her speech the following evening, she was eager to throw sand in the gears of her fellow panelists. Backstage, looking nervous and wobbly, she made a futile attempt to exchange small talk with Leslie Fiedler. "She kept remarking on my teeth with the general air of Little Red Riding Hood remarking on the dentures of the Wolf." Laying her hand on his shoulder, she said, "Be kind to Mother," words that mystified him since he was over forty and no longer considered himself particularly youthful. And her references to his teeth were totally puzzling. To Dorothy, the atmosphere of the symposium must have summoned up images of creatures with sharp teeth.

At the podium, she apologized for being alive, confessed apprehension being on the same program with such distinguished gentlemen, and warned that since she, unlike them, was not an intellectual, anything she said would be relatively worthless. Then she got down to business. She couldn't understand why the men were crabbing. Did the poor dears expect special treatment? A writer, she said, should be prepared to suffer in silence. As for the role of the writer in society, the subject of the symposium, she defined it very simply: The writer was a worker whose business it was to write. She graphically likened her proletarian writer to an Aesop walking through a forest on a dark night, when suddenly a wolf pops out of the trees and bites him on the leg.

"There!" cries the wolf to Aesop. "Go home and write a fable about that!"

She was sick of writers who always found something to bellyache about. They should shut up and get to work. She went on complaining about writers who complained until she could think of nothing more to say and tottered back to her seat.

She was, Saul Bellow thought, the most pleasant of the panelists because "she was the quietest." She was also the funniest, having taken care to deliver her barbs with humor. The audience laughed approvingly. At the close of the discussion that night, she was surrounded by autograph seekers. When she had time to look up, Bellow, Fiedler, and Morris were gone.

Arnold Gingrich sent a letter of congratulations. He thought she had been "terrific" and said, "Actually you said more in inverse proportion to the time you spent on your feet, than all the rest of the panel put together." To Dorothy's mind, she had made a "truly horrible" spectacle of herself. "I turned my face to the wall and was hostess to an attack of flu."

She made an appearance with Norman Mailer and Truman Capote, on a television program called *Open End*. In recent years, she had become friendly with Capote, whom she admired as a writer of quality, but she had never been able to forgive Mailer for the dog incident. Later, she referred to him as "that awful man who stabbed his wife."

That evening, a limousine picked her up at the hotel and dumped her at a studio in the wilds of Newark, New Jersey, a location sufficiently out of the way to put her in a bad mood. Making no concessions to the requirements of a public appearance, she had dressed herself in a black shawl and shapeless skirt and carelessly applied her makeup. The overpowdered tip of her nose suggested to Mailer the white button of a clown.

If she looked like part of a Ringling Brothers act, the appearances of her co-panelists were equally arresting. Mailer arrived wearing Cro-Magnon chin whiskers suggestive of Fidel Castro's, and Capote had the slinky air of a tiny, golden Theda Bara. Dorothy quickly rebuffed Mailer's overtures and plainly showed so much preference for Capote that Mailer was offended.

In the early part of the show, moderator David Susskind tried to put Dorothy at ease, a maneuver she fiercely resisted. In a low, quavering voice, she saluted E. M. Forster, skewered Beat writers such as Jack Kerouac, and declared that the fiction she was condemned to read for *Esquire* was trash. The sex scenes in current fiction were, she complained, "all the same."

When Susskind wondered what most disturbed her about contemporary America, she listed injustice, intolerance, stupidity, and segregation—particularly segregation.

After that, the proceedings were upstaged by a windy and aggressive Mailer and a tough Capote who demolished Mailer at every turn. As the men increasingly hogged the limelight, Dorothy contributed less and less until finally she sat silently, slumped in her chair, as if she were waiting to be cut down from the cross. *Open End* was so named because it remained on the air as long as its guests and the moderator liked. On this particular Sunday night in January 1959, *Open End* continued for almost two hours.

As they walked off the set, they noticed technicians examining a kinescope and stopped to watch. Dorothy glanced at herself and groaned in dismay.

"No," she protested to Susskind, "I really don't want to see another instant of it." He ushered her away with all the tact and delicacy of a funeral director exhibiting a decomposed corpse, and she rode back alone to Manhattan with her ego reduced to the size of a pea.

Aware that she was not telegenic, she nevertheless could not have appreciated reading one reviewer's unflattering comment that she had resembled Eleanor Roosevelt. Great as her admiration for Mrs. Roosevelt was, she did not care to look like her.

Dorothy, wrote Edmund Wilson in his diary, "had somewhat deteriorated, had big pouches under her eyes." One Saturday afternoon he visited her at the Volney.

> I was glad to see all the evidences of her having returned to her old kind of writing: a typewriter with manuscript beside it, piles of books she is reviewing for Esquire. But it is just the same kind of life that she used to live in New York before she spent so many years in Hollywood. It is as if her work in Hollywood and her twice marrying Alan Campbell had counted for nothing—she might as well have been in fairyland. Bob Benchley is dead, Campbell has left her again. She lives with a small and nervous bad-smelling poodle bitch, drinks a lot, and does not care to go out.

She served him several drinks, "as was inevitable in this atmosphere of the twenties." Wilson, feeling as if he had stepped backward in time, went away depressed.

Day to day, the friend she saw most regularly was Bea Stewart, whose East Side apartment became the scene of countless gossipy cocktail hours. A lavish dispenser of very dry martinis and a middle-aged divorcée living without a man, Bea knew about loneliness and boredom. She was a loyal friend, but Dorothy failed to appreciate her properly, devotion or no devotion. The person whose company she most prized was Lillian Hellman, even though Hellman had little time for her and eventually began to avoid her. Dorothy didn't care. Hellman was a wonderful audience who went into stitches over Dorothy's remarks, which in turn set off Dorothy's own laughter. On Saint Patrick's Day, 1957, Hellman invited her to drive to her house in Martha's Vineyard, Massachusetts. Throughout a long day of motoring, Dorothy did her best to keep Lilly entertained with stories disparaging the Irish. Hellman recalled that the invective flowing from her mouth "was amazing in variety and sometimes in length. Driving does not go with laughing too much, and the more I laughed, the more remarkable grew her anger with the Irish. By the time we got to the traffic on Major Deegan Parkway, they were even responsible for Hitler's Holocaust." When they finally arrived on the island and Hellman announced her eagerness to prepare a Saint Patrick's Day supper, Dorothy flatly told her to forget it. She couldn't possibly eat a bite in the name of Saint Patrick.

"Let's change the name to Saint Justin," suggested Hellman, who was not only passionately fond of food but also a good cook.

"Who in hell is Saint Justin?" Dorothy asked.

Hellman could not remember, but that evening she prepared a luscious meal of roast duck, green beans in a warm vinaigrette, and crepes for dessert.

On another drive to Martha's Vineyard, they broke the journey at Portland, Connecticut, where they stopped to spend the night with Hellman's close friend Richard Wilbur and his family. Hellman warned Wilbur that Dorothy was permitted only one drink at cocktail time, that this arrangement had been agreed upon between them beforehand. It was apparently a condition of taking her to the Vineyard that she limit herself to a single drink, for purposes of relaxation. This might seem sensible to a nonalcoholic, but for Dorothy it amounted to abstinence. The self-denial, the torment of being unable to assuage her craving, was the same. When drinks were served, Wilbur brought her a martini. For a long while it remained on the table, untouched, seemingly unnoticed, as she chatted easily with the others, who were busy sipping their cocktails. Then, Wilbur recalled, "suddenly she took the drink and drank it off in one motion."

Hellman's exacting such a promise may have been as much or more for her sake as for Dorothy's because her tolerance for hard drinkers was low. Dashiell Hammett's alcoholism had disturbed her greatly. As his drinking grew more self-destructive after the war, she began to see less of him. He rented an apartment in New York and later, after his release from prison, friends offered him a cottage in Katonah, New York.

Dorothy resigned herself to Lillian's restrictions. If Lilly sometimes treated her as if she were practically toothless, she managed to overlook that too. Over the years, their friendship had undergone considerable evolution as their importance in the world had somersaulted. Now it was Hellman who glittered as a literary big shot surrounded by sycophants, her bank balance bursting with the fruits of success, while Dorothy stood hungrily in the shadows.

In the early fifties, Hellman wrote a short story, a clear invasion of Dorothy's province, and presented it to her for an opinion. She hastened to praise the story highly—perhaps too highly Hellman suspected—and singled out one particular phrase as having special merit. Hellman thought she was pulling her leg. Some months later, visiting Hellman's farm in Pleasantville, New York, she inquired what had become of the story. It was pedestrian, Hellman replied. Dorothy quickly disagreed—it was original and sensitive, in her opinion. As she was saying this, she stumbled over the puppies they had brought along on their walk. Stooping to make sure the dogs were not hurt, she heard Hellman say that God must be dispensing justice by punishing puppies for the lies certain people told their friends. When Dorothy continued to insist that she really did like the story, Hellman walked on.

In silence, they continued to a lake where Hellman intended to inspect some traps that had been set for snapping turtles. Hauling a trap out of the water, she placed it on the ground and they stared at the turtle. His penis, they could see, was erect with fear.

Dorothy pinned on a catlike smile. She said prettily, "It must be pleasant to have sex appeal for turtles. Shall I leave you alone together?" Having paid her back, Dorothy was content to drop the matter.

She enjoyed her invitations to Hellman's house at the Vineyard, where the sight of the sea and the beaches transported her back to her earliest days in West End. Her apartment lacked air-conditioning and got miserably uncomfortable in summer. The only problem with staying at the Vineyard was Hammett's dislike of her, an antipathy that had grown more pronounced over the years so that he refused to be around her. When her visits coincided with his absence, everything worked out fine. When they did not, Hammett stubbornly moved out of the house and made sure he did not return until after she had gone back to New York. In the summer of 1960, a few months before he died of lung cancer, leaving was impossible and Hellman told Dorothy that she would have to stay in a guest house down the road. She was not forthright about the reason for this odd arrangement, but it was not difficult to figure out the truth. In the evenings, after Hammett had fallen asleep, Dorothy was invited to join Hellman for dinner, Hellman's second supper because she had already pretended to eat from a tray in Hammett's room. That August, Dorothy never saw Hammett once. Out of tact, she asked no questions.

What Hellman wanted, in payment for her kindness to Dorothy, was a seemingly easy favor—for anyone but Dorothy. Hellman wanted to be the sole exception to Dorothy's habit of belittling people behind their backs. As the years went by and Hellman surrounded herself with apple-polishers, she eventually convinced herself that there were two people about whom Dorothy had never made an unkind remark: herself and Robert Benchley. This fantasy was reinforced by those who wished to get on her good side. The truth was, Dorothy's nature caused her to abuse everyone except the Murphys. Although she said nothing derogatory about Benchley after his death, she had not spared him during the thirties and forties. She also poked fun at Hellman. She even did it to her face whenever she thought she could get away with it, but Hellman was determined to ignore this.

Her feelings of closeness to people who had suffered for their political beliefs—friends like Hellman, the Mostels, the d'Usseaus—emerged at the expense of certain other old friendships. No longer did she see much of Harold and Alice Guinzburg, and she also began avoiding Sara and Gerald Murphy. "To be anti-Communist," Gerald observed to Sara, "is to be anti-Dottie, apparently. Too bad." If the Murphys were far from being militants, they did happen to be liberal Democrats who believed that actors and writers were "rather poor prey" for congressional investigators. During Lillian Hellman's unsuccessful attempt to have Hammett released on bail after his arrest, Gerald emptied the Mark Cross safe of its receipts for that day and added a personal check to make a total of ten thousand dollars.

Dorothy kept Sara and Gerald at a distance. Whenever she communicated with them, which was not often, she behaved as if nothing had changed. She liked to send amusing items clipped from newspapers. Once it was a "Dear Abby" column about a couple named Dorothy and John who were celebrating fifty years of marriage but fought like tigers at their golden anniversary party. Dorothy pasted the clipping on a sheet of Volney stationery, titled it "TOGETHERNESS!" and added a few tidbits of personal information: "I have been having lumbago. Oh, my God—I have a little poodle named Cliché. I love the Murphys (the last item is not new)." Even allowing for her aversion to letter writing, this piece of mail spoke volumes about the rift that had developed, and it saddened the Murphys. Somehow Dorothy contrived to ignore everyone's feelings, including her own. To acknowledge that an estrangement had taken place would have been too painful.

Living at the Volney had serious disadvantages when she wanted privacy. Simply to venture outside could be so tricky that Dorothy developed a self-protective maneuver. If she was walking down Madison Avenue and noticed someone she knew coming toward her, she stopped at a shop window and stared fixedly at some object until the person passed by. She cut many an old friend this way. Some people decided that her desire for privacy had to be respected, others concluded that she had become a hermit. Explained an acquaintance of thirty years, "I guess she didn't want to stand on the street and pass a lot of polite gas with me."

Attacking either *The New Yorker* or the Round Table was now practically an avocation of hers. When given the opportunity, she happily announced that the cartoons were still wonderful but that the fiction had gone downhill abominably. The proof was that stories these days always seemed to be tedious accounts of the author's childhood in Pakistan. At a party given by *New Yorker* cartoonist Charles Addams, she got to talking with James Geraghty, the magazine's art editor. Under the circumstances it would have been politic to keep her mouth shut, but her tongue ran away and she proceeded to give Geraghty a complete airing of her views. He listened with equanimity. There was, she wound up tauntingly, no real wit in *The New Yorker* anymore.

This last crack proved too much for Geraghty. "You mean like 'Men never make passes at girls who wear glasses'?" he retorted.

"You son of a bitch!" she hurled back, probably as much annoyed by his misquoting of her verse as his recollection of it.

She rued the day she had written "News Item" and wished she had the power to destroy it. It was "a terrible thing to have made a serious attempt to write verse and then be remembered for two lines like those." It also made her bilious the way the same old jokes were quoted whenever anyone wrote about her. She told Tallulah Bankhead that she must "even by accident, have said other things worth repeating, if the lazy sons-of-bitches bothered to find out."

Having once begun to embrace hardship, she elevated necessity to a principle and then martyred herself over it. She was hard up but not quite as broke as she pretended. Nevertheless, she continued to simplify her existence by paying strict attention to nickels and dimes and never going to Lord & Taylor or the Chemical Bank if she could help it. She conducted banking at her favorite liquor store, which was agreeable about cashing checks. Without neo-Puritanical Hellmans or d'Usseaus keeping her on a tight rein, she arranged her days to suit herself. She read books for *Esquire*, labored over her column, and occasionally accepted invitations to read from her writings at universities or at the Ninety-second Street YMHA, where they paid a tidy hundred and fifty dollars. Her stage fright had remained incurable. Once, before going on stage to speak before a woman's group, she exclaimed, "Oh shit, what am I doing here!" She also made two long-playing records of her verse and fiction.

During these years she seldom saw Alan, who was living in Hollywood, but she continued to receive news of him from friends. He had a small amount of royalty income from his investments in *Mister Roberts* and *South Pacific*, Joshua Logan's Broadway hits. He managed a tour that the Welsh actor Emlyn Williams made of New Zealand, but beyond this he had no visible means of support. Often he had to live by his wits, aptly and sadly described by a friend as "living on the kindness of friends." When he was short of money, he stayed at his mother's house in Bucks County, usually when Horte was in Richmond, or he visited his friend Betty Moodie and her family in Erwinna. Sought after as a weekend guest, he became the unattached man that hostesses needed to round out the numbers at dinner parties. "He was a terribly witty, amusing man," said Betty Moodie. "It was pathetic but when things got tough there was no doubt that he traded on those qualities just to get by. He would play bridge and be an entertaining companion. He was staying at my place once and I remember him saying that he had to go up to Tallulah's for the weekend." Weekend visits also were made to the home of Robert Sherwood's widow, Madeline, who sometimes gave him discarded clothing—expensive outfits that he passed on to women friends. Often he was heard to remark that he wished Dorothy would stop drinking, or that he was trying to get her off the booze. "It was clear," Moodie said, "that he wasn't going to get any work without her. She had resources if she could pull herself together but he had none."

If Alan was reduced to trading on his likeability in order to live, he displayed little of this charm around Dorothy when they met. He usually had a chip on his shoulder. She would make what she believed to be a perfectly ordinary remark and he would become antagonistic (or vice versa) and they wound up quarreling. The sight of Dorothy's apartment displeased him. After a visit to the Volney, he told friends that she was living wretchedly, that he had found her wallowing in filth, and that the dog had littered the carpet.

His quickness to take offense and to belittle her made Dorothy wary about seeing him. The strain of meeting also made him uneasy. Late one night, he stopped by unannounced and brought along a casual acquaintance, Wyatt Cooper. They had run into each other earlier at a party at the home of George Kaufman and his actress wife, Leueen MacGrath, who was a friend of Alan's. Recently returned from London, Alan and Kaufman had coauthored a musical called *The Lipstick War,* a surprising collaboration because Kaufman had never particularly liked Alan—nor had he made a secret of his dislike. *The Lipstick War* was never produced, but that night Alan felt optimistic.

It was late. Since she had been expecting no visitors, Dorothy looked disheveled, and the apartment was cluttered with dog toys on the sofa and soiled newspapers where Cliché had relieved herself. More embarrassing to Dorothy, she had finished every drop of liquor and had nothing to offer guests. After apologizing for her lack of hospitality and the condition of the apartment, she could think of nothing further to say and clammed up. Wyatt Cooper felt immensely uncomfortable and stood around with a frozen smile on his face. The scene, he later wrote, struck him as unreal. "Loneliness and guilt were almost like physical presences in the space between them, and they spoke in short, stilted, and polite sentences with terrible silences in between, and yet there was a tenderness in the exchange, a grief for old hurts, and a shared reluctance to turn loose."

When all conversation petered out, Alan and Cooper finally took their leave.

Chapter 18

HAM AND CHEESE,
HOLD THE MAYO

•

1961–1964

In the spring of 1961, she agreed to join Alan in Hollywood. Unwilling to acknowledge any reconciliation, she characterized the trip as strictly business, because that was the level on which she wished to keep it. After two decades, they had been offered the chance to work together again. Their long-time friend Charles Brackett, now head of Twentieth Century–Fox, ignored Dorothy's blacklisting and decided to hire them for an adaptation of a French stage play. More precisely, Alan had sought the job and was told he could have it but only on the condition that he send for Dorothy. *The Good Soup* was not much of a play, but Fox intended the property for its biggest star, Marilyn Monroe. No doubt, this tantalizing bait tempted Dorothy, for she greatly admired Monroe's beauty and sensitivity. At the same time, she was understandably apprehensive about involving herself with Alan. Not only did it mean uprooting herself from a carefully constructed independence, but also it entailed leaving New York for a place she had always disliked and did not want to be, for a man from whom she had grown apart. Even on a temporary basis, the prospect had its disturbing aspects.

A few years earlier, Alan had invested in property, an inexpensive bungalow in West Los Angeles he was planning to remodel and sell. When he assumed that Dorothy would live with him, she indignantly objected. It was hardly suitable for them to stay together after having been as good as divorced for ten years. She had grown accustomed to privacy. At the last minute, she relented—renting a hotel room would be foolish, she decided—

but she continued to grumble lest he take her for granted. "I'm a hobo and mean to be forever." To prove she felt strongly about her single life in New York, she kept her apartment and did not even notify the Volney that she planned to be out of town. She wrote that the two things she most hated were living in suburbia and "the tedium of marriage." Moving in with Alan seemed to encompass both.

Norma Place was a block-long street in West Hollywood, named years earlier for silent-screen star Norma Talmadge, whose dressing room and servants' quarters were located there. The two-story frame building that she once had owned was now divided into handsome apartments occupied by Tuesday Weld, Estelle Winwood, and John Carlyle, among others. The rest of the street was lined with modest homes that originally had been constructed as low-income housing for streetcar workers. Alan had purchased one of these. His was a one-story, white stucco bungalow with combined living and dining room, a kitchen, and two bedrooms. It had a small front yard, a backyard, and a narrow cement walk leading up to an elaborately carved double door.

Norma Place was a sociable street. Residents visited their neighbors' homes for cocktails, ritually walked their dogs together, and cried on each other's shoulders in times of sorrow. They also were dedicated news gatherers and gossips who seemed never to have heard of minding their own business. Dorothy christened the street Peyton Place West, but more commonly it was called Swish Alps and Boys Town, because the street as well as the entire neighborhood were heavily homosexual.

Glamorous people abounded on Norma Place. Dorothy Dandridge and Carleton Carpenter owned homes. Nina Foch lived around the corner on Lloyd Place. Judy Garland frequently came to visit friends, and Oscar Levant and Hedy Lamarr attended parties. Still, Dorothy's coming, a major event, immediately established her as the street's foremost celebrity. As soon as her taxi stopped in front of Number 8983, it was obvious to her that Alan had misled his neighbors into interpreting her arrival as a romantic homecoming. As well-wishers came to the door, she found herself swept up in a sentimental greeting reminiscent of an Andy Hardy movie. After they departed, Dorothy felt fatigued and testy. Giving vent to her feeling that Alan had greatly overdone the occasion, she declared her loathing for the smell of flowers and pitched the welcoming bouquets of daisies and roses into the garbage can.

On the third of April, they began twelve consecutive weeks of employment that was followed by sporadic work, which lasted until Thanksgiving. For Dorothy, these were cheerful months, a period marked by comparative sobriety and surprisingly good relations with Alan, both at home and on the job. They found congenial company in Wyatt Cooper, who was now working as a writer at Fox and who lived a few doors down the street in Carleton Carpenter's converted garage apartment. Later, Alan splurged on a new car, a flashy dark-green Jaguar that he called his movie-star car, but at the time he and Dorothy hitched rides to work with Cooper. The young Mississippian, whom Dorothy nicknamed "the Sharecropper," exhibited a determined eagerness to please. His conduct was interpreted by other Norma Place residents as social climbing, but Dorothy considered him amusing and likeable. She also found his willingness to dance attendance on her and Alan useful, because his presence tended to create a buffer between them.

At the studio, the three of them soon fell into the habit of meeting at noon and taking long lunch breaks in which they drove toward Santa Monica seeking interesting places to eat. They giggled about the secretary the studio had assigned to Dorothy and Alan, a woman far too solemn for their taste, and promised each other sleds for Christmas if they could make her laugh. Before long, the sourpuss secretary had been transformed into a running joke. Eavesdropping on her personal phone conversations, they could hardly wait to report them to Cooper when they met at lunchtime. Dorothy enjoyed loitering in the women's room, where she picked up the latest studio dirt by listening to the secretaries gossip. All of this provided fresh fodder for a merriment that seems reminiscent of her happiness at *Vanity Fair* when she worked with Robert Benchley and Robert Sherwood.

On one of their lunch hours, they were browsing through a Santa Monica antique shop, a junky sort of place in Alan's eyes, when Dorothy spotted a set of Napoleon and his marshals, thirteen painted porcelain figurines. For reasons mysterious even to her, she found Napoleon enthralling and had begun reading everything she could find about his life. She insisted on buying the set. At home she arranged it on top of a living room bookcase and asked Alan to install a special light overhead.

All through the summer and fall of 1961 their mood continued to be gay. Having again taken over Dorothy's correspondence, Alan cheerily wrote to Sara and Gerald Murphy that they were planning a trip to New York and would be thrilled to see them. "If by any chance you come out to Carmel, let us know and we will race up." Alan wanted to believe he had rolled back the clock to 1936, when it had been possible to go larking from one amusing social engagement to another with himself as Dorothy's manager. He was counting on the box-office success of *The Good Soup*—not an unreasonable expectation for a Marilyn Monroe picture—and other assignments surely following.

During the fall, Dorothy was forced to decide whether or not she would stay in California. At first, she had been careful to mail her rent to the Volney each month. By August, feeling increasingly ambivalent, she was neglecting the rent. This lapse brought a polite note from the manager along with a reminder that her lease was due to expire at the end of September and that a renewal on 9E would mean a rent increase to $450 a month. Dorothy procrastinated. The Volney sent a telegram to notify her that if she failed to renew the hotel would be forced to charge her a monthly rate of $600. Hearing this, but still wondering about the wisdom of burning her bridges, she gave up the apartment. Life was proving sweet lately.

Wyatt Cooper noticed the immense pleasure she and Alan found in each other's company and sensed that this was how it must have been in earlier years. He was delighted to discover that this Dorothy, in marked contrast to the Dorothy he had first met at the Volney with Alan, had a mind as quick and young as a girl's. Seldom was he aware of the difference between their ages.

When Cooper's assignment at Fox ended, he applied for unemployment compensation. This was a natural step for a writer who found himself out of work, but it was not one that occurred naturally to Dorothy and Alan, who resisted his suggestions that they should apply too. No doubt they considered it demeaning, but they also expected more film work to be forthcoming at any moment. Neither was convinced that they were entitled to such payments, particularly in Dorothy's case, because she received a regular income from *Esquire* as well as royalties from Viking. In the end, Cooper broke down their reluctance. By his calculations, it would mean seventy-five tax-free dollars a week for each of them, which added up to the considerable sum of about six hundred dollars a month.

Their applications were approved, and soon they appeared every week to sign cards claiming their availability for work. Seeing the parking lot full of Rolls-Royces and sporty Cadillacs, Dorothy decided that just as many celebrities could be found at the unemployment office as at Romanoff's and, she said, "it's a much nicer set." Some months later, when signing for the checks had become a part of their regular weekly routine, they realized that

The Good Soup did not represent a comeback, in spite of their high hopes. Afterward, Dorothy said in disgust that they had written "a nice, little, innocent bawdy French farce" for Marilyn Monroe, but that Hollywood remained as always, a place where "everybody's a writer and has ideas." Fox, she said, no doubt with exaggeration, "took our script and hoked it up with dope pushers, two murders and, straight out of Fanny Hurst, the harlot with the heart of goo."

The troubles encountered by *The Good Soup* had more to do with circumstance than with the quality of their script. At that time, Monroe's contract with Fox called for two more pictures. When the studio gave her a script called *Something's Got to Give*, a remake of a 1940 Irene Dunne comedy, she indifferently agreed to do it and a starting date was set for the spring of 1962. Owing to her emotional disintegration, she proved incapable of sustained work and frequently absented herself from the set. Finally, in June, Fox fired her and suspended production on the film. Very shortly the question of whether or not Monroe would be reinstated or eventually go on to make another film became irrelevant because her life ended that August. *The Good Soup* was never produced.

Long before Monroe's death, Dorothy and Alan had to face the fact that getting another film job would not be easy. Whenever *The Good Soup* was mentioned, Alan hurried to change the subject because, a friend recalled, "he knew that he and Dottie were dead at Twentieth."

Instead of sharing Alan's double bed, Dorothy preferred the front bedroom with its twin bed and a table where she had set up her typewriter. Even though it allowed some privacy, the house with its tiny rooms felt claustrophobic. During their months at the studio, progress on Alan's home-improvement projects slowed down considerably. The unfinished kitchen where he had stripped tiles off the counter and torn out cabinets had fallen into a state of permanent rubble. Clara Lester, who had worked for the Eichel family in Richmond during Alan's childhood, now lived in Hollywood and came in several times a week to clean and cook. She and Alan engaged in a running battle about the condition of the kitchen, since it was practically impossible to cook in there. "He was hard to work for," Lester recalled, "because he was so fussy about every little thing. But Dorothy was different, so sweet and kind and she didn't bother a soul."

Dorothy regarded herself as a guest in the house. If the kitchen was cluttered, it made no difference to her. What she did mind was noise. On those days Alan worked on the repairs, she had to live with hammering. The racket in the house intensified when he decided to buy a dog, a bad-tempered male Sealyham terrier puppy whom he named Limey. It almost seemed as if he felt outnumbered by Dorothy and Cliché and sought an ally. Cliché objected strenuously to Limey. From the minute he entered the house, they were constantly at odds.

Dorothy did not feel entirely comfortable living in Norma Place. The house was Alan's house, their friends his friends, the way of life one that suited his taste. Even neighborhood parties proved tricky. At one gathering, a young man fell on his knees before her in a reverent pose and placed a notebook of his writings in her lap. Dorothy failed to find his homage touching.

At a cocktail party given by Dana Woodbury, she entered the living room to be confronted by a life-sized nude portrait of her host, which had been painted by Christopher Isherwood's talented protégé, Don Bachardy. Woodbury handed her a cocktail, then asked what she thought of the painting. She gazed at it thoughtfully. She didn't wish to offend Dana, who had once been a Buddhist monk. In the painting he was seated, facing front, and his genitals had been executed with remarkable attention to detail.

She finally cooed, "Oh, my dear, it's so real, you almost feel it could speak to you."

At another party, when some of the guests began gushing over "Big Blonde," she fumed silently. A man standing nearby apologized for his ignorance of the story. "Miss Parker," he confessed, "I've never read a word you've written."

"What's your name?" she asked.

"Rothwell."

"Well, Rothwell," replied Dorothy, "keep it that way and we'll be friends."

The nonliterary Robert Rothwell, an acting student, appealed to her because he made no pretense to being an intellectual, did not live in Norma Place, and dated beautiful fashion models. Listening to him talk about his boyhood in Santa Barbara, where he had played basketball, was refreshing to her. Other people for whom she had warm feelings included Nina Foch; an old friend from the thirties, Sally Blane Foster; and actor Clement Brace, who had appeared in *The Ladies of the Corridor.* Brace lived across the street with his friend John Dall. She also exhibited maternal feelings toward a college boy named Noel Pugh, with whom she liked to whip around town in Alan's Jaguar. To prepare for these outings, she wrapped a large scarf around her head because, she joked, she feared catching cold and dying. They drove by the Hollywood Ranch Market, where she claimed to be fascinated by a piece of California gadgetry, an immense clock whose hands never stopped revolving to indicate that the market never closed. It had been erected, she swore, as part of a cosmic plot to drive her insane. Whenever *Saboteur* happened to be playing in the area, she insisted Pugh take her to see it. It was not the film that drew her, but eagerness to watch herself on the screen in her cameo bit with Alfred Hitchcock. *Saboteur*, like all her pictures, heartily bored her. Once her scene was over she promptly nudged Pugh and announced that she was ready to leave.

A great many gay men lived in the neighborhood. Some of them went out of their ways to do her kindnesses, but she did not feel totally comfortable in homosexual society. Nevertheless, she tried to maintain good relations with her new gay friends and to retain her composure under all circumstances. Behind their backs, she made nasty digs and laughed that one of her more precious neighbors resembled Shirley Temple tossing her curls. Others she dismissed as "kiss-ass bores."

The fact that Alan elected to make his home in Norma Place and that many of his friends were now homosexual seems to lend credibility to Dorothy's old suspicions about him. Those who knew Alan at this time believed he was gay, although not sexually active. At parties, recalled Clement Brace, "He would always get drunk and make passes at all the boys," but that was the extent of his activity. Said Dana Woodbury, "Never in the whole time I knew him did I see him do anything that was bisexual or homosexual. I don't think he ever did." Another friend thought that even if he did not sleep with men, he was attracted to them. "He was not a queen, in fact was very manly, but there was no doubt he was homosexual. Having that sort of mate suited Dorothy exactly. I don't think she was ever very amorous. It was surprising how many gay people hung around their house, but it didn't have to be that way. If she had wished, there could have been an entirely different crowd."

Around the neighborhood women, Dorothy did her best to maintain a regal distance. To avoid Estelle Winwood, with whom Alan had lived before he met her, she walked Cliché on the opposite side of the street. When Winwood saw her with the dog one day and called out an invitation to tea, Dorothy declined with ill-feigned sweetness. She was afraid to cross the freeway, she yelled back. Her aversion to screenwriter Hagar Wilde (*I Was a Male War Bride*) was clearly revealed when she permitted Cliché to do her business on Wilde's lawn. Wilde turned it into a shoot-out by demanding she clean it up, which Dorothy refused to do. A tiny blonde in her fifties who owned a flock of large, aggressive cats, Wilde angrily threatened to call the police and have Dorothy arrested.

"Just who the hell do you think you are?" fumed Wilde. "The queen of Rumania? If that animal shits on my property one more time—"

"There's no need to be tasteless, my dear," Dorothy replied and ambled off.

After *The Good Soup*, Dorothy and Alan began to talk about writing for the stage, and she instructed Leah Salisbury to "find us a play to adapt—from the French or the Ukrianian or something. We'd love to do it." Salisbury took her at her word. Before a week passed, she came up with an assignment to adapt the book for a musical. Just as swiftly Dorothy rejected the job: DEAR LEAH SO SORRY BUT AFTER TWO DAYS MULLING ALAN AND I DO NOT FEEL MUSIC AT MIDNIGHT IS FOR US. PLEASE HOWEVER BEAR US IN MIND FOR SOMETHING ELSE. Salisbury continued to present writing projects, but Dorothy found none of them suitable. Nina Foch recalled that "somebody at CBS was always offering her work, but she refused. She would get very grand and turn down things she could have done." Dorothy insisted that television producers did nothing but talk because there was no contract in the end, not even "a warmly clasped hand."

Pride prevented both her and Alan from accepting work. He too felt that he had an image to maintain. Prior to Dorothy's arrival, he was offered an acting job by the producer of the Jack Benny television show. It had been necessary for Ralph Levy, a friend, to wheedle and cajole. Finally, Alan consented only because he thought it might be fun. On the Benny program, he had a special spot in which he sat in the audience and interrupted the show by pretending to represent the sponsor's advertising agency. He was, according to Levy, "very, very funny. Afterward, I know, he was offered other acting jobs," but he accepted none of them. Since his early days as a juvenile on Broadway, he associated acting with second-class citizenship.

That winter, Dorothy collected unemployment insurance and wrote for

Esquire. If anyone brought up the subject of creative writing, she claimed to have run out of ideas. "Not too long ago I tried to write a story. I got my name and address on the sheet; a title, which stank; and the first sentence: 'The stranger appeared in the doorway.' Then I had to lie down with a wet cloth on my face." Serious problems had developed with her teeth, which entailed a series of long, painful visits to the dentist and "as a result, I have been pretty languid the rest of the time." Reverting to old habits, she again allowed Alan to manage their daily lives and make decisions about when to pay the bills.

In the spring, three of her short stories were performed on New York television by Margaret Leighton and Patrick O'Neal. Dramatization of "The Lovely Leave," "A Telephone Call," and "Dusk Before Fireworks" had been arranged by Leah Salisbury and The Viking Press. For some reason, Dorothy treated the sale with complete lack of appreciation. She told *The New York Times* that she knew nothing about the forthcoming production except what she read in the papers, although she supposed it had been approved by her agent, "who reads fine type in a contract the way you would a sonnet." She went on to say that she had been troubled by financial headaches lately and resented having received no compensation for the rights to her stories.

There was not a particle of truth in this, because Talent Associates paid thirty-two hundred dollars for the rights. What made her cranky was that the money would be paid to The Viking Press and then remitted to Dorothy in her regular semiannual royalty checks, which meant that she would not see the payment for another six months. Alan, who spent a great deal of time ranting about how little income Dorothy's writings brought in, behaved as if the customary system for distribution of authors' royalties had been newly invented by Viking in order to persecute them. It was "awful," he wrote to Salisbury and wondered why the Author's League tolerated publishers who collected interest on authors' royalties. Dorothy let him bluster and compose protesting letters to Leah Salisbury. It gave him something to do.

During this period, a number of producers expressed interest in adapting Dorothy's writings for the stage. Most notable was Haila Stoddard, who had enjoyed considerable success with *A Thurber Carnival*, a Broadway revue based on James Thurber's pieces and drawings, and hoped to repeat her formula with Dorothy's material. In collaboration with director John Lehne, Stoddard arranged a half-dozen stories and a sampling of verses into a revue that she titled *There Was Never More Fun Than a Man*. To embellish the writing, she suggested including two dozen unpublished songs of Vincent Youmans. Stoddard, bubbling with enthusiasm, planned a Broadway show album and passed on to Salisbury Geraldine Page's remark that even Dorothy Parker's hiccups were actable. The project was beginning to sound like a winner.

When Dorothy received the completed script, however, she rejected it after a single reading. She felt so upset that she could not write to Leah Salisbury and instead dictated her reaction to Alan, who accordingly typed out a letter to the agent. Dorothy "hated" Stoddard and Lehne's revision of "Here We Are," its setting changed from a train to a bedroom where the newlyweds are undressing. She "hated" the additional material they had written. The closing scene in which "Dorothy" plays with a razor, nicks herself by mistake, then recites "you might as well live," did not appeal to her either. The only part to win her approval was the idea of using Youmans's tunes. In her opinion, it took a first-rate mind to do a skillful adaptation "and certainly neither Haila nor her collaborator has one." She was, in truth, deeply disappointed because of all the proposals, Stoddard's had sounded the most promising. All along she had insisted that her stories did not lend themselves to adaptation because "nothing much really happens in them." Nevertheless, her hopes were aroused.

During the summer, she and Alan took turns wringing their hands about money and seeking scapegoats—the Jaguar, the house, the renovations. Alan loaded the Jaguar with cartons of review books, some unopened, and barreled around to the Pickwick or various other bookshops to sell them. At Shermart, he purchased the cheapest brand of Scotch and poured it into Black Label bottles. Among those growing concerned about them was Parker Ladd, West Coast editor for Charles Scribner's. He noticed that Dorothy never seemed to spend any money. With the help of Frederick Shroyer, an English professor at California State College in Los Angeles, Ladd conceived the idea of Dorothy joining the English faculty there, perhaps succeeding to the chair recently vacated by Christopher Isherwood. At first, he said nothing to her but instead tested the idea on Alan, who reacted positively and allowed himself to be enlisted as an accomplice in the scheming that continued for some months. By the time they presented the plan to Dorothy, it was inflated into an honor so significant that to refuse would have been practically equivalent to rejecting the Nobel Prize. During the summer, final arrangements were made with the university for her to become Distinguished Visiting Professor of English. For teaching two courses in twentieth-century American and British literature, she was to receive a handsome salary of twenty thousand dollars. It seemed perfect.

In photographs taken that summer, she was radiant and laughing, her face unusually animated and her eyes girlishly flirtatious under the bangs. Seated behind a coffee table stacked with books, Cliché's head resting in her lap, she looked lovely.

With the Cal State salary to support them, she and Alan relinquished their unemployment benefits, and now other funds began to trickle in as well. Parker Ladd arranged for her to collaborate with Fred Shroyer on an anthology of short stories for Scribner's, a project that brought several thousand extra dollars into the Parker-Campbell bank account. Once again the Black Label bottles held genuine Black Label. Unwanted review copies were distributed to friends. Dorothy squeezed two crumpled hundred-dollar bills into the hand of a surprised Robert Rothwell and urged him to take a vacation. Despite the newfound income, she still felt poor. Ladd remembered that she continued to "bitch and complain. Clearly she loved living hand-to-mouth."

The public lectures that she occasionally delivered on the subject of literature, for a fee of four or five hundred dollars, were also motivated by fear of poverty. Her briefest speech took place at the Monterey Public Library, where she was picketed by American Legionnaires who continued to regard her as a subversive. Some thirty of them stationed themselves conspicuously in the front rows and riveted their eyes upon her, even though they said nothing. After a few minutes, she stopped talking and stared back. Fred Shroyer, who had arranged the engagement, finally had to break the impasse by coming forward and himself speaking for another twenty minutes before declaring the evening at an end.

A student from UCLA came by to interview Dorothy for the college newspaper. Alan, dapper in silk ascot and faultlessly creased trousers, made a production of serving tea and behaved like "a friendly butler who was keeping up the pretensions of a grander era." Lois Battle thought them a strange couple, and she could not help wondering why the sophisticated Dorothy Parker had chosen such a husband "when she must have had many more opportunities." Dorothy, only too eager to puncture Alan's pretensions, took delight in describing herself as "a mongrel. My father was a Rothschild; my mother was a goy; and I went to a Catholic school around the corner." Those who wished more information about her would just have to "wait 'till I'm dead." To Battle's questions about politics, Dorothy reeled out provocative replies, advocating violence of thought and declaring that people who could accept injustice might as well kill themselves.

In the presence of visitors, Dorothy and Alan donned company manners: she was gracious and animated, he came across as deferential to a preposterous degree. Remarks to each other were pointedly prefaced by "dear." Alone, they lapsed into old patterns of bickering, although the bantering tended to be gentle because they were having good times together. Dorothy likened Alan to "Betty Boop going down for the last time."

"*You* are Betty Boop," he shot back, "and as far as I'm concerned you *have* gone down for the last time." Then he added playfully, "Well, it's the end of the rainbow for both of us, I fear."

Sometimes Alan was not amusing. One evening when they had invited Cathleen Nesbitt and Wyatt Cooper for dinner, he got unpleasantly drunk and ruined the meal. Dorothy treated him with patience and quietly offered congratulations on the delicious meal.

Her behavior could be equally embarrassing. She often spoke of wanting to meet Igor Stravinsky. Since Miranda and Ralph Levy were friends of the composer, they volunteered to arrange a special dinner party. Dorothy, recalled Miranda Levy, "had had a few nippies beforehand," arrived at the party drunk, and doggedly refused to address more than a few mumbled words to Stravinsky the entire evening.

It was not unusual for her to become intoxicated at social gatherings, but she did not appreciate Alan doing likewise. She was uncomfortable and complained that he behaved like an old grump. He used to be fun when he drank, she said.

Her time was occupied by classes, the book with Shroyer, and her *Esquire* column, but Alan had nothing to do. He talked about a number of projects, including a screenplay collaboration with his friend Bill Templeton, and he also promised to reserve one day a week for work on the house. He wanted to convert the garage into a rental apartment. Little progress seemed to take place with any of these tasks. Much of the time he appeared to be at leisure, strolling about the neighborhood with the dogs or carting groceries home from Shermart, always wearing his pink sailor hat. Some afternoons he agreed to drive Dorothy to Fred Shroyer's house in Monterey Park. While they discussed selections for the anthology, Alan and Shroyer's wife Patricia passed the time playing cards. It was always Dorothy who abruptly gave the signal for their departure. "The doggies will be needing their din-din," she said.

Usually their social life depended on Alan. If he wanted to accept an invitation, they would go out; if he felt like cooking, they would have company. Otherwise they spent quiet evenings at home with Dorothy lounging on the sofa reading, chain-smoking, and sipping Scotch. She ignored ashtrays and allowed the cigarette to burn down to her fingers before knocking off the ash. Both she and Alan had so little interest in television that they did not buy a set. They owned a stereo but seldom turned it on. Questioned by a reporter about what she did for fun, she answered, "Everything that isn't writing is fun."

She continued to write for *Esquire*, but she was finding the work grueling after four years. It was not surprising that she began to miss more deadlines than ever. Meanwhile, review copies arrived almost daily and were stacked on tables and chairs until there was no place to sit. When Alan felt energetic, he opened the packages and sorted through the books, selecting those he thought she might like and sometimes even skimming them for her.

If Arnold Gingrich once had imagined the high-forceps system to be foolproof, he now realized his mistake. It was necessary to hold forms until the very last minute. Often he obtained the column only after frantic telephoning to ask when he might expect it. "I sent it days ago," Dorothy told him when she had not written a word. Sometimes, by skillful begging, he persuaded her to dictate a few paragraphs over the phone. Gingrich figured out that whenever she missed a month, she was apt to miss the next as well, but then the third month she might come through if he kept his fingers crossed. When he did get a column, it was good enough to excuse the absent ones. Eventually he was reduced to addressing playful letters to "Dear Dorothy Dix":

> I was fifty-nine on my last birthday. I publish a magazine. In
> it are what is called departments. These are about a number
> of things. One of them is about books when it is . . .

What am I to do? The lady who writes about books must not enjoy it. Maybe that just shows she is a lady.

Please advise me, dear Dorothy Dix.

Gingrich signed himself "Perplext," but "Dorothy Dix" was not disposed to advise him and did not reply. Therefore he was jolted to discover her teaching at Cal State, doing the kind of job he "could have sworn she wouldn't touch with a ten-foot pole," and he marveled that "the only thing you can expect from her is the unexpected."

Dorothy could not summon up the confidence to quit the magazine and insisted she needed the money. By now *Esquire* had been added to the list of topics that she and Alan regularly squabbled over. With relish, he nagged her about missed deadlines. She pretended that his noisy hammering and sawing prevented her from writing and sent him to Wyatt Cooper's place for the afternoon. When he returned, she announced that she had written the column and deposited it in the mailbox, when Alan knew this was certainly a lie. On leaving the house once, he carefully stretched a hair across the keyboard of her typewriter to trap her.

Innocent of the dramas taking place in West Hollywood, Gingrich continued to pay her in the hope of obtaining further columns. Her last reviews for the magazine, as it turned out, were published in December 1962.

She had imagined Cal State as "an academic paradise under the elms." Instead, she was surprised to discover "18,000 students and 150 parking spaces." The seventy-two students who registered for her classes failed to fit her picture of college kids. Most of them were over twenty-five, some were veterans with families to support, and a few appeared to be middle-aged. Fred Shroyer promised that it would be a privilege and an inspiration for them to hear her reminiscence about the writers she had known personally, about Faulkner and Fitzgerald and Hemingway. Shroyer was wrong. Dorothy's students were there to obtain three credits, not from any interest in literature. Many of them failed to get much pleasure from reading. To most of them, her name meant absolutely nothing. If at the outset that made her feel like their "grandmother's grandmother," she soon realized they were unfamiliar with practically all writers. If they had never heard of

James Joyce or read Faulkner, she reminded herself, "Why would they have heard of me?" She found their political conservatism and their general narrowness of mind to be disgraceful. When she assigned *The Grapes of Wrath*, some of them called it obscene, and one said that her mother didn't want the book in the house. While studying *Sister Carrie*, Dorothy found herself in the ridiculous position of having to defend not only Dreiser but also adultery in literature. It only stood to reason that their writing skills would disappoint her. She discovered only three of them were able to put together a sensible English sentence.

In preparation for the job, Dorothy bought new clothes. She took particular care with her hair and makeup, and she arrived at her classroom composed, patient, and sober. Sometimes, after only ten or fifteen minutes, she ran out of things to say. She confided to Sally Foster that she found the job humiliating. Teaching at a city college was fine for a younger person, she said, but she was nearly seventy, just a little too old for this sort of pressure. In an effort to maintain a benign attitude toward her students, she went to extremes. "I never give a bad mark," she told Foster, "and I never fail anyone." As Parker Ladd came to realize, "She was not a successful teacher. She had absolutely no connection with those students and couldn't figure out how to communicate with them. About a third of the time she didn't show up for class."

Ladd and Shroyer had counted on Alan's participation, because he had expressed so much initial enthusiasm for the job. They expected him to read and grade papers, or at the very least to chauffeur Dorothy back and forth to the campus, nearly an hour's commute each direction. But Alan, suddenly quite peevish, surprised them by refusing to perform these services.

By the beginning of 1963, it was not unusual for him to drink all day, starting with Bloody Marys for breakfast and continuing until bedtime, when he would finish off the day with a Scotch nightcap. To some of his neighbors, he appeared "stoned," which was an accurate impression because he was addicted to barbiturates. Dorothy had grown accustomed to his sedatives. He had used them ever since she had known him, and by now they were so much a part of his routine that questioning the habit never occurred to her. Alan even had to take a sleeping pill for an afternoon nap because, she once joked to Lillian Hellman, "he hates to toss and turn from four to six."

What concerned her now was his heavy drinking, which made him aggressive, sloppy, and sullen. She mentioned to Noel Pugh that she feared him when he was drunk. Her requests to be taken out for a ride in the Jaguar often occurred when Alan had been drinking and she needed to escape from the house for a while. Pugh noticed that

> they were fighting like hell. There were some pretty nasty
> fights about Alan's mother, and sometimes he cried. He was
> drunk most of the time, and she was drunk half the time.

Dorothy was not above needling him, aiming straight for the jugular with snipes about his being "worthless." She would tell him, "You've never been able to earn your own living." It angered her that after thirty years he still depended on her labors, her name.

Alan devised a novel means of escape. In a library somewhere he had once seen a bookcase that cleverly concealed a secret door, just the sort of gadget that he adored. Removing the door from his bedroom, he replaced it with one of the trick bookcases and filled the shelves with books. The door could be opened from either side by a hidden release if one knew where the catch was located. After a screaming quarrel with Dorothy, or when he wished to be alone, he stormed behind the bookcase door and placed himself beyond her reach.

With Alan barricaded in his room, she consoled herself with Cliché's litter of three puppies. Since they had no noticeable personalities, she began referring to them as Première, Deuxième, and Troisième, the order of their births. There were five animals in the small house, but she insisted that you could never have too many dogs. The finish on the hardwood floors was soon past redemption, and there always seemed to be a mess somewhere.

Throughout the spring, the friction in the house continued to mount. At times she humored Alan. In recent months he had championed a friend of his who wanted to make an independent film of *The Ladies of the Corridor* and asked for a ninety-day option without payment. Dorothy and Arnaud d'Usseau were agreeable, and Leah Salisbury could see no harm in giving Eugene Solow the free option, although for sixty days instead of the ninety he had requested. The option period passed before Solow could arrange financial backing. When he asked for an extension, Salisbury turned him down. Alan, upset, was unwilling to let the project drop. He and Dorothy should write a screenplay and then form a corporation to purchase the rights for five thousand dollars, he suggested. This time both Salisbury and d'Usseau reacted coolly to the plan.

To Dorothy's immense relief, the job at Cal State was nearing its end. Shortly before the close of the semester, she spouted off to the *Los Angeles Times* that her students were the stupidest people on the face of the earth. She described them as humorless, hopelessly crass, illiterate prigs who only wanted a college education so they could make lots of money. At the last minute she made a half-hearted effort to soften her indictment by saying the fault was probably hers—she was a poor teacher.

The next day she arrived at the classroom to discover that some of her students read newspapers and did not appreciate her remarks. Furthermore, they were not shy about expressing their resentment. On the blackboard they had listed every allegation they could dig up regarding her allegiance to the Communist Party. Their actions only confirmed what she had felt all along, that they hated her as much as she hated them.

The fourteenth of June began with Alan gulping a round of Bloody Marys. When Clara Lester arrived later that morning to clean, she found him "drunk as a skunk. It was pathetic how he was staggering all over the place." He insisted on going out to pick up his dry cleaning. When he got back to the house, he admitted stopping once or twice to pull himself together.

Dorothy was dressing to go out. The previous week Sally Foster had led her to a sale on good dresses and a new hairdresser. She received so many compliments that she had made another appointment with the same stylist. When she saw Alan, he was carrying his bag of dry cleaning. Saying that he planned to lie down for a while, he disappeared behind the bookcase.

She returned home in the late afternoon. When she called to Alan through the bookshelves, there was no answer. She continued to call out more urgently. Finally, with a great deal of difficulty, she managed to locate the spring release and step into the room. He was curled up on the bed with the stub of a cigarette clenched between his fingers and the plastic cleaning bag draped around his neck and shoulders. Limey jumped onto the bed and began barking and tugging at the plastic. As Dorothy bent down to shake Alan, she noticed that the floor next to his bed was sprinkled with Seconal capsules. He felt strange to her touch and only then did she realize that "rigor mortis had already set in."

The coroner's report showed that Alan had died of "acute barbiturate poisoning due to an ingestion of overdose" and listed him as a probable suicide. None of his friends believed he had intentionally killed himself. A few days earlier, he had strolled into Nina Foch's courtyard with the dogs and struck her as looking unusually sad. "I don't think he meant to kill himself, but I also felt that he'd not unaccidentally done this thing," Foch said. Dorothy told the papers that Alan had exerted himself while remodeling the house. She added that he had a history of heart trouble. To friends, she continued to maintain that the death was a mishap.

In the first hours after Alan's death, the little house was crowded with friends and neighbors. Dorothy greeted new arrivals at the door with invitations to fix themselves a drink, then repeated the details of how she had found Alan cold behind the bookshelves. Eventually, someone remembered Alan's family. A call was placed to Richmond, and Dorothy came to the phone to speak with Roy Eichel. "She asked me what should be done with the body. I told her that Horte would want Alan to come home and be buried in the family plot, next to where her grave would be." He was a little surprised when she readily agreed.

The finality and abruptness of Alan's departure at the age of fifty-nine stunned her. Torn between anguish and anger, she had a hard time responding civilly to expressions of sympathy. A woman who had been fond of Alan and who had always pretended to like her, although Dorothy doubted it, came over to offer condolences and assistance, as had many people that evening. How could she help? she asked.

"Get me a new husband," Dorothy replied without a flicker of expression.

The shocked woman said that the remark was the most vulgar and tasteless she had ever heard.

"I'm sorry," Dorothy told her. "Then run down to the corner and get me a ham and cheese on rye. And tell them to hold the mayo."

Three days later, she shipped Alan's body to his mother in a bronze casket, the most expensive one she could buy. He was buried in the Hebrew Cemetery next to his Uncle Mann and, three years later, Horte was placed on his other side. Alan's childhood friend Joseph Bryan and other friends and classmates from Virginia Military Institute served as pallbearers.

Dorothy did not attend the funeral, nor did she arrange a memorial service in Los Angeles. The whole ritual of dying, the blubbery condolences, the eulogizing of the deceased, struck her as ridiculous. It was just as well that she remained ignorant of the furor taking place in Richmond. When the coffin arrived, Roy Eichel was so shocked by Alan's appearance that he suspected the wrong person had been shipped. The corpse did not even look like his nephew. Concerned about Horte's reaction, he rushed home to find a photograph so that the embalmer might make up the face to resemble Alan as a younger man.

It was a hot, smoggy summer in Los Angeles, made all the more stifling because the living room windows, which extended down to the floor, could not be opened without the dogs' running out. That autumn she received a visit from the Associated Press because she had turned seventy in August. She certainly didn't feel seventy, she said—she felt ninety. If she had any "decency," she would be dead, she added, because "most of my friends are." During the interview, she sipped straight Scotch. Soon she would be leaving for New York where she planned to resume her *Esquire* column and publish another collection of short stories, the last an extraordinary statement because she had not written a story in five years. She wanted to be "taken seriously" as a short-story writer and "by God, I hope I make it." It was hard to make herself heard over the barking of the dogs. "Oh, children," she scolded, "please!"

Her references to Alan were limited to a fervent declaration that she and her late husband had spent "29 great years together." She made them sound like Queen Victoria and Prince Albert, and probably at the time that was the way she wished to regard their marriage.

In the months after his death, when she was numbed by intense misery, a number of good Samaritans stepped forward to look after her, but she resisted them. Perhaps the person toward whom she felt least antagonistic was Sally Foster, whom she called "my angel" and came to depend upon. In the mornings, she prepared herself tea and toast and opened cans for the animals, but that was all she could manage. Each day Foster came to the house with a casserole or freshly baked bread; she made sure that Dorothy had clean clothes, and she picked up the open cans of dog food that were spoiling in the corners; she was sensible, cheerful, and devoted. Concerned about Dorothy's drinking, she begged her to abstain at least until five o'clock. Sometimes she hid bottles on the top shelf of the kitchen cabinets where Dorothy could not reach them.

"We don't have any liquor in the house," Dorothy reminded her.

"Of course you do," Foster replied. "It's right where it always has been."

But what good was inaccessible Scotch? Instead of arguing, she made a trip to Shermart and bought more.

On the afternoons that Charles Brackett visited, he usually brought something to drink. Fred Shroyer, turning up with wine and a loaf of her favorite San Francisco sourdough bread, told her playfully, "I've got the wine and the bread and now you must supply the verses." So many friends invited her to restaurants that it seemed people were obsessed by her nutrition. Dorothy, however, was all but oblivious to food. Lack of appetite resulted in loss of weight and strength and, eventually, malnutrition. Invited to John Carlyle's house for dinner, she stared at two lamb chops on her plate but felt too weak to deal with them. Her host cut the meat for her.

She wanted to show appreciation, but the well-meaning, solicitous people got on her nerves. Sitting on the sofa while watching Sally Foster bustle around with a dustcloth gave her a seizure of guilt because she knew Sally had her own family and home to look after.

"You shouldn't be doing that," she told her.

Foster shrugged. "Somebody has to do it."

Dorothy lit another Chesterfield. Now that she was smoking two or sometimes three packs a day, her usual cough had become even worse. "My God," she murmured, "it's awful to get old, Sally."

She fiercely resisted people trying to straighten out her life, even though her helplessness provoked it. All she wanted was to be left alone so that she could drink in peace. In this goal she often succeeded. Nina Foch noticed that she looked like a sleepwalker when she walked the dogs. "When she stepped off the curb you knew she didn't even see it." On four occasions, she lost her balance and fell in the street. Once, when she was bleeding from a cut on the back of the head, she stubbornly refused to go to the hospital. In November, after she complained of severe arthritic pain in her shoulder, friends finally induced her to see a doctor. X-rays showed that it was broken. On the weekend of John Kennedy's assassination, she was in Cedars of Lebanon hospital. With the other women in her room, she kept her eyes glued to the television set the entire time. Sunk in sorrow, she scarcely noticed her surroundings or her broken shoulder.

Other physical problems arose after Alan's death. When her legs and feet began to swell, her doctor advised keeping her feet elevated to alleviate the edema. Clement Brace rigged up a special pillow that she could take wherever she went to prop up her legs. Since the broken shoulder made it painful to lift her arms, she had trouble dressing and undressing. After an evening with Christopher Isherwood and Don Bachardy, she slept in her clothing. First thing the next morning, she called Sally Foster. "You have to come over here right away and unzip my dress."

Although Sally Foster was devoted to Dorothy, her patience had limits. One day she stopped in to take care of business connected with Alan's insurance. It was after five, and Dorothy had a visitor who was taking her out for dinner. Irritated by Foster's appearance, she did not wait until her friend was out of earshot before giving vent to her feelings. "Wouldn't you know it," she said to her guest. "She had the whole day to do this and she has to get here just as I'm going out." This hurt Foster so deeply that she never returned to the house.

Various other Samaritans took her place. As always, Dorothy was adept at getting people to do favors for her.

Since the day of Alan's overdose, she refused to set foot in his room. She did not want to touch his clothing or possessions. Friends were forced to rummage through bureau drawers to learn that he had made no will and that a tiny insurance policy named Horte as his beneficiary. Dorothy, in the meantime, continued to mourn by secluding herself indoors and drinking as much as was practical. In the early months of 1964, she finally began to emerge from her lethargy and organize a departure. The house was put on the market and eventually sold to actress Peggy Sears, although most of the down payment had to be used for termite control. Cliché died, and she gave away Limey and two of the poodle puppies, keeping for herself only Troisième, whose name she shortened to Troy. As for the household furnishings, she was emphatic about getting rid of the last spoon. She wanted to make "a clean sweep" when she left California.

Since it looked as if she was going to walk away and simply abandon the furniture, Miranda Levy offered to arrange a house sale and placed advertisements in *Variety* and the *Hollywood Reporter*. On the morning of the sale, she tried to talk her into leaving the house and spending the day at Estelle Winwood's. Levy thought it would be painful for her to watch strangers handling her belongings. But Dorothy planted herself in an armchair and sat there watchfully, holding a peculiar kind of court. A sizable crowd showed up, gawkers as well as bona fide purchasers. Levy thought it strange how little visible reaction Dorothy had to the whole proceedings. Even though she obviously needed the money, she seemed determined to undermine the sale. Several times Levy heard her tell a buyer, "Here, you can have it."

Few of Dorothy's friends showed up. Some dismissed the articles as valueless, while others felt intimidated. If she had bought anything, Sally Foster said, "Dottie would have thought that I was just waiting to get hold of it. That was the way her mind worked."

At the end of March, she was escorted to the airport by Clement Brace and John Dall, who shepherded her into the plane with her foot pillow, arranged Troy on her lap, and kissed her good-bye. In her blue-and-white polka-dot dress and her red shoes, she looked like a patriotic, bedraggled sparrow.

Chapter 19

LADY OF THE CORRIDOR

◆

1964–1967

Little had changed at the Volney. Dreamlike, the fading women took up their stations in the lobby, the same bowls of fruit and trays of pastries waited expectantly in the dining room entrance, and the tiny passenger elevator continued to present hazards for corpses. The hotel looked like a stage set for a fictitious New York hotel on the Upper East Side.

She moved into an apartment on the eighth floor, a little smaller than the one she'd had before and slightly less expensive. Aside from a few pots of ivy and the addition of a shelf for her Napoleon figures, she made no attempt to alter the basic institutional look of the place. All furnished apartments, she said, tend to resemble dentists' waiting rooms anyway.

For the remainder of that year and continuing well into 1965, she was in and out of the hospital, "so sick I couldn't write a darn thing." Her broken shoulder still troubled her and she developed bursitis in the other shoulder. She made jokes about her cardiovascular problems, saying that "the doctors were very brave about it" but did not find her hospitalizations for pneumonia, broken bones, and fractures caused by various spills at all amusing. She fell a lot, no matter how careful she was. Some of these mishaps occurred while she was drinking, but by no means all of them. The dismaying truth was that she had shrunk to eighty pounds and her eyesight had deteriorated so badly that she could see little without her glasses. In August, when biographer Nancy Milford came to see her about Zelda Fitzgerald, she found Dorothy with her arm in a sling, living with a practical nurse. Health permitting, she nearly always agreed to interviews because she was all too seldom the center of attention now. Company propelled her into brief bursts of energy and provided occasions to put on one of the pretty pastel dusters that she liked to wear. Milford arrived with an armful of daisies, homage that pleased Dorothy very much. Zelda, she informed Milford, was not a particularly beautiful woman. According to Dorothy, she had the sulky kind of face usually found adorning the lids of candy boxes. In retrospect, she wished that she had been kinder to poor Zelda. She impressed Milford as "a bird in hiding. As I was leaving and going to the elevator, I could still see her peeking around the door." Others, who knew her well but had not seen her since she went west to rejoin Alan, found her physical changes shocking. Alan's death had aged her greatly. Meeting her at a party, Stella Adler was appalled to see how frail and wasted she was, as if she were "a hundred years old."

She could not get along without the nurse, a middle-aged woman who wore a frilly organdy apron over her uniform. The nurse was Dorothy's daily companion for almost a year because she could not bathe herself. Even after she had regained her strength, she still needed help with dressing and lifting. The woman's presence was probably therapeutic in other respects because it gave Dorothy a reason to complain. And she did—about the nurse's stupidity, her high-handed manner, the plastic tablecloth she had bought for the apartment, a tablecloth so dreadful that it could not even pass for pop art.

Someone pointed out that it would be prudent to put her affairs in order by making a will. One of Lillian Hellman's attorneys, Oscar Bernstien, came to the Volney to draw up the papers. It did not take long to dispose of her estate, since in her view she had no estate whatsoever, neither property nor insurance. Taking inventory, she was forced to concede that she did own fifty or sixty shares of *New Yorker* common stock that she guessed might be worth something, and she also had two savings accounts at the Chemical Bank, containing the money she had collected from the sale of the Norma Place house. Modest as these assets were, she knew exactly what she wanted done with them. When Bernstien arrived, she told him that her estate, plus any copyrights and royalties from her writings, were to go to the Reverend Martin Luther King, Jr., and in the event of his death, to the National Association for the Advancement of Colored People. This bequest did not cause Bernstien to blink an eye. As his widow, Rebecca, said, "He understood completely what she had in mind. It seemed natural because she had no heirs, and racial injustice had always affected her very deeply." Dorothy wanted Lillian Hellman to act as her literary executor. She also directed that her body was to be cremated and that there be no funeral services, either formal or informal.

After making the will, she joked to Zero Mostel that the least she could do was die. She was by no means ready, however.

For the first time in her life, she had a legitimate pretext to avoid writing. "I can't use my typewriter," she announced with the triumph of a person who has spent fifty years seeking such an excuse. Since she was unable to write, naturally she wanted to. "The people at *Esquire* have been wonderfully patient, and I hope to get back to work very soon," she said. She stacked the review copies still being sent to her on the floor behind an armchair. She also talked about writing "more stories and maybe a play. I'd love to do another play." In recent years she had become increasingly preoccupied with the idea of "making it" as a writer, whatever that term meant to her. Five years earlier, on her induction into the National Institute of Arts and Letters, it seemed as though she might have "made it," but that assurance had quickly worn off. In her own eyes, she definitely had failed to make it and probably never would, no matter what the National Institute decided about her worth. Still, the thought of dying after a lifetime of meager accomplishment filled her with shame and melancholy.

Even though holding her arms up to the typewriter for more than a few minutes was an immense effort, she managed to compose a thousand-word caption to accompany John Koch's paintings of Manhattan life. In the November 1964 issue of *Esquire*, she contributed a lyrical tribute to his graceful ladies and gentlemen, an evocation of the world of Edith Wharton and Henry James that perhaps recalled some precious shadows from her own past:

> I am always a little sad when I see a John Koch painting. It is nothing more than a bit of nostalgia that makes my heart beat slower—nostalgia for those rooms of lovely lights and lovelier shadows and loveliest people. And I really have no room for the sweet, soft feeling. Nor am I honest, perhaps, in referring to it. For it is the sort of nostalgia that is only a dreamy longing for some places where you never were.

> And, I never will be there. There is no such hour on the
> present clock as 6:30, New York time. Yet, as only New
> Yorkers know, if you can get through the twilight, you'll live
> through the night.

It was was her final magazine article but not her last piece of writing. That
was for Roddy McDowall, a talented photographer as well as actor, who was
publishing a volume of his photographs and asked her to contribute a brief
commentary for two pictures of Oscar Levant, a man she had always liked.
The four paragraphs she gave McDowall for *Double Exposure* were badly
typed and full of typographical errors, actually not even very well written,
but they were pointedly honest. In paying tribute to Levant, she became
defensive on his behalf, although it is possible to see how she may have
been identifying with him. "Over the years, Oscar Levant's image—that
horrible word—was of a cocky young Jew who made a luxurious living by
saying mean things about his best friends and occasionally playing the
piano for a minute if he happened to feel like it." Even though people said
Levant felt sorry for himself, she said, "he isn't and never was; he never
went about with a begging-bowl extended for the greasy coins of pity. He
is, thank heaven, not humble. He has no need to be."

She was uncomfortably aware of her own begging-bowl extended in
pretend meekness. Hospital bills were a great problem, because she had no
medical insurance and depended on the sudden materialization of Samaritans to bail her out. Unfortunately, Samaritans were in increasingly short
supply. It became necessary for the faithful Bea Stewart to make phone calls
notifying various people about Dorothy's plight. On one occasion, after
Stewart's canvassing had produced no results, she hesitantly sought out
Lillian Hellman. When Dorothy learned of it, she was furious and called
Bea "a damned little meddler" who had no shame calling half of New York
and describing Dorothy as "a pleading beggar." In emergencies, Hellman
was her next-to-last resort. Her final resort was The Viking Press, to which
she turned in times of extreme desperation. Harold Guinzburg was dead,
and the place was full of strangers, who no doubt found her more a burden
than an asset as an author.

Throughout these years, her royalties from books and recordings
brought in a modest income. Occasionally there would be a reprint, for
example twenty-five dollars from the *Readers' Digest,* but generally the
check was so small that it hardly seemed worth a trip to the bank. Some-

times she tossed the check into a drawer and forgot about it, an old habit that used to drive Alan crazy. Some of her friends, mystified about the source of her income, speculated that she must be receiving checks from wealthy benefactors. The list of those who were assumed to have covered her expenses included John O'Hara, Quentin Reynolds, and Joan Whitney Payson. If this was true, Dorothy never acknowledged the charitable contributions. As one who had no problem taking from the rich, she was not prepared to refuse "greasy coins of pity," but on the other hand, she saw no reason to publicize it either.

In the meantime, Leah Salisbury continued to encourage first-class producers who might successfully adapt Dorothy's work for the stage. To represent her now, especially when she was ill or depressed, a literary agent had to be inventive. Immediately after Alan's death, Salisbury was unsure of her address. She had been obliged to issue a firm warning that "this time I must hear from you, Dorothy," and suggested a novel system of communication. "To make it easy for you I send you an additional copy of this letter, and a spot below marked both 'yes' and 'no.' " Salisbury instructed her to check one and "to make the whole business still easier here is an addressed return envelope." Dorothy had meekly penned an *X* next to her name and mailed back the letter. At the Volney, when she felt unwell and asked the switchboard to hold her calls, Salisbury was screened out with the rest. She left stacks of messages. After a while, feeling pressured or guilty, Dorothy returned Salisbury's calls. It was not a particularly ideal way to conduct business, but it worked well enough.

In the spring of 1965, she began to recover and enthusiastically sent the nurse packing. For the remainder of that year and for much of the following one, she awoke in the morning feeling more cheerful than she had in a long while. Once again her name appeared in newspapers and magazines. She welcomed a reporter from the *Ladies' Home Journal* but warned she would not discuss the Algonquin. For an Associated Press photographer, she carefully dolled herself up in her polka-dot dress and pearls, posing demurely under the shelf of Napoleon generals with Troy balanced on her lap. A story on the society page of the *New York Herald Tribune* described her as "a bird that has had a tough winter, but is beginning to grow new feathers." It was true that she did feel rejuvenated. Suddenly she longed to romp in society, go to restaurants, attend new plays, even visit a discotheque. For the first time in twenty years, she made an excursion to the Algonquin Hotel, where she had made a date to meet friends. While waiting in the lobby, seated in an armchair facing the entrance to the Rose Room, she quickly drew the attention of the hotel management. Andrew Anspach came over to greet her. During their conversation, he could not resist asking her if she disliked the Algonquin because over the years she had made many derogatory remarks about the hotel. Dorothy smiled. That wasn't the case at all, she assured him, "but it's difficult to get terribly interested in food I digested forty-five years ago."

About this time, she renewed her friendship with Wyatt Cooper, who was married to Gloria Vanderbilt and living in New York. One evening she accompanied them to the United Nations to hear a recital by Libby Holman. After the concert, at a party at the singer's brownstone, Dorothy posed for photographs with Holman, Mainbocher, and Gloria Vanderbilt Cooper. In contrast to Mrs. Cooper, whose smile stretched forever, Dorothy was wearing a sour, quizzical expression, possibly reflecting her displeasure with the Coopers, who had lured her to the concert with the promise that Jacqueline Kennedy would be joining their party. The former first lady failed to show up. It turned out to be a festive evening during which many people fussed excessively over Dorothy, but her pleasure was ruined. She vented her disappointment by dressing down the Coopers for inviting her "under false pretenses."

Equally annoying was Truman Capote's oversight when he neglected to invite her to a ball he was planning at the Plaza Hotel, an event that the papers were billing as the party of the century. She lost no time telephoning Tallulah Bankhead to express her indignation, which Bankhead passed along to Capote. He admitted that he had forgotten to put Dorothy's name on the guest list. Bankhead told him that was exactly Dottie's point; she wanted to attend so that people would know she was still alive. Capote maintained that it was too late and that it would be rude to invite her at the last minute.

When a young man from radio station WBAI came to tape an interview with her, she felt extremely frisky. Richard Lamparski was just beginning a career that nostalgically chronicled the lives of celebrities past their primes. Especially adept at handling women, he captured Dorothy at her most fey by flattering her outrageously. Given an opportunity to run through her entire act, she described herself as a relic from the "long, long days ago" when she had been known as "the toast of two continents—Australia and Greenland" and professed amazement that anybody still remembered her name.

She took a liking to Lamparski, who invited her to movies at the Museum of Modern Art and entertained her with stories about the stars he met in the course of his work. When she heard that he was scheduled to visit Christine Jorgenson in the Long Island suburb of Massapequa, she expressed surprise. What on earth was Jorgenson doing in a place like Massapequa? Lamparski guessed it was because she took care of her mother, who happened to live there. Dorothy avidly pressed for more details. "Have you met her mother?"

"Not yet," said Lamparski. "Why?"

"Because I'd be very interested in knowing what sex she is," said Dorothy.

Having nothing better to do, she indulged her love of gossip. Apart from a desire to know what Jackie Kennedy ate for breakfast and the sex of Christine Jorgenson's mother, she followed the doings of the rich, the famous, and the social. As a joke, someone gave her a subscription to *Women's Wear Daily*, a fashion paper known for its coverage of such personages, but it was no joke to Dorothy, who devoured each issue with glee, mocking socialites such as Mrs. William Paley and Mrs. Winston Guest and calling model Jean Shrimpton "preposterous." She found them as diverting as fictional characters and refused to listen when anybody suggested that the "Beautiful People" were not as bad as she assumed. They were as bad, she insisted; they were "idiots" who made her feel "sick" but, she said, "I love to read about them."

Her other pastime was watching her television set, a piece of equipment she had acquired in the hopes of drowning out the nurse's chatter—"but she talked right along with it." Now the nurse was gone but the television remained. Even though she felt obliged to apologize for its presence, she did not in truth dislike the programs as much as she pretended. The set was going from morning to night.

The program that she claimed as her favorite was a comedy show, *That Was the Week That Was*. Her real favorites, however, were soap operas. Afternoon visitors were obliged to watch them with her or to hear about the latest episode of *As the World Turns*. Or, if she was not reporting on the soaps, it was the latest gossip about women like Barbara Paley, the "silly" jet-setters whose activities she followed.

Shallow conversation was hardly what people expected from Dorothy. Some of her friends found it extremely disconcerting. They had difficulty understanding that the hours crawled by, and soap operas helped pass the afternoons, until it was twilight and a waiter knocked on her door with the daily menu. An hour later, he reappeared bearing a tray. Even if she sent it back more or less untouched, it filled the void until she could settle down to Scotch and plotting the evening TV lineup. As she had written, if you can get through the twilight in New York, you'll survive the night.

On the evening of her seventy-second birthday, she was invited to Sid and Laura Perelman's Village apartment. While she enjoyed the celebration, her style was cramped because her doctor had grown increasingly tiresome about liquor, and she had meekly pledged not to touch a drop. Holding a glass of soda made her feel foolish.

"Do you know what this is?" she said to Heywood Hale Broun as she held up the glass with undisguised disgust. "Ginger ale. Isn't that awful?"

She understood that drinking had become dangerous because it increased the risk of falls. She could afford no more of them. Her periodic resolutions to go on the wagon were always short-lived. On more than one occasion, expected at a friend's house for dinner, she nipped into the Carlyle bar to fortify herself and forgot to come out. Several times she went too far with Scotch and found herself in Flower Fifth Avenue Hospital. Whenever visitors appeared, she politely offered them a drink, then guessed she would pour one for herself.

But one led to many. Parker Ladd believed that if he helped her empty a bottle, that would be the end of it, and she would be forced to stop for the day. One night shortly before Christmas 1965, he prepared highball after highball for them, swallowing a little of his own and dumping the rest down the sink. Finally he heaved a sigh of relief to find the bottle empty. To his amazement, Dorothy hauled herself up and began rummaging around on the closet floor among some old shoes. In triumph, she produced another bottle of Scotch. That year she spent the holiday in the hospital.

Increasingly, Dorothy's drinking upset her friends. Ruth Goetz discovered that even an hour's visit was "heavy going" and found herself feeling relieved when it was time to leave. Lillian Hellman only appeared when she was summoned in times of crisis, and she fled once the emergency was over.

Dorothy's alcoholism made her "dull and repetitive," she wrote, and in any case she was unable to assume "the burdens that Dottie, maybe by never asking for anything, always put on her friends." Dorothy pretended not to notice Hellman's neglect. On those rare occasions when Hellman did visit, she greeted her with, "Oh, Lilly, come in quick. I want to laugh again," instead of the reproaches Lillian was expecting. When Dorothy was on a binge, she sometimes instructed the hotel switchboard to take her calls, but more often the drinking was unpremeditated and she forgot. When Joseph Bryan telephoned to inquire how she was doing, she sounded friendly and then all at once, for no apparent reason, began to curse him as "a no-good, fascist son of a bitch."

The world seemed to be shrinking. Few new people entered her life and the political friends she once had called "my own people" had quietly dropped from sight. Some of them would have agreed with Hellman when she later wrote that Dorothy's eccentricities, once so amusing, had become "too strange for safety or comfort." Dorothy tried to accept their being dead or busy or living some new incarnation. Still remaining were the Mostels and the Perelmans, whose company she continued to enjoy. The fall she returned to New York, she was greatly saddened to learn of Gerald Murphy's death and sent Sara a telegram that simply read, DEAREST SARA, DEAREST SARA. Although Sara spent her summers at East Hampton, she kept a city apartment for the winters and now lived at the Volney with a nurse. While Dorothy saw Sara often and permitted expressions of motherly concern over her health and appetite, her closest companion continued to be Bea Stewart, who had never figured among "my own people," who cared not two cents for politics, but who had permitted Dorothy to lean on her whenever she liked for some forty years. Bea, unlike the others, never pulled a face when Dorothy reached for the Scotch.

Around close friends she did not trouble to conceal the black moods that sometimes enveloped her, times when she needed to sound off about her many afflictions and privations. She complained to Wyatt Cooper about how she really deserved to be dead because "everybody I ever cared about is dead." An afternoon with Fred Shroyer provoked a similar litany of small frustrations and major disasters. As he was leaving, she kissed him goodbye and whispered theatrically, "Listen, Fred, don't feel badly when I die, because I've been dead for a long time." He left feeling totally sorry for her. That bit of gallows humor was wicked of her, but she had few pleasures left in life.

In the early months of 1967, her situation looked bright. At last it seemed as if Leah Salisbury's years of work were going to pay off in a Broadway production. Marcella Cisney, who with her husband operated a theater company at the University of Michigan, had organized a script based on Dorothy's poems and stories as well as more recent writings from *The New Yorker* and *Esquire.* Cisney was a respected director who had conceived a similar production based on the poetry and letters of Robert Frost, a production that had been tried out at Michigan before its New York opening. Her production proposal for *A Dorothy Parker Portfolio* included Cole Porter's music, sets based on the sketches of *New Yorker* artists such as Peter Arno and William Steig, and a cast starring Julie Harris and backed up by such versatile performers as Tom Ewell and Anne Jackson.

In Salisbury's judgment, Cisney's idea was worth pursuing and encouraging. When she brought her to the Volney to read the script, Dorothy could not have been more "delighted" and gave the project her enthusiastic endorsement. She particularly liked the thought of Julie Harris as her prototype. As the months passed and the details were worked out, Dorothy's excitement mounted. Cisney planned to open the show at Ann Arbor's 1967–1968 season, give Dorothy one thousand dollars in advance royalties, and then negotiate a Dramatists Guild contract for a Broadway production. In the meantime, she asked Dorothy to attend rehearsals in Ann Arbor and offer suggestions.

The prospect of a Broadway show buoyed her spirits. She also hoped that it might alleviate her money worries. Lately she had been thinking about the future, wondering how she was going to conserve her nest egg. The result of her stewing was a decision to move to a smaller, cheaper apartment on the sixth floor. This meant a savings of twenty-five dollars a month, but having made the switch she immediately regretted it. The new apartment was not nearly as pleasant as 8E.

For a while that winter she went out frequently. Friends took her to see *Sherry*, a Broadway musical based on *The Man Who Came to Dinner.* Afterward, they went to the Oak Room at the Plaza, where she held court and was delighted to be spotted by Broadway columnist Leonard Lyons. That sort of adventure happened rarely. More often she spent quiet times with Sara Murphy or evenings at Bea Stewart's apartment six blocks away. A color snapshot taken by Bea showed that Dorothy liked to dress up for these outings. She wore a smart navy blue dress, and her hair and makeup had been obviously done with care. As always, her poodle was seated on her lap. Evenings at Bea's customarily ended with Dorothy's opening her purse and making a woebegone face. She had no change for a cab. The ritual would end with her accepting a dollar or two.

Even though she felt energetic, she continued to grumble about her terrible life. She was as good as dead. "I can't write, I can't write," she would moan. When it was proposed that she might want to reminisce about her life by dictating the story to Wyatt Cooper, she surprised everyone by agreeing. It would give her, she said, "something to live for," and she assured Cooper she would keep the narrative "gay"; otherwise there would be no point in telling it. The tapings were, in fact, somewhat of a strain. After three sessions, they gave up the project. Possibly Dorothy found them fun because she had an opportunity to demolish her father and practically every other human being whose path had crossed hers, but Cooper derived little satisfaction. Unable to accept her stories as the truth, he concluded that the recollections had to be "creative exaggerations."

In March, Gloria and Wyatt Cooper gave a party in her honor. This resulted from her having missed an earlier invitation, when a blizzard had dumped a foot of snow on the city and she had been unable to navigate the storm. Aware of her disappointment, the Coopers proposed a special party for her and promised to invite glamorous, interesting people whose company she would enjoy.

"My wife," wrote Cooper, "was, of course, fascinated by Dottie, and somewhat worshipful, an attitude that was mutual. . . . Dottie was always at her most genteel in my wife's presence, with malice toward none and charity for all." It was true that her manner toward Gloria Vanderbilt could not have been more conventionally correct, as it would have been with any of the socialites whose lives she followed in *Women's Wear Daily* and ripped to shreds with such relish. Gloria's rather imperious manner made her smile. She had taken to calling her "Gloria the Vth."

In the following weeks, invitations were extended to a dozen couples, including Mr. and Mrs. William Paley, Mr. and Mrs. Louis Auchincloss, Mr.

and Mrs. Gardner Cowles, and Mr. and Mrs. Samuel Peabody, among other notables. None of Dorothy's friends were asked.

"Have you been invited?" Dorothy demanded of Parker Ladd, who happened to be a friend of both hers and the Coopers.

"No," he answered, he had not.

"Well, I'm not going either," she swore. "Those are just not my kind of people."

In reality, nothing could have prevented her acceptance. What troubled her was having nothing to wear, at least nothing worthy of such a fine occasion. When the Coopers realized this, they quickly provided a suitable costume. Gloria Vanderbilt sent over a size-three gold-brocade caftan beaded with tiny pearls. Dorothy found it enchanting. Even though the dress was six inches too long, she refused to have it shortened, because she thought it made her look like a Chinese empress. A last-minute crisis, the realization that she lacked matching shoes and handbag, was averted by Sara Murphy, who escorted her to Lord & Taylor to purchase accessories and then treated her to tea at Schrafft's, a favor that did not prevent Dorothy from complaining afterward about the department store, Sara's taste in restaurants, and the nurse who accompanied Sara everywhere.

At the Coopers, seated between Wyatt and Louis Auchincloss, Dorothy had to admit that Gloria Vanderbilt certainly knew how to give a dinner party. The display of flowers, the red tablecloths, and silver gleaming under the candlelight looked splendid. Everyone was dressed to the teeth. Dorothy studied the details of gowns, jewels, and coiffures, the better to savor and recall later for curious friends. Although she performed her part with grace and dignity, from time to time her inhibitions loosened and she let slip an unexpected remark. When another guest delivered an accolade on the beauty of the wine goblets, pointing out that wine *always* tasted so much better in lovely glasses, Dorothy was quick to agree.

"Oh, yes," she fluted, "paper cups aren't right." It was at this moment that Wyatt Cooper, who had been finding it difficult to converse with her under these formal circumstances, was suddenly seized by an attack of nervous coughing.

On her other side, Louis Auchincloss was having a frustrating evening, because the noise at the table drowned out Dorothy's soft voice. "I could not hear a *word* she said. I have never been more sadly disappointed in a social occasion in my life. I admired her so much and we could not communicate!"

To Dorothy there was little real communication with anyone at the dinner—the percussion of all that invisible money was deafening. In the days after the fête, she expressed her disdain for the whole business by verbally garrotting practically everyone present.

Bea Stewart's telephone rang in the late afternoon on Wednesday, June 7. "She's gone," announced a desk clerk calling from the Volney.

Stewart took this to mean that Dorothy changed her mind about apartment 6F and impulsively moved elsewhere. But it was not that at all. Mrs. Parker died that afternoon, he informed her. A chambermaid discovered the body.

Stewart was astounded. The previous week Dorothy seemed tired, although not so tired that she stopped enjoying Scotch or Chesterfields. When Bea stopped by, she found Dorothy sitting up in bed and thought that all she needed was a rest. Never had she suspected the end was approaching.

She called the Volney back and asked them to enter Dorothy's apartment and remove the dog. Dorothy would not want the police to impound Troy. When Stewart arrived at the hotel, the poodle was safely stored in another apartment, and the authorities were present on the scene. Dorothy lay in bed under a sheet. When Lillian Hellman arrived a short while later, she answered the medical examiner's questions and called the newspapers—the cause of death had been a heart attack. By this time, Stewart was on her way home with Troy.

In Atlanta, Martin Luther King, Jr., was in Beaumon's Restaurant, where his Southern Christian Leadership Conference was meeting in an executive session, when he was called to the telephone. A few minutes later he made his way back to the table and announced that Dorothy Parker had bequeathed her estate to him, "which verifies what I have always said, that the Lord will provide." He was surprised because he had never met her. Afterward, he issued a formal statement saying that although she needed no monument to her memory, "this fine deed" could only add to her reputation. After deduction of expenses, the Parker estate amounted to $20,448.39.

On Thursday evening, at the Frank E. Campbell Funeral Chapel in

New York, Kate Mostel kept vigil with the body, which was laid out in the beaded caftan Dorothy had worn to the Vanderbilt-Cooper party. Mostel, raised a Catholic, thought it was awful to leave a person's body alone in a funeral parlor. The only other person present was George Oppenheimer. They sat in silence.

Lillian Hellman took charge of the funeral arrangements with her usual efficiency. On Friday morning, a day of brilliant sunshine, there was a memorial service at Frank Campbell's. In her will, Dorothy had requested no service of any kind, but Hellman believed in observing the amenities. In any case, it was going to be a very brief service. Among the one hundred and fifty friends who showed up to pay their respects were a number who expressed astonishment over the size of the obituary that had appeared in *The New York Times.* The story had begun on the front page and continued inside for almost an entire page. The paper also carried a sampling of quotes to demonstrate her "saucy wit," some of which witticisms she had written or spoken and some of which she had not.

After a violinist played Bach's "Air on a G String," Lillian Hellman and Zero Mostel came forward to deliver eulogies. Kate Mostel recalled that Hellman told Zero, " 'You take five minutes and I'll take five.' So Zero took five minutes and she took twenty." Zero Mostel tactfully pointed out that the last thing Dorothy would have wanted was this formal ceremony. "If she had her way," he said, "I suspect she would not be here at all." After the mourners had filed out, Sid Perelman remarked, "I'm sure Dorothy's foot was tapping even through as short an exercise as that because she had a very short fuse."

Many times she had rehearsed her death, imagining even the kind of weather she wanted:

> Oh, let it be a night of lyric rain
> And singing breezes, when my bell is tolled.
> I have so loved the rain that I would hold
> Last in my ears its friendly, dim refrain.

When she had written those lines she had been thirty and thinking of her mother's death, that terrifying journey across the harbor with the coffin and standing around the muddy mound at Woodlawn. On the afternoon her own life closed it was fair and warm, with temperatures in the mid-eighties. She had never been able to get what she wanted.

In Rochester, Bill Droste and Lel Iveson read of their aunt's death in the newspaper. Even though they had not heard from her in many years—not, in fact, since their mother died—they wished to acknowledge her passing out of respect. They wrote to Lillian Hellman to find out about arrangements for the funeral. When they received no reply, Bill Droste asked his attorney to write, if only to find out where she was buried. Again there was no answer.

On June 9, 1967, Dorothy was cremated at Ferncliff Crematory in Hartsdale, New York. During the following weeks, her ashes remained unclaimed. Lillian Hellman, who made the arrangements, had left no instructions about their disposition. On July 16, Ferncliff finally received word to mail the cremated remains to the legal firm of O'Dwyer and Bernstien, 99 Wall Street, New York City.

Oscar Bernstien and Paul O'Dwyer frankly did not know what to do with Dorothy's ashes. Pending further instructions from Lillian Hellman, Paul O'Dwyer stored the box in the drawer of a filing cabinet in his office. After more than twenty years, the ashes are still there.

Upon Dorothy's death, the disposition of her business affairs and her personal effects fell to her executor. Since the only business deal in progress during the last months of Dorothy's life was Marcella Cisney's *A Dorothy Parker Portfolio,* Leah Salisbury wasted no time in writing to Lillian Hellman about it. To her surprise, Hellman was unwilling to extend the necessary approval. Despite appeals from both Salisbury and Cisney asking her to reconsider, Hellman steadfastly opposed the project until Cisney was obliged to drop the matter in 1970. Hellman's attitude toward her guardianship of Dorothy's and Dashiell Hammett's estates was essentially negative. As one of her biographers later noted, she did not encourage those "who would like to keep books on Hammett and Parker, whose literary papers she keeps safely out of sight." She refused to cooperate with anyone who wished to write about Dorothy.

In 1972, over Hellman's fierce protests, the executorship of Dorothy's estate passed to the NAACP. Ownership of the Parker literary property belonged to Martin Luther King during his lifetime. After his death in 1968, it was the NAACP's position that their absolute ownership made an executor unnecessary. A court ruling in their favor terminated Hellman's fiduciary capacity, which she had assumed was for life. She was not pleased. "It's one thing to have real feeling for black people," she said, "but to have the kind of blind sentimentality about the NAACP, a group so conservative that even many blacks now don't have any respect for, is something else. She must have been drunk when she did it."

To playwright Howard Teichmann, Hellman angrily called Dorothy "that goddamn bitch." Hellman claimed that she had "paid her hotel bill at the Volney for years, kept her in booze, paid for her suicide attempts—all on the promise that when she died, she would leave me the rights to her writing. At my death, they would pass to the NAACP. But what did she do? She left them *directly* to the NAACP. Damn her!"

Hellman arranged for her secretary to be paid fifty dollars from the estate to clean Dorothy's apartment. According to Hellman's memoirs, "Among the small amount of papers she left were odds and ends of paid or unpaid laundry bills, a certificate of the aristocratic origins of a beloved poodle, a letter dated ten years before from an admirer of her poems, and the letter from me sent from Russia about six weeks before she died. [In fact, the only unpaid bills were from the Volney, Dorothy's doctor, the Zitomer Pharmacy, and a newspaper delivery service, debts amounting to less than five hundred dollars.] Around the envelope of my letter was folded a piece of paper that was the beginning, obviously, of a letter Dottie never finished. It said, 'Come home soon, Lilly, and bring Natasha on a leash. She'd be such a nice companion for C'Est Tout [Troy]. I—' "

The few personal papers, documents, or mementos that she left behind were to vanish, destroyed either when the apartment was cleaned or at some later date. As Martha Gellhorn wrote in 1981, Dorothy "might as well have left her papers to Fort Knox. Until Miss H. releases Mrs. Parker's papers, there is no way to prove how long Miss H. stayed in Spain [during 1937]."

Nothing was released. After Lillian Hellman's death in 1984, no material relating to Dorothy was found among her possessions.

. . .

Dorothy outlived nearly all the Round Tablers except Marc Connelly and Frank Sullivan. A few days after her death, Sullivan wrote to a friend,

> I could write you so much about Dotty that I don't dare get started. Jim Cagney telephoned today from Milbrook in a mild state of shock about her death. He said he just wanted to make sure I was here, as a link with former and happier days. Well, it threw me into a pensive shock too. Her departure is as much the end of an era for me . . . as the departure of the bulk of the NY papers. She was a *strong* person, Honey. And you said it, when you wrote: she was at war with herself all her life. Maybe most of us are and some negotiate cease fires occasionally, which seldom last. All the digs she took at people, friend and foe alike, were really digs at herself. . . .
>
> If there is any meaning to anything, she is now having the good time she seldom had while here, and I hope she is having it with Mr. Benchley (her name for him always).

Notes

Introduction: The Algonquin Hotel

xvi THEY SAY OF ME: Parker, "Neither Bloody nor Bowed," *The Portable Dorothy Parker*, The Viking Press, 1973, p. 117.

xvii I AM CHEAP: Edmund Wilson, *The Twenties*, Farrar, Straus & Giroux, 1975, p. 345.

xvii BUT NOW I KNOW: Parker, "Indian Summer," *The Portable Dorothy Parker*, p. 107.

xvii TIME DOTH FLIT: Author's interview with Allen Saalburg.

xvii SHE DISDAINED: Parker, *The Portable Dorothy Parker*, p. 491.

xvii AT TWILIGHT: Author's interview with Allen Saalburg.

xviii THREE HIGHBALLS: Parker, "Just a Little One," *The Portable Dorothy Parker*, p. 242.

xviii I DON'T CARE: Parker, "Morning," *Life*, July 7, 1927, p. 9.

xviii IT WAS INEVITABLE: Parker, *The Portable Dorothy Parker*, p. 483.

xviii AT LUNCH: Parker, *The Portable Dorothy Parker*, p. 510.

xix OH, HARD IS THE STRUGGLE: Parker, "Coda," *The Portable Dorothy Parker*, p. 240.

xix JUST A LITTLE JEWISH GIRL: Wyatt Cooper, "Whatever You Think Dorothy Parker Was Like, She Wasn't," *Esquire*, July 1968, p. 57.

One: The Events Leading Up to the Tragedy

3 WILD IN MY BREAST: Parker, "Temps Perdu," *The Portable Dorothy Parker*, p. 317.

3 MY GOD: Cooper, p. 57.

5 FOLK OF MUD: Parker, "The Dark Girl's Rhyme," *The Portable Dorothy Parker*, p. 78.

8 WHAT STREET: Parker, *McCall's*, January 1928, p. 4.

9 GO DOWN TO ELLIS ISLAND: Cooper, p. 57.

9 THE GREATEST SALESMAN: *Crerand's Cloak Journal*, February 1899, p. 146.

10 SILLY STOCK: Parker, "The Dark Girl's Rhyme," *The Portable Dorothy Parker*, p. 78.

11 LOVELY SPEECH: Author's interview with Ruth Goetz.

12 DIARRHEA WITH COLIC: State of New Jersey Report of Death, Eliza Rothschild, July 20, 1898.

12 PROMPTLY WENT AND DIED: Cooper, p. 57.

13   I DIDN'T CALL: Ibid.

14   WHENEVER HE'D HEAR: Ibid.

14   WOULD LAUGH: Parker, "Condolence," *The Portable Dorothy Parker*, p. 93.

14   DO NOT WELCOME ME: Parker, "The White Lady," *The Portable Dorothy Parker*, p. 90.

15   SPONTANEOUS COMBUSTION: Cooper, p. 57.

15   THEY WEREN'T EXACTLY: Ibid.

15   EIGHTY YEARS LATER: Laura McLaughlin letter to author, February 25, 1980.

15   DID YOU LOVE: Cooper, p. 57.

16   THAT YOUR SISTER?: Ibid.

16   A FOUNTAIN PEN: Parker, *Ainslee's*, October 1921, p. 156.

16   THERE'S LITTLE: Parker, "Coda," *The Portable Dorothy Parker*, p. 240.

17   SUCH ARTICLES OF JEWELRY: Eleanor Rothschild will.

Two: Palimpsest

19   SHE WAS A REAL BEAUTY: Cooper, p. 57.

20   ONE OF THOSE AWFUL CHILDREN: "Dorothy Parker," in *Writers at Work: The Paris Review Interviews*, Edited by Malcolm Cowley, The Viking Press, 1957, 1958, p. 76.

20   WONDERFUL TO SAY: Helen Rothschild letter to Henry Rothschild, July 25, 1905.

20   THIS MORNING RAGS: Henry Rothschild untitled verse, 1905.

21   DO NOT FAIL: Ibid.

22   FOR COMFORT: *Writers at Work*, p. 78.

22   LYING ON HIS FACE: William Thackeray, *Vanity Fair*, p. 347.

22   THEY SAY WHEN YOUR: Dorothy Rothschild letter to Henry Rothschild, August 6, 1906.

22   A SOCK IN THE EYE: Parker, "Inventory," *The Portable Dorothy Parker*, p. 96.

23   THE KID IS FINE: Helen Rothschild letter to Henry Rothschild, ca. July, 1905.

23   DEAR PAPA: Dorothy Rothschild letters to Henry Rothschild, Summer 1905.

24   SAY, MISS DOROTHY: Henry Rothschild untitled verse, Summer 1905.

25   ONE CAME IN HANDY: Dorothy Rothschild letter to Henry Rothschild, August 22, 1905.

25   IT'S TERRIBLY HOT: Ibid., June 23, 1906.

26   DEAR PAPA: Ibid., June 26, 1906.

27   THE TYPICAL DANA GIRL: Parker, "The Education of Gloria," *Ladies, Home Journal*, October 1920, p. 37; "The Middle or Blue Period," *The Portable Dorothy Parker*, p. 595.

28   CARRIED THE DAISY CHAIN: "Theatre," *The New Yorker*, February 28, 1931, p. 22.

28   BECAUSE OF CIRCUMSTANCES: *Los Angeles Times*, April 28, 1963.

28   THE BLACK SHEEP: "Nobody knew what happened to him," Lel Droste Iveson said of her uncle, Harry Rothschild. In "The Wonderful Old Gentleman," Parker drew the character of a scapegrace who had disappointed his father, despite everything he had done for the boy. The Old Gentleman "used to try and help Matt get along. He'd go down, like it was to Mr. Fuller, that time Matt was working at the bank, and he'd explain to him, 'Now, Mr. Fuller,' he'd say, 'I don't know whether you know it, but this son of mine has always been what you might call the black sheep of the family. He's been kind of a drinker,' he'd say, 'and he's got himself into trouble a couple of times, and if you'd just keep an eye on him, so's to see he keeps straight, it'd be a favor to me.'" Matt's wild behavior, Parker wrote, "had a good deal to do with hastening father's death." *The Portable Dorothy Parker*, p. 61.

29   MARTIN, SHE SAID: Surrogate Court, County of New York, "In the Matter of Proving the Last Will and Testament of Martin Rothschild, Deceased," May 17, 1912.

29   THREE NIGHTS LATER: Henry Rothschild's death certificate lists the cause of

death as "chronic endocarditis—chronic myocarditis—general arteriosclerosis."

30 AFTER MY FATHER DIED: *Writers at Work*, p. 72.

31 THE MOST HORRIBLE: Fred Lawrence Guiles, *Hanging On in Paradise*, McGraw-Hill Book Co., 1975, p. 87.

31 VERY NICE LIGHT VERSE: Parker, "Sophisticated Verse" speech, American Writers Congress, June 1939.

31 THERE IS NO WAY OF KNOWING: If F.P.A. published any of Dorothy's early verse in The Conning Tower, there is no way to distinguish her work from that of other contributors.

32 MY HUSBAND SAYS: Dorothy Rothschild, "Any Porch," *Vanity Fair*, September 1915, p. 32.

32 DOROTHY'S FIRST MEETING WITH FRANK CROWINSHIELD: Frank Crowninshield, "Crowninshield in the Cub's Den," *Vogue*, September 15, 1944, p. 197.

33 BUT HOW WILL WE EVER: Helen Lawrenson, *Stranger at the Party*, Random House, 1975, p. 57.

33 IF TO YOUR PAPA: Henry Rothschild untitled verse, ca. 1906.

34 I THOUGHT: *Writers at Work*, p. 72.

Three: Vanity Fair

35 FROM THESE FOUNDATIONS: *Vogue Pattern Service*, October 1, 1916, p. 101.

35 THERE WAS A LITTLE GIRL: Caroline Seebohm, *The Man Who Was Vogue*, The Viking Press, 1982, p. 60.

36 A SMALL, DARK-HAIRED PIXIE: Edna Woolman Chase and Ilka Chase, *Always in Vogue*, Doubleday & Co., 1954, p. 135.

36 IN THE WOMEN'S WASHROOM: Crowninshield, p. 197.

36 WE USED TO SIT AROUND: *Writers at Work*, p. 72.

37 I HATE WOMEN: "Henriette Rousseau" (Dorothy Rothschild pseudonym), "Women: A Hate Song," *Vanity Fair*, August 1916, p. 61.

37 FIRST AND SECOND: Dorothy Rothschild, "Why I Haven't Married," *Vanity Fair*, October 1916, p. 51.

39 SHE LIKED HIM: Parker, "Big Blonde," *The Portable Dorothy Parker*, p. 188.

41 OH LORD: Cooper, p. 113.

41 IF SHE HAD FELT: Parker, "The Dark Girl's Rhyme," *The Portable Dorothy Parker*, p. 78.

42 ONE CAN IMAGINE: Cooper, p. 113.

42 CHASE NEVER FORGOT: Chase and Chase, p. 135.

43 WHEN HE HAD UNEARTHED: Edmund Wilson, *Letters on Literature and Politics, 1912–1972*, Edited by Elena Wilson, Farrar, Strauss & Giroux, 1977, p. 405.

44 HORN-RIMMED GLASSES: Crowninshield, p. 197.

45 IN HER FIRST COLUMN: Dorothy Parker, "A Succession of Musical Comedies," *Vanity Fair*, April 1918, p. 69.

48 DOROTHY LATER SAID: Cooper, p. 113.

48 AFTER ONLY A FEW MONTHS: Parker, "The Dramas That Gloom in the Spring," *Vanity Fair*, June 1918, p. 37.

48 BY SUMMER: Parker, "Mortality in the Drama," *Vanity Fair*, July 1918, p. 29.

48 IT MAY BE: Parker, "The Fall Deluge of War Plays," *Vanity Fair*, October 1918, p. 56.

49 IT ISN'T ONLY: "Henriette Rousseau" (Dorothy Parker pseudonym), "The People Who Sit in Back of Me," *Vanity Fair*, July 1918, p. 46.

49 SINCE SHE DISLIKED: *Writers at Work*, p. 73.

49 "DEAR," HE WROTE: Edwin Parker card to Dorothy Parker, January 1919.

Four: Cub Lions

52 ALTHOUGH SHE WAS FAIRLY PRETTY: Wilson, *The Twenties*, p. 33.

53 TOLD OF HER SON'S DEATH: Nathaniel Benchley, *Robert Benchley*, McGraw-Hill Book Co., 1955, p. 28.

54 ON THE BASIS OF HIS WRITING: Parker, *New York Herald Tribune*, October 13, 1963, p. 20; Wolcott Gibbs, "Robert Benchley: In Memoriam," *New York Times Book Review*, December 16, 1945, p. 3.

54 A SORT OF MAID: Robert Sherwood letter to Nathaniel Benchley, January 4, 1955, Robert Benchley Collection, Mugar Memorial Library, Boston University.

55 SHE PUT FORTH THE THEORY: Parker, "Are You a Stopper?" *Vanity Fair*, September 1918, p. 23.

55 IN THOSE DAYS: Crowninshield, p. 200.

55 BACK AT THE OFFICE: J. Bryan III, "Funny Man" (Part 2), *Saturday Evening Post*, October 7, 1939, p. 32

55 MARK MY WORDS: J. Bryan III, "Funny Man" (Part 1), *Saturday Evening Post*, September 23, 1939, p. 10.

56 AT FIRST CROWNINSHIELD: Crowninshield, p. 199.

56 I CUT OUT A PICTURE: *Writers at Work*, p. 73.

56 I DARED SUGGEST: Crowninshield, p. 163.

56 A LOVELY MAN: *Writers at Work*, p. 73.

56 AMAZING WHELPS: Crowninshield, p. 162.

56 LATER ON: Ibid., p. 199.

57 WALK DOWN THE STREET: *Writers at Work*, p. 73.

58 THEY WOULD VIE: Robert E. Drennan, *The Algonquin Wits*, The Citadel Press, 1968, pp. 81, 129; Wolcott Gibbs, "Big Nemo," Part 1, *The New Yorker*, March 18, 1939, p. 24.

59 THEREAFTER HE PLAYED: Woollcott may have suffered from a testosterone deficiency.

59 ROSS HAD DEVELOPED: Drennan, p. 158.

59 WHERE'D YOU WORK: Jane Grant, *Ross, the New Yorker and Me*, Reynal & Co., 1968, p. 51.

60 F.P.A.'S BEAK NOSE: Drennan, p. 162.

60 NEVER MIND THE FLOSS: Bennett Cerf, Columbia University Oral History Research Office.

60 THE CLINGING OAK: Heywood Hale Broun, *Whose Little Boy Are You? A Memoir of the Broun Family*, St. Martin's Press, 1983, p. 6.

61 PERSHING, NOTICING HIM: Richard O'Connor, *Heywood Broun*, G.P. Putnam's, 1975, p. 58.

61 A FEW MONTHS EARLIER: "Helen Wells" (Dorothy Parker pseudonym), "They Won the War," *Vanity Fair*, January 1919, p. 39.

61 ALL HIS STORIES BEGAN: James R. Gaines, *Wit's End: Days and Nights of the Algonquin Round Table*, Harcourt Brace Jovanovich, 1977, p. 28.

63 IT MEANT, SHE RECALLED: Cooper, p. 113.

64 THEY RESENTED: "Policy Memorandum Concerning the Forbidding of Discussion Among Employees," to Francis L. Wurzburg from Robert Benchley, Dorothy Parker, and Robert Sherwood, October 14, 1919, in Robert Benchley Collection, Mugar Library, Boston University.

65 TO HIM THEY WERE: Frank Case, *Tales of a Wayward Inn*, Frederick A. Stokes Co., 1938, p. 61.

65 BENCHLEY'S HORROR OF LIBERTINES: Robert Sherwood letter to Nathaniel Benchley, January 4, 1955, Robert Benchley Collection, Mugar Library, Boston University.

66 ALL WE HAVE TO DO: Robert Benchley diary, Mugar Library, Boston University.

66 *VANITY FAIR* WAS A MAGAZINE: *Writers at Work*, p. 74.

Five: The Algonquin Round Table

68 HE THEN SUGGESTED: Benchley, p. 143.

68 HE LABELED THE MAGAZINE'S ACTION: Robert Benchley letter to Frank Crowninshield, Robert Benchley Collection, Mugar Library, Boston University.

68   DOROTHY WAS DEEPLY MOVED: *Writers at Work*, p. 74.

69   BENCHLEY THOUGHT: John Mason Brown, *The Worlds of Robert Sherwood*, Harper & Row, 1965, p. 138.

69   R. BENCHLEY TELLS ME: Franklin P. Adams, *The Diary of Our Own Samuel Pepys*, vol. 1, Simon and Schuster, 1935, p. 241.

69   DOROTHY WAS PROUD: *Writers at Work*, p. 74.

69   BENCHLEY, AN ARDENT: Robert Benchley diary, Robert Benchley Collection, Mugar Library, Boston University.

70   DOROTHY AND BENCHLEY: Wilson, *The Twenties*, pp. 33–4.

70   FOR A SCENE: Lillian Gish and Ann Pinchot, *Lillian Gish: The Movies, Mr. Griffith and Me*, Prentice-Hall, 1969, p. 224.

70   AN INCH SMALLER: *Writers at Work*, p. 74.

71   THERE WAS ALWAYS A LAUGH: Author's interview with Marc Connelly.

71   MRS. PARKER, HE REMEMBERED: Author's interview with Charles Baskerville.

72   HIGH SOCIETY WAS TO BE: Dorothy Parker, George S. Chappell, and Frank Crowninshield, drawings by Fish, *High Society*, G.P. Putnam's Sons, 1920.

72   "AND DOROTHY," HE SAID: Wilson, *The Twenties*, p. 48.

73   THE PREVIOUS FALL: Scott Meredith, *George S. Kaufman and His Friends*, Doubleday & Co., 1974, p. 159.

74   AT THAT TIME: Case, pp. 61–5.

74   HE SAID TO PEMBERTON: Margaret Case Harriman, *The Vicious Circle: The Story of the Algonquin Round Table*, Rinehart & Co., 1951, p. 20.

74   IN HER BOOK: Ibid., p. 21.

75   FERBER WAS SMALL: Julie Goldsmith Gilbert, *Ferber*, Doubleday & Co., 1978, p. 160.

75   SHE HAD KNOWN WOOLLCOTT: Gaines, p. 60.

76   YOU ALMOST LOOK: Harriman, p. 145.

76   THEY ALSO ENVIED HIM: Drennan, p. 16.

76   EDMUND WILSON SUSPECTED: Wilson, *The Twenties*, p. 49.

76   WELL, FRANK: Harriman, p. 145.

76   CONVERSATION WAS LIKE OXYGEN: Author's interview with Marc Connelly.

77   ONE NIGHT, MARC CONNELLY: Harriman, p. 239.

77   WHEN RAOUL FLEISCHMANN CLAIMED: Drennan, p. 82.

77   WHEN A PLAYER: Ibid., p. 88.

77   HE WOULD BE SAFELY: Parker, "Big Blonde," *The Portable Dorothy Parker*, p. 190.

78   A CHAIR FOR EVERYBODY: Author's interview with Marc Connelly.

79   SOME CHILDREN HERE: Dorothy Parker letter to Robert Benchley, September 1920, Robert Benchley Collection, Mugar Library, Boston University.

80   ANITA LOOS, NEWLY ARRIVED: Anita Loos, *A Girl Like I*, The Viking Press, 1966, p. 147.

80   IN *BUT GENTLEMEN MARRY BRUNETTES*: Anita Loos, *But Gentlemen Marry Brunettes*, Brentano's Ltd., 1928, p. 36.

81   HAVE SOME POWDER: Babette Rosmond, *Robert Benchley: His Life and Good Times*, Doubleday & Co., 1970, p. 11.

82   YOU MAY LEAD: Drennan, p. 121.

82   DID YOU EVER: Lillian Hellman, *An Unfinished Woman*, Little, Brown, 1969, p. 187 (Bantam edition).

82   SUCH DENUNCIATIONS: Wilson, *The Twenties*, p. 47.

82   DOROTHY ACKNOWLEDGED: Parker, "Not Enough," *New Masses*, March 14, 1939, pp. 3–4.

82   NOT IF IT WAS BUTTONED UP: James Gaines taped interview with Dr. Alvan Barach.

83   PARKIE WAS: Author's interview with Marc Connelly.

83   I'M ALMOST CERTAIN: Author's interview with Rebecca Bernstien.

84   IN FACT, FRANK ADAMS: Adams, pp. 305, 314, 316, 330, 440.

85   "WELL," ADAMS ANSWERED: Harriman, p. 19.

85 THAT'S ALL RIGHT, Drennan, p. 47.

85 A WAG PASSING: Gaines, p. 30.

85 SHUT UP: Harriman, p. 169.

85 PEGGY WOOD NOTICED: James Gaines taped interview with Peggy Wood.

85 I'M ENGAGED: Author's interview with Marc Connelly.

86 BUT DON'T THEY EVER SEE: Harriman, p. 85.

86 WE JUST HATED: Author's interview with Marc Connelly.

87 HE WAS, SHE NOTICED: Parker, "Not Enough," New Masses, March 14, 1939, pp. 3–4.

87 ABSOLUTELY DEVASTATING: Donald Ogden Stewart, By a Stroke of Luck! Paddington Press Ltd., 1975, p. 100.

88 MONEY CANNOT FILL OUR NEEDS: Parker, "Song for the First of the Month," Fales Library, New York University.

89 I AM ASHAMED: Dorothy Parker letter to Thomas Masson, ca. 1922, George H. Lorimer Papers, The Historical Society of Pennsylvania.

89 YOU SIT AROUND: Thomas Masson, Our American Humorists, Moffat, Yard and Co., 1922, p. 277.

90 SHE HAD EYES: Author's interview with Margalo Gillmore.

90 PENNILESS, TALKING: Nancy Milford, Zelda, Harper & Row, 1970 (Avon edition), p. 93.

90 THIS LOOKS LIKE A ROAD COMPANY: Wilson, The Twenties, p. 48.

90 SHE WAS VERY BLONDE: Milford, p. 94.

92 IT WAS FINE: Parker, "Big Blonde," The Portable Dorothy Parker, p. 193.

92 A GREAT PARTY: Adams, p. 299.

Six: Painkillers

93 I HOPE THIS PLACE: Bryan, "Funny Man," October 7, 1939, p. 32.

93 YALE CLUB: Benchley, p. 163.

94 IT'S STOPPED: Helen Thurber and Edward Weeks, Selected Letters of James Thurber, Little, Brown, 1981, p. 121.

95 MY WHOLE LIFE: Bryan, "Funny Man," October 7, 1939, p. 32.

95 HARRIS WAS SILENT: Benchley, p. 159.

96 EDMUND WILSON BELIEVED: Wilson, The Twenties, pp. 46–7.

96 HE WHISPERED: Alexander Woollcott, "Our Mrs. Parker," in The Portable Woollcott, The Viking Press, 1946, p. 180.

96 IF HE HAD BEEN A WOMAN: Sheilah Graham, The Garden of Allah, Crown Publishers, 1970, p. 109.

96 EACH TIME HE LEFT: Parker, "Big Blonde," The Portable Dorothy Parker, pp. 192–3.

97 WE'D BUILD: Parker, "Daydreams," Life, June 29, 1922.

98 IN A SEIZURE: Dorothy Parker letter to George H. Lorimer, May 1922, George H. Lorimer Papers, The Historical Society of Pennsylvania.

99 SOME SUMMER EVENING: Parker, "Such a Pretty Little Picture," The Smart Set, December 1922, p. 76.

100 A DOZEN YEARS LATER: Dorothy Parker letter to Burton Rascoe, ca. July 1934, University of Pennsylvania Library.

100 NOTHING PLEASED HER: Writers at Work, p. 79.

101 MARC CONNELLY SAID: Author's interview with Marc Connelly.

101 EVERYONE WHO KNEW HIM: New York Times, April 22, 1956.

101 HAVING CONVINCED HIMSELF: Ben Hecht, Charlie: The Improbable Life and Times of Charles MacArthur, Harper & Brothers, 1957, p. 26.

102 ADORING HIS WILD SENSE OF HUMOR: Alexander Woollcott, "The Young Monk of Siberia," in The Portable Woollcott, p. 222.

102 SINCE PLAYING MATCHMAKER: Woollcott, "Our Mrs. Parker," p. 187.

103 GOD DAMN NEW YORKER!: Hecht, p. 77.

103 MY GOOD MAN: Jhan Robbins, *Front Page Marriage*, G.P. Putnam's Sons, 1982, p. 30.

103 THE ATTRACTION: Author's interview with Marc Connelly.

103 IT SEEEMED CLEAR: Loos, *A Girl Like I*, p. 130.

103 DOROTHY, MEANWHILE: Parker, "A Well-Worn Story," *The Portable Dorothy Parker*, p. 77.

104 NEYSA MCMEIN PRESENTED: Author's interview with Marc Connelly.

104 SHE WAS DISTRAUGHT: Charles MacArthur's next publicized affair was with the English comedienne Beatrice Lillie. He and Carol Frink were divorced in 1926, after a long dispute and after Frink and MacArthur had come to a satisfactory financial arrangement. In 1928 he married actress Helen Hayes. In 1935, Frink sued Hayes for one hundred thousand dollars on the ground that the actress had alienated MacArthur's affections while he was still married to her. At the three-day hearing in Chicago, Frink declared MacArthur was getting fat and bald. She wouldn't take him now, she remarked, if he came in a box of Cracker Jack. Upon withdrawing her suit, she was ordered to pay court fees amounting to one hundred dollars.

104 LIPS THAT TASTE: Parker, "Threnody," *The Portable Dorothy Parker*, p. 74.

104 IT'S NOT THE TRAGEDIES: *Writers at Work*, p. 82.

104 FRANK CROWNINSHIELD SAID: Marc Connelly, *Voices Offstage: A Book of Memoirs*, Holt, Rinehart & Winston, Inc., 1968, p. 92.

105 EVEN WOOLLCOTT: *New York Times*, November 7, 1922.

105 HER APARTMENT: Parker, *Ainslee's*, March 1923.

106 WHISKEY: Parker, "Big Blonde," *The Portable Dorothy Parker*, p. 201.

107 A LITTLE BIT OF THEATER: Author's interview with Marc Connelly.

107 SOME PEOPLE BELIEVED: Author's interview with Margalo Gillmore.

107 WHAT'S THE MATTER: Jane Grant, *Ross, the New Yorker and Me*, Reynal and Co., 1968, pp. 120–1.

108 SHE WAS, NEYSA DECLARED: Neysa McMein, "The Woman Who Is a Design," *Arts and Decoration*, October 1923, p. 14.

109 SOMETIMES SHE FELT: Parker, "Epitaph," *The Portable Dorothy Parker*, p. 79.

109 LIKE YOUR PIE: Parker, "Too Bad," *The Portable Dorothy Parker*, p. 179.

110 WHO WAS THERE: Parker, "The Dark Girl's Rhyme," *The Portable Dorothy Parker*, p. 78.

111 A FEW MILLION: Parker, *Ainslee's*. June 1923.

111 I DON'T SAY: Parker, "What a Man's Hat Means to Me," advertising brochure for John B. Stetson Co., Philadelphia, 1923. Robert Benchley Collection, Mugar Library, Boston University.

111 "EVERYONE," MRS. FORD: Mercedes de Acosta, *Here Lies the Heart*, Reynal & Co., 1960, p. 140.

112 AMID CRIES OF GENERAL HORROR: Wilson, *The Twenties*, p. 115.

112 ONCE, THE STORY GOES: Joan Givner, *Katherine Anne Porter: A Life*, Simon and Schuster, 1982, p. 176.

113 THE WORLD AND ITS MISTRESS: F. Scott Fitzgerald, *The Great Gatsby*, Charles Scribner's Sons, 1925, p. 61.

113 HE SEEMED IRKED: Jonathon Yardley, *Ring: A Biography of Ring Lardner*, Random House, 1977, p. 261.

114 MAGGIE SWOPE: E. J. Kahn, Jr., *The World of Swope*, Simon and Schuster, 1965, p. 292.

114 SCOTT FITZGERALD: Matthew J. Bruccoli, Margaret M. Duggan, and Susan Walker, eds. *Correspondence of F. Scott Fitzgerald*, Random House, 1980, p. 135.

114 A SOCIAL SEWER: Andre Le Vot, *F. Scott Fitzgerald: A Biography*, Doubleday & Co., p. 122.

115 ADDIE KAHN: Mary Jane Matz, *The Many Lives of Otto Kahn*, Macmillan, 1963, p. 235.

116 I KNEW IT WOULD BE TERRIBLE: Parker, *Life*, July 21, 1927, p. 7.

116 NO MATTER WHERE I GO: Ibid.

116 JESUS CHRIST: Ring Lardner, Jr., *The Lardners: My Family Remembered*, Harper & Row, 1976, p. 171.

117 I WAS CHEATED: Parker, "My Home Town," *McCall's*, January 1928, p. 4.

117 FIRPO'S HOUSE: Neysa McMein as told to Dorothy Parker, "When I Painted Luis Firpo," *New York World*, September 9, 1923, p. 10.

117 IT WAS "A HORRIBLE DUMP": Robert Benchley letter to Gertrude Benchley, August 27, 1923, Robert Benchley Collection, Mugar Library, Boston University.

118 COMPELLED TO OFFER: Woollcott, "Our Mrs. Parker," p. 191.

Seven: Laughter and Hope and a Sock in the Eye

119 THINK HOW FRIGHTENED: Cooper, p. 61.

119 DECENT PEOPLE: Parker, "Such A Pretty Little Picture," *Smart Set*, December 1922, p. 77.

120 GOOD LORD: Ibid.

120 DOROTHY THOUGHT: Wilson, *The Twenties*, p. 47.

121 SHE HAD MAJESTY: Ibid.

121 HE DESCRIBED HER: Ibid., p. 345.

121 LADY, LADY: Parker, "Social Note," *The Portable Dorothy Parker*, p. 104.

122 THREE BE THE THINGS: Parker, "Inventory," *The Portable Dorothy Parker*, p. 96.

122 AFTER A PERFORMANCE: Stewart, p. 126.

123 THE DISTANCE: Case, p. 351.

123 I WAS SITTING: Author's interview with Ruth Goodman Goetz.

124 HER CHARACTERS: Elmer Rice, *Minority Report: An Autobiography*, Simon and Schuster, 1963, p. 203.

124 SHE FELT "SO PROUD": Dorothy Parker interview, Columbia University Oral History Research Office, June 1959.

125 RICE FOUND HER: Rice, p. 204.

125 WITHOUT QUESTION: Author's interview with a source who does not wish to be named.

126 THIS, NO SONG: Parker, "Ballade at Thirty-five," *Life*, June 26, 1924; *The Portable Dorothy Parker*, p. 105.

126 IT WAS A SIMPLE TALE: Rice, p. 203.

127 DON'T YOU WORRY: Elmer L. Rice and Dorothy Parker, *Close Harmony*, (Copyright 1924 under title *Soft Music*.) Samuel French, 1929.

128 GERTRUDE LATER ADMITTED: Rosmond, p. 9.

128 BENCHLEY HIMSELF LATER: James Thurber, *The Years with Ross*, Signet Books, 1962, p. 173.

129 WHICH SHOWS HOW MUCH: Benchley, p. xv.

129 LIFE COMES A-HURRYING: Parker, "For R.C.B.," *The New Yorker*, January 7, 1928, p. 21.

130 IN RETROSPECT: Rosmond, p. 11–12.

130 I'M A LATE SLEEPER: Hecht, p. 92.

132 WE DRANK OUR HEADS OFF: Dorothy Parker interview, Columbia University Oral History Research Office.

132 SHE THOUGHT: Cooper, p. 110.

132 *THE NEW YORK TIMES* THOUGHT: *New York Times*, June 2, 1925, p. 9.

133 AN ELATED ROSS: Corey Ford, *The Time of Laughter*, Little, Brown, 1967, p. 115.

134 IN HER OPINION: *New York Herald Tribune*, October 13, 1963.

134 AT FIRST HE SAT: Parker, "Book Reviews," *Esquire*, September 1959, p. 18.

134 WITH THIS "MONOLITH": Ibid.

134 ALLOWING ROSS: Grant, p. 210.

135 POLLY ADLER: Polly Adler, *A House Is Not a Home*, Rinehart & Co., 1953, p. 98.

135 THEY ONCE CHASED: Woollcott, "The Young Monk of Siberia," p. 229.

136 WHENEVER YOU OPEN: Rice, p. 205.

137 WE WERE TRAPPED: Ibid.

137 DOROTHY, HE SAID: Orville Prescott, "A Lament for the Living," *Cue*, July 10, 1937, p. 7.

138 THAT OLD FILLING: Rice, p. 207.

138 IT WAS "THE MOST EXCITING THING" : *Writers at Work*, p. 79.

138 DESPITE EXCELLENT REVIEWS: *New York Tribune*, December 1, 1924.

138 THE THIRD WEEK: Woollcott, "Our Mrs. Parker," p. 186.

138 AS ELMER RICE LATER WROTE: Rice, p. 207.

138 IN YEARS TO COME: Richard Lamparski taped interview with Dorothy Parker, 1966.

138 HE FOUND THE PLAY: Robert Benchley, "In Bad Humour," *Life*, December 18, 1924, p. 18.

139 OH I SHOULD LIKE: Parker, "Song of Perfect Propriety," *Life*, January 22, 1925; *The Portable Dorothy Parker*, p. 103.

Eight: "Yessir, the Whaddyecall'em Blues"

140 THEIR NAMES WERE EVER: Parker, "Rosemary," *Life*, August 14, 1924.

140 SHE FELL IN LOVE: Author's interview with Marc Connelly.

141 SHE DEDICATED: Rosmond, pp. 11–12.

141 BECAUSE YOUR EYES: Parker, "Prophetic Soul," *The Portable Dorothy Parker*, p. 102.

142 ONE CHRISTMAS: James Gaines taped interview with Frank Sullivan, Columbia University Oral History Research Office.

142 THEN SHE TURNED: James Gaines taped interview with Dr. Alvan Barach.

142 DONALD STEWART THOUGHT: John Keats, *You Might as Well Live: The Life and Times of Dorothy Parker*, Simon and Schuster, 1970, p. 61.

142 ALL YOUR LIFE: Parker, "Chant for Dark Hours," *The Portable Dorothy Parker*, p. 95.

143 BY THE TIME YOU SWEAR: Parker, "Unfortunate Coincidence," *The Portable Dorothy Parker*, p. 96.

144 COLLINS WAS STRICTLY: Author's interview with Marc Connelly.

144 HE SEEMED EXACTLY: Parker, "Experience," *The Portable Dorothy Parker*, p. 117.

144 IT WAS ON THE HEAD: *The Bookman*, July 1925, p. 617.

145 JANE GRANT ADMITTED: Grant, p. 220.

145 F.P.A. EXPRESSED: Adams, p. 505.

145 JAMES THURBER CALLED IT: Thurber, p. 26.

145 DESPITE THE PSEUDONYM: Parker ["Last Night," pseud.], "The Theatre," *The New Yorker*, February 21, 1925, p. 13.

145 AND WHAT DO YOU DO: Parker, *Life*, September 12, 1926.

146 SHE WAS IGNORANT: Author's interview with Allen Saalburg.

146 DOTTIE NEEDED: Ibid.

148 I UNDERSTAND FERBER: *Writers at Work*, p. 77.

149 DURING THE WAR: Jane Anderson supported Hitler and Mussolini during World War II. In 1943, after broadcasting propaganda against the Allies from Germany and Italy, she was one of several Americans indicted for treason, but later the charge was dropped for insufficient evidence. Katherine Anne Porter based her La Condesa character in *Ship of Fools* on Anderson, who eventually married a Spanish nobleman.

151 THE FIRST TIME I DIED: Parker, "Epitaph," *The Portable Dorothy Parker*, p. 79.

152 AS LARDNER ADMITTED: Ring Lardner letter to F. Scott Fitzgerald, August 8, 1925, Bruccoli et al., p. 176.

154 SABINE FARM, RECALLED: Broun, p. 41.

155 DOES ANYONE BUT MYSELF: Ibid., p. 47.

155 ROSS SAID: Thurber, pp. 27–8.

155 IF YOU CAN'T USE THESE: Frank Sullivan letter to Ann Honeycutt, June 13, 1967, in Frank Sullivan, *Well, There's No Harm in Laughing*, edited by George Oppenheimer, Doubleday & Co., 1972, p. 215.

156 CHARLIE, AS BENCHLEY LATER TOLD HIS WIFE: Robert Benchley letter to Gertrude Benchley, July 31, 1925, Mugar Library, Boston University.

156 DON'T WORRY: Adams, p. 540.

Nine: Global Disasters

157 WHAT ARE YOU HAVING: Quoted in Keats, p. 85.

157 DRINK AND DANCE: Parker, "The Flaw in Paganism," *The Portable Dorothy Parker*, p. 298.

157 WHEN JOHNNY WEAVER REMARKED: James Gaines taped interview with Peggy Wood.

157 PEOPLE, SHE WROTE: Parker, "Dialogue at Three in the Morning," *The New Yorker*, February 13, 1926, p. 13.

158 WHEN SHE WOULD BE: Author's interview with Allen Saalburg.

159 BARACH DECIDED: James Gaines taped interview with Dr. Alvan Barach.

159 SHE FELT MISERY: Parker, "Big Blonde," *The Portable Dorothy Parker*, p. 209.

159 DOROTHY CALLED HIM: Parker, "Toward the Dog Days," *McCall's*, May 1928, p. 8.

160 THEN THE TEARS: Parker, "Big Blonde," *The Portable Dorothy Parker*, p. 208.

160 INVESTIGATION REVEALED: Round Tablers treated by Dr. Barach included Heywood Broun, Frank Sullivan, and Herbert Swope. Aleck Woollcott also consulted him but did not enter treatment.

160 WHEN FRANK SULLIVAN STOPPED BY: Sullivan, p. 215.

161 THE HOSPITAL, SHE JOKED: Wilson, *The Twenties*, p. 346.

163 HIS STARK PROSE: Parker [Constant Reader, pseud.], "Reading and Writing," *The New Yorker*, October 29, 1927, p. 92.

164 SHE WOULD NOT HAVE AGREED: Milford, p. 156.

164 IN LATER YEARS: Richard Lamparski taped interview with Dorothy Parker.

165 SHE THOUGHT HER POEMS: *Brooklyn Eagle*, November 18, 1928.

166 HE JOKED ABOUT: Wilson, *The Twenties*, p. 346.

166 BENCHLEY WROTE TO GERTRUDE: Robert Benchley letter to Gertrude Benchley, February 24, 1926, Mugar Library.

168 AT HENDAYE: Parker, "Reading and Writing," *The New Yorker*, July 25, 1931, p. 55.

169 DOROTHY MOCKINGLY DESCRIBED PARIS: Parker, "The Paris That Keeps Out of the Papers," *Vanity Fair*, January 1927, p. 71.

170 MEN SELDOM MAKE PASSES: Parker, "News Item," *The Portable Dorothy Parker*, p. 109.

171 I GUESS: Rice, p. 217.

171 SHE WAS ABLE TO UNDERSTAND: Parker, "Reading and Writing," *The New Yorker*, July 25, 1931, p. 55.

171 SO I WENT: Parker, "The Garter," *The New Yorker*, September 8, 1927, p. 17.

172 WHY, THAT DOG: Parker, "Toward The Dog Days," *McCall's*, May 1928, p. 8.

173 SPANIARDS PINCHED: Ernest Hemingway, *88 Poems*, edited by Nicholas Gerogiannis, Harcourt Brace Jovanovich, 1979, p. 87.

173 DON STEWART: Stewart, p. 157.

174 THE TRANSATLANTIC CROSSING: Author's interview with Mildred Gilman Wohlforth.

174 WELL, I DON'T KNOW: Adams, *The Diary of Our Own Samuel Pepys*, vol. 2, p. 675.

174 WHAT WOULD LINCOLN HAVE DONE: Wilson, *The Twenties*, p. 346.

174 SHE KEPT "EXPECTING" : Ibid., p. 347.

174 SHE SPENT THE DAY: Elinor Wylie letter to Anne Hoyt, November 22, 1926, The Berg Collection, The Astor, Lenox, and Tilden Foundations, The New York Public Library.

175 CITING THE ELEVEN-YEAR ANALYSIS: Guiles, p. 18.

175 WHY DONTCHA: Wilson, The Twenties, pp. 344–6.

176 IT TOOK ONLY A SHORT TIME: Parker, "Reading And Writing," The New Yorker, December 31, 1927, p. 51.

176 IT WAS DEDICATED: Arthur F. Kinney, Dorothy Parker, Twayne Publishers, 1978, p. 113.

Ten: Big Blonde

177 SUDDENLY, DOROTHY: Parker, "Reading and Writing," The New Yorker, February 11, 1928, p. 78.

177 SHE WAS HORRIFIED: Adams, vol. 2, p. 706.

177 ENOUGH ROPE REVIEWS: The Nation, May 25, 1927; New York Herald Tribune, March 27, 1927; Poetry, April 1927.

178 BY FAR THE MOST THOUGHTFUL: Edmund Wilson, The New Republic, January 19, May 11, 1927.

178 DOROTHY HAD EMERGED: Wilson, ibid.; John Farrar, The Bookman, March 1928.

178 THERE IS POETRY: Parker, "Reading and Writing," The New Yorker, January 7, 1928, p. 77.

179 IF I HAD A SHINY GUN: Parker, "Frustration," The Portable Dorothy Parker, p. 231.

181 IT'S AGAINST THE LAW: Parker's arrest is based on reports in the New York World, New York Times, New York Herald Tribune, New York Telegraph, and Boston Evening Transcript for August 11, 1927. Also Jeanette Marks, Thirteen Days, Albert Boni, 1929, p. 9.

183 DOROTHY PERSUADED A NEWSPA-PER REPORTER: Upton Sinclair, Boston, vol. 2, Albert and Charles Boni, 1928, pp. 637, 648–50.

183 THEY WERE WATCHING: Ibid., p. 650.

184 THOSE PEOPLE AT THE ROUND TABLE: Richard Lamparski taped interview with Dorothy Parker.

185 THESE ADORING BUSINESSES: Gardner Jackson taped interview, Columbia University Oral History Research Office.

185 AS JACKSON REMEMBERED IT: Ibid.

185 NO FEATURES: Sinclair, p. 743.

186 MY HEART AND SOUL: Parker, "Reading and Writing," The New Yorker, December 10, 1927, p. 122.

187 FINALLY, AS AN INDIGNANT LOVETT: Gaines, p. 235.

187 THERE WAS A WONDERFUL: Parker, "Reading and Writing," The New Yorker, January 14, 1928, p. 69.

187 GARRETT WAS THE SAME AGE: Parker, "Dusk Before Fireworks," The Portable Dorothy Parker, p. 135; "Reading and Writing," The New Yorker, January 14, 1928, p. 69.

187 DOROTHY BROKE OFF: Parker, "Dusk Before Fireworks," The Portable Dorothy Parker, p. 135.

188 "LADY," DOROTHY WAS DYING: Parker, "Recent Books," The New Yorker, October 15, 1927, p. 105; The Portable Dorothy Parker, p. 452.

188 CRUDE IS THE NAME: Ibid., October 22, 1927, p. 98; The Portable Dorothy Parker, p. 455.

188 MARGOT ASQUITH'S LATEST BOOK: Ibid.

188 CONFRONTED WITH A WORK: Parker, "Reading and Writing," The New Yorker, November 5, 1927, p. 90; The Portable Dorothy Parker, p. 461. Beginning with the October 29, 1927, issue, the name of the column was changed from "Recent Books" to "Reading and Writing."

188 AND IT IS THAT WORD: Ibid., October 20, 1928, p. 98; The Portable Dorothy Parker, p. 517.

189 THE WHISTLES MEANT: Ibid., March 31, 1928, p. 97.

189 MOST OF THE TIME: Parker, "You Were Perfectly Fine," *The New Yorker*, February 23, 1929, p. 17; *The Portable Dorothy Parker*, p. 151.

190 SHE ADORED "HIS BOYISHNESS": Dorothy Parker letter to Robert Benchley, November 7, 1929.

190 LATER, TRYING TO REMEMBER: Ibid.

190 SHE HAD A FRIEND: Parker, "Reading and Writing," *The New Yorker*, April 7, 1928, p. 106; *The Portable Dorothy Parker*, p. 508.

190 SHE WOULD SIT: Parker, "A Telephone Call," *The Bookman*, January 1928, p. 501, *The Portable Dorothy Parker*, p. 119.

191 SUNK I AM: Parker, "Reading and Writing," *The New Yorker*, January 7, 1928, p. 77.

191 IT WAS A SCREAMING MATCH: Author's interview with Rebecca Bernstien.

191 A DIFFERENT CAUSE: *Hartford Courant*, January 8, 1933, p. 6.

192 THE OTHER WAS: Ibid.

192 GILMAN RECALLS: Author's interview with Mildred Gilman Wohlforth.

192 THAT SPRING: Parker, "Just a Little One," *The Portable Dorothy Parker*, p. 241.

192 BONI AND LIVERIGHT: In its fall 1928 catalogue, Boni and Liveright announced the October publication of *The Sexes*, described as a collection of satirical prose pieces that had appeared in *Life*, *The New Yorker*, and *Vanity Fair*. This book did not materialize.

192 REVIEWS WERE: William Rose Benét, "New Moon Madness," *Saturday Review*, June 9, 1928, p. 943.

193 THE SUN'S GONE DIM: Parker, "Two-Volume Novel," *The Portable Dorothy Parker*, p. 238.

193 SHE IS QUITE GIVEN: Robert Benchley letter to Mildred Gilman, May 25, 1928.

194 ALLEN SAALBURG REMEMBERED: Author's interview with Allen Saalburg.

194 INSTEAD OF REPORTING: Parker, "Reading and Writing," *The New Yorker*, March 24, 1928, p. 93; *The Portable Dorothy Parker*, p. 504.

194 I FOUND HER: Woollcott, "Our Mrs. Parker," p. 186.

195 NO RICH PEOPLE: Keats, p. 159. Dorothy repaid the loan shortly before John Gilbert's death in 1936. He acknowledged the payment with a telegram, THANK YOU MISS FINLAND, a reference to the only country in Europe that repaid its World War I debt to the United States.

195 HELL, WHILE I'M UP: Parker, "Reading and Writing," *The New Yorker*, August 25, 1928, p. 60.

196 F.P.A.'S REACTION: Adams, p. 866.

196 I DON'T SEE: Edmund Wilson, *The Thirties: From Notebooks and Diaries of the Period*, Farrar, Straus and Giroux, 1980, p. 361.

196 SHE NEVER LEARNED: Parker, "Reading And Writing," *The New Yorker*, December 31, 1927, p. 51.

196 A MOTION PICTURE THEATER: Ibid., November 26, 1927, p. 104.

197 SHE ALSO ENJOYED: Parker, "Out of the Silence," *The New Yorker*, September 1, 1928, p. 28.

197 SHE REMEMBERED THINKING: Parker, "To Richard—with Love," *The Screen Guild's Magazine*, May 1936, p. 8.

197 A TELEGRAM ARRIVED: John Gilbert telegram to Dorothy Parker, October 19, 1928.

197 IT ALWAYS TAKES: *Brooklyn Eagle*, November 18, 1928.

197 THE JOB GOT OFF: *New York Telegraph*, January 28, 1929.

197 NOW LET'S SEE: Robert Benchley letter to Gertrude Benchley, December 7, 1928, Mugar Library.

197 IT WAS A LOVELY OFFICE: Dorothy Parker speech, "Hollywood, the Land I

Won't Return To," *Seven Arts*, No. 3, 1955, p. 130.

198 A NEWSPAPER REPORTED: *New Haven Register*, January 4, 1929.

198 SHE HOPED THAT: Dorothy Parker letter to Robert Benchley, November 7, 1929.

198 DOTTIE IS SO LOW: Robert Benchley letter to Gertrude Benchley, ca. December 20, 1928, Mugar Library.

199 EVENTUALLY, THE PAGES CAME BACK: *New York Telegraph*, January 28, 1929.

199 AT HER WIT'S END: Parker speech, *Seven Arts*.

200 WHEN IT WAS ACCEPTED: "How Am I to Know?" was sung by Russ Colombo with a guitar accompaniment. This scene, using two sound tracks, proved to be one of the best in the film.

200 IN CONTRAST, GEORGIE OPP: Years later, in Hollywood, Dorothy stayed at the Chateau Marmont in a suite directly below Oppenheimer's. She was entertaining friends when suddenly a tremendous crash came from upstairs. Pay no attention, she said, "It's only George Oppenheimer dropping another name."

200 NO, SHE SAID: *Brooklyn Eagle*, November 18, 1928.

Eleven: Sonnets in Suicide, or the Life of John Knox

201 DOROTHY BLAMED THE LANGUAGE: Dorothy Parker letter to Helen Droste, September 1929.

201 FOR SIX WEEKS: Dorothy Parker letter to Helen Droste, November 28, 1929.

201 CONFINED TO HER HOTEL: Dorothy Parker letter to Helen Droste, September 1929.

201 WHEN SHE BEGAN TO FEEL BETTER: Dorothy Parker letter to Helen Droste, November 28, 1929.

202 AFTERWARD, LOOKING: Dorothy Parker letter to Helen Droste, September 1929.

202 HE SIMPLY CAN'T SPEAK: Ibid.

202 DOROTHY LEFT HER PASSPORT: Robert Benchley diary, Mugar Library, Boston University.

202 I HAVE A COLLECTION: Dorothy Parker letter to Alexander Woollcott, ca. July 1929, Houghton Library, Harvard University.

202 IT STOOD SURROUNDED: Dorothy Parker letter to Helen Droste, September 1929.

203 WHEN THE CHICKEN TURNED OUT TO BE: Dorothy Parker letter to Alexander Woollcott, ca. July 1929, Houghton Library, Harvard University.

203 NUMEROUS PAGES: Ibid.

203 THE LUCKY MAN: Dorothy Parker letter to Helen Droste, September 1929.

204 HE RESPONDED: Ibid.

204 SOMETIMES YVONNE ROUSSEL: Yvonne Luff-Roussel letter to author, August 3, 1982.

204 I DON'T KNOW: Dorothy Parker letter to Robert Benchley, November 7, 1929.

205 SHE FOUND HERSELF: Dorothy Parker letter to Helen Droste, September 1929.

205 HIS REPLY: Ibid.

205 DOROTHY PREPARED: Ibid.

205 HE WOULD NOT PERMIT: Dorothy Parker letter to Robert Benchley, November 7, 1929.

206 DOROTHY IMMEDIATELY CABLED BENCHLEY: Ibid.

206 SHE HAD ALWAYS CONSIDERED: Ibid.

207 AH, OLD BOOGLES BENCHLEY: Ibid.

207 CHRIST, THINK OF: Ibid.

207 LIQUOR, SHE FOUND: Ibid.

208 ON THANKSGIVING DAY: Dorothy Parker letter to Helen Droste, November 28, 1929.

208 IN THE EVENINGS: John Dos Passos, *The Best of Times: An Informal Memoir*, New American Library, 1966, p. 203.

208 SEE BY *PARIS HERALD*: Dorothy Parker cables to Robert Benchley, December 1929.

209 CURLED UP: *New York World*, February 1, 1930, p. 1.

209 WHEN SOMEBODY ASKED: *New York Telegram*, February 1, 1930.

209 WHEN SHE BEGAN TO TALK: Archibald MacLeish letter to Ernest Hemingway, February 10, 1930. In *Letters of Archibald MacLeish, 1907–1982*, edited by R. H. Winnick, Houghton Mifflin Co., 1983, p. 232.

210 WRITE NOVELS: Dorothy Parker letter to Robert Benchley, November 7, 1929.

210 IT WOULD HAVE BEEN SENSIBLE: Richard Lamparski interview with Dorothy Parker.

210 SUBMITTING TO *FORCE MAJEURE*: According to Thomas Guinzburg, Harold Guinzburg's son and successor at Viking Press, Dorothy's novel remained the longest unfulfilled contract in the company's history.

211 GOODBYE DARLING: George Oppenheimer cable to Dorothy Parker, May 24, 1930.

212 THE LAST TWO DAYS: Robert Benchley diary, Mugar Library.

212 GERALD SHOPPED FOR RECORDS: Unidentified newspaper clipping.

213 ALL THE REVIEWS: Dorothy Parker cable to George Oppenheimer, July 2, 1930.

213 OPPENHEIMER REPLIED: George Oppenheimer letter to Dorothy Parker, July 3, 1930.

213 ONE NIGHT AT HARRY'S: Bruccoli et al., p. 430.

214 IT PAINED STEWART: Stewart, p. 188.

214 LITTLE DROPS OF GRAIN ALCOHOL: Hemingway, p. 86.

214 AM NEARLY GONE: Dorothy Parker cable to George Oppenheimer, October 13, 1930.

214 FROM CANNES: Dorothy Parker cable to Robert Benchley, ca. October 24, 1930.

215 ARRIVING NEW YORK: Dorothy Parker cable to Robert Benchley, November 8, 1930.

215 GETTING AWAY: Parker, "Reading and Writing," *The New Yorker*, January 24, 1931, p. 62; *The Portable Dorothy Parker*, p. 527.

215 SHE WANTED TO: Parker, "Theatre," *The New Yorker*, March 7, 1931, p.33.

215 IN JANUARY: Parker, "Reading and Writing," *The New Yorker*, January 24, 1931, p. 62.

215 HER FIRST REVIEW: Parker, "Theatre," *The New Yorker*, February 21, 1931, p. 25.

216 ESCORTING HER HOME: Author's interview with Gertrude Macy.

216 A FRIEND LATER DESCRIBED HIM: J. Bryan III, *Merry Gentlemen (and One Lady)*, Atheneum, 1985, p. 115; author's interview with Allen Saalburg.

217 I AM SORRY: John O'Hara letter to Tom O'Hara, May 20, 1932, in John O'Hara, *Selected Letters of John O'Hara*, edited by Matthew Bruccoli, Random House, 1978, p. 63.

218 GIVEN HER LOVE FOR ANIMALS: Keats, 139.

218 OH, SOMEBODY SIGHED: Vernon Duke, *Passport to Paris*, Little, Brown and Co., 1955, p. 268.

219 I HAVE NO SQUASH COURTS: Prescott, p. 7.

219 *DEATH AND TAXES:* Parker, "Summary," *The Portable Dorothy Parker*, p. 313.

219 SHE DESCRIBED HIM: In Charles Brackett's 1934 novel *Entirely Surrounded*, the main character is a portrait of Dorothy at the time of her affair with McClain. Daisy Lester, a celebrated wit and nightclub singer, describes her lover as "a goddamned male whore trading on that body of his."

219 WHEN SHE ONCE LEARNED: Bryan, p. 117.

219 DEPRESSED, DOROTHY: James Thurber, *The Seal in the Bedroom & Other*

Predicaments, Harper Brothers, 1932, introduction by Dorothy Parker, p. x.

219 ANY ROYALTIES: Handwritten note, Robert Benchley Collection, Mugar Library.

220 SEND ME A SAW: Prescott, p. 34.

221 ·CAN'T FACE DECIDING: Parker, "From the Diary of a New York Lady," *The Portable Dorothy Parker,* p. 332.

221 IN THE MONTHS: *New York Herald Tribune,* December 12, 1932.

222 SHE ASKED SOME: *New York World-Telegram,* September 15, 1932.

222 LIKE HERSELF: Thurber, p. viii.

223 OH, YOU CAUGHT ME: Bennett Cerf, *At Random: The Reminiscences of Bennett Cerf,* Random House, 1977, p. 34.

223 I HAVE NO DOUBT: Woollcott, "Our Mrs. Parker," p. 190.

224 SHE CAREFULLY EXAMINED: Reprint, *Holyoke Transcript,* November 11, 1932, Tom Mooney Collection, Bancroft Library, University of California–Berkeley.

224 SHE IMMEDIATELY COMPOSED: Ibid.

224 HOW NOW, MR. PEPYS: Adams, vol. 2, p. 1121.

225 SHE AND FANNY BRICE: Author's interview with Ruth Goetz.

225 SID PERELMAN LATER WROTE: S. J. Perelman, *The Last Laugh,* Simon and Schuster, 1981, pp. 171–3.

Twelve: You Might as Well Live

227 SINCE SHE AND JOHN: Parker, "Reading and Writing," *The New Yorker,* March 18, 1933, p. 64; *The Portable Dorothy Parker,* p. 548.

227 COME ON UP: Keats, p. 160.

227 LONG I FOUGHT: Parker, "Prisoner," *The Portable Dorothy Parker,* p. 316.

228 SHE'D PICK UP: Author's interview with Clara Lester.

229 J. CLIFFORD MILLER, JR.: J. Clifford Miller letter to author, March 22, 1983.

229 ALL AT ONCE: Author's interview with Roy Eichel.

230 HE SAID YEARS LATER: William Engle, "Dorothy Parker's Rebounding Quips," *The American Weekly,* June 15, 1947, p. 14.

230 AND WHERE DOES SHE FIND THEM: Author's interview with Dorothy Rodgers.

230 ALAN WAS: Author's interview with Ruth Goetz.

230 SUNK DEEP: O'Hara, p. 88.

230 COME ALONG AT ONCE: Bryan, pp. 101–102.

231 HOW CAN THEY TELL: Ibid., p. 106.

231 SHE REFUSED TO TALK: *New York Herald Tribune,* October 27, 1933.

232 WHEN ASKED ABOUT THE ELECTION: *New York Evening Post,* October 27, 1933.

232 AN EXCITED EDMUND WILSON: Edmund Wilson letter to Louise Bogan, December 12, 1933, in Wilson, *Letters in Literature and Politics,* p. 234.

232 I DON'T KNOW WHY: Emily Hahn letter to author, February 18, 1983.

233 HER FAMILY, SHE GRUMBLED: Dorothy Parker letter to Morris Ernst, ca. February/March 1936, Humanities Research Center, University of Texas.

233 WHEN HOWARD DIETZ: Howard Dietz, *Dancing in the Dark,* Quadrangle/The New York Times Book Co., 1974, p. 77.

233 THAT SAME MONTH: Sullivan, p. 204.

234 I PICKED HIM OUT: Unidentified newspaper clipping, Dorothy Parker Scrapbook (courtesy of Susan Cotton).

234 I HAD THE PLEASURE: John O'Hara letter to Ernest Hemingway, May 1935, O'Hara, p. 107.

234 O'HARA IRRITATED HER: John O'Hara letter to F. Scott Fitzgerald, October 14–15, 1933, in Matthew J. Bruccoli, *The O'Hara Concern,* Random House, 1975, p. 95.

234 WRITING IN WHAT APPEARS: Dorothy Parker letter to F. Scott Fitzgerald, undated, F. Scott Fitzgerald Papers, Princeton University Library.

235 HE'S AWFUL: John O'Hara letter

to William Maxwell, May 16, 1963, in O'-Hara, p. 429.

236 IN ORDER TO MAKE: Author's interview with Sally Foster.

236 OTHER FRIENDS: Author's interview with Ruth Goetz.

236 WHEN DOTTIE FELL IN LOVE: Author's interview with Marc Connelly.

236 MY DEAR, SHE SAID: Cooper, p. 110.

237 AMONG THOSE: Author's interview with Marc Connelly.

237 THIS IS TO REPORT: Dorothy Parker telegram to Sara and Gerald Murphy, June 8, 1934.

238 WE ARE IN JULESBURG: *New York Evening Journal*, June 16, 1934.

238 SO WE GOT OUT: Dorothy Parker letter to Alexander Woollcott, ca. June 1934, Houghton Library, Harvard University.

238 EYEBROWS: Author's interview with Marc Connelly.

238 COMMUNICATION HAS BEEN: Dorothy Parker telegram to Helen Grimwood, June 19, 1934.

239 OH, THIS IS THE FIRST: Engle, p. 14.

239 OTHERWISE SHE WAS: Dorothy Parker letter to Alexander Woollcott, June 1934, Houghton Library, Harvard University.

239 DEAR SCOTT: Dorothy Parker telegram to F. Scott Fitzgerald, July 6, 1934, F. Scott Fitzgerald Papers, Princeton University Library.

240 BLAMING THE ALTITUDE: Dorothy Parker letter to Alexander Woollcott, June 1934, Houghton Library, Harvard University.

240 PROBABLY THIS WAS A WISE DECISION: Ibid.

240 THAT BIRD ONLY SINGS: Samuel Hopkins Adams, *A. Woollcott: His Life and His World*, Reynal & Hitchcock, 1945, p. 296.

240 GENTLEMEN: Ibid., p. 305.

241 HEARING ROSALIE STEWART'S IDEA:

Dorothy Parker letter to Alexander Woollcott, August 1934, Houghton Library, Harvard University.

242 WHEN DOROTHY CONTINUED: Ibid.

242 ONCE I WAS COMING: *Writers at Work*, p. 81.

242 WHEN THEY GATHERED: Dorothy Herrmann, *S. J. Perelman: A Life*, G.P. Putnam's Sons, 1986, p. 71.

243 THE DEVASTATING DOROTHY PARKER: Newspaper clippings, unidentified sources, Dorothy Parker Scrapbook.

243 DOUBLY FAMOUS: Caption accompanying Paramount publicity photograph.

244 SHE TOLD THE MURPHYS: Dorothy Parker letter to Sara and Gerald Murphy, ca. January 1935.

244 IT IS NOW CALLED: Dorothy Parker letter to Alexander Woollcott, ca. January 1935, Houghton Library, Harvard University.

244 BUT WOULD THEY: Ibid.

244 DOROTHY AND ALAN: Ibid.

244 DOROTHY EXPLAINED: Dorothy Parker letter to Harold Guinzburg, August 21, 1934.

245 SHE DISCOVERED: *Writers at Work*, p. 81.

245 ASIDE FROM THE WORK: Dorothy Parker letter to Alexander Woollcott, ca. January 1935, Houghton Library, Harvard University.

245 MISS PARKER, MISS PARKER: Author's interview with Joseph Schrank.

246 IN MAY MY HEART: Parker, "Autumn Valentine," *The Portable Dorothy Parker*, p. 318.

246 UPON MY HONOR: Verse attributed to Dorothy Parker, in Norman Zierold, *The Moguls*, Coward-McCann, Inc., 1969, p. 283.

247 AFTER CHRISTMAS: Dorothy Parker letter to Alexander Woollcott, ca. January 1935, Houghton Library, Harvard University.

247 WHILE REVIEWING *THE GLASS KEY*: Parker, "Reading and Writing," *The New Yorker*, April 25, 1931, p. 91.

248   A HARD MAN: Hellman, *An Unfinished Woman*, p. 186.

248   HER HABIT: Ibid., p. 187.

248   DOTTIE ADMIRED LILLIAN: Author's interview with Ruth Goetz.

249   TO INDICATE THE EMOTIONS: Author's interview with Heywood Hale Broun.

249   DESPITE HER OPPOSING: Dorothy Parker letter to Alexander Woollcott, ca. January 1935, Houghton Library, Harvard University.

249   WHEN SHE HEARD HIS VOICE: Ibid.

250   OH, GOODY: Wilson, *The Thirties*, p. 360.

250   GARBAGE THOUGH THEY TURN OUT: *Writers at Work*, p. 81.

251   DEAR HAROLD: Dorothy Parker letter to Harold Guinzburg, ca. 1935.

251   TWO YEARS EARLIER: *New York Evening Post*, October 27, 1933.

Thirteen: Good Fights

252   THEY HAVE, HE RECOUNTED: John O'Hara letter to F. Scott Fitzgerald, April 1936, O'Hara, pp. 116–17.

253   DOTTIE AND ALAN: Robert Benchley letter to Gertrude Benchley, April 27, 1936, Mugar Library, Boston University.

253   HER AMBIVALENCE: Cooper, p. 57.

253   DON STEWART RECALLED: Stewart, p. 226.

254   DOROTHY BEGAN MOVING AWAY: Parker, "Not Enough," *New Masses*, March 14, 1939, pp. 3–4.

254   SHE FLATTERED DOROTHY: Stewart, p. 234.

255   I CANNOT TELL YOU: Parker, "Not Enough," *New Masses*, March 14, 1939, pp. 3–4.

255   WITH MORE GENEROSITY: Stewart, p. 228.

256   ALAN WAS: Author's interview with Budd Schulberg.

256   AS ROBERT BENCHLEY WOULD: Robert Benchley letter to Gertrude Benchley, August 13, 1938, Mugar Library, Boston University.

256   DOROTHY MEANWHILE: Parker, "Not Enough," *New Masses*, March 14, 1939, pp. 3–4.

256   WHEN THE TRAIN: Norman Corwin, "Corwin on Media," *Westways*, November 1980, p. 64.

256   HE PAID TWENTY DOLLARS: Robert Benchley letter to Gertrude Benchley, April 27, 1936, Mugar Library, Boston University.

256   HE REACTED: Robert Benchley letter to Sara and Gerald Murphy, July 1, 1937.

257   I SAW SOME: Dorothy Parker speech, February 6, 1941, to Disney Unit of Screen Cartoon Guild.

257   EXPECTING STUDIOS: Nancy Lynn Schwartz, *The Hollywood Writers' War*, Alfred A. Knopf, 1982, p. 13.

257   AT A MEETING: Ibid., 69.

258   I DO NOT FEEL: Parker, "To Richard—with Love," *The Screen Guilds' Magazine*, May 1936, p. 8.

258   HER ANGER: Parker, Screen Cartoon Guild speech.

258   THAT SONOFABITCH: Schwartz, p. 124.

258   NOW, LOOK, BABY: Parker, Screen Cartoon Guild speech.

259   WE HAVEN'T ANY ROOTS: Perelman, p. 173.

260   THERE WAS NO CELLAR: Dorothy Parker, "Destructive Decoration," in *20th Century Decorating, Architecture, and Gardens: 80 Years of Ideas and Pleasure from House and Garden*, Mary Jane Pool, ed., Holt, Rinehart and Winston, 1980, pp. 178–9.

260   ALAN, LITHE: Author's interview with Lester Trauch.

260   IT WAS AUGUST WEATHER: Parker, "Destructive Decoration."

261   THAT'S THEIR PROBLEM: Perelman, p. 176.

261   IT WAS THE DEPRESSION: Author's interview with Lester Trauch.

262   SOME YEARS LATER: David O. Selznick, *Memo from David O. Selznick*, Rudy

Behlmer, ed., The Viking Press, 1972, p. 96.

262 THEY WOULD SPRING: Parker interview, Columbia University Oral History Research Office.

262 SHE SAID HAPPILY: Newspaper clipping, April 24, 1937, unidentified source.

263 SHE ALSO LIKED TO PRETEND: Parker interview, Columbia University Oral History Research Office.

263 AT THE OSCAR PRESENTATIONS: Ronald Bowers, The Selznick Players, A.S. Barnes and Co., 1976, p. 27.

263 OVER THE YEARS: Author's interview with Frances Goodrich.

263 HOW DID YOU KNOW: New York American, December 15, 1936.

263 GOODRICH FOUND: Author's interview with Frances Goodrich.

264 SHE WAS GREAT: Author's interview with Ruth Goetz.

264 ANOTHER SKEPTIC: Author's interview with Allen Saalburg.

264 HE WOULD BE WITH US: Thomas Guinzburg taped interview with Columbia University Oral History Research Office.

264 DICK MYERS WROTE: Richard E. Myers letter to Alice Lee Myers, January 14, 1937.

265 THEY DECIDED IT WOULD BE: Parker, "Destructive Decoration."

266 NEAR THE HOUSE: Ibid.

266 WRITER JOSEPH SCHRANK OBSERVED: Author's interview with Joseph Schrank.

266 FIFTY-SECOND STREET: Parker, "Destructive Decoration."

266 SID PERELMAN GAZED: Author's interview with Allen Saalburg.

267 HE WAS, JOSEPH SCHRANK RECALLED: Author's interview with Joseph Schrank.

267 I'M AWFULLY LAZY: Dorothy Parker letter to Fred B. Millett, May 27, 1937, Beinecke Rare Book and Manuscript Library, Yale University.

267 RUTH GOETZ NOTICED: Author's interview with Ruth Goetz.

267 WHEN THE CAMPBELLS: Ibid.

268 IT WAS THE WEIRD HOURS: Author's interview with Roy Eichel.

268 AS MARC CONNELLY REMEMBERED: Author's interview with Marc Connelly.

268 THROUGHOUT THE VISIT: Dorothy Parker letter to Morris Ernst, ca. February/March 1936, Humanities Research Center, University of Texas.

268 THE OTHER MRS. CAMPBELL: Author's interview with Marc Connelly.

268 SHE FIRED OUR FARMER: Dorothy Parker letter to Alexander Woollcott, September 2, 1942, Houghton Library, Harvard University.

268 HORTE FELT: Ibid.

269 IT'S AS HOT AS HELL: Hellman, An Unfinished Woman, p. 188.

269 FROM NOW ON: Author's interview with Ruth Goetz.

269 USUALLY THE GROUP: Ibid.

270 IN APRIL 1938: Daily Worker, April 28, 1938, p. 4. The list of signatories supporting the Soviet trial verdict included Nelson Algren, Langston Hughes, Harold Clurman, Lillian Hellman, Malcolm Cowley, and Irwin Shaw.

270 IT WAS QUITE BRIEF: Author's interview with Ring Lardner, Jr.

270 EVERYONE AT THAT TIME: Author's interview with Budd Schulberg.

271 THE FOLLOWING SIX PIECES OF EVIDENCE: Federal Bureau of Investigation, files.

272 OF THIS NUMBER: The Hollywood Nineteen included writers Bertolt Brecht, Richard Collins, Gordon Kahn, Howard Koch, and Waldo Salt; actor Larry Parks; actor-director Irving Pichel; directors Lewis Milestone and Robert Rossen; along with the Hollywood Ten: writers Alvah Bessie, Lester Cole, Ring Lardner, Jr., John Howard Lawson, Albert Maltz, Samuel Ornitz, and Dalton Trumbo, writer-producer Adrian Scott, and directors Herbert Biberman and Edward Dmytryk.

272 DOROTHY LOOKED PUZZLED: Hellman, *An Unfinished Woman*, pp. 190–1.

272 IN 1937 SHE WROTE: Dorothy Parker, "Incredible, Fantastic . . . and True," *New Masses*, November 23, 1937, pp. 15–16.

274 SHE SUSPECTED: Lillian Hellman, *Scoundrel Time*, Little, Brown, 1976 (Bantam edition), p. 41.

274 A MEMBER AT LARGE: U.S. Congress, House Committee on Un-American Activities, *Communist Infiltration of Hollywood Motion Picture Industry*, Hearings, Eighty second Congress, Part 4, September 19, 1951. Lillian Hellman was the only one of the five writers named by Martin Berkeley to respond to his charges. She denied knowing him and being present at the meeting.

275 I HAVEN'T THE FAINTEST: Parker interview, Columbia University Oral History Research Office.

275 HE DESCRIBED THEIR NEW QUARTERS: Alan Campbell letter to Harold Guinzburg, ca. July 6, 1937.

276 GARSON KANIN REMEMBERED: Garson Kanin, *Hollywood*, The Viking Press, 1974, p. 284.

277 OH COME, MY LOVE: Dorothy Parker, "The Passionate Screen Writer To His Love," Marc Connelly estate.

278 DOROTHY THOUGHT: Parker speech, Screen Cartoon Guild.

278 BUT SHE ALSO BELIEVED: Parker speech, *Seven Arts*, p. 135.

Fourteen: Bad Fights

279 NATHANAEL WEST FINISHED: S. J. Perelman, "And Did You Once See Irving Plain?" in *The Most of S. J. Perelman*, Simon and Schuster, 1958, p. 599.

280 HAVING ALWAYS FOUND HER: F. Scott Fitzgerald to Gerald Murphy, September 14, 1940, in *The Letters of F. Scott Fitzgerald*, Andrew Turnbull, ed., Charles Scribner's Sons, 1963, pp. 429–30.

280 IT'S A LONG STORY: Hellman, *An Unfinished Woman*, p. 57.

281 BENCHLEY TOLD HIS WIFE: Robert Benchley letter to Gertrude Benchley, August 14, 1937, Mugar Library, Boston University.

282 DOROTHY WOULD RATHER: Dorothy Parker letter to Alexander Woollcott, December 1940, Houghton Library, Harvard University.

282 IT TURNED OUT: Hellman, *An Unfinished Woman*, p. 87.

282 THE RICH AND FAMOUS: Hellman, *Pentimento. A Book of Portraits*, Little, Brown and Co., 1973 (New American Library edition), pp. 102–3.

283 THE LOYALIST CAUSE: Leland Stowe letter to author, September 15, 1982.

284 I COULDN'T IMAGINE: Dorothy Parker, "Spain, For Heaven's Sake!" (originally titled "Who Might Be Interested"), *Mother Jones*, February/March 1986, p.42; Parker, "Not Enough," *New Masses*, March 14, 1939, pp. 3–4.

284 DOTTIE PARKER IS HERE: Martha Gellhorn, "Guerre de Plume," *The Paris Review*, Spring 1981, pp. 280–301.

284 ALL DAY LONG: Parker, "Not Enough," *New Masses*, March 4, 1939.

284 SHE PREFERRED NIGHT RAIDS: Parker, "Incredible, Fantastic . . . and True," *New Masses*, November 23, 1937.

285 THEY DON'T CRY: Parker, "Spain, For Heaven's Sake." *Mother Jones*, February/March 1986.

285 DESCRIBING HER TRAVELS: Hellman, *An Unfinished Woman*, p. 88.

285 DESPITE HER *COJONES*: Lillian Hellman's first writings about the Spanish Civil War appeared two years after Dorothy's death. In 1981, Martha Gellhorn published a long article in *The Paris Review*, accusing Hellman of substituting fiction for fact, and combed newspaper clippings and her own notes from the period in an attempt to show that Hellman's stories were apocryphal. Hellman, Gellhorn charged, had written a great part for herself throughout. "She is the shining heroine who overcomes hard-

ship, hunger, fear, danger—down stage center—in a tormented country."

In 1980, Hellman had filed a defamation suit against Mary McCarthy for calling her a dishonest writer, but she failed to sue Gellhorn, whom she said had written the article out of pique because Hellman had been "not pleasant" to her in *An Unfinished Woman*.

285 MISS H. BROUGHT NOTHING: Gellhorn, p. 296.

285 SHE GAVE NEWSPAPER INTERVIEWS: *New York Post*, October 22, 1937.

285 YOU KNEW DARN WELL: Parker interview, Columbia University Oral History Research Office.

285 AT PARTIES: *Mother Jones*.

285 IN PIPERSVILLE: Author's interview with Lel Droste Iveson.

285 SHE IMAGINED: Dorothy Parker letter to Alexander Woollcott, September 2, 1942, Houghton Library, Harvard University.

286 DEAR MISS KENNEDY: Dorothy Parker letter to Sheelagh Kennedy, November 1937, Spanish Refugee Collection, Rare Book and Manuscript Library, Columbia University Libraries.

287 SHE MANAGED TO GET A LAUGH: *New York Herald Tribune*, December 4, 1937.

287 PERELMAN WAS CURIOUS: Perelman, *The Last Laugh*, pp. 186–7.

289 IN A LETTER: Alan Campbell letter to Toni Strassman, April 1938.

289 AS ALWAYS: Dorothy Parker letter to Sheelagh Kennedy, March 21, 1938, Spanish Refugee Collection.

289 KOBER LATER CLAIMED: Richard Moody, *Lillian Hellman, Playwright*, Pegasus Division of Bobbs-Merrill Co., 1972, p. 113.

289 HER WORK HABITS: Author's interview with Budd Schulberg.

290 AND THEN WHAT: Author's interview with Frances Goodrich and Albert Hackett.

290 AT A PARTY: Writers Guild of America West *News*, March 1982.

290 YOU COULD HAVE: Dorothy Parker interview, Columbia University Oral History Research Office.

290 NOW LISTEN: Ibid.

290 TO AN INTERVIEWER: Ibid.

291 ONE DAY, SHE LOOKED OUT: Siegfried M. Herzig letter to author, January 31, 1983.

291 A REPORTER ASKED HER: *New York Times*, "Miss Parker Never Poses," January 8, 1939.

291 SHE INSISTED: Richard Lamparski interview with Dorothy Parker.

292 IF YOU HAD SEEN: *Time*, January 16, 1939, p. 55.

292 TWENTY-FIVE YEARS LATER: Richard Lamparski interview with Dorothy Parker.

292 THOUGH THE WORLD: William Rose Benét letter to Dorothy Parker, May 15, 1939, Spanish Refugee Collection.

292 MEANWHILE, DOROTHY WENT ON: Dorothy Parker letter to Evelyn Ahrend, May 19, 1939, Spanish Refugee Collection.

293 NOT UNTIL 1942: Dorothy Parker note to Marshall Best, The Viking Press, received August 21, 1942.

293 DOT, CHARLES MACARTHUR REMARKED: Janet Flanner letter to Alexander Woollcott, ca. 1939–1940, Houghton Library, Harvard University.

294 PRESENTS, SHE GROWLED: Cooper, p. 112.

294 WHY IS IT: Parker, "One Perfect Rose," *The Portable Dorothy Parker*, p. 104.

295 THE WHOLE WORLD: Alan Campbell letter to Ruth and Augustus Goetz, undated.

295 DOROTHY PERKED UP: Dorothy Parker telegram to Helen Grimwood, June 16, 1939.

295 JOHN DAVIES THOUGHT: John Davies letter to author, December 12, 1979.

296 HELEN WALKER ALSO NOTICED: Author's interview with Helen Walker Day.

296 THAT SUMMER, JANET FLANNER: Janet Flanner, *Paris Was Yesterday, 1925–1939*, The Viking Press, 1972, p. 220.

296 ALAN IMPRESSED HELEN: Author's interview with Helen Walker Day.

297 ALAN ADMITTED: Alan Campbell letter to Alexander Woollcott, August 1939, Houghton Library, Harvard University.

297 KNOWLEDGE OF THE FIBROIDS: Dorothy Parker letter to Alexander Woollcott, December 1940, Houghton Library, Harvard University.

298 HE WAS ASTONISHED: Alan Campbell letter to Alexander Woollcott, December 1940, Houghton Library, Harvard University.

298 CONVALESCING: Dorothy Parker letter to Alexander Woollcott, December 1940, Houghton Library, Harvard University.

298 ROBERT BENCHLEY DESCRIBED HIM: Robert Benchley letter to Gertrude Benchley, December 29, 1940, Mugar Library, Boston University.

299 THE POOR SON-OF-BITCH: Frank Scully, *Rogues Gallery*, Murray and Gee, 1943, p. 269.

299 SHE HAD MADE POSSIBLE: Author's interview with Albert Hackett.

299 BENCHLEY TOLD THE MURPHYS: Robert Benchley letter to Sara and Gerald Murphy, July 1, 1937.

300 SCRATCH AN ACTOR: Author's interview with Albert Hackett.

300 WHAT AM I DOING WITH HIM: Author's interview with Ruth Goetz.

300 WHAT AM I DOING IN HOLLYWOOD: Author's interview with Albert Hackett.

300 IT'S THE CURVED LIPS: Author's interview with Henry Ephron.

300 GROWING RECKLESS: Author's interview with Ruth Goetz.

300 SAID RUTH GOETZ: Ibid.

301 DOROTHY HAS BEEN HEARD TO SAY: Sid Perelman letter to Ruth and Augustus Goetz, April 10, 1940.

302 RUTH GOETZ CALLED HIM: Author's interview with Ruth Goetz.

302 SID PERELMAN, SPECULATING: Sid Perelman letter to Ruth and Augustus Goetz, April 10, 1940.

302 SHE BITTERLY DESCRIBED: *Writers at Work*, p. 75.

303 SHE WAS, AFTER ALL: Brendan Gill, *Here at The New Yorker*, Random House, 1975, p. 264.

303 CLEARLY HER SO-CALLED FRIENDS: Prescott, p. 7

304 NEGLECTING TO MENTION: Harold Guinzburg letter to Dorothy Parker, July 12, 1937.

304 TO ALAN,: Harold Guinzburg letter to Alan Campbell, July 12, 1937. Even though Dorothy felt no need of a literary agent, some of the tasks that an agent ordinarily handles were taken care of by Harold Guinzburg or Alan. In his agent role, Alan tended to be quite haughty. When, for example, a biographical dictionary asked for information, he forwarded the request to Toni Strassman at Viking with a disdainful note saying that he simply could not imagine his wife writing "an informal, first-person autobiographical sketch of about five hundred words."

304 GOD DAMN IT: Parker, *New Masses*, March 14, 1939.

305 HE "THOUGHT IT WAS A SCREAM" : Dorothy Parker letter to Helen Bugbee, March 24, 1939, in *Mother Jones*, February/March 1986, p. 41.

305 THEIR VILLAGE: Parker, "Soldiers of the Republic," *The Portable Dorothy Parker*, p. 168.

306 SHE SAID: Dorothy Parker telegram to Harold Guinzburg, April 25, 1938.

306 HE SCOLDED HER: Harold Guinzburg letter to Dorothy Parker, April 27, 1938.

306 HE HAD SENT HER: Harold Guinzburg letter to Dorothy Parker, November 3, 1936.

307 THE MAN SAID: Hellman, *An Unfinished Woman*, p. 188.

307 IN THE SUMMER OF 1941: Robert Benchley to Gertrude Benchley, July 2, 1941, Mugar Library, Boston University.

307 ON HER BIRTHDAY: Dorothy

Parker letter to Harold Ross, August 22, 1941.

308 "MY," DOROTHY REMARKS: From *Saboteur.*

308 SHE CALLED HIS VALUES: Dorothy Parker to Alexander Woollcott, September 2, 1942, Houghton Library, Harvard University.

308 I WAS TOO GREEN: Author's interview with Helen Deutsch.

309 SHE WOULD JUST HOLD OUT: Author's interview with Joseph Bryan.

309 OUR OLD FRIEND DOTNICK: Sid Perelman to Ruth and Augustus Goetz, December 1941. Prudence Crowther, editor of *Don't Tread on Me: The Selected Letters of S.J. Perelman,* dates this letter March 1942.

310 NOW THE WHOLE WORLD: Author's interview with Sally Foster.

310 WE WERE WORKING VERY HARD: Author's interview with Henry Ephron.

311 SHE ASSURED ALECK: Dorothy Parker letter to Alexander Woollcott, September 2, 1942, Houghton Library, Harvard University.

311 AFTER CONFUSING THE ISSUE: Ibid.

311 HER PHILOSOPHY: Ibid.

Fifteen: The Leaking Boat

312 RELATIONS WITH HER SISTER: Dorothy had difficulty imagining her sister's life. After Helen separated from Victor Grimwood and considered renting a small apartment in Manhattan, Dorothy was full of encouragement. She sent her a check to have "a little fun" but wondered if Helen really wished to live in the eighteen-dollar-a-week room she described. It sounded "dreary" to Dorothy, who instead recommended the Fairfax Hotel, where she could have "a great big room that sort of divides itself into a sitting room, and a sort of kitchenette—at least, with a nice ice-box, so you could give people a cocktail." (Dorothy Parker letter to Helen Grimwood.) The rates at the Fairfax were probably beyond Helen's means because in the end she decided to live with her daughter.

312 DESPITE HER COMPLAINTS: Ibid.

312 HER NIECE LEL: Author's interview with Lel Iveson.

313 SHE WAS DETERMINED: Dorothy Parker letter to Alexander Woollcott, September 2, 1942, Houghton Library, Harvard University.

313 HE LATER JOKED: Harold Ross letter to Marc Connelly, September 22, 1942.

314 FIVE THOUSAND DOLLARS: Author's interview with Thomas Guinzburg.

315 ALAN LATER RECALLED: Alan Campbell letter to Alexander Woollcott, in "P.S. He Got the Job," *As You Were,* The Viking Press, 1943, p. 637.

316 DESPITE HIS PRECONCEIVED NOTIONS: Joshua Logan, *Movie Stars, Real People, and Me,* Delacorte Press, 1978, p. 250-1.

316 THEY WERE TERRIBLY INTIMATE: Author's interview with Joshua Logan.

316 A BELOVED LITTLE MOUSE: Logan, p. 251.

317 WE HAVE THE ROUND TABLE: Gaines, p. 237.

317 HARPO MARX: Harpo Marx, *Harpo Speaks!,* Bernard Geis Associates, 1961, p. 432.

317 DOROTHY, SEATED: Ted Morgan, *Maugham,* Simon and Schuster, 1980, p. 472.

318 HIGGLEDY PIGGLEDY: Parker untitled verse, in W. Somerset Maugham, "Variations on a Theme," introduction to *The Portable Dorothy Parker,* p. 600.

318 ALTHOUGH DOROTHY LATER: Morgan, p. 473.

318 IN AN ARTICLE: Excerpt reprinted in *New York Times Book Review,* June 24, 1945, p. 21. On the Sunday that the excerpt appeared in the *Times,* Dorothy was to be a weekend guest at the Kaufman farm in Bucks County. Beatrice Kaufman, shortly before her death, thought the feud between George and Dorothy was silly and hoped to

reconcile them. That morning, Dorothy saw the newspaper before George came down for breakfast. Dismayed, she tucked it under her arm and thumped back to her room where she locked it in her suitcase. Kaufman, upset over the disappearance of the paper, spent the morning interrogating the servants for clues to its whereabouts.

318 ON THE OTHER HAND: Parker, "The Middle or Blue Period," *Cosmopolitan*, December 1944, in *The Portable Dorothy Parker*, p. 594.

319 PEOPLE OUGHT TO BE: Parker, "The Middle or Blue Period."

319 WHEN SHE WAS NOTIFIED: Rosmond, p. 11.

320 AFTER BENCHLEY'S DEATH: Bruccoli, p. 181.

320 WHENEVER PEOPLE ASKED: Case, p. 60.

320 DOROTHY WAS HAPPY TO SPREAD: Richard Lamparski taped interview with Dorothy Parker.

320 THREE DECADES LATER: *New York Times*, October 27, 1979.

320 THOSE EYES: Benchley, p. 17.

321 BOB, DON'T YOU KNOW: Sheilah Graham, *The Garden of Allah*, Crown Publishers, 1970, p. 111.

322 HIS SON TIMOTHY: Author's interview with Timothy Adams.

322 BRENDAN GILL RECALLED: Author's interview with Brendan Gill.

323 WHEN SHE KNEW: Parker, "The Lovely Leave," *The Portable Dorothy Parker*, p. 5.

323 THE LETTERS SPELLED OUT: Logan, p. 252.

323 SHE MADE IT HOMIER: Author's interview with Mary McDonald.

324 AT *THE NEW YORKER*: Author's interview with E. J. Kahn, Jr.

324 EVERYONE MAKES A SWELL FUSS: Helen Grimwood letter to Bill Droste, ca. 1943.

324 HE HAD GAINED: Parker, "The Lovely Leave."

325 WE GUESSED: Author's interview with Marge Droste.

326 YOU SEE THAT: Author's interview with William Targ.

326 DOROTHY FELT: Dorothy Parker, "Who Is That Man?" *Vogue*, July 1944, p. 67.

327 ONLY, FOR THE NIGHTS: Parker, "War Song," *The Portable Dorothy Parker*, p. 370.

327 ALAN EXPECTED HER: Author's interview with Joshua Logan.

328 I CAN COMPETE: Charles Addams letter to author, February 23, 1983.

328 I'M SORRY IT'S OVER: Engle, p. 14.

328 TO HIS UNCLE: Author's interview with Roy Eichel.

328 A COUNTRY RESIDENCE: Dorothy and Alan sold Fox House in July 1947. Over the years the farm has changed hands several times. Its present owner is Robert Yaw III.

Sixteen: Toad Time

330 HE WAS A CONFIRMED ALCOHOLIC: Author's interview with Joshua Logan.

330 LATER HE DESCRIBED HIMSELF: *Newark News*, October 15, 1961.

331 THERE WERE QUITE A FEW: Keats, p. 250.

331 COMPARED WITH ALAN: Author's interview with Joshua Logan.

331 SHE WAS CONSTANTLY: Author's interview with Joseph Bryan.

332 DON'T WORRY ABOUT THAT: A. E. Hotchner, *Choice People: The Greats, Near-Greats, and Ingrates I Have Known*, William Morrow, 1984, pp. 20–32.

334 REFERRING TO A FILM: Dorothy Parker/Ross Evans letter to Margo Jones, August 12, 1949, Dallas Public Library.

335 IN LETTERS: Margo Jones letters to Dorothy Parker and Ross Evans, June 6, 30, 1949, Dallas Public Library.

335 NOW WE KNOW: Dorothy Parker and Ross Evans letters to Margo Jones, Feb-

ruary 17, March 25, 1949, Dallas Public Library.

335 CRIES FOR AUTHOR: *Dallas Morning News*, April 5, 1949.

335 WE'VE TASTED BLOOD: *Time*, April 18, 1949.

336 I SAID IT WOULDN'T WORK: Norman Mailer, "Of a small and Modest Malignancy, Wicked and Bristling with Dots," *Esquire*, November 1977, p. 133.

336 IN POOR HEALTH: Ross Evans letter to Margo Jones, August 12, 1949, Dallas Public Library.

336 ONE OF HER DOCTORS: Ibid.

337 BIT BY BIT: Despite extensive revisions, further productions of *The Coast of Illyria* failed to materialize. In England, it was rejected by every first-rate director, all of whom disliked the script. Dame Flora Robson, insufficiently impressed, could barley recall the play in 1982. (Dame Flora Robson letter to author, March 15, 1982.)

338 THE REPORT: Files of the Federal Bureau of Investigation, Los Angeles Field Office.

338 HE SAID LATER: Ross Evans letter to Margo Jones, January 27, 1951, Dallas Public Library.

338 SHE HAD NOT EXPECTED GRATITUDE: Ross Evans remained in Cuernavaca, where he eventually married and had a child. In the late 1950s, returning to the United States, he fell upon hard times and worked as a dishwasher in San Francisco and then as a Macy's salesclerk in New York. For a time he had an affair with singer Libby Holman and lived at her Connecticut estate. An autobiographical novel begun in 1950 finally appeared in 1961 as *A Feast of Fools* but did not prove a critical or commercial success. When Evans died in 1967, he was 51.

339 WHO IN LIFE: Author's interview with Albert Hackett.

339 HE QUERIED FRIENDS: Ibid.

339 A WOMAN HE HAD BEEN DATING: Author's interview with Bob Magner.

339 YOU NEVER KNOW: Newspaper clipping, unidentified source, August 15, 1950.

339 THEY HAD NO PLANS: *Doylestown Intelligencer*, August 18, 1950.

339 INCLUDING THE BRIDE: Cooper, p. 112.

339 BUDD SCHULBERG DESCRIBED: Author's interview with Budd Schulberg.

339 ALAN WAS HEARD TO REMARK: Author's interview with Sally Foster.

339 AS THE EVENING WORE ON: Dietz, p. 237.

340 IN JANUARY, HE REPORTED: Alan Campbell letter to Sara and Gerald Murphy, ca. January 1951.

341 FRANKLY, SHE FINALLY SAID: Author's interview with Albert Hackett.

341 LISTEN, I CAN'T: Ibid.

341 DURING THE COURSE OF THIS INTERVIEW: Federal Bureau of Investigation files.

341 DEAR MR. HOOVER: Ibid.

341 SHE COULD THINK OF: Dalton Trumbo, *Additional Dialogue: Letters of Dalton Trumbo*, M. Evans and Co., 1970, p. 133.

342 IN 1947: *New York Daily News*, June 13, 1947.

342 IN NEW YORK: *New York Herald Tribune*, November 3, 1947.

342 STILL SHE WAS NOT CALLED: Federal Bureau of Investigation files citing 1952 speech at Abraham Lincoln Brigade/Joint Anti-Fascist Refugee Committee meeting.

342 RED APPEASER: *New York Times*, June 9, 1949.

342 THE ACCUSATION MADE HER FEEL: Ibid.

342 NO DENIAL: *New York World Telegram*, June 8, 1949.

342 BY 1950: Federal Bureau of Investigation files, memo dated August 28, 1950.

343 THE BUREAU ALSO QUOTED: Ibid., memo dated July 19, 1950.

343 I WAS BLACKLISTED: Parker interview, Columbia University Oral History Research Office.

344 SHE KNEW NOTHING: *New York Times*, February 26, 1955.

344 A FOUR-PAGE MEMORANDUM: Federal Bureau of Investigation files. Even though FBI Headquarters closed her file in 1955, the New York Field Office continued to maintain its records until May 1956.

344 MR. TAVENNER: U.S. Congress, House Committee on Un-American Activities, *Communist Infiltration of Hollywood Motion Picture Industry*, Hearings, Eighty-second Congress, Part 1, March 8, 1951.

345 MANY HE KNEW: S. J. Perelman letter to Leila Hadley.

345 DOROTHY LIKENED: Parker speech, *Seven Arts*, p. 139.

346 A DISGUSTED SID PERELMAN: Sid Perelman letter to Leila Hadley, 1951.

346 BY SEPTEMBER 1952: *New York World Telegram and Sun*, October 16, 1953.

346 ALL SHE WANTED: Ibid.

347 WE DROPPED IT: *New York Herald Tribune*, October 18, 1953.

347 WE HAD BEEN THINKING: Dorothy Parker, untitled typescript, Leah Salisbury Collection, Columbia University Library.

348 WE'D ARRIVE: Quentin Reynolds, *By Quentin Reynolds*, McGraw-Hill Book Co., 1963, p. 2.

348 SHE EDUCATED HIM: Author's interview with Kate Mostel.

349 THEY HAVE TO ASK QUESTIONS: Kate Mostel and Madeline Gilford, *170 Years of Show Business*, Random House, 1978, p. 129.

349 AN ADORING KATE MOSTEL: Author's interview with Kate Mostel.

350 TO NORMAN MAILER: Mailer, p. 132.

350 THAT WAS REALLY THE DRUNKEST: Author's interview with Kate Mostel.

350 ANOTHER EVENING AT THE MOSTELS: Author's interviews with Ian Hunter, Kate Mostel.

350 BY THE TIME: *New York Herald Tribune*, October 18, 1953.

351 WALTER MATTHAU REMEMBERED: Walter Matthau letter to author, May 3, 1982.

351 THE FIRST DAY OF REHEARSAL: Harold Clurman interview, Columbia Oral History Research Office.

351 DOROTHY THOUGHT IT WOULD BE INSANE: Dorothy Parker interview, Columbia Oral History Research Office.

351 SOME OF THE REVIEWS: Mostel and Gilford, p. 130.

351 IT WAS, HE THOUGHT: *New York Journal-American*, April 4, 1954.

352 WHEN THE GOOD NEWS: Office memo dated October 14, 1955, Leah Salisbury Collection, Columbia University Library.

352 THE SUBJECT OF HOMOSEXUALITY: Author's interview with Robert Whitehead.

Seventeen: High-Forceps Deliveries

354 FOR COMIC RELIEF: William Maxwell letter to author, February 21, 1983.

355 I HAVEN'T GOT: Malcolm Cowley, *—And I Worked at the Writer's Trade: Chapters of Literary History, 1918–1978*, The Viking Press, 1978, p. 181.

355 IN 1955: *Writers at Work*, p. 80.

355 IN HER DEALINGS WITH WILLIAM MAXWELL: Author's interview with William Maxwell.

356 SEEING THE REVIEW: Author's interview with Harold Hayes.

357 BUT, RECALLED GINGRICH: Arnold Gingrich, *Nothing but People: The Early Days at Esquire, A Personal History 1928–1958*, Crown Publishers, 1971, p. 301.

357 HE VIEWED HIS OWN JOB: Arnold Gingrich letter to Bernard Geis, August 30, 1962, Michigan Historical Collections, Bentley Historical Library, University of Michigan.

359 BERNARD GEIS ADMITTED: Bernard Geis letter to author, March 17, 1982.

359 DOROTHY CONFIDED IN QUENTIN REYNOLDS: Reynolds, p. 6.

359 DEAR BERNIE: Dorothy Parker letter to Bernard Geis, ca. 1960.

360 GEIS FELT HAPPY: Bernard Geis letter to author, March 17, 1982.

360 DEAR DOROTHY: Leah Salisbury letter to Dorothy Parker, September 11, 1957, Leah Salisbury Collection.

360 I HAD ONLY ONE LYRIC: Richard Lamparski interview with Dorothy Parker.

361 LEONARD BERNSTEIN RECALLED: Leonard Bernstein statement to author, January 26, 1983.

361 I'VE GOT TROUBLES: Lillian Hellman. *Candide: A Comic Operetta Based on Voltaire's Satire*, score by Leonard Bernstein, lyrics by Richard Wilbur, other lyrics by John Latouche and Dorothy Parker, Random House, 1957. "Gavotte" lyrics by Dorothy Parker, Act 2, Scene 2, pp. 127–8.

361 THE SHOW WAS, SHE THOUGHT: Richard Lamparski interview with Dorothy Parker.

362 AFTER FRIENDS ADVISED HER: Dorothy Parker letter to Malcolm Cowley, April 4, 1958, American Academy and Institute of Arts and Letters.

362 TO DOROTHY PARKER: American Academy and Institute of Arts and Letters citation.

362 IN 1958 STANDING OVATIONS: Malcolm Cowley to author, November 17, 1982.

363 MY DRIVING IDEA: Dorothy Parker letter to Elizabeth Ames, April 11, 1958, Yaddo.

363 THE TWO YOUNG LADIES: Dorothy Parker letter to Morton Zabel, October 27, 1958, Joseph Regenstein Library, University of Chicago.

364 I CAN ONLY SAY: Dorothy Parker letter to Morton Zabel, ca. November 1958, Joseph Regenstein Library, University of Chicago.

364 ALTHOUGH THE ENTIRE EXPERIENCE: Dorothy Parker letter to Elizabeth Ames, ca. November 1958, Yaddo.

364 BROOKS TERMED HER: Van Wyck Brooks, "Nomination of Candidate," National Institute of Arts and Letters.

364 THE INSTITUTE INSISTED: *Writers at Work*, p. 77.

364 DEAR MISS GEFFEN: Dorothy Parker letter to Felicia Geffen, 1959, American Academy and Institute of Arts and Letters.

365 I NEVER THOUGHT I'D MAKE IT: Richard Wilbur letter to author, July 26, 1982.

365 AFTERWARD, THORNTON WILDER: Thornton Wilder letter to Frank Sullivan, undated, quoted in Gilbert A. Harrison, *The Enthusiast: A Life of Thornton Wilder*, Ticknor & Fields, 1983, p. 319.

365 HER GAFFE: Richard Wilbur letter to author, April 28, 1982.

366 SHE KEPT REMARKING: Leslie Fiedler letter to author, May 24, 1982.

366 THERE! CRIES THE WOLF: Dorothy Parker draft of speech, R. G. Davis Collection, Rare Book and Manuscript Library, Columbia University Libraries.

367 SHE WAS, SAUL BELLOW THOUGHT: Saul Bellow letter to author, June 16, 1982.

367 HE THOUGHT SHE HAD BEEN: Arnold Gingrich letter to Dorothy Parker, October 23, 1958, Bentley Historical Library.

367 I TURNED MY FACE: Dorothy Parker letter to Morton Zabel, ca. October 27, 1958, Joseph Regenstein Library.

367 THAT AWFUL MAN: Author's interview with Noel Pugh.

368 NO, SHE PROTESTED: Mailer, p. 134.

368 DOROTHY, WROTE EDMUND WILSON: Edmund Wilson, *The Fifties: From Notebooks and Diaries of the Period*, Leon Edel ed., Farrar, Straus & Giroux, 1986, p. 531.

369 HELLMAN RECALLED: Lillian Hellman and Peter S. Feibleman, *Eating Together: Recipes and Recollections*, Little, Brown and Co., 1984, p. 76.

370 THEN, WILBUR RECALLED: Richard Wilbur letter to author, April 28, 1982.

370 SHE SAID PRETTILY: Hellman, *An Unfinished Woman*, p. 192.

371 TO BE ANTI-COMMUNIST: Gerald Murphy letter to Sara Murphy, quoted in Honoria Murphy Donnelly and Richard N.

Billings, *Sara and Gerald: Villa America and After*, Times Books, 1982, p. 211.

372 DOROTHY PASTED THE CLIPPING: Dorothy Parker letter to Sara and Gerald Murphy, July 1, 1958.

372 EXPLAINED AN ACQUAINTANCE: Author's interview with William Lord.

373 THIS LAST CRACK: Charles Addams letter to author, February 23, 1983.

373 IT WAS A TERRIBLE THING: Bob Thomas, "Feminine Wit Mourns State of U.S. Humor," Associated Press, January 15, 1951.

373 SHE TOLD TALLULAH: Kiernan Tunney, *Tallulah, Darling of the Gods*, E.P. Dutton and Co., 1973, p. 11.

373 HER STAGE FRIGHT: Author's interview with Shepperd Strudwick.

374 OFTEN HE HAD TO LIVE: Author's interview with Betty Moodie.

375 LONELINESS AND GUILT: Cooper, p. 111.

Eighteen: Ham and Cheese, Hold the Mayo

377 I'M A HOBO: *Los Angeles Times*, June 18, 1962.

377 SHE WROTE THAT THE TWO THINGS: Parker, "Books," *Esquire*, June 1961, p. 38.

378 IF BY ANY CHANCE: Alan Campbell letter to Sara and Gerald Murphy, November 29, 1961.

379 SEEING THE PARKING LOT: Cooper, 111.

380 AFTERWARD, DOROTHY SAID IN DISGUST: *New York Herald Tribune*, October 13, 1963.

380 WHENEVER *THE GOOD SOUP* WAS MENTIONED: Author's interview with Dana Woodbury.

380 HE WAS HARD: Author's interview with Clara Lester.

381 SHE FINALLY COOED: Author's interview with Dana Woodbury.

381 MISS PARKER, HE CONFESSED: Author's interview with Robert Rothwell.

382 AT PARTIES, RECALLED CLEMENT BRACE: Author's interview with Clement Brace.

382 SAID DANA WOODBURY: Author's interview with Dana Woodbury.

382 HE WAS NOT A QUEEN: Author's interview with Parker Ladd.

383 JUST WHO THE HELL: Author's interview with Dana Woodbury.

383 AFTER *THE GOOD SOUP*: Dorothy Parker letter to Leah Salisbury, January 25, 1962, Leah Salisbury Collection.

383 DEAR LEAH: Dorothy Parker telegram to Leah Salisbury, February 13, 1962, Leah Salisbury Collection, Columbia University.

383 NINA FOCH RECALLED: Author's interview with Nina Foch.

383 DOROTHY INSISTED: *New York Times*, May 6, 1962.

383 HE WAS, ACCORDING TO LEVY: Author's interview with Ralph Levy.

384 NOT TOO LONG AGO: *New York Times*, May 6, 1962.

384 SERIOUS PROBLEMS: Dorothy Parker letter to Leah Salisbury, March 9, 1962, Leah Salisbury Collection.

384 SHE TOLD *THE NEW YORK TIMES*: *New York Times*, May 6, 1962.

384 IT WAS AWFUL: Dorothy Parker/Alan Campbell letter to Leah Salisbury, September 19, 1962, Leah Salisbury Collection.

385 DOROTHY HATED: Ibid.

385 ALL ALONG SHE HAD INSISTED: *New York Times*, May 6, 1962.

386 PARKER LADD ARRANGED: Dorothy Parker and Frederick Shroyer, *Short Story: A Thematic Anthology*, Charles Scribner's, 1965.

386 LADD REMEMBERED: Author's interview with Parker Ladd.

386 ALAN, DAPPER IN SILK ASCOT: Author's interview with Lois Battle.

387 DOROTHY, ONLY TOO EAGER: Lois Battle, "A Wink at a Cock-eyed World," *UCLA Daily Bruin*, February 16, 1962.

387 DOROTHY LIKENED ALAN: Author's interview with Dana Woodbury.

387 DOROTHY, RECALLED MIRANDA

LEVY: Author's interview with Miranda Levy.

388 THE DOGGIES: Author's interview with Frederick Shroyer.

388 QUESTIONED BY A REPORTER: *Los Angeles Times*, June 18, 1962.

388 I SENT IT: Cooper, p. 112.

388 DEAR DOROTHY DIX: Arnold Gingrich letter to Dorothy Parker, February 4, 1963, Bentley Historical Library.

389 THEREFORE, HE WAS JOLTED: Arnold Gingrich to Arthur Kinney, May 10, 1963, Bentley Historical Library.

389 SHE HAD IMAGINED: *Los Angeles Times*, April 28, 1963.

390 I NEVER GIVE A BAD MARK: Author's interview with Sally Foster.

390 AS PARKER LADD CAME TO REALIZE: Author's interview with Parker Ladd.

390 TO SOME OF HIS NEIGHBORS: Author's interview with Bob Tallman and Bob Magner.

390 ALAN EVEN HAD TO TAKE: Hellman, *An Unfinished Woman*, p. 193.

391 PUGH NOTICED THAT: Author's interview with Noel Pugh.

391 DOROTHY WAS NOT ABOVE: Ibid.

392 WHEN CLARA LESTER ARRIVED: Author's interview with Clara Lester.

392 HE FELT STRANGE: Cooper, p. 113.

393 THE CORONER'S REPORT: Certificate of Death No. 63-084891. State of California Dept. of Public Health.

393 I DON'T THINK: Author's interview with Nina Foch.

393 SHE ASKED ME WHAT SHOULD BE DONE: Author's interview with Roy Eichel.

393 GET ME A NEW HUSBAND: Hellman, *An Unfinished Woman*, p. 199.

394 IF SHE HAD ANY DECENCY: *New York Herald Tribune*, October 13, 1963.

394 PERHAPS THE PERSON: Author's interview with Noel Pugh.

395 WE DON'T HAVE ANY LIQUOR: Author's interview with Sally Foster.

395 FRED SHROYER: Author's interview with Frederick Shroyer.

395 YOU SHOULDN'T: Author's interview with Sally Foster.

395 WHEN SHE STEPPED: Author's interview with Nina Foch.

396 YOU HAVE TO COME OVER HERE: Author's interview with Sally Foster.

396 WOULDN'T YOU KNOW IT: Ibid.

396 SHE WANTED TO MAKE A CLEAN SWEEP: *New York Herald Tribune*, April 8, 1965.

397 SEVERAL TIMES LEVY HEARD HER: Author's interview with Miranda Levy.

397 IF SHE HAD BOUGHT: Author's interview with Sally Foster.

Nineteen: Lady of the Corridor

398 FOR THE REMAINDER: Richard Lamparski interview with Dorothy Parker.

398 SHE MADE JOKES: New York *World-Telegram*, August 3, 1965.

399 SHE IMPRESSED MILFORD: Author's interview with Nancy Milford.

399 MEETING HER AT A PARTY: Author's interview with Stella Adler.

399 AS HIS WIDOW: Author's interview with Rebecca Bernstien.

400 I CAN'T USE MY TYPEWRITER: *New York Herald Tribune*, April 8, 1965.

400 I AM ALWAYS A LITTLE SAD: Dorothy Parker, "New York at 6:30 P.M.," *Esquire*, November 1964, p. 101.

401 OVER THE YEARS: Dorothy Parker, "Oscar Levant," in Roddy McDowall, *Double Exposure*, Delacorte Press, 1966, p. 42.

401 WHEN DOROTHY LEARNED OF IT: Hellman, *An Unfinished Woman*, pp. 194–5.

402 SHE HAD BEEN OBLIGED: Leah Salisbury letter to Dorothy Parker, March 9, 1964, Leah Salisbury Collection.

402 A STORY ON THE SOCIETY PAGE: *New York Herald Tribune*, April 8, 1965.

403 THAT WASN'T THE CASE: Author's interview with Andrew Anspach.

403 SHE VENTED: Cooper, p. 114.

403 GIVEN AN OPPORTUNITY: Richard Lamparski interview with Dorothy Parker.

404   AS A JOKE: *New York Herald Tribune*, April 8, 1965.

404   THEY WERE AS BAD: Richard Lamparski interview with Dorothy Parker.

404   HER OTHER PASTIME: Ibid.

405   DO YOU KNOW WHAT THIS IS: Author's interview with Heywood Hale Broun.

405   RUTH GOETZ DISCOVERED: Author's interview with Ruth Goetz.

406   DOROTHY'S ALCOHOLISM: Hellman, *An Unfinished Woman*, pp. 193–4.

406   WHEN JOSEPH BRYAN TELEPHONED: Author's interview with Joseph Bryan.

406   FEW NEW PEOPLE: Dorothy Parker, "Not Enough," *New Masses*, March 14, 1939, p. 4.

406   SOME OF THEM WOULD HAVE AGREED: Hellman, *An Unfinished Woman*, p. 194.

406   THE FALL SHE RETURNED: Dorothy Parker telegram to Sara Murphy, October 20, 1964.

406   SHE COMPLAINED: Cooper, p. 114.

406   AS HE WAS LEAVING: Author's interview with Frederick Shroyer.

407   WHEN SHE BROUGHT HER: Leah Salisbury letter to Lillian Hellman, July 5, 1967, Leah Salisbury Collection.

408   I CAN'T WRITE: Author's interview with Parker Ladd.

408   IT WOULD GIVE HER: Cooper, p. 57.

408   THE TAPINGS: Wyatt Cooper quoted from these 1967 tapes in his *Esquire* profile written the year after Dorothy's death. Upon Cooper's death in 1978, the tapes passed into the possession of his widow, who declines to make them public.

408   MY WIFE, WROTE COOPER: Cooper, p. 114.

409   HAVE YOU BEEN INVITED: Author's interview with Parker Ladd.

409   OH, YES, SHE FLUTED: Cooper, p. 114.

409   I COULD NOT HEAR A *WORD*: Louis Auchincloss letter to author, May 1982.

410   SHE'S GONE: Guiles, p. 285.

410   A FEW MINUTES LATER: Unidentified newspaper clipping.

411   THE STORY HAD BEGUN: *New York Times*, June 8, 1967.

411   KATE MOSTEL RECALLED: Author's interview with Kate Mostel.

411   IF SHE HAD HER WAY: *New York Times*, June 10, 1967.

411   AFTER THE MOURNERS: Ibid.

411   OH, LET IT BE: Parker, "Testament," *The Portable Dorothy Parker*, p. 92.

412   AS ONE OF HER BIOGRAPHERS: Moody, p. 347.

413   IT'S ONE THING: Nora Ephron, "Lillian Hellman Walking, Cooking, Writing, Talking—" *New York Times Book Review*, September 23, 1973, p. 51.

413   TO PLAYWRIGHT HOWARD TEICHMANN: William Wright, *Lillian Hellman, the Image, the Woman*, Simon & Schuster, 1986, p. 311.

413   ACCORDING TO HELLMAN'S MEMOIRS: Hellman, *An Unfinished Woman*, pp. 196–8.

413   AS MARTHA GELLHORN WROTE: Gellhorn, p. 296.

414   I COULD WRITE YOU SO MUCH: Frank Sullivan letter to Ann Honeycutt, June 13, 1967, in Sullivan, pp. 214–15.

Index

INDEX

Grateful acknowledgment is made to each of the following for permission to reprint previously published material:

THE CONDÉ NAST PUBLICATIONS, INC.: excerpt from "Any Porch" by Dorothy Parker from the September 1915 issue of *Vanity Fair*. Copyright 1915, renewed 1943, 1971 by The Condé Nast Publications, Inc. Courtesy of *Vanity Fair*. Excerpt from "Crowninshield in the Cubs Den" from the September 1944 issue of *Vogue*. Copyright 1944, renewed 1972 by The Condé Nast Publications, Inc. Courtesy of *Vogue*.

MALCOLM COWLEY: letter dated November 17, 1982. Reprinted with his permission.

DOUBLEDAY & COMPANY, INC.: excerpt from *Elinor Wylie* by Stanley Olson. Reprinted by permission of Doubleday & Company, Inc.

ESQUIRE MAGAZINE: excerpt from "Whatever You Think Dorothy Parker Was Like, She Wasn't" by Wyatt Cooper from the July 1968 issue of *Esquire*. Copyright © 1968 by Esquire Associates. Reprinted with permission of *Esquire*.

M. EVANS AND COMPANY, INC.: excerpt from *Additional Dialogue: Letters of Dalton Trumbo 1942–1962* by Dalton Trumbo and Helen Manfull. Copyright © 1970 by Dalton Trumbo. Reprinted by permission of the publisher, M. Evans and Company, Inc., New York.

FARRAR, STRAUS & GIROUX, INC.: excerpts from *Letters on Literature and Politics*, 1912–1972 by Edmund Wilson. Copyright © 1957, 1973, 1974, 1977 by Elena Wilson. Also, excerpts from *The Twenties* by Edmund Wilson. Copyright © 1975 by Edmund Wilson. Reprinted by permission of Farrar, Straus & Giroux, Inc.

SAMUEL FRENCH, INC.: excerpt from Act III of *Close Harmony or The Lady Next Door* by Elmer L. Rice and Dorothy Parker. Copyright 1924 by Elmer L. Rice and Dorothy Parker. Reprinted by permission of Samuel French, Inc.

HARCOURT BRACE JOVANOVICH, INC.: excerpts from *88 Poems* by Ernest Hemingway. Copyright © 1979 by The Ernest Hemingway Foundation and Nicholas Gerogiannis. Reprinted by permission of Harcourt Brace Jovanovich, Inc.

HOUGHTON MIFFLIN COMPANY: excerpt from *The Enthusiast: A Life of Thornton Wilder* by Gilbert A. Harrison. Copyright © 1983 by Gilbert A. Harrison; excerpt from *Letters of Archibald MacLeish 1907–1982*, edited by R.H. Winnick. Copyright © 1983 by the Estate of Archibald MacLeish and R.H. Winnick. Reprinted by permission of Houghton Mifflin Company.

NATALIA MURRAY: letter from Janet Flanner to Alexander Woolcott, ca. 1939–1940. Permission granted for Janet Flanner by Natalia Murray, Literary Executor.

RANDOM HOUSE, INC.: excerpts from *Sara and Gerald: Villa America and After* by Honoria Murphy Donnelly and Richard N. Billings. Published by Times Books, a division of Random House, Inc. Copyright © 1982 by Honoria Donnelly and Richard N. Billings; excerpts from *Correspondence of F. Scott Fitzgerald*, edited by Matthew J. Bruccoli and Margaret M. Duggan. Copyright © 1980 by Frances Scott Fitzgerald Smith; excerpts from *Candide: A Comic Opera Based on Voltaire's Satire* by Lillian Hellman. Copyright © 1957 by Lillian Hellman; excerpts fr m *Selected Letters of John O'Hara*, edited by Matthew J. Bruccoli. Copyright © 1978 by United States Trust Company of New York, as Trustees of the will of John O'Hara; excerpts from *The O'Hara Concern: The Biography of John O'Hara* by Matthew J. Bruccoli. Copyright © 1975 by Matthew J. Bruccoli. Reprinted by permission of Random House, Inc.

CHARLES SCRIBNER'S SONS AND HAROLD OBER ASSOCIATES, INC.: excerpts from *The Letters of F. Scott Fitzgerald*, edited by Andrew Turnbull. Copyright © 1963 by Francis Scott Fitzgerald Lanahan. Reprinted by permission of Charles Scribner's Sons and Harold Ober Associates, Inc.

SIMON AND SCHUSTER, INC.: excerpts from *The Diary of Our Own Samuel Pepys* by Franklin Pierce Adams. Copyright 1935 by Franklin Pierce Adams. Copyright renewed 1963 by Anthony, Jonathan, Timothy, and Persephine Adams. Reprinted by permission of Simon and Schuster, Inc.

LELAND STOWE: excerpt from a letter from Dorothy Parker to Leland Stowe. Reprinted with his permission.

ROSEMARY C. THURBER: excerpt from *Selected Letters of James Thurber* by Helen Thurber and Edward Weeks. Copyright © 1981 by Helen Thurber. Published by Atlantic–Little Brown.

VIKING PENGUIN, INC.: excerpts from *The Portable Dorothy Parker*, revised and edited by Brendan Gill. Copyright 1926, 1928, 1929, 1933, 1938, 1943, 1944 by Dorothy Parker. Copyright renewed 1954, 1956, 1957, 1961, 1966 by Dorothy Parker. Copyright renewed 1971, 1972 by The Viking Press, Inc.; excerpts from *Don't Tread on Me: The Selected Letters of S. J. Perelman*, edited by Prudence Crowther. Copyright © 1987 by Abby Perelman and Adam Perelman; excerpts from the interview with Dorothy Parker by Marion Capron in *Writers at Work: The Paris Review Interviews, 1st Series*, edited by Malcolm Cowley. Copyright © 1957, 1958 by The Paris Review, Inc. Reprinted by permission of Viking Penguin, Inc.